THOMAS
EARL OF DANBY

SIR THOMAS OSBORNE, AFTERWARDS EARL OF DANBY
From an engraving by Blooteling, after the portrait by Sir P. Lely

National Portrait Gallery

THOMAS OSBORNE
EARL OF DANBY
AND DUKE OF LEEDS

1632–1712

BY

ANDREW BROWNING, M.A., D.Litt.

PROFESSOR OF HISTORY IN THE UNIVERSITY OF GLASGOW

VOLUME I

LIFE

GLASGOW
JACKSON, SON & CO.
PUBLISHERS TO THE UNIVERSITY
1951

PRINTED IN GREAT BRITAIN BY ROBERT MACLEHOSE AND CO. LTD.
THE UNIVERSITY PRESS, GLASGOW, FOR JACKSON, SON AND CO.
(BOOKSELLERS) LTD., PUBLISHERS TO THE UNIVERSITY, GLASGOW

PREFACE

MORE than thirty years ago, when publishing an Oxford Prize Essay on the subject of this study, the author expressed a hope that at a later stage he might be able to develop it into something more worthy of the great statesman with whom it deals. Since then wars and rumours of wars have twice led to the abandonment of the project for years at a time, and with each successive resumption of work its scope has been expanded and its arrangement been recast. That it has eventually been completed is largely due to the encouragement and assistance of others.

Foremost among these must be mentioned the late and the present Duke of Leeds, who most courteously and generously allowed the author unrestricted access to the very valuable Leeds Manuscripts formerly preserved at Hornby Castle ; and the late Earl of Lindsey, who similarly permitted a thorough examination of the Danby papers formerly preserved at Uffington House, Stamford.

At different stages the *Life* has had the inestimable advantage of being read and criticised by three great historians who are no longer with us—Sir Charles Firth, Sir Richard Lodge and Sir Robert Rait. The author's indebtedness to all three is deeper than he can well express.

The task of recognising obligations to friends and colleagues, however agreeable, is always a difficult one. Mr. E. S. de Beer has not only been unsparing of advice and assistance, but has also placed his own extensive researches in the same field at the author's disposal. Mr. David Ogg has read the typescript throughout, and has made many helpful suggestions. Professor G. O. Sayles has not infrequently interrupted his own mediaeval studies in order to help in the elucidation of some difficult problem. Dr. J. J. Sutherland Shaw and Dr. Dorothy Somerville have contributed valuable references. Mr. C. Douglas

PREFACE

Chandaman has read the proofs with meticulous care. To all these the author offers his most sincere thanks.

Finally the author has to thank the Carnegie Trustees for their generous assistance with the work of publication.

University of Glasgow,
  March 1950

CONTENTS

PART I

SIR THOMAS OSBORNE AND THE DUKE OF BUCKINGHAM

1632-73

PART II

MY LORD TREASURER THE EARL OF DANBY

1673-9

PART III

A STATESMAN OUT OF OFFICE

1679-89

PART IV

CARMARTHEN AND LEEDS
1689-1712

NOTE ON DATES

UNLESS otherwise indicated all dates in the text are given according to the Old or English Style, but with a year calculated as beginning on January 1. Letters and documents, however, whether printed or referred to, are given the actual dates they bear. Thus letters from foreign representatives in England to their superiors at home normally appear to have been written ten days (in the eighteenth century eleven days) after the date on which according to the English reckoning they were written.

ABBREVIATIONS

Manuscript

B.M.Add.MSS. British Museum, Additional Manuscripts.

Leeds MSS. Manuscripts of the Duke of Leeds formerly preserved at Hornby Castle, now in the British Museum.

P.C.Reg. Privy Council Register.

Printed

A.H.R. American Historical Review.

Bulstrode Papers. Catalogue of the Collection of Autograph Letters and Historical Documents formed by Alfred Morrison. Second Series. The Bulstrode Papers.

Burnet. Gilbert Burnet, History of My Own Time, ed. O. Airy for the reign of Charles II, and ed. 1833 thereafter.

C.J. Journals of the House of Commons.

Cal. S. P. Dom. Calendar of State Papers, Domestic.

Cal. S. P. Ire. Calendar of State Papers, Ireland.

Cal. Treas. Books. Calendar of Treasury Books.

Campana de Cavelli. Marquise Campana de Cavelli, Les Derniers Stuarts à Saint-Germain en Laye.

D.N.B. Dictionary of National Biography.

Dalrymple. Sir John Dalrymple, Memoirs of Great Britain and Ireland.

Doebner. Richard Doebner, Memoirs of Mary Queen of England.

E.H.R. English Historical Review.

Evelyn. Diary of John Evelyn.

Grey. Anchitell Grey, Debates of the House of Commons.

Hist. MSS. Com. Historical Manuscripts Commission Reports.

Kennet. White Kennet, A Complete History of England, ed. 1719.

L.J. Journals of the House of Lords.

x

Luttrell. Narcissus Luttrell, A Brief Historical Relation of State Affairs.

Macaulay. T. B. Macaulay, The History of England from the Accession of James II, ed. C. H. Firth.

Mignet. F. A. M. Mignet, Négociations relatives à la succession d'Espagne.

Morrison Catalogue. Catalogue of the Collection of Autograph Letters and Historical Documents formed by Alfred Morrison, ed. A. W. Thibaudeau.

Pepys. Diary of Samuel Pepys.

Ranke. Leopold von Ranke, A History of England principally in the Seventeenth Century.

Rawdon Papers. The Rawdon Papers, ed. E. Berwick.

Reresby. Memoirs of Sir John Reresby, ed. 1936.

PART I

SIR THOMAS OSBORNE AND THE DUKE OF BUCKINGHAM

1632-73

CHAPTER I

ANCESTRY AND EARLY LIFE

THE rise of the family of Osborne to prominence was a result of the social and economic changes of the sixteenth century. In May 1547 Edward, eldest son of Richard Osborne of Ashford, whose family had for some centuries remained undistinguished among the gentry of Kent, was induced by the magnificent prospects opening up in the world of trade and commerce to enter the service of William Hewett, clothworker, of London, one of the most successful merchants of the day. His career thereafter, if tradition may be trusted, resembled that of the industrious apprentice of romance. From a window of his master's house on London Bridge a careless nurse allowed Hewett's infant daughter Anne to fall into the river beneath. Osborne immediately plunged in and rescued her, and in spite of the crowd of suitors who later came forward was rewarded in due course with her hand in marriage.[1] Shortly afterwards, on January 21, 1567, his father-in-law died, leaving to Anne, his only surviving child, the greater part of his immense wealth.[2]

This legacy is important, not merely as laying the foundation of the fortunes of the house of Osborne, but as first establishing the connection between it and the part of England with which for more than three centuries it was to be intimately associated. Although his family had long been seated in Derbyshire, William Hewett was himself a native of Wales, a hamlet in the extreme

[1] In 1562, when the bride was about eighteen years old. The story of the events leading to the marriage rests on the authority of John Strype, who obtained it, according to his own account, through the Rev. John Hewyt from the first Duke of Leeds himself, and embodied it in his edition of Stow's *Survey of London* (ed. 1720, ii. 133). At a later date, Hewett's house was certainly in Philpot Lane.

[2] Sir William Hewett's will, dated January 3, 1567, is printed in *North Country Wills* (Surtees Society), ii. 46.

south of the West Riding of Yorkshire. From there he had migrated at an early age to make his fortune in London ; but although he amassed an estate estimated at £6,000 a year, filled the highest offices in the City, became Lord Mayor in October 1559, and received the honour of knighthood from Queen Elizabeth herself, he never lost interest in the place of his birth. Much of his wealth was expended in purchasing lands at Wales and in the neighbouring parish of Harthill, all of which on his death passed into the keeping of his daughter and her husband.

Edward Osborne, however, was little disposed to retire, as he might have done, from the world of commerce, and live the life of a country gentleman on his Yorkshire estates. At least as early as 1554 he had been admitted to the freedom of the Clothworkers' Company, and since then he had built up for himself a considerable reputation as a merchant. On the death of his father-in-law he succeeded not only to his estates, but also to his business, which he proceeded to develop and extend. Scarcely an important commercial venture was launched in the reign of Elizabeth without his participation. He was deeply interested in the trade with Spain and the Mediterranean, and on the Turkey Company, largely as a result of his exertions, obtaining its charter, he became its first governor. It was his ambition to extend his commercial activities as far as the East Indies, and when Ralph Fitch and his fellows undertook the exploration of the overland routes which started from the seaports of Syria he was largely responsible for providing the necessary financial support.

In the affairs of the City of London he was equally prominent. Alderman in 1573, he became Sheriff in 1575, and Lord Mayor eight years later. During his period of office in the last capacity he received the honour of knighthood at Westminster.[1] In national affairs, however, he played a small part. The only Parliament in which he served was that of 1586,[2] and he does not appear at any time to have held office under the Crown.

By his first wife, who predeceased him in July 1585,[3] he had a

---

[1] On February 2, 1584 (W. A. Shaw, *Knights of England*, ii. 82).

[2] For London City (*Return of Members of Parliament*, i. 418).

[3] Buried at St. Martin Orgar, July 14 (*Register Book of St. Dionis Backchurch*, Harleian Society, p. 199).

numerous family. Two sons, the elder appropriately named
Hewett [1] and the younger Edward,[2] were born in 1567 and
1572. Of three daughters Alice, goddaughter of Sir William
Hewett, was born in 1563,[3] Anne in 1570 [4] and Jane in 1578.[5]
A second marriage, however, with Margaret Chapman, of St.
Olave's, Southwark, proved fruitless, Osborne himself dying
only three years later in 1592.[6]

Of Sir Edward's son and successor, Hewett, singularly little is
known. Embarking on a military career, he served, it is said
with some distinction, under Lord Willoughby in France and
under the Earl of Essex in Ireland. By the latter he was
knighted at Maynooth on July 24, 1599 [7]; but a month later
he was slain in battle when only thirty-two years of age. During
his father's lifetime he had married Joyce, daughter of Thomas
Fleetwood, of the Vache, Buckinghamshire, by whom he had
had four children, Hewett, who died in infancy ; Edward, his
successor ; another son, William ; and a daughter, Alice.[8]

Throughout these years the Yorkshire estates of the family
had been somewhat neglected. Sir Edward Osborne the Lord
Mayor had found Harthill too far from London for his purposes,
and had made his country seat at Parsloes in Essex, another of
the estates which he had inherited from his father-in-law. Sir
Hewett Osborne had also preferred Parsloes, and in any case
was so frequently out of England as to be unable to devote
much attention to any of his estates. Sir Hewett's son Edward,

[1] Baptised March 13, 1567 (*Register Book of St. Dionis Backchurch*, p. 80).

[2] Born November 27, baptised November 30, 1572 (*ibid.*, p. 82).

[3] Baptised March 4, 1563 ; married June 29, 1580, to John Peyton, of
Isleham, Cambridgeshire (*ibid.*, pp. 9, 79).

[4] Baptised March 25, 1570 ; married February 3, 1589, to Robert Offley,
haberdasher, of London (*ibid.*, pp. 11, 81).

[5] Baptised November 9, 1578 (*ibid.*, p. 83).

[6] The marriage took place on September 15, 1588 ; Sir Edward was buried
on February 15, 1592. His widow married, on April 10, 1592, Robert Clarke,
Baron of the Exchequer, but died without issue by him, and was buried on
May 20, 1602 (*ibid.*, pp. 11, 12, 201, 206).

[7] Shaw, *Knights of England*, ii. 96.

[8] Alice was born January 5 and baptised January 15, 1593, at Isleham ;
Hewett was baptised August 23, 1594, at St. Giles, Cripplegate ; William was
baptised February 20, 1599, at Dagenham, Essex (Foster, *Pedigrees of York-
shire Families*, vol. ii. ; Collins's *Peerage*, ed. 1812, i. 254). An abstract of
Sir Hewett Osborne's will, dated March 28, 1599, is printed in *North Country
Wills*, ii. 224.

however, was destined to be associated with Yorkshire almost from the cradle to the grave. At the time of his father's death he was not yet three years old, having been born in London towards the close of 1596.[1] His mother apparently preferred her Yorkshire residence, and in 1604 made her connection with the north permanent by marrying as her second husband Sir Peter Frescheville of Staveley. Although in Derbyshire, Staveley lies only some seven miles from Harthill, and it was in this district accordingly that Edward passed his early years, in the company of his sister Alice and his mother's children by her second marriage.

Thus it was inevitable that as he grew to manhood he should find himself taking his place in the ranks of the Yorkshire gentry. London and commerce meant little or nothing to him. Scarcely had he attained his majority when, in February 1619, he sold Parsloes to the Fanshawe family and used the funds so obtained to extend his possessions in the parish of Harthill. During the reign of Henry VIII Nicholas Kiveton had sold the estate from which he took his name to William Hewett, through whom it had passed to the Osbornes. To this were now added the mansion and lands at Kiveton owned by Anthony Eyre.[2] On the enlarged estate Osborne established his principal seat, and it was as Sir Edward Osborne of Kiveton that he was created a baronet on July 13, 1620.[3]

In the local politics of Yorkshire the Osbornes were without traditional alliances, and their outlook was largely determined by the marriages which they contracted. Sir Edward himself, by his marriage on October 13, 1618, to Margaret, daughter of Sir Thomas Belasyse, later Viscount Fauconberg, formed a connection with the Fairfaxes, the Darcys, and other important families of the north ; but after bearing him an only son, who received the name of Edward, the first Lady Osborne died on November 7, 1624. More significant was the marriage of Sir Edward's sister Alice, on September 22, 1614, to Christopher Wandesford of Kirklington, the life-long friend and associate

[1] Baptised December 12, 1596, at St. Benet's, Gracechurch, London (G.E.C., *Complete Baronetage*, i. 153).

[2] J. Hunter, *South Yorkshire*, i. 142.

[3] *Cal. S.P. Dom.*, 1619-23, p. 161 ; *Complete Peerage*, vii. 507.

of Sir Thomas Wentworth, later Earl of Strafford. As Sir Peter Frescheville had long been on friendly terms with the Wentworths,[1] and as their seat at Wentworth Woodhouse was only a few miles from Kiveton, Sir Thomas Wentworth and Sir Edward Osborne were presumably well acquainted already ; but this marriage established between them a closer intimacy, which was to prove the chief determining factor in Sir Edward's career.[2] Before his dramatic fall Strafford was to have one of the brothers-in-law acting as his representative in the government of Ireland and the other serving him as deputy in the north of England.

From the very beginning, however, the Osbornes, like so many of the great families of City origin, were thorough loyalists, and with the earlier part of Wentworth's career, in which his zeal for efficient government drove him temporarily into opposition to the Court, Sir Edward had little connection. The death of his wife had left him almost entirely free from domestic ties, and had induced a restlessness for which foreign travel seemed the appropriate cure. Immediately after the accession of Charles I, accordingly, he obtained permission to reside abroad for three years, and in July 1625 left the country.[3] The quarrel between King and Parliament thus grew to a head during his absence and without his participation on either side. That he was regarded with some favour at Court may be assumed from his appointment as Sheriff of Nottinghamshire in the November following his departure from England [4] ; but the appointment itself came to nothing, as in his continued absence another Sheriff had to be chosen in his place.[5]

---

[1] He was godfather to William, younger brother of Sir Thomas (*Strafford Letters*, i. 1).

[2] The *Strafford Letters* contain evidence of a long and intimate correspondence between them. Unfortunately few of their letters to each other are printed (vol. i., pp. 19, 81 ; vol. ii., pp. 193, 232, 281).

[3] *Cal. S.P. Dom.*, 1625-6, pp. 55, 160. Nothing whatever is known of his travels.

[4] It seems impossible to connect this appointment with the King's policy of getting rid of his parliamentary opponents by creating them sheriffs. Sir Edward was assessed at £25 for the forced loan of 1626, and his name appears on a contemporary list of those who failed to pay. The reason given, however, is his absence from the country (J. J. Cartwright, *Chapters in the History of Yorkshire*, p. 234).

[5] Hist. MSS. Com., *Cowper MSS.*, i. 236.

His first incursion into the political arena was in consequence postponed until 1628, when he was returned to Charles I's third Parliament as member for East Retford.[1] But in the events of the tempestuous sessions which followed he played little part. His name does not appear among the speakers on either side in the debates and negotiations which led eventually to the Petition of Right. Anxious, presumably, not to quarrel with Wentworth and Wandesford, who were among the foremost advocates of the reforms demanded by the Commons, and yet unwilling to appear in opposition to the King, he thought it best to remain discreetly in the background.

Fortunately the conflicting interests which he had to consider were already on the point of being reconciled, and a more congenial sphere of activity than the House of Commons was about to be opened up to him. Towards the close of 1628 Wentworth, who had become alarmed at the growth of Puritanism, and at the claims of some members of the parliamentary opposition to practical control over the executive, boldly threw in his lot with the King, and was created first Baron and then Viscount Wentworth. One of the most serious problems which confronted Charles was that of enforcing law and order in the turbulent districts beyond the Humber, and the determination and ability of his new supporter, as well as his acquaintance with the Yorkshire gentry, marked him out for the task. On December 15, accordingly, he was created Lord President of the Council in the North, and in June of the following year secured the appointment of Sir Edward Osborne as a member of the Council.[2]

Sir Edward's elevation was followed almost immediately by his second marriage, to Anne, widow of William Middleton of Stockeld, Yorkshire, and a descendant, though not a representative, of the family of Danvers and of the Nevills Lords Latimer.[3] Early in the morning of February 20, 1632, Anne's

---

[1] *Return of Members of Parliament*, i. 477.

[2] R. R. Reid, *The King's Council in the North*, pp. 406, 498.

[3] The new Lady Osborne's ancestry is important as explaining the titles later borne by her son. Her father was Thomas Walmesley, of Dunkenhalgh, Lancashire. Her mother, whose rights did not descend to her, was Eleanor, third daughter of Sir John Danvers and sister of Henry, Earl of Danby. Eleanor's mother in turn was Elizabeth, fourth daughter and coheiress of John Nevill, fourth and last Baron Latimer. *Cf.* Danvers pedigree in the *Letters of Dorothy Osborne*, ed. G. C. Moore Smith, p. 321.

first child, the future Duke of Leeds, was born, and was called Thomas after his maternal grandfather.[1] Next year followed another son, Charles, and later a daughter, Joyce, who died in infancy.[2]

During their earliest years Sir Edward's children appear to have spent the greater part of their time at Kiveton, or on the neighbouring estate of Thorpe-Salvin, which Sir Edward purchased from the Sandford family in 1636.[3] But as the reign of Charles I progressed, circumstances made any prolonged period of residence in the country increasingly difficult for them. Early in 1632 Wentworth's success in England had induced the King to appoint him to the still more onerous post of Lord Deputy of Ireland. The Presidency of the Council in the North, however, was not taken away from him, and a Vice-President had therefore to be appointed to execute his functions in his name. This important post was conferred upon his supporter, Sir Edward Osborne, who, especially after the actual departure of Wentworth for Ireland in the summer of 1633, found himself practically confined by his duties to the President's official residence, the Manor House at York.[4]

As far as the younger Osbornes were concerned the disadvantages of staying in town were in some measure counterbalanced by the greater facilities for education which could there be enjoyed. Sir Edward was very anxious for the proper training of his children, and in particular had engaged a tutor whose chief function it was to give instruction in the French language both to Edward and to Thomas. The change of residence, however, was to prove the herald of tragedy. On the morning of October 31, 1638, as Edward and his tutor were

[1] The generally accepted date places his birth a year too early. For the correct date see B.M. Add. MSS. 28040, f. 65 ; *Portland MSS.*, v. 202 ; J. Aubrey, *Brief Lives*, ii. 105. The time is given precisely by Aubrey as 3.53 a.m. The baptism was on February 28 (*Bulletin of the Institute of Historical Research*, xi. 137).

[2] Died May 11, buried May 13, 1636, at St. Olave's, York (Foster, *Pedigrees of Yorkshire Families*, vol. ii.).

[3] Hunter, *South Yorkshire*, i. 143.

[4] Sir Edward removed with his family and belongings to the Manor House about Christmas, 1632 (*Strafford Letters*, i. 81). Kiveton was forty miles away, and though he visited it frequently his correspondence makes it clear that he was never long resident there while the Council in the North remained in existence. His family, however, may have been more fortunate.

engaged in their studies, a stack of chimneys was dislodged by a high wind, and the heavy masonry, crashing through the roof, killed Edward on the spot. Accident alone preserved the future Duke of Leeds from the same fate. Shortly beforehand he had been dispatched by his nurse to join his elder brother, but while he was passing through the great chamber a chance encounter with the family cat delayed his progress, and on search being made by the distracted household he was discovered with his pet hiding below the table.[1]

Before he had reached his seventh birthday Thomas Osborne had thus become the heir of his house and the chief object of his father's care. Nevertheless he passed a troubled and somewhat neglected boyhood. Already in the summer of 1638 alarming rumours of disaffection in Scotland had begun to spread abroad, and the Yorkshire militia had been ordered to hold itself in readiness. During 1639 and 1640 the entire north was thrown into a turmoil by the Bishops' Wars. Sir Edward Osborne was incessantly occupied in endeavouring to provide men, supplies and quarters for the English armies which were being mustered near the Border, and had no time to devote to the care of his own family. Not merely was his work extremely exacting in itself, but it involved him in a host of petty troubles of the most exasperating kind. In civil affairs he was Wentworth's representative, and as Vice-President of the Council in the North ruled with almost despotic authority in his name. But in military matters he was only one of many deputy lieutenants, all of whom claimed to be invested with equal authority by Wentworth as Lord Lieutenant of Yorkshire. Of this the opponents of the Court and those who were jealous of the pre-eminence assigned to him took full advantage, questioning every step he made and endeavouring to bring business as far as possible to a standstill.[2]

[1] J. le Neve, *Lives and Characters of the most illustrious Persons who died in the year* 1712, pp. 20-21 ; *Strafford Letters*, ii. 231, 232 ; *Diary of Ralph Thoresby*, i. 406-7, ii. 108-9 ; *Diary of Sir Henry Slingsby*, pp. 1-2, where a very favourable account of Edward Osborne is given. He was buried on November 1 in York Minster. The Manor House was so badly wrecked that for some months it was practically uninhabitable.

[2] Details of these rather wearisome intrigues can be found scattered through the *Calendar of State Papers Domestic*, the *Strafford Letters*, and the *Fairfax Correspondence*.

Among the most obstinate contemners of his authority were Sir John Hotham and Sir William Savile, to both of whom Wentworth dispatched strong remonstrances on their conduct. But no amount of remonstrance could obscure the fact that Osborne was being called upon to fill a position to which he had been given no legal title, and a proposal was accordingly made that Lord Clifford, who was Lord Lieutenant of Northumberland, Cumberland and Westmorland, should be associated with Wentworth in a special commission for raising levies in the north. As this would have meant that Lord Clifford, being on the spot, would have superseded both Wentworth and Osborne, it received the support of all the discontented elements in Yorkshire ; but Wentworth protested so strongly to the King that the whole project was dropped, the military administration of Yorkshire was left entirely in his hands, and he was authorised to issue a commission to his Vice-President, making him his representative in this sphere also, with the title of Deputy-Lieutenant-General.[1]

This increase in power and dignity marks the highest point to which Sir Edward Osborne was to attain. For some months he was practically supreme throughout Yorkshire. But the duties and responsibilities involved, especially during the spring of 1639, when the King himself was in the north, were absolutely overwhelming. Discontent and disaffection confronted him on every side ; his own subordinates could not be relied upon ; the civil and military machinery which he was called upon to operate was rusty and out-of-date ; above all, money was always lacking. Even the settlement with the Scots effected in the Treaty of Berwick brought no relief, for it was almost immediately apparent that little regard was going to be paid to it, and during the winter of 1639-40 he was as busy as ever, preparing for the operations of the following summer.[2]

By that time he had come to be regarded as indispensable.

---

[1] Wentworth's letter enclosing the commission is dated Dublin, February 10, 1639 (*Strafford Letters*, ii. 281). *Cf.* Wentworth's letter to the deputy lieutenants (*ibid.*, p. 284).

[2] Much information about his activities can be obtained from his own letters to the Secretaries of State and others, which are preserved in the Public Record Office and among the Cowper MSS. at Melbourne Hall (Hist. MSS. Com., *Cowper MSS.*, vols. i. ii.).

When Charles in the spring of 1640 so far capitulated to his people as to summon what became known as the Short Parliament, he was chosen, upon Strafford's recommendation, as one of the members for the city of York ; [1] but scarcely had he reached Kiveton on his road south to London when he was met by an express from Secretary Vane commanding him to return to York and resume his duties there.[2] Upon the other local officials, however, no similar commands were laid, and Sir Edward, deprived of the help of many colonels and deputy lieutenants who were attending Parliament, found the burden imposed upon him heavier than ever.

It is significant of the change in the temper of the country which took place during the summer of 1640, that when Charles in the autumn summoned another Parliament, and Sir Edward once more sought election at York, the mere fact that he was Strafford's representative and had Strafford's recommendation earned him an unhesitating refusal.[3] Many of the smaller boroughs, however, were more open to influence, and a few days later Strafford contrived to secure the return of his supporter for Berwick-on-Tweed.[4] But again the King's service came in the way. Sir Edward apparently was not allowed to leave the north, and in justice to his constituency felt it his duty to resign. On December 7, accordingly, his election was declared void and a new writ was issued, without, as far as can be ascertained, his having been present in Parliament at all.[5]

Nothing could have been more fortunate for him. Had Sir Edward attended Parliament he could scarcely in honour have refrained from doing his best to defend his patron from the attacks levelled against him, and had he appeared on behalf of Strafford he might very possibly have shared his fate. Even as things were his immunity is a matter for some surprise. But

---

[1] March 16, 1640 (*Return of Members of Parliament*, i. 484).

[2] *Cal. S.P. Dom.*, 1640, p. 10; *Hist. MSS. Com.*, v. 331.

[3] *Cal. S.P. Dom.*, 1640-1, p. 158. Strafford himself was in York at the time.

[4] October 3, 1640 (*ibid.*, p. 258 ; *Return of Members of Parliament*, i. 491). Strafford's other candidate at York, Sir Thomas Widdrington, was returned along with him.

[5] *C.J.*, ii. 47 ; *Return of Members of Parliament*, i. 491.

the energies of the opposition were so completely concentrated upon effecting the ruin of Strafford that every grievance was laid at his door, and the convenient assumption was made that his Vice-President had been only his mouthpiece.[1] Moreover in the intricate local rivalries of Yorkshire, which did not a little to bring Strafford to the block, Osborne's position was by no means the same as that of his patron. It is not without significance that Strafford's most inveterate opponent, Lord Fauconberg, was Sir Edward's father-in-law, while Sir Edward's most jealous rival, Sir William Savile, was Strafford's own nephew.[2]

The fall and execution of Strafford, followed as they almost immediately were by the abolition of the Court and Council in the North, deprived Osborne of the exalted position which he had for some time occupied, and reduced him to the level of his fellows among the Yorkshire gentry. His duties, however, cannot have been greatly lightened. As a result of the presence of two hostile armies, one of them at least ill-organised and badly disciplined, the north had been thoroughly upset, and in his capacity of deputy lieutenant and justice of the peace he had to play his part in reducing it once more to order. Scarcely had that been partially accomplished when the outbreak of the Civil War made a new call upon his energies. For more than ten years he had been captain of one of the three militia troops supplied by the West Riding, and for a somewhat shorter time lieutenant-colonel of the horse of the whole county ; [3] but he had enjoyed no real military experience, and in his forty-sixth year was scarcely of an age to desire or take any part in active hostilities. Far from pressing on the conflict, he lent all his weight to the side of peace, and was one of the signatories of the Treaty of Rothwell, by which the opposing factions provided for a suspension of arms within Yorkshire. But on the collapse of

---

[1] The *Strafford Papers* make it fairly clear that Sir Edward was never really independent. The most arbitrary acts of the Council in the North belong also to the period before he was Vice-President.

[2] Sir William's father, Sir George Savile, had married Strafford's eldest sister Ann, and until his death in 1614 had been on very intimate terms with him. Strafford had been one of Sir William's guardians (H. C. Foxcroft, *Life of Halifax*, i. 6).

[3] B.M. Add. MSS. 28082, f. 80 ; 28094, f. 3.

this agreement his acknowledged administrative ability inevitably brought him to the fore, and serious trouble had scarcely begun when he was summoned to play his part in raising men and money to maintain the royalist cause. The Yorkshire Cavaliers, however, soon proved unable to withstand their fellow countrymen under Lord Fairfax, and had to appeal for assistance to the Earl of Newcastle, who had raised a large body of troops in the border counties. Towards the close of October 1642 Sir Edward Osborne was appointed a member of a small committee to arrange terms with the Earl, hastened north to join him at Newcastle, and then marched with him to the relief of York.[1] For nearly two years thereafter he was incessantly engaged in the administrative work of providing for Newcastle's army.

With the disastrous defeat of the Royalists at Marston Moor in 1644 that army ceased to exist, Newcastle fled to the Continent, and the whole north was rapidly overrun by the Parliamentarians and their Scottish allies. York itself capitulated on July 16. Many of the northern Royalists had drawn off after the battle with Rupert, and had gone to join the King in the south ; but for a civilian like Sir Edward Osborne there was little inducement to accompany the army, and as an older man he was loath to leave his home. Relying, as so many others did, on the kindness of his kinsman Lord Fairfax, he retired to Kiveton, and took no further part in the struggle. For the first time for six years, although in somewhat disastrous circumstances, he was at leisure to attend to his own family and affairs.

What had been happening during that strenuous period to his son and heir, where he had been living and how he had been educated, are matters for conjecture. At the time of the unhappy accident at York Manor the French tutor had contrived to escape by clinging to a window out of which he happened to be looking ; but soon afterwards he must have retired to some less perilous post, for nothing more is heard of him. Many years later, when writing to the Corporation of the city, Thomas Osborne, then Lord Latimer, referred with some affection to

---

[1] *Memoirs of the Duke of Newcastle*, ed. Firth, p. 191 ; *Portland MSS.*, i. 70.

York as " the place of my education," [1] and the probability is
that he lived with his father at the Manor House and was either
educated at home or attended the ancient grammar school of
St. Peter, which in spite of its intimate association with the
cathedral church continued to perform its functions, under its
master, Christopher Wallis, right through the period of the
Civil War and Commonwealth.[2] If the latter supposition is
correct, one may credit Wallis with that clear and regular handwriting, that lucid and forceful style of expression, which make
the Earl of Danby's letters even at the present day a pleasure
to read. But the loss of the French tutor was never to be
entirely repaired. Throughout his official career Danby
exhibited an unfamiliarity with the French language scarcely
to be expected in a statesman of the seventeenth century.[3]

That his education was seriously defective can hardly
occasion surprise. York during the course of the Civil War was
no place in which to invoke the arts and sciences, and if young
Thomas, as seems probable, retired with his parents to Kiveton
in 1644, even the training he was receiving there must have
come to an abrupt conclusion when he was twelve years of age.
Sir Edward Osborne was scarcely in a position to provide edu-
cational advantages for his sons. Shortly after Marston Moor
his personal property was sequestered by the county committee,
his corn and cattle were sold, and he was reduced to living at
Thorpe-Salvin on the fraction of his former income reserved by
parliamentary ordinance for the support of the wife and
children of delinquents. Even his person was not safe. In the
autumn of 1644 he obtained a formal protection from Lord
Fairfax on condition of his giving no further cause of offence to

[1] Latimer to the Mayor and Corporation of York, September 6, 1673 (*infra*,
ii. 41).

[2] *Victoria County History, Yorkshire*, i. 423. Wallis was appointed in 1637,
just before the accident at the Manor House, and in 1639 became also
Rector of Harthill. It would have been quite natural, therefore, for Sir
Edward Osborne to entrust the care of his children to him. In October 1641,
however, Sir Edward settled upon a certain Mr. Rushton an annuity of £30 in
return for his services in the education of the children, and this annuity was
still being paid in 1646 (J. W. Clay, *Yorkshire Royalist Composition Papers*,
ii. 159).

[3] He could almost certainly read and speak French, but he appears never to
have written it. Even his earliest letters to William of Orange, written while
he was still on the most distant terms with the Prince, are in English.

the existing Government ; but on at least one occasion thereafter he was informed that a warrant had been issued for his
arrest, and deemed it prudent to go into hiding, thus bringing
down on his unfortunate wife the suspicion of the neighbouring
soldiery, who threatened her with a plundering raid.[1] On the
mind of young Thomas the hardships of these months must have
made an indelible impression, which was to be responsible many
years later for a rancorous hatred of everything associated with
Puritanism and the parliamentary cause.

In the autumn of 1645 the position was somewhat eased by
the issue to delinquents of a general permission to compound
for their estates, of which Sir Edward immediately endeavoured
to take advantage. One condition, however, was that the
delinquent should first take the Covenant and the Negative
Oath, by which he promised never again to bear arms against
Parliament, and Sir Edward's petition of November 29 was
accordingly respited until he could produce evidence that he
had fulfilled this requirement. Unlike many Royalists he
immediately complied, taking both Oath and Covenant on
December 4, but even then it was more than a year before a
settlement was reached. On March 30, 1647, the value of his
estate previous to the outbreak of the war was finally assessed
at £16,490, and his fine was fixed at the moderate proportion of
one tenth. The sum of £649 was to be paid immediately in the
customary two instalments, but the remainder was to be
remitted on condition that out of the rectory of Seaton Ross,
which was in his hands, the sum of £100 a year should be settled
on the church there.[2]

Even on these terms Sir Edward was unable to secure the
restoration of all his property. In the North Riding his own
tenant, Ralph Rymer, having come into possession of lands at
Yafforth and Wickmore of which he had a lease, refused to give
them up, and being one of the receivers of compositions employed by the Government was sufficiently influential to be able

---

[1] Lady Osborne to Lord Fairfax, April 23, 1645 (*Fairfax Correspondence,
Civil War*, i. 199).

[2] *Calendar of the Committee for Compounding*, p. 1027. The formal ordinance pardoning his delinquency and taking off the sequestration of his estate
passed the Commons only on August 26 and the Lords on September 8, 1648
(*C.J.*, v. 683 ; *L.J.*, x. 493).

to persist in his attitude.[1]   Lands and property elsewhere were no doubt lost in much the same manner.[2]   The recovery of the remainder was the last important act of Sir Edward's life. For ten years or more he had known little rest, and his constitution had been undermined by incessant work and anxiety.   On September 9, 1647, he died at Thorpe-Salvin,[3] in his fifty-first year, and was buried in the church at Harthill, where his widow erected a monument in his memory.[4]

[1] *Cal. S.P. Dom.*, 1663-4, p. 117.

[2] Nearly thirty years later it was stated in the House of Commons that Sir Edward's losses amounted to £1,000 per annum (*Grey*, iii. 93).   This, however, is probably a gross exaggeration, as his entire estate was valued in 1646 at about £970 per annum, made up as follows : Lands in Kiveton, Harthill, Woodhall, Tretton, Thorpe-Salvin, Wales and Anstan, £318 ; manor and lands of Seaton Ross, settled by him on his wife at the time of their marriage, £260 ;   rectory of Seaton Ross, £100 ; lands in Yafforth and Wickmore, his wife's jointure by her first husband, £293 (Clay, *Yorkshire Royalist Composition Papers*, ii. 159).

[3] According to one account, of a surfeit of melons (*Autobiography of Alice Thornton*, Surtees Society, p. 54).

[4] The inscription is printed in Hunter, *South Yorkshire*, i. 146.

CHAPTER II

YORKSHIRE POLITICS, 1647-65

IT is perhaps not altogether fanciful to find in the immediate ancestry of Sir Thomas Osborne an explanation of the part which he was to play during the course of his own life. To his father he certainly owed his general political outlook, and his interest in local if not in national affairs. From his grandfather he may have derived that military capacity, slight no doubt, which yet enabled him to play with credit his part as an officer in the militia and as leader of the northern insurrection against James II. To his great-grandfather may with more confidence be traced the business ability and command of figures which raised him twice to the highest position in the state, and secured for him a distinguished place among those to whom the control of his country's finances has been entrusted.

In 1647, however, there was little suggestion of what the future held in store. At the age of fifteen Sir Thomas found himself fatherless and largely friendless, in possession of an impoverished and encumbered estate, and regarded with suspicion by the existing Government. Having been debarred by his youth from taking any part in the Civil War, he had formed no associations with the Cavaliers of his father's generation, many of whom were already drifting abroad; and yet there appeared to be no place for him at home. Too old to return to school, he was too young to enter any of the professions open to a man of his rank, and too stout a Royalist to be attracted to either of the universities, where the reforming activities of the Puritans were then reaching their height.

For more than a year he remained quietly in Yorkshire, hoping for better times, while the details of his inheritance, somewhat complicated by the fact that his father had died intestate, were adjusted between his mother, himself, and the

Government. The principal difficulty was caused by the annual payment to Seaton Ross Church, for the parsonage was part of Lady Osborne's jointure, and she not unnaturally argued that the burden should fall on the estate as a whole, and not on her own particular portion of it. A fresh order, dated January 4, 1649, had accordingly to be issued requiring her, during her son's minority, to continue the payment, in the form of £50 to Seaton Ross Church and £50 to Gunthwaite Chapel. But even then trouble continued to arise, and in the end the whole arrangement had to be abandoned. The £1,000 originally re-mitted to Sir Edward Osborne was exacted from the estate, and this sum was handed over to trustees as an endowment from which the annual payment to the churches could be made.[1]

Long before this conclusion was reached, however, the failure of the Royalists in the second Civil War, followed by the trial and execution of the King, had convinced Sir Thomas Osborne of the impossibility of any rapid reversal of fortune, and early in 1649 he determined to follow the prevailing fashion, and complete his education by a lengthy period of travel on the Continent. Of this tour, unfortunately, practically nothing is known. In April 1649 Sir Thomas was at Rouen.[2] For some time during his travels in France he was accompanied by William Temple, upon whose friendship and diplomatic ability he was later to place such reliance.[3] It appears practically certain that he visited Italy and Rome ;[4] but by the autumn of 1650 he was back in Paris, living on intimate terms with John Evelyn and other Royalist exiles whom he met at the house of

---

[1] *Calendar of the Committee for Compounding*, pp. 1027-8. A final settlement was not reached until April 19, 1654.

[2] *Hist. MSS. Com.*, vii. 457.

[3] T. P. Courtenay, *Memoirs of Sir William Temple*, i. 423. When it is remembered that Sir Thomas was only seventeen or eighteen years of age it can scarcely be imagined that he set out on his travels alone. Temple, who was nearly four years his senior, was also touring Europe, and they may very possibly have joined forces at an early stage. Unfortunately Temple's move-ments are themselves involved in complete obscurity.

[4] See the sheet headed, " As to religion," in B.M. Add. MSS. 28043, f. 35 : " with that aversion as not to bee gott once to the curiosity of seeing the Pope himselfe att mass." In the British Museum copy of the first edition of Sir John Reresby's *Memoirs* there is also a manuscript note, " The Duke of Leeds got a great illness by his Italian travell." The references cannot apply to any period but this.

Sir Richard Browne, father-in-law of the diarist and ambassador of Charles II to the French court. On November 8, 1650, he left Paris for England, never again during his long life of eighty years to set foot outside his native land.[1]

His return home, as well as the approach of his majority, naturally raised the problem of his marriage, and Lady Osborne, in accordance with the custom of the day, endeavoured to find him a suitable wife. Her first choice fell upon her own cousin, Dorothy Osborne,[2] with whose brother Henry she entered into negotiations on February 6, 1652.[3] During March Sir Thomas himself was in London making " formall adresses " to Dorothy, though, one must suspect, without much enthusiasm.[4] On April 8 Lady Osborne broke off the match. Relations between the parties were thereafter somewhat strained ; but no permanent ill-feeling resulted.[5] Smallpox had just broken out at the house of Sir Thomas Peyton, with whom Dorothy was staying, and in the midst of the alarm which this occasioned other matters passed almost unnoticed. Sir Thomas Osborne himself had the misfortune to contract the disease,[6] in a form sufficiently severe to affect him for the rest of his life. To the after-effects of his sickness at this time may almost certainly be ascribed those curious bodily infirmities which later excited

[1] *Evelyn*, October 15, November 6, 1650 ; June 19, 1673.

[2] As has frequently been pointed out the relationship between Sir Thomas and Dorothy Osborne was not on the Osborne but on the Danvers side. Dorothy's mother, Dorothy Danvers, was a younger sister of Eleanor, the mother of Lady Osborne.

[3] *Diary of Henry Osborne* under that date. Extracts from this *Diary* have been printed by G. C. Moore Smith in the *Times Literary Supplement*, 1920, p. 616, in *Notes and Queries*, 12th series, vol. vii., and in his *Letters of Dorothy Osborne*.

[4] According to Dorothy Osborne it was Sir Thomas himself who took the initiative in this affair (*Letters of Dorothy Osborne*, p. 7) ; but even she does not suggest that he pressed his suit with any vigour, and the facts of the case as well as the entries in her brother's *Diary* render it highly improbable that he was following his own choice. While he was barely twenty years of age she was nearly twenty-five. Moreover it is quite possible that he was aware of the understanding she already had with his friend William Temple, whom she was eventually to marry.

[5] *Letters of Dorothy Osborne*, pp. 7, 49. There appears to have been more than one good story connected with this curious tangle, but while Henry Osborne sent a full account to his Aunt Gargrave, and Dorothy retailed it all to Temple, they have both unfortunately proved more reticent with posterity.

[6] On April 10 (*Notes and Queries*, 12th series, vii. 304).

the ill-natured mirth of his opponents and proved a constant handicap when he had risen to eminence.

As her next choice Lady Osborne turned to Lady Bridget Bertie, second daughter of the Royalist leader Montague, Earl of Lindsey. Of the negotiations on which she embarked no record can be found, but it seems probable that Sir Thomas had begun his new suit as early as January 1653, and the marriage itself took place on May 1 of the same year, at Rycote, the Oxfordshire seat which the Earl of Lindsey had acquired by his own second marriage.[1] To contemporaries the match seemed to be dictated by interest rather than by sentiment, and it was certainly to prove of considerable assistance in promoting the fortunes of the bridegroom. While the Osbornes were a family of comparatively recent origin, with few immediate connections even among the gentry of the north, the Berties were allied to half the noble houses of England. The Earl of Lindsey had been twice married, to Martha, daughter of Sir William Cockaine of Rushton, and to Bridget, daughter and sole heir of Edward Wray, by Lady Elizabeth Norris, daughter and sole heir of Francis, Earl of Berkshire. Lady Bridget Bertie, a child of the first marriage, had eight brothers and three sisters, who by their own marriages, and later by the marriages of their children, were to provide Sir Thomas Osborne with an ever increasing band of influential relatives. Her father could procure him immediate admission to social circles in which by himself he would scarcely have ventured to appear.

Yet in spite of the fact that the bride was somewhat older than the bridegroom [2] the marriage was destined to be as happy [3] as

---

[1] Note in the Duke of Leeds's handwriting in Leeds MSS. ; *Letters of Dorothy Osborne*, pp. 4, 41.

[2] Lady Bridget was baptised on June 6, 1629 (*Complete Peerage*, vii. 509).

[3] In this connection Dorothy Osborne's remark has been too often repeated, " that nothing tempted my cousin O[sborne] to marry his lady (soe much) as that shee was an earl's daughter " (*Letters of Dorothy Osborne*, p. 97). In view of the fact that she had once been nearly engaged to Sir Thomas herself, and that the match had been broken off from Sir Thomas's side, it is impossible to regard Dorothy as providing reliable evidence on this point ; but in any case she gives the comment only as what she has heard from some one else, and appears to lay little stress upon it. Lady Bridget Osborne had many peculiarities, which her husband's enemies were quick to seize and use against him ; but the fragments of their correspondence printed in the second volume of this work show that their relations remained affectionate to the end.

it unquestionably proved fruitful. Of the three sons and eight daughters with whom it was blessed, the eldest, born probably at Thorpe-Salvin in 1654, was named Edward after his paternal grandfather.[1] In the following year was born another son, Thomas, who however died in infancy.[2] Next came two daughters, Elizabeth [3] and Anne ; [4] while immediately before the Restoration appeared the third son and eventual heir,[5] called Peregrine after his mother's great-grandfather, the famous Lord Willoughby of Elizabeth's reign.

From the care of this growing family Sir Thomas had little to distract his attention. Excluded from all participation in local or national affairs, he spent his time looking after his domestic concerns, administering his estates, visiting the country seats of his friends and relatives, and taking occasional trips to London.[6] During these years of waiting, however, he must have made the acquaintance not only of his wife's connections but of many of the northern nobility and gentry with whom he was afterwards to be closely associated. Sir George Savile, later Marquis of Halifax, the son of his father's old rival, was sufficiently friendly to stand godfather to one of his daughters.[7] Henry Cavendish, Lord Mansfield,[8] who was to

[1] The exact date of Edward's birth is uncertain, but there is a letter amongst the Leeds MSS. (Packet 5), written by P[eregrine] B[ertie] from the Camp before Arras to Lady Bridget Osborne at Thorpe-Salvin, and dated 1654, which concludes, " Remember me to Sir Thomas and little Ned and all our friends at Thorpe-Salvin."

[2] Born at Thorpe-Salvin, March 26, 1655, and baptised there April 5 (Foster, *Pedigrees of Yorkshire Families*, vol. ii.).

[3] Born October 21, 1656 (*ibid.*).   [4] Born December 28, 1657 (*ibid.*).

[5] Baptised at Harthill, December 29, 1659 (*ibid.*).

[6] His name frequently appears in such connections in Henry Osborne's *Diary*, but the individual entries have no particular significance. The best picture of the life which he and his fellows were leading is to be found in Dorothy Osborne's *Letters*. That he was not regarded as an irreconcilable opponent of the Government is shown by the grant to him from Cromwell of a fortnightly fair at Seaton, dated September 8, 1656 (*Leeds MSS.*, p. 41).

[7] Sir George Savile to Sir Thomas Osborne, July 20, 1667, printed in Foxcroft, *Halifax*, i. 52. Could the daughter be identified some indication would be obtained how early this friendship began. The two baronets were certainly on intimate terms by June 1661 (Sir Thomas to Lady Osborne, June 1, *infra*, ii. 8).

[8] He preferred to be known as Lord Ogle, a title which came to him from his grandmother. Welbeck Abbey, the Nottinghamshire seat of the family, is only six or seven miles from Kiveton.

become Duke of Newcastle in 1676, began at this time an intimate correspondence with him which he continued for thirty years.   More important than either of these was George Villiers, Duke of Buckingham, whose patronage was to form the chief determining factor in Sir Thomas's rise to eminence.   In 1657 Buckingham, tiring of exile, had returned to England, and had married Mary, only child of Lord Fairfax, to whom Parliament had granted much of the Villiers property in Yorkshire and elsewhere.   Since early in 1659 he had been living quietly with his wife at Nun Appleton, the home of his father-in-law, and had formed a natural centre of attraction for all the younger members of the Yorkshire gentry.   When his connection with Osborne commenced is not clear, but it is at least as likely to have begun before the Restoration as after it.

Thus the proclamation of Charles II on May 8, 1660, found Sir Thomas not ill prepared to take advantage of changed conditions.   For such men as himself the Restoration meant a complete reversal of fortune.   The governed suddenly became the governors, and with fifteen years of pillage, insult and oppression fresh in their minds were not slow in seeking reparation and revenge.   Osborne had fewer injuries to remember than many of his fellows.   No near relative of his had been executed, or even slain in battle ; he had never been reduced to absolute penury ; the fine imposed upon his father had been moderate in amount.   Nevertheless a considerable amount of Osborne property had been compulsorily alienated, which he hoped might now be restored ; while he confidently expected the share in the dignity and emoluments of office to which he considered his rank entitled him.

In the spring of 1660, accordingly, he hastened with thousands of other Cavaliers to London, to wait upon his sovereign and join in the general scramble for place and favour which immediately broke out.   A few months were sufficient to show him the vanity of most of his hopes.   Faced with the tremendous task of deciding conflicting claims to half the land in England the predominantly Presbyterian Convention which had recalled the King adopted a policy of compromise.   The lands of the King, the Church and certain Royalist magnates, as well as all lands which had been confiscated by the revolutionary

Governments, were required to be restored ; but where land had been sold by private bargain in order to pay a fine or finance the Royalist cause no redress was offered. On the whole this arrangement was highly satisfactory to the older Cavaliers and those who had gone into exile, but extremely unsatisfactory to the younger Cavaliers and those who had stayed at home. To Sir Thomas Osborne it gave nothing whatever.

Nor was the position much better as regards office under the Government. Buckingham, it is true, was immediately taken into favour. The Earl of Lindsey had his claim recognised to the post of Lord High Chamberlain, was admitted to the Privy Council, and was chosen a Knight of the Garter. But for every position to which Sir Thomas could advance any pretension there were at least half a dozen aspirants, and in the end he had to be content with what he could secure in Yorkshire itself. As his first Lord Lieutenant of the West Riding Charles selected the old Cavalier leader, Marmaduke, Lord Langdale, whose friendship twenty years earlier with Sir Edward Osborne induced him not merely to nominate Sir Thomas one of his deputies but to give him the command of the particular regiment of militia which he desired.[1] With the duties of these offices Osborne was kept sufficiently busy for the remainder of the year. In order that the army of the Commonwealth might be safely disbanded the militia had to be hastily organised ; the territorial settlement decreed by the Convention, involving a considerable redistribution of land, had to be put into force ; the ordinary administration of the county had to be provided for, and all this by officials the majority of whom were quite new to the positions they occupied. Not until the following year was Sir Thomas able to resume the prosecution of his claims.

Even then his interest in the north was insufficient to justify him in seeking election to the House of Commons ; but in the spring of 1661, when many of his neighbours were journeying south to take their place in the first regular Parliament of the

[1] F. H. Sunderland, *Marmaduke Lord Langdale*, pp. 223-9 ; Langdale to Sir George Wentworth, July 14, 1660, printed in Hunter, *South Yorkshire*, ii. 247. Osborne was a deputy lieutenant of the West Riding at least as early as January 25, 1661, when a view of arms was held by him in that capacity at Rotherham (B.M. Add. MSS. 28082, f. 15).

reign, he travelled up to London to put his fortune once more to the test. His immediate object was to recover the fine of £1,000 paid by the Osborne estate which had been converted into a permanent endowment for Seaton Ross Church and Gunthwaite Chapel. This sum had been seized by the Crown, and Sir Thomas not unnaturally considered that if it did not belong to the churches it ought to belong to himself or his mother. Legal advice, however, convinced him that while he might compel the Crown to restore the money to the churches he had no right to insist on its restoration to himself, and he accordingly began to consider the possibility of some accommodation with the King, by which the money might be shared between them.

How exactly the matter was determined cannot be discovered, but the negotiations connected with it had the advantage of bringing Osborne into personal touch with Charles and influential members of his Court, through whose favour some compensation for his losses might be obtained. A project for an advantageous farm of the Yorkshire Excise floated before his mind, somewhat nebulously, it is true, for as yet he confessed he knew little of such matters. Lord Ossory, eldest son of the Duke of Ormonde, was preparing to cross over to Dublin as lieutenant-general of the horse in the Irish army, and " some good peniworths in Ireland " were offered if he would join his train ; but to the practical exile which this implied he hesitated to condemn himself until at least he had consulted his wife. Meanwhile he was not above diverting his leisure by occupying a box at the theatre with Lady Dorothy Savile, although he repudiated all connection with the " vast gallantry " which he saw around him, and professed to be " more weary then ever of this towne." [1]

From this combination of business and pleasure he was recalled by a further increase in his family. On June 1, 1661, was born a third daughter, Bridget, who was followed at intervals of little more than a year by three others, Catherine,[2] Martha,[3] and Sophia.[4] To the family cares which this involved

---

[1] Sir Thomas to Lady Osborne, June 1, 1661, *infra*, ii. 8.
[2] Born June 20, 1662 (Foster, *Pedigrees of Yorkshire Families*, vol. ii.).
[3] Born October 10, 1663 (*ibid.*).
[4] Born March 23, 1665 (*ibid.*).

may be attributed the failure of Sir Thomas to accept the offers made to him in Ireland or to push with any vigour his fortunes in London. One achievement which he must have found particularly gratifying was the recovery of a sum of £346 from his father's old enemy Ralph Rymer ; [1] but this appears to have been the only recompense awarded him, and proved insufficient to encourage him to further efforts. For some years after the Restoration he hesitated to travel far or remain long from home, and his career during this period is connected in consequence almost entirely with local Yorkshire politics.

In this sphere his position was considerably improved by the death of Lord Langdale on August 5, 1661, and the appointment as his successor of the Duke of Buckingham. In spite of the favour which he had shown to Sir Thomas, Langdale was after all a Catholic, and belonged to an older generation. Buckingham, on the other hand, was just sufficiently Osborne's senior to be able gracefully to assume the lead, and was both more willing, and, owing to the influence which he had already established with the King, more able to advance him. In October the new Lord Lieutenant made his formal entry into his province,[2] and about the same time nominated his principal subordinates. Sir Thomas Osborne was continued in his former positions of deputy lieutenant, justice of the peace, and colonel of one of the foot regiments of the West Riding militia. In November, no doubt through the influence of Buckingham, he was appointed High Sheriff of Yorkshire for the ensuing year. On February 19, 1662, he and other prominent Yorkshiremen were united by letters patent in a commission for enforcing the recently passed Corporation Act throughout the county.[3]

These appointments were by no means purely honorary. It was the function of Osborne and his fellows to restore order and stability, and at the same time to secure the ascendancy in local affairs for the long neglected supporters of monarchy. In the discharge of their duties they had much open and still more secret hostility to face. Many irreconcilable republicans had

[1] *Cal. S.P. Dom.*, 1663-4, pp. 117, 133. Osborne's petition to the King on the subject is printed in full in T. D. Hardy, *Syllabus of Rymer's Foedera*, I.i.p. cxiii.

[2] Reresby's *Memoirs* (ed. 1875), p. 52, note.

[3] *Hist. MSS. Com.*, viii. 275.

always opposed the Restoration.   Others with more moderate views became alienated when they found that the Restoration meant practically proscription for themselves.   Inevitably the change injured many people—soldiers of the Commonwealth army, which was rapidly disbanded ; purchasers of Crown or Church lands, who had to surrender them without compensation ; ministers who were deprived of their livings ; officials who lost their posts.   From these and similar classes was built up a large discontented element which formed a serious danger to the peace of the country and which it was the chief business of the local officials to hold down.

In Yorkshire and the north discontent was specially strong, and Sir Thomas Osborne acquired a considerable reputation by his activity in suppressing it.   During his period of office as Sheriff of Yorkshire he had six informers in his pay, to whom he allowed £15 each " for intelligence among the old soldiers of the late disbanded army ; " and on this service he relied when petitioning, though unsuccessfully, for a renewal of his appointment as Sheriff at the close of 1662.[1]   When the trouble eventually came to a head in the autumn of 1663 his place lay with the militia, whom the Duke of Buckingham hastened north to bring into the field.   The general rendezvous was at Pontefract, where the bulk of the Yorkshire gentry gathered together, but his own particular regiment was summoned to meet at Doncaster, where no doubt he shared in the alarm caused by the abortive gathering of the conspirators at Farnley Wood, with which the danger practically came to an end.[2]

Thereafter he was incessantly occupied, as deputy lieutenant, in investigating the ramifications of the conspiracy, procuring the arrest of suspects, and preparing depositions for the special commission of judges who were sent down in the following January to try them.   The task was not a pleasant one. The *agent provocateur* had been busy, and it was freely declared that some of the accused had become involved in the plot " not soe much from inclination as persuasion of thos that evidenced

[1] *Cal. S.P. Dom.*, 1661-2, pp. 537-8.
[2] Sir Thomas Osborne to the Marquis of Newcastle, October 9, 1663, in *Portland MSS.*, ii. 144 ; *Reresby*, pp. 46-9 ; *Depositions from the Castle of York* (Surtees Society), p. 102 *et seq.* ; W. C. Abbott, " English Conspiracy and Dissent, 1660-1674," in *A.H.R.*, vol. xiv.

against them." Along with Ralph Rymer and even more
extreme supporters of Commonwealth ideals, for whom the
Royalist magistrates cannot be supposed to have had much
sympathy, were involved several men of standing in the county,
such as Sir John Hotham. But the Government determined
that it must have victims, and with this attitude Osborne was
in thorough agreement. Scarcely had the special commission
completed its labours when he made a formal representation to
the Government of the very unsatisfactory results. Several
suspects had not been examined at all ; others had not been
tried, and some had even been acquitted because of the lack of
two witnesses against them. Investigation was proceeding so
slowly that there was little prospect of more effective prosecutions, and the rebels were only being encouraged to persist in
their designs.[1]

Probably as a result of this representation stringent orders
were issued to Sir Thomas himself and the other deputy
lieutenants for a further investigation to prepare material for
the coming assizes.[2] These orders were zealously obeyed, but
with so little practical result that the deputy lieutenants felt
constrained to defend themselves by elaborating a point which
Osborne had already brought out. The more influential among
the conspirators, they declared, were able by persuasion and
bribes to keep the rest silent, and no rewards were offered to
informers sufficient to counteract this influence. The Government, however, proved unwilling to accept this view of the
matter, and about the middle of April the investigation came
to an end with some dissatisfaction on both sides.[3]

Nevertheless the complete failure of the plot and the execution
of a number of the malcontents had the effect of relieving somewhat the tension in the north, and Sir Thomas, whose children
were now emerging from infancy, began to dream of appearing

---

[1] Osborne's paper is printed *infra*, ii. 26. Although undated it clearly comes
after the special gaol delivery, which was in January 1664, and before the
assizes, which were in March. There are long accounts of the trials in Carte
MSS. 81, ff. 218-222.

[2] The orders are dated February 24, 1664 (*Cal. S.P. Dom.*, 1663-4, p. 493).

[3] The case of the deputy lieutenants, dated April 9, 1664, is printed *infra*,
ii. 27. Although signed by four of them it is entirely in Osborne's handwriting and was probably drawn up by him.

upon a wider stage. His recent activities had brought him prominently to the notice of the Government, which rewarded him by bestowing upon him a share in the estate which Ralph Rymer had possessed at Brafferton. He was granted a lease of the estate at the nominal rent of 20s. a year, redeemable on payment of £2,000 ; while Sir Jordan Crosland was granted the estate itself, subject to his paying the redemption money.[1]

The services of Sir Thomas, however, had also commended him to the party which was now in the ascendant in the local affairs of Yorkshire, and to the Duke of Buckingham, whom he had relieved of many of the cares of his high office. It is not surprising therefore that when John Scott, one of the parliamentary representatives of the city of York, died during the autumn his name was put forward as that of a possible successor.[2]

Opposition was offered by Sir Roger Langley, the retiring Sheriff of Yorkshire, who appears to have been the Government candidate, and who received the support of many of the local gentry. But Buckingham was whole-heartedly in Osborne's favour, and his influence, if indeed it was needed, was sufficient to bring over most of the citizens and aldermen. On November 24, 1664, the first day of the new session, order was given for the issue of a writ for an election at York. On January 16, 1665, Sir Thomas was returned with a majority of 185 votes. Towards the close of the month he took his seat for the first time in the House of Commons.[3]

---

[1] *Reresby*, pp. 48-9 ; *Cal. S.P. Dom.*, 1664-5, p. 4 ; Sir Thomas to Lady Osborne, November 8, 1664, *infra*, ii. 9. The estate was said to be worth £300 a year (*Cal. S.P. Dom.*, 1670, p. 694).

[2] He had been admitted to the freedom of the city in the previous year (*Register of the Freemen of York*, Surtees Society, ii. 128).

[3] Unpublished passage in Evelyn's Diary, January 2, 1665 ; *Newes*, January 26, 1665, p. 57 ; *C.J.*, viii. 567 ; *Return of Members of Parliament*, i. 532. Osborne's letter acknowledging his indebtedness to Buckingham for his election is printed *infra*, ii. 18.

CHAPTER III

IN OPPOSITION, 1665-7

At the time of his entrance upon the stage of national politics Sir Thomas Osborne had passed his first youth, and according to the standards of the seventeenth century had already, in his thirty-third year, reached the very prime of life. Nature had endowed him with a striking and noble appearance,[1] and a restless and acute intelligence ; but ill health had already begun to mar the one, while his early training had done little to develop the other. As yet there was nothing to distinguish him in the eyes of the world from the crowd of needy and greedy Cavaliers who since the first days of the Restoration had been clamouring incessantly round the throne. Rumour, it is true, credited him with the considerable income of £1,200 a year, but also with debts amounting to many thousands. His Yorkshire reputation went for nothing in London. To the few honest administrators still left at Whitehall he was simply a late comer in the importunate throng, who all considered that services rendered by themselves or their fathers twenty years earlier entitled them to a well paid post the duties of which they were quite incompetent to perform.[2]

Sir Thomas, however, differed from his fellows in realising that claims of twenty years' standing would carry little weight unless he could do something at the moment to support them. Even during the period of the Protectorate he had never resigned himself to the life of idle debauchery led by so many of

---

[1] " A comely gentleman " (*Pepys*, November 5, 1668).

[2] *Ibid.*, February 14, 1669 ; *Burnet*, ii. 14. That this was Pepys's first estimate of Sir Thomas is abundantly clear, although he later saw good reason to modify it. Allowing for some addition to the family fortunes due to Sir Thomas's marriage the estimated yearly income of £1,200 agrees fairly closely with the parliamentary valuation of Sir Edward Osborne's estate.

the Cavaliers who remained at home, and since the Restoration he had done his best to remedy the defects in his early training by diligent application to the local business entrusted to his care. Fortune perhaps was kind in forcing him, after his wasted youth, to serve such an apprenticeship to affairs of state ; yet it is difficult to examine his career without feeling that he himself fully appreciated the dangers of rushing precipitately forward, and deliberately tried to qualify himself for the position he hoped to fill. Ambition no doubt was his guiding star, but even when reaching towards the greatest prizes he preferred to stand on a firm foundation.

It is in keeping with this attitude that on his first appearance in Parliament he made no effort to push himself immediately to the front. Were it not for two unimportant entries in the Journal his very presence in the House of Commons during the early weeks of 1665 might indeed be questioned.[1] Parliament was a new sphere to him. The policy which he was to pursue in it and the attitude which he was to adopt to the existing Government had to be carefully considered before he would venture to move.

The situation which confronted him was certainly not without promise for a politician with his way still to make. For five years Lord Chancellor Clarendon had maintained without serious challenge the position of first minister of the Crown. His conservative outlook, legal knowledge, and studied moderation had admirably fitted him to carry through the immediately necessary work of restoration and settlement. His skill in reconciling discordant interests had laid a solid foundation for the new system. His ascendancy over the King, to whom he had made himself indispensable during the years of exile, had protected him in some measure from the intrigues of a jealous and unprincipled Court.

But by 1665 the work for which Clarendon was specially suited had been largely accomplished, and his day was drawing to a close. The coalition of old Cavaliers and Parliamentarians on which his whole system was founded had been badly shaken

[1] On February 7 he was added to the Committee of Privileges and Elections (*C.J.*, viii. 596). On February 20 he was made one of a committee to whom was entrusted a private bill sent down from the Lords empowering Lord Henry Paulet to sell part of his estate (*ibid.*, p. 605).

by the so-called Clarendon Code, and many of his Presbyterian allies had begun to desert him. A rapidly increasing body of opponents had appeared among the younger Cavaliers, who complained that while much had been done for those who had fought in the Civil War and gone into exile with the King, the next generation, who had remained at home and suffered under the Commonwealth, had been entirely neglected.[1] Charles himself was becoming restive under his mentor's somewhat tactless control, and was surrounded by men and women who saw their own advantage in making the most of his dissatisfaction. Even at the exiled court Clarendon had had his enemies, the ablest of whom were William Coventry and Sir Henry Bennet, since created Lord Arlington. These were now putting themselves at the head of all the other elements of discontent and endeavouring to bring about the fall of the Lord Chancellor.[2]

For the young politician opposition is the regular path to power, and Osborne, whose ultimate object was to force himself upon the attention of the Government, would probably have joined the malcontents in any case. But while his general political outlook, as his later career clearly showed, was not dissimilar to that of Clarendon, he was also one of the younger generation who were bitterly jealous of the favour shown to the older Cavaliers. To him and his fellows the Restoration had on the whole been a disappointment, and the blame for this he naturally laid at the door of the chief minister, who, he declared, had monopolised all power and office for himself and his associates.[3]

Moreover his whole political attitude was necessarily dependent on that of his patron, the Duke of Buckingham, and

[1] The Long Parliament as originally constituted contained an unusual proportion of old men, whose decease led to a surprisingly large number of by-elections during the early years of the reign. Professor W. C. Abbott points out that during the seven years of Clarendon's administration no fewer than 129 new members were introduced into the House of Commons, and the great majority of these were naturally of the younger generation (" The Long Parliament of Charles II," in *E.H.R.*, xxi. 45).

[2] Clarke, *Life of James II.*, i. 398.

[3] Osborne's attitude is well expressed in the speech which he made two years later during the impeachment of Clarendon : " No man ever had more employments—Threatens any man that gave advice—No vessel to swim without his hand at the rudder " (*Grey*, i. 23).

Buckingham was one of Clarendon's most inveterate foes.   The
breach had begun shortly after the execution of Charles I, when
Buckingham, in spite of all the staunch Anglicans among the
exiles could do, had persuaded Charles II to come to terms with
the Covenanters and embark on his disastrous expedition to
Scotland.   Earl and Duke thereafter had been almost constantly at variance, the one endeavouring to induce the King to
take a serious and statesmanlike view of his position and duties,
the other delighting to engage him in erratic adventures and
distract his mind with frivolous and unworthy pleasures.
Since the Restoration Clarendon had done his utmost to exclude
Buckingham from all participation in the management of
affairs.   Buckingham had retaliated by forming alliances with
all the opposition factions, disparaging the Chancellor with the
King, and making him the butt of unsparing ridicule.[1]   At this
particular moment the situation was unusually strained.   In
the preceding years several petitions had been presented to the
King for the re-establishment of the Court and Council in the
North, and for these the apprehension roused by the Farnley
Wood conspiracy had secured considerable support.   A bill had
accordingly been introduced into Parliament to revive the
Court, of which it was generally assumed that Buckingham,
whose work in Yorkshire had brought him great credit, would
be made President.   As early as November 1664 Sir Thomas
Osborne believed his appointment to be as good as made, and
by the following February it had apparently been carried
through.   But in the end the bill, on which everything depended, was dropped, and the appointment lapsed with it.
Buckingham, probably with justice, blamed the Lord Chancellor for his disappointment and was very bitter indeed.[2]

Nevertheless the decisive factor in determining Osborne's
resolution to throw in his lot with Clarendon's enemies was
probably an almost simultaneous disappointment of his own.
The project which he had contemplated three years earlier of

[1] *Burnet*, i. 444-5.

[2] Sir Thomas to Lady Osborne, November 8, 1664, *infra*, ii. 9; Lord
Mansfield to Sir George Savile, quoted in Foxcroft, *Halifax*, i. 33 ; Reid, *The
King's Council in the North*, pp. 454-7.   It is just conceivable that Osborne
was hoping to have his father's old position of Vice-President, but popular
opinion assigned this post to Lord Belasyse or Sir George Savile.

C   D.L. I.

farming the Yorkshire Excise had come to nothing. The lowest sum which the Government would accept had proved to be nearly £1,000 more than any of the Yorkshire gentry were prepared to offer, and in the summer of 1662 the farm had been entrusted for three years to Francis Wetherhead, the Comptroller of Works.[1] The Excise, however, was always unpopular, and in the hands of a stranger to the county it proved doubly so. Wetherhead and his officials were accused of ruining whole families by their oppression and extortion, and were declared to have raised from the tax-payers twice as much as they had paid to the King. As the expiration of his agreement drew near, accordingly, Osborne and several others among the Yorkshire gentry began to consider the possibility of supplanting him, and taking the farm into their own hands.

At least as early as October 1664 Sir Thomas was maturing his scheme and endeavouring with the assistance of his mother and her family to raise the quarter's rent which all farmers were required to pay in advance.[2] But it was not until March 1, 1665, that he formally presented his project and explained it in person to the King.[3] As his first serious essay in the sphere of finance it has a very real importance, and the general ingenuity of its provisions cannot be denied. Every interest was considered. To the King Sir Thomas offered £14,000 a year nstead of £13,500 paid by Wetherhead. To his fellow countrymen in Yorkshire he offered a reduction of £1,000 a year in the amount that could be required of them Finally in the interests of order and good government he proposed to raise and maintain under his own command a troop of horse with officers according to the establishment laid down for the regiment of horse commanded by the Earl of Oxford.[4] The annual cost of this last item he estimated at £3,700 ; but if the King decided against raising the troop he could offer instead only a further

[1] *Cal. Treas. Books*, i. 425.

[2] Sir Thomas to Lady Osborne, November 8, 1664, *infra*, ii. 9. The earliest reference to his plans that has been found is contained in a letter to him from Edward Turner of Rotherham, dated October 11, 1664, in Leeds MSS., Packet 2.

[3] His own draft of the paper which he presented to Charles is printed *infra*, ii. 29.

[4] By some slip he describes these troops in his paper as consisting of 100 men. The troops in Lord Oxford's regiment were of 60 men.

advance of £2,500 in the rent of the Excise, as he would then lose the advantages which he hoped to derive from the command.

Charles was so far impressed with the scheme as to promise that unless others should bid considerably more Sir Thomas should have the farm,[1] but the latter thought it advisable, in view of the King's notorious instability, to make his interest elsewhere as well, and turned to Sir Philip Warwick, the Secretary to the Treasury, who was in a much more real sense the head of that department than was his nominal superior, Lord Treasurer Southampton. With Warwick Sir Thomas had a somewhat distant connection, of which he did not fail to remind him in explaining his proposals,[2] and having made himself, as he thought, secure in that quarter, he awaited the result with some confidence.

Southampton, however, was one of the closest associates of Clarendon, and Clarendon regarded all Buckingham's Yorkshire satellites with suspicion. Accordingly when the matter came up for decision on April 21, not merely Sir Thomas's proposals but several others from different groups of Yorkshire gentry were rejected, and Wetherhead was continued as farmer for a further period of three years. His offer had been £16,000, none of his rivals had risen higher than £16,500, and this difference was declared to be insufficient to justify a change.[3] On July 7 the new agreement with him was formally approved, and although Osborne in a last desperate effort tried to get the grand juries at the Yorkshire assizes to petition against it the decision of the Government was not to be altered.[4]

For the moment, however, Osborne's resentment was denied an outlet, and his attention was distracted for some time

[1] Sir Thomas to Lady Osborne, February 25, March 11, 1665, *infra*, ii. 10-12.

[2] Warwick's son Philip had married Elizabeth, second daughter of John, Lord Frescheville of Staveley, who was Sir Edward Osborne's half-brother. Sir Thomas's letter to Warwick is printed *infra*, ii. 29, and it is significant that in it Osborne is at pains, quite unnecessarily, to mention Lord Frescheville's name.

[3] Sir Philip Warwick's letter explaining and excusing the decision is printed *infra*, ii. 30.

[4] *Cal. Treas. Books*, i. 638. There is a draft of the petition in Osborne's handwriting in Leeds MSS., Packet 2. His suggestion in it is that the collection of the Excise should be entrusted to the justices of the peace. It does not appear whether it was ever adopted or presented. At a later date Clarendon's obstruction of the scheme, which may have embraced other counties besides Yorkshire, appears to have been one of the charges brought against him by the younger Cavaliers, who assured the King that it would both " have raised his authority and . . . increased his revenue " (*Burnet*, i. 451).

elsewhere.   The year 1665 was made memorable, partly by the formal declaration of war against the Dutch,[1] partly by the outbreak of the Great Plague.   The former revived the hopes of the revolutionary party in England, which had been shattered by the failure of their plot a year earlier ; the latter made London and its neighbourhood a very unsafe place of residence for the Court.   Accordingly as the summer advanced and the Plague reached its height it was resolved that while the King and Queen should retire into the west of England, the Duke and Duchess of York should take up residence in the north.   By this means the restraining influence of the royal family would be spread as widely as possible over the most disaffected parts of the country, and the Duke, who had only recently surrendered command of the fleet, would be enabled to keep closely in touch with its movements in the North Sea.[2]

During the early days of August James was slowly making his progress northward, feasted and entertained at every point on his route.   On August 6, amid great acclamation, he made his formal entry into York itself, where he remained for nearly two months.   The precise movements of Sir Thomas Osborne at that time cannot be determined ; but it may be assumed that he played his part, as colonel of militia, in the ceremonies connected with the Duke's reception, and thereafter remained, like the rest of the gentry, in frequent if not constant attendance upon his Court.   If so, this provided him with his first opportunity of becoming intimately acquainted with the Duke's character, and his impressions seem to have been not unfavourable. James gained many friends during his stay in the north.   When towards the close of September he set out to attend the meeting of Parliament, which had been adjourned on account of the Plague to Oxford, it was part of Sir Thomas's regiment which formed his guard at Pontefract, where he lay the first night, while the remaining companies received him next day at Doncaster.[3]

It was thus, strangely enough when one considers the later

---

[1] February 22.   Actual hostilities had begun some months earlier.

[2] Clarke, *Life of James II.*, i. 421-2 ; Clarendon, *Continuation of Life* (ed. 1759), pp. 520-2.

[3] *Reresby*, p. 55 ; *Hatton Correspondence*, i. 47 ; Buckingham to Osborne, September 18, [1665], in B.M. Add. MSS. 28053, f. 9; *Morrison Catalogue.* i. 247.

relations of the two men, as a supporter of James that Sir
Thomas first came forward in Parliament. Shortly before his
visit to York the Duke, in command of the English fleet, had
won great reputation by his victory over the Dutch off Lowes-
toft,[1] and the Commons, after having provided for the requirements of the war itself by a vote of £1,250,000, proceeded to
recognise his services by a personal gift of £120,000. Osborne,
who had been detained in the north by business connected with
the Duke's visit, did not reach Oxford until October 12, when
the former vote had already passed. But the latter vote was
proposed by Sir John Goodricke, member for York County,
seconded by Lord Ogle, who represented Northumberland, and
supported so enthusiastically by the northern members,
Osborne included, as to earn them in a very special sense the
reputation of being the Duke's servants.[2]

Support of James, however, did not necessarily imply in
Sir Thomas's eyes support of the Government, and an opportunity of manifesting his dislike of the existing regime soon
presented itself. During the course of the session was passed
the Five Mile Act, the last of the persecuting statutes directed
against the Dissenters, which forbade all ejected ministers to
approach within five miles of any corporate town, or of any
parish in which they had preached, unless they first took an
oath by which they declared it unlawful, under any pretence
whatever, to take up arms against the King, and promised not
to attempt any alteration in the government either of Church
or of State. To this measure Osborne presumably offered no
opposition, but when a bill was introduced with the object of
imposing the same oath upon the whole nation his attitude
completely changed. The effect of such a provision would be
to strengthen the hands of the existing Government rather than
to promote the interests of Anglicanism, and he accordingly
joined with those who rejected the bill by a majority of six.[3]

[1] June 3.

[2] Sir Thomas to Lady Osborne, October 13 and 25, 1665, *infra*, ii. 12-13.

[3] *Parliamentary History*, iv., App., p. xl. The " Bill for enjoining the taking
the oath and declaration therein mentioned " was read a first time in the
Commons on October 26, 1665. On the following day it was read a second
time, but the proposal that it should be committed was rejected by 57 votes
to 51. The tellers for the Noes were Sir John Talbot and Sir Thomas
Littleton (*C.J.*, viii. 621-2).

Among those associated with Sir Thomas on this occasion were two of his brothers-in-law, Robert, Lord Willoughby de Eresby, and Peregrine Bertie. The former had represented Boston since the first assembling of the House of Commons in 1661, the latter had only recently been returned at a by-election as member for Stamford.[1] As yet these three, together with the Earl of Lindsey in the House of Lords, formed the entire Bertie-Osborne connection in Parliament, but from that small nucleus was to develop in due course a considerable parliamentary faction, of which Sir Thomas himself was eventually to assume the leadership.

At the moment, however, little time was given him to consolidate his alliances, whether with his relatives or with his " countrymen " of Yorkshire. On October 31, after a session of only three weeks, Parliament was prorogued, and immediately thereafter Osborne returned to Kiveton. Since the Duke of York's visit the situation in the north had changed decidedly for the worse, and he was almost immediately confronted with his old task of discovering plots and hunting down malcontents. The heavy taxation caused by the war had proved a new source of disaffection ; the Dutch had soon shown that they had by no means been crippled by their defeat in the spring ; a combination against the Government of rebels within the country and enemies without was a serious possibility, and in the inflamed state of public feeling was perhaps regarded even more seriously than it deserved. Alarming reports were received of a conspiracy designed for the first day of the following year. On December 16 twelve suspects were committed at York, and a few days later, on information received from the Duke of Albemarle, others were added to their number.

To deal with the prisoners a large number of examiners were appointed, among whom were Sir Thomas Osborne, Sir George Savile, and Sir Godfrey Copley. The memory of their treatment after the Farnley Wood conspiracy, however, was still fresh in the minds of Buckingham's deputy lieutenants, and these three politely but firmly asked to be excused, Osborne on the ground that his wife was ill, the others for more general reasons. A few weeks later Sir Thomas was even prepared to

[1] October 21, 1665 (*Return of Members of Parliament*, i. 524, 525).

assert that no danger need be feared from their enemies in the country, and to hint that the Government was being misled by interested information supplied by his former opponent Sir Roger Langley, through his son Richard, who was an ensign in Albemarle's regiment of guards.[1]

Possibly this estimate of the situation was correct, but as the year advanced the position became much more serious. In January 1666 France had entered the war on the side of the Dutch, and little though Louis XIV intended to do on behalf of his allies, the possibility of an effective combination between the French and Dutch fleets was sufficient to fill England with renewed alarm. Towards the close of June, accordingly, commissions were hurriedly issued for raising additional forces, and the militia were ordered to hold themselves in readiness to protect the coasts.[2] The Duke of Buckingham and Sir George Savile were both authorised to raise troops of horse, which were to be stationed at York ;[3] but when on Buckingham's advice Sir Thomas Osborne endeavoured to secure a similar favour, even his offer to buy out any one who had a better claim failed to secure him success, and he had to be content with the prestige given him by his position in the militia.[4]

So great was the competition for places in the new-raised troops that many men of good family were to be found even in the ranks, and the preparations for defence as a whole led to a vast concourse of noblemen and gentlemen at York, where they remained in comparative inactivity for more than two months. Of this Buckingham took full advantage for the exercise of that lavish hospitality in which he delighted. A chance visit of the Earls of Cardigan and Shrewsbury was made the excuse for a series of entertainments which lasted for weeks, and frequently ran on right through the night into the following day. But Buckingham could never continue long without rousing the enmity of some of those with whom he was associated. Strange rumours

---

[1] Osborne to Buckingham, December 25, 1665, and March 17, 1666, *infra*, ii. 18, 20.

[2] *Infra*, ii. 19-20 ; Hist. MSS. Com., *Various Collections*, ii. 122-3.

[3] Foxcroft, *Halifax*, i. 44-6.

[4] A draft of Osborne's letter petitioning for the appointment, dated July 9, 1666, is in Leeds MSS., Packet 2. His lieutenant was to have been Sir Ralph Knight, " who comanded the army into England under the Generall."

began to spread abroad of his connection with the Countess of Shrewsbury, although for the moment the husband was induced to believe that all was well. A few words spoken at table gave great offence to Lord Fauconberg, Lord Lieutenant of the North Riding, and provoked a hasty answer, which in turn led to a challenge. Buckingham chose Sir George Savile as his second, but on the field being reached showed little inclination to engage, and accepted some verbal satisfaction with a readiness which roused much adverse comment. When at the beginning of August he set out for London it was a very heated atmosphere indeed which he left behind.[1]

Had Sir Thomas Osborne been present at York during these intrigues it is scarcely to be supposed that he would have failed to play his part as a supporter of his patron ; but for the greater part of the summer his presence was required elsewhere by domestic troubles of his own. On July 25, after an illness lasting many weeks, his father-in-law, the Earl of Lindsey, died at Kensington.[2] Scarcely had he been buried in the family vault at Grimsthorpe when Sir Thomas had to hasten to the bedside of his own mother, who died on August 18 and was buried two days later at Harthill.[3] Not until the beginning of September was he in a position to resume his public duties, and then just in time to meet a renewed scare caused by the outbreak of the Great Fire of London on September 2. Popular opinion was unanimous in declaring the fire to be the work either of the Catholics on the one hand or of the Republicans and Dissenters on the other, and the general expectation was that it would be followed by an insurrection, aided very probably by the Dutch. As soon as the news reached the north the militia was called out, and Sir Thomas was ordered to assemble his regiment of foot at Doncaster.[4] The alarm, however, was of short duration, and about the middle of the month, while the special levies were being disbanded, he was able to

---

[1] *Reresby*, pp. 57-60.

[2] B.M. Add. MSS. 28040, f. 3 ; Carte MSS. 222, f. 107.

[3] B.M. Add. MSS. 28040, f. 3.

[4] September 4 (*ibid.*). The order presumably came from the deputy lieutenants at York. Buckingham's own instructions arrived later (Burghclere, *Buckingham*, p. 154).

dismiss his regiment and ride south to attend the meeting of Parliament on September 21.[1]

There he was almost immediately caught up in the whirlpool of intrigues and animosities from which he had hitherto remained comparatively free. Lord Fauconberg still considered himself entitled to some satisfaction ; and although he dared not pick a deliberate quarrel with Buckingham himself he had no such hesitation as regards Buckingham's followers. Probably by mere chance he selected Sir Thomas Osborne as the object on which to vent his ill-humour, and little more than a fortnight after the opening of the session, without having received any provocation whatever, challenged him to a duel. The result was disastrous to himself. On October 6, supported by Sir John Talbot, he met Osborne and Captain Daniel Collingwood at Islington, and was so severely wounded in the thigh that his opponents thought it prudent to go into hiding. It soon appeared, however, that the wound was not likely to prove mortal. By October 11 Sir Thomas was back in the House of Commons, watching the usual futile attempt of Parliament to prevent by legislation the kind of incident in which he had just been involved. By October 20 Lord Fauconberg was out of bed and apparently out of danger.[2]

Had the matter ended there it would have had none but a personal and temporary significance, and would have been of moment chiefly as enabling Osborne to put his patron under an obligation. But Buckingham had many enemies in London as well as in the north, and circumstances, by uniting both groups of opponents, were soon to give to the affair a real political importance. In the long parliamentary session of 1666-7

---

[1] Osborne was certainly in the House of Commons on September 22, when he was appointed a member of two committees, one to prepare proposals for the relief of London, and the other to consider means for advancing the manufactures of the nation and preventing excess in the use of foreign commodities (*C.J.*, viii. 626).

[2] B.M. Add. MSS. 28040, f. 3 ; 33413, ff. 6-15 ; Carte MSS. 72, f. 105 ; *Cal. S.P. Dom.*, 1666-7, p. 191 ; Sir Thomas Osborne to Lady Campden, October 20, 1666, *infra*, ii. 16. Sir Thomas protested that Lord Fauconberg mentioned no cause of quarrel before the duel, and that even afterwards he could not find where his offence lay. This is probably true, but the accompanying statement that the Duke of Buckingham was not involved cannot be allowed much weight. The prevailing opinion certainly was that the duel was a result of the quarrels in the north.

opposition to Clarendon and the Government at length showed signs of coming to a head. The war, the Plague and the Fire formed a triple national burden sufficient to shake the allegiance even of firm supporters of the existing regime. For the two last it was difficult directly to blame the Chancellor ; but many miscarriages had occurred in connection with the first, and these there was an increasing tendency to lay at his door. In the summer of 1665 an attack on the united merchant fleets of the Dutch at Bergen had been badly mismanaged. In the following June an ill-advised division of the English fleet had led to Albemarle being caught by a much superior force in the Downs and very severely handled. Peculation also had been rife, and there was a general impression that of the vast sums voted for the war a considerable proportion had found its way into the pockets of politicians and courtiers. Meanwhile the ordinary seamen were reduced by lack of pay to the utmost destitution, and paraded the streets in mutinous throngs which excited pity and alarm in all beholders.[1]

Of the general discontent which resulted it was Buckingham's object to make himself the champion and spokesman. In the House of Lords he had no real following, but in the House of Commons his Yorkshire adherents provided him with the nucleus of a party, round which he proceeded to gather all the malcontents he could find. Prominent among these were men with whom Sir Thomas Osborne was to be constantly associated in alliance or hostility, and who were to play a great part on both sides of the House during the next dozen years—Sir Richard Temple, Edward Seymour, William Garroway and Sir Robert Howard.[2] At the instigation of Buckingham, and with the approval of a considerable section among the unattached members in the House, this motley array then proceeded to attack the Government, denouncing its failure to suppress popery, criticising the administration of the finances and the government of Ireland, and questioning the integrity of individual ministers.

[1] *Pepys, passim.*

[2] " Who were all bold speakers, and meant to make themselves considerable by saying upon all occasions what wiser men would not, whatever they thought " (Clarendon, *Continuation of Life*, pp. 701-2).

In these proceedings Osborne played a considerable, but by no means outstanding part. He was one of the examiners employed by the committee appointed at the beginning of the session to inspect the accounts of the navy, ordnance and stores. He was among those entrusted with the task of questioning persons suspected of setting fire to London, although he gave it as his opinion that " the allegations are very frivolous, and people are generally satisfied that the fire was accidentall." He certainly voted for the bill prohibiting the importation of Irish cattle and meat, by which Buckingham hoped to embarrass Clarendon's ally Ormonde, the Lord Lieutenant of Ireland.[1] He was not deterred by the hostility of a section of the courtiers from championing the personal and family claims of Lady Osborne's eldest half-brother, James Bertie, who had inherited the title of Lord Norris through his mother.[2] He opposed the general Excise proposed by Government spokesmen as the best means of raising the supplies voted for the war, declaring instead for the poll tax and the assessment on land advocated by the opposition.[3] When on December 11 a measure was introduced nominating a commission to examine the accounts of all war taxation, he was one of the twenty-four commissioners appointed.[4] But with the more extravagant proposals of his associates he had nothing to do. It was William Garroway who endeavoured to tack the provision for the inspection of accounts to the Poll Bill, and thus force the King to accept it. It was Sir Robert Howard who insisted on the inclusion of the word " nuisance " in the Irish Cattle Bill, because the use of that word would prevent the King from employing his dispensing power in connection with it.[5] Osborne was ready enough to

---

[1] Sir Thomas to Lady Osborne, September 29, October 2, 1666, *infra*, ii. 14-16. The importation of Irish cattle was regarded as specially disadvantageous to the northern counties, so this vote may have been quite in consonance with his own opinions (Clarendon, *Continuation of Life*, p. 704).

[2] *L.J.*, xii. 93, 95, 108-9 ; *C.J.*, viii. 663 ; *Hist. MSS. Com.*, viii. 109 ; *Diary of John Milward* (ed. Robbins), pp. 66, 72.

[3] *Infra*, ii. 32 ; *Diary of John Milward*, pp. 21-5, 33-6, 38-9 ; *C.J.*, viii. 647.

[4] *C.J.*, viii. 661. Garroway and Temple were also included.

[5] *Pepys*, December 8, 1666 ; January 9, 1667 ; *Diary of John Milward*, p. 56 ; *C.J.*, viii. 659, 671.

attack the Government, but he was no opponent of the prerogative.

In this moderate policy he was fully justified by the event, for Buckingham, it soon appeared, had badly over reached himself. The proposal to tack the provision regarding the inspection of accounts to the Poll Bill, although never actually carried out, inflamed the House of Lords, which in the interests of the prerogative petitioned the King to have the accounts examined by a commission of his own,[1] and when the Commons sent up a separate bill upon the subject returned it with amendments which the Lower House absolutely refused to accept. The attack upon the ministers was so indiscriminate as to force them, although bitterly hostile to each other, to form a temporary alliance for mutual defence. Scarcely an official could have faced with equanimity a strict investigation into the administration of the finances. Arlington, by supplying erroneous information to the Government, had been mainly responsible for the disastrous division of the fleet. Sir William Coventry had failed to secure the immediate dispatch of the orders by which that division was countermanded. Every member of the Government would willingly have saved himself at the expense of the rest, but in face of a danger which seemed to threaten all alike their only course was to hang together and seek salvation by destroying the credit of their principal opponent. A tacit alliance was accordingly struck, not only among them, but between them and all Buckingham's other enemies, and before the close of the session a conspiracy against him was in course of formation, which had roots in the north, at Whitehall, and in the Duke's own disorderly household.

According to Clarendon the first move in the conspiracy was made by Buckingham's steward Richard Braythwaite, who having access to the royal person informed Charles himself that the Duke " was of late very much altered, and was fallen into the acquaintance and conversation of some men of very mean condition but of very desperate intentions, with whom he used to meet at unseasonable hours and in obscure places, where

---

[1] In reply the King on December 29 actually nominated such a commission, composed of six peers and twelve of the twenty-four commissioners appointed by the Commons, but the matter went no further at that time (*Pepys*, January 2, 1667 ; *Cal. S.P. Dom.*, 1666-7, pp. 365-6 ; *L.J.*, xii. 54, 57).

persons of quality did not use to resort, and that he frequently received letters from them ; all which made him apprehend that there was a design on foot, which, how unreasonable soever, the Duke might be engaged in." Clarendon, however, also refers somewhat vaguely to other information which at the same time was reaching Lord Arlington, and it is in this that the real origin of the conspiracy is almost certainly to be found. The truth appears to be that the Lord Chancellor, who was superior to the base arts employed by many of his colleagues, was unconnected with the initial stages of the affair, and that Braythwaite was simply a cunning rascal who learned that an accusation against his master was coming from another source and endeavoured to profit by being first in the field.[1]

From depositions made after the whole affair had somewhat blown over it appears that the originator of it all was that same Sir Roger Langley with whom Sir Thomas Osborne had several times already come into collision. At some point Langley entered into a close alliance with Lord Arlington, and these two together, by means of bribes, enlisted the services of three informers, Middleton, Leving and Freer. When the story which they were to tell had been perfected it was committed to writing and formally laid before Langley, who in turn carried it to Arlington.[2]

The main point in the accusation was the existence of a treasonable intercourse between Buckingham and John Heydon, an astrologer. On January 24, 1667, Heydon was arrested, carried to the Tower, and there examined by Sir William Coventry, Sir Thomas Clifford, and the two Secretaries of State, Arlington and Sir William Morice. Among his papers were found several letters to the Duke, which " gave him the style of Prince, and mentioned what great things his stars promised to him ; " while there was also one letter to the astrologer, which the King declared was in the handwriting of Buckingham himself. Most ominous of all, there was discovered a horoscope of the King's nativity which informers were prepared to swear had been cast at the Duke's desire.[3]

---

[1] Clarendon, *Continuation of Life*, pp. 813-6 ; *Diary of Sir Henry Slingsby*, pp. 375-6.
[2] B.M. Add. MSS. 27872, ff. 12, 15.
[3] Clarendon, *Continuation of Life*, p. 817 ; *Hist. MSS. Com.*, xii. 7, p. 44.

Had Buckingham been in his usual favour at Court he and Charles would probably have made merry together over these disclosures ; but the Duke was experiencing one of his frequent periods of eclipse. The King had been bitterly incensed by his behaviour in Parliament ; he was for the moment on the worst possible terms with Lady Castlemaine ; and he had seriously discredited himself by two disgraceful quarrels with the Earl of Ossory and the Marquis of Dorchester. On February 25, accordingly, after a further examination of Heydon, Charles formally declared in Council his great dissatisfaction with the Duke and his resolution to deprive him of all his posts, as a Privy Councillor, as a Gentleman of the Bedchamber, and as Lord Lieutenant of the West Riding. Warrants were then issued for his arrest and imprisonment in the Tower.[1]

If, however, the matter was taken seriously it might prove very serious indeed. Casting the King's horoscope might quite conceivably be construed as compassing or imagining the King's death ; and Buckingham's wild utterances no less than his constant association with the most disaffected elements in Church and State could easily provide corroborative evidence of any treasonable designs imputed to him. The Duke, accordingly, evaded Sergeant Barcroft, who was sent to effect the arrest, and went into hiding.[2] On March 8 a proclamation was issued for his apprehension on a charge of having held secret and seditious correspondence and raised mutinies among the forces.[3] For the next three months his activities and whereabouts can only be conjectured.

Had Osborne chosen to save himself in this apparent wreck of his patron's fortunes he could easily have done so. It is to the credit, certainly of his head and possibly of his heart, that he resolutely declined. In the West Riding of Yorkshire Buckingham's opponents came into power with the Earl of Burlington as Lord Lieutenant at their head. Burlington, whose personal influence in his new Lord Lieutenancy was small, would gladly have retained his predecessor's officials ;

---

[1] *Cal. S.P. Dom.*, 1666-7, p. 532.

[2] Barcroft's strange experiences in his attempt to execute his warrant are fully related by himself in Clarendon MSS. 85, f. 96. He also told Pepys his adventures (*Diary*, March 3, 1667).

[3] P.C.Reg. 59, p. 329 ; *Cal. S.P. Dom.*, 1666-7, p. 553.

but Osborne, Savile and others, who probably knew fairly well how their patron's ruin had been effected, absolutely refused to serve along with his·enemies and resigned all the commissions they held.[1]   The summer of 1667 was a time of great activity in the north owing to fear of a Dutch descent.   Throughout it all Osborne remained quietly at Kiveton, with no duties whatever to perform.

Charles also would willingly have bought over Buckingham's more moderate supporters.   Scarcely had Parliament been prorogued on February 8 when he appointed a commission of his own to examine the public accounts, in which Osborne and several of the more reasonable members of the opposition were included.[2]   His object was to take advantage of the absence of Buckingham and the abeyance of Parliament to carry through an investigation which would pacify the malcontents and yet bring nothing serious to light.   Osborne, however, insisted on a real examination or none at all.   Along with others he first questioned the right of the commission to act, then maintained that its powers were insufficient to enable it to produce any real result, and finally succeeded in depriving it so completely of all credit that its members were no more desirous of meeting than Government officials were of appearing before it.[3]

Even a personal appeal from the King himself failed to shake his attitude.   On June 8 Charles in a long conversation endeavoured to convince him of the ill intentions of the Duke of Buckingham, and remonstrated with him on his attempt to reduce the commission to impotence and so bring the whole question of the accounts once more into the hands of

[1] *Reresby*, pp. 64-5 ; *Diary of Sir Henry Slingsby*, pp. 369-72 ; S.P. Dom., Charles II., vol. 196, No. 93, gives a list of Lord Burlington's deputy lieutenants as approved by the King, April 5, 1667.   This list includes both Sir Thomas Osborne and Sir George Savile, but it seems clear that they refused their commissions.   Their action in doing so is too often represented as a protest against Clarendon and the Government.   It was mainly a matter of local Yorkshire politics.   The Government, however, considered the whole affair so serious that it sent Lord Belasyse down into Yorkshire to try to pacify them (*Pepys*, April 7, 1667).

[2] The members were the same as those nominated on December 29, 1666. For the rather complicated history of this commission see *Calendar of Treasury Books*, ii., pp. xxxiv-xlix.   Sir Thomas gives the date of his appointment as April 17, the day on which the commission was opened (B.M. Add. MSS. 28040, f. 3 ; *Kennet*, iii. 286).

[3] *Pepys*, May 1, June 5, 1667.

Parliament. Osborne would admit none of the charges against his patron, and protested that his own conduct on the commission was designed, not to diminish the royal prerogative in financial matters and increase the powers of Parliament, but simply to make the investigation a reality. Other men, he admitted, might have more sinister aims, but he and his immediate associates had refused to give them any countenance. In truth Sir Thomas was by no means at ease in the company of some of the allies with whom Buckingham had provided him, and it was probably with real gratitude that he received Charles's parting promise of favour if he would reconsider his policy. He would not abandon his patron, or cease his attack upon the existing Government, but he had no quarrel with monarchy or with the King.[1]

Had Sir Thomas been able to foresee the events of the next few days his attitude might have been even more determined, for the balance of parties was on the verge of being completely reversed, and the apparent triumph of the Government was about to end in disastrous failure. In the early spring negotiations for peace had been begun, and in May plenipotentiaries from all the powers involved in the war had assembled at Breda. Lulled into a false security by these means the English ministers had resolved to seek relief from their financial embarrassments by laying up the fleet. To the Dutch this offered a splendid opportunity of forcing a speedy peace upon better terms than they could otherwise have obtained. On June 7 they appeared off the North Foreland, and on the evening of the same day anchored in the Gunfleet. On June 10 they occupied Sheerness. Two days later they sailed up the Medway, broke the chain with which the English had tried to bar the passage, burned or seized several men-of-war, and bombarded Chatham.[2]

For some time the panic was extreme, and even when the Dutch had retired from Chatham to the Buoy of the Nore the fear of what they might still do united with a very deep sense of national humiliation to produce a furious demand

---

[1] Osborne's account of this conversation is printed *infra*, ii. 31.

[2] *Cal. S.P. Dom.*, 1667, pp. xiv-xxvii ; *Pepys*, June 8, 1667, and following days.

for the punishment of those responsible for so disastrous a miscarriage. Of this Buckingham resolved to take advantage by emerging from a concealment of which he was now heartily tired. On June 26 Parliament, which stood prorogued to October, was hastily summoned to meet on July 25.[1] The next day Buckingham appeared openly in London dining with his followers at a tavern in the Strand. On June 28 he wrote to the King announcing his intention to surrender himself and asking for an interview, gave himself up to Secretary Morice and was forthwith committed to the Tower.[2]

At such a time any attempt at severity on the part of his opponents would have been suicidal. The King's anger was never lasting, and had already begun to evaporate. Popular opinion, taking Buckingham at his own valuation, regarded him as a martyr for the national cause. So much so, in fact, was this the case that he had no sooner surrendered himself than a report spread abroad that he had been released and restored to favour.[3] On July 1 he was examined in the Tower by the same committee as had formerly examined Heydon, but the proceedings were very formal. The only serious point was the letter which he was alleged to have written to Heydon, and this he offered to bet Arlington £100 he had not written at all.[4] Exactly a week later he was brought before the Council, and the letter was there produced ; but immediately he saw it he declared that it was in the handwriting of his sister, the Duchess of Richmond, and the King in some confusion at his own mistake had to admit that this was the case. With that admission the whole charge practically collapsed, and on July 14 Buckingham was set at liberty.[5] The meeting of Parliament to which he had been looking forward, however, came to nothing. When the Houses assembled on the appointed day they were

[1] *Cal. S.P. Dom.*, 1667, p. 235. The summons of Parliament was opposed to the last by Clarendon and the Duke of York (*Savile Correspondence*, p. 17 ; *Pepys*, June 25, 1667).

[2] *Cal. S.P. Dom.*, 1667, p. lxiv. ; *Hist. MSS. Com.*, xii. 7, p. 51 ; Carte MSS. 222, f. 160.

[3] *Cal. S.P. Dom.*, 1667, p. xxxvi. ; *Lindsey MSS.*, p. 367.

[4] A full account of the examination is in B.M. Add. MSS. 27872, f. 13.

[5] *Cal. S.P. Dom.*, 1667, p. 294 ; Clarendon, *Continuation of Life*, pp. 822-4 ; *Lindsey MSS.*, p. 369 ; *Savile Correspondence*, p. 18 ; *Pepys*, July 12, 17, 1667.

required to adjourn until July 29.   In the interval the King came to terms with the Dutch, and having no longer any immediate need for their services waited only for their reassembling to prorogue them to October 10.[1] Sir Thomas Osborne, who had returned to Kiveton about the middle of June, appears to have come all the way from Yorkshire solely to attend the Parliament. If he did so he must have shared in the discontent felt by scores of country gentlemen, who had put themselves to great inconvenience to come up to London in the height of summer only to learn that they might just as well have stayed at home.[2]

Sooner or later, however, Parliament would have to be reckoned with, and the mere prospect was sufficient to destroy that temporary unity among the ministers which had led to Buckingham's fall.   Sir William Coventry, anxious to secure reforms and concessions which he knew the Chancellor would obstruct, urged that Clarendon should be dismissed.[3] Lord Arlington, determined at whatever cost to others to save himself, advocated the same course.[4] Even to honest men the sacrifice of the Lord Chancellor might well seem the best method of silencing the popular clamour, and his many enemies at Court and in the Council hailed the suggestion with delight. On August 30 Secretary Morice was sent to demand the great seal, and King and ministers for a moment breathed more freely in the hope that discontent had been in some measure appeased.   By the rabble at Whitehall news of the Chancellor's dismissal was received with an extravagant and indecent joy[5] which found a more decorous counterpart in many manor houses throughout the country.   To Sir Thomas Osborne in retirement at Kiveton it came with greater significance than to most.   The first necessary step towards his own rise to power had been accomplished.

[1] *Cal. S.P. Dom.*, 1667, pp. lv-lvii ; *Hastings MSS.*, ii. 154.

[2] *Pepys*, July 25, 29, 1665.   Pepys asserts that on July 25 more than 300 members of the House of Commons were present, a most unusual attendance at such a time.

[3] *Pepys*, September 2, 1667.

[4] V. Barbour, *Arlington*, pp. 111-3.

[5] *Pepys*, August 26, 27, 31, 1667.

CHAPTER IV

RISE TO OFFICE, 1667-9

THE fall of Clarendon marks in a very real sense the beginning of the reign of Charles II. Not merely did it free the King from the position of practical tutelage in which he had hitherto been held, and enable him to develop, as was shortly to appear, a policy of his own, but it flung wide the door for the entrance of all those new influences which were to be specially characteristic of the Restoration period. Before 1667 the government of England was largely in the hands of statesmen who had been prominent under Charles I, and clung to the ideals of their early years. After 1667 the way was clear for younger men, who knew little of conditions before the Civil War, to come rapidly to the front.

For Sir Thomas Osborne the prospects opened up were particularly bright. Originally a comparatively unimportant figure in the brilliant group who acknowledged Buckingham as their leader, he had by diligent and faithful service raised himself in his patron's esteem until he occupied a foremost place. During the preceding months he had given conspicuous proofs of loyalty to his leader's cause. Not merely had he fought Lord Fauconberg on his behalf, resigned all his offices as a protest against his dismissal, maintained his principles on the Commission of Accounts, and resisted all the attempts of the Court to win him over, but at some point which cannot now with certainty be determined he had saved him from imprisonment by proving one of the documents produced against him to be a forgery.[1] Ingratitude was not one of

[1] Sir Thomas's own reference to the matter is extremely cryptic—" 1667, February 25th—Duke of Buckingham was put out of all his offices and was sent for by a messenger, and I saved him from imprisonment by proveing his hand to have been counterfitted in a letter which was giving to the King " (B.M. Add. MSS. 28040, f. 3). The letter in question may possibly be the one

Buckingham's failings, and it was confidently anticipated that Sir Thomas would be the first to benefit by his restoration to power and favour.

Of that restoration there could no longer be the faintest doubt, for Buckingham had suddenly become the most popular figure in the country. Apart from occasional periods when he was under a cloud, he had always enjoyed immense influence with the King. Recent events had enabled him to add to this an almost incredible reputation with the people and with Parliament. Not merely was he the only prominent politician who had had no share in the miscarriages of the previous two years, but he had, in appearance at least, suffered severely for denouncing those responsible for them. The fall of Clarendon thus almost inevitably meant his reappearance at Court and in Council.[1] On September 4 jealous eyes noticed that he and Charles had a conference of two hours' duration alone together.[2] On September 15 he was openly restored to favour.[3] Eight days later he formally took his seat at the Council Board and waited on the King at dinner as Gentleman of the Bedchamber.[4]

For Buckingham to effect a revolution in the north was a comparatively simple matter. Towards the close of October the Earl of Burlington was persuaded to surrender his commission as Lord Lieutenant of the West Riding, the Duke was reinstated in his place, and a corresponding change was made

which Buckingham declared to have been written by the Duchess of Richmond ; but this letter was in no sense a forgery, nor can it be supposed that Osborne was better acquainted with the Duchess's handwriting than Buckingham himself was. Moreover, it should be noted that at the time when Buckingham was before the Council Sir Thomas was in Yorkshire. It is probably to this matter that Charles Bertie refers in his letter of July 30 to Lady Osborne—" As Sir Thomas Osborne . . . pretends [*i.e.* claims to have performed] a service to the Duke of Buckingham " . . . (*Lindsey MSS.*, p. 369. *Cf.* Lord Ogle to Sir George Savile, September 20, 1667, in Foxcroft, *Halifax*, i. 55, note 6).

[1] Pepys, who was certainly no friend of Buckingham, is mainly responsible for the common statement that the Duke owed his restoration to the good offices of Lady Castlemaine, who wished for an ally against Clarendon ; but even he realised that this explanation did not account for everything (*Diary*, July 12, 17, 22, 1667). The French ambassador had no doubt of the strength of Buckingham's position (Ruvigny to Louis XIV, October 6 and 10, 1667, quoted in Barbour, *Arlington*, pp. 113, 114).

[2] *Savile Correspondence*, p. 21.

[3] *Ibid.* ; *Lindsey MSS.*, p. 370 ; *Hist. MSS. Com.*, xii. 7, p. 53.

[4] P.C. Reg. 59, p. 593 ; *Hist. MSS. Com.*, xii. 7, p. 53.

among the subordinate officials, Osborne becoming again
deputy lieutenant, justice of the peace, and colonel of militia.[1]
A revolution at Whitehall, however, could not be so easily
accomplished. Clarendon, although dismissed, refused to admit
the justice of the accusations levelled against him, and believed
he could vindicate himself in Parliament. He had still many
supporters, chief of whom was his old friend Ormonde, the
Lord Lieutenant of Ireland. His son-in-law, the Duke of
York, was understood to be bitterly resentful of the treatment
meted out to him, and to be working in his favour. Thus it
was by no means impossible that he might be restored to power,
or at least allowed to exercise very considerable influence
within the Government. The revolution at Whitehall could
not be considered complete or even secure until he had been
finally ruined, his supporters swept from office, and the influence of the Duke of York as far as possible diminished.

So little attraction had this triple task that Buckingham's
first idea was to come to terms with Clarendon, and form an
alliance for the ruin of Arlington, whose part in bringing about
his own disgrace and imprisonment he had neither forgotten
nor forgiven.[2] But the complete rejection of his overtures
forced him to adopt an attitude of determined hostility, and he
resolved instead to form an alliance with Arlington against
Clarendon and all his connections. Arlington was himself
sufficiently hostile to the ex-Chancellor, and in any case was
so afraid of a parliamentary enquiry into his own conduct
that he dared not refuse whatever Buckingham asked. Thus
the two enemies, for the moment working in unison, set themselves at the head of popular discontent, and when Parliament
met on October 10 stirred up the Commons to proceed against
Clarendon by impeachment.

In this impeachment Sir Thomas Osborne played a part
sufficiently prominent to make a deep impression on contemporaries,[3] and to be remembered against him eleven years later

---

[1] *Cal. S.P. Dom.*, 1667, p. 547, 1667-8, p. 2 ; B.M. Add. MSS. 36916, f. 6.

[2] With this object in view Buckingham approached Clarendon shortly
after his dismissal, but without success (Clarendon, *Continuation of Life*, pp.
837-8 ; *Pepys*, November 13, 1668).

[3] Reresby describes Sir Thomas as the Chancellor's greatest enemy in the
House of Commons (*Memoirs*, p. 71).

when he was called upon to face a similar accusation. Clarendon credits him with preventing any intervention of the King on his behalf, and asserts that even before Parliament met he was openly declaring " that the Chancellor would be accused of high treason, and if he were not hanged he would be hanged himself." [1] Nevertheless it is not easy, from the imperfect accounts of the proceedings which have survived, to discover what precise form his activities assumed. When the impeachment was moved by Edward Seymour, Sir Thomas certainly spoke in favour of the motion, declaring that Clarendon " had scandalized the King as not to be a true protestant but a papist in heart, and that the Earle did endeavour to subvert the laws both of Church and State." [2] Later he returned to the matter of the King's religion, denounced the Chancellor's monopoly of office, and accused him of neglecting Parliament. [3] But his recorded speeches are few and short compared to those of Edward Seymour and Sir Robert Howard among Buckingham's followers, or Sir Thomas Littleton among the supporters of Arlington. Osborne was not yet, and indeed was never going to be, one of the recognised orators of the House of Commons. It was not by his speeches that he contributed to the ruin of Clarendon.

Apparently he found his proper sphere in the semi-administrative work of committees. He was one of those entrusted with the task of drawing up the address of thanks for the King's speech, in which special gratitude was expressed for the dismissal of the Lord Chancellor. [4] He was placed upon committees to consider the former bill for the examination of the public accounts, to enquire into the miscarriage of affairs during the war, and to investigate the reasons for the sale of Dunkirk. [5] He was a member of the committee appointed to determine the proper method of proceeding against Clarendon, and also of that which drew up the formal accusation. [6] Throughout the early stages of the trial he showed himself

---

[1] Clarendon, *Continuation of Life*, pp. 847-8.

[2] October 26 (B.M. Add. MSS. 33413, f. 35). According to another account Sir Thomas Littleton seconded Seymour's motion, and Sir Thomas Osborne " thirded " it (B.M. Add. MSS. 35865, f. 13).

[3] November 7 (*Grey*, i. 23). [4] *C.J.*, ix. 1, 2.

[5] *Ibid.*, pp. 3-5. [6] *Ibid.*, pp. 8-9.

ready to go as far as any of his fellows,[1] and when the charge
was considered clause by clause he was prepared to undertake
that at least two of them should be fully made out.[2] The
refusal of the Lords to commit upon a general charge of treason
he regarded as a plain denial of justice, and although not among
those originally entrusted with the task of managing the conference with the Upper House on the subject he was soon added
to their number.[3] Almost immediately thereafter, however,
probably as a result of some illness, he ceased to attend Parliament.[4] When towards the middle of December he once more
appeared in the Commons, Clarendon had fled to France, and
he was just in time to assist in passing a bill of banishment
against him.[5]

Even before this the attack on Clarendon's supporters had
been begun, in which Osborne was destined in the end to be
just as deeply involved. As early as October 31 the administration of Ireland had been called in question, when Alderman
Barker presented a petition to the House of Commons complaining of injuries done him there.[6] A few days later it became
matter of general knowledge that Sir Richard Temple was ready
with articles of impeachment against the Lord Lieutenant,
Ormonde, and that a movement was on foot to deprive the
Duke of York of his position of heir presumptive by securing

[1] He was teller for the majority when the Commons resolved that the
charges against Clarendon should not be referred to a committee for proof,
and teller for the minority when it was resolved that the first head of the
accusation did not amount to treason, on both occasions in company with
Edward Seymour (*ibid.*, pp. 15, 18).

[2] Osborne undertook, singly or in conjunction with others, for Article 3
(receiving money for procuring the Canary Patent), Article 11 (advising the
sale of Dunkirk), and probably also Articles 9 and 10 (introducing arbitrary
government in the plantations, and frustrating proposals for the defence of
Nevis and St. Christopher). There are many lists of those who offered to
make the various charges good, but considerable discrepancies among them.
See *Diary of John Milward*, pp. 112-6 ; *State Trials*, ii. 338 *et seq.* ; B.M. Add.
MSS. 33413, f. 39 ; 35865, ff. 18, 23 ; 38175, f. 63 ; Carte MSS. 36, f. 86 ;
72, f. 29 ; Clarendon MSS. 85, f. 428.

[3] *C.J.*, ix. 20-23.

[4] Sir Thomas constantly appears in the Commons' Journal until November
19, and then not once till December 14.

[5] He served on the committee to whom the bill was remitted (*C.J.*, ix.
40-41). Osborne's own papers regarding the impeachment are B.M. Add.
MSS. 28045, ff. 1-17.

[6] *C.J.*, ix. 10 ; Carte, *Life of Ormond*, iv. 314-8.

for the King either a divorce or a decision that his favourite son, the Duke of Monmouth, was legitimate.[1] For the moment, however, the controversies roused by the impeachment of Clarendon absorbed all attention, and these designs had to remain in abeyance. On December 19 Parliament adjourned for the Christmas recess, and the members of both Houses hastened to join their families in the country. A tacit truce was established between parties; but the breathing space could be only a short one. No supplies had yet been granted, while popular indignation had been only very partially appeased by the dismissal and flight of the Chancellor. Thus the re-assembling of Parliament could not long be postponed, and as soon as it met the attack upon the Government was bound to be resumed.

Clarendon had left a considerable party behind him, but it was temporarily discredited, loosely bound together, and without a leader of conspicuous ability. Few of the rising generation had enrolled themselves among his followers, with the exception of his own sons Henry and Laurence, neither of whom had yet attained the age or acquired the experience necessary to enable him to take a prominent part in affairs. Thus the Clarendonians, as they were somewhat vaguely called, were in no position to offer serious resistance to a determined assault, and their only hope of retaining their place in the Government lay in the rise of divisions among their opponents. Of such divisions there seemed every prospect, for the chief motive force which had inspired many of the enemies of Clarendon was a desire for the sweets of office, and no sooner had their first success been won than they began to quarrel over the spoils.[2]

The seal which had been taken from the Lord Chancellor had been immediately entrusted to the Chief Justice of the Common Pleas, Sir Orlando Bridgeman, with the title of Lord Keeper. But Bridgeman was a lawyer rather than a statesman,

---

[1] Carte MSS. 36, f. 25 ; *Pepys*, November 4, 1667.

[2] " There is a stop put upon the disposall of offices at Court with which they thought to have gratified severall of the House of Commons before next session, but there are so many pretenders for every place that they finde they shall disoblige more then they shall gaine by it " (Conway to Ormonde, January 14, 1668, in Carte MSS. 36, f. 104).

and was quite unable to fill the place in the Government
vacated by his predecessor. Of the three most prominent
opponents of Clarendon, any one of whom might have aspired
to be his real successor, Sir William Coventry was in general
estimation the most honest and the most capable ; but his
honesty made him more enemies than friends, while his capacity proved insufficient to counterbalance a complete lack of
that personal charm without which few statesmen went far
at the Court of Charles II. The King disliked him ; the Duke
of York had been alienated by his attitude to Clarendon ; even
with his own colleagues he was never popular. As a result
the real struggle for supremacy lay between Buckingham and
Arlington.[1]

Of these two Arlington unquestionably had the greater
credit with the King, but Buckingham had, or at least was
believed to have, much more influence in the House of Commons, and as matters then stood that was almost bound to be
the decisive factor. Buckingham at least imagined that he
had the ball at his feet, and proceeded, with cheerful optimism,
to apportion the principal Government offices in accordance
with his own ideas. For himself he claimed all the positions
held by Ormonde, the Stewardship of the Household in England and the Lord Lieutenancy of Ireland. By subordinate
posts in his Irish government he hoped to gratify the less
important among his followers ; but for the two most capable
of them something better was reserved. Sir Robert Howard
was to replace Sir William Morice as Secretary of State. Sir
Thomas Osborne was to have the Earl of Anglesey's post of
Treasurer of the Navy, one of the most lucrative offices at the
disposal of the Crown. At the same time, in order to silence
all rivals, the Commission to which the Treasury had been
entrusted on the death of Southampton was to be dissolved,
Arlington was to be appointed Lord High Treasurer, and Sir
William Coventry was to succeed him as Secretary.[2]

Throughout the period when this grandiose scheme was
under discussion Sir Thomas Osborne was detained in the
north by the first real tragedy in his family, the death on

---

[1] Clarke, *Life of James II*, i. 433 ; *Pepys*, December 7, 1668.
[2] Carte, *Life of Ormond*, iv. 321-5 ; *Cal. S.P. Dom.*, 1667-8, pp. 258-9.

January 14, 1668, at the age of eleven, of his eldest daughter Elizabeth. For a time Lady Osborne was inconsolable. Sir Thomas remained with her at least till the end of January and probably longer. Not until the meeting of Parliament on February 6 does he appear to have come up to London, and even then he was constantly distracted by the melancholy letters which he received from his wife.[1]

His preoccupation during these weeks, however, was not without its advantages, for it enabled him to escape all connection with one of those discreditable episodes by which Buckingham constantly contrived to ruin his own prospects. The intrigue between the Duke and the Countess of Shrewsbury, which had begun at York in the summer of 1666, had continued throughout the following year, and had even been brought prominently to public notice by the frantic behaviour of Henry Killigrew, one of the Countess's discarded lovers, who received a public beating from the Duke.[2] The result of this scandal was a challenge from the injured husband, followed by a duel at Barn Elms, near Putney, on January 16. Buckingham was accompanied to the field by Sir Robert Holmes and Captain William Jenkins ; Shrewsbury's seconds were his own relatives, Sir John Talbot and Bernard Howard. Of the six combatants only two escaped serious injury. Buckingham thrust Shrewsbury through the right breast and shoulder. Holmes and Talbot wounded each other. Howard killed Jenkins on the spot.[3]

The duel caused a great sensation, partly because of the scandalous circumstances which had given rise to it, partly because of the unusually ferocious character of the contest itself. All the survivors deemed it prudent to obtain pardons from the King, for the coroner's jury which investigated the death of Jenkins brought in a verdict of manslaughter.[4]

[1] B.M. Add. MSS. 28040, f. 4 ; *Lindsey MSS.*, pp. 370, 371. Elizabeth was buried at Harthill on January 17 (Foster, *Pedigrees of Yorkshire Families*, vol. ii.).

[2] *Pepys*, July 22, 1667 ; *Hist. MSS. Com.*, vii. 486.

[3] Lady Burghclere, *Buckingham*, pp. 190-7 ; B.M. Add. MSS. 36916, f. 58 *et seq.* ; *Pepys*, January 17, 1668.

[4] *Cal. S.P. Dom.*, 1667-8, pp. 192, 193, 198, 205, 233. The pardons were accompanied by the usual " resolution never to pardon duellists for the future," and were regarded with such distaste that Lord Robartes refused to let them pass the privy seal (B.M. Add. MSS. 36916, ff. 63, 77).

Shrewsbury was for some time confined to bed; but by January 23 he was believed to be out of danger, and about the beginning of February Buckingham appeared openly at Court again. Nevertheless when Shrewsbury eventually died on March 16 the testimony of the surgeons, that his wound was perfectly healed and that death was due to some disease of the heart or liver, went for nothing. In popular estimation Buckingham had killed him, and the horror which this occasioned was soon intensified by the fact that the Duke openly continued his relations with the widowed Countess.[1]

No more unfortunate time could have been selected for such an incident than the days immediately preceding the reassembling of Parliament. Buckingham's personal following in the Commons was never really large, and his recent successes had been mainly due to purely fortuitous circumstances, which had gained him the support, on the one hand of the considerable Presbyterian group which had been alienated by the repressive Anglicanism of Clarendon's Government, and on the other of the large body of country gentlemen who viewed all officials and courtiers with suspicion and dislike. With both these bodies, among the most solid and respectable in the House, his influence was now severely shaken,[2] and by a serious mistake in tactics he weakened his position even further. Parliament as a whole was still intent on a thorough investigation of the miscarriages during the war, and his obvious course was to restore his credit by urging on the investigation, and leading the hue and cry after incompetent ministers which had served him so well before. Instead of this he made a premature attempt to inaugurate a policy of his own by supporting a project, foreshadowed in the King's opening speech, for giving relief to Protestant dissenters. By this means he no doubt recovered some of his reputation with the Presbyterians; but among the Anglican majority the mere suggestion of toleration or comprehension was sufficient to provoke an

---

[1] *Bulstrode Papers*, pp. 22, 23, 30; *Diary of John Milward*, pp. 230-1. *Cf.* the scandalous story told by Pepys (*Diary*, May 15, 1668), which whether true or not illustrates public opinion. Buckingham obtained further pardons after Shrewsbury's death and again in 1671 (*Cal. S.P. Dom.*, 1667-8 ,p. 400; 1671, p. 226).

[2] There was even a rumour that his pardon would be questioned in Parliament (*Pepys*, February 6, 1668).

outburst of feeling which gave new life to the Clarendonian party and produced in Buckingham's personal following the most serious divisions. Sir Thomas Osborne in particular regarded with extreme disfavour the influences under which his leader was falling. One of the results of the dismissal of Clarendon had been the release of several political prisoners who had been detained since shortly after the Restoration, among them John Wildman, the republican and leveller. Wildman now secured a large share in Buckingham's counsels, and brought others of like mind with him.[1] To the policy they advocated in Church and State Osborne was irreconcilably opposed, and he accordingly took as little part as he possibly could in the work of the House of Commons during the session.[2]

The meeting of Parliament, in consequence, brought Buckingham nothing but disappointment. He had staked his credit as a statesman on his ability to procure an adequate supply for the Government ; but all he could obtain was a vote of £310,000 towards the equipping of a fleet in the spring, about half the amount required for that purpose.[3] Not merely were no concessions made to Dissenters, but a new and more stringent measure dealing with conventicles was passed through the Commons, and prevented from becoming law only by a quarrel which broke out between the two Houses. The honours of the early months of 1668 went indeed to Arlington rather than to Buckingham. During the previous year Louis XIV had alarmed the whole of Europe by overrunning the Spanish Netherlands, which he claimed in right of his wife. In January 1668, however, Sir William Temple was dispatched by Arlington to the Hague, and there arranged with the Dutch an alliance for resistance to French aggression, which Sweden also shortly joined. This Triple Alliance, in appearance at least, forced Louis to accept terms at Aix-la-Chapelle, and

[1] " The Duke of Buckingham is the great favourite, and his cabal are Major Wildman, Dr. Owen and the rest of that fraternity, so that some say we are carried in Oliver's basket " (*Cal. S.P. Dom.*, 1667-8, p. 238. See also pp. 89, 259).

[2] His name does not appear at all in the Commons' Journal. Grey records one speech of his, on February 26, in committee of supply (*Debates*, i. 94).

[3] *C.J.*, ix. 62, 91. Buckingham's followers in the Commons became known as the Undertakers, and fell into complete discredit owing to a belief that they had been won over by the Court (*Pepys*, February 14, 1668).

secured for Arlington a temporary reputation far beyond that
of his rival.[1]

It is not surprising, therefore, that when, after the adjournment of Parliament on May 9, Buckingham endeavoured to
reconstruct the anti-Clarendonian faction, he found himself in
a much weaker position than he had occupied six months
earlier. The prestige which he had drawn from his supposed
control over the House of Commons had largely vanished.
Arlington, no longer in such deadly terror of a parliamentary
enquiry, refused to admit the same subordination as formerly.
Above all, the Clarendonians had received a considerable
increase of strength, so much so indeed that the arrival of
Ormonde in London on May 6 was the signal for a rumour that
he was to be made Lord High Treasurer of England, and was
to surrender the Lord Lieutenancy of Ireland to his son the
Earl of Ossory.[2] An unexpected but powerful ally for their
party had also appeared in Sir William Coventry, who had
been thoroughly disgusted by the erratic course recently pursued by the Government, and had for some time been dis-
sociating himself from Buckingham and Arlington.[3]

The prospect of a Clarendonian revival, however, was
sufficient to restore a measure of unity to the opposing factions,
and during the course of the summer a new cabal came into
being, the leading members of which were Buckingham,
Arlington and Lord Keeper Bridgeman. In the debates at the
Council Board the principal point at issue was the attitude
which should be adopted towards Parliament, and over this
problem the two groups drew definitely apart. The Clarendonians wished to retain the existing Parliament, to allow it to
reassemble in the autumn, and even perhaps to recall Clarendon
himself. The Buckinghamians, as they are occasionally called,
viewed with disfavour the Anglican zeal of the House of
Commons, and wished for a dissolution, or at least a long
prorogation. In the end something of the nature of a compromise was effected. Parliament, which stood adjourned to
August 11, was not dissolved, but was required to adjourn first

---

[1] Arlington's part in carrying through the Triple Alliance is fully discussed
in Barbour, *Arlington*, chap. vii.

[2] B.M. Add. MSS. 36916, f. 101.

[3] *Ranke*, iii. 482-4.

to November 10, then to March 1 of the following year, and was then finally prorogued to October 19, 1669.[1]

How far Sir Thomas Osborne agreed with his patron in his attitude to Parliament cannot now be determined ; but in the efforts to reconstruct the ministry on which Buckingham was at the same time engaged he certainly gave him all the assistance that was in his power, and played a very important though unfortunately very obscure part. It is significant of the altered balance of forces that the early successes of the new cabal were won at the expense of the Albemarle group rather than of the Clarendonians, and benefited Arlington rather than Buckingham. The sole achievement of the latter was to persuade Albemarle himself to sell to him his position of Master of the Horse, which Arlington had apparently destined for Ossory.[2] On the other hand the death of the Treasurer of the Household, Lord Fitzharding, was followed by the appointment of Arlington's henchman, Sir Thomas Clifford ; [3] while Albemarle's factotum, Sir William Morice, when at length he was induced to sell his post of Secretary of State, was persuaded to dispose of it to Arlington's nominee, Sir John Trevor, rather than to Buckingham's, Sir Robert Howard.[4]

These changes, however, were in Buckingham's eyes merely incidental to what throughout was his main object, the dismissal of Ormonde. In the long intrigue which had this end in view it was Osborne's function apparently to act as a unifying element, binding Buckingham and his allies together and galvanising them into activity. The task was far from

[1] *C.J.*, ix. 97. The struggle in Council over the summons of Parliament can be traced in B.M. Add. MSS. 36916, f. 103 *et seq.*

[2] Buckingham owed Albemarle £10,000. In repayment of this debt and in return for the place of Master of the Horse he gave him an estate worth £1,800 a year. He was sworn in on June 4 (B.M. Add. MSS. 36916, f. 102 ; *Bulstrode Papers*, p. 43 ; *Cal. S.P. Dom.*, 1667-8, pp. 411, 435 ; *Hist. MSS. Com.*, xii. 7, p. 56).

[3] B.M. Add. MSS. 36916, ff. 104, 105. The warrant for Clifford's appointment is dated June 14 (*Cal. S.P. Dom.*, 1667-8, p. 436).

[4] " Sir John Trevor is looked on by all now as Secretary of State, but is not yet sworn. Tis said the Duke of Buckingham endeavoured to bring Sir Robert Howard into that place, but the Lord Arlington was too hard for him " (newsletter of September 19, 1668, in B.M. Add. MSS. 36916, f. 114). Trevor paid Morice a sum variously estimated at £6,000 and £8,000, and was sworn in on September 29 (*ibid.*, f. 113 ; *Bulstrode Papers*, p. 61 ; *Hist. MSS. Com.*, xii. 7, p. 59).

being an easy one. Buckingham could never be relied upon to pursue a settled policy, and was constantly neglecting the most important negotiations for the sake of some erratic adventure. Bridgeman was timorous to the last degree, and was incessantly turning ill at the most inopportune moments. Arlington was an incalculable quantity, for though he was in general sympathy with the aims of the confederates he was attracted in the other direction by his long friendship with Ormonde, and by the fact that his wife, Isabella of Beverweert, was the sister-in-law of Ossory.[1]

It is to be doubted, therefore, whether Osborne could have secured any effective co-operation among his principals had it not been for the appearance of a new ally, who was to exercise a considerable influence over his political career during the next ten years. Roger Boyle, Earl of Orrery and Lord President of Munster, had hitherto been regarded by Ormonde as a friend, but about the beginning of 1668 he began to intrigue against the Lord Lieutenant, and when Ormonde came over to England in May he followed in June and joined his assailants.[2] The special contribution which he was able to make to their cause was his skill in dealing with figures, and his intimate acquaintance with the unfortunate financial condition of Ireland, where the expenditure ever since the Restoration had seriously exceeded the revenue. Finance was not directly subject to Ormonde's control, but as head of the administration he might be held responsible for anything that happened in Ireland, and it was determined to make a charge of financial maladministration the chief weapon of attack against him.

At the time of Orrery's arrival Bridgeman had retired for the sake of his health to Tunbridge Wells, and thither on July 17 the King was persuaded to dispatch Buckingham and Osborne to consult with the Lord Keeper about the removal of Ormonde from his position. The result of the conference which took place on the following day is to be seen in the appointment, almost exactly a month later, of a special commission to

---

[1] Clarke, *Life of James II*, i. 435 ; Carte, *Life of Ormond*, iv. 343.
[2] Carte, *Life of Ormond*, iv. 330-7 ; *Pepys*, May 3, 1668 ; B.M. Add. MSS. 36916, ff. 100, 107.

examine the Irish accounts.[1]　The original intention was that
Osborne should be a member of the commission, but Ormonde
protested so strongly against him as a confidant of Buckingham
that his name was omitted, and the commissioners appointed
were Bridgeman, Buckingham, Albemarle, Lord Robartes,
Sir Heneage Finch, Sir Edmund Wyndham, William Garroway
and Edmund Waller.　Garroway, however, petitioned that he
might be excused from sitting, and when the commission was
opened on August 20 the King with his own hand inserted
Osborne's name in his place.[2]

The investigation brought little to light,[3] and its main effect
was to divert the wrath of the confederates for a time to Lord
Anglesey, former Vice-Treasurer of Ireland, who had failed to
make the revelations about Ormonde which had been expected
of him.　Buckingham had already come into collision with
Anglesey over the affairs of the navy, of which he was now
Treasurer,[4] and a resolution was at last taken that he must be
driven from the ministry.　Throughout October Osborne was
busily engaged in pressing forward this new intrigue.[5]　The
King and Court were absorbed in a round of amusements at
Newmarket and Audley End ; the Lord Keeper was lying ill
in his house at Teddington ; Osborne himself and Orrery were
detained in London.　Yet by steady persistence Sir Thomas at

[1] This conference did not pass unnoticed at the time (*Bulstrode Papers*,
p. 52), and its meaning was fairly accurately surmised.　On Sunday, July 19,
one of Ormonde's correspondents wrote to him, " Fryday night the Duke of
Buckingham went to Tunbridge to speake with the Keeper.　Tis suspected
that the commission for the examination of your Graces administration in
Ireland was then sealed.　He is return'd this morning.　If it is not now done
it will be presently " (Carte MSS. 36, f. 406).　Osborne himself puts the matter
beyond doubt (B.M. Add. MSS. 28040, f. 4).

[2] B.M. Add. MSS. 28040, f. 4 ; 36916, ff. 111, 112, 113 ; *Cal. S.P. Ire.*,
1669-70, pp. 639-40 ; *Cal. S.P. Dom.*, 1667-8, pp. 543, 557, 564 ; *Hist. MSS.
Com.*, vii. 486.

[3] A considerable number of Osborne's own papers connected with the
investigation are in Leeds MSS., Packet 12.

[4] During the discussion of the affairs of Ireland and the navy at the time
of Clarendon's fall criticism had been concentrated largely upon Anglesey,
Vice-Treasurer of Ireland, and Sir George Carteret, Treasurer of the Navy.
In the summer of 1667 these two endeavoured to save themselves by changing
places, with the result that each of them was now in danger of being called
to account not only for his own faults but for those of the other as well.

[5] A good idea of his activities can be obtained from his letters to Buckingham
of October 7 and 8, printed *infra*, ii. 21-4.

length secured that action should be taken. On October 17 the King returned somewhat unexpectedly to Whitehall. On October 28 Anglesey was dismissed the Council, and suspended from the execution of all his offices. In vain he presented a petition setting forth that the post of Treasurer of the Navy had been given him by patent for life and could not be thus summarily taken away. The King did not deny him the benefit of the law in testing any title he might consider he had, but " saw no reason upon his petition to alter what he had already done." [1]

Apparently the original idea was that Arlington's follower Sir Thomas Littleton should have Anglesey's place ; [2] but Osborne's services by this time were much too great to be ignored. His appointment some weeks earlier to the reconstituted Council of Trade [3] could not be considered more than an earnest of something better to follow. On November 5, accordingly, he and Littleton were given a joint commission to execute Anglesey's office during his suspension, and being introduced by Lord Arlington kissed the King's hand upon it. [4]

This, however, was not the full extent of the reward intended for Sir Thomas. One of the things which had enabled Ormonde to retain his post in Ireland for so long was the difficulty of providing a successor. From the very first Buckingham had intended the place for himself, and this idea prevailed at least as late as the beginning of October. [5] But what Buckingham wanted was the dignity and emoluments of the office rather than the duties connected with it, and the problem was thus merely altered into one of finding a suitable deputy. As early

[1] Carte, *Life of Ormond*, iv. 340-1 ; *Pepys*, October 29-November 5, 1668 ; *Bulstrode Papers*, pp. 70, 72 ; *Hastings MSS.*, ii. 376-7 ; *Rawdon Papers*, pp. 233-7.

[2] B.M. Add. MSS. 36916, ff. 116-9.

[3] September 2, according to his own account (B.M. Add. MSS. 28040, f. 4). A copy of the commission and instructions to the Council of Trade, dated October 20, 1668, is in Leeds MSS., Packet 12.

[4] B.M. Add. MSS. 28040, f. 4. Pepys ascribes the formal ceremony both to November 4 and to November 5. There can be no doubt that the latter date is correct.

[5] Carte MSS. 36, ff. 25, 201. In his letter of October 8, 1668, Osborne clearly implies that the design was still to make Buckingham Lord Lieutenant (*infra*, ii. 23).

E

as March Lord Berkeley of Stratton had been put forward, but at the same time it was apparently suggested that Osborne might be associated with one or two others in a commission to act in Buckingham's name.[1] Still more when Arlington's remonstrances induced Buckingham to modify his pretensions did Osborne's name keep cropping up. Arlington wished to soften the dismissal of the Lord Lieutenant by handing over the government of Ireland to a number of Lords Justices, among whom possibly Ormonde and certainly Ossory should be included. Buckingham replied by putting forward his own chief supporters as their colleagues, and at the close of October a commission of five was confidently anticipated, consisting of Ossory, Orrery, Lord Berkeley of Berkeley Castle, Sir Thomas Osborne and Sir Robert Howard.[2]

Probably as a result of the nice balance of forces which they involved these elaborate schemes had eventually to be abandoned. On February 14, 1669, Charles was at length brought to the point of dismissing Ormonde ; but his successor was found, not among Buckingham's immediate followers, but in the Privy Seal, Lord Robartes, one of the Presbyterian group who were counted among Buckingham's associates.[3] At the same time, however, another prospect of advancement was opened up before Osborne. Apart from the Duke of York himself the sole remaining prop of the Clarendonian cause was Sir William Coventry, whose influence had for some time been steadily declining. At the beginning of March Coventry was induced by a caricature of himself intended by Buckingham for the London stage to send the Duke a challenge, and this was seized by his enemies as a pretext for ruining him.[4] On March 3 he was ordered to be committed to the Tower, and on March 5 was dismissed from the Council.[5] The most important office he had to lose was that of Commissioner of the Treasury,

[1] Carte MSS. 36, f. 212. There can be little doubt that the space after " Sir Thomas " should be filled by " Osborne."

[2] B.M. Add. MSS. 36916, f. 117 ; *Rawdon Papers*, p. 237.

[3] B.M. Add. MSS. 28040, f. 4 ; *Hist. MSS. Com.*, xii. 7, p. 61 ; *Cal. S.P. Ire.*, 1669-70, p. 627 ; Carte, *Life of Ormond*, iv. 348-52.

[4] B.M. Add. MSS. 36916, ff. 128, 129 ; *Pepys*, March 1, 4, 6, 1669 ; Christie, *Life of Shaftesbury*, ii. 3-4.

[5] *Cal. S.P. Dom.*, 1668-9, p. 222 ; B.M. Add. MSS. 28040, f. 4 ; *Hist. MSS. Com.*, xii. 7, p. 62 ; *Portland MSS.*, iii. 311.

and it was generally expected that one of the Treasurers of the Navy, probably Osborne, would have this post conferred upon him. Buckingham and the Lord Keeper united to press his appointment ; Orrery urged him to accept, and plans were even discussed for filling the place in the naval administration which his promotion would leave vacant.[1] Again, however, the difficulty of balancing contending factions proved an insuperable obstacle. Arlington took alarm at the threatened increase of Buckingham's influence, and exerted himself to prevent it. When on March 20 a new commission for the Treasury was issued, it merely reappointed Coventry's former colleagues without nominating any one in place of Coventry himself.[2]

These were serious disappointments. Nevertheless the outcome of the attack on the Clarendonians was highly satisfactory for Sir Thomas. It is true that he and Littleton were not allowed the traditional commission of threepence in the pound on all money passing through their hands which had made the post of Treasurer of the Navy one of the recognised prizes at the disposal of the Government ; but even the fixed salaries of £1,250 granted to each of them[3] enabled them to take their place among the more highly paid officials of the Crown. Osborne's income was certainly more than doubled, and relief was thus offered from the financial embarrassments which had hitherto been troubling him.

That relief came at a most opportune moment. On September 3, 1669, occurred the second bereavement in his family, the death at the age of two or three years of his youngest daughter Penelope.[4] On the following day was born the last of his many children, another daughter, to whom out of compliment to his wife's family he gave the name of Norris. Two years

---

[1] *Pepys*, March 11, 1669 ; *Cal. S.P. Ire.*, 1666-9, pp. 694-5, 697.

[2] *Cal. S.P. Dom.*, 1668-9, p. 240. Coventry was released the same day.

[3] Apparently the traditional poundage was still paid to Anglesey (*Cal. S.P. Dom.*, 1668-9, pp. 403, 589). The actual value of their appointment to the new Treasurers was estimated at £1,500 each (Lansdowne MSS. 805, ff. 86, 88).

[4] B.M. Add. MSS. 28040, f. 4. The date of Penelope's birth cannot be exactly determined, but the autumn of 1667 seems the most probable time. She was buried at Harthill on September 12 (Foster, *Pedigrees of Yorkshire Families*, vol. ii).

later little Norris was to follow her elder sister to the grave ; [1] but the remaining seven children were all destined to reach at least their majority, and were already attaining an age where serious provision had to be made for them. In the autumn of 1668 the eldest son Edward had been sent to school at West-minster.[2] Early in 1671 he and his brother Peregrine were to set out in the company of their governor to complete their education by a period of residence and travel in France.[3] The day was not far distant when the marriage portions of the daughters would have to be considered.

Moreover, Osborne's whole way of life had for some time been steadily changing. For the first six years of the reign or more he had been essentially a country gentleman whose interests lay almost entirely in Yorkshire. His visits to the south were few and short ; his wife, encumbered with the cares of her large family, never accompanied him ; he had no lodgings of his own in London, but resided while there either at his mother's house in Holborn or at his father-in-law's in the Old Palace Yard, Westminster. The death of his mother and father-in-law in the summer of 1666, however, followed by the long parliamentary session of 1666-7, had made some alteration in this practice almost imperative. Towards the close of October 1666 Lady Osborne was at length induced, very probably by news of the duel in which her husband had just been engaged, to come up to London,[4] where Sir Thomas was detained by his appointment as a commissioner of public accounts until the following June. In 1668 a further advance was made. After the first shock of her grief for the death of her daughter was

---

[1] She was born on September 4, baptised at St. Margaret's, Westminster, on September 29, 1669, and died at Hampstead on August 15, 1671 (B.M. Add. MSS. 28040, f. 5 ; *Register of St. Margaret's*, Harleian Society, p. 92, where her name is given as Morris and she is said to have been a boy).

[2] October 23, 1668 (B.M. Add. MSS. 28040, f. 4).

[3] Edward and Peregrine, together with one Hopkins, their governor, set out for France on March 16, 1671. On October 13 Lady Osborne went to join them at Saumur, and returning on November 22 brought Peregrine with her. Edward did not come back until February 18, 1672, recalled no doubt on account of the impending war with the Dutch (*ibid.*, ff. 5, 6).

[4] Sir Thomas Osborne to Lady Campden, October 20, 1666, *infra*, ii. 16. Sir Thomas had previously pressed his wife to come up on account of the anticipated length of the session (Sir Thomas to Lady Osborne, October 2, 1666, *ibid.*, p. 15).

over, Lady Osborne brought her family to London, and Sir
Thomas, leaving Lindsey House, set up with her an establishment of his own.[1] Thereafter he and his family abandoned
the simple life of the country for the more expensive life of the
town, and for the remainder of his life he had to face the
burden of maintaining two establishments.[2]

The concluding stage in this change was his appointment as
joint Treasurer of the Navy, which gave him permanent duties
requiring his presence in the south practically throughout the
year. That appointment and the change itself, however, have
a significance quite apart from their effect upon his private life.
Until 1668 Osborne's whole political outlook was that of the
typical country gentleman, and apart from personal and family
ties his natural allies were to be found among what was later
to be called the country party. After 1668 his residence in
London and association with other officials opened up to him
a new set of ideas by which he allowed himself to be gradually
dominated. No material exists to illustrate the change, which
was to occupy the four following years ; but its effect was to
secure that Sir Thomas Osborne always thereafter regarded
politics, even when himself out of office, from the official rather
than from the popular standpoint.

[1] In February 1668 Lady Osborne was being urged by her brother Peregrine to come to London and occupy half of Lindsey House, where Sir Thomas
was at that time residing (*Lindsey MSS.*, p. 371). Under date March 6 Sir
Thomas notes, " I removed my family from Lindsey House " (B.M. Add.
MSS. 28040, f. 4). Probably the word " family " here means only servants,
and Sir Thomas removed in order to receive his wife and children. It is not
clear where he went to, but it was to some place sufficiently commodious to
enable him to invite his " cousin " Frances Frescheville to stay with him
(Harleian MSS. 7001, f. 270). Two years later he was living in Tuttle Street.
On May 23, 1670, he returned to Lindsey House, apparently occupying the
whole of it, as he was able to entertain his brother-in-law, Lord Norris, there
for nearly a year. On December 16, 1672, he and his family left Lindsey
House for the Treasury Office in Broad Street (B.M. Add. MSS. 28040, ff. 5-7).
He was still living there in April 1673 (*Cal. S.P. Dom.*, 1673, p. 193).

[2] Another result of the change is noted in a frequently quoted passage in
the *Diary of Dr. Edward Lake* (*Camden Miscellany*, vol. i), p. 16. It should
be observed that the remarks there made originate with a lady who considered
she had been ill-used by the Osbornes.

CHAPTER V

DEPARTMENTAL DUTIES, 1669-72

In the spring of 1669 Sir Thomas Osborne may well have congratulated himself on the foresight that had led him to associate his political fortunes unswervingly with those of Buckingham. The supremacy of the Buckingham faction in the state and his own position as one of the leading men within that faction seemed to be growing steadily more assured. The suspension of Anglesey and the dismissal of Ormonde, followed so rapidly by the disgrace of Coventry, produced an immense impression, and marked their author out, in the eyes of contemporaries, as unquestionably the foremost politician of the day. It is true that they alienated some of the more reputable among Buckingham's supporters, notably Coventry's nephew, Sir George Savile, now Viscount Halifax, whose early friendship with Sir Thomas Osborne comes in consequence to an end about this time.[1] But they also attracted able men of a more self-seeking type, whose object it was to enlist under whatever leader could best further their ambitions. As early as April 28 Ralph Montagu was writing to Arlington warning him that Sir John Trevor was no longer to be trusted,[2] and during the summer the junior Secretary came to be generally recognised as one of the partisans of Buckingham.

With politicians of the second rank such as Trevor and Orrery it was now Osborne's privilege to associate. The days when he had to reckon Sir Robert Howard and William Garroway as serious rivals were fast fading into the background. Orrery in particular, a much older and more experienced man, proved very ready to advance his interests, and during the summer of 1669 the high degree of favour which

[1] Foxcroft, *Halifax*, i. 63-4.
[2] Hist. MSS. Com., *Buccleuch MSS. at Whitehall*, i. 423, 487.

he established with the King gave him every opportunity of
doing so. On July 5, at the express desire of Charles himself,
a firm alliance was established between Buckingham, Bridgeman, Orrery and Sir Thomas Osborne.[1] For the next three
years these four, with the addition of Trevor, were to form
the core of the Buckingham faction.

The more closely Sir Thomas was brought into touch with
the centres of political activity, however, the more he was
compelled to realise the handicap from which his own group
suffered. Although perhaps the most brilliant, Buckingham
was also the most erratic and unreliable of all the courtiers
who surrounded the throne of Charles II. Although numbering
within its ranks many able and pushing men, his following
contained far too many discordant elements to be able to work
harmoniously together in the pursuit of any policy. So long
as the task of the moment was the purely destructive one of
driving the Clarendonians from office these weaknesses might
remain hidden in the background. But the Clarendonians
had now been dealt with, and the adoption of a constructive
policy could no longer be postponed. The financial position
of the Government, as the Treasurer of the Navy could
not but know, was going from bad to worse. Money
somehow or other had to be procured, and the real problem
confronting those in authority was from whom it should be
sought and on what terms.

Since his failure at the beginning of 1668 Buckingham had
evaded this problem, and had pursued a policy of a very negative character. As against the Triple Alliance concluded
under Arlington's auspices he had advocated a French alliance ;
but while he had by this means secured a great reputation at
the French court he had done nothing definite to justify it.
As against the aggressive Anglicanism of the Clarendonians
he had advocated a measure of toleration or comprehension
for Dissenters ; but beyond conniving at a lax administration
of the penal laws he had taken no active steps in that direction
either. From both the French Government and the English
Dissenters financial assistance might in certain circumstances
be anticipated. The French king, intent on overrunning as

---

[1] Orrery to Conway, July 10, 1669, in *Cal. S.P. Ire.*, 1669-70, pp. 637-8.

much as possible of the Netherlands, was ready to pay heavily for English neutrality, and still more heavily for English assistance in a war with Holland or Spain. The Dissenters, just freed from the oppressive provisions of the Conventicle Act, which had expired on March 1, were growing in numbers and audacity.[1] If Parliament were dissolved, and they secured a majority in its successor, they might be expected to assist those responsible for the dissolution, though their assistance was only too likely to be given at the expense of the Church.[2]

Sir Thomas Osborne may have been influenced by that hostility to the Dutch which was still strong among those interested in trade,[3] or he may simply have regarded Buckingham's French intrigues as the lesser of two evils. Whatever the reason, he appears not merely to have known of Buckingham's connection with France but even in some measure to have lent it his countenance.[4] His natural inclination, however, was to reject the overtures both of France and of the Dissenters, and to secure relief for the necessities of the Government by coming to terms with the existing Parliament. It was probably at his instigation, therefore, that in the autumn

---

[1] The original Conventicle Act of 1664 was passed for a period of three years, counting from the close of the session in which it received the royal assent, and for one parliamentary session thereafter. The three years expired on May 17, 1667, and as Parliament in 1668 failed to renew the Act it lapsed with the first prorogation. The consequent growth of conventicles was so striking that the Government took the opinion of the judges on the legal restrictions still in force against them (*Cal. S.P. Dom.*, 1668-9, pp. 256-7, 398).

[2] The project most commonly put forward was that the lands of the Deans and Chapters should be confiscated and sold for the benefit of the State. This had already been proposed and debated in Parliament (B.M. Add. MSS. 36916, f. 80 ; *Cal. S.P. Dom.*, 1668-9, pp. 320-1).

[3] The anti-Dutch attitude is fully set forth in *A Letter to Sir Thomas Osborne, one of H.M. Privy Council, upon the reading of a Book called The present Interest of England stated*. This pamphlet, published in 1672, was frequently attributed to Buckingham, and presumably its main contentions are at least such as Osborne was not inclined openly to deny.

[4] According to Buckingham's secretary, Sir Ellis Leighton, who acted as intermediary in the French intrigues, Osborne and Orrery were employed in an attempt to modify the anti-French attitude of Bridgeman and gain his support. " Leyton dit aussy que ledit Duc presse et Milord Orory, dont il est si fort assure, et Asborn, quy est aparement en grand credit dans le Parlement, de faire agreer cette alliance au Garde des Sceaux, sur lequel ils ont grand credit " (Colbert de Croissy to Louis XIV, October 5, 1669). It is significant, however, that Osborne is hardly ever mentioned in the French dispatches at this time.

of 1669 Buckingham once more took up the project he had
abandoned nearly two years earlier, of an alliance with the
Clarendonians, whose foreign policy had also been based on
friendship with France.　During the reign of Charles I Buckingham and his younger brother Francis had been educated
in the company of the royal princes, Charles and James, under
the supervision, among others, of Thomas Howard, first Earl
of Berkshire.　This nobleman, or more probably his son
Charles, the second Earl,[1] was now employed as intermediary
in laying before James a scheme which presumably involved
a general confirmation of the existing Anglican ascendancy,
together with some concessions to Catholics and Dissenters,
as the basis of a great coalition of Courtiers, Clarendonians and
followers of Buckingham in support of the Crown.[2]

Such a coalition, Osborne felt confident, could command
more than sufficient support in the House of Commons to
ensure the grant of supplies, and in his desire to demonstrate
this clearly to his patron he embarked on an elaborate survey
which constitutes, so far as can be ascertained, his first essay
in the art of party organisation.　Even Clarendon had not
disdained to keep in touch with some of the leading members
of the Commons, holding occasional meetings with them, where
policy and tactics were discussed, and directions were agreed
upon which they in turn passed on to the rank and file among
the supporters of the Government.　Arlington had gone much
further, setting himself at the head of the younger men who
disliked the Chancellor's patronising attitude, forcing himself
and some of his followers into the inner circle of advisers, and
extending the scope of the conferences in a way which Clarendon felt was bound to earn them a large amount of very
unfavourable attention.[3]　For some years the practice had
been followed of conferring positions at Court upon members

[1] The first Earl died on July 16, 1669.

[2] Clarke, *Life of James II*, i. 436-7.

[3] The leaders of Clarendon's organisation, according to his own account,
were himself and Lord Treasurer Southampton.　Its inner ring of influential
politicians included Sir Hugh Pollard, Henry Coventry, Sir Orlando Bridgeman
and Sir Geoffrey Palmer.　The chief point carried by Arlington was the
admission of himself, Sir Thomas Clifford, Sir Winston Churchill and perhaps
Sir William Coventry to this inner ring (Clarendon, *Continuation of Life*,
pp. 343-5, 347-56).

of the Commons, and procuring seats in the Commons for servants of the King. By these means there had been built up, even before the fall of Clarendon, a very loosely knit and unreliable Court party, consisting of many different sections —royal officials, who were expected to vote as the Government directed ; personal adherents of the leading politicians on the Government side ; and the considerable group of west-country-men who had been enlisted in the service, first of Clarendon by Sir Hugh Pollard, then of Arlington by Sir Thomas Clifford. After Clarendon's fall this party had largely resolved itself into its component elements ; but at least a considerable nucleus continued to be held together by the combined efforts of Clifford and Arlington's indefatigable secretary, Joseph Williamson.[1]

During the frequent alliances between Buckingham and Arlington Sir Thomas Osborne, as representing the former, must have been brought into close touch with this organisation, and it was on the experience of its managers that his calculations were based. Government officials in the House of Commons were estimated at 92, and the Duke of York's servants there at 9. Members of Parliament whose support might be enlisted by James and his friends were believed to number 45, and those who might be similarly engaged by Buckingham and his friends to number 39. Finally it was hoped that reliance might be placed on those members, estimated at 106, who had previously manifested their readiness to grant supplies. For the proposed coalition there was thus shown a grand total of 291 probable supporters.[2]

The coalition, however, never became a reality, and when Parliament was at last permitted to assemble on October 19 Osborne's calculations proved to have singularly little bearing on the actual course of events. Far from accepting the proffered co-operation of Buckingham, the Duke of York, when it

[1] In an anonymous paper headed " The Alarum," scattered in Westminster Hall on October 20, 1669, Arlington is described as the " great instrument " of corruption in Parliament, " who, besides promises of this or that place, tells out ready money to hirelings, who engage to betray their country for it." Clifford is recognised as his chief assistant and probable supplanter (*Cal. S.P. Dom.*, 1668-9, pp. 541-2).

[2] The list of names, in the handwriting of Sir Thomas Osborne, is printed *infra*, iii. 33-42.

came to the point, showed an unexpected readiness to join with Arlington,[1] and the support of his friends, in consequence, could no longer be hoped for. With him went the Clarendonians, the older Cavaliers and the Church party in general, who united in recognising the leadership of Buckingham's inveterate enemy, the Duke of Ormonde.[2] Even Buckingham's personal following grew strangely thin.[3] With a view to enlisting the support of the large body of unattached members in the Commons he had recourse to his old policy of denouncing corruption, and organised a successful attack on Sir George Carteret. But the Clarendonians were now strong enough to strike back, and under the inspiration of Ormonde countered with an impeachment of Orrery, which the Buckingham group proved too weak to ward off. Meanwhile the problem of supply received only the most perfunctory attention, and after nearly two months of futile bickering the prorogation of Parliament was decided upon through the influence of the Duke of York, Ormonde, Arlington and Prince Rupert at a meeting at which Buckingham was not even present.[4]

Osborne was bitterly disappointed, and not altogether un-justly inclined to blame his patron both for the failure of his proposed coalition and for the very unsatisfactory position in which he now found himself. While still loyally supporting Buckingham in Parliament, and readily taking part in such personal matters as the assault on Carteret and the defence of Orrery,[5] he could not but feel that so far as the major issues of the day were concerned he was on the wrong

---

[1] Clarke, *Life of James II*, i. 444.

[2] Among the Carte MSS. (vol. 36, f. 320) is a paper endorsed by Ormonde, " Lyst of such as my Lord Aungier conceived to bee my friends in the House of Commons, 11 May 1668." If Lord Aungier himself be included, this gives the names of 57 supporters of the Duke. Of these no fewer than 47 are to be found among the 291 names on Sir Thomas Osborne's list. The details are indicated *infra*, iii. 34-44.

[3] According to one observer Buckingham's following in the Commons during this session numbered no more than 8 (F. R. Harris, *Life of Sandwich*, ii. 312). Even of these only 5 are included among the 39 supporters whom Buckingham was to enlist. The names are noted *infra*, iii. 34-43.

[4] There is a good description of the events of this session in a letter printed in Harris, *Sandwich*, ii. 313-7.

[5] *Grey*, i. 169, 214 ; Marvell, *Poems and Letters* (ed. Margoliouth), ii. 88 ; Carte, *Life of Ormond*, iv. 381-2.

side of the House. At a private meeting early in the session
the Clarendonians had adopted, as the chief planks in their
political platform, the preservation of the existing system of
Church government, the promotion of the Cavalier interest,
and the institution of a test to exclude from Parliament all
those of contrary opinions. These were precisely the principles
which Osborne himself favoured, and to which he was to endeavour when in power to give effect. Yet he was debarred
from supporting them by the fact that he had thrown in his
lot with Buckingham, and Buckingham apparently had so
grievously offended York, Ormonde and other leaders of the
Clarendonians that even an alliance with them was impossible.

Nor was it merely Buckingham's policy that raised doubts
in Osborne's mind. Still more trying was the complete irre-
sponsibility of his behaviour, at this particular moment
threatening to be productive of more than usually serious
consequences. The problem of Ireland, mainly as a result of
Buckingham's unsteadiness, had never been satisfactorily
settled. The morose Lord Robartes entirely failed to satisfy
the Irish, quarrelled with the Government at home, and towards
the close of 1669 wrote asking to be recalled.[1] Coming immediately after the impeachment of Orrery this raised a very
difficult situation for the Buckingham group ; yet after calling
on Buckingham, writing to him, and calling again several
times the next day, Osborne was unable to obtain even an
interview in which to discuss the steps that should be taken.
If business of such moment was to be given so little attention,
he bitterly declared, he would prefer to be excused from all
participation in public affairs, and would confine himself to
the duties of his office.[2] Buckingham, who for once was
genuinely incapacitated by illness,[3] had some difficulty in
pacifying him, and although on the recall of Lord Robartes
the Duke was able to demonstrate his power by securing the

---

[1] B.M. Add. MSS. 36916, f. 162. His letter is dated December 7, 1669
(*Cal. S.P. Ire.*, 1669-70, p. 50).

[2] His second letter to Buckingham, dated December 18, 1669, together
with Buckingham's reply, is printed *infra*, ii. 24.

[3] He was seriously ill from about this time to the beginning of February
(B.M. Add. MSS. 36916, ff. 161, 162, 164 ; *Cal. S.P. Ire.*, 1669-70, pp. 59,
651-2).

appointment of his own nominee, Lord Berkeley of Stratton, this incident may be taken as marking the rise of a definite suspicion within Osborne's mind that his patron was more a hindrance than a help to him, and the first faint beginning of the breach which was to follow more than four years later.

So far as Parliament is concerned Osborne's threat to abandon public affairs seems to have been largely fulfilled. When the Houses reassembled on February 14, 1670, the main factor in the political situation was a renewal of the uneasy alliance between Buckingham and Arlington, and the main work of the session proved to be an indirect attack on the Duke of York. Both Buckingham and Arlington viewed with genuine apprehension the probability that James and eventually the grandchildren of Clarendon himself might sit upon the throne, and as a preliminary step towards a divorce and remarriage for Charles united to pilot through Parliament a bill enabling the divorced Lord Roos to marry again. In this Osborne appears to have taken no part whatever.[1] Even when Parliament at last made a serious effort to meet the financial needs of the Crown by granting, for a period of eight years, additional duties on wine and vinegar, and providing for the sale of the fee farm rents and other fixed revenues deemed too expensive to collect, he does not appear to have come forward on behalf of the Court. Indeed his only recorded intervention in Parliament during the spring session of 1670 was in favour of a new and more severe Conventicle Act which Buckingham can scarcely have approved.[2]

At Court, on the other hand, Sir Thomas continued to exert himself to maintain his patron's ascendancy, for on that ascendancy his own position was still dependent. Especially after the refusal of the King to profit by the Divorce Bill the influence of the Duke of York, Ormonde and the Clarendonians increased, Arlington showed a growing inclination to join with them, and Buckingham was compelled to seek allies elsewhere. These he might hope to find among the more prominent politicians who were without strong party ties of their own.

[1] Harris, *Sandwich*, ii. 318-33 ; *Grey*, i. 251-63. If Osborne had seriously supported Buckingham in this matter his name could hardly have been omitted from every account of it.

[2] *Grey*, i. 250. His name is not once mentioned in the Journal.

With the Chancellor of the Exchequer, Lord Ashley, he had already established some kind of understanding ; but more important even than Ashley was the Earl of Lauderdale, whose success in upholding the royal authority in Scotland had confirmed the influence he had long enjoyed with the King. As late as March 1670 Lauderdale's position in English politics was still uncertain. He had, however, offended the Duke of York by supporting the Divorce Bill, and alienated Ormonde and Arlington by advocating the claims of Lord Berkeley in Ireland as against those of Lord Ossory. About the beginning of the month, accordingly, Ormonde, Arlington and Clifford combined in an attempt to diminish his credit with the King, and at a meeting held in the house of Lord Kingston attacked him so fiercely as to produce an open breach. Several days of feverish intrigue followed, in which Orrery and Osborne appear to have played their part, and the royal sanction was then secured for the establishment of a new " governing cabal," consisting of Buckingham, Ashley, Lauderdale, Kingston, Berkeley, Trevor, Orrery and Osborne. For the first time Sir Thomas came to be recognised as a member, however unimportant, of the inner circle of the King's advisers.[1]

Even when thus reinforced, however, the Buckingham group was far from being in a position to impose its own policy upon the King. The associates of Ormonde and Arlington were almost equally powerful, and continued to exercise a strong rival influence at Court. The result was two years of extraordinary confusion, during which the only genuine thread of connection is the policy which Charles himself devised and somewhat fitfully pursued.

The origin of that policy is to be found in a meeting on January 25, 1669, in the Duke of York's closet, where Charles in the presence of the Duke, Lord Arlington, Sir Thomas Clifford and Lord Arundell of Wardour, declared his belief in

---

[1] Conway to Rawdon, March 15, 1670, in *Rawdon Papers*, pp. 239-41. One may question whether the inclusion of Osborne among the members of this cabal is not due to the partiality of a friend. Marvell gives substantially the same list of names, but omits Kingston, Berkeley and Osborne (*Poems and Letters*, ii. 303). Another account agrees with Marvell, but substitutes Bridgeman for Ashley (B.M. Add. MSS. 36916, f. 179). It is, however, abundantly clear from many sources that Bridgeman's influence by this time had greatly declined.

the Roman Catholic religion, and requested their opinion how it could best be promoted within his dominions. The conclusion reached after long debate was that the most effective method would be to enlist the assistance of the French King, and secret negotiations were accordingly entered upon with this object in view.[1] The intrigue was a protracted one, for when it came to a question of terms each King was bent on overreaching the other, and it was not until the summer of the following year that an agreement was concluded through the mediation of Charles's sister, Henrietta, Duchess of Orleans, who enjoyed the confidence of both monarchs. In the middle of May Henrietta crossed the Channel, ostensibly on a friendly visit to her brother, and on the 22nd of the month a secret treaty was signed at Dover by the French ambassador Colbert on the one side, and by Arlington, Arundell, Clifford, and Sir Richard Bellings on the other. Charles undertook to declare himself a Catholic, and make war on the Dutch in alliance with France. Louis promised, in the event of trouble in England, to assist his ally with money and troops, and agreed to pay him an annual subsidy so long as the war with Holland continued. Provision was made for a division of conquests between the two kings.[2]

Meanwhile Buckingham, who knew nothing of these developments, had become alarmed at the increasing favour shown to Arlington, and had been induced to initiate a parallel series of negotiations with France, by which he hoped to maintain his own credit at Court. Of these advantage was now taken by the King to enable him to make known to a wider circle of ministers just as much of the real treaty as he considered necessary and politic. The death of Henrietta immediately after her return to France was made the excuse for sending Buckingham on a special embassy to Versailles, as a result of which a second treaty was negotiated, substantially the same as the first, except for the omission of all reference to the King's profession of Catholicism. This *traité simulé* was signed on December 21, 1670, by Clifford, Arlington, Buckingham, Ashley and Lauderdale, and, the declaration of war against

[1] Clarke, *Life of James II*, i. 440-2.
[2] *Mignet*, iii. 186-99.

Holland having been delayed by the unprepared condition of England, was redrawn in practically the same terms and signed once more by the same men on February 2, 1672.[1] The entrusting to their hands of so important an affair marked them out as forming in a very special sense the " cabal " or inner circle of ministers, and the singular fact that the initials of their names could be arranged to form the word itself earned for them in a very short time an unenviable notoriety as *the* Cabal of the reign.[2]

Neither Buckingham nor Arlington was really in favour of the policy which these treaties embodied. As a politician Buckingham had a great admiration for Louis XIV and the system of government which he represented, but his religious associations throughout his life were with Puritanism rather than with Catholicism. Arlington, on the other hand, was inclined to Catholicism, but as a result of his Dutch marriage and his embassy to Madrid before the Restoration his political sympathies lay with the United Provinces and with Spain. Nevertheless so acute was the rivalry of these two statesmen that neither dared endanger his favour with the King by any backwardness in supporting the royal wishes, and the zeal of both was inflamed by rewards skilfully dangled before them. Arlington was deluded with the hope that he would be made Lord Treasurer. Buckingham, among whose many ambitions a desire for military glory held a foremost place, believed that he was to be given command of the English troops employed against the Dutch.

No similar prospect of personal gain, however, obscured the judgment of Sir Thomas Osborne, who from the first regarded these developments with complete disapproval. How much exactly he knew of what was going on can only be surmised.

---

[1] *Ibid.*, iii. 256-65, 699-701. The sole object of the last treaty was to make it possible to publish the agreement with France while at the same time concealing how long the French intrigue had been in progress. As early as October 1671 it was matter for common discourse that a war against the Dutch in alliance with France was to be anticipated (B.M. Add. MSS. 36916, ff. 231, 232, 235 ; *Hist. MSS. Com.*, vii. 489).

[2] The Cabal was not a ministry which was in power from 1667 to 1673. The only intelligible way in which the word can be used is to denote the men who were primarily responsible for the policy initiated by the Treaty of Dover and the *traité simulé*.

On May 30, 1670, three days before the Duchess of Orleans left for France, he waited on the King at Dover, returning with him later by sea to London, and it is just conceivable therefore that he may have had some suspicion of the real meaning of Henrietta's visit and of Arlington's side of the intrigue.[1] Buckingham almost certainly told him all he knew, and before the Duke set out for France on July 21 Sir Thomas did his utmost to dissuade him from having anything to do with the affair, declaring that it would inevitably mean his ruin. The Duke, however, somewhat gloomily replied that if he refused to go York and Arlington would certainly ruin him in three months, whereas if he complied with the King's wishes he might postpone the evil day for two or three years. The assimilation of England to France, he argued, was bound to happen in any case, and he might as well join in forwarding it and gain what he could for himself.[2]

From this despondent attitude Buckingham was effectually aroused by the magnificent reception which Louis XIV accorded him in France, and by the apparently complete success of his negotiations there.[3] For the moment he became an enthnsi-astic supporter of the French alliance, and after his return to England on September 10 the favour which he had hitherto shown to Sir Thomas Osborne appreciably declined. This change came at a most inopportune moment. Since the beginning of the year Lord Anglesey had been steadily recover-ing credit with the King, and was endeavouring to secure the removal of his suspension from the office of Treasurer of the Navy. As early as April he had been summoned once more to the Privy Council. At the end of June it was popularly reported that he had been restored to his old post, and since then the danger threatened by his claims had increased.[4] Without Buckingham's support Osborne felt quite unable to stand against him, and accordingly took the desperate step of

---

[1] It may or may not be significant that he considered his visit to Dover worth recording in the brief notes of important events in his life which he drew up more than thirty years later (B.M. Add. MSS. 28040, f. 5).

[2] B.M. Add. MSS. 28042, f. 30, printed *infra*, ii. 92.

[3] Burghclere, *Buckingham*, pp. 220-7.

[4] B.M. Add. MSS. 36916, ff. 179, 185 ; *Cal. S.P. Dom.*, 1670, pp. 162, 175, 185 ; *Rutland MSS.*, ii. 14-15 ; *Finch MSS.*, ii. 191.

coming to an agreement, in return for some compensation, not to oppose his claims. About November he wrote to Buckingham announcing what he had done, and expressing his resolution to lay down all his employments and retire into private life.[1]

How far exactly this trouble was patched up is not clear. The suspension of Anglesey certainly was not removed, nor did Osborne resign any of his places. On the other hand Sir Thomas persisted in his determination not to be associated with the policy on which Buckingham and the Government had embarked. The main object of the King in permitting the Houses to reassemble on October 24 was to obtain sufficient supplies to enable him to make preparations for his attack on the Dutch. With discreditable disingenuousness, however, he allowed Lord Keeper Bridgeman, who knew little or nothing of the French intrigues, to represent the supply as needed in order to fulfil the terms of the Triple Alliance, and the Commons, among whom that league was immensely popular, responded with unusual generosity. From October 1670 to April 1671 Parliament remained almost constantly in session, and during that period granted a special subsidy, calculated to produce £800,000 ; an additional Excise on beer, ale and other liquors, to continue for six years from June 24, 1671 ; and certain duties on proceedings at law, which were to remain in force until May 1, 1680.

For its success in securing these very considerable grants the Government had to thank the better organised Court party which had by this time been brought into existence. The failure of Osborne's attempt in the autumn of 1669 to gather together a party in support of Buckingham had left the way clear for Clifford and Williamson to perform a similar service for Arlington, and with Arlington's original organisation to work upon they had been much more successful. The prorogation of December 1669, for which Arlington was largely responsible, had been intended at least in part as a warning to the more neglectful among the " Courtiers and indebted members " that they must either show greater readiness to assist the Government or risk the loss of their parliamentary

---

[1] His letter, undated, is printed *infra*, ii. 25.

privileges by a dissolution.[1] The effect was seen in the spring
of 1670, when Williamson first began the practice of drawing
up instructions for the guidance of his followers,[2] and the
Courtiers were so successful in working together that on one
occasion the country gentlemen to the number of nearly 80
left the House in a body as a protest.[3] In the autumn it was
widely believed that bribery was being used by Clifford,[4] and
it was noted that the Buckingham group had thrown in its
lot with the Court.[5] It is significant, however, that while
Seymour, Howard and others among Buckingham's satellites
became extremely active on behalf of the Government Osborne
remained obstinately aloof. Knowing only too well how the
money being voted would be employed, and yet unwilling to
force an actual breach with his patron, he preferred to attend
Parliament as little as possible.[6] His purely official duties were
already sufficient to occupy the whole of his time, and to these
he confined his attention, not merely during the session but
for more than a year after its close. Probably his relations
with Buckingham were never quite the same again.

Not a little of his time during these months was devoted to
the problem of the relations of England and Scotland. As a
Yorkshireman he had a certain natural interest in the affairs of
the sister kingdom, which had led, as early as the beginning
of 1668, to his inclusion in a special commission, appointed by

[1] B.M. Add. MSS. 36916, f. 159.

[2] *Cal. S.P. Dom.*, 1670, pp. 71, 76.

[3] B.M. Add. MSS. 36916, ff. 166, 167.

[4] Looking back on this session in the summer of 1672 Charles was able to
assure the French ambassador that the majority of the Commons " were tied
to his interests either by offices or by pensions, and all by the fear of a dissolution of the Parliament which would expose them to free pursuit by their
creditors " (Christie, *Shaftesbury*, ii. p. xvi ; Harris, *Sandwich*, ii. 334-5 ;
Lansdowne MSS. 805, ff. 83-9 ; Harleian MSS. 7020, ff. 33-48, where Clifford
is described as the " bribe-master general ").

[5] Marvell, *Poems and Letters*, ii. 305.

[6] Between the assembling of Parliament on October 24, 1670, and its prorogation on April 16, 1671, he is mentioned only three times in the Journal
(*C.J.*, ix. 161, 172, 188). Grey records four unimportant speeches of his
(*Debates*, i. 287, 327, 354, 357), and Sir Edward Dering records a fifth (*Parliamentary Diary*, ed. B. D. Henning, p. 73). His failure to play a more prominent part is the more remarkable inasmuch as the supply was required for
the navy, in which he was personally concerned, and the estimates for which
he presented, by order of the Commons, on October 31, 1670 (*Bulstrode Papers*,
p. 157).

the King to discuss with a similar Scottish commission the establishment of freedom of trade between the two countries.[1] When negotiations had broken down over the refusal of the English to exempt Scotland from the Navigation Act, he played an active part in a further commission, which considered, with little more success, proposals for the political union of England and Scotland.[2]

But his most important duties were those which devolved upon him as joint Treasurer of the Navy along with Sir Thomas Littleton. The Treasurer of the Navy was the most considerable of the four " principal officers " who, together with a varying number of " commissioners ", constituted the Navy Board, or advisory council of the Lord High Admiral in the discharge of his functions as governor of the navy. Nominally the mere channel through which the Lord Admiral issued his commands, this Board had in practice a considerable degree of independence in administrative affairs, for its official superior, as befitted a great minister of state, was constantly engaged elsewhere, and in his absence all ordinary business, and even by special direction extraordinary business, could be transacted by it on its own initiative. Its most energetic member was the indefatigable Clerk of the Acts, Samuel Pepys, but on the whole it was a committee of experts, with a creditable record behind it of good work done under very difficult circumstances.[3]

Into this body Littleton and Osborne had been thrust as representatives of the reforming faction in Parliament and in the country. The supreme governor of the navy, the Duke of York, had not even been consulted about their appointment.[4] They were mere civilians, without any special knowledge of naval affairs.[5] Their sole function was to correct the abuses

[1] Osborne gives the date of his appointment as December 30, 1667 (B.M. Add. MSS. 28040, f. 3). The warrant is dated January 4, and the commission January 7, 1668 (Cal. S.P. Dom., 1667-8, pp. 156, 158).

[2] Terry, The Cromwellian Union (Scottish History Society), p. 187 et seq.; B.M. Add. MSS. 28040, ff. 5, 9.

[3] J. R. Tanner, Catalogue of Pepysian MSS., i. 6 et seq.

[4] Clarke, Life of James II, i. 436 ; Pepys, October 29, 1668 ; Hist. MSS. Com., xi. 5, p. 32.

[5] In his Naval Minutes (ed. J. R. Tanner, p. 257) Pepys includes them both among those " brought into the navy for want of other ways of gratification."

which had been denounced in the navy during the course of
the war with Holland, and at the same time to advance in
every possible way the interests of the group to which they
belonged. As a natural consequence they were highly unpopular both with their colleagues and with their official superior,
while their proceedings savoured distinctly of faction. Instead
of finding remedies they indicated faults, and gave the whole
Board the impression that their object was to spy out its
weaknesses in order to hand it over in due course to the mercy
of its parliamentary critics.[1] They declared themselves dissatisfied with the precedence assigned them, endeavoured to
dismiss their subordinates and bring in new men, and opposed
to the best of their ability every appointment advocated by
the Duke of York in naval affairs. Only as the wave of reform
which followed the dismissal of Clarendon gradually died away
did they fall into their proper sphere, acquire a better knowledge of the difficulties which confronted those in charge of
the navy, and earn even among their colleagues a high reputation for energy and ability.[2]

In addition to his duties as a member of the Navy Board,
however, the Treasurer of the Navy had special duties of his
own to perform. It was his function to receive money by
order of the Lord Treasurer or Treasury Commissioners, and
pay it away to the uses of the navy. In doing so he was
nominally a mere subordinate executing the instructions of the
Lord Treasurer, the Lord Admiral or the Navy Board ; but
in practice, partly owing to having too many superiors, partly
as a result of the extraordinary financial confusion which prevailed, he had a very considerable degree of independence.
The navy had its own financial system and its own debt, and
it was his business to keep it from financial collapse by the best
methods he could find. In default of assistance from the
Treasury he might have to act very much on his own responsibility, and stave off the constantly impending catastrophe by
pledging his own credit in support of that of the Government.

How precisely these various duties were divided between

---

[1] Cf. especially Pepys, December 4, 15, 1668 ; February 12, 14, May 10,
1669.

[2] Clarke, Life of James II, i. 445 ; Pepys, passim. A number of Osborne's
navy papers are in Leeds MSS., Packet 12.

Littleton and Osborne is by no means clear, but it seems certain that Osborne had nothing to do with purely financial matters,[1] and highly probable that Littleton was the senior partner all round. The result was not satisfactory. On the one hand the Lord Admiral and the Navy Board both resented the independent attitude assumed by the Treasurers ; on the other hand Osborne chafed at the subordinate position which he was required to occupy in the partnership, and as Buckingham and Arlington drifted apart he and Littleton inevitably fell out with each other. In the early summer of 1671 a crisis was reached. Osborne accused Littleton of serious malversations in connection with the funds entrusted to his care,[2] and those who wished to diminish the Treasurer's importance seized the opportunity to urge upon the King that both Osborne

---

[1] *Cal. S.P. Dom.*, 1671, pp. 469, 514 ; 1672-3, p. 268 ; 1673, pp. 584-5. Many corroborative expressions could be quoted from Osborne's own papers.

[2] The following document, preserved among the Leeds MSS. (Packet 16), and endorsed, "Memorial concerning Sir Thomas Littleton about the Treasury of the Navy," must have been drawn up at a somewhat later date, but seems to embody the charges made at this time :

Sir Thomas Littelton, late employ'd in the Treasury of the Navy, has been the occasion of very great disservice to his Majestie in the following particulars, viz.

1. There being a very great strait for mony in the navy in *anno* 1669, and the goldsmiths then insisting upon their having old navy bills and tickets in their hands, which they would have taken in by the Treasurers of the Navy and allow'd them out of such mony as they should advance to them, a warrant was obtained from his Majestie to permitt the borrowing mony of the goldsmiths upon these termes, provided the said bills and tickets were not above a tenth part of the mony to be advanced. Nevertheless it was left to the particular care and prudence of Sir Thomas Littelton and his brother to borrow what mony they could without giveing that liberty or letting the goldsmiths know it was in theire power, who accordingly did so. But instead of improoveing that care (as they ought) to his Majestie's advantage, the said brother, Mr. James Littelton, bought bills and tickets to the value of neere 100,000 l. at great profitt, and brought the same to account as if taken in with the loans of mony from the goldsmiths, who never had the like allowance in any proportion to the mony by them lent. And this was so well knowne that Sir Thomas Littelton could not bee ignorant of it, and may reasonably bee concluded to have had a share therein.

2nd. The said Sir Thomas Littelton singly disposed of sundry considerable payments in the navy by his written and verball orders, which were irregular and ought not to have been paid out of the treasure then supply'd for the use of the navy.

3rd. The said Sir Thomas Littelton hath not to this day made account of the monys received for the use of the navy, and in the last eight weekes of his management certified to the Navy Board the payment of about 80,000 l. in old bills and tickets, and yet notwithstanding is a considerable debtor to

and Littleton should be dismissed and a subordinate official with the title of Cashier appointed instead.[1] On July 11 both Treasurers and the entire Navy Board were summoned to give evidence before the Privy Council, where the whole problem was debated. As between Osborne and Littleton no decision was reached, but it was resolved that in future there should be only one Treasurer, who should be brought under much stricter subordination than formerly.[2] There, however, the matter was allowed to stand for some time. Charles set out on a lengthy voyage among the sea-ports of the south, and it was not until September 6 that the new instructions for the Treasurer of the Navy were formally approved, nor until September 20 that Buckingham's influence prevailed over Arlington's and the post was conferred upon Sir Thomas Osborne.[3] A few days later Littleton was consoled by being joined with four others in a new contract for victualling the navy.[4]

It is tempting to suppose that Osborne's victory may have been partly due to the support of Samuel Pepys, with whom he had struck up some sort of alliance.[5] If so Pepys's judgment was not at fault. The new regulations were decidedly stringent. The Treasurer of the Navy in future was to consider himself an ordinary member of the Navy Board, all meetings of which he was to attend ; he was not to dispose of any money without

his Majestie on that accompt, haveing particularly lent 9,000 l. of the King's mony since his being in the victualling to his partners in that affaire in other men's names.

All which undue diversions of the King's mony from the use it was appointed to was at times of the King's being very much straitned for mony in all his offices.

Besides his joint miscarriage in the victualling matters.

[1] By June 28 the King had been prevailed with to decide in favour of a Cashier, but a week later he promised Osborne that if the change were made he should continue with the same salary as he had as Treasurer (B.M. Add. MSS. 28040, f. 9).

[2] P.C. Reg. 63, p. 46 ; *Cal. S.P. Dom.*, 1671, p. 379 ; *Hist. MSS. Com.*, xiii. 6, p. 265.

[3] B.M. Add. MSS. 28040, ff. 5, 9, 12 ; *Hatton Correspondence*, i. 71. Osborne was appointed to execute the office at a salary of £2,000 a year, and at the same time was granted the reversion of it after the Earl of Anglesey (*Cal. S.P. Dom.*, 1671, pp. 498-9, 537).

[4] B.M. Add. MSS. 36916, f. 231 ; *Cal. S.P. Dom.*, 1671, pp. 506-7 ; 1671-2, p. 37.

[5] *Pepys*, May 14, 1669 ; *Cal. S.P. Dom.*, 1671-2, p. 154.

their order, nor, once their order had been given, was he to delay in carrying it out; he was to deliver every week a certificate of his receipts and payments, and he was not to have any vote in making contracts or bargains.[1] But all these rules Osborne faithfully observed,[2] and even his enemies admitted his success in his new post. His principal achievement appears to have been the introduction of more businesslike methods not only in his own department but in the proceedings of the Navy Board as a whole. Scarcely had he entered upon his duties when he prevailed with the Board to keep a minute book for recording their orders, warrants and other transactions. To contemporaries, however, his most striking characteristic was his skill in borrowing money. The Osbornes, apparently, had never entirely dropped their City connections, and Sir Thomas was sufficiently well known in business circles to be able to secure accommodation from the bankers when scarcely any one else could do so. Within five days of taking over Littleton's money orders he had borrowed £9,000 upon orders on which it was supposed nothing could be had, and that at a lower rate of interest than had been paid for two years.[3]

It was perhaps in the Buckingham tradition that Osborne showed himself at the same time unusually careful to prevent frauds on the seamen, whose interests were largely in his hands, but opportunity was denied him to carry his work in this connection to a fitting conclusion. The outbreak of war with the Dutch shortly after his entrance upon his duties threw a heavy strain upon the Navy Office and postponed radical reform indefinitely. By the time the war came to an end and reform was once more practicable, Sir Thomas had been removed to another sphere.

[1] P.C. Reg. 63, p. 63 ; *Catalogue of Pepysian MSS.*, i. 24-6.

[2] There is, however, at least one instance of an item in his weekly certificate being questioned (*Cal. S.P. Dom.*, 1671, pp. 579-80).

[3] " My Journall commencing 20th September, 1671, and ending 2nd December, 1672, relating to the business of Treasurer of the Navy," in Osborne's own handwriting (B.M. Add. MSS. 28040, ff. 11-32). This journal is concerned almost entirely with official details, but it brings out fairly clearly the essential features of Osborne's work.

CHAPTER VI

THE REWARD OF INDUSTRY, 1672-3

THE success of Sir Thomas Osborne in dealing with the administrative duties entrusted to his charge greatly improved his standing at Court. From a mere member, however prominent, of the Buckingham group it raised him to the position of a trusted official, and gave him a status and reputation of his own quite independent of his patron. Charles himself, and still more the Duke of York, were quick to recognise good service, especially in connection with the navy ; and the constant attendance of Sir Thomas upon them, during the course of their visits to the fleet,[1] enabled him to efface the bad impression created by his earlier behaviour in Parliament, and gain for himself a comparatively high place in their favour. Between him and speedy promotion the only obstacle which intervened was his continued and determined aloofness from the whole world of politics.

Nevertheless the actual moment at which Sir Thomas allowed himself to be brought back to the political arena may seem to have been singularly ill-chosen. At the beginning of 1672 Charles, after much hesitation, at length embarked on his great design. On January 2, by the Stop of the Exchequer, he suspended for a year all payments on assignments, thus practically admitting bankruptcy, and threatening the bankers, who had advanced the money on these assignments, with immediate ruin. On March 15 he gave his sanction to a Declaration of Indulgence, which in virtue of the King's supreme power in ecclesiastical matters suspended all penal laws against all dissenters from the Church of England.[2] Two days later,

[1] Osborne's diary (B.M. Add. MSS. 28040) contains frequent references to his visits to the fleet with the King or the Duke or both.

[2] The precise object of this declaration has frequently been debated, and no doubt it appeared in a somewhat different light to every one of the ministers who supported it ; but Osborne was later assured by Clifford that it " was designed only in behalfe of the papists " (*infra*, ii. 91).

after an unsuccessful attempt to seize the Dutch Smyrna fleet
in time of peace, he issued a formal declaration of war against
Holland.   On April 16 he prorogued Parliament, which had
not met for nearly a year, to October 30.   With these measures
Osborne had no connection, and to all of them he was strongly
opposed.   Yet on April 29 he was offered a seat on the Privy
Council, and on May 3 he was formally sworn in.[1]

The object of Charles in making the offer is not difficult to
discern.   In the interests of his great design he was anxious
to enlist as many supporters as possible, and throughout 1672
was busily engaged in distributing places and titles not only
to those who favoured his policy, but to all who he thought
might be won over, or whom he deemed it worth his while to
conciliate.   During the last fortnight of April Lauderdale was
made a Duke in the Scottish peerage and was given the Garter,
Arlington was made an Earl, Lord Ashley became Earl of
Shaftesbury, and Sir Thomas Clifford Lord Clifford of Chud-
leigh.   On April 17 four influential lords were admitted to the
Council, Worcester, Essex, Fauconberg and Halifax ; while
at the same time Essex was nominated to take the place of
Berkeley as Lord Lieutenant of Ireland.[2]   Towards the close
of May the death of Sir John Trevor was followed by the
appointment of Henry Coventry as Secretary of State, and a
rumour spread abroad that his brother, Sir William, was also
to be given a place in the ministry.[3]   The promotion of Sir
Thomas Osborne was only a small item in a very much wider
policy.

The object of Sir Thomas in accepting the King's offer, and
thus associating himself to some extent with a policy which he
had hitherto refused to consider, cannot be so easily determined.   It seems at least possible that he may have regarded
it as an earnest of something much better to come, for in spite

---

[1] B.M. Add. MSS. 28040, f. 9 ; P.C. Reg. 63, p. 231.   Almost at the same
time he was gratified by a small appointment for his brother Charles, who was
made Commissioner of Prizes for Hull (B.M. Add. MSS. 28040, f. 6).

[2] B.M. Add. MSS. 28040, f. 6 ; *Kennet*, iii. 313-4.

[3] Trevor died on May 28 and the appointment of Coventry was immediately
decided upon.   As Coventry was then on an embassy to Sweden, however, he
was not actually sworn in till July 3 (Lord Halifax to Henry Coventry, June 3,
1672, in Foxcroft, *Halifax*, i. 69 ; *Hatton Correspondence*, i. 89 ; B.M. Add.
MSS. 28040, f. 6).

of his lack of diplomatic experience his claims to succeed Trevor as Secretary were at least considered.[1] More probably, however, he was inspired by a very different motive. Signs were already apparent that the great design was not going to prove the complete success which had been anticipated, and Buckingham especially had begun to regard it with some disfavour. The Duke's heart had been set on securing the command of the English auxiliary land force provided for in the Treaty of Dover, and he had been bitterly aggrieved by an arrangement made between Charles and Louis that this force should be dispensed with for a year.[2] His ill-humour had been increased by the failure of his own lieutenant, Sir Robert Holmes, in the attack on the Dutch Smyrna fleet, and by the course which the war had taken during its early months. While the French on land had overrun half of the United Provinces, the English at sea had won no striking successes whatever, and the part of the Netherlands assigned by treaty to England remained untouched. Since the beginning of the year Buckingham had been on bad terms with the Government,[3] and he was now considering the possibility of making peace.[4] When Osborne allowed himself to be sworn of the Council it was not improbably with the idea that a change of policy was imminent, and that he might as well be in a position to take advantage of it when it occurred.

If such was his belief he was doomed to disappointment. Towards the close of June Buckingham and Arlington were dispatched to Holland to discuss terms with the States and the French King ;[5] but the resolution of William of Orange, who

---

[1] Orrery to Osborne, June 14, 1672, in Leeds MSS., Packet 4.

[2] Colbert to Louis XIV, November 9, 1671, in *Dalrymple*, ii. 86 ; *Buccleuch MSS. at Whitehall*, i. 501-7.

[3] *Hatton Correspondence*, i. 77-9.   [4] Foxcroft, *Halifax*, i. 77-8.

[5] On their arrival they were joined by Lord Halifax, who had been dispatched somewhat earlier to congratulate the French King on the birth of a son. A full account of the embassy is contained in Foxcroft, *Halifax*, i. 70-97, and Barbour, *Arlington*, pp. 193-9. It has not been generally noticed, however, that the ambassadors were accompanied by Edward Seymour, who was entrusted with the task of conveying to William of Orange the terms agreed upon between them and the French King (B.M. Add. MSS. 29577, f. 123 ; *Correspondentie van Willem III en Bentinck*, part ii., i. 65-6). On his return to England Seymour sent an account of the embassy to Sir Thomas Osborne (B.M. Add. MSS. 28053, f. 43, dated London, July 16, 1672).

had just been appointed Stadtholder, precluded all possibility of their demands being accepted ; Buckingham, unstable as usual, swung violently over to the French side, and the war continued to be prosecuted as vigorously as ever. Possibly with the failure of this embassy may be connected Osborne's retirement, about the beginning of July, into the north on the plea of ill-health. Not until September did he return to London,[1] and by that time the continued success of the French and comparative failure of the English had made him even more hostile to the war. Hitherto there had at least been the prospect that England might obtain territorial advantages or trading concessions at the expense of the Dutch which would serve as some compensation for the growth in power of France, but it was now becoming very doubtful whether she could hope to gain anything at all.[2] The decision of the King to prorogue Parliament once more, announced in Council on September 17,[3] was the signal for a further period of retirement on his part, this time to Chatham, where he busied himself with the affairs of the navy.[4] It is significant that from June 28 to November 8 he was scarcely ever present in Council.[5]

Other statesmen also, however, were now becoming alarmed at the ill-success of the great design. Arlington had always hoped that a few victories over the Dutch would make the war popular and untie the purse strings of the House of Commons ; but of these victories there was no sign, and he was becoming very apprehensive of what might happen when financial necessity should again compel a summons of Parliament. Bridgeman had never approved of the great design at all, and

[1] He left London on July 9 and returned on September 5 (B.M. Add. MSS. 28040, ff. 25, 26). His illness appears to have been real, though not very serious, and his time was spent mainly at Knaresborough, until towards the close of August he went south to Bath.

[2] *Cf.* Seymour's comment, " I beleeve wee are and shall bee most danably gull'd, that the whole power of Holland will fall into the hands of the French King, and that at the latter end of the yeare the striking of sayle and a little money will bee our portion."

[3] " September 17th. The Parliament was prorogued to the 4th February next, and I was then at the Bath " (B.M. Add. MSS. 28040, f. 6). In reality Sir Thomas attended the meeting of the Privy Council in London on that day (P.C. Reg. 63, p. 243).

[4] *Cal. S.P. Dom.*, 1672-3, pp. 5, 27, 66, 73.

[5] P.C. Reg. 63, *passim*.

was highly doubtful of the legality of many of the Government's proceedings. For support in his schemes Charles had to rely mainly on Shaftesbury, who would not abandon the Declaration of Indulgence, and Clifford, whose object all along had been to raise his own credit by diligent advocacy of a policy which he knew to be acceptable both to the King and to the Duke of York. In the autumn what was practically a trial of strength took place between the two factions, and the resolution to prorogue Parliament was essentially a victory for Shaftesbury and Clifford. Their firm support of the Government was speedily rewarded. On November 16 the refusal of Bridgeman to put the great seal to a commission establishing regulations for the troops raised during the war led to his dismissal,[1] and on the following day Shaftesbury was created Lord Chancellor in his place. Sir John Duncombe was immediately appointed Chancellor of the Exchequer ;[2] but as Shaftesbury had also been a member of the Treasury Commission a further reorganisation of the financial department seemed inevitable, and Arlington hoped at last to realise his ambition of being made Lord High Treasurer. Charles and James, however, had been much impressed by the greater determination of Clifford, who now definitely broke away from his patron, and on November 28 was given the post which Arlington had hoped to fill. Party dissentions were thereafter embittered by personal jealousy, for Arlington and Clifford hated each other with a deadly rancour.[3]

[1] Osborne's own statement is quite explicit—" 1672, November 16th. The great seal was taken from the Lord Keeper Bridgeman upon the Earl of Shaftsbury's accusation to the King that he would not put the great seal to a comission for marshchall law " (B.M. Add. MSS. 28040, f. 7). The commission was presumably that issued on December 4, of which complaint was later made in Parliament (*Cal. S.P. Dom.*, 1672-3, p. 243 ; *C.J.*, ix. 276 ; *Parliamentary History*, iv. 581). A somewhat different reason for Bridgeman's dismissal is given in *Hatton Correspondence*, i. 101-2, and in the *Lives of the Norths*, i. 115. Osborne, however, believed he knew all the facts. More than thirty years later, when Duke of Leeds, he noted against p. 289 of Kennet's *History* (ed. 1706), " Lord Bridgman's resignation not true. Memorandum also to relate that story, and note the expression of Shaftsbury's uninterupted good services " (B.M. Add. MSS. 28042, f. 112).

[2] *Cal. S.P. Dom.*, 1672-3, p. 171.

[3] The story that Arlington deliberately forwarded the Test Act with the object of driving Clifford from office (*Mignet*, iv. 236) is almost certainly a reasoning backward from events, but it gives a fair idea of the relations

In the comparatively equal balance of forces at Court much naturally depended on the attitude of the Duke of Buckingham, while in the parliamentary session which would soon have to be faced it was believed that his dangerous following might have a decisive voice. During the winter of 1672-3, accordingly, Charles and James made a determined effort to conciliate the whole Buckingham group. The prospect of high military command in an expedition against the Dutch was again dangled before Buckingham, and a pension of £2,400 was conferred upon him.[1] Lord Orrery was invited over from Ireland and very favourably received by the King.[2] Edward Seymour was gratified by being made a Commissioner of the Navy,[3] and the project was mooted of securing his election as Speaker of the House of Commons. The problem presented by Sir Thomas Osborne, however, could not be so easily solved. So long as he refused adhesion to the policy of the Court he could hardly be given a higher official position than the one he occupied, while the grant of any English title would have the effect, undesirable at the moment, of withdrawing him from the House of Commons. In the end, accordingly, it was determined to confer upon him a Scottish title, and on February 2, 1673, just two days before Parliament met, a warrant was

between the two men. Arlington, however, had been quite willing to contemplate Clifford's appointment as a possibility, and had even planned that if it should occur his own followers should secure an advance all round, Lord Newport taking Clifford's place as Treasurer of the Household, Sir Robert Carr succeeding Newport as Comptroller, and Sir Joseph Williamson securing Carr's position as Chancellor of the Duchy (Williamson's Diary under date November 21 in *Cal. S.P. Dom.*, 1672-3, p. 629). Arlington's real grievance was probably his failure to secure any compensation for his disappointment either by the promotion of Carr and Williamson or by the grant of a Dukedom, of which he had some hopes at this time (Thomas Thynne to Sir William Coventry, December 4, 1672, quoted in Christie, *Shaftesbury*, ii. 98). The post of Treasurer of the Household was given to Lord Newport, but that of Comptroller to Lord Maynard (*Cal. S.P. Dom.*, 1672-3, p. 219).

[1] *Hatton Correspondence*, i. 95 ; *Cal. S.P. Dom.*, 1672-3, p. 510.

[2] *Cal. S.P. Dom.*, 1672-3, p. 499. On his leaving Charles after a conference lasting more than an hour he met Sir Thomas Osborne, who enquired whether he had been persuaded to support the designs of the Court, and received a reply in the negative. "Then," said Sir Thomas, "you are the honester man, but will not be worth a groat" (T. Morrice, *Memoirs of the Earl of Orrery*. p. 41).

[3] Osborne gives the date as October 19, 1672 (B.M. Add. MSS. 28040, f. 6), but see *Cal. S.P. Dom.*, 1672, pp. 91, 429.

issued for his elevation to the Scottish peerage as Viscount Osborne of Dumblane.[1]

If Charles hoped by this means to secure his support in any shape or form for the Declaration of Indulgence he was speedily undeceived. Towards the close of 1672 several meetings of Government supporters had been held to discuss the policy which should be adopted towards Parliament, and in these Osborne had taken part; [2] but there is no evidence that the meetings had led to the consolidation of any considerable party in support of recent measures, or even that those who attended viewed these measures with approval. In spite of the King's assertion, in his opening speech on February 5, that he was resolved to stick to his Declaration, the new Lord Osborne[3] immediately, though in the most respectful manner, let it be seen that he was opposed to it. Some members of the Commons would have replied to the King's speech with a simple vote that the Declaration was illegal. In opposition to this, Osborne first proposed and carried a motion that the customary thanks should be given for the speech, together with an intimation that the matter contained in it would be considered two days later, and then in the main debate on February 10 joined with others to persuade the House to proceed by the milder method of a formal address to the King. Partly no doubt as a result of his efforts on the committee which drew up the address, the terms in which it was couched were made as conciliatory as possible, and when an evasive answer was returned he was instrumental in persuading the Commons to give thanks for the " gracious assurances and promises " contained even in that. Of the committee which drew up the address of thanks he was not a member, but it is possible to discern his influence in its respectful tone no less than in

---

[1] *Cal. S.P. Dom.*, 1672-3, p. 511.

[2] *Ibid.*, pp. 629, 630.

[3] The title is used with some hesitation. It was very rarely given him by contemporaries, whether strangers, friends or relations, and never by the House of Commons. Even the first announcement of his appointment as Lord Treasurer in *The London Gazette* (No. 792) described him as Sir Thomas Osborne, Baronet, though the mistake was corrected in the next number. Not a few contemporaries took the correction in the *Gazette* as meaning the grant of a new title, although the title was then four months old (*Letters to Williamson*, i. 62 ; *Hatton Correspondence*, i. 108).

its continued insistence that the Declaration could not be accepted.[1]

Short of abandoning the interests of his Church, however, Osborne was ready to give the Government all the assistance in his power, and with that object in view he exhibited in this, his last session in the House of Commons, greater activity than he had ever displayed before. Since the last time he had been prominent in the House, during the attack on Clarendon, his whole position and outlook had altered. Not merely was he now a trusted official, but he was also a privy councillor, and every speech he uttered was weighted with a new sense of official responsibility.

The reply of the opposition to the Declaration of Indulgence was the introduction of two bills, one to give ease to Protestant dissenters, the other to prevent the growth of popery. Towards the former Osborne adopted a very suspicious attitude. While professing a desire to comprehend within its scope as many dissenters as possible he showed himself irreconcilably opposed to any proposal to suspend even for a year the renunciation of the Covenant which was the principal test used against them. Such a suspension, he asserted, would merely " encourage the wickedness of these men," and incite them to " return into rebellion." " If there be any one," he declared, " that thinks himself under the obligation of this Covenant, he is no good man." [2]

Towards the bill against popery, which provided that all office-holders and members of the royal household should take the oaths of allegiance and supremacy, receive the sacrament according to the rites of the Church of England, and subscribe a declaration denying transubstantiation, Osborne's attitude was more complicated. In principle he was in favour of the bill, and he was a member of the committee which drew it

---

[1] C.J., ix. 248, 251, 252, 256-7 ; Parliamentary Diary of Sir Edward Dering, pp. 107, 116, 119, 131-3 ; Grey, ii. 24, 54-69.

[2] Grey, ii. 45, 47. Cf. Secretary Coventry's speech—" As for removing the Covenant, if we are to increase our garrison, would not do it with those that have the plague " (ibid., p. 43). Many years later Sir Thomas Osborne, then Earl of Danby, declared that he opposed the Indulgence solely because of the favour it showed to Catholics (B.M. Add. MSS. 28043, f. 35). His speeches on the bill for the relief of dissenters hardly support this statement.

up ; [1] yet all his efforts in the House of Commons were directed towards securing the modification of what appeared to him as an official to be objectionable features in it. A rigid exclusion of all but Anglicans from military command he considered unnecessary and likely to impair the efficiency of the army. Previous to the outbreak of the war with the Dutch, he pointed out, an investigation inaugurated by the King had shown that there were at most sixteen Catholics holding commissions, all of whom had been appointed as efficient soldiers and not on account of their religion.[2] If the restrictions proposed must pass he hoped they would be confined to the land forces. In the fleet there were only two Catholic captains, and these young men of no particular eminence. At the very least, he argued, the word " officers " should be confined to those holding superior positions. Among the masters, boatswains and gunners the proportion of fanatics was unusually large, and too strict a test applied to them would mean the complete ruin of the navy.[3]

So long as religion was under review Osborne was torn by conflicting considerations, but in the debates on supply his sole aim was to secure from the Commons as large and speedy a grant as possible. The best safeguard against the growth of popery, he declared, would be a subsidy for the use of the navy, for if lack of money should cause the fleet to fall short popery would stand upon the very threshold of the country.[4] To the proposal to postpone the final stages of the bill of supply until that against popery had passed into law he was completely opposed. The task of guarding against popery, he argued, could if necessary be handed over to a later session ; but the summer's campaign had to be provided for at once or not at all. Supply should be granted as rapidly as possible, and a little trust should be placed in the King and the House of Lords to deal fairly thereafter with the religious measure.[5]

In the end Osborne's efforts on behalf of the Government

---

[1] *C.J.*, ix. 260. [2] *Grey*, ii. 75. [3] *Ibid.*, p. 86.

[4] *Ibid.*, p. 83. This was really a direct condemnation of the Government's foreign policy, for it was the French, not the Dutch fleet that was likely to bring popery into England. Foreign affairs, however, were not at the moment under discussion.

[5] *Ibid.*, pp. 109, 115, 137 ; *Parliamentary Diary of Sir Edward Dering*, p. 140.

proved of little avail. Although supported by all the principal ministers with the exception of Arlington, the Declaration of Indulgence had to be unconditionally cancelled,[1] while the bill against popery, with very few alterations, became the first Test Act.[2] Only when the King had made a complete surrender did the Commons carry to a conclusion their grant of an Eighteen Months' Assessment, calculated to produce £1,238,000, for the purposes of the war. But the activity which he had shown greatly increased Osborne's credit at Court, and enabled him to commend himself in particular to the Duke of York. One of the minor problems raised during the debates in the Commons was whether the test provided by the bill against popery should be applied to the household of James as well as to that of the King, and on this point Osborne had definitely taken the Duke's side, arguing that he was merely a subject like any one else, and should not be placed under any special disability.[3] James was not ungrateful, and this incident marks the completion of that reconciliation between the Lord Admiral and the Treasurer of the Navy which had been steadily developing for some time. For more than five years Osborne was to find one of his firmest supporters in the Duke of York.

When Parliament adjourned on March 29, however, it could scarcely have been anticipated that the favour of the Duke would prove of immediate value. The passing of the Test Act had not been expected to produce any sudden or serious changes in the ministry. Few members of the Government, if any at all, were credited with a greater attachment to the Catholic faith than to their places,[4] and even those who hesitated between the claims of conscience and interest were not required to make

[1] The seal was broken by the King with his own hand on March 7, and the cancellation was announced to the Commons on the following day (*Cal. S.P. Dom.*, 1673, p. 24 ; *Parliamentary Diary of Sir Edward Dering*, p. 134 ; Colbert to Louis XIV, March 20, 1673, in *Dalrymple*, ii. 93).

[2] On the King's giving the royal assent " there was the greatest hum amongst the Commoners that ever was heard " (*Cal. S.P. Dom.*, 1673, p. 101).

[3] *Grey*, ii. 144.

[4] The common statement that the Test Act was intended to drive Catholics from office rather misses the point. It would be nearer the truth to say that its object was to compel those in office to repudiate Catholicism. Many even of those who had formerly been counted Catholics complied with the provisions of the Act (*Letters to Williamson*, i. 24).

a final decision until June 15. Throughout the month of April the principal statesmen were steadily observing the provisions of the Act amidst singularly little comment from any quarter.[1] Public interest was concentrated rather on the formal negotiations for peace, which led to the dispatch early in May of Sir Leoline Jenkins and Sir Joseph Williamson as plenipotentiaries to a congress at Cologne, or on the preparation at the same time of an immense armament against the Dutch, of which the supreme command was given to the Duke of York, with Prince Rupert as his subordinate in charge of the fleet, and the Duke of Buckingham as lieutenant-general in charge of the army.[2] Buckingham was greatly delighted with his appointment, and hurried into the north to see to the raising of six hundred recruits for his own regiment.[3] Other politicians retired into the country.[4] Domestic affairs sank completely into the background.

Suddenly and without warning the whole position changed. Clifford had allowed it to be understood that he would take the sacrament at St. Martin's Church on Whitsunday,[5] and had insisted on being left undisturbed the previous day in order that he might make fitting preparation. In reality he spent the Saturday at the Queen's palace, Somerset House, which he left towards evening in a coach, accompanied by her almoner, Father Patrick McGinn. Unfortunately as the coach turned into the Strand it upset, and the occupants were thrown among the passers-by, who assisted them to pick themselves up and recover their hats and wigs. Next day the congregation at St. Martin's looked for the Lord Treasurer in vain. The obvious suggestion was that he was still indisposed after his accident, but this was immediately disproved by his appearance the same evening at Council, and the whole town forthwith concluded

---

[1] *Hist. MSS. Com.*, xii. 7, pp. 100-1.

[2] *Cal. S.P. Dom.*, 1673, pp. 175, 243 ; Colbert to Louis XIV, May 25, 1673.

[3] Buckingham left London on the morning of May 16 (*Cal. S.P. Dom.*, 1673, p. 258). On May 24 he wrote to Osborne from York and on June 1 from Halifax (*Hist. MSS. Com.*, ix. 2, p. 449; *Morrison Catalogue*, i. 128).

[4] Edward Seymour, for instance, with no idea of what was coming, took up residence at Maiden Bradley in Wiltshire, where he proposed to stay for the rest of the summer (*Cal. S.P. Dom.*, 1673, p. 299).

[5] May 18.

that he was a determined Catholic and would refuse the Test.[1]

That Clifford was not a Catholic in any real religious sense is perfectly clear from the evidence of his most intimate friends.[2] But as a politician he had gambled on the chance of a Catholic revival, and fortune having declared against him he was sufficiently honest to be ready to forfeit his stake. It was by casting aside the half-hearted Catholicism of Arlington that he had raised himself to eminence, and it was almost impossible for him to retreat without incurring the contempt of the King, the Duke of York, and his own former patron. The wholly unexpected revelation of his intimate connection with the Catholics, and the reception of that revelation by popular opinion, probably decided his wavering counsels. For the next month the problem which confronted the politicians was not so much whether he was going to resign as who should have his place.

One possible solution was the appointment of Arlington, who still considered that he had claims on the post. Clifford, however, had no intention of resigning for Arlington's benefit, and sought a successor among the members of the opposing faction, with which he had for some months been associated. During his period of office at the Treasury he had been much impressed by the financial ability of the Treasurer of the Navy, and he now took the lead in indicating Osborne as the only man fit to fill his place. The attention which Osborne had devoted to his departmental duties then at length bore fruit. The Duke of York was easily induced to join with Clifford in urging his claims on the King, who was himself most favourably inclined. The very first rumour that the Treasury was about to become vacant was accompanied by a confident assertion that he was designed for the post.[3] All Arlington

[1] *Cal. S.P. Dom.*, 1673, p. 255 ; *Letters to Williamson*, i. 2, 4, 6.

[2] Evelyn was certain that Clifford had no religious objection to the Test (*Diary*, June 19, July 25, 1673), and the decision of the Lord Treasurer to resign came as a great surprise to Sir William Coventry (Foxcroft, *Halifax*, i. 108) as well as to many others (*Letters to Williamson*, i. 57, 60). At the very moment when the problem of his resignation was being most furiously debated he was having " dayly prayers in his chappell after the forme of the Church of England " (*ibid.*, p. 24).

[3] *Cal. S.P. Dom.*, 1673, p. 266 ; *Letters to Williamson*, i. 2.

could do in opposition was to urge the desirability of a Treasury Commission, on which he and his henchman Sir Robert Carr might hope for places, and even this compromise there was little prospect of his obtaining.[1]

Before the close of May matters had gone so far that Osborne's own post of Treasurer of the Navy had, it was generally believed, been promised to Edward Seymour, and Seymour himself had come up to London to prosecute his claims.[2] But at this point a check occurred. Clifford's resolution to resign his places rather than take the Test appears to have been instrumental in determining the Duke of York's decision to do likewise, and as the Duke not unnaturally wished to have the credit of acting first Clifford's resignation had to be postponed. Provision also had now to be made not merely for the post of Lord High Treasurer, but also for that of Lord High Admiral and for the command of the expedition against the Dutch.[3] The result was three weeks of incessant intrigue, during which Osborne's fortunes now rose, now fell, and the most varied reports were current. Clifford was to be made Lord Lieutenant of Ireland ; he was to be given command of the army against the Dutch ; he was not to resign after all ; he was to be replaced by a commission.[4]

On June 11 the Duke of Buckingham returned to London,[5] and his presence may have done something to bring about a decision. It is not unlikely that Buckingham, in whose

[1] The intrigues which led up to Osborne's appointment as Treasurer are variously described, but there seems no doubt that the lead was taken by Clifford and the Duke of York. The frequently quoted statement of the French ambassador that the appointment was due to York, Buckingham, Clifford and Lauderdale is true only in the general sense that these four at the time were closely united together and had a large share in determining the King's policy. During the greater part of the intrigues Buckingham was in Yorkshire, and however strongly he may have favoured Osborne's appointment, cannot have done very much to forward it (Colbert to Louis XIV, June 1, 1673 ; *Hist. MSS. Com.*, ix. 2, p. 449 ; Clarke, *Life of James II*, i. 484 ; *Burnet*, ii. 14 ; Christie, *Shaftesbury*, ii. 312-3).

[2] *Cal. S.P. Dom.*, 1673, p. 299 ; *Letters to Williamson*, i. 10.

[3] For some time James entertained the idea that after he had resigned a special commission might be given him appointing him generalissimo for that particular expedition, but the lawyers would not agree that this could legally be done (*Letters to Williamson*, i. 55-6, 60).

[4] *Ibid.*, i. 34 and *passim*.

[5] *Ibid.*, p. 42.

exuberant imagination nothing was impossible, may have
pictured himself as winning glory at the head of the English
forces in France, while his faithful follower Osborne laboured
to provide the sinews of war at home. He certainly gave
Osborne what assistance he could, and took some part in
arranging the compensation which was to be given to Clifford
for the surrender of his place.[1] On June 15 the Duke of York
resigned all his offices.[2] On the morning of June 19 Clifford
delivered his white staff to the King, who immediately handed
it to Lord Osborne.[3] Exactly a week later the new Lord
High Treasurer was formally sworn in at the Exchequer Bar
as Treasurer of the Exchequer, and made the customary round
of visits to all the offices. By a strange irony the Lord Chancellor who administered the oath was the Earl of Shaftesbury,
who was to spend the greater part of the next six years in
trying to drive him from the offices to which he was now being
admitted. In a short speech delivered by Shaftesbury, which
gave some amusement to contemporaries and considerable
offence to Osborne, the Treasurer was reminded that the
talents which enable men to rise to high place are often very
different from those which enable them to maintain themselves
there.[4] The words were to prove curiously prophetic, though
not quite in the sense in which Shaftesbury intended them.

[1] The arrangement made is variously stated. According to Reresby
(*Memoirs*, p. 88) Osborne was to pay Clifford half the salary of his office.
The popular belief was that he was to give Clifford £20,000 at once, and £4,000
a year thereafter (*Letters to Williamson*, i. 48). Another account, however,
speaks only of a single payment of £10,000 (*ibid.*, p. 59). There was nothing
in the least discreditable or unusual in such a bargain. A retiring official,
provided he retained the King's favour, always expected compensation for
the post he surrendered. This compensation might come either from the
King, or from his successor, or from both. *Cf.* the statement of the position
drawn up by Osborne himself when Earl of Danby, *infra*, ii. 110.

[2] *Cal. S.P. Dom.*, 1673, pp. 374, 377 ; *Letters to Williamson*, i. 44, 46.

[3] *Letters to Williamson*, i. 50, 51.

[4] *Ibid.*, pp. 66-7, 71, 77. The speech is printed in Christie, *Shaftesbury*, ii.
App., p. lxxi.

PART II

MY LORD TREASURER THE EARL OF DANBY

1673-9

CHAPTER VII

THE FALL OF BUCKINGHAM, 1673-4

THE appointment of Osborne as Lord Treasurer was not in appearance a matter of very great significance. The protégé of Arlington, who had endeavoured upon a somewhat insufficient basis to break away from his patron and establish an independent interest of his own, was removed from office, and the protégé of Buckingham was substituted in his place. A slight readjustment was effected in the balance of power within the Cabal. But Arlington and Buckingham did not cease to be the leading ministers of the Crown, nor did the policy of the Government experience any immediate alteration. Time was needed to show that Osborne had the ability and determination to succeed where Clifford had failed, and that his elevation really marked the opening of a new era in the reign of Charles II.

So far was the Duke of York from attributing to Osborne's appointment the significance which is now associated with it, that he appears to have entertained some hope of converting the new Lord Treasurer to Catholicism and continuing the policy of the Cabal under his auspices.[1] James himself, however, had already by his resignation from the Admiralty made the ultimate dissolution of the Cabal inevitable. That resignation had only confirmed the worst fears of the Protestant majority, and roused throughout the country a fever of indignation before which the entire ministry quailed. Arlington,

---

[1] James certainly made an effort about this time to persuade Osborne to alter his religion, offering him the example of the Duke of Buckingham, who he said had been reconciled to the Church of Rome, or, if that would not suffice, " the example of a greater man." Osborne replied that " that was not a thing to bee done by example " (*infra*, ii. 92-3).

disappointed for the second time of his ambition to be Lord Treasurer, would risk nothing further for a policy of which he had never really approved. Buckingham was now to find himself in similar case. The appointment of Prince Rupert to succeed the Duke of York in the supreme command of the expedition against the Dutch was not a serious cause of offence, for it was assumed that Rupert would remain with the fleet. But a very different situation was created when the famous Huguenot leader, Frederic Count of Schomberg, was brought over from France and associated with Buckingham as Lieutenant-General in the command of the land forces. Finally when Schomberg was given precedence as Captain-General Buckingham threw up his commission in disgust and refused to serve against the Dutch at all.[1]

Not unnaturally, perhaps, Arlington and Buckingham blamed each other for their separate disappointments, and Buckingham especially was so bitter as to be prepared to sacrifice everything in order to accomplish his rival's ruin. Shaftesbury and Lauderdale were already alarmed by the rising tide of popular feeling, and the outbreak of this dissension between their colleagues only increased their uneasiness. Shaftesbury began to contemplate coming to terms with the opposition. Lauderdale reflected that his real interests lay in Scotland. The whole Cabal began to go to pieces.

When thieves fall out honest men come by their own. Among those who wished for a change of counsels the promotion of Osborne roused not a shadow of hope; but the almost simultaneous return to the Cabinet Council of the Duke of Ormonde, "a good Protestant and Englishman," was hailed with enthusiasm as heralding the complete collapse of the Cabal and all it represented.[2] Arlington and Buckingham, it was declared, were both discontented and afraid to await the next meeting of Parliament. The former would resign his secretaryship to

---

[1] The debates over these appointments occupied some weeks, and can be traced in *Letters to Williamson*, i. *passim*; *Hatton Correspondence*, i. 109-11; *Burnet*, ii. 5. Rupert's commission as generalissimo and Schomberg's as lieutenant-general are dated July 4; Schomberg's commission as captain-general is dated July 13 (*Cal. S.P. Dom.*, 1673, pp. 422-3, 434).

[2] Every writer at the time seems to insist on the significance of this event (*Letters to Williamson*, i. 48-77, *passim*).

Sir Joseph Williamson or Sir Robert Carr, and retire to the safer and less exacting post of Lord Chamberlain. The latter would surrender his position of Master of the Horse to the Duke of Monmouth, or to Monmouth's young half-brother Don Carlos, later Earl of Plymouth, and on his retirement from office would take Osborne with him. Lauderdale, if not displaced by Monmouth in Scotland, would at least abandon all interference in English affairs. Shaftesbury also might resign, and be succeeded as Lord Chancellor by the Earl of Bridgewater. The "old Protestants" would then come to their own again under the leadership of the Duke of Ormonde, the Treasury would be entrusted to Sir William Coventry, Parliament would meet in August, and there would be a great reckoning for all that had gone amiss.[1]

Something of this nature might well have happened had it not been for the capacity soon displayed by the new Lord Treasurer. As the holder of any other office Osborne might have continued for some time longer to occupy a subordinate position, but the Treasury gave him an unrivalled opportunity of pushing himself immediately to the front. In financial ability he far surpassed any other minister of the day, and on the successful management of finance, it was becoming increasingly apparent, the whole fate of the Government, if not indeed of the dynasty, depended. Charles II had come to the throne heavily encumbered with debts of all kinds—debts incurred by his father before and during the Civil War, debts contracted by himself while in exile, debts inherited from the governments of the Commonwealth period. Not merely had Parliament, in spite of repeated undertakings to repay these debts, shrunk in the end from making any adequate provision for doing so, but it had failed to supply the King even with a sufficient revenue for the ordinary expenses of government. Nominally the regular annual revenue was £1,200,000 as against an average peace expenditure of rather more than £1,300,000. Actually in the years preceding 1673 the regular revenue had amounted only to about two thirds of what it

[1] These rumours were incessantly floating about from the middle of June to the middle of July (*ibid.*, i. 73-119, *passim*; *Hist. MSS. Com.*, vii. 491 ; B.M. Add. MSS. 29571, ff. 226, 228).

was supposed to be, and every year had been marked by a heavy deficit.[1]

Thus the financial position of Charles II, bad from the very beginning, grew steadily worse. The Government was always working upon money borrowed at ruinous rates of interest, always making extravagant concessions for accommodation, always paying high prices because it could not pay cash, and steadily falling deeper and deeper into debt. Only by handing over to the national Exchequer his wife's dowry and the purchase price of Dunkirk was Charles able to postpone even for a few years an open confession of bankruptcy. The finishing stroke was the first Dutch War of the reign. Immense though the grants in aid of that war appeared to be, they fell short of the expenses by about £1,500,000, and the Government thereafter remained on the verge of collapse. On October 31, 1670, an official statement made at the request of the Commons estimated the interest-bearing debt alone at £2,100,000, and the sum necessary to set the Government upon its feet at more than £3,000,000.[2] But the response to this and other indications of the Government's needs was disappointing. Convinced that peculation and unjustifiable expenditure on the part of the Court were the main cause of the trouble, Parliament consistently refused to give adequate assistance ; and although the ministers of the Crown were well aware of the general deficiency of the revenue,[3] the cumbersome methods of accounting then in use made it impossible for them to draw up a complete statement of their position, or even defend themselves with success against the accusations they were called upon to face.

In its financial aspect the policy embodied in the Secret Treaty of Dover was a last desperate effort to escape from the toils in which the Government was involved. Since money could not be obtained from Parliament it had to be got from

---

[1] The financial history of the post-Restoration period has been elaborately investigated by W. A. Shaw in "The Beginnings of the National Debt" (*Owens College Historical Essays*), and in his introductions to the various volumes of the *Calendar of Treasury Books*.

[2] *C.J.*, ix. 159 ; B.M. Add. MSS. 36916, f. 74.

[3] As early as February 29, 1664, Sir Philip Warwick was able to convince Pepys that the revenue was £300,000 short of its nominal level (*Diary* under that date).

France. War on the Dutch was the price paid for the money ; but it was also hoped that if the war was as successful as it promised to be it would lead to an expansion of trade, commercial concessions, or war indemnities which would more than repay its cost. Finally the war provided some semblance of an excuse for the inevitable bankruptcy at length admitted in the Stop of the Exchequer. The hopes of the Court, however, were woefully disappointed. Scarcely had the war been running for half a year when the King was reduced to the necessity of pressing France in desperation for an advance on the subsidy promised him.[1] Far from gaining anything by his policy, he succeeded only in ruining completely the credit of the Government, and entangling it in an expensive struggle for which Parliament, in its irritation at the alliance with a Catholic against a Protestant power, was not in the least likely to make proper provision.

Thus Osborne on his appointment as Lord Treasurer was called upon not merely to solve a problem which had baffled all his predecessors, but to clear up the confusion which this last misguided attempt at solution had left behind. The general belief that the task was beyond human capacity contributed not a little to his elevation, for there was not much competition for the post, and the enemies who might otherwise have opposed his advancement were satisfied that it would ruin him.[2] It was Osborne's success in disappointing all such gloomy expectations that laid the permanent foundation for his own supremacy, and saved, so long as he chose to lend it his countenance, the dwindling credit of the Cabal.

For some weeks after his appointment Osborne had little connection with the Treasury. The actual demission of office by Lord Clifford and his removal from Wallingford House

[1] Colbert to Louis XIV, September 15, 1672, quoted in Barbour, *Arlington*, p. 203.

[2] " Your enemies had so embroiled the management of your office that they looked on your advancement as the instrument of your ruin " (Dedication of Dryden's *All for Love*). The same idea can be found repeated in many places. It was believed at the time that the King, when he made Osborne Treasurer, warned him " that he ought to take care of himselfe, for he had but two friends in England ; which startled him, till his Majesty explained himselfe by saying he was one himselfe and his owne meritts was the other " (*Letters to Williamson*, i. 64).

required time,[1] and meanwhile Osborne could do little but secure statements of the actual financial position and provide for the appointment of his subordinate officials. It says much for the good relations which existed between the new and the retiring Treasurer that these statements were drawn up with Clifford's friendly assistance, and that the majority of the existing officials were retained ; but a difficulty arose regarding the Secretary to the Treasury, Sir Robert Howard. Although they had both risen to prominence as members of Buckingham's motley following, Howard and Osborne were men of very different temperament and were already on bad terms with each other. It seemed therefore a fortunate chance when on July 13 the death of Sir Robert Long rendered vacant the office of Auditor of the Exchequer, and Howard, who had been granted the reversion of the post four months earlier, was sworn in his place. The new Auditor, however, endeavoured to retain his old post as well, and Osborne's success in defeating his attempt was the beginning of a long and bitter enmity between them. For the place which he vacated two candidates appeared, Charles Bertie, who had already gained some reputation as envoy to Denmark, and Sir Thomas Meres, one of the more moderate opponents of the Court, who it was suggested might be won over. Not unnaturally Osborne secured the post for his brother-in-law, who was to remain until his death his most faithful and most trusted henchman.[2]

By July 20 preliminaries had been completed, and on the following day the Lord Treasurer was to enter upon the execution of his office. Just at this moment, however, he, the Lord Chancellor and Secretary Coventry were simultaneously attacked by serious illnesses, which gave rise to all sorts of alarming rumours in town. Some blamed the red wine of

---

[1] While waiting on Clifford to vacate Wallingford House, Osborne was apparently living at Hampden House, near the Cockpit (*ibid.*, i. 56, 157, 198).

[2] *Letters to Williamson*, i. 67, 104, 106, 108, 138. Bertie's appointment was on July 17 (*ibid.*, p. 117). The significance of this contest is brought out in a letter from Robert Benson to Osborne, dated York, July 21, 1673 : " The newes of the seasonable removall of Sir Robert Howard was very welcome to all your Lordshipps freinds that know him. We doe beleeve your Lordshippe before stood upon your guard, and now sitts at ease with a freind to guard your Lordshippe " (B.M. Add. MSS. 28053, f. 65).

which they had partaken at an entertainment. Others darkly
hinted at poison, and spoke of a barrel of figs sent over from
France. Whatever the explanation of this curious incident,
its effect upon the Lord Treasurer was sufficiently unfortunate.
For some days his life was believed to be in danger. Not until
August 4 was he able to walk across his chamber. A fortnight
later he began to drive abroad in a coach, and on August 20
he appeared for the first time since his illness at a Council
meeting ; but it was the end of the month before he had fully
recovered.[1]

So unpromising a start upon his new duties might well have
proved fatal had Osborne served a more exacting monarch
than Charles II. But the autumn was in any case the quietest
season of the year, and the King was content to wait until his
Treasurer recovered. The business of the Treasury remained
practically at a standstill, with little disadvantage to any one
but the " poore petitioners," who anxiously attended " in
droves." The Cabinet rarely met, the King seldom appeared
in Council, the pretensions of Ormonde and his followers, and
even the quarrels within the Cabal, fell temporarily into
abeyance.[2]

Meanwhile a step was being taken which greatly altered
Osborne's standing at Court. His official promotion had
led to a natural expectation of his elevation to the English
peerage, and various titles had been suggested—Viscount
Leeds or Latimer, Earl of Leigh, or Earl of Danby.[3] Shortly
before his illness the final choice had been made, and while he
was confined to bed the grant of his new dignities was actually
carried through. It was thus as Baron Osborne of Kiveton
and Viscount Latimer of Danby that he resumed his place in
public life.[4] No longer could even his enemies affect to regard

---

[1] *Buccleuch MSS. at Whitehall*, i. 319 ; *Letters to Williamson*, i. 121-98
passim ; *Cal. S.P. Dom.*, 1673, pp. 465, 467, 477 ; P.C. Reg. 64, p. 83.

[2] *Letters to Williamson*, i. 146, 151.

[3] *Ibid.*, pp. 34, 48, 51, 62-3, 90. That these were something more than
mere rumours is shown by the titles later conferred upon the Lord
Treasurer.

[4] The warrant for his grant is dated July 23 (*Cal. S.P. Dom.*, 1673, p. 456),
and the patent August 15 (*L.J.*, xii. 586). His choice of title caused some
grumbling among other families more closely related to the early Barons
Latimer (*Letters to Williamson*, i. 63, 157).

him as the mere factotum of Buckingham. As one of the highest officials in the land and a member of the House of Lords he was on something of an equality with his patron and in a position even to grant him favours.[1]

Lord Latimer himself, however, was well aware that in spite of his title his future was bound in the end to be determined by his success or failure in his new office, and no sooner was he able to attend to business than he attacked its problems with his wonted energy. His immediate object was to effect a balance of revenue and expenditure, and to that end he now subjected to a searching scrutiny the financial statements prepared before his illness. The position they disclosed, though not substantially different from what had been anticipated, was disquieting in the extreme. Not merely had a semi-permanent debt of more than £1,000,000 been created by the Stop of the Exchequer, but the three main branches of the revenue, Customs, Excise and Hearth Money, stood charged with sums totalling roughly £470,000, the lesser branches were pledged for a full year ahead, advances made by the farmers of the various taxes stood to be repaid, and salaries in general were heavily in arrear. Worst of all, it was calculated that even when allowance had been made for the special war taxation already imposed the current year would show a deficit of £563,000.[2]

So far as expenditure was concerned the Government had clearly three problems to face—the growth of small but unnecessary expenses due mainly to the weakness and ineptitude of Charles and his ministers, the heavy interest charges due to the accumulated debt, and the staggering burden imposed by the hostilities against the Dutch. The first of these

---

[1] See Buckingham's letter of August 21, 1673, desiring his assistance to procure for some friends the governorship of the Isle of Wight (*Hist. MSS. Com.*, ix. 2, p. 449).

[2] *Infra*, iii. 10-15. This calculation was made by Sir Robert Howard. In his later controversy with the Treasurer Sir Robert endeavoured to make the whole position look better by quoting a financial statement drawn up on June 10, 1673, according to his account by Sir Philip Lloyd. The statement is substantially accurate, and a copy appears to have been given to Osborne (B.M. Add. MSS. 28078, ff. 65, 90). It was, however, drawn up for Clifford to assist him in making his final adjustments, and serious changes were effected before Osborne took over (*Memoirs of the Earl of Danby*, pp. 72-5, 123-32, 164-70, 201).

problems had been tackled without success before, and could not in any case be adequately dealt with at short notice; the second was beyond the capacity of any body but Parliament to solve; but the last and most pressing was faced without the slightest delay. From the returns in the Treasurer's hands it was apparent that expenditure on the army had more than doubled since the outbreak of war, and as the failure of the English fleet to secure command of the sea had rendered impossible the projected descent on Holland there seemed no need for keeping so large a force in existence. Orders were accordingly issued for a reduction of companies by forty men each, and by September 20, only three weeks after Latimer's entrance upon the execution of his office, a saving of nearly £70,000 per annum had in this way been effected. Meanwhile the declaration of the Emperor and Spain against France had forced Louis XIV to appeal to Charles for assistance, and advantage was taken of this to dispatch across the Channel three complete regiments and twelve companies drawn from other regiments. By the middle of November this force of about 4,000 men had come into the pay of the French King, and a further annual saving of nearly £60,000 had been made.[1]

There can be little doubt that Latimer would have liked to conclude peace with the Dutch and attack in a similar fashion expenditure on the navy and ordnance. As early as July he had indeed calculated that if he could secure peace by Michaelmas the accounts of the following twelve months, during which a considerable amount of war taxation had still to come in, would actually show a surplus of £813,100.[2] But his influence in the Government was not yet sufficiently strong to give him much hope of carrying his point, and so long as there remained any prospect of a fleet being required in the ensuing spring the experience of 1667 warned him against pressing his reductions

---

[1] B.M. Add. MSS. 28082, ff. 47, 57; *Letters to Williamson*, ii. 21, 32, 37, 39, 42. The estimated annual charge of the army at Michaelmas 1671 was £223,000; in July 1673, £471,731 3s. 1d.; on September 20 of the same year, £403,052 9s. 0d.; and on November 18, £347,806 7s. 0d.

[2] *Infra*, iii. 15-16. The calculation is obviously somewhat fanciful, inasmuch as it assumes, not merely that peace might be concluded, but that army and navy might be reduced to a peace establishment by September 29, 1673. It indicates, however, the direction in which the Treasurer's mind was working.

too far.[1] Nevertheless he had demonstrated his capacity to find something of the nature of a path through the financial maze, and completely justified his appointment. Immediately after his elevation to the Treasury he had been appointed to the Admiralty Commission which took over the greater part of the Duke of York's functions as Lord Admiral,[2] as well as to a new Tangier Commission,[3] and on these bodies also he was beginning to make his influence felt. The idea that his tenure of office was likely to be short was altogether abandoned. The pretensions of Ormonde and Coventry were allowed to sink completely into the background.

Certainly the existing Government had good reason to be grateful to the Treasurer, for it was his success alone that enabled them to avoid an immediate and abject surrender to Parliament. Three inconclusive engagements with the Dutch during the summer had destroyed any enthusiasm for the war that had ever existed in the country. The last engagement had been marked by the signal failure of the French fleet to give any assistance to the English, and the French alliance, always unpopular, had thus been rendered the object of fresh execration. Fear of Catholicism, which had been made a serious political force by the failure of the Duke of York to take the Test, had been immensely increased since then by his negotiations for a Catholic wife, ending in his marriage by proxy, on September 20/30 at Modena, to Mary Beatrice, sister of Francesco II, the reigning Duke. News of the marriage reached London on October 3, and was received with the bitterest resentment by the large number of members of Parliament who had already come to town and were consulting excitedly together.[4] A change of policy, a change of ministers,

---

[1] Even as matters stood the prospect of the Government being able to set out a fleet in 1674 was none too bright. In their return to the Lord Treasurer, dated September 22, 1673, the Ordnance Office admitted a debt of nearly £240,000, and declared that if the whole fleet was to be put to sea in the following year a further expenditure of nearly £150,000 would be absolutely necessary. As the debt already incurred was due mainly to those who would have to furnish stores for 1674 nothing could be accomplished without ready money (B.M. Add. MSS. 28082, ff. 49, 51 ; *Cal. S.P. Dom.*, 1673, p. 561).

[2] July 9 (*Catalogue of Pepysian MSS.*, i. 38).

[3] Warrant dated August 6 (*Cal. S.P. Dom.*, 1673, p. 480).

[4] *Cal. S.P. Dom.*, 1673, p. 566 ; *Letters to Williamson*, ii. 24, 26, 29, 36.

or even a change in the succession to the throne was certain to
be demanded when the Houses assembled,[1] and had Latimer
not been able to discover a gleam of hope in the financial
situation the Government would have been unable to offer any
resistance.   Even as matters stood apprehension among the
members of the Cabal was so great that they all obtained
pardons from the King ; [2] Lauderdale sought refuge in Scotland;
while Clifford retired into the country, and perished, it was
generally believed, by his own hand.

The immediate object of Parliament was to prevent, if
possible at this late date, the full completion of the marriage.
The object of the Court, on the other hand, was to hasten the
arrival of the new Duchess of York in England, and present
Parliament with an accomplished fact before it could interfere.
Unfortunately the Duchess was delayed by indisposition in the
course of her journey through France, and it was therefore
considered best by the King to let Parliament assemble on the
day to which it stood adjourned, but to prorogue it immediately
on technical grounds for a week.[3]   By a real or pretended
oversight, however, the prorogation was entrusted to Lord
Chancellor Shaftesbury and a commission, of which the new
Lord Treasurer, although he had never yet appeared in the
Lords, was a member.   On October 20, accordingly, when the
Houses met, Shaftesbury had some excuse for proceeding first
with the formal introduction of new peers, and this, in spite
of a bitter remonstrance from the Duke of York, he insisted on
doing.[4]   Latimer was introduced by Viscounts Stafford and
Fauconberg, and took his seat.   Two other peers followed.
Meanwhile the Commons were given ample time to overcome
the obstructive tactics of the Speaker, who did not even make
his appearance until half past ten, and to resolve upon an
address to the King against the consummation of the Duke

---

[1] The various elements in the opposition are skilfully analysed by Sir
William Temple in a letter to the Earl of Essex (*Essex Papers*, i. 130-3).

[2] *Cal. S.P. Dom.*, 1673, pp. 418, 567 ; 1673-5, pp. 11, 26 ; *Letters to Williamson*, ii. 42, 46.

[3] The grounds for the prorogation, sound enough, though probably not the
real reasons, are set forth in *Letters to Williamson*, ii. 51, 72.

[4] Clarke, *Life of James II*, i. 485-6 ; *Parliamentary Diary of Sir Edward
Dering*, pp. 149-51 ; *Burnet*, ii. 36.

of York's marriage.[1] Only after the gage of battle had thus
been thrown down were they summoned to the Lords to hear
the prorogation formally pronounced.[2]

The session which opened on October 27 was thus doomed
from the beginning to be productive of little good. The Commons were suspicious and thoroughly discontented, too dis-
united among themselves to force any policy on the Government, and yet ready at a moment's notice to burst into violent
denunciations of the favour shown to Catholics, the existence
of a standing army, the alliance with France and the presence
of evil counsellors round the throne.[3] The ministers were
jealous of each other, uncertain of their position, and quite
incapable of giving any satisfactory guidance to Parliament.
Buckingham, although himself standing on sufficiently slippery
ground, was intent only on instigating a parliamentary enquiry,
in the hope that it would lead to the ruin of his fellow sinner
Arlington.[4] The latter, timorous as usual, was anxious mainly
to save himself. Shaftesbury was preparing to abandon the
Court altogether and throw in his lot with the popular party.
Neither in Council nor in Parliament did there appear to be
any stable foundation on which a durable policy might be built.

In this bewildering confusion Lord Latimer moved at first
with the greatest circumspection, seeming to an acute observer
" to bee yett but discovering the coosts, and not resolved what
course to steere." [5] The House of Lords was not the scene of
any special activity, and in its comparatively peaceful atmosphere he could easily maintain a reserve which would have
been distinctly difficult in the Commons. Before the session
came to an unlamented end on November 4, however, he had
apparently made up his mind, and in a brief memorandum
which dates probably from about this time he outlined the

---

[1] *Letters to Williamson*, ii. 49, 51-3 ; *Essex Papers*, i. 130 ; Colbert to Louis
XIV, October 20, 1673, in *Campana de Cavelli*, i. 124.

[2] *L.J.*, xii. 586-7.

[3] These are enumerated as the four principal grievances in letters written
shortly after the prorogation of Parliament (*Letters to Williamson*, ii. 70, 76 ;
see also *Parliamentary Diary of Sir Edward Dering*, pp. 155-61).

[4] " Like the envious man hee could have been contented to loose an eye
himselfe to leave his enemie none " (*Letters to Williamson*, ii. 62).

[5] *Essex Papers*, i. 132-3.

policy he intended to pursue.[1] Protestantism at home and
abroad, the maintenance and extension of the Triple Alliance,
the observance of rigid honesty and economy in financial
matters—these were the main aims which he set before himself.
In essentials they are the aims he endeavoured to pursue all
through his life.

Such a policy had little in common with that of the Cabal
or of Buckingham, but Latimer believed the time had come to
sever completely his association with the former, while even
the tie which had long bound him to the latter was beginning
to wear dangerously thin. The irresponsible behaviour of
Buckingham during the preceding months had not merely
demonstrated his lack of capacity as a constructive statesman, but had cast serious doubt on his ability even as a party
leader. Far from giving his followers the guidance which they
might reasonably expect from their chief in a time of such
general disintegration, he had left them to shift for themselves,
and had devoted his energies to purely personal and profitless
animosities which seemed only too likely to involve his own
fortunes and those of his supporters in one common ruin.

At this particular moment Latimer had just received convincing proof of the disadvantages of his connection with the
Duke. His own elevation to the House of Lords, together with
the deaths of Sir Francis Goodricke and Sir Robert Long, had
opened up vacancies in the parliamentary representation of
York, Aldborough and Boroughbridge, and caused something
like a miniature general election in the north. Latimer was
most anxious to secure the election of his own son Edward at
York,[2] and not only wrote more than once to the Corporation
strongly advocating his claims, but induced Buckingham also
to write.[3] A similar policy was pursued at Aldborough, where
the Treasurer's henchman, Robert Benson, was put forward.
Buckingham's influence in Yorkshire, however, had been
greatly diminished by his support of the French alliance and

[1] The memorandum is printed *infra*, ii. 63.

[2] Edward Osborne at this time was certainly not twenty-one years of
age.

[3] Latimer's letters are printed *infra*, ii. 41-5. Buckingham's have been
published in his *Works* (ed. 1775), ii. 210-11. Correspondence about the election is in B.M. Add. MSS. 28051, ff. 12-31.

the Declaration of Indulgence. During his visit to the north in the summer the suspicion that he was inclined to Catholicism had risen so high that he had been unable to procure any recruits for his regiment until he had taken the sacrament " almost in all the churches of his lieutenancy." [1] As a result the candidates he supported were now defeated, Sir Henry Thompson being returned at York, Sir John Reresby at Aldborough, and Sir Henry Goodricke, Reresby's life-long friend, at Boroughbridge.[2] Not only so but the opposition, ready to seize any weapon against Buckingham, threatened a parliamentary enquiry into the whole proceedings, which might have had serious consequences for Latimer as well.[3]

It is scarcely surprising, therefore, that in the autumn of 1673 the Treasurer began to form, within the Buckingham group, a party of his own, whose aims were by no means identical with those of his patron. The little circle of older statesmen with whom he had originally cast in his lot had practically vanished from the field of politics. Trevor was dead, Bridgeman in retirement, Orrery almost incapacitated by gout. His new associates were younger men, who had risen to prominence at much the same time as he had himself and were not unwilling to accept him as their leader. Among them were Orrery's nephew, Richard Jones, Viscount Ranelagh ; Orrery's intimate confidant, Edward, Viscount Conway ; Lady Conway's numerous relatives of the Finch family ; and Lord Conway's cousin, Edward Seymour.[4] Of these the most important was the last. Since their association with each other in the session of 1666-7 Latimer and Seymour had been drawn steadily closer together by a certain similarity in their ambitions and ideals. Together they had climbed the political ladder, Latimer, on account of the greater favour shown him by Buckingham, usually slightly in advance. The elevation of the one to the Scottish peerage as Lord Osborne had been

---

[1] *Letters to Williamson*, i. 24, 28, 58.

[2] *Return of Members of Parliament*, i. 531, 532 ; *Reresby*, pp. 88-92. All these elections were the subject of petitions to the House of Commons (*C.J.*, ix. 290, 291).

[3] *Letters to Williamson*, ii. 38, 44-5.

[4] Some light is thrown on the personal relations of this group in M. H. Nicolson, *Conway Letters*.

followed almost immediately by the promotion of the other to
the lucrative and influential post of Speaker of the House of
Commons. They had been admitted to the Privy Council
within a few months of each other. They had been for some
time associated on the Navy Board, and the resignation of the
Treasurership of the Navy by the one had been followed at
once by the appointment of the other. A definite alliance was
now struck between them which was to be an important factor
in the political situation for the next five years. Seymour had
gone much further in support of Buckingham than Latimer had
done, but he was equally quick to mark the decline in the Duke's
prestige and the increasing fatuity of his political conduct.
Like Latimer he realised that the time had come to look to his
own position and prepare at least for the possibility of his
patron's fall.

Scarcely had Parliament been prorogued when the new
coalition made its influence felt. On November 9 Shaftesbury,
whose activities had for some time been regarded with increasing suspicion by the Court, was dismissed from the Chancellorship. By unremitting exertions Latimer and Seymour persuaded the King to appoint as his successor, though only with
the title of Lord Keeper, the attorney-general, Sir Heneage
Finch, and these three thereafter regularly worked in unison.[1]
Although they formed no mean element of strength in the
Buckingham group, however, the leaders of that group still
remained Buckingham himself and his ally Lauderdale.
Against them was arrayed a most miscellaneous coalition, con-
sisting of Arlington, Anglesey, Ormonde, Henry Coventry,
Shaftesbury and the Duke of York.[2] Passions ran high.
Arlington's follower, Ralph Montagu, was sent to the Tower for
an unseemly quarrel with the Duke of Buckingham in the
King's presence.[3] Sir Thomas Littleton told the Lord Treasurer,

[1] *Essex Papers*, i. 140. It shows the extraordinarily unstable position which
existed at the time that the King was believed to have altered his mind
regarding the appointment six times in six hours, and that before it was two
days old Latimer and Seymour were beginning to fear that Finch had struck
up an alliance with Arlington. The disappointed competitor appears to have
been Latimer's old rival Anglesey (*Cal. S.P. Dom.*, 1673-5, p. 13).

[2] *Essex Papers*, i. 140, 142 ; *Letters to Williamson*, ii. 92.

[3] *Infra*, ii. 50 ; P.C. Reg. 64, p. 138 ; *Letters to Williamson*, ii. 89-91 ; *Cal.
S.P. Dom.*, 1673-5, pp. 43-6 ; *Buccleuch MSS. at Whitehall*, i. 522.

at a meeting of the Admiralty Commission, that he was a cheat, and the whole Board rose up in confusion.[1]

Arlington, however, was fatally handicapped by his own timidity and irresolution, and by the complete lack of unity among his associates. Torn this way and that by conflicting considerations he could not come to a definite decision even as regards the main problem then before the Government. The French ambassador believed he was trying to conciliate Parliament by sacrificing France.[2] English observers thought his object was to obtain money from France in return for a prorogation or dissolution of Parliament.[3] Buckingham it is true was equally uncertain in his attitude, but Seymour and Latimer had a perfectly definite policy to pursue. The former was recognised by Colbert as one of the most bitter opponents of France.[4] The latter had several times openly declared that he would break either the French alliance or his own white staff.[5] Moreover in one sense the Treasurer held the key to the whole position. Wherever and however it might be obtained a supply of money, unless very considerable in amount, would be of little use without a competent financier to administer it, and no other competent financier had yet been found.

It was possibly a recognition of this fact that induced the Duke of York, about the beginning of December, to abandon all pretence of friendship with Arlington and give his support to Buckingham and Latimer.[6] Thereafter Arlington's influence steadily declined. The Treasurer even hoped to drive him from office and secure his place for the Earl of Orrery.[7] Before the close of the year Buckingham, Latimer and Seymour shared the chief power in the kingdom, and Arlington had ceased to be one of the principal advisers of the King.[8]

[1] *Essex Papers*, i. 146; *Letters to Williamson*, ii. 91-2; *Hist. MSS. Com.*, xiii. 6, p. 276.

[2] *Mignet*, iv. 232 *et seq.* The French dispatches at this point must be used with the greatest caution. Every statesman in England was trying to deceive the French ambassador.

[3] *Essex Papers*, i. 132, 133, 140.   [4] *Mignet*, iv. 241.

[5] *Ibid.*, 249-50.   [6] *Essex Papers*, i. 150.

[7] *Ibid.*, p. 153; *Letters to Williamson*, ii. 87, where " Ossory " should be " Orrory " (*Cal. S.P. Dom.*, 1673-5, p. 36).

[8] *Essex Papers*, i. 155.

In endeavouring to secure the adoption of his policy, however, Latimer encountered an unexpected check. With unanswerable logic he demonstrated to the King the only path of deliverance from the unfortunate condition in which he found himself. The suggestion which had been made more than once during the year that the Government should maintain itself by force he rejected as impracticable. If help were summoned from abroad nothing short of a total conquest of England would suffice. If, on the other hand, reliance were placed exclusively on the existing English army, it would be necessary, in order to retain the loyalty of the troops, to supply them with regular and sufficient pay, and of that, in the depleted state of the Exchequer, there seemed little prospect. Unless, therefore, the King could face the " infinite reducement of expence " which might enable him to live within his income, the only possible course appeared to be to come to terms with Parliament. The existing Parliament could be conciliated only by an open breach with France and the enforcement of the laws against popery and nonconformity. A new Parliament would be even more bitter against France and popery, would desire some relief for the nonconformists, and might endeavour to satisfy the needs of the Crown at the expense of the Church. A dissolution therefore might be regarded as a hazardous expedient, and the Treasurer let it be seen that he favoured instead a reconciliation with the existing Parliament.[1]

His analysis of the situation was in substance accepted. A resolution was taken that Parliament should meet on January 7, the day to which it stood prorogued, and on December 10 a proclamation requiring the attendance of members was approved in Council.[2] At the same time all Catholics were forbidden the Court, orders were issued requiring the enforcement of the laws against them, and preparations were made for disbanding what remained of the newly raised forces.[3] But on the all-important matter of the alliance with France Charles

---

[1] " State of the present condition of the Crowne, which cannot bee amended but by force or by compliance " (infra, ii. 63-4). There cannot be much doubt about the date.

[2] P.C. Reg. 64, p. 147. The proclamation appeared on December 12 (Letters to Williamson, ii. 94).

[3] Letters to Williamson, ii. 70 et seq. ; Mignet, iv. 251.

dared not give the satisfaction required. If he abandoned France altogether it was only too likely that Louis in revenge would reveal to the English nation the whole truth about the Treaty of Dover.[1] A compromise was therefore suggested by Buckingham and Latimer, approved by Charles, and sanctioned by the French King.[2] The treaty of February 2, 1672, was to be shown to Parliament, and an assurance was to be given that it was the only treaty with France. By this means it was hoped that the more serious suspicions which were current would be allayed,[3] and Parliament would be induced to support the war at sea for one year more. As an inducement to it to do so Charles allowed private information to be spread abroad that he would withdraw from the French alliance by the following Michaelmas.[4]

Of the four main grievances which had been raised in the previous session of Parliament three had been to some extent remedied by these measures. But the jealousy of evil coun-sellors remained as strong as ever, and it could scarcely be doubted that one of the first things the Commons would do when they met would be to call to account those who had been responsible for the policy they condemned. Among these the most seriously threatened were Lauderdale, who was extra-ordinarily unpopular in England, and Buckingham, whose ostentatious embassies to France had earned him the undeserved reputation of being the originator of the French alliance. Nevertheless both of them supported the summons of Parlia-ment. Lauderdale considered himself to a certain extent exempt from the operation of English public opinion. Buck-ingham believed he could turn the hunt off upon his rival Arlington, and by that means reinstate himself with both King and people. To that end he sedulously courted the favour

---

[1] *Essex Papers*, i. 154-5. Sir William Temple was clear that this con-sideration made it impossible for the King to risk a complete breach with France ; yet even Temple did not know what good ground Charles had for apprehension. As late as 1680 the French ambassador believed that his power to disclose the truth gave him a real hold over Charles (*Dalrymple*, App., i. 80-1).

[2] *Mignet*, iv. 253-9.

[3] Some of these suspicions came surprisingly near the truth (Colbert to Louis XIV, January 1, 1674, in *Mignet*, iv. 253).

[4] *Essex Papers*, i. 159.

of the members of the House of Commons, " the debauchees by drinking with them, the sober by grave and serious discourses, the pious by receiving the sacrament at Westminster."[1]

It is doubtful whether Latimer shared Buckingham's optimism, although he was doing the best he could, in conjunction with Seymour, Finch and Secretary Coventry, to secure a favourable issue from the meeting of Parliament.[2] Probably he would have liked to retain Buckingham as his nominal leader at least until Arlington had been finally disposed of, but circumstances and the Duke's own behaviour made this impossible. With the meeting of Parliament on January 7, 1674, all Buckingham's difficulties accumulated upon him. A quarrel with the King's most powerful favourite, the Duchess of Portsmouth, intensified the hatred which that lady had always borne him,[3] and greatly weakened his position at Court. A petition presented to the House of Lords by the relatives of the young Earl of Shrewsbury brought down upon him the wrath of the peers, who, whatever they may have thought of his relations with Lady Shrewsbury, were bitterly incensed at his conduct in having his illegitimate son by her buried in the family vault in Westminster Abbey.[4] Meanwhile in the Commons the King's speech offering to submit his treaty with France to inspection had produced no permanent effect. The attack on evil counsellors, it was clear, was to be proceeded with. On January 13 an address was resolved upon requesting the King to remove the Duke of Lauderdale from his presence and councils for ever, and there could be little

---

[1] *Letters to Williamson*, ii. 105-6.

[2] *Essex Papers*, i. 152. Conway was asked to request Essex to restrain his brother, Sir Henry Capel, who had been prominent in opposition to the Court. Influence was brought to bear on others by similar methods.

[3] *Reresby*, pp. 93, 94. The hatred of the Duchess of Portsmouth for Buckingham dates from the Duke's visit to France in 1670. Buckingham persuaded Louis XIV to allow her to come over to England, intending to use her influence to support his own credit at Court. Having brought her as far as Dieppe, however, he sailed for England and there forgot all about her. In the end it was Arlington who came to her rescue, and so secured her support, at least for a time (Burghclere, *Buckingham*, pp. 228-30).

[4] March 12, 1671. The statement frequently made, that he was buried as Earl of Coventry, seems to be without foundation. The burial register describes him only as " a young male child . . . related to that family " (*Westminster Abbey Registers*, Harleian Society, p. 173).

doubt that similar addresses were in preparation against Buckingham and Arlington.

In endeavouring to meet this last danger Buckingham seems to have completely lost his head. Without obtaining permission either from the King or from the House of Lords, which as a Privy Councillor and a peer he should first have done, he desired the House of Commons that he might be heard in his own defence. The effect was only to rouse further resentment without securing any corresponding advantage. The Commons, after patiently listening to him on two successive days, remained quite dissatisfied with his explanations, which consisted of little more than an attempt to lay everything at the door of Arlington, and were disfigured by some most unseemly reflections on the King and the Duke of York. Thus when on January 14 the Commons resolved upon an address requesting the King to remove Buckingham from his presence and councils, and from all employments which he held during pleasure,[1] their desire was immediately granted. Although not actually struck off the Council the Duke ceased to attend it or to appear at Court, while his Yorkshire Lieutenancy and his position as Gentleman of the Bedchamber were taken from him.

There is no reason to suppose that Latimer could have prevented this catastrophe, or was in any way remiss at this early stage in his efforts on the Duke's behalf. It is true that he benefited considerably by his patron's fall. On February 12 the King granted him the vacant Lieutenancy of the West Riding,[2] and shortly afterwards his brother-in-law the Earl of Lindsey was given Buckingham's place in the bedchamber.[3] But nothing would have been gained by allowing these posts to fall into the hands of enemies. Throughout the spring of 1674 Latimer was actively engaged in saving what he could out of the wreck of his patron's fortunes. The main problem centred round the post of Master of the Horse, which the King wished to confer upon the Duke of Monmouth. Buckingham pointed out that he had bought the place, that it had been given

---

[1] *C.J.*, ix. 293.

[2] B.M. Add. MSS. 28040, f. 9. The warrant for his commission is dated February 28 (*Cal. S.P. Dom.*, 1673-5, p. 184).

[3] *Hist. MSS. Com.*, vii. 491 ; *Campana de Cavelli*, i. 138.

to him for life, and that even the House of Commons in their address against him had been careful in consequence not to include it among the places of which they desired he should be deprived. Charles, however, was too deeply incensed against him to pay much attention to such arguments. He suspended the Duke from the execution of his office, refused Latimer's request to grant him an interview, appointed Monmouth in his place, and practically forced him to surrender his patent on what he considered very unsatisfactory terms.[1] It was the failure of Latimer to procure better terms which first made Buckingham doubt his good faith, but in spite of a certain amount of suspicion the Duke and the Treasurer remained friendly with each other at least till the close of the year.

The charge of ingratitude so frequently brought against Latimer is therefore not altogether deserved. He neither benefited so much by his association with Buckingham, nor failed so conspicuously to make any return, as his enemies were inclined to declare. Between two men so different in character and inspired by such different ideals a rupture was sooner or later inevitable. It is perhaps to the Treasurer's credit that it was postponed for so long, and came in the end from the Duke's side as much as from his own.

[1] Buckingham's letter to the King in *Fairfax Correspondence*, iv. 249 (draft in B.M. Add. MSS. 18979, f. 285), the date of which is certainly about January 1674, and his letter to Latimer, dated May 21, 1674, in Leeds MSS., Packet 5. The grant to Monmouth is dated April 14 (*Cal. S.P. Dom.*, 1673-5, p. 224), but negotiations between the King and Buckingham were still proceeding at the end of May. As compensation for the loss of his post and of his existing pension of £2,400, Buckingham was eventually granted two pensions, one of £1,500 a year for life and the other of £2,500 a year for 21 years, out of the Excise (*Cal. Treas. Books*, iv. 232, 500 ; *Bulstrode Papers*, p. 266). He estimated the value of the post alone at £5,000 a year.

CHAPTER VIII

THE LAST RIVAL, 1674-5

THE complete collapse of Buckingham's fortunes was a distinct though temporary check to Lord Latimer, for his long association with the Duke made it impossible for him to avoid some share of the discredit which it involved. A report even spread abroad that he was going to surrender his place as Treasurer to the Earl of Essex, and retire into private life.[1] Popular opinion had failed to mark his growing independence of his patron, and found difficulty in believing that he could stand when Buckingham fell. Amidst the ruin of the Buckingham group, however, his own immediate circle of friends and allies remained comparatively unaffected, and waited only opportunity to establish their influence securely with the King.

In the eyes of the Lord Treasurer the really ominous feature in the situation was the partial recovery of Lord Arlington, which almost as a matter of course followed Buckingham's disgrace, for the re-establishment of Arlington's ascendancy would almost certainly mean his own dismissal from office. To the House of Commons as a whole Arlington was scarcely less obnoxious than Buckingham, but in dealing with his accusers there he was careful to avoid all the mistakes made by his rival, and suffered in consequence a very different fate. When on January 15 articles of impeachment were introduced against him, he first obtained permission from the King and Lords, and then delivered in the Commons a moderate and reasoned defence which greatly enhanced his reputation. Possibly his position was improved by the fact that among the foremost of his

---

[1] *Essex Papers*, i. 164.

accusers were the partisans of Buckingham.[1] More certainly
he benefited from the countenance shown him by Ossory and
the Ormonde group in the House. In the event a proposal that
an address should be made to the King for his removal was
rejected by a majority of thirty-nine,[2] and the impeachment
was referred to a committee which never made any report.

This success alone would greatly have improved Arlington's
standing at Court, but he was also buoyed up by the fact that
his knowledge of foreign affairs was for the moment too valuable
an asset to be readily laid aside. The intractable attitude of
Parliament had convinced the King that peace must at all costs
be concluded with the Dutch. Nothing was to be expected
from the congress at Cologne, the futility of which had
long been recognised ; but in the autumn of 1673 another
avenue to peace had been opened up by Spain, which while
declaring war on France had endeavoured to avoid a similar
declaration against England by sending the Marquis del Fresno
to Whitehall charged with proposals for a settlement between
England and Holland. So long as any hope remained of an
agreement with Parliament Fresno had been largely ignored,
but now Arlington was allowed to enter into negotiations with
him, and obtain from him the conditions of peace which he was
empowered by the Dutch to offer. On January 24 the proposed
terms were laid before Parliament, and an address in favour of
a speedy peace with Holland having been obtained from both
Houses, the Treaty of Westminster was concluded with that
country on February 9.[3]

Latimer had a much better appreciation of parliamentary
tactics than Arlington had. The resolution to submit Fresno's
proposals to the consideration of the Houses was taken on his
advice, and the unexpected action of the Government produced,
as he had anticipated, widespread confusion in the opposition.[4]

[1] The impeachment was introduced and largely prosecuted by Sir Gilbert
Gerard and Sir Charles Wheeler, two of Buckingham's minor satellites (*ibid.*,
pp. 163-4 ; *Grey*, ii. 270-329). Wheeler, at Buckingham's desire, had been
ready with articles against Arlington in the previous November (*Letters to
Williamson*, ii. 62).

[2] January 20 (*C.J.*, ix. 296).

[3] *Ranke*, iii. 557-9 ; Barbour, *Arlington*, pp. 237-8 ; *Cal. S.P. Dom.*, 1673-5,
pp. xi-xii.

[4] *Essex Papers*, i. 167-8.

He took a prominent part in piloting through Parliament the
address in favour of peace,[1] and was one of the six commissioners entrusted by the King with the task of concluding the
treaty.[2] But the settlement was not in any real sense his work,
and such credit as could be derived from it went to Arlington.
Even his hope that the Commons might be so far conciliated as
to relieve the financial necessities of the Government was disappointed, for they continued to devote their time to grievances, and when the King on February 24 at length prorogued
Parliament they had voted no supplies whatever.

Scarcely, however, had peace been concluded and Parliament
dismissed when finance took the place of foreign affairs as the
most pressing concern of the Government, and a rapid change
began in the balance of forces at Court. Hitherto Latimer had
been compelled to devote most of his attention to the political
struggle, and had done little more than touch the fringes of the
financial problem. A complete readjustment was impossible
so long as the country remained at war and his own influence
on policy was slight. Now, however, he felt himself in a position to make really comprehensive plans, and about the beginning of March inaugurated a series of financial reforms which
were to have immediate and indeed startling success.

Had the whole revenue and expenditure of the Crown been
under his personal supervision his task would have been
arduous enough. Unfortunately as Lord Treasurer he was
head only of one out of several spending departments, and even
in that capacity was merely an official, whose function it was
to carry out, in accordance with the regulations of his office,
the orders he received from the real head of the Government,
the Privy Council. He had no authority to make a complete
survey of the finances, to construct anything of the nature of a
budget, or to control the activities of the Treasurer of the Navy,
the Paymaster of the Forces or the Cofferer of the Household.

Everything therefore turned on the influence which he could
exert over his sovereign and in Council, and to that point he immediately addressed himself. All the troubles of the reign, he
represented to Charles, could be traced in the end to the financial

[1] *L.J.*, xii. 618-28 *passim*.
[2] B.M. Add. MSS. 28040, f. 9 ; *Letters to Williamson*, ii. 152.

situation. No doubt by using his own credit he could borrow enough to tide the Government over its immediate difficulties, but that would merely mean postponing the evil day. At all costs an effort should be made to place the finances once and for all on a sound basis. In order to do so retrenchment would be necessary, and that retrenchment would have to be strictly adhered to, or it would prove as valueless as earlier efforts which had been made in the same direction. Only three years at most could be allowed for recovering " the sinewes of the monarchy," for at the end of that period the special taxes granted in 1670 and 1671, amounting to more than £300,000 a year, would come to an end, and the Government, if it could not do without them, would have to submit to the wishes of Parliament in order to have them renewed.[1]

It says much for the position which Latimer had already established that he was able to convince Charles, and secure at least some semblance of the " steddy and unalterable resolutions to assist him " for which he asked. Against any turn of fortune's wheel at Court he endeavoured to safeguard himself by forming an alliance with the Duchess of Portsmouth,[2] and then proceeded to attack unnecessary expenditure with a hardihood which left contemporaries aghast. The primary problem was still that of the army and navy, the latter of which alone, so long as it remained on a war footing, involved an unnecessary drain upon the resources of the Government of about £1,500 a day. Arrangements were accordingly made for the disbandment of all new raised regiments by March 6,[3] and the reduction of the army to what was coming to be considered its normal peace establishment of about 6,000 men.[4] On March 7 the Treasurer formally laid the problem of the navy before the Admiralty Commission, advising

---

[1] Memorandum dated March 17, 1673/4, printed *infra*, ii. 64-5.

[2] *Essex Papers*, i. 199, 255; ii. 3. Latimer's original connection, as a follower of Buckingham, was rather with Nell Gwyn (*ibid.*, i. 146), and this connection was continued for some time longer (*infra*, ii. 40; *Morrison Catalogue*, iii. 172-3).

[3] B.M. Add. MSS. 28082, f. 84; Coleman to Rizzini, March 2/12, 1671 [really 1674], in *Campana de Cavelli*, i. 135.

[4] *Cal. S.P. Dom.*, 1673-5, pp. 490-4. The disbandment of the new raised regiments meant a saving of £97,518 17s. 8d. a year, and further reductions in the number of men in each company were expected to bring the annual expenditure on the army down to £203,653 4s. 7d. (B.M. Add. MSS. 28082, ff. 87, 89, 93).

I

that ships as they came into port should be immediately paid off, asking for suggestions how this might be done with least inconvenience to the Government and the seamen, and strongly urging that every effort should be made to reduce naval expenditure to the neighbourhood of £200,000 a year.[1] For these purposes large sums of ready money were necessary,[2] and to assist in raising them a temporary stop was put to all salaries and pensions, even the secret service money, which Arlington regarded as indispensable, being cut off. In vain the courtiers grumbled. In vain the opposition started a run upon the bankers to whom the Treasurer was looking for immediate supplies. Latimer was determined that his schemes should be carried through.[3]

At the same time as expenditure was thus reduced every effort was made to increase the revenue. Here Latimer was singularly favoured by fortune, for he could count not merely on the new taxation imposed in 1670 and 1671, the effect of which on the revenue was not yet fully apparent, but also on a rapidly developing wave of prosperity in the country. The years 1673 and 1674 witnessed a remarkable expansion of English trade, due partly to the contemporary embarrassments of the Dutch, and partly to a gradual recovery from the exhaustion which had followed the extravagances of the Commonwealth. Of this development Clifford had already endeavoured to take advantage, shortly before his demission of office, by letting the entire Excise to farm for three years at an annual rent of £530,000, an increase of about £60,000 on the return previously enjoyed by the Government.[4] The farm was to date from June 24, 1674, and the whole benefit of it was therefore a gift from the retiring Treasurer to his successor. Nevertheless, urged on by

---

[1] *Catalogue of Pepysian MSS.*, iv. 17-22, 25, 28-30.

[2] *Cf.* B.M. Add. MSS. 28078, f. 150, " Fonds for raising money to discharge seamens wages, &c., 10th March, 1673/4." The total fund available is shown as £327,600. According to a statement later made by the Treasurer the cost of disbanding the military and naval forces raised for the war was about £800,000 (*Memoirs of the Earl of Danby*, p. 5).

[3] *Essex Papers*, i. 174, 181, 199-200.

[4] The warrant for the indenture is dated June 7, and the indenture itself July 15, 1673 (*Cal. Treas. Books*, iv. 155-6, 538, 606-7). Of the previous return as much as £104,000 had been derived from the new duties (*ibid.*, iii. 736, 833: iv. 65, 552-3).

the representations of previous farmers,[1] and by the competing
offers of a rival group who promised £30,000 a year more,[2]
Latimer refused to recognise it, and in March 1674 negotiated
a new farm with the same group of financiers at an annual rent
of £550,000. The Hearth Money he also farmed out for five
years at a rent of £151,000,[3] about £16,000 more than the previous return. Only the receipts from the Customs were left to
grow of themselves. Since 1671 the Customs had been under
" management," or subject to direct collection by Government
officials at fixed salaries, and with this system Latimer did not
for the moment care to interfere. He therefore contented himself with an elaborate investigation into the cost of collection,
and a reduction of expenses wherever possible.[4] Altogether he
might reasonably calculate that the regular revenue at his
disposal would exceed that at the disposal of Clifford by
£150,000 at the very least,[5] while in the immediate future he
would be able to count in addition upon a large lump sum
derived from the advance payments of not less than £345,000
for which he had covenanted with his farmers.[6]

[1] *Cal. S.P. Dom.*, 1673-5, pp. 72-3.　　　[2] *Infra*, iii. 20-1.

[3] The farm was to date from March 26, 1674 (*Cal. Treas. Books*, iv. 540).

[4] *Cal. Treas. Books*, iv. 233. A calculation endorsed by Latimer, " About
regulateing the charge of management of the Customes," gives the saving in
the 21 outports of England as £2,666 a year (B.M. Add. MSS. 28078, f. 133).

[5] An increase of £110,000 had been anticipated even before Latimer's
measures had been adopted (*infra*, iii. 15).

[6] An exact figure for this lump sum is difficult to give. Clifford had agreed
with his Excise farmers for an advance of £180,000. Latimer increased this
figure to £245,000, and required from the farmers of the Hearth Money
£100,000, with a further £25,000 if necessary. All these payments were to be
completed by the autumn of 1674. On the other hand the first instalments of
the advance from Clifford's farmers had become due even before Latimer's
appointment as Treasurer, and sums totalling £34,000 had actually reached
the Exchequer (*Cal. Treas. Books*, iv. 381, 608) ; while there were, of course,
advances on previous farms, though on a much smaller scale, which had to
be repaid. A paper in Williamson's handwriting, which analyses the income
of the Government from midsummer 1673 to midsummer 1675 (*Cal. S.P. Dom.*,
1678, p. 610), appears to put the total lump sum at £340,000, but this probably makes no allowance for the repayment of previous advances on the
Excise. The same paper puts the ordinary revenue for each of these two years
at £1,358,000, and notes, as items of income not likely to recur, £106,000 from
the sale of fee farm rents, £40,000 from the Dutch indemnity provided for in
the peace treaty, and £76,000 from the sale of prizes taken during the war.
Including the special war tax of £1,238,000, which fell due during this period,
but excluding the money received from France, which did not pass through the
Treasurer's hands, Danby had at his disposal during these two years rather
more than £4,500,000.

By these means the Government was not merely rendered solvent, but put in a position to liquidate some of its debts. The cost of the war, which had exceeded by nearly £400,000 the supplies voted by Parliament to maintain it,[1] was duly met. A temporary settlement was reached with the bankers who had been defrauded by the Stop of the Exchequer, the sum of £140,000 being assigned them as interest at 6 per cent from January 1, 1672, to January 1, 1674, and arrangements being made for the actual payment of the money in eight quarterly instalments during the years 1675 and 1676.[2] Alarming rumours became current among the opponents of the Court. It was declared that expenditure fell short of the revenue by £10,000 a week, and that it was the intention of the King, by laying up half a million in specie every year, to bring about a fall in rents, and so reduce the nobility and gentry to complete dependence on himself.[3]

Unfortunately the Treasurer was unable to stop here. So inextricably had the financial problem become connected up with all the problems of Government, that in trying to solve the one he was almost necessarily, though perhaps not unwillingly, compelled to attack the others. His attempt, in virtue of his favour with the King, to extend his control even over all purely financial matters had already brought him into collision with every financial official who repudiated subordination to the Treasury, and had led to a renewed quarrel with Sir Robert Howard.[4] His efforts to deal with related problems were now to involve him in conflict with the Secretaries of State.

As yet Latimer remained quite unconnected with the intrigues to obtain money from France, but his supervision of finance inevitably brought him into contact with William of Orange and Holland. William had a long-standing claim upon Charles for money lent during the period of the Civil War and the exile, while the Dutch by the Treaty of Westminster had undertaken to pay the English King an indemnity of 800,000

---

[1] This is Dr. W. A. Shaw's calculation (*Cal. Treas. Books*, iv. pp. xxxix-xl).

[2] *Ibid.*, iv. 303, 540, 546.

[3] *Essex Papers*, i. 259, 260.

[4] *Ibid.*, p. 176 ; *Cal. S.P. Dom.*, 1673-5, pp. 153, 185.

crowns. On the adjustment of claim and counter-claim was to be based Latimer's first serious introduction to foreign affairs. Either before or during the negotiations for the peace he had entered into friendly relations with William's secretary, Frederic van Reede,[1] and had even sent the Prince a general message of compliment by his hands. It is not surprising, therefore, that when towards the close of March William dispatched van Reede to England to discuss the matter of his debt he gave him special instructions to apply to the Treasurer.[2] The result was a lengthy negotiation which led eventually to the last three instalments of the Dutch indemnity being assigned to William in satisfaction of his claim.[3] The Prince freely admitted his obligation to Lord Latimer for obtaining so favourable a settlement, and marked his gratitude by appointing the Treasurer's eldest son as his agent to carry through the necessary legal formalities.[4]

It was inevitable, however, that in the course of these negotiations Latimer should advance beyond the consideration of purely financial questions. At the time when he received the Prince's first letter rumours were current of a proposed marriage between William and the Princess Mary, elder daughter of the Duke of York. While sending a most complimentary reply by the hands of Sir Walter Vane, he accordingly instructed his envoy to supply him with information regarding the whole situation in Holland, including the inclination of the Prince towards the marriage.[5] A few weeks later a further temptation

---

[1] It is not clear when the friendship between Latimer and van Reede began. It may conceivably date from 1672, when van Reede was twice in England as an emissary partly to the King and partly to the opposition. The earliest extant letter written by him to Latimer is dated London, April 15/25, 1674 (Leeds MSS., Packet 5).

[2] William of Orange to Lord Latimer, April 3, 1674, *infra*, ii. 381.

[3] Danby to William of Orange, February 2, 1674/5, *infra*, ii. 384.

[4] William of Orange to Danby, February 20, 1675, March 10, 1676, and to his son, Lord Latimer, March 31, 1676, *infra*, ii. 385, 387.

[5] Latimer to William of Orange, April 30, 1674, *infra*, ii. 382, and Vane to Latimer, May 20, 1674, in *Morrison Catalogue*, vi. 299. Latimer intimated to the King his entire approval of the suggested marriage, but did not care to go further in view of the bitter opposition of the Duke of York. The French ambassador Ruvigny, in almost prophetic words, warned James " que de fortes raisons l'obligeaient à craindre comme la mort la conclusion de ce mariage, qu'il devait regarder le prince d'Orange comme l'idole de l'Angleterre, et qu'un tel gendre serait infailliblement sa ruine " (*Mignet*, iv. 323).

presented itself to seek some foothold in the sphere of foreign policy. In the interests of European peace Charles determined to send Sir William Temple to the Continent to offer his mediation to all the combatants. Latimer thereupon renewed the friendship with Temple which he had dropped nearly twenty years earlier, and was kept informed by him of what was going on.[1]

In commerce also there existed a natural connecting link between finance and foreign affairs. The abolition of the feudal incidents in 1660, the sale of the fee farm rents, and the growing tendency of Parliament, when making special grants, to rely on indirect taxation, were only the last stages in a long process by which direct taxation had been reduced to a minimum. When Latimer assumed the direction of the finances fully five-sixths of the revenue was derived from Customs and Excise duties, and there was little prospect of this proportion diminishing. The commercial well-being of the country was therefore of immediate and vital importance to him, and he lost no time in making his influence felt on those negotiations with foreign powers by which trade might be affected. In July 1674 he was added to a committee engaged in arranging a treaty of commerce with France. In August he was appointed to a similar committee to conclude a treaty with Sweden.[2]

All this gave great offence to Arlington, who felt that his province was being invaded ; but Latimer's incursion into the sphere of foreign policy was not yet very serious, and it was rather over the affairs of Ireland that the real conflict took place. As Lord Treasurer of England Latimer claimed the right to supervise the finances of Ireland as well, and interpreted his duties in a somewhat liberal manner. Arlington, on the other hand, insisted that all Irish affairs should pass through the hands of the Secretaries of State, and was warmly supported in this attitude by his colleague, Henry Coventry. The Earl of

---

[1] The connection between Temple and Latimer had been renewed at the time of the Treaty of Westminster (Temple, *Works*, ed. 1740, i. 376-7) ; but the first of the long series of letters from Temple to the Treasurer is dated June 7, 1674, shortly before the former set out for Holland (*infra*, ii. 447). In foreign affairs Temple was to be Latimer's mentor. See especially the letter of October 26, 1674, in which, like a pedagogue instructing a pupil, he " opens the scene " to the Treasurer (Temple, *Works*, ii. 311).

[2] *Cal. S.P. Dom.*, 1673-5, pp. 314-5, 336.

Essex, who had no desire to quarrel with either side, tried to satisfy them both ; but their attitudes were really irreconcilable, and the only result was that Essex and Latimer, who had originally been on good terms, gradually drifted into hostility.[1] Latimer knew little about the problems of Ireland, and was handicapped by the connection which he had formed, during the days of his association with Buckingham, with some of the less reputable among the leading Irish politicians. His principal adviser on Irish affairs was now Lord Ranelagh, who became one of his most intimate confidants, and steadily poisoned his mind against Essex. In 1670 Ranelagh had entered into an engagement to collect the entire revenue in Ireland and defray all the expenses of government, and had been given in consequence complete control of the finances for a period of five years. So huge an undertaking provided endless opportunities for malversation, and Ranelagh and his agents were constantly accused not only of extortion in collecting the revenue, but of misapplication of it when it was in their hands. Latimer felt himself bound to support his associate, and in this way became involved in a whole host of Irish animosities which were to have a disastrous effect on his later career.

In the summer of 1674, however, these Irish troubles were still largely in the future, and all Arlington could see was a further successful encroachment on what he considered to be his own sphere. For more than a year he had been on the verge of resigning his post, and now general dissatisfaction induced him to take the final step. On September 11 he surrendered his office of Secretary of State to Sir Joseph Williamson, and retired to comparative obscurity as Lord Chamberlain of the Household.[2] His successor was nominally one of his own followers, but really Williamson was no more than a laborious official, without capacity or desire to maintain an interest independent of those at the head of the Government.[3] The last serious obstacle to the ascendancy of the Treasurer was thus removed. Within a fortnight of his rival's resignation a pro-

[1] *Essex Papers*, ii. 5-6 and *passim*. A number of the Treasurer's letters to Essex are printed *infra*, ii. 48 *et seq*.

[2] P.C. Reg. 64, p. 272 ; B.M. Add. MSS. 9798, f. 51.

[3] He was already suspected of inclining to the other side (*Essex Papers*, i. 236, 242).

clamation was issued postponing the meeting of Parliament to the following spring.[1] That proclamation was not in accordance with his policy and did not meet with his approval,[2] but only his success had made it possible.

It was scarcely to be expected in those days that a statesman should perform great services for his King and country without at the same time doing what he could to benefit himself, and the Treasurer's activity in the latter direction was such as to expose him to a good deal of criticism from jealous and disappointed competitors. Before the close of June royal gratitude for his success in dealing with the finances was manifested by the grant to him of the title by which he has since been generally known, that of Earl of Danby.[3] Almost at the same time more tangible rewards were conferred upon him in the advowson of the church of his own parish of Harthill,[4] fee farm rents in Wales to the value of £723 a year,[5] and the immediate possession of other fee farms, to the annual value of more than £1,200, of which he had already purchased the reversion.[6]

His increase of dignity came at an opportune moment for his eldest son, who was now able to assume the courtesy title of Viscount Latimer. Although barely twenty years of age, Edward Osborne had married, only a few weeks earlier, Elizabeth Bennett, eldest daughter of Simon Bennett, of Beachampton, Buckinghamshire.[7] The marriage had an obvious political

[1] The first announcement was made on September 18, and the definite decision was reached on September 23, when a proclamation was approved in Council proroguing Parliament to April 13 (P.C. Reg. 64, pp. 275, 276 ; Cal. S.P. Dom., 1673-5, p. 365 ; Essex Papers, i. 259-60).

[2] As late as August 24 he was confident that Parliament would assemble in November (Carte MSS. 243, f. 134).

[3] The patent is dated June 27, 1674. He was introduced in the Lords on November 10, 1674, when Parliament held a formal meeting to hear the official prorogation (L.J., xii. 650).

[4] February 28 (Cal. S.P. Dom., 1673-5, p. 184 ; Cal. Treas. Books, iv. 495).

[5] Cal. Treas. Books, iv. 541-2. The grant itself, dated July 8, 1674, is in Leeds MSS., Packet 5.

[6] These fee farms, mainly in Yorkshire, were part of the jointure of the Queen, who was compensated out of the hereditary Excise (Cal. Treas. Books, iv. 542-3). Danby had given £10,000, or eight year's purchase, for the reversion (Grey, iii. 92-4).

[7] Earl of Orrery to the Lord Treasurer, May 25 ; Lord Ogle to Lady Latimer, May 31, 1674, in Leeds MSS., Packet 5. Both these letters offer congratulations on the marriage, which presumably must have taken place a few days before.

significance, for Simon Bennett was a half-brother of Lady Conway, and therefore a connection of the Finches. Its successful
conclusion, after two years of negotiation,[1] meant that some
separate provision had now to be made for Latimer, and Danby
endeavoured to secure his appointment as Gentleman of the
Bedchamber to the King, with the customary salary of £1,000
a year. At the moment there was no vacancy, but Latimer was
promised the first place, and towards the close of October was
sworn in, although without fee until a vacancy should occur.[2]

Edward's younger brother Peregrine presented a more
difficult problem, for in his fifteenth year he was scarcely of age
to fill any position whatever. Rumour declared that he was
to be made an English viscount ; but the absurdity of summoning him to the House of Lords before his elder brother, and
giving him in his own right a rank which that brother held only
by courtesy, could scarcely fail to be apparent, and the project,
if it was ever seriously entertained, had to be dropped.[3] Instead, the Earl of Danby, who had never had any great liking
for his own Scottish title, obtained permission from the King
to surrender it, and in December a warrant was issued creating
Peregrine in his own right Viscount Osborne of Dumblane.
It seems to have been felt, however, that this title bore too
much resemblance to some of Danby's remaining titles, and
in the patent it was eventually altered to Viscount Dumblane.[4]

More than a year earlier some provision had been made
for the future maintenance of the new peer when the office of
Clerk of the Patents in the Court of Chancery had been granted
to him for life, in reversion after the holder, Sir Richard
Piggott.[5] But the post which Danby desired ultimately to

[1] *Conway Letters*, pp. 364-5.

[2] *Cal. S.P. Dom.*, 1673-5, p. 386. Latimer waited on the King for the first
time as Gentleman of the Bedchamber on September 21, 1674 (*Essex Papers*,
i. 260). His regular appointment did not take place till a vacancy had been
created by the death of the Earl of Rochester in the summer of 1680. Rochester died on July 26, and the warrant for Latimer's appointment was drawn up
on July 29 (Leeds MSS., Packet 16 ; *Cal. S.P. Dom.*, 1679-80, p. 580).

[3] Carte MSS. 72, ff. 235, 253.

[4] Danby in his diary dates the appointment November 26, 1674 (B.M. Add.
MSS. 28040, f. 9). The warrant for the grant is dated December 5 (*Cal. S.P.
Dom.*, 1673-5, p. 449). The patent is dated July 19, 1675.

[5] The warrant is dated October 22, 1673 (*Cal. S.P. Dom.*, 1673, p. 591), and
the grant December of the same year (*Cal. Treas. Books*, iv. 446).

secure for him was that of Auditor of the Exchequer, then held
by Sir Robert Howard. The work of the Auditor was very intimately associated with that of the Treasurer, and Danby
had already been seriously inconvenienced by the obstacles
placed in his way by Sir Robert. On December 20, accordingly, he persuaded Charles to bestow the reversion of Howard's
place on Lord Dumblane,[1] and on the last day of the year the
grant was formally made.[2] This Sir Robert believed, probably
quite rightly, to be merely a first step towards his own dismissal.

In securing this grant Danby was giving rise to an involved
sequence of events which was not to come to an end until
thirty years later ; but the complications it produced were
simplicity itself compared to those which flowed from his
attempt at the same time to find for Dumblane a suitable marriage alliance. Among the most important of the Treasurer's
friends and allies in the business world was the great London goldsmith and banker, Sir Robert Viner, who had married
Mary, daughter of John Whitchurch of Walton, Berkshire,
and widow of Sir Thomas Hyde of Albury, Hertfordshire. By
her first husband Lady Viner had had one child, Bridget, who,
partly as heiress to the Hyde estates,[3] and partly owing to such
expectations as she might have from her step-father, was
regarded as one of the most brilliant matches of the day. On
her, accordingly, Danby's choice fell, and he entered with every
prospect of success on negotiations with Sir Robert and Lady
Viner to secure her hand for his son.

Unfortunately Lady Viner had other relatives of a very
different type. Some years before her marriage with Sir
Thomas Hyde her two sisters, Susan and Sara, had married
two brothers, Richard and William Emerton, who were Sir
Thomas's bailiffs. Both these sisters desired to keep the Hyde

[1] B.M. Add. MSS. 28040, f. 9.

[2] Doubts having arisen as to the validity of the grant, on account of Dum-
blane's extreme youth, it was renewed a year later to Lord Latimer, Charles
Bertie and Charles Osborne, who were to hold it in trust for him (B.M. Add.
MSS. 28086, f. 1 ; Cal. Treas. Books, iv. 641, 868). A pension of £500 a year
was also given to Dumblane until the grant should become effective (Cal. S.P.
Dom., 1703-4, p. 389).

[3] Her inheritance is variously stated—£3,000 a year with £20,000 in standing
timber (B.M. Add. MSS. 28072, f. 1), £100,000 in all (ibid., f. 83 ; Pepys,
September 7, 1665).

estates within the family, and if the report of their enemies may
be believed proceeded about their task with diabolical ingenuity. Having secured by false representations the dismissal of
Ursula Hobson, who had been Bridget Hyde's nurse almost
since her birth, Susan Emerton obtained charge of the child
herself, and proceeded, by strict discipline and training, to
establish a complete ascendancy over her, with a view to marrying her, when she was old enough, to her own son Richard.
This aroused the jealousy of Sara Emerton, who had hoped to
marry Bridget to her second son John, but after a short conflict
Susan and Sara came to an agreement, and brought their
united influence to bear on Lady Viner, skilfully playing upon
her fear of the corruptions of Whitehall, and her consequent
distaste for any courtier as a husband for her daughter.

In the end a real or pretended marriage took place on October
1, 1674, between Bridget Hyde and John Emerton. The bride
was then just twelve years of age, and did what she was told
without appreciating the significance of the ceremony in the
least. The proceedings were secret ; Lady Viner was not
present ; there is no proof whatever that she had given her
consent, and it is probable that she was not even informed
afterwards of what had been done.[1] A more unsuitable marriage could scarcely have been devised. The bride was a gentle-
woman and a great heiress ; the bridegroom was of the degree
of yeoman, the son of a servant of the bride's father, " a pittifull
boy going to prentice and christned the day before to qualify
the marriage, for the father was an Annabaptist." [2]

For some weeks nothing was suspected, but towards the close
of the year the death of Lady Viner brought matters to a head.[3]
Bridget Hyde had naturally been brought to London to be with
her mother at the last, and Sir Robert Viner, finding his step-
daughter on his hands, proceeded in all good faith to complete
the negotiation for her marriage to Lord Dumblane. The

---

[1] B.M. Add. MSS. 28072, f. 3 et seq.

[2] Sir Robert Southwell to the Duke of Ormonde, January 16, 1674/5, in
Carte MSS. 72, f. 255. The description appears to be substantially just. Some
years earlier Sir Robert Viner himself had spoken of Richard Emerton as " a
plain bumpkin, and not worth 150 l. a year, and a rank Anabaptist " (Cal.
S.P. Dom., 1670, p. 524 ; 1671, p. 511).

[3] Her death took place on December 31, not, as stated in the D.N.B., on
March 9, 1674 (Bulstrode Papers, p. 274 ; Carte MSS. 72, f. 253).

Emertons replied by proclaiming that she was already married, and demanding that she should be surrendered to her husband. Inevitably their statement was received with a good deal of scepticism. Danby obtained from Williamson a warrant for the arrest of John Brandling, the minister by whom the marriage ceremony was alleged to have been performed,[1] and Brandling, when examined, admitted, either willingly or under duress, quite enough to invalidate the whole proceeding.[2]

In a practical sense the position was largely one of stalemate. As bailiffs the Emertons had little difficulty in securing control of the Hyde estates. On the other hand Sir Robert Viner had possession of Bridget Hyde herself, and that young lady, who had now some appreciation of the issues at stake, allowed no doubt to be entertained that she was on the side of her step-father and still more on that of Lord Dumblane. At the beginning of February a report spread abroad that Dumblane had tried to solve the problem by marrying her,[3] but Danby probably felt that there were already complications enough, and restrained his son from so imprudent a course. The whole matter was therefore left to the Ecclesiastical Courts, which were to determine the validity of the marriage, and the King's Bench, which was to deal with the estates.

The proceedings of the former are a dreadful story of eight years' procrastination and delay,[4] but the King's Bench showed the greatest activity, assigning temporary possession of the estates to John Emerton, and issuing at his instance a writ of Habeas Corpus requiring Sir Robert Viner to produce Bridget Hyde.[5] The reply of Sir Robert, that Bridget was under no

[1] January 11, 1675 (*Cal. S.P. Dom.*, 1673-5, p. 527).

[2] *C.J.*, ix. 324 ; *Grey*, iii. 77-82 ; Carte MSS. 72, f. 255—" The parson who plaid this pranck is in custody, and ownes enough, as is said, to make the marriage void."

[3] Carte MSS. 38, ff. 253, 260.

[4] The Emertons maintained that the delay was due to the obstructive tactics of their opponents, but one principal cause appears to have been that all their own witnesses were declared excommunicate for having been present at a clandestine marriage, and could not give evidence until they had been absolved (*Finch MSS.*, ii. 91-3).

[5] January 25, 1675 (Carte MSS. 72, f. 259 ; *English Reports*, lxxxiv. 89, 289, 298, 807-8). These proceedings are described by Lord Keeper Guilford as a glaring instance of political partiality on the part of Chief Justice Hale (*Lives of the Norths*, i. 85).

detention, and was free to go where she pleased, was treated as an equivocation, and he was compelled to bring her into Court. There " she behaved herselfe very briskely, and at utter defyance with Mr. Emerton or anything of marryage, and that she was in full liberty with my Lord Mayor and would be noe where else." So determined, in fact, was her attitude that the Court ordered Viner to give bonds for £40,000 that she should not enter into any marriage while the case in the Ecclesiastical Courts remained undetermined, but the law term being then almost at an end the order was not carried out. Meanwhile the intimacy between Dumblane and Bridget Hyde grew apace, and contemporaries had little doubt what the end was likely to be.[1]

Dumblane was thus too preoccupied, and was as yet too young, to play any serious part in politics, but towards Latimer the Lord Treasurer was already beginning to look for assistance in his political schemes. In spite of his retirement to the post of Lord Chamberlain Arlington had never intended to abandon his interest in foreign affairs or to resign himself to exclusion from the inner secrets of the Government, and as the year 1674 drew to a close he made a desperate effort to maintain his waning influence at Court by a brilliant stroke of diplomacy abroad. So long as the war in Europe continued Charles felt himself in constant danger of being compelled by Parliament to intervene in opposition to France. He had also been much annoyed by intrigues into which the Prince of Orange had entered with the parliamentary opposition in England, and with discontented subjects in Scotland. Arlington accordingly proposed that he should be dispatched on a special mission to the Hague, to urge upon the Prince the desirability of peace, and to obtain from him the names of his correspondents in Britain. If William proved ready to give satisfaction in these matters an effort might be made to bring him entirely over to the King's side by bringing forward once more the project of his marriage to the Princess Mary.

The immediate effect of these suggestions was to ruin Arlington's credit with the Duke of York, who agreed only with

---

[1] " The Lord Dunblane is dancing with his mistris day and night, and she dotes on him, and soe that good worke is as good as done " (Southwell to Ormonde, February 13, 1674/5, Carte MSS. 38, f. 260).

the greatest reluctance to the marriage of his daughter, and with the French King and ambassador, who regarded the whole project with deep suspicion.[1] But the real struggle began when Danby and Lauderdale, who were kept in ignorance to the very last, obtained some knowledge of what was going on. The Treasurer complained bitterly to the King, " saying that it was very unkind to good and faithful servants to see that a man who had ill served him enjoyed his confidence to their prejudice." [2] So strong were his remonstrances that Charles was forced to pacify him by allowing Lord Latimer to accompany the embassy ; but in spite of that he was not admitted to the inner secret of the negotiation, and had to guess as well as he could the precise purpose it was intended to serve.[3]

The result was practically a trial of strength between Danby and Arlington at William's Court. The Lord Chamberlain placed his reliance on the credit he believed he had with the Prince himself, and on the influence among the Dutch nobility of the Countess of Arlington, her brother Odyck, her sister Charlotte of Beverweert, and her brother-in-law the Earl of Ossory, all of whom accompanied him to the Hague. The Lord

---

[1] *Mignet*, iv. 323-4 ; Clarke, *Life of James II*, i. 500-2.

[2] Ruvigny to Louis XIV, November 19, 1674, quoted in Barbour, *Arlington*, p. 245.

[3] It is curious to find Danby, the chief English minister at home, and Temple, the English representative at the Hague, writing anxiously to each other in an effort to understand the origin and meaning of the embassy. Temple's letters are printed or referred to *infra*, ii. 450-6 ; and his account of the embassy is given in his *Works*, i. 394-8. Danby's notes for the guidance of Lord Latimer, endorsed, " The Kings instructions, [16]74," and headed, " To Monsieur Rhede," are preserved in Leeds MSS., Packet 5 :

1. That since his going Monsieur Odyke has made himselfe a very busy minister here, and has undertaken great things which shall bee done by my Lord Arlington with the Prince, which I should bee glad of, only I would rather the good things (if any bee) should come by his Lordships hands.

2. That Odyke has been the sole cause of this journey. and has made much use of the Princes name to procure it.

3. That these Lords have nothing but verball instructions.

5. That if hee pleases to lett me know what they do there hee shall have a true account what result itt meetes with here att theire returne.

4. That if anything should be moved to them about the match with the Dukes daughter itt will bee placed in wrong hands to effect that businesse.

6. That I desire a good correspondence with his Lordship by which wee may both of us do our masters good service.

That finding Monsieur Odyke not to bee much his freind I had comanded you to give him private notice.

Treasurer made what he could of his own interest with the
Prince, and hurriedly called upon the help of his allies van
Reede and Sir William Temple.[1] Arlington practically ignored
the regular English embassy, lived with Odyck and waited on
the Prince without introduction beyond that contained in his
credentials. Latimer on his arrival at the Hague made his
home with Temple, was formally presented by him to the
Prince, and though he did not himself discuss political affairs
brought his influence to bear through van Reede. William
behaved with delightful impartiality, showing himself equally
gracious to all the candidates for his favour, and entertaining
them with a round of festivities in which Latimer at least took
his full share.[2]

Arlington, however, had made a bad miscalculation. William
had never really forgiven him for his conduct during the time
of the Cabal, and believed that the embassy, if not actually
engineered in concert with France for the purpose of introducing dissension between him and the States, was only too
likely in practice to produce that effect. No one could be
induced to believe that so important a mission had been
dispatched without some great object in view, and as the
ostensible objects were quite insufficient, secret objects of the
most sinister character were imagined instead. Among
William's enemies at home and confederates abroad a suspicion spread that he was in treaty with the Kings of England
and France to secure selfish aims of his own, and the Prince
began heartily to wish that Arlington would cut his negotiation
short and return to England before worse evil followed.[3] The
one thing which the ambassadors had to offer, a marriage with
the Princess Mary, would, he was assured, be fatal to him, if
brought about by Arlington's interest.

It is not surprising, therefore, that the embassy made little

[1] Letters to all three, dated November 9, 1674, were entrusted by him to
Lord Latimer, and are printed *infra*, ii. 383, 451.

[2] Among the Leeds MSS. (Packet 5) are the drafts of two letters written by
Latimer at this time, one dated Hague, December 15, 1674, to his uncle
Charles Bertie, the other to the Lord Treasurer. They suggest that Latimer's
own interests lay in the social rather than in the political side of the embassy,
and that he played no direct part in the intrigue which was going on.

[3] Temple's confidential report in his letter to Danby of December 10, 1674,
probably gives a fair idea of the situation (*infra*, ii. 454).

progress, and that William's answers to the representations
made to him were extremely evasive. He refused to compromise his friends in England. The terms of peace he suggested were such as France would not consider. The projected
marriage, he declared, would require that he should first visit
England in order to make sure that his person was not dis-
pleasing to the Princess, and for the moment a visit to England
was impossible.[1] By the beginning of December Arlington would gladly have abandoned his unhappy undertaking
and returned home ; but contrary winds detained him for
some weeks in Holland, and gave his enemies in England a
splendid opportunity to profit by his discomfiture. Not until
January 6, 1675, did he reach Whitehall, and even then he was
anticipated by Lord Latimer, who with the energy of youth
outdistanced him on the last stages of the journey, and nearly
twenty-four hours before his arrival was delivering to Danby
the messages with which he had been entrusted by van Reede
and Sir William Temple.[2]

The effect of Danby's triumph was not immediately apparent
in England, for Charles was reluctant to desert old friends.
Even to such a keen observer as Sir Robert Southwell, Arlington on his return seemed as well with the King as ever.[3] But
when faced with the united hostility of the Duke of York,
Danby and Lauderdale he had literally nothing but the King's
friendship to fall back upon, and that was not in the least
likely to stand a prolonged strain. He had no skill in finance,
no capacity for dealing with Parliament, and, his enemies might
now insinuate, no knowledge of foreign affairs. Hitherto he
had always been able to pose, when he so desired, as the chief
representative in England of the Orange and Dutch interest,
and had derived not a little of his strength from that fact. But
his pretensions in that direction were now decisively rejected
by those most intimately concerned, and he found himself

---

[1] *Mignet*, iv. 325-6.

[2] *Cal. S.P. Dom.*, 1673-5, p. 518. The gentleman who accompanied Latimer
in this dash for home was almost certainly Sir William Temple's son John
(*infra*, ii. 458).

[3] " My Lord Chamberlain is as close in his Majesties favor as at any tyme
before, and having skill in suting the King's genius, tis not beleived that the
many contrary winds wil be able to shake him " (Southwell to Ormonde,
January 16, 1674/5, Carte MSS. 72, f. 255 ; *cf. Essex Papers*, i. 286, 288).

excluded from both camps, a friend neither of Holland nor of France. For four years more he was to remain a constant thorn in Danby's side, but after his return from his Dutch embassy he was never able seriously to dispute with him the control of the policy of the Government.

CHAPTER IX

CHURCH AND KING, 1675

By the beginning of 1675 Danby had attained to a position such as no one could have anticipated eighteen months earlier. The King had succumbed to the glamour of his financial successes ; the Duke of York had been conciliated by his determined championship of the interests of the Crown ; his former superiors and rivals, with the exception of his Scottish colleague Lauderdale, had been reduced to a position of definite inferiority. It is true that the edifice of his power was built upon the most unstable foundations. He had many enemies and scarcely one trustworthy friend. Nevertheless for the moment he was unquestionably the principal minister of the Crown, and for the first time in his political career was able to develop a real policy of his own.

The only power with which he had not yet reckoned was Parliament, and the main object of the policy which he devised was to establish permanently good relations with that body. Not merely was his own inclination strongly in favour of the Cavalier and Church interest, but he was confident that the same was true of the attitude of the nation as a whole. His aim, therefore, was a firm alliance of Anglicans and Royalists against Catholics, Dissenters, and all opponents of the prerogative.[1] On the basis of such a policy, he believed, a genuine reconciliation might be effected between the King, the Parliament, and the majority of the nation, and a new era of peace and prosperity might be inaugurated under his own leadership. It is true

[1] " The aim you have to settle the Church and State ; to defend the one against schismatics and papists, and the other against Commonwealths men and rebels " (Earl of Lindsey to Danby, August 25, 1675, in *Lindsey MSS.*, p. 376).

that, like many of his contemporaries, he was always inclined to regard religion as a branch of politics, and he was certainly not above making party capital out of his beliefs ; but these beliefs were sincere, and the charge so freely advanced at the time, that his sole idea was to maintain himself in office, has no real foundation. Whatever may be said against them his proposals constituted a more honest and statesmanlike attempt at a national policy than had been made since the time of Clarendon.

The first step towards the realisation of the new ideas had already been taken about the middle of October 1674, when Danby paid a visit to Bishop Morley of Winchester at Farnham Castle, " and in his Majesty's name told the bishop of a consultation which would be necessary among the fathers of the Church and with some of the Privy Council how to propose some things that might unite and best pacify the minds of people against the next session of Parliament." [1] Nearly a fortnight later Secretary Williamson dispatched formal letters to Morley and to other bishops desiring their presence in London for the purpose of such a consultation, [2] and on their arrival those who were able to attend were required to meet and consider the most efficacious methods for the suppression of popery and for the support and preservation of the Church of England. [3] During the closing weeks of the year several conferences were held among them, the result of which appeared in a paper presented by them to the King at the beginning of the following January. Existing legislation, they unanimously declared, was sufficient for the purposes propounded to them. All that was necessary was that the law should be enforced, and that those who obstructed its operation should be rigorously discountenanced. [4]

From the very beginning Danby had endeavoured to keep the

[1] Southwell to Ormonde, October 24, 1674, in Carte MSS. 72, f. 229.

[2] *Cal. S.P. Dom.*, 1673-5, p. 390. The letters are dated October 31 an l November 3, 1674.

[3] *Ibid.*, p. 548.

[4] Southwell to Ormonde, January 2, 1674[/5], in Carte MSS. 72, f. 253. The paper mentioned in this letter is clearly that summarised in *Cal. S.P. Dom.*, 1673-5, pp. 548-9, the date of which should presumably be January 1 or 2.

threads of this affair in his own hands, with a view to securing for himself all the credit which might arise out of it. To his annoyance he now found Lauderdale insinuating himself into the negotiation, and dared not run the risk of giving offence by trying to exclude him.[1] He had therefore to take him into partnership, and these two ministers were united with the Lord Keeper and the Secretaries of State in a small committee to discuss the matter with the bishops and give greater precision to the somewhat vague suggestions they had made. On January 21 bishops and Privy Councillors met for the first time at Lambeth, and five days later they had agreed upon a number of conclusions which they embodied under six heads. The conviction of Roman Catholics, they considered, should be encouraged and made more effectual ; the celebration of mass should be suppressed except in the Queen's chapel and in those of foreign ministers, and the resort of English subjects to these chapels should be prevented ; all English priests should be banished ; English subjects being educated at popish seminaries abroad should be recalled ; papists should be prevented from coming to Court ; conventicles should be suppressed, and the licenses issued at the time of the Declaration of Indulgence should be declared void.[2]

It remained to secure the approval of the Council Board, but this presented little difficulty. On January 27 the precise methods were considered by which the ends aimed at might be secured. Two days later the King announced his policy to the Council, and the Lord Keeper explained the whole scheme in detail.[3] Some Lords to whom the proposals came as a complete surprise desired time for consideration, and were given a week for that purpose ; but the ultimate decision was never in doubt. On February 3 an order in Council was adopted substantially embodying the points which had been agreed upon, and on February 10 a declaration was issued requiring the order

[1] " The bishops were treated withall in this matter first by my Lord Treasurer, who has not been over pleased with the Duke of Lauderdale for affecting to concern himself therein " (Southwell to Ormonde, *ut supra*).

[2] Carte MSS. 72, ff. 257, 259 ; *Cal. S.P. Dom.*, 1673-5, pp. 549-50 ; Danby to the Earl of Essex, January 28, 1675, *infra*, ii. 54-5.

[3] Ruvigny to Louis XIV, February 11, 1675, in *Campana de Cavelli*, i. 146-8 ; Carte MSS. 72, f. 261 ; *Cal. S.P. Dom.*, 1673-5, pp. 550-1.

to be strictly observed.[1] At the instigation of the Lord Treasurer, who had some appreciation of the value of an appeal to popular sentiment, more spectacular measures followed. The rebuilding of St. Paul's cathedral, destroyed by the Great Fire, was pressed forward. Old Cavalier memories were stirred by preparations for the erection at Charing Cross of a brass statue of Charles I.[2] A proposal was even made that the body of the Martyr King should be taken up and " reinterred with great magnificence." [3]

All these measures were intended to rouse the enthusiasm of Anglicans and Royalists and so pave the way for what was Danby's main object, the introduction of a test which was to be taken by members of both Houses of Parliament and by all office holders. By means of this test he proposed to confine political power to the friends of monarchy and the establishment, and to unite them in support of the King's authority and his own supremacy.[4] Not merely would an Anglican test, he believed, make the existing Parliament more tractable, but it would enable the King, if he so desired, to dissolve that Parliament and summon another, without running the risk of being confronted by a Dissenting and republican assembly.

Had this whole policy been brought forward six or seven years earlier it is conceivable that it might have proved a triumphant success. In essentials it was a repetition of Clarendon's policy, shaped on more up-to-date lines and with a greater regard for practical political considerations. But events since the fall of Clarendon had greatly weakened popular confidence in the good faith of the Court, and the new measures were received with widespread suspicion. Even Danby himself had been just sufficiently connected with the Cabal to make his sincerity, in general estimation, distinctly doubtful, while about the insincerity of his chief associate, Lauderdale, there

[1] P.C. Reg. 64, p. 372 ; Cal. S.P. Dom., 1673-5, pp. 568, 578.

[2] The statue had been cast in 1633, and was bought by Danby specially for his purpose. Months, however, were spent on the preparations for its erection, and the delay laid the whole project open to ridicule (see " The Statue at Charing Cross " in Marvell, Poems and Letters, i. 189-91).

[3] Ibid., ii. 319 ; Burnet, ii. 61-2.

[4] Danby appears to have had more than one idea of how this might be accomplished. A semi-voluntary scheme is suggested in his notes for an " Association of Lords," printed infra, ii. 65.

could be no doubt whatever. The King was simply reversing a policy which he had insisted upon with the greatest emphasis only two years earlier, and, although his subjects were not fully aware of the fact, was at the same time continuing his negotiations with the French King in order to have a way of retreat should his new venture prove unsuccessful.[1] The Duke of York, as a Catholic, could scarcely be supposed to favour an Anglican domination, and had in reality for some time been endeavouring to introduce a very different policy, involving a prorogation of Parliament and the issue of a new Declaration of Indulgence.

In this way was introduced an element of weakness in Danby's position, of which his numerous enemies were not slow to take advantage. Since the failure of his embassy to Holland Arlington had allowed his personal enmity to the Lord Treasurer to incline him more and more towards the opposition, and during the coming session was to take his place as a rule among those arrayed against the Court.[2] Ormonde, who might otherwise have supported an Anglican policy, had also a long tradition of enmity with Danby, and was united by intimate ties to Arlington. Buckingham rather unexpectedly chose this moment for a breach with his former follower, determined very possibly by the declaration of the latter against the nonconformists.[3] Shaftesbury, in spite of great efforts made by the King to secure his support, was already beginning to come forward as the real leader and inspirer of the opposition. All these statesmen had considerable parliamentary followings of their own, but their principal strength lay in their capacity to play on the general

[1] *Ranke*, iv. 7.

[2] At the height of the discussions on the religious problem meetings of the Council had to be suspended because Danby, Lauderdale and Finch refused to give their advice regarding the policy which the Government should pursue towards Parliament if Arlington was present (Ruvigny to Louis XIV, February 4, 1675). A strongly worded remonstrance against the behaviour of Arlington's associates, which Danby may have presented or read to the King, is printed *infra*, iii. 1-2.

[3] As late as January 1675 Buckingham appears still to have been on friendly terms with Danby. The last letter which has been found of those he wrote to the Lord Treasurer is dated York, January 27, 1674[/5], and requests his assistance in securing an appointment for a friend. The only discordant note it strikes is contained in a complaint that earlier letters have not been answered (Leeds MSS., Packet 5).

distrust of the Government entertained by the vast body of unorganised opinion in the House of Commons.

It was an additional difficulty in Danby's path that the proceedings of the English Parliament had become a matter of acute concern to the principal powers of Europe. France was now being fairly well held in check by Austria, Spain, and the German princes who had come to the assistance of Holland, and England was in a position to cast the balance to whichever side she chose. So long as King and Parliament remained at variance, however, England was practically powerless, and the object of the French King, who had no serious hope that they could be persuaded to intervene in his favour, was therefore to perpetuate the disagreement between them, either by subsidising the King to neglect Parliament, or, where that course had to be abandoned, by stirring up Parliament to attack the King. The allies, on the other hand, set their hopes on a reconciliation between King and Parliament which might lead to intervention against France, and exerted themselves to the utmost to bring about that result. All the principal ambassadors in England, Austrian, Spanish, Dutch and French, were entrusted by their governments with funds, to be employed in influencing the House of Commons to suit their views, and a series of cross currents were thus set up in an already sufficiently complicated situation which made exact political calculations impossible.[1]

Under these conditions the only thing which could have ensured success for Danby was the organisation of a large body of Government supporters in Parliament ; but the efforts made in this direction were ridiculously inadequate. The existing Court party was not of Danby's creation, and it was doubtful how far it could be trusted. A few personal letters were accordingly written by the King and by Danby himself, desiring the presence at Westminster of influential loyalists in both Houses.[2] A certain number of more official invitations were

---

[1] *Mignet*, iv. 333-4 ; Ogg, *England in the Reign of Charles II*, ii. 530. As early as March 17 Secretary Coventry was complaining that " it seems the Spanish Ambassador is to come to wait on the Parliament, not the King " (*Cal. S.P. Dom.*, 1675-6, p. 25).

[2] Danby to the Earl of Essex, February 15, 1674/5, *infra*, ii. 56 ; same to the Earl of Ogle, April 1, 1675, in *Portland MSS.*, ii. 150. Essex in his reply entrusted Danby with his proxy (*Letters of the Earl of Essex in the year* 1675, pp. 89-91).

issued by Secretary Coventry to men of less importance.[1]
Otherwise reliance was placed almost entirely on the attractiveness of the new policy, and although that policy unquestionably brought over a large number of supporters, its effect was
liable at any moment to be discounted by a wave of feeling
from some unexpected quarter which might put the Government in a minority even on the most important questions.

That a determined opposition would have to be encountered
was made manifest almost as soon as Parliament met. The
principal point in the King's speech, delivered on April 13, the
opening day, was to raise the problem of additional securities
for the established religion, which he declared himself resolved
to maintain. Of this Shaftesbury, in the debate which followed,
endeavoured to take advantage, with a view to detaching the
Catholic peers from their customary alliance with the Government. The Duke of York, however, although he had hitherto
resisted all the attempts of Danby and Lauderdale to secure
his support for their policy, was not readily to be drawn into
actual opposition.[2] Religion, he pointed out, might be secured
by mildness and moderation as well as by rigour and severity,
and the King had not prescribed any method. As a result of
this speech all the Catholics with the exception of the Earl of
Powis supported the Government, and although both Arlington and Ormonde joined the opposition, thanks were voted to
the King in the usual form.[3]

This, however, was a mere preliminary to the appearance of
the real issue. On April 15 the Earl of Lindsey introduced in
the House of Lords " an Act to prevent the dangers which may
arise from persons disaffected to the Government," which in
substance repeated Clarendon's unsuccessful bill of ten years

[1] Feiling, *History of the Tory Party*, p. 158, referring to B.M. Add. MSS.
25124 ; Ogg, *Charles II*, ii. 483, referring to the Coventry papers at Longleat.
The ten members of the Commons who were summoned by Coventry are indicated *infra*, iii. 57-60.

[2] Clarke, *Life of James II*, i. 499-500. Undoubtedly James at this time came
very near throwing in his lot with the malcontents, who made him the most
extravagant offers. Possibly the representations of the French ambassador,
that any breach between him and the King would be fatal, decided his wavering counsels (Ruvigny to Louis XIV, April 8, 1675).

[3] *Bulstrode Papers*, p. 284. Opposition came from 26 lords, of whom 10
entered a formal protest (Schwerin, *Briefe aus England*, p. 19 ; J. E. T. Rogers,
Protests of the Lords, i. 43).

earlier, proposing to exact from all members of Parliament and
officials under the Crown the declaration of the unlawfulness of
resistance to the King, and the oath not to endeavour any
alteration of the government in Church or State, which had
already been imposed by several statutes on clergymen, officers
in the militia, and members of corporations. Such a test could
be really acceptable only to extreme Anglicans, and it was
accordingly opposed by many different interests. Presbyterians and men of moderate views were reinforced by a section
of the Catholics, and by personal enemies of the ministers, such
as Arlington, Ormonde and the remaining Clarendonians.[1]
The result was a furious contest which continued until June 2,
and was accompanied by unprecedented scenes. For seventeen
days in all the bill was before the Lords, the debates upon it
running on repeatedly until nine or ten in the evening and once
actually until midnight. Every stage in its progress was marked
by formal protests, for the most outspoken of which the protesters were called to account, and even threatened with
imprisonment in the Tower. After the debate of April 23,
when a proposal to consider whether the bill infringed the
privileges of the House was rejected only by a single vote, the
Government was never really sure of a majority, and several
times had to accept amendments rather than risk a defeat.

Foremost among the supporters of the measure were naturally those who had taken a prominent part in the Lambeth conferences, Danby, Lauderdale and Finch, Bishops Morley and
Ward and their brethren. Finch was the principal speaker for
the Court, and did not a little to weaken its case by that flowery
style of oratory which his enemies knew so well how to ridicule.[2]

---

[1] It has often been pointed out that Danby, the promoter of the new bill, and
Lindsey, its sponsor in the Lords, had opposed Clarendon's bill (*supra*, pp. 37-8).
It is scarcely less remarkable that Clarendon's eldest son, who had supported his
father's bill, opposed Danby's, and was dismissed in consequence from his place
of Chamberlain to the Queen (*Bulstrode Papers*, p. 288; *Essex Papers*, ii. 1, 30).

[2] Even at the beginning of the session one of his phrases had caused a good
deal of unfavourable comment. "The Lord Keeper, haveing a hole in his
speech which no word but ' trifle ' would fill exactly, was pleased for sweet-
sounding sake and the beauty of oratory advize that they would not ' trifle
away their time,' at which expression both Houses tooke great exceptions and
will, some thinke, be at it againe hereafter, so that perhaps his Lordship may
find some inconveniencie in musical rhetorick when made use of to rough men "
(*Bulstrode Papers*, p. 284).

On Danby fell the task of directing the debate, marshalling the Government forces, and deciding what amendments might safely be accepted,[1] a task which even his opponents admitted he performed with skill and resolution. Only once was he caught napping, when he allowed himself to countenance the suggestion that the words " by force or fraud " should be added to the oath not to endeavour any alteration of the government in Church or State. As a result of this slip, a motion to that effect made by Lord Grey of Rolleston was seconded both by the Duke of York and by the Bishop of Rochester, and it was not till the last moment that Danby realised how completely the inclusion of these words would destroy the value of the oath for his purposes, and by giving " the word and sign " to his followers secured with difficulty the rejection of the proposal.[2]

In general estimation the opposition, led by Shaftesbury, Buckingham, Winchester, Halifax and Salisbury, had much the better of the arguments, and it was only the steadfast refusal of the Duke of York to desert the Court,[3] together with the influence exerted by the regular attendance of the King himself at the debates, that deprived them of success. Nevertheless it was early anticipated that the bill would probably pass the Lords, and every effort was accordingly made to impose a check by stirring up trouble in the Commons. There the King's speech was criticised much more openly than in the Lords, Henry Powle declaring that " if they should thanke in general they must thanke for the convention at Lambeth, and for a few lords and bishops advising that which the Parliament never yet desired and which in very truth was plaine

[1] " The Lord Treasurer, whose authority easily obtained with the major vote."

[2] The most complete account of the proceedings of the Lords is given in the contemporary pamphlet, " A Letter from a Person of Quality to his Friend in the Country," reprinted in *Parliamentary History*, iv. App., p. xxxvii. See also *Journals of the House of Lords ; Hist. MSS. Com.*, ix. 2, pp. 51-2 ; *Burnet*, ii. 81-4 ; Carte MSS. 79, f. 17.

[3] " Duke and Papists divided and Papists and Presbyterians united. For Duke sees a necessity of using other hands and will be the first that shall take the Test " (Conway to Essex, May 4, 1675, in *Essex Papers*, ii. 8). To some extent James seems to have played the part of a mediator between the Court and the opposition (*Bulstrode Papers*, p. 289). A division list is printed *infra*, iii. 122-5.

persecution." In the end the House reserved its opinion of the
Government's policy by thanking the King, not for his speech
as a whole, but for the " gracious promises and assurances "
contained in it, and turned instead to the more congenial task
of denouncing the King's ministers. During the debate on the
speech there had been ominous references to Lauderdale, but
these had no connection with his recent activities at Lambeth
and elsewhere ; and the actual attack upon him, delivered on
the following day, was simply an echo from the session of 1674,
which affected the Lord Treasurer only in so far as his loyal
efforts to defend his colleague involved him in the odium of
which he was the object.[1] The impeachment of Danby himself which followed was quite another matter. Although in
origin merely an attempt on the part of Arlington to discredit
his rival, it secured the support of many of the discontented
factions in the House of Commons, and became the basis of a
real trial of strength between the Government and the opposition.

The impeachment was not in any sense a surprise to Danby.
At least as early as the close of March he had been informed of
what was meditated, and had urged the King to dismiss Arlington, as the only means of preventing the divisions in the House
of Commons which it would inevitably produce.[2] Before
Parliament met he knew who his accusers would be, and had
seen at least some of the articles which would be produced
against him.[3] But he had no reason to suppose that his
opponents could substantiate, or would even advance, any
charge of real importance, and he believed his credit with the

[1] On April 14 Sir Nicholas Carew attacked Lauderdale, " and voted to
make the same address against him now which they made the last sessions,
to remove him from the King's person and all employments under him."
A resolution to that effect was adopted, and the address was presented on
April 26 (C.J., ix. 316; Bulstrode Papers, pp. 284-5, 288; Essex Papers,
i. 318).

[2] " Il [le Grand Tresorier] m'a dit que Milord Arlinton et ses amis ont tout
remué contre luy et contre le Duc de Lederdail, qu'il en advoit donné advis au
Roy son maistre, et qu'il l'avoit asseuré sur sa teste que s'il esloignoit ce
ministre il trouveroit le Parlement dans toutes les bonnes dispositions que sa
Majesté pouvoit desirer " (Ruvigny to Louis XIV, April 8, 1675. See also
Burnet, ii. 73, note 2).

[3] Essex Papers, i. 319, which gives " Litleton, Powell [not Powys], Meeres,
Candish, Sir John Coventry, &c.," as the authors of the articles.

Commons was sufficiently good to maintain him against vague denunciations.

His confidence was fully justified by the event. On April 26 William Russell, later to become famous as " the patriot," opened the attack in the House of Commons, denouncing Danby's conduct at the Treasury, and moving that he should be deprived of his employments and proceeded against by impeachment. Sir Samuel Barnardiston immediately followed with definite articles against him, the general tenor of which he explained to the House ; and he in turn was supported by Henry Powle, Sir Thomas Meres and Sir Thomas Littleton. The articles themselves, however, proved to be " pitifull stuff." In an endeavour to enlist the support of as many sections as possible in the House of Commons, matters of the most incongruous character were grouped together. By the first and most important article, which declared that Danby had " overthrown and violated the ancient course and constitution of the Exchequer," it was hoped to conciliate all those who had suffered by his financial reforms. The charge that he had " assumed to himself the management of the Irish affairs, which were in precedent times dispatched always by the Secretaries and passed in Council," was intended to win over the Coventries and their connections. A reference to the " great gifts and grants from the Crown " which he had received would, it was believed, rouse the country gentlemen ; while a statement that he was responsible for the continued stop of the Exchequer might influence commercial interests. Coupled with these more or less serious charges were the usual vague reference to secret service money, a foolish statement that Danby had once declared " that a new proclamation is better than an old Act," and an article dealing with the negotiations for Dumblane's marriage, in the course of which undue pressure was alleged to have been brought to bear on John Brandling.[1]

In meeting these charges Danby had no need to rely on such personal friends and followers as Lord Ogle, Sir Charles Wheeler and Sir Edmund Jennings, all of whom hastened to speak on his behalf. The first to come forward in his defence, indeed,

---

[1] The articles of impeachment are printed *infra*, ii. 72-4.

were William Garroway and Sir Richard Temple, once his associates among the partisans of Buckingham, but now for some time connected rather with the opposition. Colonel Titus objected to the character of the whole proceedings. " This," he declared, " is to seeke an offender and then looke if it bee an offence." Colonel Birch was confident that from all his accusers could say the Treasurer would " come out purified like gold." Sir Charles Harbord bore strong testimony to his success in his office, and expressed his surprise " that a young man, and a country gentleman, should understand it so soon." That stout Cavalier and Churchman, Colonel Giles Strangways, reflected so bitterly on the conduct of Sir Thomas Littleton in supporting the accusation that some would have called him to the bar,[1] but confident that the House as a whole agreed with him he refused to explain his words away, and " went to his pipe of tobacco without any further concernment." [2]

The resolution ultimately arrived at was that the impeachment should be considered article by article,[3] but the proceedings of the two following days, during which the first article was debated, clearly demonstrated the weakness of those who supported it. Two patents were produced as the instruments

[1] The expression complained of was, " I am not for a generall accusation when I have heard some gentlemen speake one way when they have offices and another when they have none, and fall out when they cannot agree aboute shareing the revenue among them." On Littleton ejaculating, " I presume the worthy member meanes me, and if reflected on I may speake," Strangways replied, " I intended no particular reflection, but if any gentleman will take it to himselfe he may."

[2] Essex Papers, ii. 1-2; Grey, iii. 40-49. There is a very full account of the entire proceedings on the impeachment preserved among the Lindsey MSS., and a fragment of the rough notes for that account in Leeds MSS., Packet 6. The writer was not present on the first day when the impeachment was moved, and his account begins with Garroway's speech recorded in Grey, iii. 42-3. His notes of the speeches are not always so full as those in Grey, but he gives many speeches and details which Grey does not record at all. There is also a hastily written list of the speakers on the first day (B.M. Add. MSS. 28047, f. 142), with each name marked " con " or " pro " according as the speaker was against or for Danby. It reads, " Russell began, con ; Sir Bernard Diston presents the articles, con ; Powell explains, con ; Sir Thomas Meares, con ; Ogle, pro ; Sir John Coventry, con ; Garway excuses, pro ; Sir Thomas Littleton, con ; Vaughan, pro ; Sir Thomas Lee, con ; Sacheverell, con ; Sir Nicholas Carew, con ; Herbert, pro ; Burch, pro ; Reeve, pro ; Williamson, pro ; Strangways, pro."

[3] C.J., ix. 324.

by which the Treasurer had " engross'd the revenue into his owne hands . . . and alter'd the ordinary course of the Exchequer." On April 27 it was resolved that the first did not contain matter for an impeachment, and on April 28 the decisive struggle took place over the second. A proposal that the patent should be declared " contrary to the course and constitution of the Exchequer " was rejected by 181 votes to 105, and it was then resolved without a division that the patent was not illegal, that it provided no ground for an impeachment of the Treasurer, and that no matter for such proceedings could be found in the first article of the charge against him.[1]

So decisive a result deprived Danby's enemies of all hope that the remaining articles might be carried, and at this point they would gladly have allowed their accusation to drop, and remained content with such weight as their unproved assertions might have in the country as a whole.[2] But the Treasurer's friends insisted on a thorough examination, and the unattached members, anticipating perhaps some interesting revelations in connection with the second article, which concerned Dumblane's marriage negotiations, gave them their support. On April 30, accordingly, after a delay required for the production of witnesses, the investigation was resumed, and Sir Robert Viner, now Lord Mayor of London, was examined concerning the arrest of Brandling. The Treasurer's enemies, however, were unable to make the faintest impression,[3] and on the question being put whether there was any ground for an impeachment in this article only six ventured to vote in the affirmative.[4] This practically meant the end of the whole affair.[5] On May 3

---

[1] *Ibid.*, pp. 325, 326 ; *Bulstrode Papers*, p. 288.

[2] " Thinking this would be sufficient to bespatter him " (*Essex Papers*, ii. 2).

[3] According to one account Danby's friends were " so much too strong for his enemies that they would hardly hear anybody, either member or witness, speake against him " (*Bulstrode Papers*, p. 289).

[4] *C.J.*, ix. 326-8 ; *Grey*, iii. 51-2, 58-82 ; *Essex Papers*, ii. 6 ; Marvell, *Poems and Letters*, ii. 146-7.

[5] At this point, indeed, Sir Nicholas Carew and Lord O'Brien, two of the most resolute supporters of the impeachment, proposed that all the remaining articles should be grouped together and made the subject of a similar vote, but the House preferred an adjournment.

the remaining articles were hastily debated, and dismissed apparently without a division.[1]

The disappointed supporters of the impeachment did not scruple to attribute this result to " great bribing " on the part of the Court,[2] or to the use of " the most unparliamentary means imaginable ; "[3] but their unreadiness to come to a division, and the small number of votes they could muster when they did so, clearly show that the Treasurer had no need to use bribery or undue influence, while such evidence as exists suggests that all the bribery was on the other side.[4] The articles of impeachment were extremely weak, and their origin was not regarded with favour. It seems probable that Danby profited to an appreciable extent by the old hatred of the Bucking-

---

[1] *C.J.*, ix. 328-9 ; *Grey*, iii. 83-96. In a short speech delivered after the final decision Sir Joseph Tredenham endeavoured to improve the occasion. " Wee ought both to punish and protect. None of the greivances complayned of last Parliament cann bee layd to this man's charge. Noe favourer of popery ; an honest, just and good man. And am of opinion hee was great cause of our meeting and continueing here. And if wee use great men thus 'twill hinder any good and just man from takeing employment hereafter " (Lindsey MSS.).

[2] Marvell, *Poems and Letters*, ii. 320.   [3] *Essex Papers*, ii. 7.

[4] On May 4 Sir Thomas Littleton complained to the Commons of a report that he had offered £4,000 to a certain Thomas Salter if he would sign a statement that Danby in his hearing had declared a new proclamation to be better than an old law. The House was not much interested, but summoned Salter to appear before it the following day, when he denied that Littleton or any other member had endeavoured to bribe him, but admitted signing a paper at the instance of Littleton and Powle. Both these members asserted that Salter's information and signature were given with the utmost willingness, and the House allowed the matter to drop (*C.J.*, ix. 329-30 ; *Grey*, iii. 96, 102-3 ; Lindsey MSS.). That the behaviour of the two members was not absolutely blameless, however, is suggested by the following letter, addressed to Danby and endorsed by him, " Mr. Salters letter about Sir Thomas Littletons and others contrivances against mee in Parliament, 20 January 1676/7 " :

London, January 20th, 1676/7.—Right Honourable Sir, I hope you will not judg me troublesome, though my present condition I must confess is not extreamly easie ; yett that which most disturbs me is that expression of yours, you know not of any kindness done because you are left upon record in the House of Commons. I am very sorry my letter to Captain Mead had no better success, when I went into the countrey and absented myself from all mine own affaires on purpose with one person more, eight or ten dayes, with full intent to be servicable to you in not appearing. And when I did, pray give me leav to ask where was my fault. Is it because I answerd not to that broad word " bribe." If so, 'twas your freinds in the House. I could not, nor did it become me, for it was the work of the House to give it that name if what I had to evidence deserved it. Had I bin askt whither I was offerd repaires of losses, and sattisfaction for damages I received in case I would give testemony against

ham group for Arlington and all his works.[1] Nevertheless the triumphant acquittal of the Lord Treasurer was in essentials a vote of confidence in the domestic policy for which he had made himself responsible, and as such it was an event of very real significance.

The rock on which Danby was to suffer shipwreck was his inability to give any similar satisfaction regarding foreign affairs. Apart from the question of securities for religion, the chief point in the King's speech had been to recommend to the consideration of the Commons the condition of the fleet. In the absence of any guarantee how the fleet might be used, however, the Commons hesitated to make any satisfactory response, and far from voting an additional supply resolved in the end to appropriate the greater part of the existing Customs duties for three years to the use of the navy.[2] The main cause of their distrust was the continued presence of English troops in the French army. Not merely had those sent to France during the war been allowed to remain, but since the conclusion of peace with Holland they had been extensively recruited. On April 19, accordingly, the Commons resolved on an address to the King for the recall of all his subjects in the service of France.[3] Some

you, I could have chearfully answerd, and still can. And because your Honour was pleased to desire me to gett some reputable men should attest that those offers were made me by Sir Thomas Littleton and others, Captain Mead has promised me he will not be wanting to wittness the truth thereof, he being then present, who is knowne in this part of the Citty to be a man of creditt and reputation ; and I can show and prove myself an honest man, although providence hath brought me low to what I was, and that I am, Sir, Your Honours most humble and obedient servant, Thomas Salter. I shall wait on your answer and pleasure herein. (Leeds MSS., Packet 8. See also *Supplement to Lindsey MSS.*, pp. 9-12.

[1] He was supported even by Sir Robert Howard.

[2] " So that the great favour they intend the King at present is onely to tell him how to use what he has already " (*C.J.*, ix. 330 ; *Grey*, iii. 34-40, 96-102 ; *Bulstrode Papers*, p. 289).

[3] The matter was introduced by Sir Thomas Littleton, who estimated the King's subjects in the French army, English, Scottish and Irish, at 10,000 men. In the extreme attitude it adopted the opposition, according to the French ambassador, was influenced largely by the representations of " M. Van Beuninghen et les autres ministres des confédérés, qui se trouvaient tous les jours à l'entrée et à la sortie du parlement et qui sollicitaient comme les parties sollicitent leur procès au palais." The address was presented by the Speaker, attended by two hundred members, on April 21, and was received by the King with an assurance that he would consider it (*C.J.*, ix. 319, 321 ; *Grey*, iii. 3-9 ; Ruvigny to Pomponne, April 29 and May 2, 1675, in *Mignet*, iv. 345).

three weeks later the King's reply, that he would prohibit the departure of fresh troops for France, but could not in honour recall those who had been in the French service before the peace, provoked a furious debate in Grand Committee of the whole House. On a division being taken over the proposal that a further address should be made to the King for the recall of his subjects, the votes were 135 on each side ; but the figures were questioned, the tellers could not agree as to whether there should be a recount, and a scene of unparalleled disorder followed. Insults were exchanged, swords were half drawn, some members set their feet upon the mace to prevent the Speaker taking the chair, and had not Seymour with great address contrived to frustrate this manoeuvre and assume control of the House bloodshed would certainly have ensued. Even on the following day, when the same subject was debated in a calmer atmosphere, and the Secretaries of State made an official intimation that the King was prepared to recall his subjects who had entered the French service since the peace with Holland, a strong undercurrent of opposition prevailed. A motion was made for an address that he should recall all his subjects, and on a division being taken over the word " all " it was decided only by 173 votes to 172 that it should be omitted.[1]

As a result of these debates feeling in the House of Commons had become as heated as in the House of Lords, and a splendid opportunity was offered, by playing on the general excitement, to bring all business to a standstill. Of this Shaftesbury was not slow to avail himself. In an appeal carried by a certain Dr. Thomas Sherley from Chancery to the House of Lords it happened that the defendant, Sir John Fagg, was a member of the House of Commons. The formal order of the Lords, that Fagg should put in an answer to Sherley's petition, was accordingly regarded with the deepest suspicion by the Commons, who not only requested the Lords to have regard to their privileges in the matter, but on receiving what they considered

---

[1] The King's answer to the original address was delivered to the House on May 8. The debates followed on May 10 and 11 (*C.J.*, ix. 333-5 ; *Grey*, iii. 115-39 ; *Essex Papers*, ii. 8-9, 11 ; Ruvigny to Louis XIV, May 23, 1675, in *Mignet*, iv. 350-1).

an unsatisfactory answer forbade Fagg to proceed in the case without their permission.[1]   Immediately Shaftesbury took up the cudgels on behalf of his own House, and vigorously endeavoured to fan the flames of discord, hoping by such obstructive tactics to force a prorogation if not a dissolution.[2]

With characteristic audacity Danby met this move by coming forward as the champion of the House of Commons.   At his instigation the King lent the Commons his countenance, the Speaker pressed their claims to the utmost, and the Duke of York worked in unison in the House of Lords.[3]   The policy of the Court, Danby believed, was certain of a majority in the Lords.[4]   If by this astute move he could only conciliate the Commons and make them look to the Crown for support, his non-resisting test would pass, and he might obtain the vote of supply without which he was loath to bring the session to a

[1] The original order of the Lords was made on April 30, and the first remonstrance of the Commons on May 5 (*L.J.*, xii. 673-4, 679 ; *C.J.*, ix. 329-35).

[2] If Shaftesbury did not, as is sometimes stated, actually create his opportunity, he at least recognised it at a very early stage.   It is significant that the report of the Lords' committee on the Commons' remonstrance was presented by his intimate associate the Earl of Berkshire, and that a formal protest against the reply sent by the Lords to the Commons, on the ground that it was too conciliatory, was made by nine peers, at least seven of whom were united with him in opposition to the non-resisting test (*L.J.*, xii. 680-1).

[3] " Un differend touchant les privileges dont on est icy fort jaloux estant survenu entre les Seigneurs et les Communes, le Grand Tresorier a tourné son maistre du costé de celles-cy, de sorte que ceux-la sestans unis ensemble sa Majesté Britanique n'a plus le credit quelle avoit aupres d'eux.   Ce que voyant le Grand Tresorier, il a persuadé ce Prince que cette perte ne luy devoit pas estre considerable, puisqu'il avoit gagné par ce moyen l'affection des Communes, qui ne manqueroient pas de luy donner de l'argent à la prochaine session " (Ruvigny to Louis XIV, June 27, 1675).   William Harbord seems to have had some idea of what was going on (*Essex Papers*, ii. 18, 23-4, 27) ; but other observers were hopelessly puzzled.   When a further address was proposed in favour of recalling the King's subjects in the French army, and the Commons again divided equally, it was noted with astonishment that the Speaker gave his casting vote in favour of the address (*C.J.*, ix. 343 ; *Grey*, iii. 184 ; *Bulstrode Papers*, p. 295).

[4] Owing to the unwavering support of the bishops, this was practically the case.   During the contest over the non-resisting test the number of bishops present in the Lords rose as high as eighteen, and of the absentees four had given proxies.   Not without reason was the bill establishing the test called the Bishops' Bill, and a proposal made in the Lords that they should withdraw while it was being discussed, as they had no right to vote in their own case (*L.J.*, xii. *passim.* ; *Bulstrode Papers*, p. 286).

close.[1] The resolution adopted by the Commons on May 17
that no new bills should be introduced except such as came down
from the Lords, precluding, as it appeared to do, all likelihood
of a money bill, was a serious disappointment to him;[2] but as
late as June 1 he was still hopeful of obtaining some of his ends.[3]

Thereafter, however, it became increasingly apparent that
the quarrel between the two Houses had reached a stage which
made parliamentary business absolutely impossible and actual
bloodshed only too likely. Possibly the initial fault lay with the
Commons, who very arbitrarily ordered the arrest of Sherley,
and whose under-sergeant foolishly endeavoured to effect that
arrest in the lobby of the House of Lords. The outraged
magnates retaliated in kind by taking the officer's warrant
from him and sending it to the Commons with a message in
which it was described as " a paper signed Edward Seymour."
Stung to fury by what they regarded as a piece of gratuitous
insolence the Commons showed themselves most intractable
at the ensuing conference between the two Houses, and, even
after the Whitsun vacation had given them time for reflection,
proved sufficiently determined to resolve " that there lies no
appeal to the judicature of the Lords in Parliament from courts
of equity." Four eminent lawyers who presumed to plead
before the Lords in defiance of this resolution they committed
to the custody of their Sergeant. The Lords immediately
insisted on their release. The Commons then rearrested them
with an alarming display of force, Seymour himself apprehend-
ing Francis Pemberton in Westminster Hall, and on his hesitating to submit ordering his officers " to shove him before the

---

[1] It was tactics such as these, rather than any use of corruption, that laid
the basis of Danby's immense reputation as a parliamentary manager.

> " Zounds! What meant the Parliament?
> Sure they were drunk with brandy,
> When they thought to circumvent
> Thomas Earl of Danby."

[2] The resolution did not make the introduction of a money bill impossible.
In order to keep the way open the Courtiers proposed to add to the resolution
the words " unless it be upon extraordinary occasion ; " but Henry Powle,
Sir William Coventry and Sir Thomas Meres explained in the clearest possible
manner that the House was not bound by its own orders, and that if such an
occasion arose the resolution could be annulled. It was on this understanding
that the addition was then rejected by 169 votes to 121 (*C.J.*, ix. 340 ; *Grey*,
iii. 156-66).

[3] Danby to Essex, June 1, 1675, *infra*, ii. 58-9.

mace " towards the Speaker's Chamber, while the Sergeant, backed by thirty members,[1] took the remaining three from the bars where they were pleading, one of them, Sir John Churchill, actually from the Court of Chancery, where in legal theory the King himself was present.[2]

In the midst of the passions aroused by such high-handed actions an immediate settlement of any kind was impracticable, and Danby's hopes of some good issue from Parliament had to be transferred to another session. By the autumn, he believed, the ill-feeling which had been aroused would have had time to die down, and the part which the Court had played in favouring the pretensions of the Commons would then bear its appropriate fruit. On June 9, accordingly, Parliament was prorogued to October 13, and preparations were immediately begun for the new session.

This prorogation was in no sense a confession of defeat, nor did it in any way lessen Danby's credit with the King. Never indeed had his reputation stood higher than in the summer of 1675. Arlington had finally ruined himself by his conduct during the session.[3] Lauderdale had been weakened by the repeated evidence of the irreconcilable hatred with which he was regarded by the House of Commons. To the French ambassador Danby appeared to possess a virtual monopoly of the royal favour even to the exclusion of the Duke of York.[4] James, however, was by no means content with a subordinate position in the King's counsels, and was highly distrustful of the policy which the Court was pursuing. Of this Shaftesbury and the other opponents of the non-resisting test took immediate

[1] " Who came down to see their orders executed, and who, perhaps, would have done it with blows in case of any resistance " (*Bulstrode Papers*, p. 299).

[2] *L.J.*, xii. and *C.J.*, ix. *passim* ; *Bulstrode Papers*, pp. 290-300 ; *Essex Papers*, ii. 15-16, 23-27 ; *Hist. MSS. Com.*, xii. 9, p. 65. A resolution to commit the lawyers to the Tower was carried by 152 votes to 147, the tellers for the majority being Danby's followers, Sir Edmund Jennings and Francis Gwyn (*C.J.*, ix. 353).

[3] " Vostre Majesté ne pourra pas croire a quel point est tombé le credit de Milord Arlinton. Le Roy son maistre ne luy parle que tres peu, et lorsque ce ministre luy dit quelque chose il n'en est presque pas escouté " (Ruvigny to Louis XIV, May 23, 1675).

[4] " La retraite de Milord Arlinton la persuadé qu'il possede si bien l'esprit de son maistre qu'il traite seul avec luy les affaires et mesme sans en faire part a Monsieur le Duc d'York " (Same to same, June 27, 1675).

advantage, representing in the strongest possible terms to
the Duke that the effect of that measure would be to establish
the rule of the bishops at the expense of the King, the Lords,
and the nonconformists of all kinds.   By these arguments
James was more than half convinced, and his alliance with the
Treasurer was seriously shaken.[1]

A union between James and the Catholics on the one hand
and the Presbyterians on the other had already several times
been foreshadowed, but had always broken down over the anti-
monarchical tendencies of the latter and the refusal of the Duke
to desert the King.   In bringing the alliance now to a successful
conclusion the principal influence was that of France.   Danby
had been much impressed during the session by the handicap
imposed upon him by the French proclivities of the Court, and
the prorogation had scarcely been pronounced when he secured
the King's assent by undertaking that supply would thus be
made certain, and in a series of interviews with the principal
leaders of the Commons gave them an assurance that he would
destroy every vestige of the French connection.   To this there
could be only one reply.   The summer of 1675 was not a happy
one for the French.   The death of Turenne, the success of the
Austrian commander Montecuculi in Alsace, and the defeat of
their allies, the Swedes, on land and sea, formed a chapter of
misfortunes which it was feared might be followed by insur-
rectionary movements in France itself.   A reconciliation between King and Parliament, leading quite possibly to the
active intervention of England in the war on the side of the
Confederates, could not be risked.   The French ambassador
Ruvigny accordingly entered into close relations with the
opposition, and by playing on their hatred of the domestic
policy of the Court persuaded them, in return for a promise of
Louis's good offices with Charles, to moderate their anti-French
zeal.   At the same time he promoted in every possible way a
reconciliation between them and the Duke of York.   To assist
in building up an effective coalition the Duke and his former
secretary, Edward Coleman, were even supplied with 100,000
crowns to be distributed among members of Parliament.[2]

[1] *Ibid.*; *Essex Papers*, ii. 32; *Bulstrode Papers*, p. 302.
[2] *Mignet*, iv. 364-6.

Had the King, the Treasurer, and the Church party remained determined and united they should have had little difficulty in meeting the utmost efforts of Catholics, Nonconformists and France combined. But Charles as usual could not give his resolute adhesion to any one line of policy, and allowed himself to be drawn by the French ambassador into a negotiation which was almost directly contradictory of his engagement to Danby. In Ruvigny's opinion the surest method of guaranteeing England's neutrality and damping the hopes of the Confederates was to secure the dissolution or prorogation of Parliament, and he accordingly lost no opportunity of urging on Charles the undesirability, in his own interests, of permitting the Houses to meet. His representations suggested to Charles at least the need for a way of escape in case Danby's schemes should fail, and with the beginning of August he was authorised by the English King to lay two alternatives before his master. Either Charles would prorogue Parliament to the following April, or he would undertake, while meeting it in October, to dissolve it altogether if it failed to vote supplies or proved hostile to France. In the one case he would expect a lump sum of 500,000 crowns, in the other a similar subsidy annually so long as Parliament remained in abeyance. Louis, who had no hopes of any good effect from a short prorogation, immediately chose the second alternative, and towards the close of August the bargain was concluded, the annual subsidy being fixed at £100,000.[1]

Although Danby had no share in this bargain it is scarcely to be supposed that he was ignorant of it, but his only course was to make the best he could of the extremely uncertain position in which it left him. The open declaration against France on which he had rested his hopes was no longer possible, but his original Anglican policy had still a good prospect of success, especially if he could enlist in its support a better organised party than he had had at his disposal during the previous session. Immediately after the prorogation tentative efforts had been made to establish something of the nature of party discipline. To show the readiness of the Court to reward good

[1] *Ibid.*, pp. 367-70.

service Colonel Strangways had been admitted to the Privy
Council, an honour which he had long desired, but lived to
enjoy only for a few weeks.　At the same time Shaftesbury,
Cavendish and Newport had been forbidden the King's presence.[1]　But as the day for the meeting of Parliament drew near
more elaborate and far-reaching methods were recognised to be
necessary, and a genuine effort at the reconstitution of an effective Court party was begun.

The problem of party organisation, as it originally presented
itself to Danby, was not one of securing as large a number of
supporters as possible for his policy.　Like many another politician before and since, he found it difficult to conceive that
his policy could lack supporters ; while he believed the Commons to be specially bound to him by the favour he had shown
them in the previous session.　The problem was rather one of
ensuring that his supporters, whose numbers he did not doubt,
should attend Parliament with regularity and vote in a consistent manner.　So careless were many members, and so varied
the influences which might at any moment determine their vote,
that even a policy which met with general approval was by no
means certain of being accepted by the Commons.　To Danby,
accordingly, the first essential step towards an effective party
organisation appeared to be the formation of a solid core of
members who would be ready to follow implicitly the directions
he gave, and who might exercise some controlling influence
over those outside their own body.

With material for this task he was already well supplied.　He
could count on the personal loyalty of his own relatives and
immediate friends, on the party loyalty of that section of the
Buckingham group which had adhered to his standard, and on
the local loyalty of Osborne partisans in Yorkshire, Bertie
partisans in Lincolnshire, and Seymour partisans in the south-
west.[2]　But he was also tempted to rely on a very different type

---

[1] Marvell, *Poems and Letters*, ii. 320 ; *Bulstrode Papers*, pp. 302-3.　" Diese
Verfügungen werden alle dem Mylord Schatzmeister zugeschrieben " (Schwerin,
Briefe aus England, p. 31).　Strangways was admitted to the Council on
June 23.

[2] " This man (Danby) is as remarkable in the north as somebody (Clifford)
was in the west " (*Grey*, vi. 437).　Seymour had succeeded to much of Clifford's
influence.

of loyalty exhibited by quite another group of men, whose
association with him was largely due to his official position of
Lord Treasurer. It is on his dealings with these men that many
of the worst charges of corruption made against him, both at
the time and since, have been based.

The key to the whole problem of corruption under Charles II
is to be found in the single word " compensation." Representatives of Cavalier families which had suffered in the service of
Charles I expected compensation. Representatives of Round-
head families which had been required (unjustly in their
opinion) to restore part of their gains also expected compensation. Everybody who had held a lucrative office of any kind
and had been deprived of it expected compensation. The
innumerable creditors of the Government expected payment,
which in practice was apt to be indistinguishable from the compensation accorded to others. In the whole of England there
must have been few men of position without claims on the
Crown such as their own age would have admitted, while
thousands had claims which would be considered valid according to the standards of any age.

Compensation might take many forms—a lump sum of
money, a grant of land, a title, a well-paid post, active or sinecure, an occasional gift, a regular pension. Whatever the form,
the recipient was apt thereafter to consider himself under an
obligation to the ruler, minister or Government who had
recognised his claims ; and if the compensation was one of
which he could at any moment be deprived the tie thus created
might be very strong indeed. Inevitably the bulk of the quite
inadequate compensation at the disposal of the Government
fell to the share of courtiers and members of Parliament, who
were in a position to make their claims heard, and probably
without conscious purpose on the part of anybody what was in
effect a system of corruption thus grew up.

The centre of the most obnoxious features of the system was
to be found in the big revenue farms, and more particularly in
the Excise farm. During the early years of the reign, when Sir
Thomas Osborne had himself proposed to farm the Yorkshire
Excise, the Government had been anxious to engage as many
as possible of the country gentry in this beneficial employment,

which it hoped might provide them with some compensation
for their losses under the Commonwealth, attach them to its
service, and render more generally acceptable what from the
first was a most unpopular tax. Time, however, had shown
that the gentry had not the resources to compete successfully
with the London financiers, and even when they could offer the
same annual rent could not undertake to pay as large a sum by
way of advance. Thus the gentry had gradually to retire in
favour of the financiers ; but while doing so they expected
compensation for what they were losing, and very generally
obtained it from their rivals, in the shape either of pensions or
of subordinate posts under them. When Clifford farmed the
entire Excise to one group of individuals in 1673 the successful
financiers found themselves engaged to pay as much as £20,000
a year by way of pensions, while other financiers, who had not
been successful, had entered into similar engagements, which
they might or might not be able to fulfil.[1]

A system under which a small number of private individuals
had in their pay a large number of men of position, many of
them courtiers and members of Parliament, was obviously most
undesirable ; but the only people with any personal animus
against it were the pensioners of unsuccessful financiers, who
had the same claims as their more fortunate fellows, and were
now confronted with the danger that they might get nothing.
It was, accordingly, one of these, Sir Richard Wiseman,
representative for Maldon since 1661, who drew Danby's
attention to the whole situation, and by so doing was indirectly
responsible for the reorganisation of the Excise farm effected in
1674. That reorganisation was something more than a mere
financial operation. In substance it meant that Danby added
to the annual rent of the farm the sum which the farmers had
proposed to disburse in pensions, and undertook that the
pensions, so far as they were considered justifiable, would be
paid in future by the King.[2]

It is at least doubtful whether Danby, in making this change,
had any intention of creating a new group of dependants in
Parliament. The first list of pensioners which he approved

---

[1] Edward Hughes, *Studies in Administration and Finance*, chap. iv.

[2] Wiseman's own account of this is printed *infra*, iii. 19-20. *Cf. ibid.*, p. 28.

contained only sixteen names, of which only ten were those of members of Parliament. The total disbursement provided for was only £4,700 a year, and this seems to be a reduced figure, reached under pressure from Danby himself.[1] On the other hand it is significant that Danby immediately added two new names, those of his faithful follower Daniel Collingwood and of Sir Richard Wiseman himself, whom he now accepted as his principal personal adviser on the organisation of Government influence in the House of Commons.[2] In truth the number of perfectly genuine claimants to a pension on the Excise was so large, and the temptation to find among them recruits for the Government party in consequence so great, that it was inevitable Danby should extend the list. During the year 1674 the number of pensioners was increased by seven, and the total annual disbursement was raised to £7,900. At the same time the practice seems to have been adopted of using fictitious names for those who were specially anxious that their receipt of a pension should not become known. Three of the new pensioners were members of Parliament who were prepared to use their own names, and at least three more were members who preferred to conceal their identity under false names. One of the latter group, indeed, appears to have been Sir Richard Wiseman, who was thus permitted to enjoy two pensions.[3]

The real organisation of the system, however, was effected in the summer of 1675. About that time eleven new pensioners were created, at least eight and possibly all of whom were members of Parliament, while four other members of Parliament had pensions promised, if not actually granted, to them. Thus by the autumn of 1675 between twenty-three and thirty-four members of Parliament were in receipt of pensions on the

[1] The list is printed *infra*, iii. 44-5. The inclusion in it of a seventeenth name, that of Sir Thomas Carew, who died in September 1673, some months before Danby reorganised the Excise at all, seems to indicate that it was not in origin Danby's work, but was based on arrangements made by Clifford or the Excise farmers. Danby's influence appears in a reduction of two of the pensions.

[2] There are indications that Wiseman was originally a dependant of Arlington and Williamson (*Cal. S.P. Dom.*, 1671, pp. 402, 421).

[3] The list is printed *infra*, iii. 45-6. See also "John Knight," "Thomas Peirce," and "John Wood," *infra*, iii. 52-5.

Excise, and approximately £10,000 a year was being distributed among them.[1]

The particular point which made the Excise pensioners so important was that their pensions were paid as secret service money under a general Privy Seal which did not specify individual items. Thus although it was widely known that there were such pensioners, their precise identity and the amounts paid to them were matters only for conjecture, and they could act on behalf of the Government with much greater readiness and much more effect.[2] Danby, in consequence, made them the very centre of his organisation ; but other similar groups were by no means neglected. Of the seven much-envied Commissioners of Customs, with salaries of £2,000 each, five were members of Parliament ;[3] of lesser officials, and of officials of the Irish revenue, unquestionably a very considerable number. Unfortunately the majority both of these and of the general body of office-holders had been appointed before Danby's rise to power, and it was uncertain how far they could be relied upon. The principle acknowledged almost from the beginning of the reign, that when Government business was under discussion in the Commons all office-holders should attend and vote, seems to have been reiterated at this time,[4] but, one may conjecture from divisions in the succeeding session of Parliament, without any striking success.

Danby, however, was not entirely blind to the advantages of a wider appeal than one addressed merely to Government dependants, and about the middle of September had recourse to an

[1] *Infra*, iii. 46-9, where Sir Stephen Fox's list shows the final position at this time. It is worthy of note that about half the members of Parliament appearing on these lists had in actual fact been associated with early Excise farms, and might quite honestly consider themselves entitled to compensation.

[2] In the *Seasonable Argument*, for instance, they are not all recognised even as supporters of the Government, the fact that they enjoyed pensions is noted only in a few cases, and even in these cases the amount given is generally incorrect.

[3] *Cal. Treas. Books*, iv. 71. The existing organisation for the collection of the Customs had been established in 1671 under the influence of Ashley and Clifford, who appointed some 763 subordinate Customs officers in addition to the Commissioners (Hughes, *Studies in Administration and Finance*, pp. 139-40). Danby later reduced the salary of the Commissioners to £1,200.

[4] The earliest list of officials printed *infra*, iii. 62-5, was probably drawn up just before the meeting of Parliament.

expedient, in appearance new, but in reality only an extension of a familiar practice. For some time it had been the custom for the Secretaries of State to summon to Parliament by special letters any members whose presence there was particularly desired by the Government. The names of more than a hundred members of the House of Commons who it was hoped might be willing to support the Government were now put together,[1] and assigned, apparently on a basis of personal acquaintance, to one Secretary or the other. The Secretaries then wrote, usually in formal terms, but sometimes in a more intimate manner, to those assigned to them, requesting their presence in London at or before the opening of Parliament on October 13. In a number of cases very favourable replies were received.[2] Special letters were sent to more prominent individuals.[3] Where members of the House of Lords did not intend to be present their proxies were carefully collected.[4]

Even to unprejudiced contemporaries who grasped what was going on these appeared to be developments of a highly undesirable kind. A body of men who habitually voted together must, it was believed, be inspired by some sinister motive, or united by some disgraceful bond, and such a body it was obviously Danby's object to build up. Hence the extravagant charges of bribery and undue influence which were immediately hurled at his head. But there is no clear proof that he was as

[1] It would be a mistake to regard the members included in this list as the most assured supporters of the Government. They were rather those whose attendance in the previous session had been most unsatisfactory. But no rigid principle appears to have been observed in compiling the list.

[2] *Infra*, iii. 56-61.

[3] *Cal. S.P. Dom.*, 1675-6, p. 341. Danby seems to have taken some personal part in this canvass. On September 21 Lord Orrery wrote to him from London, " I had the oportunity to speake with one of our House since I had the honour to see your Lordship, who has undertaken to me for four who your Lordship could not depend upon in the list you marked. My Lord Bishops of Winton and Sarum wrott to me last night they will both be heere this day sennight, and that they have not bin idle " (Leeds MSS., Packet 6).

[4] Williamson wrote in the King's name to the Earl of Suffolk at Newmarket asking him to sign a blank proxy which was to be given to Lord Maynard, and enclosing another blank in case any other lord could be persuaded to sign it. Suffolk replied that he and Lord Oxford had already sent their proxies to Lord Maynard, and apparently persuaded Lord Crofts to sign one of the blanks (*Cal. S.P. Dom.*, 1675-6, pp. 343, 347). Lord Keeper Finch secured Lord Huntingdon's proxy (*Hastings MSS.*, ii. 169).

yet indulging in any practices which can be unreservedly condemned. His Excise pensioners were undoubtedly much too
numerous ; but even a modern Government requires a certain
number of salaried " whips " to supervise the conduct of its
business in Parliament. His officials in the Commons were also
too numerous ; but even in modern times it is recognised that
the principal ministers of the Crown ought to be members of
Parliament, and in that capacity should place their entire
influence at the disposal of the Government. His letters of
summons to individual members were open to criticism only by
reason of their apparent novelty. In spite of some distinctly
dubious features Danby's attitude on the whole was still very
much that of the modern party Whip, who summons to the
assistance of the Government those who he believes approve
of its policy and organises them in its support.

Unfortunately Danby had not the experience of a modern
Whip, and was probably greatly surprised to find that in
building up one party he was inadvertently helping to consolidate another. Members of Parliament who had not received a
summons from the Court or been approached by it found a
certain bond of unity in that very fact,[1] of which Shaftesbury
took full advantage to increase his own parliamentary following
and connect it up with other discontented groups. One of the
features of the session which began on October 13 was in consequence the practical disappearance of the unattached member
and the division of the House of Commons into two fairly well
defined parties with a voting strength of rather more than 150
each.

Whether as a result of hostility to Danby's tactics, resentment at his failure to fulfil his undertaking regarding France,
or underlying distrust of the King and Court, the opposition
party proved slightly the stronger. Having given every
assurance in his power that the policy to be pursued by the

---

[1] Even before the meeting of Parliament the opposition groups were aware
of what was going on. Lord Cavendish was informed that Sir Robert Thomas
had been seen at the Lord Treasurer's and had been " taken off." Cavendish
protested that he did not believe it ; but some remarks he made on the subject
to Sir Thomas Littleton roused such resentment as to induce Sir Robert to
absent himself from meetings of the group, and on October 8 Cavendish had to
write to him urging him to resume his attendance (Leeds MSS., Packet 6).

Government would be such as he believed the country to desire, Danby appealed to Parliament for the financial support to which he considered the advocate of a genuinely national policy was entitled. Only a considerable grant of supply obtained under his auspices, he well knew, would secure for his policy the continued favour of the King. Only such a grant, he had long been convinced, would enable him to free the Government from the many embarrassments in which he had found it involved, and establish the finances on a reasonably secure foundation.

The particular source of embarrassment about which he was most anxious was the heavy anticipations on the revenue. As a result of the financial reforms instituted nearly two years earlier he had contrived to place revenue and expenditure substantially on a level, and effect a temporary settlement of the semi-permanent debt held by the bankers. But the final problem with which he was confronted, the problem of the large floating debt represented by these anticipations, he had scarcely touched. Clifford's charges on the revenue had, it is true, been duly met ; but as this had been done other payments had had to be charged on the revenue in their place, and the general position had remained substantially unaltered. Between receipts in advance, obtained from the farmers of the revenue, and payments in arrears, taking the form of charges on items of taxation not yet due, the Government was living steadily ahead of its income to the extent of about £1,000,000, and for this there seemed to be no remedy except in Parliament. The principal points in the speech with which the King opened the session on October 13 were accordingly a recommendation of additional securities for the established religion, and a request for a sufficient supply to discharge all anticipations on the revenue and enable a fresh start to be made.[1]

Almost immediately it was made clear that the supply demanded was more than the Commons would readily consider. So uncertain were the leaders on both sides as to the best tactics to pursue that on their return to their own House members " sat almost an houre lookeing upon one another in a

[1] *C.J.*, ix. 357.

profound silence."[1] For some days beforehand Danby had
been endeavouring to gauge the temper of the Commons in
frequent consultations with such approved loyalists as Sir
Philip and Sir Christopher Musgrave, Sir Edward Dering, Sir
Philip Warwick and Lord Gorges.[2] He had learned that his
following was going to prove considerably less numerous than
he had anticipated, and had begun to doubt his ability to carry
any of his measures before the arrival of other supporters
whom he knew to be on their way up from the country. The
opposition was similarly doubtful, and similarly hopeful of
recruits. After an aimless debate, accordingly, it was resolved
with little opposition to adjourn the consideration of the King's
speech to October 18.[3]

On that day some indication of the relative strength of parties
was given when Danby, through the agency of Sir Edward
Dering and Sir Philip Musgrave, tried to give the question of
religion precedence over that of supply and failed to carry his
point ;[4] but the real test came in Grand Committee a day later,
when the problem of the anticipations was formally taken into
consideration. Some members refused to believe that there
were any anticipations. Others declared that to discharge the
anticipations would be to condone the Declaration of Indulgence, the alliance with France, and the war with the Dutch
out of which the anticipations had arisen. Others argued that
if anything was to be done the first claim on the generosity of
the House lay with those who had been defrauded by the
Stop of the Exchequer. Little personal hostility was shown
to Danby, but here as elsewhere he had to suffer for the sins of
his predecessors. In vain his followers strove to postpone a
decision to a time when the House was in a more favourable
mood. After " many curst speeches " had been made upon the
subject of the anticipations Lord Cavendish moved for the
question whether an aid should be granted for taking them
off. The previous question was first put, and led to an equal

---

[1] *Grey*, iii. 290 ; *Bulstrode Papers*, p. 315. There is a very full account of
the debates among the Lindsey MSS.

[2] *Cal. S.P. Dom.*, 1676-7, p. 480.

[3] *C.J.*, ix. 358.

[4] *Grey*, iii. 293-6 ; *Bulstrode Papers*, pp. 316-7.

division, 166 voting on each side. Sir Charles Harbord, the chairman of committee, rather weakly gave his casting vote for proceeding, and some members of the opposition having meanwhile come in, the Government was then defeated on the main question by 172 to 165.[1]

Danby, however, had provided himself with a second avenue towards a money grant by securing the inclusion in the King's speech of a request for a special supply for the navy, and on this the Commons were inclined to look with more favour. It is true that on October 18 and 21 they gave a first and second reading to a bill appropriating the Customs for three years to the use of the navy ; that they refused to consider Sir John Cotton's motion for a grant of £500,000 on the strange ground that " to ascertain a summe might be a prejudice to the King ; " and that they showed themselves distinctly niggardly on such matters as the number and size of the ships for the con-struction of which it was proposed to provide. But they were not prepared to refuse supply altogether, and on October 26, after a debate lasting till five o'clock, even rejected by 171 votes to 160 a motion that what they should grant should be lodged in the Chamber of London instead of paid into the Exchequer. Danby began to hope, while " the angry Commons, . . . being very much disturbed that they loss'd the question, and fearing that everything would be carried against them by the Treas-urists," indulged in a bitter attack on the methods by which they alleged the Court victory had been secured. The letters of summons sent to individual members before the opening of the session, which had already been repeatedly criticised, were freely condemned, and a test was introduced and referred to a committee by which all members were to purge themselves from any suspicion of having received rewards for their votes.[2]

[1] *Grey*, iii. 301-11 ; *Burnet*, ii. 86-7 ; Marvell, *Poems and Letters*, ii. 160. The Spanish ambassador, who feared that Charles, if made independent, would throw in his lot with France, claimed the credit of having secured the defeat of the Court (*Ranke*, iv. 15-16). Harbord's conduct would now be regarded as correct ; but Danby did not consider it so, and never really trusted him again. According to Lord Conway, Harbord " gave it against the King " (*Hastings MSS.*, ii. 383).

[2] *C.J.*, ix. 359-65 ; *Grey*, iii. 317-20, 323-33, 354-72 ; Marvell, *Poems and Letters*, ii. 161-3 ; *Bulstrode Papers*, pp. 318-20. According to Sir Charles Wheeler " there were letters on both sides " (Lindsey MSS.).

There is no real reason to suppose that the division of October 26 was the result of any unusual pressure on the part of the Court. The point involved was one of prerogative, on which some of the less determined malcontents were bound to desert the opposition.[1] It seems clear, however, that immediately thereafter Danby endeavoured to remedy his mistake in not concentrating more on numbers, and embarked on a great effort to increase his voting strength in the Commons. On the one hand he saw a genuine prospect of a considerable supply, and brought renewed pressure to bear on Government dependants to induce them to vote solidly for it.[2] On the other hand he was seriously alarmed by the proposed test, and persuaded the King to speak personally to members who might thus be engaged to oppose it.[3]

His effort, however, was made too late, and probably did more harm than good. Far from diminishing, the small majority hitherto enjoyed by the " confederates or anti-Treasurists " slightly increased. The test for members of Parliament was quietly dropped, for a strict investigation might have unearthed some strange facts about the opposition no less than about the Court party ; but bills to prevent illegal imprisonment and the illegal exaction of money were pressed forward, complaint was made of the methods employed in the collection of the Excise, and the practice of summoning before the Council justices of the peace who endeavoured to protect the subject from the receivers of that most unpopular tax was freely condemned. At the same time the controversy over the King's subjects in the French service, which had caused so much trouble in the spring, was revived. On May 19 the King had fulfilled his promise to Parliament by issuing a proclamation

[1] Some influence was also exercised by provincial jealousy of London. Sir Winston Churchill declared that if the money were lodged in the Chamber of London the ships would be built in the port of London, and other ports would be neglected (*Grey*, iii. 359-60).

[2] The second list of dependants, printed *infra*, iii. 65-8, was almost certainly drawn up during the course of this session of Parliament.

[3] *Infra*, iii. 74-7. This list also appears to have been drawn up during the course of the session. The identity of the test to which it refers is not absolutely certain, but of several possibilities this seems the most likely. It was regarded by contemporaries as a personal insult to the King that those whom he favoured should be viewed with suspicion by the Commons, and his personal intervention in opposition to such a test was therefore not unnatural.

M   D.L. I.

recalling all his subjects who had entered that service since the establishment of peace with the Dutch, and prohibiting others from entering it in future. This proclamation, it was now asserted, had been habitually disregarded, and on October 23 a resolution was adopted that all soldiers remaining in or entering the French service contrary to the proclamation should be " taken to be contemners of his Majesty's royal authority and opposers of the interest of their country." A bill was ordered to be prepared imposing heavy penalties on those who persisted in their disobedience, and this bill, having been introduced on November 4, was read a second time on November 10 and committed.[1]

By the discussion of these and kindred topics, deliberately brought forward by the opposition with the object of rousing hostility to the Government, an atmosphere was created little favourable to a grant of supply, and Danby soon found that he would have to exert himself to the utmost to secure anything at all free from conditions which would make it valueless in his eyes. Having at length decided, on November 2, to provide for one ship of the first rate, five of the second and fourteen of the third,[2] the Commons spent three days in elaborate calculations, and on November 4, in Grand Committee of the whole House, resolved that a supply not exceeding £300,000 should be granted " for the building, and towards the guns, rigging and other furnishing, of the twenty ships." [3] This was

---

[1] *C.J.*, ix. 362, 367, 371 ; *Grey*, iii. 334-6.

[2] The Court party tried to secure nine ships of the second rate, but were defeated by 182 votes to 170 (*Grey*, iii. 378 ; *Bulstrode Papers*, p. 321).

[3] *C.J.*, ix. 368, 369. The unusual wording of this resolution was the result of a dispute whether the " ships " for which the House had undertaken to provide were ships equipped with guns and rigging or merely hulls without any furnishings. " The Treasurists said ships were not ships without all necessaries ; but yet were so little willing to trust the Committee with the exposition of the word ' ship ' that they desired the House might give the Committee further instructions in the point, ... which the others opposed ; and so about two o'clock it came to a question whether the Committee should be further instructed or no, upon which the House was divided, and the question carried to the negative by six voices, 163 against 157 " (*Bulstrode Papers*, p. 321). No exact calculations appear to have been made of the cost of the furnishings ; but the sum granted was of the nature of a compromise, the cost of the hulls alone having been estimated at £208, 050, and the " rigging, sailes, gunns and other furniture, with provisions and setting out for six moneths, amounting," according to Samuel Pepys, " to full as much " (Lindsey MSS.).

much less than Danby had hoped for, and when the resolution
was reported to the House he accordingly fixed on the word
" towards " as conveying a suggestion that some further supply
was intended to meet the ends the Commons had in view, and
instructed his followers to reopen the whole question.   Sir
Robert Holt moved for £380,000 as the smallest sum that
would prove sufficient, and was supported by Sir Edward
Dering and others.

This was probably a mistake in tactics.   Within a week of
the unhappy vote of October 19 Danby had contrived to substitute Sir John Trevor for Sir Charles Harbord as chairman
of committee ; but Trevor was neither an intimate associate
of his nor as yet a skilled parliamentarian, and he therefore
believed his " strength greater in a House, by reason of the
dexterity of the Speaker," and sought an immediate decision
there.   Not unreasonably, however, it was argued that no
change in the sum granted should be made without a reference
back to the committee responsible for the grant, and on this
point the Court party proved unable to maintain a united front,
Williamson and the more cautious members openly advocating
such a reference.   In consequence when a division was taken
on the question whether the House should agree with the
resolution of the committee it was carried in the affirmative by
176 votes to 150.[1]

This was a heavy defeat for Danby, and the opposition, now
confident of their majority, seized every opportunity of driving
it home.   On November 8, having adopted a resolution that
the proposed supply should be raised by means of a land tax,
they carried by 145 votes to 103 a motion adding the words,
" and that no other charge be laid upon the subject this session
of Parliament."   On November 11 they brought forward a
proposal that the bill of supply and the bill appropriating the
Customs to the use of the navy should be joined together, and
when the Court party endeavoured to evade the issue by
moving the adjournment of the House defeated them by 150
votes to 136.   Danby then made one last effort to save something from the wreck of his hopes by proposing that the anticipations on the Customs should first be taken into consideration ;

[1] C.J., ix. 369 ; Grey, iii. 411-7 ; Bulstrode Papers, pp. 321-2.

but this was rejected without a division, and the motion for uniting the two bills was carried by 151 votes to 124.[1]

Meanwhile the Court had fared little better in the House of Lords. Among the lay peers the resentment aroused by the high-handed proceedings of the Commons in support of Sir John Fagg, and still more by the countenance shown to these proceedings by the Court, had by no means died away, and the session had scarcely begun when the opposition endeavoured to take advantage of it by introducing a petition from Dr. Sherley for the hearing of his case. In vain the House was reminded that the King in his opening speech had warned them against the fatal consequences of allowing former differences to revive. In vain Danby with doubtful wisdom declared " that the King had advis'd Sherly to delay the presenting his petition for some time, to which he answer'd he could not, for that he was oblig'd by some persons of honour to bring it in." The Lords did not at all like the introduction of the King's name into the debate, and were more influenced by the argument, repeatedly put forward by the opposition and coming only too near the truth, that they were being required " to sacrifice the honour and right of the House to the Commons for mony." After debates lasting for six days it was proposed that November 20 should be appointed for the hearing of the case. The previous question was first put and carried by 43

---

[1] *C.J.*, ix. 370, 373-4 ; *Grey*, iii. 425-30, 446-59 ; *Bulstrode Papers*, pp. 323, 324. The main objection raised by the Court against the appropriation of the Customs to the use of the navy was that the Customs were already charged by anticipation for other uses. The main argument employed by the opposition in favour of the appropriation was the traditional one that the expenses of defence by sea were a natural charge upon maritime commerce. But the motives underlying the controversy had little connection with these arguments. The opposition were anxious to secure better provision for the navy, of which they approved, at the expense of the army and pensions, of which they disapproved. Danby was anxious to keep the revenue, and ultimately the royal authority, free from parliamentary control, and was specially anxious about the Customs, because for various reasons they were the part of the revenue most open to attack. It was indeed his deliberate policy to keep the Customs charged as far as possible in advance in order to have a sound practical argument against any attempt to appropriate them. Much was made in the debates of the possibility that all sources of revenue might similarly be appropriated to particular uses, and that the King might thus be left with nothing wherewith " to buy bread ; " but it is doubtful whether this argument was taken seriously (Lindsey MSS.).

votes to 23, and the motion was then accepted without a division.[1]

By naming so distant a date the Lords had clearly shown their inclination towards moderate courses,[2] and the same spirit of moderation characterised their proceedings throughout. They refused to agree with the rather extravagant vote of the Commons concerning the King's subjects in the French service, and adopted instead an address praying the King to renew and reinforce his proclamation dealing with the matter.[3] They refrained from becoming entangled in a controversy regarding the proper method of recording protests which might have produced confusion within their own body.[4] But the fixing of any date, however distant, for the hearing of Sherley's appeal inevitably established a period beyond which the mis-understanding between the two Houses could no longer be ignored, and owing to the failure of the Commons to proceed more rapidly with their business that period was reached before anything of moment had been achieved. When the Commons took notice of the action of the Lords, accordingly, it was the obvious policy of the opposition, which saw every prospect of carrying its measures, to postpone any quarrel between the two Houses, while the Court party was tempted to force on a quarrel under cover of which it might conceal its own failure.

At first the opposition, being in the ascendant, was able to dictate the course of events, and the Commons displayed a reluctance to face the issue in startling contrast to the

---

[1] *L.J.*, xiii. 8-12 ; *Bulstrode Papers*, pp. 317-21.

[2] This was not in accordance with expectations. Popular opinion had anticipated strong pressure for " the speediest day that can be, and that nothing may be done in that House before that business be determin'd."

[3] *L.J.*, xiii. 14 ; *C.J.*, ix. 371-2 ; *Grey*, iii. 435-6.

[4] No doubt was cast on the right of protesting and entering dissent even by a single peer ; but the Court party argued that the protesters " ought not to add the reasons for that dissent, because then the reasons of the minor part appearing upon record, and not those of the other side," everybody would be apt " to censure the major part of the House." The opposition, on the other hand, declared that to countenance protesting without reasons given would be " to encourage any opiniative to protest at any time without cause or reason." The general expectation was that the dispute would be decided in favour of those who wished to give reasons ; but as a result of repeated postponements no conclusion was reached at this time (*L.J.*, xiii. 18, 23, 28 ; *Bulstrode Papers*, pp. 323-4).

eagerness they had shown in the spring. On November 15 they merely resolved that the prosecuting of the appeal by Sherley was a breach of the privilege of their House, and forbade Sir John Fagg to make any defence. On November 17 they decided, by 158 votes to 102, not to put the question " that there lies no appeal to the judicature of the Lords in Parliament from courts of equity." On November 18 they refused to renew their insulting votes of the previous session, resolved to desire a conference with the Lords " for avoiding the occasions of reviving the differences between the two Houses," and agreed by 130 votes to 84 to omit from their message all expressions which might conceivably give offence.[1] But underneath this seeming moderation there lay a very real jealousy of the other House, and when the Lords after the conference failed to send any answer to the Commons' request that proceedings in connection with the appeal might be postponed until more important measures had been completed the atmosphere suddenly changed. Late on November 19 news reached the waiting Commons that the Lords had risen after confirming their order for hearing Sherley on the following day, and the leaders of the opposition found no course open to them but to abandon their policy of conciliation and acquiesce in the more violent measures advocated by the Court party. Without a dissentient voice it was resolved " that whosoever shall sollicit, plead, or prosecute any appeal against any commoner of England from any court of equity before the House of Lords shall be deemed and taken a betrayer of the rights and liberties of the Commons of England, and shall be proceeded against accordingly."[2]

In a sense, therefore, Danby had achieved a success. During the spring session the opposition, led by Shaftesbury, had successfully obstructed the measures on which he had set his heart by raising trouble between the two Houses of Parliament. Now he had obstructed the measures of the opposition in precisely the same way. But in doing so he had laid himself open to a most damaging imputation, that he was maintaining in existence, to serve his own ends, a House of Commons which

[1] C.J., ix. 376-9 ; Grey, iv. 9-15, 27-39, 42-9.
[2] C.J., ix. 380-1 ; Grey, iv. 50-3.

had become altogether unmanageable.   On November 20,
when the resolution of the Commons was brought to the notice
of the Lords, it was unanimously declared to be " illegal, unparliamentary, and tending to the dissolution of the government ; " and advantage was taken of the indignation it aroused
to propose, as the only way of escape from an impossible situation, that an address should be made to the King for the dissolution of Parliament.[1]

True to the alliance into which he had entered during the
summer, the Duke of York joined the opposition, and it soon
became apparent that if the Court party were to avoid defeat
it could only be by mustering every available supporter.   For
five hours, in consequence, Danby prolonged the debate, while
messages were hastily dispatched summoning to his aid all
those of whom he had any hope.   Towards nine o'clock Lauderdale and Lord Maynard were brought up, and a motion was
then carried that the question should be put.   In favour of the
address there voted 41 peers ; against it 20 peers and 13
bishops.[2]   Here, however, Danby's care in collecting proxies at
length bore fruit.   The Government held 15 proxies, the
opposition only 7, and when proxies were called the voting thus
stood equal, with 48 on each side.

At this moment the Earl of Ailesbury entered the House.
He had not heard the debate, and was not believed to have
strong views either for or against the address ; but the opposition hoped that his friendship with the Duke of York would
incline him one way, while the Court lords hoped that his care
for the prerogative would incline him the other.   The decision
was therefore left to him, and he gave his vote against the
address.   As he also had a proxy in his hands this meant that

[1] *L.J.*, xiii. 32-3.   As early as October 25 the Master of the Rolls, Sir Harbottle Grimston, one of the members specially summoned by the Court, had
made a similar proposal in the Commons.   " Frequent Parliaments," he
declared, " are the right of the subject.   A standing Parliament, a standing
army ; a standing army, a standing Parliament.   I like noe such thing."   He
failed to find a seconder, however, and was somewhat severely dealt with
by the Speaker (Lindsey MSS. ; *Grey*, iii. 341-9, 368 ; *Bulstrode Papers*,
p. 319).

[2] These were all the bishops present in the House.   Their solid vote against
the address was considered as helping to discredit the Government (B.M. Add.
MSS. 29555, f. 261).

the Government secured a precarious victory by 50 votes to 48.[1]

Such a victory was little better than a defeat. In view of the attitude of both Lords and Commons even Danby could scarcely maintain that any useful purpose was to be served by keeping Parliament in session any longer. At the same time the opposition had unwittingly done much to defeat its own end. Charles had promised the French king to dissolve Parliament if it proved recalcitrant, and in other circumstances he might have kept his promise. But having just frustrated an attempt to force him to dissolve he was naturally reluctant to make the apparent surrender involved in doing so. A long prorogation was therefore determined upon instead. On November 22 Parliament was prorogued for the unprecedented period of fifteen months,[2] and Danby was left to review the situation and decide what could be saved from the apparent ruin of his plans.

[1] *Cal. S.P. Dom.*, 1675-6, pp. 413-4 ; Schwerin, *Briefe aus England*, pp. 41-2. The division list is printed *infra*, iii. 125-6.

[2] To February 15, 1677 (*L.J.*, xiii. 35).

CHAPTER X

PREPARATION, 1675-7

THE long interval during which Parliament remained in abeyance after November 1675 was a period of comparative eclipse for Danby. His personal credit with the King, it is true, remained substantially unaltered,[1] for it could scarcely be denied that his skilful management alone had prevented the Commons from exhibiting the same hostility to the Court, and inflicting the same humiliations upon it, as had marked the sessions of 1673 and 1674. But his policy was in some measure discredited. It had not produced the results anticipated, either by effecting a complete reconciliation between King and Parliament, or even by doing so sufficiently to secure a reasonable vote of supply. In consequence the King was thrown back on the policy which he always liked to keep in reserve, reliance upon France. Danby's schemes, however, had not failed so badly as to be abandoned by their author. Thus for more than a year two distinct and even contradictory lines of policy were pursued by the Government, one favoured by Charles and the Duke of York, the other by Danby and his immediate associates, each line of policy being in the most curious way tolerated and even connived at by the supporters of the other.

The most pressing problem was that of finance. The revenue was already showing a tendency to decline from the level it had reached in 1674, and Danby, quick to distrust a prosperity of which he scarcely understood the explanation, had been extremely anxious to secure a parliamentary grant.[2] Nobody

---

[1] Early in 1676 a rumour was current that he was to be made a Duke (B.M. Add. MSS. 29555, f. 288).

[2] William Harbord is a very prejudiced witness where Danby is concerned, but his evidence seems to make it clear that throughout 1675 the Treasurer was very uneasy about the financial situation (*Essex Papers*, i. 293, 294; ii. 20).

knew better than he did that his success hitherto had been made possible only by the enormous advances obtained from the farmers of the different branches of the revenue. These advances were now falling due to be repaid with interest,[1] and if this operation had to be carried through in a time of declining revenue the results would be serious indeed. Normally Danby might have hoped to repay the advances obtained from one farm with the assistance of the advances provided by the succeeding farm ; but a long prorogation following an unfavourable session of Parliament was not, in his opinion, productive of a good atmosphere for negotiating a fresh agreement, and it seemed that the greater part of the old advances would have to be repaid before any new advances could be expected.

Faced thus with the practical certainty that there would be a shortage of money in 1676, Danby determined on a drastic, if temporary, reduction of expenditure, and at the very first meeting of Council after the prorogation induced the King to appoint a special committee, which was to embark forthwith on the preparation of a scheme of expenses not exceeding £1,000,000 per annum.[2] The difficulties encountered, however, proved insuperable,[3] and after deliberations lasting more than two months the scheme finally adopted provided for an expenditure of £1,175,315, not counting the establishment for Jamaica and the Leeward Islands. Even this result was achieved only by suspending the payment of one half of all fees, salaries and

[1] The regular method of repayment was by deduction from the concluding instalments of the farm. Of the advance on the Excise £112,500 stood to be repaid during the course of 1676, and £132,500 early in 1677. The farm of the Hearth Money had still some time to run.

[2] November 24, 1675 (P.C. Reg. 65, p. 43). This was not merely a special expedient designed to meet a special emergency but also the culmination of a long series of efforts at general economy. Almost every page of the *Calendar of Treasury Books* from the summer of 1673 to the end of 1675 bears evidence of Danby's methodical checking of expenditure. His " office hours " as Treasurer are set forth in *Cal. Treas. Books*, iv. 326-7, 347.

[3] The following may be taken as typical : " Yesterday his Majesty had a petition presented to him by the Greene Cloth and all the officers of the Howsehold in relation to the intended retrenchments of the family, setting forth that there are many which will not be able to eate bread if those retrenchments be putt in execution, and recomendinge it to his Majestyes consideration whither the advantage expected from it will countervayle the dishonour which it will bring " (Richard Langhorne to Lord Hatton, January 11, 1675[/6], B.M. Add. MSS. 29555, f. 298).

pensions from January 1, 1676, to March 31, 1677, the period during which the shortage of money was expected to continue and the scheme in consequence was to remain in force.[1]

At the same time some relief was sought from a reorganisation of the finances of Ireland. Ranelagh's contract was due to expire on Christmas Day, 1675, and in the previous August offers had accordingly been invited for a farm of the whole Irish revenue.[2] Negotiations were protracted, for the estrangement between Danby and the Duke of York had gone far, and James did not scruple to assure Charles that Danby was no longer to be trusted. Since his impeachment, he declared, the Treasurer had shown more concern for his own interests than for the King's, and as farmers was recommending his personal dependants rather than those who offered the best terms.[3]

Apparently James favoured the proposals of George Pitt and partners, which were also supported by Ormonde ;[4] and the question of the farm was debated with some acrimony by the committee appointed for the purpose. On September 23 and 24 Pitt spoke " in most rude and indecent termes " both to Coventry and to Danby, and in the case of the latter " with most unworthy reflections." So wild were his accusations of underhand practices, and so slight his evidence in support of them, that he was dismissed from his post of comptroller of the household to James, and reduced to petitioning Danby to ask for his reinstatement. In the end the farm was let for a period of seven years to the Lord Lieutenant's candidates, Sir James Shaen and others, at an annual rent of £240,000, with an

---

[1] The scheme was adopted on January 28, 1676, by an order of the Privy Council, printed in *Cal. Treas. Books*, v. 116-8. It should be compared with the estimate of expenditure drawn up on September 29, 1675, and printed in *Cal. S.P. Dom.*, 1675-6, p. 324. This shows the total expenditure, before the reduction, as £1,362,770. Danby's preliminary notes on the reduction are printed *infra*, iii. 22-3. In B.M. Add. MSS. 28078, f. 227, there is an elaborate schedule showing not only each main item of expenditure but also the sources of income against which it was to be charged. This schedule clearly indicates the principal cause of trouble. The total amount charged against the Excise, which in a normal year should have produced £550,000, is only £374,247.

[2] *Cal. Treas. Books*, iv. 326.

[3] Schwerin, *Briefe aus England*, p. 34. *Cf. Burnet*, ii. 111.

[4] *Cal. Treas. Books*, iv. 329-33 ; Carte, *Life of Ormond*, iv. 501 ; *Hist. MSS. Com.*, ii. 212 ; *Bulstrode Papers*, pp. 313-5.

advance payment of £60,000 and a further advance, if necessary, of £20,000.[1] Immediately afterwards, as a counterpart to this adjustment of the revenue, was drawn up a scheme of expenditure providing for a permanent Irish establishment, to date from March 25, 1676, of roughly £200,000.[2] As the establishment itself included a sum of £20,000 for the King's privy purse, this meant that Danby could count on drawing from Ireland anything up to £140,000 in the first year and £60,000 in succeeding years which he could use to assist the English Exchequer. The advance money would eventually have to be repaid, but this would be done by deduction from revenues in Ireland and so would not affect England. Bitter protests were naturally made by responsible Irish officials, and Danby's conduct in this connection undoubtedly did much to antagonise still further his enemies in Ireland. Nevertheless it was on substantially English objects that the Irish surplus was spent.[3]

Finally Danby turned, as he had done two years earlier, to a consideration of those economic factors on which all taxation ultimately depends. The main subject of debate, as so often before, was the trade between England and France, which was declared to be highly prejudicial to the former country, inasmuch as her exports to France were small, while her imports from France[4] were quite disproportionately large and consisted

---

[1] The warrant is dated November 28, 1675, but the formal agreement was not carried through till the following April (*Cal. Treas. Books*, iv. 853-5, 858-60; v. 173-4, 181; *Cal. S.P. Dom.*, 1676-7, pp. 115-6). Some notes in Williamson's handwriting on the points at issue are printed in *Cal. S.P. Dom.*, 1675-6, pp. 480-1. Danby's own notes are B.M. Add. MSS. 28042, ff. 41-3. Conway makes it clear that Shaen and his partners owed their success to Essex. Danby did not like the agreement with them, and soon found reason to express dissatisfaction with their performance (*Hastings MSS.*, ii. 383; *Cal. Treas. Books*, v. 188, 483-4, 495-6).

[2] Read and adopted in Council on March 10 (P.C. Reg. 65, p. 141; *Cal. S.P. Dom.*, 1676-7, pp. 39-40).

[3] Danby's own notes on the disposal of the first year's surplus, amounting, together with the privy purse money, to £130,000, are printed *infra*, iii. 24-5. Apart from £60,000 allowed for the repayment of debts in Ireland the entire sum was assigned to the navy, the ordnance, Tangier, building at Windsor and the redemption of Lady Portsmouth's jewels, the last two items being specifically charged upon the privy purse (*Leeds MSS.*, p. 13).

[4] Imports and exports for the year 1674 are tabulated in *Parliamentary History*, iv. pp. cxv-cxviii.

almost entirely of luxuries. In the previous autumn attention had been drawn to this matter by some serious rioting
among the English weavers, who declared that they were
being deprived of employment by French competition,[1] and
Danby found himself compelled to come to a decision on what
for him was a very difficult problem. As Lord Treasurer he
was reluctant to condemn the French trade, for a large
part of the Customs revenue was derived from it. On the other
hand he greatly disliked any form of dependence on France,
and was well aware that in the quite probable event of trouble
with that country trade with it would be prohibited altogether.
In the end, therefore, he gave all his support to regulations
designed to make England self-sufficing as regards commodities
imported from France, hoping no doubt that the inevitable
decline in the Customs would eventually be more than balanced
by an improvement in the Excise.[2]

In all these schemes of financial reorganisation Danby could
count on the ungrudging, if not very resolute, support of the
King ; but in spite of that Charles at heart favoured and was
endeavouring to give effect to an entirely different solution of
the financial problem. At the same time as Danby's committee
of retrenchment was being set up the Duke of York was demanding from the French ambassador the payment of the subsidy of
£100,000 promised by Louis XIV in the event of a dissolution.
Louis in reality was highly pleased with the long prorogation,
but relying on the letter of his promise he considered that, as
Parliament had only been prorogued, and even that for reasons
unconnected with France, he was entitled at least to a reduction
in the sum payable, and accordingly instructed his ambassador
to press for better terms. Of this partial rebuff to the English
King Danby endeavoured to take advantage, making a last
desperate effort to keep Charles out of the clutches of France.
At a secret meeting, where the only others present were Charles,
James, and Lauderdale, he strongly argued that a treaty of

---

[1] *Cal. S.P. Dom.*, 1675-6, pp. 252-9, 329, 513-4 ; *Bulstrode Papers*, pp. 310-
11.

[2] Little evidence survives for Danby's economic ideas, which do not seem
to have been in any way in advance of his time. His notes on this particular
point are printed *infra*, iii. 25-7.

alliance should be concluded with the United Provinces in order to forestall Louis XIV, who would otherwise in all probability conclude such an alliance himself and so put England at a disadvantage at sea. Charles, however, declared that it would ill become him, after having deserted France in the war, to join the enemy against her, and professed to have too many obligations to Louis XIV to be able to consider such a suggestion. He then laid the whole matter before Ruvigny, and used it as a weapon to extract from him the full subsidy which had originally been promised.[1]

Danby's arguments indeed produced a result the very opposite of what he had intended. When reminded of the danger of an alliance between France and Holland, Charles preferred to provide against it by allying with France himself, and at the very close of 1675 proposed to the French ambassador that he and Louis should enter into a reciprocal engagement not to assist each other's enemies or rebellious subjects, and not to enter into any treaty with any state whatever without each other's consent. Louis was delighted with the suggestion, and dispatched to England a draft treaty, which Charles immediately submitted to the consideration of his brother, Danby and Lauderdale. For some weeks Danby excelled himself in the art of obstruction. He criticised every article, suggested that Louis might already have made a secret treaty with Holland, and insisted that that country must be specifically named among those with which an alliance was not to be established.[2] He demanded further time for consideration, and his request having been granted wasted ten days in doing nothing at all. Finally he represented in the strongest terms to Lauderdale the danger which they would incur if they alone signed such a treaty, and at a meeting in the King's cabinet proposed that the matter should be laid before his ally Heneage Finch, now Lord Chancellor, and all the other ministers. Charles, however, pointed out that as long as he was acting the part of mediator in Europe he could not allow it to become known that he was

[1] *Mignet*, iv. 375-8. Payment was to be made quarterly, beginning with the close of the following March.

[2] His representations on this point were given effect to in Article 5 of the treaty.

forming an alliance with one of the parties in the struggle, and on February 16, 1676, solved all difficulties by writing out the treaty, signing and sealing it with his own hand, and entrusting it to Ruvigny for dispatch to France. In return, he received a copy of the treaty signed and sealed by Louis.[1]

Some such result was probably inevitable, and Danby may have been well enough pleased at heart that the engagement with France did not take a more objectionable form or involve him more deeply. His own hopes were set upon a meeting of Parliament which even in the most fortunate circumstances could not take place for a considerable time, and his principal task was by careful preparation to secure that when at length it met it should be as favourable to the King as possible. A secret treaty with France, all the terms of which were of a negative character, was not likely to be a serious handicap, or even to prove of long duration. When his preparations for a Parliament were complete he would probably be able to induce the King to break it and adopt a policy more fitted to win popular support.

The autumn session of 1675 had clearly demonstrated the inability of the new Court party to outvote the opposition, and convinced Danby of the need for paying more attention to mere numbers. The Clarendonian idea of a House of Commons engaged to support the King by general approval of his policy, and guided in its individual measures by a group of influential members in close touch with the ministers, was obviously out of date. At the same time, by making the dissolution question a serious issue, the session had provided a most effective means by which additional supporters for the Government might be secured. Many members of the existing Parliament knew they could never hope to be chosen again, and being dependent on their membership and privileges for their social position, or even for freedom from the attentions of their creditors, regarded any proposal to summon a new Parliament as threatening practical ruin. To these it was represented that their only resource lay in throwing all their weight on the side of the King

---

[1] *Dalrymple*, App., pp. 99-107 ; *Mignet*, iv. 378-86.

and so enabling him to avert a dissolution.[1] To others, whose position was less insecure, more substantial rewards were offered. Direct bribery was rarely attempted, if for no other reason than that the resources of the Government could scarcely have stood the strain ; but every conceivable " gratification " was dangled before the eyes of those whose votes the Government desired to gain—titles, pensions, places, local offices, the favour of the King or some great minister, for themselves, their relatives, personal friends or servants. In some cases, indeed, the prospective recruit for the Court party was simply asked to suggest what the Government might do for him.[2]

The task confronting Danby was not the unsavoury one of inducing genuine opponents of his policy to deny their principles, for the genuine opponents of his policy were neither very numerous nor at all open to influence. His task was rather that of persuading the careless and indifferent to devote regular attention to their parliamentary duties, of inducing personal enemies to abate their hostility, of convincing the suspicious that his policy was seriously intended, and of opening the eyes of all to the little-recognised fact that nothing could be accomplished unless they would agree to vote solidly together. So far as the official dependants of the Government were concerned this task had already been largely performed, and although a fresh survey of " officers and servants " was made at this time,[3] it is improbable that Danby expected any particular result from it. But much remained to be done among the ordinary members of Parliament. In December 1675, accordingly, Sir Richard Wiseman drew up and presented to Danby an estimate of probable Government supporters outside official circles.[4]

[1] *Burnet*, ii. 89. As early as December 18, 1675, Sir Robert Holt, member for Warwickshire, found it necessary to appeal to Danby for assistance. As a result of his sufferings on behalf of Charles I, he declared, his financial position had always been bad, and the support he had given to the Government during the preceding session had made it worse. Many of his creditors were persons of less loyalty than he could have wished, and on the expiration of privilege of Parliament threatened to take proceedings against him (Leeds MSS., Packet 6).

[2] Some idea of how this process of solicitation was conducted is given by the documents printed *infra*, iii. 71-111.

[3] Danby's own list, printed *infra*, iii. 68-71, was almost certainly drawn up at the very end of 1675.

[4] *Infra*, iii. 86-93.

His list was divided into three portions, the first giving the names of 79 members of the House of Commons for whose future good behaviour he was prepared to undertake himself, the second giving the names of 90 members who were equally open to influence but might best be approached by somebody else, and the third indicating 22 members of whom some hopes might be entertained. For months thereafter this list formed the basis on which Danby and his agents worked. Every person mentioned in it was approached in what was believed to be the most effective manner, and his support for the Government if possible secured. Where he proved impervious to argument or influence a cross was entered against his name, and in that way Danby was able to calculate, probably by the spring of 1676, that 130 of those mentioned in the list were engaged to support him, 64 from the first section, 60 from the second, and 6 from the last.[1] The process, however, did not stop there. Other recruits for the Court party were suggested, and where application to them proved successful their names were added to the roll.[2] Before the middle of June Danby was able to assure the King that he had gained 150 votes since the last meeting of Parliament.[3]

[1] See the notes in Danby's handwriting, " 64 good " and " 66 good." The figures correspond exactly with the names in Wiseman's handwriting which have not a cross opposite them.

[2] Six names have been inserted in Wiseman's list by Danby himself.

[3] " Le Roy d'Angleterre me fit l'honneur de m'informer, il y a deux jours, des raisons qui l'obligent à ne pas casser le Parlement. Les principales sont qu'il prétend avoir gagné depuis la dernière assemblée plus de 150 personnes, et qu'avec ce nombre et les gens qui sont attachez à ses intérests il croit se pouvoir faire donner de l'argent, parce qu'il ne s'en fallut qu'une voix dans la dernière séance qu'il n'eut sur ce point la satisfaction qu'il désiroit " (Courtin to Louis XIV, June 22, 1676). This statement seems to make it clear that apart from the Excise pensioners Danby had not seriously engaged before 1676 in what would then have been called corruption. Government officials in the House of Commons were, of course, expected to support the Court, but for additional supporters Danby had relied mainly on his personal following, and had done little more in 1675 than issue whips to those who he hoped might favour his policy. He had now gone beyond that, and by using the inducements at his disposal had persuaded 150 additional members of Parliament to promise him their assistance, giving him a total voting strength of about 250. The 150 " engaged " men were to some extent the same people as those to whom whips had been issued a year earlier, but the identification cannot be carried very far. There were undoubtedly a number of members of Parliament whose sympathies as a rule inclined them to Danby's side, but who would not engage themselves to anybody.

Danby's object, however, was not merely to increase and consolidate his own party, but also to destroy that of his opponents. The Court party always had a permanent centre for its organisation in the Court itself ; but the opposition had to rely largely on the coffee-houses, where coffee, chocolate, sherbet and tea were consumed, news of all kinds was retailed, and politics were discussed. At Danby's instigation, accordingly, a proclamation was read and approved in Council on December 29, 1675, ordering the suppression after January 10 of all public coffee-houses, and the withdrawal of their licences, on the ground that they had become the resort of idle and disaffected persons, and had occasioned the spreading of false reports to the defamation of the Government.[1] Unfortunately the consequences of this step had not been adequately considered beforehand. A storm of opposition was immediately aroused, which found a colourable pretext in the hardship imposed on the coffee-house keepers, many of whom would be left with great and unsaleable stocks on their hands. The legal problem involved was examined from every angle, and the power of the Government to withdraw licences granted for a specified time was seriously called in question.[2]

On January 7, 1676, a petition from the coffee sellers was presented to the Privy Council, praying that they might at least be allowed time to get rid of the stocks they had,[3] and a long debate ensued. So uncertain were the law officers of the Crown about the legality of the recall of the licences that the matter was referred to the judges, who on the following day gave an equally hazy opinion.[4] On the question of practical expediency, however, there was greater unanimity. The Government

[1] P.C. Reg. 65, p. 79 ; *Cal. S.P. Dom.*, 1675-6, p. 465. The coffee-houses did not stand alone as centres of disaffection. From a document printed *infra*, iii. 2-3, it is clear that they had rivals among the booksellers' shops. The regular meeting places of the parties were, of course, the taverns, where members could dine together ; and in addition meetings were sometimes held in private houses.

[2] " Wee are now in a mutinous condition in this towne upon the account of coffee-howses. The suppression of them will prove a tryall of skyll. All wytts are at worke to elude the proclamation, and I am doubtfull they will doe it. If soe then the advice was ill, and if the Government shew itselfe to feare the people I suspect the people will hardly feare the Government " (Richard Langhorne to Lord Hatton, January 1, 1675, B.M. Add. MSS. 29555, f. 288).

[3] P.C. Reg. 65, p. 86.   [4] *Cal. S.P. Dom.*, 1675-6, pp. 496-7, 500.

freely admitted the hardship to the coffee sellers, while the coffee sellers on their part had no desire to quarrel with the Government. A compromise was therefore reached by which the time limit for the sale of coffee, chocolate, sherbet and tea was extended from January 10 to the following midsummer, the coffee sellers in return entering into recognizances not to allow any scandalous papers, books, or libels to be brought into their houses, to prevent all persons from declaring there any false and scandalous reports against the Government, and to give information of any such papers or reports. On January 8 a proclamation embodying the agreement was ordered to be prepared by the Attorney-General,[1] and when the period of grace had expired it was found convenient to extend it first to Christmas 1676 and then to midsummer 1677.[2] Thereafter the efforts of the Government were directed towards the control of the coffee-houses rather than their suppression.[3]

The partial defeat of the Government's attempt to strike at the root of the opposition movement made it all the more necessary in Danby's eyes that individual opponents of his policy should be strictly dealt with. On January 7 Halifax and Holles, who had endeavoured to champion the cause of the coffee sellers, were struck off the Council,[4] and a fortnight later Danby's faithful follower Henry Compton, who had been promoted by his influence from the bishopric of Oxford to that of London,[5] was sworn in their place.[6] On January 19 Sir Stephen Fox, who had been too closely connected with Arlington to be really trusted by Danby, was required to surrender his post of

---

[1] *Ibid.*, p. 503 ; P.C. Reg. 65, p. 88.   [2] P.C. Reg. 65, pp. 439, 442.

[3] Ogg, *England in the Reign of Charles II*, i. 101-2.

[4] Burnet's explanation of this, as the result of a personal quarrel between Danby and Halifax (*History of my Own Time*, ii. 111), must be received with some caution. Secretary Coventry, who was Halifax's uncle, asked the King the reason for his dismissal, " aber darauf keinen andern Bescheid bekommen, als dass Seine Majestät diese beiden Herren ihrem Interesse jederzeit entgegen gefunden " (Schwerin, *Briefe aus England*, p. 45). The obviously significant facts are that Halifax and Holles were forbidden to appear at Council on the day on which the petition from the coffee sellers was presented and discussed, and in their absence were dismissed from the Board (B.M. Add. MSS. 29555, f. 296 ; P.C. Reg. 65, p. 87).

[5] *Burnet*, ii. 98-100. " He was as a property to Lord Danby, and was turned by him as he pleased."

[6] January 21 (P.C. Reg. 65, p. 102).

Paymaster of the Forces to Sir Henry Puckering ;[1] and shortly afterward the secret service expenditure, which had hitherto been largely in his hands, was transferred to Charles Bertie. About the middle of February an attempt was made to put an end to Shaftesbury's intrigues with discontented factions in London[2] by sending Williamson to him with a formal message that he would do well to retire into the country.[3] Had the attempt succeeded a similar effort might have been made to get rid of Buckingham, who had recently taken a house in the City,[4] and possibly of others as well. Shaftesbury, however, protested that private business made his presence in town absolutely necessary, and remained where he was. Danby would have sent him to the Tower ; but the utmost pressure he could exert failed to induce Williamson to sign a warrant, and when Charles with his usual kindliness took the distracted Secretary's part[5] the whole matter had to be dropped.

This was a distinct check to Danby, but in spite of it he proceeded resolutely on his way. The local magistracy was remodelled where necessary.[6] In April, Sir John Duncombe, who had presented the petition of the coffee sellers,[7] was deprived of his position as Chancellor of the Exchequer, and the Treasurer's creature, Sir John Ernly, was given his

[1] Schwerin, *Briefe aus England*, p. 46 ; *Cal. Treas. Books*, v. 126, 128, 145 ; *Evelyn*, January 14, 1682. Puckering's position was a sinecure, and his only reward a pension of £400. The real paymaster was his nominal subordinate, Lemuel Kingdon.

[2] Some idea of these intrigues may be obtained from Williamson's notes in *Cal. S.P. Dom.*, 1675-6, pp. 562-3.

[3] L. F. Brown, *Shaftesbury*, pp. 235-6. Williamson's own account is in *Cal. S.P. Dom.*, 1675-6, pp. 559-61.

[4] B.M. Add. MSS. 29555, f. 309.

[5] " Warum soll er es unterschrieben, wenn er es nicht zu verantworten weiss " (Schwerin, *Briefe aus England*, p. 54).

[6] *Cal. S.P. Dom.*, 1675-6, p. 577. There was, of course, nothing new about this. The principal purpose of the association of lords which Danby had contemplated some months earlier was apparently to reserve all local offices strictly for members of the Church of England (*infra*, ii. 65-6). In B.M. Add. MSS. 28088, f. 3, there is a list of lords lieutenants, drawn up about this time in Danby's handwriting, with crosses opposite the names of those who were regarded with disfavour. Two of those whose names are so marked were dismissed in February 1676.

[7] " I heare Sir J[ohn] D[uncomb] is the person who undertakes to present the petition. Methinkes this lookes ₁yke an opposition to the Treasurer " (Richard Langhorne to Lord Hatton, January 6, 167⸗ , B.M. Add. MSS. 29555, f. 292).

place.[1] Rumour forthwith assigned Ernly's post as commissioner of the navy to one of Danby's followers, Sir Francis Lawley or Sir Richard Wiseman; but the Treasurer had been able to get rid of Duncombe only by enlisting the support of the Duke of York, and had to leave to him the nomination of Ernly's successor. Who would fall next could only be surmised. Sir Robert Howard seemed the most probable victim;[2] but Arlington, Coventry, Sir Robert Carr and the Attorney-General Sir William Jones were all believed to be in danger, and few felt really secure except the immediate supporters of the Lord Treasurer.[3]

It would have profited Danby little, however, to clear the Court of his adversaries and build up a party in the House of Commons had the King obstinately refused to consider his policy and allow Parliament eventually to assemble. Throughout the greater part of 1676, accordingly, the Treasurer's best efforts were directed to keeping prominently in the foreground the feasibility of an early session. One of the criticisms levelled by the King and by others as well against his Anglican policy was that it would lead to a union in self-defence of the nonconformists of all types, who might then prove equal or even superior in number to those who were endeavouring to suppress them.[4] To demonstrate the fallacy of this contention Danby and his allies among the bishops resolved upon a religious census of the Province of Canterbury, and on January 17 Archbishop Sheldon, who was now old and failing, issued a formal letter to Compton of London requiring him to undertake the task.[5] Instructions were to be sent by Compton to all the bishops, and by the bishops in turn to their archdeacons. The archdeacons were to hold conferences with the ministers and churchwardens in each parish and find out from them how many persons there were in the parish over sixteen years of age, how

---

[1] Duncombe was dismissed on April 21 and Ernly sworn in on May 8 (*Hatton Correspondence*, i. 122, 123; *Cal. S.P. Dom.*, 1676-7, p. 91). The Lord Chancellor had been hoping to secure the appointment of Sir Edward Dering.

[2] *Rutland MSS.*, ii. 28.

[3] "Many of our great ones apprehend they heare their bells tolling for them" (William Longueville to Lord Hatton, April 25, 1676, B.M. Add. MSS. 29555, f. 423).

[4] Bishop Morley to Danby, June 10, 1676, in *Leeds MSS.*, p. 14.

[5] The letter is printed in Wilkins, *Concilia*, iv. 598. A copy is in Carte MSS. 79, f. 22.

many of them were popish recusants, and how many nonconformists of any other type. The figures were then to be gathered
together by the archdeacons, sent by them to the bishops, and
by the bishops to Compton. In the whole proceeding it is not
difficult to discern Danby's guiding hand.

During the spring the returns were steadily coming in, and
the figures they disclosed were extremely favourable to the
Anglicans. Out of a total of almost exactly two and a quarter
million persons over the age of sixteen less than 12,000 were
declared to be papists, and rather more than 93,000 nonconformists of some other type. No exact census was taken
for the Province of York, but it was assumed that the same
proportions would hold good there, and that the number of
conformists, nonconformists, and papists might safely be taken
as one sixth of the corresponding figure for the Province of
Canterbury. A grand total was thus shown of 2,477,254 conformists, 108,676 nonconformists, and 13,856 papists. There
were, it was calculated, 23 conformists for every nonconformist,
179 conformists for every papist, and only 4,940 papists in the
whole of England fit to bear arms.[1]

For the purposes of modern investigation these figures cannot
be regarded as altogether reliable. The mere inauguration of
the enquiry frightened many weaklings back into the Church.
Presbyterians who sometimes attended the established service
were not counted as nonconformists, and it was admitted that
many of the so-called conformists did not receive the sacrament.
The bishops and their subordinates, it may be assumed, inclined to interpret every doubtful case in their own favour.
Nevertheless the returns demonstrated beyond possibility of
dispute the immense preponderance of the Anglicans, and so
strengthened Danby's hands at a most opportune moment.
Towards the close of May the Duke of York and Arlington
united in a determined effort to secure a dissolution of Parliament, the latter with the object of embarrassing his old rival,

[1] At some later period a copy of this return found its way among the papers
in King William's Chest, and the return in consequence has been printed in
Dalrymple, App. ii. pp. 11-15, and in *Cal. S.P. Dom.*, 1693, pp. 448-50, as
belonging to the reign of William III. The figures in this copy, however, are
identical with those in Bishop Morley's letter, Bishop Ward's abstract (*Leeds
MSS.*, pp. 14-15, 18) and a short summary in Leeds MSS., Packet 7.

the former in the hope of securing from a new Parliament some measure of toleration for the Catholics and Dissenters. Prince Rupert, Ormonde and Williamson gave them their support ; Secretary Coventry and the Lord Chancellor adhered to Danby, and a genuine trial of strength took place at Court.

The position, however, was now very different from what it had been some months earlier. Danby could demonstrate, with the aid of actual figures, on the one hand that the measure of toleration expected from a new Parliament was not in any vital sense necessary, on the other that the vote of supply which he had undertaken to obtain from the existing Parliament was practically certain. Charles, in consequence, adopted an unusually determined attitude, refused to listen to the proposal made by James that the problem should be debated in Council, and declared in the most positive manner that he was resolved on a further attempt in February to secure a satisfactory settlement of the revenue from the old assembly. In order to create a favourable atmosphere he even encouraged the Treasurer and his associates in a display of anti-French activity, and allowed the impression to spread abroad that a complete breach between the Crowns of England and France was imminent.[1]

So serious were the divisions at Court brought to light by this struggle that Charles thought it advisable, in view of the coming session, to aim at a general reconciliation among his chief ministers. Danby, who was now strong enough to be magnanimous, offered no opposition, and came to some kind of agreement not merely with the Duke of York, but with his earliest enemies, Ormonde and the Clarendonians. Arlington alone stood out, with the result that he weakened his own credit still further, and succeeded merely in strengthening the position of the Lord Treasurer.[2] A special committee was set up, consisting of the Treasurer, Chancellor, Ormonde and Lauderdale, for the sole purpose of making preparations for the meeting of Parliament. Shortly afterwards the two Secretaries of State and some of the bishops were added to their number, and a

[1] Courtin to Louis XIV, June 8, 1676 ; Schwerin, *Briefe aus England*, p. 60 ; *Hatton Correspondence*, i. 128-9 ; *Essex Papers*, ii. 49-50.

[2] Courtin to Louis XIV, June 4, 1676.

general unanimity seemed to be assured among the principal
ministers of the Crown in support of Danby's policy.[1]

It was thus in a spirit of quiet optimism that Danby entered
upon the uneventful period which even in the political world
usually occurred during the autumn. Towards the close of
July he contracted a serious illness, and on his recovery in
August [2] ventured to take one of the few holidays which he
enjoyed during his strenuous period of office as Lord Treasurer.
Nearly two years earlier the future of his many daughters had
become a subject of anxious consideration, and he had begun
that series of brilliant alliances for them which were to cause
his family to be compared to the House of Austria.[3] On November 26, 1674, he had married his eldest surviving daughter,
Anne, to Robert Coke of Holkham, Norfolk, who had inherited
nearly all the estate amassed by his great-grandfather, the
famous lawyer of the reign of James I.[4] He was now engaged
in negotiations for the marriage of his third daughter, Catherine,
to James Herbert, of Kingsey, Buckinghamshire, grandson of
Philip, fourth Earl of Pembroke ; and his fourth daughter,
Martha, to Charles, Lord Lansdowne, son and heir of John, Earl
of Bath, or to Charles, grandson and eventual heir of John, Lord
Robartes.[5] It was not unnatural, therefore, that while his wife
paid a visit to Holkham, he should take up residence at Rycote,
the Oxfordshire seat of his brother-in-law, James Bertie, Lord
Norris, which was within a short distance of Kingsey. There he
spent his time hunting, attending the races at Woodstock, and
making calls upon the neighbouring nobility and gentry.[6]

At the beginning of the year considerable anxiety had been
caused by an accident to Lord Dumblane, which threatened to

[1] *Cal. S.P. Dom.*, 1676-7, p. 480.

[2] Danby and the King turned ill at the same time and in the same manner,
but the latter recovered more quickly (Carte MSS. 38, f. 357 ; Lord Maynard
to Danby, August 14, 1676, in Leeds MSS., Packet 7).

[3] Airy's note in *Burnet*, ii. 101.

[4] *Bulstrode Papers*, pp. 271-2 ; *Hastings MSS.*, p. 166 ; C. W. James, *Chief
Justice Coke*, pp. 126-8. The portion was £7,000, and the jointure estates were
worth £1,500 a year.

[5] Robert Robartes to Danby, July 6, 1676, in Leeds MSS., Packet 7. Charles
Robartes, according to his father, was heir to more than £7.000 a year.

[6] Danby to Lady Danby, September 16, 23, 1676, *infra*, ii. 38-9 ; Danby to
Conway, September 21, 1676, in *Cal. S.P. Dom.*, 1676-7, p. 334.

make him lame for life, and as the summer advanced his
gradual recovery was hailed with relief. Even the skill in
dancing for which he was already famous was not, apparently,
to be impaired.[1] But the principal event of the autumn was
the expected birth of a child to Lord Latimer. In the middle
of April Lady Danby had been hurriedly summoned to attend
upon her daughter-in-law,[2] and as the year drew to a close hope
rose high that an heir would be provided for the House. The
result was only disappointment. Early on December 27 the
child was born, and was given his grandfather's name of
Thomas. Within a few hours he was dead, and Lady Latimer
herself was saved only with the greatest difficulty.[3]

Long before this, however, Danby had returned to the world
of politics to find a somewhat less satisfactory situation confronting him. His anticipation that the close of the year would
find the Government in urgent need of money was proving only
too correct. Under pressure of sheer necessity, assisted by the
careless generosity of the King, the establishment laid down in
January had been exceeded at almost every point.[4] Several
fresh causes of expenditure had arisen. An expedition was
required against Algiers. A rebellion had taken place in Virginia, which would not only involve the dispatch of ships and
men to North America, but would produce a diminution in the
revenue from tobacco for some years to come.[5] When to all
these was added the consideration that the additional Excise
on beer granted in 1671 was due to expire in a few months it
was obvious that the only thing which could avert a catastrophe
was the meeting of Parliament in a mood favourable to the
Government.

Unfortunately the general course of events in 1676 had not
been such as to reassure those who were inclined to regard

[1] George Evans to Lady Danby, January 29, 1676, in Leeds MSS., Packet 7 ;
Hastings MSS., ii. 170.

[2] B.M. Add. MSS. 29555, f. 409.

[3] Danby to Latimer, December 25, 1676 (*infra*, ii. 39), to Lord Ogle, and to
Lord Montagu, December 27, 1676 (*Portland MSS.*, ii. 152 ; *Buccleuch MSS.
at Whitehall*, i. 323). The child was buried in Westminster Abbey on December 29 (*Westminster Abbey Registers*, Harleian Society, p. 190).

[4] *Cal. Treas. Books*, v. pp. xxxviii-xxxix.

[5] Courtin to Louis XIV, October 12, 1676 ; *Cal. S.P. Dom.*, 1676-7, pp. 347,
358 ; *Mignet*, iv. 430 ; *Grey*, iv. 225.

the Court with suspicion. At Easter the Duke of York had removed the last lingering doubts about his religion by absenting himself altogether from the English Church service, and not even the remonstrances of the King proved sufficient to make him reconsider his decision.[1] During the summer France had recovered from the temporary check imposed by the Allies in the previous year. A French army had seized Condé and Bouchain in the Netherlands. A French fleet had successfully met de Ruyter in the Mediterranean, and the death of the great Dutch admiral had been followed by a most alarming development of French sea-power. English public opinion, always sensitive regarding France and Catholicism, had become seriously inflamed,[2] and a particular point upon which to concentrate had been provided by the depredations of French privateers at the expense of English shipping. Innumerable stories were current of hardships imposed by the French Government and tortures inflicted by French seamen on English subjects, and an uneasy suspicion prevailed that the English Court, if it did not actually connive at such incidents, at least did not resent them as it ought to have done.

The problem which confronted Danby, as it was to confront him again and again during the next two years, was that of giving adequate satisfaction to popular feeling on these points without completely alienating the Duke of York. James had no liking for Danby's policy, and although he was well aware of the storm he had roused by his open avowal of Catholicism still hoped both to safeguard himself and to secure some sort of toleration for his co-religionists by an alliance with his most determined opponents, Shaftesbury and the Presbyterians. The opposition for their part were not unready for such an alliance, for they were anxious to detach James from Danby, and hoped to use his influence with the King to effect a dissolution of Parliament. Both James and the opposition were much influenced by the French ambassador, who feared that the

---

[1] *Campana de Cavelli*, i. 166-7, 173 ; *Mignet*, iv. 405-6.

[2] " Toute l'Angleterre est allarmée de voir l'heritier présomptif de la couronne faire profession d'une religion contraire a celle du royaume, et il n'y a pas un ministre qui ne presche toutes les semaines ou dans les villes ou dans les villages que la religion protestante est en grand peril, et que la France la veut ruiner " (Courtin to Louis XIV, December 3, 1676, in *Campana de Cavelli*, i. 185).

alliance of Danby, the King, and possibly the greater part of the nation might mean war between England and France, and was desperately anxious with their assistance to secure at least a further prorogation.[1]

Over the question of the French privateers no real difficulty arose, for Louis himself adopted a most conciliatory attitude, and made what even Danby regarded as generous concessions.[2] As regards the attitude which the Government should adopt towards the Catholics, however, it was almost impossible for Danby and the Duke of York to agree. On October 3, at the Treasurer's instigation, an attempt was made to allay Protestant feeling by the issue of an Order in Council forbidding the abuse of the religious privileges enjoyed by the Queen and foreign ambassadors, and warrants were issued to messengers to watch the entrances to the Queen's chapel and the ambassadors' houses and report the names of any English subjects who frequented them.[3] This gave considerable offence to the Duke of York, who was further incensed by a rumour that Danby was endeavouring to separate the Presbyterians from the other nonconformists by offering them permission to build churches outside the limits of the principal towns.[4] In spite of his strong loyalist principles it seemed possible that the alliance between James and the opposition might become an accomplished fact.[5]

---

[1] Courtin to Louis XIV, October 3, November 12, 1676.

[2] Courtin to Louis XIV, November 26, December 3, 1676 ; Ogg, *Reign of Charles II*, ii. 538-9.

[3] P.C. Reg. 65, pp. 349, 361 ; *Cal. S.P. Dom.*, 1676-7, pp. 349, 386 ; Courtin to Pomponne, October 15, 1676, in *Campana de Cavelli*, i. 180-1.

[4] It is not clear whether this proposal was ever definitely made or seriously intended. The Presbyterians at any rate resolved not to trust Danby (Courtin to Louis XIV, January 21, 1677).

[5] Courtin was not very confident of James. " Monsieur le Duc d'York ne veut entrer dans aucune cabale qui soit contraire aux interests et aux intentions du Roy son frère. Je ne crois pas aussy qu'il fust de la bienséance que je prisse un autre party. Mais mon dit Sieur le Duc d'York se déclare qu'il n'a aucun engagement particulier avec le Grand Tresorier, et qu'il demeurera toujours (selon les occasions qui se présenteront) en estat de conseiller au Roy son frère ce qu'il croira le meilleur pour son service, sur quoy les Presbytériens doivent estre persuadés qu'il sera toujours d'avis de convoquer un nouveau Parlement, puisqu'il en a esté dans la dernière sceance, et que depuis il a fait tous ses efforts pour obtenir cette convocation " (Courtin to Louis XIV, January 21, 1677).

The need for averting, if possible, this danger did much to determine Danby's attitude on all but the main issues of the day. One of the problems coming to the front in the summer of 1676 was that of finding a successor for the Archbishop of Canterbury, whose life was obviously drawing to a close. Danby's candidate was the Bishop of London, and for some time it was considered extremely probable that Compton would be appointed ; but the Protestant zeal which commended him so strongly both to the Treasurer and to the nation as a whole was regarded with great disfavour by the Duke of York, who exerted himself to the utmost to oppose his pretensions, advocating instead the claims of Nathaniel Crew, Bishop of Durham. The struggle was a long one, for the death of Archbishop Sheldon did not actually take place until November 9, 1677 ; but at no time did Danby care to risk a quarrel with the Duke of York by using all his influence on Compton's behalf, and the decision ultimately reached by the King was in effect a compromise, all the bishops being passed over and William Sancroft, Dean of St. Paul's, appointed.[1]

Even more difficult of adjustment was the problem of the government of Ireland which arose about the same time. The reconciliation effected in the summer between Ormonde and Danby had not been a mere formality, but a recognition by both statesmen that in essentials their policies were the same. Differences of character and personal outlook, however, still remained, and Danby could ill endure the advantages which greater age, wider experience and more illustrious ancestry conferred upon his rival. From the very first, accordingly, his idea seems to have been to secure the recall of Essex, with whom he had been on bad terms since the reorganisation of the Irish revenue, and bring about the restoration of Ormonde to the post of which he had helped only eight years earlier to deprive him. A friendly Lauderdale in Scotland and a friendly Ormonde in Ireland would do much, he believed, to strengthen his own ascendancy in England.

No sooner had his plan been laid, however, than he found it obstructed by an entirely different scheme devised by his own followers. Ranelagh was even more anxious than Danby to

[1] *Burnet*, ii. 100 ; *Essex Papers*, ii. 51 ; *Ormonde MSS., N.S.*, iv. 381-91.

get rid of Essex ; but he was on the worst possible terms with Ormonde, and had to seek a successor elsewhere. His plan, accordingly, was that the Duke of Monmouth should be given the dignity and emoluments of Lord Lieutenant, while the actual duties of the office should be performed by Conway with the title of Lord Deputy. Danby was not particularly friendly with Monmouth, but he could hardly oppose on an Irish question his own chief partisans in Ireland, and so was relegated to a neutral position between contending claimants.

Again the determining factor in his policy was the attitude of the Duke of York. James was completely opposed to any project which would give increased importance to Monmouth, and threw all his weight on the side of Ormonde. For the sake of appearances Danby maintained a display of activity on behalf of his own supporters, but virtually acquiesced in what James was doing ; and after another lengthy intrigue Ormonde was able to declare himself sure of appointment by the spring of 1677.[1]

While complaisance in such matters, however, did much to keep the Duke of York out of the hands of the opposition, it did not contribute in any other way towards diminishing the strength of that opposition, and as the meeting of Parliament drew nearer and became more certain Danby grew increasingly anxious about the capacity of his own following in the Commons to secure that victory for the Court on which he had practically staked his political future. Towards the middle of 1676, possibly as a result of the party conferences held in June, Sir Richard Wiseman had been commissioned to draw up a more elaborate survey than had yet been attempted of the political attitude of members. A complete list of the House of Commons was prepared, and opposite the name of each member of whom he knew anything Wiseman entered a note of his previous behaviour in Parliament, and an estimate of what might be made of him for the future.[2] Wiseman's suggestions were now put in force, and a final campaign was begun to secure adherents for the Government.

[1] *Essex Papers*, ii. 126-8 and *passim*; *Ormonde MSS.*, N.S., iv. 21 ; Carte, *Life of Ormond*, iv. 525.

[2] What remains of this list is printed *infra*, iii. 96-111.

At the same time great attention was paid to by-elections, of which, owing to the long prorogation, there promised to be a large number.[1] As early as October 27 the Court was calculating that out of 23 constituencies rendered vacant by death it should be able to carry 16, while even the opposition conceded it a majority of the seats concerned.[2] It was noticed also that of the Court candidates put forward an increasing proportion were personal adherents of the Lord Treasurer. In April 1675 Danby had secured the return of his son-in-law, Robert Coke, for King's Lynn, at a famous election which cost nearly £8,000.[3] In May of the same year he had supported without success the candidature of Lord Ranelagh.[4] He was now working on behalf of his brother Charles and his sons Latimer and Dumblane, all of whom were to be elected, together with James Herbert, shortly after Parliament reassembled.[5]

[1] On the assembling of Parliament order was given for the issue of writs for no fewer than 28 constituencies (*C.J.*, ix. 383-4).

[2] *Clarendon Correspondence*, i. 3.

[3] Coke's opponent, Simon Taylor, threatened to petition the Commons against the return, and had to be bought off by an arrangement, engineered by Danby, that his election expenses should be paid for him. The new member's estate was in such disorder as to make immediate payment of the double expenses impossible, and parliamentary privilege was invoked to enable it to be evaded ; but Danby supervised the reorganisation of the estate, and met the difficulty with a personal loan of £5,000 at 6 per cent, which remained outstanding till 1708 (*Return of Members of Parliament*, i. 525 ; *Seasonable Argument* ; James, *Chief Justice Coke*, pp. 126-8).

[4] *Essex Papers*, ii. 15.

[5] *Return of Members of Parliament*, i. 520, 522, 526 ; *Cal. S.P. Dom.*, 1677-8, pp. 78, 80, 87, 90 ; *Buccleuch MSS. at Whitehall*, i. 326. As he grew more powerful, and his difficulties in Parliament multiplied, Danby became increasingly arbitrary in his attitude to elections (*Reresby*, pp. 148-9, 155). Dumblane and Herbert were both under age when they were elected. Dumblane's opponent was John Rushworth, the historian, who later petitioned Parliament against the return (*C.J.*, ix. 400, 485). It was obtained largely through the influence of the Duke of Newcastle, and the activity of the sheriff, Sir Richard Stote, who acknowledged great obligations to Danby, and secured a promise from the mayor of Berwick that there would be " nothing refused him that is leagell." The methods Stote employed are set forth in his own letters.

On February 25, 1676/7, he wrote to Newcastle, " I finde the opposite party still exceed us in votes, notwithstanding our endeavours, so the game I have now to play is to make use of the exceptions we have to disallow many, yea most, of their votes. And to this purpose I have applyed to the mayor, who seemed very much startled therewith at first ; but after long discourse and

Meanwhile with the turn of the year members had started to drift up to town, where pressure upon them increased. Sir John Reresby, who had hitherto inclined towards the opposition, was invited by the Treasurer to call upon him, and given an account of the political situation which convinced him of the evil designs of his former associates. His conversion to the Court party was completed by a personal interview with the King, and was followed almost at once by that of his " brother " Sir Henry Goodricke.[1] Other members of the House of Commons were similarly approached by the Chancellor, the Speaker, or whoever was deemed to have most credit with them. Nor was the House of Lords neglected. Proxies were collected as zealously as in the autumn of 1675, both in semi-official fashion by Williamson and in a more personal manner by Danby himself.[2]

One thing alone remained which might assist towards the creation of a favourable atmosphere in Parliament. The stop of the Exchequer had never been forgiven by the commercial community or by the nation as a whole, and the continued failure of the Government to reach a permanent settlement with the victims of that transaction was a grievance which provided the opposition with one of its most effective weapons of attack. In August 1675 the bankers had presented a petition pointing

many arguments used he seemed content. Yett for all that, untill I have better assurance from him, as also from the bailiffes (whom I doe not so much doubt), the writt shall not be delivered, nor the election day appointed. I tell them all the blame will lye upon me (as in truth it will) if I misleade them in matter of law, and I will owne it ; and it is now talked here, they cannot loose it but by trickes in law. I care nott what is said so long as my owne judgement and reason is satisfyed in what I shall doe, though perhaps such things have beene rarely if ever practized."

On March 3, 1676/7, he wrote to Danby, " After a troublesome contest with an unreasonable party opposite to us we found many of them stood excommunicate for nott repaireing to divine service and nott receiveing the sacrament, and haveing procured an authenticke copy we did except against their votes as nott legall and so to be disallowed. And then my Lord haveing the greater number the mayor and bailiffes, upon my declaration of my opinion in point of law publiquely and giveing it under my hand, were at last perswaded this day to declare my Lord Dunblaine their burgesse lawfully elected for this towne, and the indentures were this day sealed accordingly, and the returne made and delivered to the bearer who brought the writt first to us " (Leeds MSS., Packet 7).

[1] *Reresby*, pp. 111-3.

[2] *Cal. S.P. Dom.*, 1676-7, pp. 459, 544 ; *Cal. Treas. Books*, v. 425.

out that the existing arrangement made with them had only eighteen months to run, insisting on the great advantages to the country in general which would follow a more lasting settlement, and suggesting as a possible basis that interest for the three years 1674, 1675 and 1676 should be added six-monthly to the principal sum originally due, and that at the close of 1676 the stop of the Exchequer should be taken off.[1] Some such arrangement remained thereafter a constant object of Danby's policy;[2] but inasmuch as any payments to the bankers were almost bound to be charged on the Excise, no progress was possible until a settlement of that source of revenue had also been effected, and as the Excise produced nearly half the total income of the Crown such a settlement was too near a general declaration of financial policy to be lightly undertaken.

It is characteristic of Danby's whole attitude as a statesman that while hastening to introduce order and method in the administration of the finances, he shrank from innovations of a revolutionary character. The sphere within which it was in his power to effect financial changes was indeed strictly limited. Not merely was his control of expenditure incomplete, but he had practically no control whatever over taxation. He could, it is true, represent to Parliament what sums were necessary, and even indicate how these sums might best be raised ; but there was little chance of his representations producing much effect, for the ultimate decision on these points lay with a House of Commons which was dominated by traditional ideas and deeply resentful of any interference from without. A genuine readjustment of the finances to suit the circumstances of the country and meet the legitimate needs of the Government was therefore a vain ambition. In theory existing taxation was equitable in its incidence, fixed in amount, and sufficient to defray the ordinary expenses of government. In practice it was none of these things. It fell much too heavily on the commercial elements in the community and on the poorer classes ; it was so dependent on Customs and Excise as to be

---

[1] The petition, endorsed by Danby, " Paper from the goldsmiths att Windsor, August [16]75," is preserved among the Leeds MSS., Packet 6.

[2] In a paper headed, " Memorandums in [16]75," Danby has noted, " To acquainte the King with my designe about the banquers debt " (*ibid.*).

subject to violent fluctuations ; and it was still on the whole insufficient.

There is nothing to suggest that Danby was much troubled by the first of these defects ; but he was always conscious of the other two, and in his determination to devise a remedy is to be found the origin of the principles he came to advocate in revenue collection, the only operation connected with the revenue where he had a reasonably free hand. What was wanted, in his opinion, was a system which would produce not merely as large but also as steady a return as possible. To a " management," accordingly, he had early shown himself opposed, as unlikely to serve either of these ends. Under a system of direct collection, he argued, nobody had any interest in increasing the return, while it was obviously impossible to say with certainty what the return would be. On the other hand, the alternative method of farming the main branches of the revenue, to which he at first had recourse, had its own disadvantages. The farmers could be required to guarantee a fixed advance payment and a fixed annual return, which the bidding of rival groups might be expected to raise to the highest level possible ; but in spite of all precautions experience suggested that they always contrived to make too much for themselves out of their farms, and that the leading financiers, by combining together, could on occasion force the Government to accept practically what terms they liked.

The system towards which Danby gradually inclined, accordingly, was a compromise, which sought to combine the best features of the " farm " with those of the " management." The farmers were to be required as before to pay a large sum in advance and guarantee a fixed annual rent ; but instead of being allowed to enrich themselves with any surplus they might collect they were to be compelled to account for that too. In return they were to be paid an agreed amount for the work of collection, and also a percentage of the surplus sufficient to induce them to collect as much as possible. The certainty and productiveness of the " farm," it was hoped, would thus be secured, without the wastefulness which too often characterised it.[1]

[1] An account of the development of Danby's financial ideas, written and presented to him at his own request, is printed *infra*, iii. 27-31.

The first important financial operation in which Danby gave effect to these ideas was the Excise farm of 1677. With a view to gratifying the Cavalier interest, and increasing his voting strength in Parliament, a very different scheme was pressed upon him, which provided for direct collection of the Excise by a body of well-paid commissioners, most of whom were to be members of the House of Commons ;[1] but it is doubtful whether this plan of wholesale bribery was ever seriously considered. Offers for the farm of the Excise were invited by August 25, 1676, and the invitation apparently provoked considerable competition.[2] After prolonged negotiation, however, an agreement was reached in February 1677 with George Dashwood and a somewhat different group of partners from those associated with him in 1674. Their farm was to run for three years from June 24, 1677. On the assumption that the additional Excise granted in 1671 would be continued by Parliament the advance money was fixed at £250,000, on which interest at 6 per cent was to be allowed, and the annual rent at £560,000. Of money collected beyond the annual rent the farmers were to be allowed £55,000 for the pay of their inferior officers, £5,000 for bad debts, and £10,000 for " their hazard and reward for management ; " but any further surplus was to go to the King, subject only to a deduction by the farmers of $3\frac{3}{4}$d. in the £.[3]

By the middle of February £100,000 of the advance money had actually been received, and the financial position of the Government had been made so much the stronger ; but the great advantage which Danby hoped to derive from his farm of the Excise was a settlement with the bankers. Since April 1676 calculations on which such a settlement might be based had been proceeding, and on February 8 Danby's final report was

---

[1] A letter which accompanied and seeks to explain the proposal is printed *infra*, iii. 4-6. Apparently there were to be 66 commissioners, all of them if possible members of Parliament, at a salary of £500 a year each. Those who already had places or pensions of less value were to surrender them, and the money thus made available was to be distributed among others of the Cavalier interest, so that a total of about 80 might be secured for the Crown. There were also to be 400 sub-commissioners, who were to be appointed on a similar basis.

[2] *Cal. Treas. Books*, v. 64, 86.

[3] *Ibid.*, pp. 830-2, 902-3.

placed before the King. Four computations of what might be considered due were set forth, the first increasing the original principal by simple interest at 6 per cent per annum, the second allowing compound interest calculated yearly at 6 per cent per annum, the third allowing compound interest calculated half-yearly at 6 per cent per annum, and the last allowing not only the interest but also a gratuity of 4 per cent per annum. Of these computations Danby recommended the second, his recommendation was accepted, and on February 9 it was ordered by the King in Council that part of the Hereditary Excise should be assigned in perpetuity towards the payment of interest at 6 per cent from January 1 on the sum of approximately £1,400,000 thus recognised as due.[1] The settlement came just in time. Six days later Parliament was to meet.

[1] *Ibid.*, pp. 36-8, 42, 201, 427, 542-6.

CHAPTER XI

WITHIN SIGHT OF SUCCESS, 1677

WHEN Parliament assembled on February 15, 1677, Danby rested his hopes of a successful issue partly on the larger and better organised Court party which he had built up, partly on the attractiveness of the domestic policy which he had inaugurated two years earlier and pursued ever since, and partly on the satisfaction which he believed he could now induce the King to give regarding foreign affairs. Before any of these factors could be put to the test, however, his position was immensely strengthened by an act of almost incredible folly on the part of the opposition. While he had been working assiduously for the meeting of Parliament on the day to which it stood prorogued, his opponents had been exerting themselves to the utmost either to secure a dissolution, or alternatively to maintain that by a prorogation exceeding the period during which the King could legally dispense with Parliament a dissolution had *ipso facto* been pronounced.[1] In June they had endeavoured to secure an address to the King from the City in favour of a new Parliament.[2] Throughout the year, in spite of

---

[1] Their arguments were based upon two statutes, 4 Edw. III, c. 14, and 36 Edw. III, c. 10, which required that Parliament should be held at least once a year. On the other hand it was maintained that these statutes had been superseded by the Triennial Acts of 1641 and 1664 (*Cal. S.P. Dom.*, 1677-8, p. 544).

[2] *Cal. S.P. Dom.*, 1676-7, pp. 184, 194, 253-6 ; *Essex Papers*, ii. 60-1, 63. According to the French ambassador it was Buckingham who was responsible for this, and the project was condemned by Shaftesbury as inopportune (Courtin to Louis XIV, July 9, 1676 ; *cf. Hatton Correspondence*, i. 132-3). When the proposer of the address, Francis Jenks, a linen-draper, was summoned before the Council and asked who had inspired him to his attempt, he replied that no one had done so ; but " le Roy d'Angleterre luy dit en riant que c'estoit l'Alderman Georges qui estoit l'autheur de ceste enterprise " (Courtin to Louis XIV, July 23, 1676).

the handicap imposed by the Government censorship, they had been using the press to set forth their arguments.[1] Finally, about December, when it became clear that the Houses were going to reassemble on the appointed day, they determined to maintain in Parliament itself that a dissolution had already taken place.[2] In vain Lord Halifax and other moderate members of the opposition argued that a legal quibble was a poor basis on which to build, that the proposed contention was not likely to be well received in Parliament, and that the Commons, who stood to suffer by it, were certain to be bitterly offended if it was put forward in the House of Lords.[3] From their comparative success in the sessions of 1675 Buckingham, Shaftesbury and Holles had derived an altogether exaggerated idea of the strength of their following in the Lords, and nothing would restrain them from pressing their point ; [4] while even the Duke

[1] *Cal. S.P. Dom.*, 1676-7, pp. 528, 543, 577 ; 1677-8, p. 11 ; *Hist. MSS. Com.*, ix. 2, pp. 69-79. By the long continuance of the existing Parliament, it was pointed out, men between the ages of 21 and 37 had been practically disfranchised.

[2] *Rutland MSS.*, ii. 33-5 ; B.M. Add. MSS. 29556, f. 94.

[3] *Burnet*, ii. 115-7. " We would gladly be disolved, but not by the Lords nor at their pleasure " (Harbord to Essex, December 17, 1676, in *Essex Papers*, ii. 86).

[4] At the last moment Shaftesbury began to have misgivings, and endeavoured, though without success, to come to some agreement with Danby and so turn the tables on the section of the opposition which was refusing to accept his leadership. As intermediary he chose the newly appointed Deputy-Paymaster of the Forces, who wrote to one of Danby's associates :

" My Lord, I was this morning sent for by my Lord of Shaftesbury. The maine of his businesse was to desire Mr. Bridges, who is employed by me, might have my leave to take care of his lordships Citty concernes. This over, his lordship asked me for newes. I telling him I neither knew nor looked after any, my Lord began and told me that he wondered my Lord Treasurer did not observe where he was, and who were his freinds. For his part, he declared he had noe personall anger with any man, and though my Lord Treasurer was angry with him he wisht my Lord Treasurer well and that he might keep his staffe, and that he had rather it should be in his hands then his owne, for my Lord Shaftsbury said he aimed not at particular things but publick good ; but for my Lord of Ormond, there was my Lord Treasurers danger, and he wondered he did not see it, for Sir William Coventry and my Lord of Ormond were in councells together against my Lord Treasurer to bring in Sir William Coventry and their party, and could not but wonder that my Lord Treasurer did not observe that my Lord of Ormond advised in all his secretts with my Lord of Hallifax and my Lord Marquis of Winchester, who were my Lord Treasurers profest enemies. And my Lord Shaftsbury said for his part he was apprehensive of nothing more than thet these councells would take effect to destroy my Lord Treasurer, for whatever my Lord Treasurer thought he

of York appeared to imagine that he might have something to gain by giving it his countenance.[1]

Had the scheme of the opposition been sprung upon Danby as a surprise it might conceivably have met with some success ; but the Treasurer had ample warning of what was intended,[2] and his preparations to turn it to his advantage, as shown in the course of events, suggest that he had a much better appreciation of the parliamentary situation than his opponents. Scarcely had the Commons withdrawn from the House of Lords after hearing the King's speech, when Buckingham rose, " in great bravery in liveries of blue," and in a set speech of considerable length moved that as the Parliament then sitting was not legally in existence an address should be made to the King for a new one.[3] Immediately Danby's cousin Lord Frescheville, presumably by preconcerted arrangement, replied

would certainly be attackt this session by the aforesaid persons, and for his part he vowed he would support him all he could, for though he could not love my Lord Treasurer while he used him thus, yet he had noe personall prejudice for him. He added that he dreaded nothing more then Sir William Coventrys comming into my Lord Treasurers place, which he was sure was intended, and the thing soe confident of that they had among themselves setled all places already, and if they should effect their designe they having a great interest in the nation would ride everybody. This was [the] purport of what he told me, and I thinke it is word for word. I thought it my duty to acquaint your Lordship with it, that my Lord Treasurer might be acquainted with it ; but I beg of my Lord Treasurer and your Lordship that noe use might be made of it to my hurt. I remaine, My Lord, Your Lordships most obedient and most humble servant, Lemuel Kingdon.—February 13th, 1676[/7]." (Leeds MSS., Packet 7.)

[1] Courtin to Louis XIV, December 10, 1676. Courtin correctly anticipated what would happen, and warned James. " Ma responce [to the Duke's mention of the project] fut que j'estois desja informé du dessein de Milord Hollis, que je n'estois pas assez instruit de la disposition des loix et de l'usage observé en Angleterre pour juger si son opinion estoit bien ou mal fondée, mais que ce qui me faisoit appréhender que sa proposition ne fut pas bien receue, c'estoit parce que tous les membres du Parlement seroient juges en leurs propre cause ; qu'ils avoient tous un grand interest de se maintenir dans leurs députations par les advantages utiles et honorables qu'ils en retiroient, et qu'il ny avoit guere d'apparence de croire qu'ils voulussent se degrader eux-mesmes ; que cela me faisoit craindre que si on faisoit d'abord une proposition qui vraysemblablement seroit rejettée, le party de Mylord Tresorier ayant recognu ses forces par l'advantage qu'il auroit remporté n'en devint plus fier."

[2] At least as early as December 20 he was acquainted with the design, and in anticipation of it was summoning his supporters to be present on the first day Parliament met (*Cal. S.P. Dom.*, 1676-7, p. 459).

[3] This speech has frequently been printed, and may be read most conveniently in the *Parliamentary History*, iv. 815-23.

with a motion that Buckingham should be called to the bar to answer for his reflections on the Parliament. Two motions were then before the House, and in spite of an attempt on the part of Buckingham to explain away anything which might have given offence, the debate centred impartially round both. Lord Arundell of Trerice seconded Frescheville's motion. Salisbury, Shaftesbury and Wharton opposed it and supported Buckingham. Ailesbury, Halifax, Berkshire, Winchester and Dorchester steered a middle course, arguing that Parliament was not dissolved, but that the lords who had raised the question were deserving of thanks rather than condemnation.

After the first hour's debate, however, the proposal to call Buckingham to the bar dropped out of sight, and for four hours more the contest raged over the problem of dissolution. Meanwhile Danby himself remained inactive, awaiting the course of events in the House of Commons. There the same problem had been raised in a much more cautious manner by Sir John Malet, Sir Philip Monckton, and Lord Cavendish ; but the suggestion that the existing assembly was not a true Parliament received little support, the general opinion was that if the prorogation was invalid it must be taken as equivalent to an adjournment, and without a division having been challenged or even a formal motion made the House about three o'clock read a bill and proceeded to private business.[1]

Immediately on receiving news of this very satisfactory result Danby rose in the Lords and proposed that the House should " consider about punishing those that argued for dissolving." An edge was thus given to the debate which it had hitherto lacked. Buckingham declared that it " was hard that a man in that power should drive a thing so," and " some high and bitter clashings " followed between him and the Treasurer. Salisbury endeavoured to start a counter-attack by moving for the names of those who had advised the long prorogation. Wharton desired to have the opinion of the judges. Shaftesbury excelled himself in his exposition of the legal situation. But the supporters of Buckingham's original motion were in a

---

[1] *Grey*, iv. 64-72 ; Marvell, *Poems and Letters*, ii. 172-3 ; *Essex Papers*, ii. 101. The arguments in favour of assuming that Parliament had been adjourned were particularly clearly set forth by William Sacheverell (*Grey*, iv. 66-7, 81-2).

hopeless minority, and when the question was finally put that the debate should be laid aside it was carried without difficulty in the affirmative. Danby then once more moved " that it might be considered what to do with those lords who had asserted the Parliament was dissolved." Ormonde, with the insults and injuries of nearly twenty years to avenge, took the lead by naming Buckingham ; the Treasurer, who had perhaps shrunk from making a direct personal attack on his own former patron, then named Salisbury, Shaftesbury and Wharton ; and an exhausted House sought relief in an adjournment of the debate.[1]

The following day provided the first effective trial of strength between parties among the Lords. Having had time to review their position, the four peers whose proceedings had been called in question came forward with precedents of similar proceedings in Parliament to which no exception had been taken ; but in a debate lasting two hours they were unable to make any serious impression, and on the question being put that they should be required to withdraw 53 voted for the affirmative as against 30 for the negative. The case of each lord was then considered separately. Salisbury and Wharton, who had argued that the prorogation was illegal, but not that Parliament was dissolved, were merely called in to their places and required to ask pardon of the King and the House. Shaftesbury, on the other hand, who had gone much further, was called in to the bar and required to acknowledge that his endeavouring to maintain that Parliament was dissolved was an ill-advised action, for which he begged pardon. Buckingham had meanwhile retired on the plea of illness, but on the following day, when he appeared in the Lords, he was dealt with in the same way as Shaftesbury. Each of the culprits in turn refused to obey the direction of the

---

[1] Holles was also in the House, and " argued for the dissolution ; " but he spoke late and briefly, and presumably in a way which gave no offence. According to Burnet he was incapacitated by gout. The fact seems to be that he came to doubt the wisdom of proceedings which he had originally approved, and withdrew from them as far as loyalty to his allies permitted. " On observa que Milord Hollis n'avoit rien dit pendant les deux dernières séances, et qu'il n'avoit pas jugé a propos de se commettre, préveoiant bien que la tentative que ces messieurs avoient résolu de faire contre le sentiment de tous leurs amis n'auroit aucun succés " (Courtin to Louis XIV, March 1, 1677).

House,[1] and for that contempt was sentenced to kneel at the bar as a delinquent and be imprisoned in the Tower during pleasure.[2]

Even then Danby was not satisfied. The similarity of the speeches made by the four lords, he declared, showed that there had been collusion if not an actual conspiracy between them, and it was therefore necessary that they should be separately confined. An order was accordingly made that they should neither see nor send to each other in the Tower, nor receive any visits without leave except from their wives, children, and necessary servants.[3] Danby was not being vindictive. His object was simply to emphasise the dangerously revolutionary character of his opponents' proceedings, and so strengthen the reaction in favour of the Government which he was expecting. Nevertheless the eventual result of these high-handed actions was to appear some years later, when his own period of tribulation arrived, and he was to receive as little mercy as he had shown.[4] At the moment their most important effect was to

---

[1] Great efforts were made to induce Salisbury to obey, and he would probably have done so had not Shaftesbury dissuaded him. Wharton declared he had changed his opinion during the debate and had already asked pardon for what he had said at the beginning, but he refused to admit the justice of the House's proceedings by asking pardon again.

[2] *Cal. S.P. Dom.*, 1676-7, pp. 555-6 ; *Rutland MSS.*, ii. 38-9 ; *Hist. MSS. Com.*, xii. 7, pp. 132-3. The request made by all the lords except Wharton that their cooks might accompany them to the Tower was inspired by Shaftesbury. There are three elaborate and closely related accounts of the proceedings in Carte MSS. 79, ff. 31-44. The first seems to consist of rough notes taken in the Lords at the time ; the others are based upon it.

[3] *Cal. S.P. Dom.*, 1676-7, p. 564 ; *Rutland MSS.*, ii. 39 ; Courtin to Louis XIV, March 1, 1677. On their first Sunday in the Tower the lords met at divine service and talked to each other all the time, but measures were taken to prevent even that.

[4] " The Earl of Danby's long imprisonment afterwards was thought a just retaliation for the violence with which he drove this on " (*Burnet*, ii. 118). For the moment, however, there was a very real lack of sympathy with the imprisoned peers. In requiring them to admit their error and ask pardon the House of Lords had considered that it was acting leniently, and it was much incensed by their obstinate refusal to obey. On March 20 Lord Delamere moved the House for their release ; but his contention, that they were confined upon a mere punctilio, was so badly received as almost to lead to his being sent to join them. With some justice Danby declared " qu'il ne lui paroissoit pas raisonnable qu'on mist en liberté des gens qui ne le demandoient pas, et qui se faisoient un point d'honneur de ne pas presenter une requeste a leurs juges naturels." His arguments had the complete approval of the House, and Delamere's only supporters were Halifax, Clarendon and Berkshire (*Hist. MSS. Com.*, vii. 469 ; Courtin to Louis XIV, April 1, 1677).

bring down upon him the implacable hostility of the Duke of
Buckingham. Hitherto Buckingham, although definitely in
opposition, had shown little personal enmity towards his former
follower ; but the humiliation inflicted upon him at this time
he never forgot. Probably Danby, who knew better than most
men the Duke's infirmities, and the extent to which he had
declined in the estimation of the King, imagined that he was a
spent force. If so he was soon to be undeceived. Although
he had greatly degenerated since the time of Clarendon and the
Cabal, Buckingham was by no means negligible either as a
courtier or as a statesman, and the last expiring flashes of his
brilliant intellect were to be devoted almost entirely to accomplishing the Treasurer's ruin.

Of this, however, there was as yet no serious premonition,
and Danby's success seemed for the moment assured. Shaftesbury had many excuses for his failure. He had counted
on the support of the Duke of York and the Catholic interest,
and had received no help whatever from them. The resolution even of his most determined followers had been badly
shaken by the appearance, just before the session began,
of the Government pamphlet, *A Pacquet of Advices and
Animadversions sent from London to the Men of Shaftesbury.*[1]
But no amount of explanation could obscure the fact that by
his ill-advised scheme [2] he had reduced his party to temporary
impotence.[3] In the House of Lords the Duke of York, alarmed

---

[1] By Marchamont Needham, 1676 (*Cal. S.P. Dom.*, 1677-8, pp. 226-7).

[2] " Une affaire mal entreprise et plus mal soustenue " (Courtin to Louis XIV,
March 1, 1677).

[3] Some anonymous notes on the whole enterprise are preserved in B.M. Add.
MSS. 28047, f. 199 :

" The league was as well with the Roman Catholick interest as the independ-
ant, and some assurance it is confest they had in his Royall Highness who
seem'd to concur with them till the very last.

" They adjudge the distruction of theire whole designe to that pamphlit cald
A Packet of Animadversions, which the Earle of Shaftsbury hath bin heard to
say was as politickly contriv'd, and as unluckey tim'd to the prejudice of him,
as ever anything was, for indeed sixteen of twenty who were but three or four
dayes before the Parliament satt in as firme a league as could be dropt off upon
peruseall and well digestion of that booke, assertening the point of prudentialls
to be the safest principall, for that booke did intimate to the rest those dangerous consequences which those that declin'd the four now in the Tower did
avoyd and shun by acquiessing with the sence of the House, and those four are
by the rest charg'd with a mighty imprudence in not doeing the like.

by so open an attack on the prerogative, resumed his alliance with Danby, and even consented to the introduction of a bill limiting the powers of a Catholic sovereign in Church matters,[1] by which the Treasurer hoped to remove some of the apprehension with which the possible accession of the Duke was regarded, and so secure his inclusion in the Cavalier-Anglican coalition on which he was endeavouring to base his power. In the House of Commons so many members were alienated from the opposition that the first definite trial of strength between parties showed a large majority in favour of the Government. On February 17 the whole question whether the long prorogation was legal or not was raised by a proposal that the House should proceed to name the committees usually appointed at the beginning of a new session. The previous question having been put, the Government mustered 193 votes against 142 for the opposition, and the committees were then named.[2] Danby was probably disappointed, after all his efforts, that the voting strength of his party was not greater, but his majority appeared to be sufficient, and the experience of some weeks suggested that it was fairly reliable.

" They have since privately declard that in the issue they would have given the King a million of mony, to the end he should see that the comand of the nation lay in them, and not the interest his Majesty hath espousd, by which means he would soone have declind the Lord Treasurer, &c.

" It is confest they are at a loss now what to doe, and the Earle of Shaftsbury particularly dreads an impeachment for what accumilations may be charg'd against him since he was Lord Chancellor, at which time he past his own pardon.

" That he hath sent particularly to Mr. Symson the councellor and others is well known to advice upon the statute Edw. 3d for dissolution of the Parliament, but he and they denied giveing theire opinions therein.

" The Earle of Shaftsbury declared privately that Sir William Coventry was to come into play before he could."

[1] " Il esté proposé de concert avec Monsieur le Duc d'York, qui m'advoua qu'il avoit crû estre obligé de se relascher sur ce point pour rasseurer les esprits des députés des deux chambres, et pour empescher (en ceddant quelque chose de ses droits) qu'ils n'allassent plus avant sur ce sujet " (Courtin to Louis XIV, March 8, 1677). Nevertheless James was one of fourteen who entered a protest when the bill finally passed the Lords (L.J., xiii. 75). By one of the perversities of politics this bill, which granted so much of what the opposition then wanted, failed to secure the approval of the Commons ; " but the scheme was the first feeble adumbration of that Tory policy of limitations on a Catholic successor, which was to do battle, in 1680-1, with the Whig scheme for entirely excluding such a successor from the throne " (Feiling, Tory Party, pp. 166-7).

[2] C.J., ix. 384 ; Grey, iv. 81-95 ; Essex Papers, ii. 101-2 ; Courtin to Louis XIV, March 1, 1677.

These weeks Danby employed in obtaining from the Commons the first votes of supply granted since he had become Lord Treasurer. The alarm caused by the development of the French fleet encouraged him to ask for £800,000 for the use of the navy; but it was almost immediately apparent that this sum was more than the Commons would consider, and in order to defeat the opposition, who argued in favour of £400,000, his supporters had to moderate their demands. When the House went into Grand Committee on February 21 it was only with difficulty that the chairmanship was secured for his candidate,[1] and the debate which followed was marked by much outspoken criticism of the Government. In the end, however, the sum of £400,000 was rejected as inadequate by 199 votes to 165, and in accordance with the revised proposals of the Court a sum of £600,000 was then voted for the construction of thirty ships.[2] On March 2 it was resolved by a majority of 49 that this sum should be raised by a land tax based upon a monthly assessment; on March 5 an attempt on the part of the opposition to incorporate in the bill of supply a clause appropriating the Customs to the uses of the navy was defeated by 51 votes;[3] and a week later a slightly reduced majority of 33 resolved that the additional Excise, which Danby had been so anxious to have renewed, should be continued for a further period of three years.[4] Charles was delighted. On April 9 the bill for £600,000 passed the Commons, and on the following day was sent up to the Lords.[5] At the King's request the huge document, swollen to an enormous bulk by the lists of commissioners contained in

[1] Sir Richard Temple and Sir John Trevor were both put forward, and the voting was 127 to 104 in favour of the former (*C.J.*, ix. 386 ; Marvell, *Poems and Letters*, ii. 175).

[2] *Grey*, iv. 103-30 ; *Reresby*, p. 111 ; Courtin to Louis XIV, March 4, 1677. There is an elaborate account of the proceedings of the Commons during this session in B.M. Add. MSS. 28091, f. 29 *et seq.* From the disproportionate amount of space given to the speeches of Thomas Neale, who had represented Petersfield since 1668, it seems probable that Neale himself was the compiler.

[3] " Worüber der Hof über alle Massen zufrieden ist " (Schwerin to Frederick William, March 16, 1677, in *Briefe aus England*, p. 96).

[4] The voting on these three occasions was 214 to 165, 175 to 124, and 189 to 156 (*Grey*, iv. 177, 237 ; *C.J.*, ix. 392).

[5] *C.J.*, ix. 417 ; *L.J.*, xiii. 107.

it, was unrolled, and stretched from the throne to the lower end
of the House. Handing his stick, which he said was just three
feet long, to one of the lords, Charles seized the white staff from
Danby, and joyfully ticked off the yards as they were measured
along the bill.[1]

Even before that, however, the characteristic weakness of
Danby's party had become apparent. It had now the numbers
necessary to carry a division, but few of its members shone in
debate or possessed any capacity for managing the business of
the House.[2] The opposition, in consequence, by confusing the
issues, could interpose innumerable obstacles in the path of the
Government, and by taking advantage of the feeling roused by
events abroad was able in the end to bring the majority over to
its side.

Popular opinion in England was extremely sensitive regarding the course of events in Flanders, and there the early months
of 1677 witnessed a series of almost uninterrupted successes on
the part of Louis XIV. Operations commenced at the beginning of February. Early in March Valenciennes fell, and towards the close of the month Cambray followed. On April 9
St. Omer capitulated, after William of Orange, in a vain attempt
to relieve it, had suffered a disastrous defeat at Cassel. The
reply of the House of Commons was to introduce a bill for the
recall of the English troops in the French service,[3] and to vote

---

[1] *Buccleuch MSS. at Whitehall*, i. 326. Even the representative of Branden-
burg was interested in the size of " das Dokument, welches 1½ Schuh breit und
210 Schuh lang ist " (Schwerin, *Briefe aus England*, p. 126).

[2] *Burnet*, ii. 79, 125-6. Like many another resolute statesman, Danby had
a reputation for surrounding himself with incapable subordinates. A curious
story is told by Le Neve (*Lives and Characters*, pp. 34-5) of the method he
adopted in dealing with the leading men of the opposition. He first made
them the lowest offer that there was any chance of their accepting. If they
agreed to it, all was well. If not, Danby presently gave out that £100 more
would have bought them, and so made them odious to their own party. This
story is on a level with that of Cardinal Morton's fork, but it receives at least a
partial confirmation from Reresby (*Memoirs*, p. 112).

[3] In spite of proclamations forbidding the King's subjects to enlist in the
French army, recruiting had continued during 1676, not merely in England,
but also in Scotland, where it was encouraged by Lauderdale, and in Ireland,
where it was connived at by Essex. The indignation this aroused was increased
by reports that many of the recruits had been practically kidnapped (*Cal. S.P.
Dom.*, 1675-6, p. 126 ; 1676-7, pp. 58, 60-1, 64. 69 ; 1677-8, pp. 12-17, 24, 57 ;
Essex Papers, ii. 41-2, 119 ; Danby to Lauderdale, December 18, 1677, in
Lauderdale Papers, iii. 240).

address after address to the King, requesting him, in increasingly urgent terms, to take steps for the preservation of Flanders.

With these addresses Danby was in complete agreement, and there is no doubt that he gave them at least underhand encouragement. In the interests of his own domestic policy he had long desired to induce the King to make a definite declaration against France, and the time had now come, he believed, for the accomplishment of his design. It was neither to be expected nor desired, however, that the King should take such a step without first receiving a promise of adequate support, and when the first address was sent up by the Commons to the Lords for their concurrence Danby accordingly took the lead in proposing that such a promise should be embodied in it. In spite of a conference between the two Houses, in which the Treasurer himself acted as one of the managers, this proposal had to be abandoned, owing to the jealousy entertained by the Commons of any interference by the Lords in matters of supply ; [1] but the alternative course remained of bringing the matter forward in the House of Commons itself, and after the King had given a somewhat colourless answer to the first address, promising to take all care for the preservation of Flanders which could " consist with the peace and safety of the kingdom," Danby accordingly engineered a second address, which gave a definite promise of " aids and supplies " in the event of the measures recommended leading to a war with France. For such a war, it was declared amidst the applause of the entire House of Commons, " les Anglais donneraient tout, jusqu'à leur chemise." [2]

---

[1] This first address was voted on March 6, referred for preparation to a committee on the 7th, presented to the Commons and adopted by them on the 10th, sent up to the Lords the same day, debated by them on the 12th, made the subject of a conference between the two Houses on the 13th and 15th, and finally presented to the King and answered by him on the 16th (*L.J.*, xiii. 68-76 ; *C.J.*, ix. 393-401 ; *Grey*, iv. *passim* ; *Essex Papers*, ii. 110 ; Schwerin, *Briefe aus England*, pp. 96-103).

[2] Courtin to Pomponne, April 8, 1677, in *Mignet*, iv. 443. The original motion for this second address was made in the Commons on March 20. On the 26th the motion was debated, and the framing of the address was entrusted to a committee, which reported on the 29th. As finance was involved the concurrence of the Lords was not asked for, and the address was presented to the King by the Commons alone on the 30th. According to the French ambassador it received support both from Danby's friends and from those of Lauder-

The terms of the address were by no means entirely to the satisfaction of the Court, and some time was spent in considering the precise answer that should be made to it. Before a decision could be reached on this point, however, the whole position had been appreciably altered by the appearance upon the political scene of the sinister figure of Ralph Montagu. Hitherto the chief difficulty which Danby had been called upon to face was the influence exerted over Charles and the Duke of York by Louis XIV and the French ambassador in England. He was now summoned to deal, in addition, with the intrigues and suggestions of the English ambassador in France.

Like so many of the English representatives abroad, Montagu had originally been a follower of Arlington, and in that capacity had not hesitated to disparage Sir Thomas Osborne with his patron.[1] Early in 1676 he had even joined in a last desperate attempt to overthrow Danby and secure the restoration of Arlington to favour by bringing the Duchess of Mazarin to Court as a rival of the Duchess of Portsmouth.[2] The complete failure of that attempt, however, convinced him that Arlington's star had finally set, and with characteristic disregard of the claims of gratitude or consistency he turned immediately to make his court where most was to be gained. Three years earlier he had married the widowed Countess of Northumberland, and had thus become the step-father of the sole heiress to the Percy estates, Lady Elizabeth, then a child six years old.[3] It was with this highly valued matrimonial prize more or less at his disposal that in the autumn of 1676 he approached Danby, ostentatiously consulting him about her future, and suggesting as a possible husband Charles, Earl of Plymouth, the King's natural son by Catherine Pegge, with whom the Lord Treasurer

dale, and was first proposed by " un nommé Forert, parent du Grand Tresorier." This appears to be James Herbert, father of Danby's son-in-law, who proposed the motion of March 20, and was seconded by Sir Nicholas Carew, Henry Powle, and Sir Thomas Meres (B.M. Add. MSS. 28091, f. 59 ; Courtin to Louis XIV, April 5, 1677 ; *C.J.*, ix. 402-9 ; *Grey*, iv. 304-15, 331-4).

[1] *Buccleuch MSS. at Whitehall*, i. 423, 484.

[2] Barbour, *Arlington*, pp. 253-4, and the French dispatches there quoted ; *Cal. S.P. Dom.*, 1675-6, pp. 474-5.

[3] Lady Elizabeth Percy, born on January 26, 1667, not only inherited immense wealth, but held in her own right six of the oldest baronies in England, including that of Latimer.

had already struck up an alliance.[1] The suggestion was well received, but on the matter being proposed to the King Charles preferred to put forward the claims of his youngest son by the Duchess of Cleveland, to whom he had already given the title of Earl of Northumberland. Moreover the legal guardian of the child was not her mother, but her grandmother, who wished to marry her to the young Lord Ogle, son of Danby's old friend.[2] The result was a most complicated situation, from which Montagu sought relief by pointing out that Lady Elizabeth was still two years short of marriageable age, and urging the desirability of delay.[3]

The negotiations over his proposal, however, had gained him considerable intimacy with the Lord Treasurer, and paved the way for the introduction of a more serious affair. Few men knew better than Montagu the advantages which England might derive from intrigue with France, and had it not been for the attendant dangers he would probably have entered into direct relations with Charles II and organised such an intrigue himself. As it was, he considered it more prudent to induce or even compel Danby to take up the matter, confident that if all went well he would profit by the Treasurer's gratitude, while if anything went ill he would be able to shelter behind him. Towards the close of March, accordingly, he wrote to Danby, insisting on the complete inability of the French Government to refuse any reasonable demands which the English King might make. The compliant attitude of Parliament, he de-

---

[1] As early as November 21, 1674, Lord Plymouth, who had not then been given his title, wrote from Paris to Danby : " When I consider in whose hands all my concerns are placed, I cannot butt reverence his Majestie's judgement in the choice, and your Lordship's goodnesse in the care of them. I was ever sensible of the reallity of your kindness to me whilst I was in England, and will still believe your Lordship will not desert the interest of one you have soe generously undertaken to assist. The confidence of this leaves me no apprehensions of any injuries from my enemies, of what sort soever, especially since I am resolved uppon all occasions to show the gratitude of " etc. (Leeds MSS., Packet 5 ; *cf.* also *Leeds MSS.*, p. 18). Danby's idea was to use the influence of Lord Plymouth to counterbalance that of the Duke of Monmouth.

[2] The will of the Earl of Northumberland had provided that if his widow married again the custody of his daughter was to go to his mother. There was a long struggle over the matter (*Letters to Williamson*, i. 180-98 *passim* ; *Letters of Lady Russell*, i. 13-14).

[3] See the early correspondence between Danby and Montagu printed *infra*, ii. 257-61.

clared, followed by the address for the preservation of Flanders, had caused serious alarm at Versailles, and so encouraged the Confederates that they needed only a confirmatory declaration from the King to make them offer a really effective resistance to the French armies. The continued progress of the French was therefore made possible only by the favour of the English King, and so obviously was this the case that every one in France, except the inner circle of ministers, believed that Charles was being paid three or four million livres a year for his neutrality. If the King would only insist upon it he could have without difficulty from the French sufficient money to free him from all trouble in his domestic affairs.

This letter was enclosed by Montagu in a short covering note, in which he expressed a hope that Danby might be able to use his suggestions to his own advantage, and invited him, as he thought proper, to show the letter to the King or suppress it altogether.[1] Its arrival, just at the moment when Charles was considering his reply to the Commons' second address, was most inopportune, and it is to Danby's credit that he immediately and unhesitatingly suppressed it. Far from showing it to the King he drew up, in opposition to it, his own statement of the existing position, and on April 4 laid that before Charles as the basis of an answer to the address. One of the main causes of the comparative success of the Government during the session, he declared, was the belief which he had been able to spread abroad of the King's firmness to the Protestant religion and determination to withstand the undue aggrandisement of France. To such a height, however, had fear of that power risen, that nothing short of an open declaration against it would any longer satisfy the people. Failure to make such a declaration would involve the Government, when again it should have to look to Parliament for assistance, in a stormier session than it had ever yet experienced, and might so completely alienate popular opinion as to lead to something of the nature of a revolution. The adoption of an anti-French policy, on the other hand, would unloose the purse-strings of the Commons, would enable the King to secure what commercial concessions

[1] The letter and the covering note, dated March 25/April 4, are printed *infra*, ii. 261-4.

P   D.L. I.

he desired from Spain and Holland, and would win him a great reputation as the saviour of Europe from domination by one despotic power. The enmity of France need not be feared, for the fleet which Parliament would enable the King to put to sea would be sufficient to ward off invasion, and any diminution of the Customs duties which might result from the activities of French privateers would have to be made good by the House of Commons. Nor need it be supposed that after being involved in an expensive war the Crown might be deserted by Parliament, for even in the unlikely event of the Commons falling away the people were so unanimously in favour of war that they would support the King in bringing pressure to bear on their own representatives. War would mean the raising of an army and the strengthening of the fleet, which would enable the King to adopt an independent attitude towards Parliament ; and if the worst came to the worst he might even in the end offer to disband his army in return for the payment of his debts and the provision of a sufficient revenue for the future. Some such method seemed to be the only practicable means by which the King could escape from his precarious financial position and cease to " depend rather upon his subjects then they upon him."[1]

Nothing reveals more clearly than these arguments the essential weakness of Danby's position. The idea that the King might derive some financial advantage from war had been at least partly responsible for the two contests with the Dutch, and had been shown to be without foundation. The suggestion that an army might be raised on account of the war and then sold to Parliament in return for a revenue hardly looks as if it was seriously meant. But Danby was faced with the task of showing that the policy he advocated was calculated both to benefit the nation and to advance the personal interests of the King, and the conflict of interests was in reality so great that

---

[1] The memoranda in which Danby embodied his views, dated April 4, are printed *infra*, ii. 66-9. There is no actual proof that they constitute his answer to Montagu's letter, but the dates are almost conclusive, and it is a significant fact that the Duke of Leeds, judging by the alterations he made, later considered the idea of printing the memoranda with his published *Letters*. The inference that Montagu's letter was never presented to the King is drawn from the memoranda, which contain no reference whatever to the suggestions it makes.

he could not afford to be very particular about the arguments he used. All through his memoranda two separate lines of thought seem to be running, one leading to sound and the other to unsound conclusions. It is typical of his own limitations as a statesman and of the essential selfishness of Charles that he makes no serious attempt to argue that the interests of King and people must in the end be the same.[1]

Nevertheless Danby's reasoning prevailed for the time with Charles, and it was determined to embark upon the course he had suggested. The immediate problem was that of obtaining sufficient money in advance to enable preparations to be made for the war which would probably result, and this the Lord Treasurer proposed to solve by a declaration to the House of Commons that unless they could first provide an adequate supply it would be impossible for the King to enter into the alliances their recent address required, lest he should make enemies against whom he was in no condition to defend himself. On April 11, accordingly, Charles sent a message to the Commons insisting on his need of supply in order to make fitting preparations, and suggesting an immediate adjournment in order that the Houses might meet after Easter to deal with the matter.[2]

The result was disappointing. If the King was fearful that he might become involved in a war for which Parliament would grant no supply, the Commons were equally fearful that they might grant supply only to find it used by the King for other purposes than a war.[3] Resolute leadership by any representatives of the Court interest in the Commons would probably have swayed the balance in favour of the Government, but such leadership was conspicuously lacking. Secretary Williamson, who delivered the King's message in writing, delivered also a

[1] It should be noted that Danby appears to regard Parliament as a third interest which cannot be identified with either King or people.

[2] *C.J.*, ix. 418 ; *Cal. S.P. Dom.*, 1677-8, p. 85. There can be no doubt that this message is based on the second-last paragraph of Danby's memoranda.

[3] This suspicion was in the minds of many members of the House of Commons even when the first address was being drawn up. " Soe much the argument of distrust prevailed, and that example of Harry the 7th, who got aids for the warr and presently struck up a peace and remained with all those materials at his arbitrement, that for fear of a pickpocket warr they would not name assistance " (*Essex Papers*, ii. 110).

verbal explanation of the proposed adjournment which proved
utterly irreconcilable with it. Secretary Coventry had to admit
that he had not seen the King for three days and had no particular acquaintance with the message. Whether through sheer
ineptitude, or through lack of faith in the King's good
intentions, the leaders of the Court party entirely failed to
indicate a clear line of action, and it was a thoroughly mysti-
fied House that adjourned the debate until the following
day. The only constructive suggestion had come from Sir
William Coventry, who in an impressive speech emphasised the
dangers of delay, and urged that the difficulties of the moment
should be tided over by authorising the King to anticipate
the taxes already voted to the extent of £200,000.[1] The vital
decision was to be reached, not by the Government, but by
a conference of the opposition leaders held later on the same
day.

The determining factor in the outlook of that conference was
a conviction, for which there was only too much justification,
that Charles had no intention of going to war with France, and
was using the possibility of war only as a pretext for extorting
money from Parliament. It was therefore resolved to require
from the Government a statement what preparations the King
could make for the security of his kingdoms without special
supply, to insist that an ordinary summer guard for this purpose was chargeable upon the regular Customs duties, and to
complain of the ill management which had reduced the fleet
and stores far below the level necessary for safety. The royal
demand for a special supply, it was felt, could not be entirely
ignored ; but any such supply should be granted only for six
weeks at a time. Meanwhile the best course appeared to be
that indicated by Sir William Coventry. A clause should be
inserted in the bill continuing the additional Excise, empowering the King to borrow the sum of £200,000 at 7 per cent
interest on the security of it, and an undertaking should be
given that if any part of this sum was expended in making
preparations pursuant to the Commons' addresses it would be
repaid when Parliament next met.

Scarcely had the conference come to an end when its resolu-

[1] *Grey*, iv. 343-51.

tions were betrayed to Danby by Sir John Trevor ; [1] but although the Treasurer now knew what to expect he had no means whatever of averting it. Nobody knew better than he the impossibility of giving any absolutely convincing assurance of the King's hostility to France, and nothing less would suffice. On the following day, accordingly, the borrowing clause was proposed and accepted in the Commons, and on April 13 a third address was adopted and presented to the King, in which the House gave renewed assurances of their readiness to provide him with supplies in support of whatever engagements he might find it necessary to make. [2]

Danby's objection to this ingenious solution of the financial difficulty was partly that the sum granted was insufficient, and partly that it was only an advance upon a fund already given to the King for other uses. A fresh message was therefore drawn up by him and sent to the Commons on April 16, in which the King, while undertaking to devote all his resources to the preservation of his kingdoms, insisted that the objects of the Commons themselves could not possibly be secured without a grant of £600,000 of new money. To this the reply of the House, embodied in a fourth address, was that so many of their members had already retired into the country in expectation of the Easter recess that they did not consider it parliamentary to vote money, but that if the King would permit a short adjournment, during which he might conclude his alliances, they would assist him when they next met as the situation required. With this the Government had perforce to be content, and permission was given for an adjournment to May 21. [3]

Unfortunately it was impossible for the Government to do anything to meet the wishes of the Commons. The £600,000 granted for the use of the navy would not begin to

[1] Trevor's information is B.M. Add. MSS. 28053, f. 118. A few lines scribbled on the letter by Danby himself appear to indicate those who attended the conference—"Candish, Sir William Coventry, Sir Thomas Clargis, Sir Thomas Meeres, Mr. Powell, Sir John Trevor and Sir Thomas Littleton. They denied Sir Thomas Lee to bee with them."

[2] C.J., ix. 419-21 ; Marvell, *Poems and Letters*, ii. 191-2.

[3] C.J., ix. 422-3 ; *Cal. S.P. Dom.*, 1677-8, pp. 93-4. The message of April 16 was certainly Danby's work. A much corrected draft in his own handwriting is in Leeds MSS., Packet 8. It differs only in some verbal points from the version printed in the *Journals*.

come in for some months.[1] Even the £200,000 which the King
had been authorised to borrow could not for some time be
obtained, for the Commons' guarantee of repayment was
dependent on the use to which the money was put, and this
made lenders reluctant to come forward.[2] Army and navy were
both unprepared for war, and every responsible minister recognised that in such circumstances it would be madness to take
any steps which might entangle England in the European conflict.[3] Thus when Parliament reassembled, and the question
was raised what alliances had been made, no satisfactory
answer was forthcoming. Rightly or wrongly a report had
spread abroad that Danby was hoping for a thin House in
which he might carry what votes of supply he pleased by means
of his own followers, and members in consequence had appeared
in great numbers and in a highly suspicious humour.[4] An
attempt to revive the request for an additional grant which had
been made just before the adjournment was ruthlessly swept
aside, and on May 23, after the King had again insisted on his
inability to act unless put in a better condition to do so, it was
resolved with only two dissentient voices that a further address
should be made to him.[5]

In the terms of this address it is possible to discern the
influence of the Confederate ministers then in London. Anxious
though they were to secure the intervention of England on their
side, they were even more anxious to safeguard themselves
against the possibility that Charles, if well supplied with money,

---

[1] The first small payment into the Exchequer was actually made on June
15, 1677, but the final payments were not due until September 16, 1678 (*Cal.
Treas. Books*, v. pp. xlvii-xlix).

[2] *Mignet*, iv. 474.

[3] Sir John Ernly, speaking presumably with a full sense of his responsibility
as a Privy Councillor, declared in Parliament, " The King has neither stores,
nor money, nor ships. Twenty or thirty privateers may easily burn all our
ships and master the Channel " (*Grey*, iv. 345).

[4] Courtin to Louis XIV, June 3, 1677. Much irritation had also been caused
by continued recruiting on behalf of the French king in Ireland. " Indessen
sind aus Irland wieder 900 Mann nach Frankreich gegangen, welches einer von
des Königs Räthen dadurch entschuldigt, dass der König es gern sieht, wenn
die Papisten in Irland sich in fremde Dienste begeben " (Schwerin to Frederick
William, May 7, 1677, in *Briefe aus England*, p, 128).

[5] *C.J.*, ix. 423-4 ; *Grey*, iv. 355-74 ; B.M. Add. MSS. 28091, ff. 107-8 ;
Marvell, *Poems and Letters*, ii. 194-6.

might throw his weight on the side of France. Just before the meeting of Parliament they had taken part in a conference with the opposition leaders, at which it had been resolved that supply should be absolutely refused unless Charles joined the Confederates, and that a grant of £1,200,000 should be made if he did. Since then they had been busily engaged in extending their influence among the members by arguments designed to inflame their hatred of France and suspicion of Charles, and by a lavish distribution of the money provided by their Governments for that purpose. Under their inspiration a lengthy address was now drawn up desiring the King " to enter into a league, offensive and defensive, with the States General of the United Provinces . . . and to make such other alliances with such other of the Confederates " as he should think useful, after the conclusion of which such supplies would be granted as would answer the occasion.[1]

So confident were the opposition of success that when this address was reported to the Commons on May 25 they endeavoured to secure the adoption of it by acclamation, meeting the arguments of the Court with concerted shouts of " Agree, agree." While in general sympathy with the address, however, Danby was unable to countenance the attack it involved on the royal prerogative of determining war and peace, and he therefore directed his followers in a series of criticisms which made a deep impression. Sir Jonathan Trelawny denounced the cries of the opposition as " savouring to him like club-law," and a genuine debate followed, in which the principal opposition leaders found it necessary to take part. Eventually a division was challenged on the question whether the words " offensive and defensive with the States General of the United Provinces " should stand, and it was determined by 182 votes to 142 that they should ; but even this result was made possible only by the fact that some forty or fifty members did not vote at all. The success of the opposition was not as impressive as had been anticipated.[2]

The address was presented on May 26, and received by the King with the answer that it was long and would require time

[1] *C.J.,* ix. 425 ; *Mignet,* iv. 473-5.
[2] *Grey,* iv. 374-88.

for consideration ; but in reality Charles had already made up his mind how to deal with the situation. He disliked what he was being called on to do ; he disliked the peremptory manner in which he was being called on to do it ; and he disliked the interference of foreign ministers in English politics which had led to his being required to do it. Immediately after the departure of the representatives of the Commons he summoned his Council and announced his intention of dismissing Parliament, an intention from which no arguments of the Confederate ministers could move him. On May 28 he summoned the Commons before him, rebuked them very sharply, and bade them adjourn to July 16. On their return to their own House Henry Powle would have spoken, and was supported by Sir Thomas Lee ; but the Speaker declared that having been commanded to adjourn they had no course but to obey, and although Lord Cavendish offered to show precedents to the contrary, declared the House adjourned, secured the mace, and amidst loud shouts of " Sit on, sit on," passed through the door with his friends around him.[1]

This unhappy ending to a session which had begun so well might seem to suggest that the Treasurer had failed, but in reality he had achieved a considerable measure of success. Not merely had he obtained for the King one of the largest grants of supply ever accorded him in time of peace, but he had almost contrived to establish a genuine reconciliation between King and Parliament on the basis of a truly national policy. No thought that he had failed entered his own mind. All that was necessary, he believed, was that some means should be devised of giving the Commons more definite satisfaction regarding foreign affairs than had yet been found possible, and the reconciliation at which he was aiming would become an accomplished fact.

Possibly William of Orange appreciated the situation. More probably he had been convinced by the reverses of the earlier part of the year, the increasing dissensions among the Allies, and the development of a strong opposition to his authority in

---

[1] *C.J.*, ix. 426 ; *Grey*, iv. 389-91 ; *Cal. S.P. Dom.*, 1677-8, pp. 137-49 ; *Essex Papers*, ii. 141-3 ; Marvell, *Poems and Letters*, ii. 196-8 ; *Reresby*, pp. 123-4. There is an early draft of the King's speech of May 28 in Leeds MSS., Packet 8.

Holland itself, that his only hope lay in obtaining some assistance from his uncles in England. This, at any rate, was the moment which he chose for the dispatch of his chamberlain and intimate friend, William Bentinck, on a complimentary mission, with instructions to assure Charles of his dependence upon him and readiness to be directed by him in the conclusion of peace or conduct of the war.[1] The real object of the Prince, however, was to secure permission to come over to England himself, and to that end Bentinck was specially instructed to approach the Treasurer, to whom he carried a letter of recommendation,[2] take his advice as regards making such a request, and beg his support for it.[3]

It shows the reputation which Danby had gained, that although neither William nor Bentinck had ever met him he was singled out in this way. Without hesitation he threw all his weight on their side, and seized this opportunity to draw up for the King's consideration a complete analysis of the situation at home and abroad. In domestic affairs, he insisted, all that was necessary was firmness in the pursuit of the policy already laid down, together with a resolute determination to favour those who supported it and discountenance those who did not. In foreign affairs the best course would be to arrange for a peace which would satisfy the Prince of Orange, and form a strict alliance with him. This might bring many advantages in the way of trade, whereas no benefit whatever could be derived from an alliance with France. The argument that decency required some consideration for the French King need not be given any weight, as that King in similar circumstances would not show the slightest regard for the King of England.[4]

By these representations Charles was at least so far convinced that he received Bentinck's assurances with the utmost civility, and gave a general assent to William's proposed visit, although he expressed an opinion that it should not take place

---

[1] Bentinck reached London on June 4. His memoranda and correspondence at this time are printed in *Correspondentie van Willem III en Bentinck*, part 1, i. 4-9.

[2] William of Orange to Danby, June 9, 1677, *infra*, ii. 388.

[3] Danby to Temple, June 14, 1677, *infra*, ii. 485.

[4] Danby's " memorandums " are dated only June, 1677 (*infra*, ii. 69-71), but it is impossible to avoid connecting them with Bentinck's visit.

while Parliament was in session. The terms of a satisfactory settlement were certainly considered, and as it was deemed inadvisable that Bentinck should wait long in England, a promise was given that an emissary should shortly be sent over to Holland to discuss matters further with the Prince.[1] About who that emissary should be Danby had no doubt whatever. The growing importance of foreign affairs had for some time convinced him of his need for a Secretary of State who should be thoroughly conversant with the condition of Europe, and at the same time such as he personally could trust. Even before Bentinck's arrival advantage had been taken of Secretary Coventry's frequently repeated desire to be relieved of the burden of his office, the King's support had been obtained for the claims of Sir William Temple, and the terms of a surrender by one to the other had been discussed. Now Sir William's son John was hurriedly dispatched to Nimeguen to lay the terms before his father, with the idea that he should return home, undertake the mission to Holland, and then settle down as Secretary. So determined indeed was the Treasurer that when Temple endeavoured to excuse himself, on the ground that he could not pay the price which Coventry demanded, his representations were ignored, and a positive command was sent to him to return to England at once.[2]

With the dispatch of this command Danby reached the greatest height of power he was ever to attain. His control of domestic affairs was already practically complete. With Temple by his side he would be able to establish a similar control over foreign affairs,[3] and monopolise the Government. Contemporaries marvelled at the ascendancy which his positive and energetic nature had enabled him to establish, not merely

[1] Danby to William, June 11 ; Danby to Bentinck, June 29 ; Bentinck to Danby, June 25 and July 16; William to Danby, June 25, 1677, *infra*, ii. 389-93.

[2] Danby to Temple, June 14 ; Temple to Danby, June 25, 1677, *infra*, ii. 485-9 ; Temple, *Works*, i. 448-9.

[3] The French ambassador watched his efforts with an amused incredulity. " Monsieur Temple aura toujours la principale direction des affaires estrangères, parce que ce ministre [i.e. le Grand Tresorier], qui ne les cognoist pas, croit les pouvoir apprendre de luy. Je scais qu'il cherche a s'en instruire, mais il me semble que c'est un peu tard, et il est difficile qu'un homme qui n'a point voyagé puisse a l'aage de 50 ans devenir un grand personnage sur cette matière " (Courtin to Louis XIV, July 26, 1677).

over the King but even to some extent over the Duke of York. His most active enemies were in the Tower, and their fall had terrified the more timid. No serious rivals threatened his position. Lauderdale was slipping into the background, and was entirely in his interest.[1] Ormonde was preparing to succeed Essex as Lord Lieutenant of Ireland.[2] The mainspring of the Government, then and for some time afterwards, was a triumvirate composed of Charles, James and Danby,[3] and in this inner council it was generally Danby's policy that prevailed, for he could usually induce either Charles or James to join with him, and having secured the support of the one he could nearly always overbear the opposition of the other.

In this very fact, however, lay the seeds of future trouble. It was one of Charles's incurable weaknesses as a monarch, repeatedly exhibited throughout his reign, that while he could rarely bestir himself sufficiently to take the control of affairs into his own hands, he could never give his whole-hearted confidence to any one who would manage them on his behalf.[4] Thus no sooner had Danby attained apparent supremacy in the Government than the King began to chafe under his domination, and look round for some counterpoise to his influence, if not among his statesmen at least among his courtiers.

That counterpoise he was to find, as so often in similar circumstances before, in the Duke of Buckingham, now the Treasurer's most inveterate foe. Shortly after the adjournment of Parliament in April the lords in the Tower had petitioned the King for their release ; but in view of the speedy reassembling of the Houses Charles had refused to grant more than a few weeks' leave of absence, for special reasons, to Lord Wharton.[5] The adjournment of May 28, however, opened up a prospect of indefinite imprisonment for the lords, and made

---

[1] *Reresby*, p. 121.

[2] After many delays Ormonde actually set out for Dublin at the very beginning of August.

[3] Nothing more strongly emphasises this point than the dispatches of Barillon, who succeeded Courtin as French ambassador in the summer of 1677. Barillon always consulted these three, and rarely any others.

[4] According to Lord Ailesbury (*Memoirs*, i. 104, 146) this was the result not of weakness but of policy, and was an attempt on the part of Charles to imitate the methods of Louis XIV.

[5] *Hist. MSS. Com.*, xii. 7, p. 136 ; *Cal. S.P. Dom.*, 1677-8, pp. 92, 96.

them take more vigorous action.   Salisbury, the least dangerous of the four, secured a temporary release on the ground that his wife was about to be delivered.[1]   Shaftesbury had his case brought by Habeas Corpus before the King's Bench, only to find that the judges were of the opinion that they had no jurisdiction in the matter, his commitment having been by order of a higher court.[2]   Buckingham, with better judgment and more success, invoked the assistance of his allies among the revellers at Whitehall, by whom his enforced absence had been deeply deplored.

It was one of the many difficulties which beset the path of Charles's statesmen that they could neither with safety ignore the " buffoones and ladys of pleasure,"[3] nor find among them any stable support for their authority.   Danby's alliance with the more respectable section which centred round the Duchess of Portsmouth was effective only so long as he could satisfy the demands of the Duchess[4] and she in turn could retain her favour with the King.   Meanwhile it inevitably earned him the hatred of the less reputable section led by Nell Gwyn.

At this particular moment the Duchess of Portsmouth was under a cloud, while Nell Gwyn had been rendered particularly bitter against the Lord Treasurer by a recent refusal on his part to support her claim to be made a countess.   An intrigue was thus easily set on foot.   Nell Gwyn first mollified the royal wrath against the Duke, and then Buckingham sought a personal interview with the King.   To contrive this with the necessary secrecy under the very eyes of watchful opponents was no easy task, but a stratagem suggested by Lord Middlesex proved effective.   On June 21 a warrant was signed permitting the Duke to leave the Tower for two days under the escort of

[1] *Hist. MSS. Com.*, xii. 7, p. 137 ; *Cal. S.P. Dom.*, 1677-8, pp. 166, 214, 215.

[2] *Savile Correspondence*, pp. 62, 63.

[3] This is the phrase applied by Evelyn to the enemies at Court who did so much to ruin Clarendon (*Diary*, August 27, 1667).

[4] These demands presented a serious financial problem.   A return giving the individual items for the period March 26, 1676, to March 25, 1678, shows that during these two years the Duchess of Portsmouth was paid £55,198 7s. 11d., and Nell Gwyn £16,041 15s. 6d. (B.M. Add. MSS. 28094, f. 54 ; letters of the Duchess to Danby, partly printed in *Hist. MSS. Com.*, ix. 2, pp. 450-1).

Sir John Robinson, in order to examine the building which he was erecting at Cliveden, near Maidenhead. Care was taken, however, that his departure from the Tower should not take place till six o'clock on the evening of June 22, so that he had to lie that night at his own house in the City. There he was almost certainly visited by the King, and a reconciliation was effected.[1]

Danby, however, was well served by his spies, and it is scarcely to be supposed that he was long in guessing what had occurred. Unfortunately the reappearance of Buckingham as a political force came at the most inopportune moment possible. Since the adjournment of May 28 Charles and James had been inclining more and more to look to France for help, and it had required all the Treasurer's vigilance to prevent undesirable developments in that direction. Having spent some days in drawing up a statement of revenue and expenditure, he insisted that if the meeting of Parliament was to be postponed, as the French desired, until the spring of the following year, a subsidy of at least £200,000 would be absolutely necessary. This sum, as he had probably hoped, was found to be more than the French were prepared to give, and the whole negotiation came temporarily to a standstill.[2]

But the project of an advantageous agreement with France, when presented from another quarter, proved less easy to ward off. About the middle of June Ralph Montagu, becoming tired of waiting, and guessing fairly accurately no doubt what had happened to his earlier letter, tried to force Danby's hand by writing direct to the King, explaining once more the ease with which a large subsidy could be extorted from France, and making a definite offer to procure, in addition to the existing subsidy, a million livres a year while the war should last and four millions six months after the conclusion of peace. All he desired was that the King would send him a note authorising him to embark upon his undertaking, and that thereafter the

---

[1] Burghclere, *Buckingham*, pp. 324-9, and the authorities there quoted ; *Cal. S.P. Dom.*, 1677-8, p. 205.

[2] *Mignet*, iv. 476-98. Louis XIV and the French ambassador were much annoyed at Danby's attitude to the negotiation, which they were convinced it was his object to wreck. The demand he put forward amounted practically to doubling the existing French subsidy.

matter might be entrusted to the care of the Treasurer. On July 1, accordingly, the King handed the letter to Danby and desired his opinion upon it.[1]

It was at this point that Danby made his fatal mistake. Hitherto he had avoided all direct participation in the intrigues with France, and had pursued a policy which, if not always of the most exalted type, had on the whole been consistent, and such as the majority of his fellow countrymen would have approved. His best course now would unquestionably have been to adopt the same attitude as in the previous year, refuse to take any personal part in the negotiation, and allow the King, if he persisted, to manage it himself through Montagu or through some other agent. But he had come so near complete success that he hoped a little humouring of Charles's weaknesses might bring him finally over to his views, while at the same time, with a vague danger from Buckingham looming on the horizon, he feared that too stubborn an attitude might involve the complete repudiation of his schemes, if not his own dismissal from office.[2]

Even so, the struggle was a sharp one. Although haste was imperative, if any supply was to be obtained from the French before the close of the campaigning season rendered them indifferent to the policy pursued by England, a week elapsed before Danby, at the King's command, drafted a letter to Montagu approving of his suggestions. For yet another week the affair remained at a standstill while the Treasurer lay in real or pretended sickness in Sir William Temple's house at Sheen, hoping against hope that Temple would arrive in time to give him his advice and assistance. Some decision, however, had to be reached before the day to which Parliament stood adjourned, and on July 15 Temple had not arrived.[3] That

---

[1] The letter, dated Paris, June 21, 1677, is printed *infra*, ii. 265-8.

[2] " It begins now to be taken for graunted here that a white staff will not long support a great officer, Sir William Coventry talkt of for the Treasury, that my Lord Roberts must have his seale again, and that my Lord Bridgewater, Mr. Pierpoint and some other will be sodainly of the caball " (Charles Godolphin to Sir William Godolphin, London, July 11, 1677, B.M. Add. MSS. 28052, f. 87). This almost suggests that rumours of Buckingham's return to favour were becoming common property.

[3] He left the Brill on July 14/24 (*Cal. S.P. Dom.*, 1677-8, p. 251), but it is not quite clear when he reached London.

evening, accordingly, Danby reluctantly completed his letter, and sent it off to Montagu by express. An additional subsidy of a million livres during the war and four millions after the conclusion of peace would, he informed him, be welcomed by the King, but the additional million alone would not be sufficient, and unless the four millions after the peace could be guaranteed, a total subsidy of £200,000 a year during the war would be absolutely necessary.[1] Three days later Charles himself wrote confirming what his Treasurer had said.[2]

A decision in favour of France meant a decision against Parliament, and on July 16 the House of Commons was adjourned by the Speaker to December 3 amidst scenes of disorder similar to those which had characterised the adjournment of May 28.[3] A few hours later Danby dispatched to Montagu a personal letter which offers a startling contrast with his official note of the previous day. In the plainest possible language he declared his satisfaction that Chiffinch was to be the receiver of any subsidies obtained, and his desire to have nothing to do with France except in the way of hostility. So little faith had he in French promises that he expected " the noise rather then the benefitt of theire money." He would be greatly obliged if Montagu would send him some illustrations of the way in which France neglected the interests of England in order that he might use them to influence the attitude of the King.[4]

There is no doubt whatever that this second letter represents Danby's real sentiments, and its bitter tone may perhaps be accounted for by his consciousness that the French intrigue had seriously jeopardised the chances of his own projected agreement with William of Orange. If so, his fears were soon justified. Coventry suddenly discovered that he did not wish to part with his place after all, unless he were given permission to recom-

---

[1] The letter is printed *infra*, ii. 269.

[2] *Infra*, ii. 273. In the light of later events it is difficult to avoid a suspicion that Montagu had been deliberately angling for these written authorisations from the King and Danby with the object of using them, if necessary, to shield himself, or even employing them for purposes of blackmail.

[3] *Cal. S.P. Dom.*, 1677-8, p. 149 ; *Grey*, iv. 391 ; Marvell, *Poems and Letters*, ii. 198, 327-8.

[4] *Infra*, ii. 270-2.

mend his successor, and Temple, when he arrived, accordingly found little opposition to his expressed desire not to be made Secretary. An unlucky letter from William of Orange was made the excuse for arguing that his ideas were too different from those of the English King for a reconciliation to be possible, and Danby had to perform the melancholy task of writing to the Prince to inform him that Sir William Temple would not be sent over after all.[1]

The chagrin of the Treasurer at this collapse of his plans was made all the greater by his discovery that his complaisance regarding the French intrigue was not even going to safeguard him from Buckingham. Towards the close of July Salisbury and Wharton, upon making full submission, were finally discharged from their imprisonment, and at the same time Buckingham, on the ground of " a very dangerous distemper " which he had contracted by his confinement, was set at liberty for a month.[2] The Duke immediately took up residence in the Earl of Rochester's lodgings at Whitehall, was received by the King at a private supper in Chiffinch's lodgings, and on August 5 obtained a complete release, upon condition of his giving satisfaction to the Lords when Parliament should again meet. Rumour even declared that he was to be made Lord Steward, and eagerly anticipated the changes he might bring about at Court.[3]

News of what had occurred came as a terrible blow to Danby, and led to a dramatic scene, in which he declared to the Duke of York that it was impossible to serve a King who treated his faithful ministers in such a manner, and threatened to retire altogether from public life. With some difficulty James contrived to appease him, and the two then united in a determined effort to dissuade the King from the course on which he had embarked. For several days the battle raged, but in the end Buckingham was ordered to leave Whitehall, and immediately

---

[1] Danby to William of Orange, August 1, 1677, *infra*, ii. 393 ; Temple, *Works*, i. 449-50.

[2] *Cal. S.P. Dom.*, 1677-8, pp. 260-2, 274. From letters preserved among the Leeds MSS. (Packet 8) it is clear that Salisbury consulted Danby about the steps he took to secure his release, and was largely indebted to him for a favourable result.

[3] *Cal. S.P. Dom.*, 1677-8, pp. 290-2 ; Carte MSS. 79, f. 112.

afterwards the King set sail for Portsmouth on a fortnight's voyage of inspection among the seaports of the south.[1]

Danby's victory, however, was a purely superficial and temporary one. Buckingham remained excluded from the Court, but Charles had scarcely returned to London [2] when he was meeting him elsewhere as frequently as ever. September was marked by a series of entertainments at Nell Gwyn's house, where the mannerisms of Lady Danby were mimicked, to the great delight of the King. Events began to bear an ominous resemblance to those which had preceded the fall of Clarendon.[3] The Duke of York argued with Charles, the Lord Chancellor brought all his eloquence to bear, but without result. The King " would not deny himself an hour's divertisement for the sake of any man."[4]

Buckingham's complete failure as a constructive statesman should not be allowed to obscure his immense importance as a leader of opposition. His " peculiar faculty of turning all things into ridicule," [5] an effective weapon against any government, was doubly effective where a light-minded King and frivolous courtiers had as much influence as serious statesmen. His instability, fatal to him while in power, was scarcely even a handicap when his sole business was to criticise others. Contemporaries all bear witness to the " infinite credit " which he had with the Dissenters, the merchants, and the discontented of all classes. To Danby he was specially dangerous, for he knew all the Treasurer's personal weaknesses, and was inspired against him by a bitter resentment which he rarely showed towards anybody.

Danby's alarm, therefore, was by no means extravagant, and

[1] Marvell, *Poems and Letters*, ii. 328-9 ; Carte MSS. 79, f. 114 ; Clarke, *Life of James II*, i. 544-5.

[2] August 21 (B.M. Add. MSS. 28040, f. 38).

[3] The parallel, if pursued in detail, is surprisingly close, as was noticed at the time. Buckingham had returned from a similar disgrace and imprisonment in the Tower to bring about Clarendon's fall. He had done so mainly through his influence with the King and at Court, and against the wishes of the Duke of York. Danby, however, differed from Clarendon in being a man of the age in which he lived, and in having the support of the Duchess of Portsmouth.

[4] *Ormonde MSS., N.S.*, iv. 106, 376. Danby appears to have attempted a reconciliation with Nell Gwyn, but nothing came of it (*infra*, ii. 40).

[5] *Burnet*, i. 182.

it is scarcely surprising that with such a danger threatening him he felt quite unable to withdraw from the French intrigue, or even to offer any remonstrance against it. His sole object, in fact, came to be to make it as profitable as possible, and to that end he insisted unceasingly on the absolute necessity for a total subsidy of at least £200,000. Courtin, however, had no authority to promise so large a sum, and after a struggle with Danby which lasted for three days he persuaded the King and the Duke of York, in the Treasurer's absence, to be content with two million livres. In return Charles undertook not merely to adjourn Parliament, when the time came, from December 3 to the following April, but to make known immediately to the ambassadors of the Allies that it was his intention to do so.[1]

Meanwhile Montagu had been endeavouring to carry out the instructions which Danby had given him. His own original suggestion of a large subsidy after the conclusion of peace he had abandoned on the ground that it would be difficult to find any adequate security for the payment of it ; but he had every hope of obtaining £200,000 a year during the course of the war, and that too without making any definite promise about Parliament.[2] It came therefore as a shock to him to be informed by the French Secretary, Pomponne, that Charles had agreed to be content with two million livres, especially as he was assured that the agreement had been reached " de concert avec le Grand Tresorier." Not merely, he pointed out, was this sum considerably less than £200,000, but by their control of the exchanges the French would probably make it £12,000 less than it appeared to be.[3]

Montagu's remonstrance was apparently the first intimation which Danby received that any agreement had been concluded,[4] and he immediately took steps to retrieve the position.

[1] Courtin to Louis XIV, August 5, 1677, in *Dalrymple*, App. 112-4, and *Mignet*, iv. 499. The fact that Danby was not present at the decisive conferences is clearly brought out in Courtin's letter to Pomponne of August 19, 1677. Montagu later saw this letter and informed Danby of the admission (*infra*, ii. 292).

[2] Montagu to Danby, August 7, 1677, *infra*, ii. 274-6.

[3] Montagu to Danby, August 12, 12, and 30, 1677, *infra*, ii. 276-80, 282-3. Montagu apparently estimated two million livres as about £145,000 (*infra*, ii. 291).

[4] Danby to Montagu, August 10, 1677, *infra*, ii. 280-1.

The King and Duke of York being then on their voyage to the seaports of the south coast, he approached Courtin himself and argued that the two million livres must be considered as an addition to the sum of 100,000 crowns which had already been paid in accordance with the agreement of 1676. This contention the French ambassador refused to accept,[1] and when Charles and James returned they had to admit the justice of his attitude.[2] Danby then changed his ground, and insisted on his original statement that nothing short of £200,000 would be of any use. For this he had no difficulty in making out a good case, and the King admitted he had been somewhat careless in concluding his agreement ; but when the Duke of York failed to persuade Courtin to reconsider the matter, Charles refused to discuss it himself, and instructed Danby instead to order Montagu to press for the £200,000 at the French Court.[3]

Thus Courtin handed over his embassy to his successor, Barillon, and returned to France under the impression that all was settled, only to find when he arrived there that Montagu had reopened the whole question. The English ambassador showed considerable dexterity in excusing his master's rather shifty conduct, and never entertained any doubt of his ability to obtain the sum required ; but it was not to his interest to take the negotiation into his own hands, and it was very probably at his suggestion that it was remitted for final settlement to England.[4] There Barillon did his best to keep the King to his word, but Charles, with the desperate resolution of a weak man caught in an untenable position, refused even to listen to him, insisted he must speak to the Treasurer, and in the end practically hustled him out of his presence.[5] Danby apparently went so far as to offer to split the difference with him ;[6] but before any final agreement could be reached on the disputed point the whole question of the French subsidy had been

---

[1] Courtin to Pomponne, August 19, 1677. This dispatch gives a useful survey of the whole affair from the French standpoint.

[2] *Mignet*, iv. 501.

[3] Danby to Montagu, September 3/13, 1677, *infra*, ii. 284-5.

[4] Montagu's letters to the King and to Danby, September 25, October 12, 1677 (*infra*, ii. 286-97).

[5] Barillon to Louis XIV, October 4, 1677, in *Dalrymple*, App. 114-6.

[6] *Mignet*, iv. 519.

swallowed up in a much wider issue which was soon to absorb all attention.

The year which had opened with such bright prospects for the success of the Treasurer's policy thus drew to a close in an atmosphere of dubiety or even of gloom ; but for Danby as an individual the same year had been a brilliant one indeed. On March 24 his services to the Crown had been recognised by his election as Knight of the Garter in place of the deceased Earl of Bristol,[1] and on April 19 he and his old friend Lord Ogle, now Duke of Newcastle, were installed together at Windsor with great splendour.[2] Early in the summer arrangements were concluded for the most distinguished alliance which he had yet attempted, and on June 25 his youngest surviving daughter, Sophia, then only twelve years of age, was married to Donatus, son of Henry, Lord O'Brien, and grandson of the Earl of Thomond, who could claim kinship with the King himself.[3] For twelve days after the ceremony one festivity followed another, in which the Treasurer himself did not disdain to take part, dancing country-dances with Secretary Williamson till five o'clock in the morning.[4] Later in the year Danby

---

[1] *Essex Papers*, ii. 112 ; Marvell, *Poems and Letters*, ii. 185. The honour must have been doubly gratifying to him if Schwerin's statement is correct, that the first vacant stall had been promised to Arlington's son-in-law, the Duke of Grafton (*Briefe aus England*, p. 117).

[2] " Duty, curiosity and friendship brought 150 coaches thither " (*Essex Papers*, ii. 122). According to Reresby no fewer than 46 coaches attended the Lord Treasurer alone (*Memoirs*, p. 117). A bill for work done at the installation, showing a total of £47 5s. 8d., is preserved among the Leeds MSS. (Packet 8). Buckingham wrote a bitter invective against Danby on the occasion. St. George, presented with the two new knights, lets Newcastle pass " for his father's sake,"

> " But whisper'd thus in pale Sir Os——n's ear,
> Away thou worthless rogue, what makes thee here."

The main point of the verses is Danby's physical appearance, but there is a reference also to his " base ingratitude," and to his alleged subjection to his wife,

> " the Treasuress,
> Who, though my Lord to govern things may boast,
> Does with her honour's prudence rule the roast "
>   (*Works*, ed. 1775, ii. 164).

[3] Stowe MSS. 212, f. 212 ; *Cal. S.P. Dom.*, 1677-8, p. 217. On May 26, 1679, the marriage was celebrated a second time (*Ormonde MSS.*, N.S., v. 116).

[4] Courtin to Pomponne, July 15, 1677. It is curious to find Courtin wondering what French people would say if they saw Pomponne and Colbert behaving in the same indecorous manner.

entered into occupation of the town residence which he had for some months been building at the Cockpit, near St. James's Park,[1] and also satisfied his ambition, common in the official world, to have a country seat near London, by purchasing Wimbledon House, in Surrey, where he was to spend a great part of his time for the rest of his life.[2]

Danby's only personal disappointment, in fact, was connected with Lord Dumblane. The legal proceedings concerning Bridget Hyde still dragged on, and for some time the whole position had been rendered more complicated by the very equivocal course pursued by Sir Robert Viner. While he had much to gain from the Treasurer in the shape of favourable treatment for his own vast claims on the Government, Viner could also hope by agreement with the Emertons to secure for himself or his son Charles some share of the Hyde estates. Lady Viner had kept all her relatives in mind, and had provided that in the event of her daughter being without legitimate issue part of her estate should go to her nephew William, the elder brother of John Emerton, and part to her husband.[3] On this basis Viner had come to some composition with the Emertons as early as April 1675,[4] and since then he had purchased a further share in the reversion of the Hyde property. His ambition appeared to be to maintain a foot in both camps, and in that case it was of the first importance that proper provision from some other source should be found for Dumblane.

In September 1677, accordingly, Danby revived the scheme he had first meditated nearly three years earlier, and delivered his long-expected attack upon Sir Robert Howard, formally accusing

---

[1] The grant of the Cockpit to him was made in February 1676. Repairs to existing buildings and additions to them were expected to cost about £1,600, and actually cost £1,856 5s. 4½d. The Treasurer removed from Wallingford House to his new home before October 1677 (*Cal. Treas. Books*, v. 135-6, 1152 ; Carte MSS. 79, f. 130).

[2] The negotiations occupied some months, but were apparently concluded about the end of July. The Treasurer paid the Earl of Bristol either £11,000 or £12,000 for his purchase, and took Evelyn's advice about the altera ions he should make (B.M. Add. MSS. 29577, ff. 159, 161 ; Carte MSS. 79, f. 114 ; *Savile Correspondence*, p. 66 ; *Evelyn*, December 20, 1677, February 18, 1678).

[3] B.M. Add. MSS. 28042, f. 88.

[4] Marvell, *Poems and Letters*, ii. 146.

him in Council of conniving at the misuse of Government funds by the Tellers of the Exchequer, employing his knowledge of their irregularities to compel them to lend him money, and trying to defeat an investigation by exhibiting false bags, in which were lead blanks or pieces of iron with only a little silver on top. The charge appears to have been substantially true, and the best Howard could do in his defence was to interpose one delay after another. Serious doubt was entertained, however, whether he could be proved guilty of any legal offence, and when his case was finally settled in Council on November 9 he was allowed to escape with a severe reprimand.[1] Charles declared his great satisfaction with the vigilance exercised by Danby, and required Howard to make his submission to him ; but all prospect of an early promotion for Dumblane had to be abandoned.[2]

[1] P.C. Reg. 66, pp. 109, 120-3, 158 ; Carte MSS. 79, ff. 126, 128, 139, 142 ; *Cal. S.P. Dom.*, 1677-8, pp. 368, 448 ; *Ormonde MSS., N.S.*, iv. 377, 383-4, 386. The Teller primarily involved appears to have been Sir William Doyley, who himself gave evidence against Howard (*Cal. Treas. Books*, v. 306, 788 ; *Leeds MSS.*, pp. 13-14).

[2] As Dumblane was not yet eighteen years of age it is scarcely to be supposed that Danby intended him actually to take over the functions of Auditor of the Exchequer. An odd note to Danby's memoranda of the previous June (*infra*, ii. 69) suggests that the post was to have been given, probably temporarily, to Sir Philip Warwick.

CHAPTER XII

A GAMBLER'S THROW, 1677-8

LOOKING back from the vantage point of two years later the Duke of York noted the restoration of Buckingham to favour as the first event which seriously shook Danby's confidence, and inclined him to devote more attention to securing his own safety than to advancing the interests of the King and the Government.[1] This criticism, however, just fails to meet the case. Danby certainly was badly shaken, and it can scarcely be denied that in the end he allowed selfish anxieties to blind his vision and warp his judgment. But the immediate effect of Buckingham's reappearance was rather to inspire him to stake everything on one last great effort. The closing months of 1677 were to witness the most resolute and comprehensive attempt which he had yet made to secure the permanent adoption of a Protestant and anti-French policy with himself in control.

Hitherto the chief obstacle to his success had been, not popular opposition to his political principles, nor even the personal jealousy and animosity which he had inspired in so many of his rivals, but general distrust of the master whom he served and the heir presumptive with whom he was in alliance. Few believed that Charles really supported Danby's policy, or would lend it his countenance any longer than he found convenient. Nobody imagined that James, if he succeeded to the throne, would fail to reverse it at the earliest possible moment. Thus there was a widespread disinclination to accept the Treasurer's projects at their face value, lest they should prove to be only a screen behind which the royal brothers were meditating something entirely different.

[1] Clarke, *Life of James II*, i. 544-6 ; *Morrison Catalogue*, iii. 118.

By the middle of 1677 Danby had exhausted every possible means of dispelling this suspicion, with one exception. The marriage of James's elder daughter, Mary, to her cousin William of Orange would, it was generally recognised, be a declaration on the part of the English King in favour of Protestantism and against France which it would be impossible to belittle or ignore, while at the same time it would hold out a fair prospect that even if the Duke of York succeeded to the throne he would himself be succeeded in due course by a Protestant line of sovereigns who might be expected to remedy anything he had done amiss. But in spite of these attractions Danby had long hesitated to take the marriage into serious consideration. It was a rock on which not a few of his predecessors had wrecked their careers. The mere suggestion of it, he feared, would alienate the Duke of York, while he doubted very much his capacity to make it acceptable even to the King. It was bound also to involve England in the whirlpool of European politics in ways which he could not foresee and would have preferred to avoid.

Such considerations as these probably explain Danby's attitude to the question of the marriage during 1676. In April of that year the Prince of Orange consulted Sir William Temple, and as a result of his representations entrusted Lady Temple, who was going over to England, with letters to Charles and James, asking leave to come over after the close of the campaign and discuss the marriage with them.[1] Danby alone among the ministers was honoured by being informed of the design, and was requested to furnish information which might help it forward ;[2] yet he appears to have taken no active part in it, and the reply eventually sent to William was not favourable.[3] Again in the autumn there were incessant rumours of an intended marriage, and the French ambassador deemed it pru-

---

[1] Temple, *Works*, i. 415-6.

[2] Temple to Danby, April 23, 1676, and the " remarkes " of the Duke of Leeds (*infra*, ii. 477-8, 516). The statement made by the Duke of Leeds that he alone was entrusted with the secret, to the exclusion even of the King, is entirely erroneous. Not only did William write to both Charles and James, but Temple did so too (*Works*, ii. 395-6).

[3] Temple to the Prince of Orange, May 29, 1676, *ibid.*, p. 410 ; *Mignet*, iv. 503-4.

dent to keep a watchful eye on the movements of Lady Temple,
" une femme d'intrigue," of whose activities as intermediary
between the Prince and the King he had received some intimation from the Duke of York.[1] But whatever he might suspect,
he saw no reason for associating Danby with it. Even in June
1677, when the Treasurer was doing all he could to assist
Bentinck's mission and establish a good understanding between
Charles and William, he appears to have mentioned the marriage only as a tentative suggestion, which he had little hope
would be approved.[2]

During August, however, as his position at Court became
less assured, Danby began to consider the desirability of playing
his last and in some ways his highest card. Charles was anxious
for the establishment of a general peace in Europe, and could
be deluded with the hope that the proposed marriage would
induce William to moderate his terms and enter more readily
into negotiations for a settlement. James knew quite well the
dangerous position in which he had placed himself by his open
profession of Catholicism, and could be persuaded that the
marriage of his daughter to a Protestant was the only means by
which he could reassure the nation and safeguard himself.
Both Charles and James were aware of William's connection
with the English opposition, and realised the advantages they
might derive from breaking that connection and attaching him
to the interests of the Crown.

To what extent Danby put forward these considerations at
this early date cannot well be determined, but he succeeded at
least in persuading Charles to reopen negotiations with the
Prince of Orange. The failure of the English King to send the
promised envoy to Holland in July had to a large extent destroyed the effect of Bentinck's mission. At the very end of
August, accordingly, Laurence Hyde, on his way back to
Nimeguen, was instructed to wait upon the Prince and repeat
the assurance originally given him of Charles's readiness to

[1] Courtin to Louis XIV, November 16, 1676. The French dispatches at this
time are full of apprehensions concerning the marriage.

[2] *Infra*, ii. 516. The Duke of Leeds gives the date as May, which, if it has
any significance at all, suggests that he mentioned the marriage before the
actual arrival of Bentinck.

receive him in England in the autumn.[1] William immediately
made all needful preparations,[2] embarked at the Brill on a
yacht sent to bring him over, landed at Harwich on October 9,
and drove the same day to Newmarket, where the Court was
engaged in the customary autumn diversions.[3]

News of his coming had caused " great alarmings everywhere ; " but it is clear that nobody really knew what to make
of it. The French ambassador naturally connected it with
Bentinck's visit, and feared that William's real object was to
secure the hand of the Princess Mary ; but Charles and James
succeeded in convincing him that even if they were prepared to
consider the marriage they were determined it should be carried
through in such a way as to safeguard the interests of France.[4]
The ambassadors of the Allies, on the other hand, were afraid
that the Prince was seeking his own advantage at the expense
of his associates, and the English malcontents agreed so far as to
declare that the whole project was " a thing of the French
King's making." Meanwhile so well placed an observer as
Secretary Coventry wondered whether it might not end, after
all the commotion, in a " bare visit," and believed that if so
" it would have ill consequences." [5]

Danby, however, knew quite well what course he intended to
pursue. At the very outset he received an unexpected check
from the pretensions of his old rival Arlington, who still claimed
to be the chief representative of Dutch interests at the English
Court, met the Prince as he stepped from his coach, and

---

[1] Danby to the Prince of Orange, Danby to Bentinck, August 27, 1677,
infra, ii. 396. That the proposal on which William finally acted came from
England, and not from Holland, is confirmed by a conversation between the
Duke of York and the French ambassador. " Jusques là M. le Duc d'York
ne m'avoit pas dit que la proposition de ce voyage vint du Roy d'Angleterre "
(Barillon to Louis XIV, September 27, 1677).

[2] William of Orange to Danby, Bentinck to Danby, September 18, 1677,
infra, ii. 397.

[3] *Cal. S.P. Dom.*, 1677-8, pp. 381, 384, 391 ; B.M. Add. MSS. 28040, f. 39
Ormonde MSS., N.S., iv. 53 ; Temple, *Works*, i. 454.

[4] Barillon knew that William was coming over at least as early as Septem·
ber 11, and constantly thereafter discussed the matter with Charles and James.
Charles assured him, " Je ne me laisseray pas tromper par mon nepveu ;
j'espere plustost luy faire faire ce que je crois advantageux." Barillon, however, could see no sign that even the Duke of York had any aversion to the
marriage (Barillon to Louis XIV, September 23, 27, 30, 1677).

[5] *Ormonde MSS.*, N.S., iv. 48, 376.

endeavoured to monopolise him thereafter.[1] But William had
no faith whatever in Arlington, and at his very first meeting
with the Treasurer, a chance encounter on the stairs, contrived
in a few whispered words to strike up a firm alliance with him.[2]
Temple acted as a useful intermediary, and thus the whole
conduct of the ensuing negotiations rested in the hands of
Charles, James, William, Danby and Temple.[3] Of these five
the three last wished to proceed at once to the question of the
marriage ; but Charles and James, true to their promises to
France, insisted that the terms of peace must first be settled,
and especially after the return of the Court to London on
October 13 several days were spent in rather aimless discussions
to that end. Meanwhile William became more and more restive,
until on October 17 he made a formal request to the Duke of
York for the hand of the Princess Mary, only to have it evaded
on the same ground as his earlier hints.[4]

In this " punctilio," as Temple strangely calls it, lay the
real crux of the whole affair. If the peace were first considered,
William during the negotiations would be in a weak position,
he would have to be content with unsatisfactory terms for his
people and his Allies, and would lay himself open to the charge
that he had sacrificed others in order to obtain an alliance with
the English royal house for himself. If, on the other hand, the
marriage were first concluded, he might hope, with the assistance
of his uncles, to obtain better terms of peace, and in any case
could not so readily be accused of having been bought over. The
one course would imply his subordination to the English King,
the other his alliance with, or even ascendancy over him. William
accordingly took up a resolute attitude, and declared that unless
the King altered his mind he would return home in two days.

---

[1] Arlington had a considerable initial advantage, for his duties as Lord
Chamberlain brought him into close personal touch with the Prince, while his
possession of Euston Hall, near Newmarket, enabled him to entertain him as
a guest (*Ormonde MSS.*, *N.S.*, iv. 53 ; Danby to Lady Danby, October 11,
1677, *infra*, ii. 40-1). The Duke of York, however, strongly supported Danby,
although he believed, curiously enough, that Arlington would prevail. His
principal objection to the Chamberlain was that he was " un homme timide et
incertain, qui tremble toujours " (Barillon to Louis XIV, October 25, 1677).

[2] Temple, *Works*, i. 454.

[3] *Ormonde MSS.*, *N.S.*, iv. 381.

[4] Barillon to Louis XIV, October 28, 1677, in *Mignet*, iv. 508-9.

Charles always disliked a crisis, and by bringing matters to a head in this way the Prince gave Danby his opportunity. In the strongest possible language the Treasurer pointed out the evils which would follow both at home and abroad if William went away dissatisfied, without accomplishing anything. At the same time he reiterated all the arguments he had formerly brought forward in favour of the marriage, especially the effect it would have in allaying discontent at home. His representations were ably seconded by Sir William Temple, and proved sufficient to convince Charles.[1] Early on October 21 the King informed the Duke of York of his resolution to conclude the match at once, and obtained his consent all the more readily perhaps because the Duchess of York was then expecting a child, who, if a boy, would come before Mary in the succession.[2] In the afternoon Mary herself was informed, in the evening the Cabinet Council, and on the following day the Privy Council. The effect was instantaneous. Congratulations poured in from every quarter. The whole night of October 22-23 was spent in London " in ringing of bells and bonfires, and the greatest expressions of joy " manifested since the Restoration.[3] Arlington and the French ambassador alone appeared displeased, the one because it destroyed completely his pretence of being in the special confidence of the Prince, the other because he had assured his master to the very last that the marriage would not be arranged before the peace settlement.[4] Meanwhile in France Louis XIV received the news " as he would have done the loss of an army." [5]

[1] Temple takes the whole credit of the King's change of front to himself (*Works*, i. 454-5). Montagu, who was still abroad at the time, gives it entirely to Danby (*Burnet*, ii. 129-32). The matter is not of very great consequence, as Temple and Danby were certainly working together, but the fairest conclusion seems to be that Temple completed what Danby had begun.

[2] The importance of this point was fully recognised at the time. At the marriage ceremony itself the King " desired that the Bishop of London would make haste, lest his sister should bee delivered of a son, and so the marriage be disappointed " (*Diary of Dr. Edward Lake*, p. 6).

[3] *Hatton Correspondence*, i. 151-3 ; Carte MSS. 79, f. 136 ; 243, f. 313 ; *Ormonde MSS., N.S.*, iv. 54 ; Clarke, *Life of James II*, i. 508-10.

[4] Temple, *Works*, i. 455. " Monsieur le Duc d'York me dit . . . que je pouvois asseurer vostre Majesté qu'il ne seroit point question du mariage de Madame la Princesse Marie avant que la paix ne fust conclue, et qu'il ne feroit rien que de concert et par l'avis de vostre Majesté " (Barillon to Louis XIV October 30, 1677, the day before the marriage was announced).

[5] *Burnet*, ii. 132.

For the moment Danby's triumph was complete. His attempt to identify the Prince still more closely with his wife's countrymen by securing for him an English peerage was, it is true, defeated by the opposition of Catholic interests, but no report of this spread abroad at the time.[1] To all appearance the general reconciliation so long aimed at had been accomplished. Even the Duke of York had gained a temporary popularity by his ungrudging acquiescence in the marriage and his straightforward declaration in Council that he hoped by means of it to satisfy the nation that his religion was a purely private affair. As the creator of the new atmosphere the Treasurer enjoyed unbounded prestige. When the marriage was privately celebrated, by his ally the Bishop of London, on the Prince's birthday, November 4, he was one of the three English nobles summoned to be present.[2] A round of festivities followed, and the last and most sumptuous of these, previous to the great Court ball from which the happy pair were to take their departure, was given at Wimbledon House.[3] The relations between Danby and the Prince assumed a new character, with results of immense importance in later years. Hitherto they

---

[1] *Clarendon Correspondence*, ii. 222.

[2] The others were the Duke of Albemarle and the Earl of Ossory (*Hatton Correspondence*, i. 154). The private character of the ceremony, however, was not altogether intentional. Immediately after the marriage had been arranged William dispatched a messenger to Holland to announce the coming event to the States and bring back the family jewels. In anticipation of the messenger's return by that time the ceremony was fixed for November 4, but owing to his movements having been delayed the date was altered to November 14. On the evening of November 3, however, the Dutch post came in with news which made the King alter his resolution, and the marriage was hurriedly arranged for November 4 after all, " so suddenly and privately that the Dutch ambassadors themselves knew nothing of it till it was over." William's messenger returned the next day with the jewels, which were presented to Mary (Carte MSS. 79, ff. 136, 138, 140). It was noted, as symptomatic of the real situation, that when the Bishop of London asked the formal question, " Who gives this woman to this man," it was the King who replied, " I do " (Schwerin, *Briefe aus England*, p. 163).

[3] The entertainment at Wimbledon House was on November 14 (Carte MSS. 79, f. 143). The following day, being the Queen's birthday, was set apart for the ball, at which the Princess took her leave of her relatives about eight o'clock in the evening. Easterly winds, however, prevented the Prince and Princess from actually setting out till November 19, and even then the weather was so troublesome that they did not reach Holland till November 29 (*Diary of Dr. Edward Lake*, pp. 9-12 ; *Hatton Correspondence*, i. 157-8 ; B.M. Add. MSS. 28040, ff. 40-1 ; Carte MSS. 243, f. 274).

had been distant acquaintances, united only by a community of ideals the extent of which they did not themselves appreciate. Now, at the desire of the Prince, all ceremony was abandoned between them, and they became, if never perhaps intimate friends, at least unswerving allies. Again and again during the course of his journey back to Holland, and after his arrival there, William insisted on his deep sense of the obligation under which he lay to Danby, an obligation which he never perhaps entirely forgot.[1]

None knew better than Danby himself, however, that permanent success had not yet been won. Even before the marriage was announced there were not wanting those who declared that William of Orange was really a papist and an emissary of France.[2] In the midst of the enthusiasm roused by the engagement, a discordant note was struck by the King's announcement that Parliament was to be adjourned from December 3 to April 4.[3] The effect of the marriage itself was partly discounted by the birth, just three days later, of a son to the Duke of York.[4] Discontented people could find just sufficient ground for casting suspicion on the policy of the Government, and as early as November 3 some of the members of the parliamentary opposition were applying to Barillon for assistance to obstruct it.[5]

[1] William of Orange to Danby, November 23/December 3, November 26, November 28/December 8, December 10, 1677, *infra*, ii. 398-401.

[2] " Your Lordship would wonder more if you were here to see how coldly our malecontents looke upon and how malitiously they speake of that Prince. The whole may be wound upp in this short character, that he is a papist, and will certaynly declare himselfe to be soe whenever the French King shall give him his directions for that purpose. At his coming to Whitehall he saluted the Queene, and there is a great remarque upon that by way of confirmation of the other character " (Richard Langhorne to Lord Hatton, October 16, 1677, in B.M. Add. MSS. 29556, f. 243).

[3] The decision to postpone the meeting of Parliament was taken as early as October 23 (Carte MSS. 243, f. 314), and declared in Council on October 26 (P.C. Reg. 66, p. 152 ; *Cal. S.P. Dom.*, 1677-8, p. 422). The object of the King was probably to conciliate Louis XIV, whom he was trying to convince that the marriage was not really contrary to his interests ; and although the postponement was only part of the bargain made with France in the autumn, Barillon thought it advisable, in the altered circumstances, to give special thanks for it (Barillon to Louis XIV, November 4, 1677). In accepting the King's decision Danby's idea was probably to retain the French subsidy as long as possible.

[4] Charles, Duke of Cambridge, who died on December 12 following. William of Orange himself stood godfather along with the King (*Diary of Dr. Edward Lake*, pp. 6-7, 14).

[5] *Dalrymple*, App. 129-30 ; *Mignet*, iv. 521.

The marriage, in fact, was bound in the end to be judged by its fruits. Taken by itself it could still be interpreted as implying merely that William of Orange had been bribed into throwing in his lot with the Court. To show beyond possibility of dispute that it was the Court which had taken the side of William of Orange, it was essential that favourable terms of peace should be secured for the Dutch, and that pressure, if necessary, should be brought to bear on France to that end. It was here that Danby completed his triple triumph. Having first persuaded Charles to invite William to England, and then induced him to agree to the marriage before peace was concluded, he now summoned the Prince and Temple to his assistance, and in the interval between the marriage and the departure of William for Holland prevailed with the King to sanction terms of peace much more advantageous to the Allies than the military situation warranted.[1] With these Lord Feversham was dispatched to Paris, authorised to insist on unconditional acceptance or rejection within two days.[2]

On December 1 Feversham was back in England with what amounted to a rejection of the proposed terms,[3] and at a meeting on the following day of the committee for foreign affairs more strenuous measures were determined upon. The adjournment of Parliament was to be shortened, and Ralph Montagu, who had just returned home for a brief visit, was to be sent to France to press more vigorously the same demands as had been entrusted to Feversham. On December 3, accordingly, when the Houses met, they were required to adjourn only to January

---

[1] The only sphere of war in which the English were much interested was the Netherlands. There France was to retain Franche-Comté, Aire, St. Omer, and Cambray, but to restore Maastricht to Holland, and Charleroi, Ath, Tournay, Oudenarde, Courtray, Valenciennes and Condé to Spain (Louis XIV to Barillon, November 30, 1677, in *Mignet*, iv. 516).

[2] Danby expressed his readiness to carry the terms of peace to France himself, and considered that the only alternative messenger was Temple. The latter was decided upon, but was almost immediately replaced by Feversham, whom Charles and James believed less likely to prove obnoxious to Louis (Temple, *Works*, i. 455-6).

[3] Louis was prepared to restore Maastricht, Charleroi, Ath and Oudenarde, but declared he could not answer it to his own kingdom if he gave more (Danby's copy of Williamson's diary in B.M. Add. MSS. 28040, f. 41).

15,[1] and four days later Montagu hurriedly left for France, accompanied by Lord Dumblane, who was to be instructed by him in the art of diplomacy and possibly exercise some supervision, in Danby's interest, over his conduct.[2] At the same time preparations were made for raising troops, strengthening the navy, and improving fortifications, with a view to a possible war.[3] The English forces in France were hastily recalled, and tacit permission was given to English subjects to enter the service of the States.[4] Even the Duke of York began to adopt a bellicose attitude.[5]

Unfortunately, as Danby was to find to his cost, it was easier to effect a breach with France than to bring about any satisfactory agreement with the Allies. On November 13 Laurence Hyde, who had continued at Nimeguen since September, had been given permission, as uncle of the Princess Mary, to pay his respects to the newly married pair on their arrival in Holland.[6] Advantage was now taken of his presence at the Hague to make him the channel of a proposal to the Prince that if the United Provinces would join with the King to oblige Spain, the King would join with them to oblige France to

---

[1] *L.J.*, xiii. 128 ; *C.J.*, ix. 426 ; *Ormonde MSS., N.S.*, iv. 387-8. A proclamation intimating the new date of meeting was approved in Council on December 7 (P.C. Reg. 66, p. 175 ; *Cal. S.P. Dom.*, 1677-8, p. 497). The fact that the adjournment was for a much shorter period than was originally intended induced the Commons to accept it without serious opposition, but even so there were signs of discontent. " As soone as this [the King's] message was read Mr. Sacheverill stood up to have spoke something to the House ; but the Speaker, spying him, immediately (without putting the question) declared that according to his Majesties pleasure the House was adjourned to the 15th of January next, and soe left the chaire. Tis said that as the Speaker was goeing out of the House Sir Francis Rolles said to him, Well, Sir, for all this we shall putt you out of the chaire when wee meet " (B.M. Add. MSS. 32095, f. 52).

[2] Carte MSS. 79, ff. 148, 154 ; Montagu to Danby, December 27, 1677, *infra*, ii. 299.

[3] *Cal. S.P. Dom.*, 1677-8, pp. 516-8 ; B.M. Add. MSS. 10115, f. 1 *et seq* ; *Mignet*, iv. 529.

[4] *Infra*, ii. 411. Louis XIV replied that he was entitled to keep the troops until thirty days after an actual declaration of war between England and France, and did everything he could to postpone their departure from the country.

[5] Danby assures William of this in almost every letter at this time (*infra*, ii. 399-410 *passim*).

[6] B.M. Add. MSS. 28040, f. 40.

accept the conditions originally laid down.[1] This was precisely the agreement which William himself had repeatedly advocated while he was in England,[2] and he accordingly made no difficulty about accepting it ; but it is significant that both he and Charles insisted that their mutual engagement must as yet remain a secret, not merely from the French and the Confederates, but even from the States themselves.

So unsubstantial an agreement, even if it could be divulged when Parliament met, would certainly do little to satisfy the thirst of that body for treaties of alliance, and on December 15, accordingly, the committee for foreign affairs drew up a project for a formal offensive league, based on the same principles, between England and Holland.[3] Danby, whose ideas of foreign policy were still very much those of the average country gentleman, was unquestionably aiming at a revival of the Triple Alliance, the mere name of which carried immense weight in England ; and for the actual work of negotiation he was equally unquestionably looking to the author of that alliance, Sir William Temple. But Temple with some asperity pointed out that the day of the Triple Alliance was past,[4] argued that what was wanted was a league with all the Confederates, and finally, on the pretence of urgent private business, begged to be excused from having anything to do with the matter. After some delay, in consequence, instructions had to be sent by Henry Thynne to Laurence Hyde,[5] whose conduct of the negotiation was not altogether fortunate. On the last day of the year the treaty was signed, but with alterations which proved so objectionable to the English Government that it was sent back to the Hague for reconsideration, and not re-signed until

---

[1] Williamson to Hyde, December 4, 1677, *infra*, ii. 571-3.

[2] Danby to the Prince of Orange, December 4, 1677, *infra*, ii. 402-4.

[3] C. L. Grose, " The Anglo-Dutch Alliance of 1678," in *E.H.R.*, xxxix. 354.

[4] " That being a great original, of which this seem'd but an ill copy (Temple, *Works*, i. 457).

[5] Danby to the Prince of Orange, December 24, 1677, *infra*, ii. 406-8. The main purport of the instructions is clearly set forth by Danby—" to gett some such thing perfected as may justify the King to say truly to his Parliament that an alliance is already made betwixt his Majestie and Holland for the preservation of Flanders." Williamson in a letter to Hyde describes the alliance as " the foundation all the King's businesse at this time in the Parliament must rest upon " (B.M. Add. MSS. 10115, f. 187).

January 16. Even then it was not quite what was desired,[1] but Charles was content to accept it on January 21, although the formal ratification did not take place till nearly a month later.[2]

This offensive treaty, however, was intended to be only part of a general settlement with Holland, and at the same time as it was remitted for reconsideration a project for a permanent defensive treaty was drawn up and dispatched with it.[3] Unfortunately there were still too many points in dispute between England and Holland for a general settlement to be an easy matter, and after negotiations lasting many weeks the defensive treaty fell through.   Meanwhile the problem had been raised of co-operation between England and the Allies in the event of war.   The chief desire of the English Government was to secure a base of operations in Flanders, and the most suitable port appeared to be Ostend, which was itself in grave danger from the French.   The Spanish habit of procrastination, however, combined with a fear that the English occupation might prove permanent, put endless obstacles in the way, and although the cession of Ostend was suggested as early as the beginning of December, it was the end of February before the first English contingent, under Lord Howard of Escrick, was allowed to land there.[4]

These delays and uncertainties gave the French their opportunity.   So completely had the change in England's attitude taken them by surprise that a resolute pursuit of the advantage gained might have found them seriously at a loss.   But a very short time enabled them to recover.   Even when dealing with Feversham, who was under precise orders, they had endea-

[1] Hyde apologised to Danby and explained the difficulties with which he had had to contend in a letter of January 16/26, 1678, printed *infra*, ii. 573.

[2] B.M. Add. MSS. 28040, ff. 43-8 *passim*.

[3] " Itt. will bee of use in the Parliament to lett them know that such a treaty is made as well as the present treaty of alliance " (Danby to William of Orange, January 8/18, 1678, *infra*, ii. 410-2.

[4] Danby to William of Orange, January 8, 9, 23, February 8, 1678, *infra*, ii. 410-9 *passim*.   Monmouth, who was in supreme command of the English force, gives a deplorable picture of the position at Ostend.   " For the Spaniards that ar hier, they ar the miserablest creaturs that ever I saw, and their is but 400 of them, and that is all the garison that is in Osten exsept thoss that I braught " (B.M. Add. MSS. 32095, f. 81).

voured to gain time by giving indefinite answers, and suggesting, instead of a peace, a suspension of arms in Flanders, with
the result that they had induced him to stay considerably longer
than the two days to which he had been restricted.[1] In dealing
with Montagu, whose instructions were not so exact, they
carried the same policy much further. Every town became the
subject of a separate discussion. As a necessary preliminary
to peace a general truce was proposed for a year or fourteen
months, and endless negotiations were made to centre round
the problem of a temporary suspension of arms while the truce
was being arranged. To counteract the effect on Charles of the
marriage of one niece to William of Orange hints were dropped
that another niece, Marie Louise, daughter of Charles's favourite sister Henrietta, might find a husband in the Dauphin.
Financial considerations were not forgotten. The whole resources of the French King, " even to the engaging of his
jewells," were put at the disposal of Charles, if only he would
prevent Parliament from drawing him into a war ; and lest
the payment of so large a subsidy as he might need should
attract attention, it was promised that " it should be put into
wedges of gold, and soe put into bales of silk, and sent over
in a yacht." Danby himself was assured of all he needed to
make his fortune, " in diamonds and pearles, that noebody
could ever know it," if he would exert his influence on the side
of France.[2]

By representations such as these, which were not merely sent
through Montagu but repeated in the most persuasive accents
by Barillon,[3] the resolution of the English King, none too great
even at the beginning, was steadily sapped. Danby, no longer
supported by the presence of the Prince, and without even the
assistance on which he had counted from Sir William Temple,
found it impossible to maintain the wavering counsels of

[1] Temple, *Works*, i. 457. Temple regarded the failure of Feversham to
follow his instructions precisely as the beginning of all the trouble.

[2] The best account of Montagu's negotiations is contained in his three long
letters to the King of December 29, 1677, January 5 and 10, 1678 (*infra*, ii.
299, 306, 310). There is no doubt that on this occasion and on others as well
Danby could have had any sum of money he pleased from France in return for
the surrender of his principles, but unlike many of his opponents he never
stooped to receive bribes from the enemy of his country.

[3] *Mignet*, iv. 521-8.

the Court, and in order to prevent worse happening deemed it
necessary to connive at much of which he thoroughly disapproved.[1] Quite possibly the whole scheme would have had
to be abandoned had it not been for the unexpected conduct of
the Duke of York, who, having once thrown in his lot with the
war party, was inclined to see its policy through to the end. A
war against France was the only war in which there was any
chance of his being allowed to take command. By setting himself at the head of the armed forces of the nation in so popular
a conflict he hoped both to satisfy his love of military glory
and to confirm the good impression he had made by assenting
to the marriage of William and Mary.[2]

Meanwhile the French, having secured the breathing space
they required, did everything in their power to sow dissension
among their opponents. To the Allies they insinuated suspicions of the separate agreement made between England and
Holland. In Holland they played upon the commercial jealousy of England and the fear of the increasing importance of
the House of Orange entertained by the republican party. In
England itself they spread doubts of the good faith of the
Government, harped upon the danger to popular liberties involved in the creation of a large army, and lavished bribes upon
all members of Parliament who could be induced by such means
to oppose the Court. By an unlucky chance Barillon had in his
hands the greater part of the subsidy due to the English King
in December, and this he was now instructed to employ among
the opposition.[3] At the same time a valuable ally was dispatched to his assistance in the person of Henri de Massue, son
of the old Marquis de Ruvigny, who as a Protestant and a
relative of the Russells could penetrate into Presbyterian circles

---

[1] A good illustration of Danby's difficulties, even at an early stage, can be
obtained by comparing his letter of December 24, written in accordance with
the King's instructions to Montagu (*infra*, ii. 304), with his more personal
letter of the same date to William of Orange (*ibid.*, p. 406). They give two
entirely different impressions of the same facts.

[2] *Campana de Cavelli*, i. 207-8; *Ormonde MSS., N.S.*, iv. 396.

[3] The payment of the French subsidy was stopped as soon as Louis XIV
heard of the summons of Parliament for January 15 (*Mignet*, iv. 522-3).
According to Danby £18,000 had then been paid out of £50,000 which was due,
and Barillon had about £30,000 in his hands (Danby to Montagu, January 9,
1678, *infra*, ii. 326).

where money had little power and the ambassador's religion was a constant barrier to free intercourse.[1]

That the representations of the French found ready acceptance was largely the result of one unfortunate incident, the precise responsibility for which it is difficult to determine. Nothing had given greater satisfaction in England and among the Allies, or had caused more alarm in France, than the summons of Parliament for January 15 ; but when that day arrived the treaty with Holland had not yet been perfected, and it was considered advisable to require the Houses to adjourn to January 28. The effect was to revive the atmosphere of the previous July. No sooner had Seymour read the message declaring the King's pleasure than several members stood up to speak, and when he insisted on pronouncing the adjournment and leaving the House it was actually proposed to elect another Speaker in his place and sit on without him.[2] No such revolutionary course was in the end adopted ; but dislike of the manner in which the adjournment had been effected combined with dislike of the adjournment itself to produce widespread dissatisfaction. All the suspicion and unrest which Danby had been at such pains to lull to sleep sprang into renewed activity, and the belief prevalent in certain quarters from the very beginning, that a deception of some kind was being practised on the nation, gathered strength and spread with alarming rapidity.[3]

Of this, full advantage was taken by the leaders of the opposition when the session actually began. Following the tactics

---

[1] Montagu warned Danby of Barillon's intrigues as early as December 31, and informed him immediately afterwards of the object of young Ruvigny's visit to England (*infra*, ii. 315, 319). Ruvigny arrived on January 15 (*Ormonde MSS.*, *N.S.*, iv. 88).

[2] Schwerin, *Briefe aus England*, p. 190; *Finch MSS.* ii. 38.

[3] Danby gives a gloomy picture of the effect of the adjournment in his letter to Montagu of January 17. He certainly implies that the adjournment was not his work (*infra*, ii. 332 ; *cf.* also Danby to William of Orange, January 9, 1678, *ibid.*, p. 412). Contemporaries, however, believed that he wanted a few more days to strengthen his parliamentary organisation, which had somewhat fallen into neglect. "Il est vraysemblable que le Grand Tresorier a voulu gagner du temps pour redoubler ses caballes, et essayer de gagner plus de gens qu'il n'en a " (Barillon to Louis XIV, January 24, 1678). Danby had already called Lord Dumblane home to take his place in Parliament, and had endeavoured to enlist the good offices of the ambassadors of the Allies with that assembly (*infra*, ii. 305, 407).

which they had adopted with such success in the previous year, they waged at first a guerilla warfare, avoiding as far as possible an open trial of strength with the Court, but doing everything they could to delay business, rouse dissensions and confuse issues. Now that the alliances insisted upon by the Commons had been concluded, the Court naturally considered that it was the business of Parliament to fulfil its part of the bargain by voting the supplies it had repeatedly promised. This, indeed, was the main point made in the King's opening speech, and no sooner had the Commons returned to their own House than one member of the Court party after another rose and insisted that the speech should be taken into immediate consideration. The opposition, however, led by Sir Thomas Lee, proposed a delay of three days, and when some weighty arguments from Secretary Coventry [1] had shamed them into accepting a postponement of only one day, contrived to divert the attention of the House for the remainder of its sitting to a consideration of the alleged irregular conduct of the Speaker at the last four adjournments. [2]

On the following morning similar tactics led to an equally unsatisfactory debate. By skilfully playing on the general ignorance of foreign affairs [3] the opposition first prevailed with the House to give instructions for an absurd address desiring the King not to admit of any peace which should leave France in a stronger position than at the Treaty of the Pyrenees. [4] Then, lest Royalist susceptibilities should have been aroused, they gave their support to a motion for supply, not, however, for the army or the navy, but for the decent interment of

[1] " The putting off the consideration of this great affair for three days will seem strange, when a conquering Prince is marching, who considers neither holidays nor workdays."

[2] *Grey*, v. 4-17. That the Court had been expecting this question to be raised is clear from Williamson's notes in *Cal. S.P. Dom.*, 1677-8, pp. 518, 579-80, 587-8.

[3] No better illustration of this ignorance can perhaps be given than the speech of Colonel Birch some weeks later on the fall of Ghent—" I know not this Ghent, but 'tis said to be a great place " (*Grey*, v. 205).

[4] *C.J.*, ix. 428 ; *Grey*, v. 17-32, 37-46 ; *Cal. S.P. Dom.*, 1677-8, pp. 608-9 ; *Ormonde MSS., N.S.*, iv. 396-8. The address itself, approved by the House on January 31 and presented to the King on the following day, was much more absurd than the instructions for it. The King's reply on February 4 tore it in pieces, but a dialectic victory was of no value to the Court (*C.J.*, ix. 429-32).

Charles I.[1] On February 4, a full week after the opening day,
the Court was able to carry it by 193 votes to 151 that the
House should resolve itself into committee of supply ; [2] but
even then obstructions were encountered at every turn. With
the object of forcing the King to disclose the actual terms of his
alliances, or at least of safeguarding themselves against the
possibility that the terms were not such as they would approve,
the opposition, in accepting the formal vote of supply on
February 5, insisted that its purpose must be defined as " for
the support of the present alliances made with the States
General of the United Provinces, for the preservation of the
Spanish Netherlands, and lessening the power of France."
They then tried to maintain that of the 90 ships of war which
the King had demanded in his opening speech, 50 should be
provided out of the ordinary Customs duties. On this claim
being negatived by 178 to 146, they endeavoured to secure a
reduction in the vote of 30,000 troops which the King had
required, but were again beaten by 107 to 85. Finally, on
February 18, they concentrated on an effort to reduce the vote
of £1,000,000, which the calculations of a special committee of
the House showed to be necessary to maintain the war for six
months, to one of £800,000 ; but the larger sum was carried by
186 to 166.[3]

The Court thus had a fairly steady majority, but it was so
small that an untoward incident might at any moment destroy
it altogether, and such incidents, owing to the address of the
opposition,[4] were of daily occurrence. Meanwhile business
proceeded with painful slowness, and Charles, whose whole-
hearted support for Danby's policy could have been purchased
only by immediate and easy success, became steadily more
disgusted at its failure and more irritated at the efforts of
Danby and the Duke of York to keep him loyal to it. The
effect was seen on February 7, when the Duke of Buckingham,

---

[1] This, of course, was an old idea of Danby's, and the motion was introduced
by the Court, but the opposition found it as good a side-issue as any other
(*Grey*, v. 32-4).

[2] *C.J.*, ix. 432.

[3] Marvell, *Poems and Letters*, ii. 205-9 ; *Ormonde MSS., N.S.*, iv. 398-405.

[4] " Having a greater number of able and contentious speakers, though they
are outdone in votes " (*ibid.*, p. 399).

who had made his peace with the Lords on the day Parliament met,[1] was openly received at Court and waited on the King at supper. A half-hearted effort was made by Charles to reconcile him with the Treasurer, but he refused all association " with one whom he despised not only as an ungrateful but an ignorant man." His confident assertion that he was " as well with the King as ever " was accepted by many as heralding Danby's fall. In a loyal effort to serve his patron, the Bishop of London preached before Charles a special sermon on " the dangers of ill conversation, or the showing any degree of countenance or delight in those who were under marks and blemishes of evil life ; " but even he " looked on the Treasurer as a lost man." [2]

Even before Parliament met Buckingham had been working for the ruin of Danby, and had tried to form an alliance between his " cabal " and the French ambassador to that end.[3] The real importance of the Duke, however, lay not in his parliamentary following, the size of which he habitually exaggerated, but in his personal influence with the King. Left to himself Charles would scarcely have had the hardihood to withstand the pressure exerted upon him by his brother and Danby combined, but with Buckingham to encourage him he had little hesitation in initiating a policy of his own, of which neither of them approved. Modified terms of peace were worked out, with which Ruvigny

[1] Salisbury and Wharton followed his example on February 4 and 7 respectively (*Cal. S.P. Dom.*, 1677-8, pp. 606, 624, 631).

[2] *Ormonde MSS., N.S.*, iv. 105-6, 401 ; Barillon to Louis XIV, February 17, 19, 1678.

[3] Barillon to Louis XIV, January 24, 1678 ; Montagu to Danby, March 12, 1678, *infra*, ii. 341-2. On April 30 Sir Robert Thomas wrote to Danby, " My associates discoursed much of Buckingham being reconciled to the King further then your Lordshippe designed, for you onely intended his enlargement, and not to have him a courtier, which highly discomposes you. But this is a certeinty, that it is not onely Nell Gwyns interest that brings him in, but the King of France, which Crequi and Ravignie procured, for Buckinghan declared himselfe to us and to all in the Tower himselfe a Frenchman, and soe are his commonwealthmen Wildeman and Harry Nevile. This you may relye on, that the French King sticks to him. Moreover they say your Lordshippe and the Duke and Ormonde dislike it, and my companions thinke it will ferment good, as they tearme it, and if any hardshippe be pushed by the Spaniard or any other accident, it is then they expect a difference in Councell. They believe your Lordshippe will be compelled to appeare for the Confederates rather then to truckle the third or fourth hand for France . . . Rochester, Middlesexe, Sheppard are but distant assistances to Buckingham. The French King is closer. Be pleased to burne this " (B.M. Add. MSS. 28051, f. 41).

was dispatched to France, while Godolphin was hurried over to Holland to press them upon the Prince of Orange.[1] Danby began to despair,[2] and although in an extraordinarily outspoken letter he urged the Prince not to accept the terms brought by Godolphin, his only hope appears to have been that in the time gained by the new negotiation the position of the Allies might be improved.[3] Charles had promised not to make any declaration of war against France until after he had received a reply to Ruvigny's proposals, on condition that the French King during the same period should not lay siege to any town in Flanders.

Unfortunately Louis paid no attention either to the new terms of peace or to the conditions under which they were to be discussed. During the weeks of delay which had elapsed since Feversham's original mission he had been steadily preparing for a decisive blow, and he now struck. On February 22 he appeared in person before Ghent with an army of 70,000 men. On February 27 the town surrendered, and two days later the citadel, whither the garrison had retired, followed its example. Ypres was immediately invested, and capitulated on March 15. Within less than a month the whole military situation had been changed, and the terms of peace on which negotiations had hitherto been based had been rendered completely out of date.

The fall of Ghent meant the collapse of Danby's policy. French intrigues had done their work among the Allies, and mutual recriminations took the place of opposition to the common foe. In Holland an insistent demand for peace arose,[4] which even the Prince could scarcely ignore. In England sus-

---

[1] The principal difficulty in the original terms had proved to be Tournay. Charles suggested Charlemont in exchange for it. The negotiation was kept secret from all but Charles, James, Danby and the French ambassador. Ruvigny was supposed to be returning permanently to France, and Godolphin was believed to be entrusted with a mission regarding Ostend (Danby to William of Orange, February 8; Godolphin's instructions, February 8; Danby to Montagu, February 11, 1678, *infra*, ii. 334, 418, 598).

[2] Danby to Laurence Hyde, February 8, 1678, *infra*, ii. 574.

[3] Danby to William of Orange, February 9, 1678, *infra*, ii. 420. The Treasurer asked the Prince for two replies, one for himself and one which he could show to the King. William's personal letter, dated February 25, is equally frank (*infra*, ii. 422).

[4] " Tant soit peu seure." This phrase is repeated again and again in Danby's orrespondence and in Williamson's diary (B.M. Add. MSS. 28040, f. 49).

picion and discontent came to a head. The Court endeavoured
to find the cause of the disaster in the reluctance of Parliament
to vote supplies; but the opposition with more justice declared that the real fault lay in the policy which the Government had been pursuing for some years.[1] On February 26 a
premature report that Ghent had fallen was laid before the
Commons by Secretary Coventry, and " stirred up a very cloudy
and ungrateful repetition of things passed," in the course of
which the need for the removal of evil counsellors was freely
mentioned.[2] That a grant of money should immediately be
made was not denied, and the next few days, somewhat to the
general surprise, were spent by the Commons in perfecting
a Poll Bill, which was calculated to produce about half the
sum already voted.[3] But this was only a lull in the storm. On
March 14 a carefully prepared attack was delivered on the
Government.[4] By a bare majority of five the Court defeated
a motion for the removal of those counsellors who had advised
the adjournment of the previous May; but on the question of
the moment they were not so successful. Apparently without a
division it was resolved that an address should be presented to
the King, desiring that he would immediately declare war on
France, recall his representatives from Paris and Nimeguen,
and dismiss the French ambassador from England. On March
15 the address was submitted and approved, and the best the
Courtiers could do was to secure a short time for reconsideration
by persuading a somewhat reluctant House that it should be
sent to the Lords for their concurrence.[5]

　In allowing this last proposal to be adopted the opposition

---

[1] Danby endeavoured to start a counter-attack by going back still earlier.
" Le Grand Tresorier a suscité des gens de sa cabale qui doivent accuser ceux
qui ont conseillé au Roy d'Angleterre de rompre la triple alliance et de faire
la guerre de 1672." Buckingham and Arlington, however, made light of his
efforts (Barillon to Louis XIV, March 10, 1678).

[2] *Ormonde MSS., N.S.*, iv. 407; *Grey*, v. 202-9; *Reresby*, pp. 133-4. " They
named noe man then, but it was plane that they pointed at the Duke of
Yorke and my Lord Tresorer."

[3] The Poll Bill passed the Commons on March 8 and received the royal
assent on March 20 (*C.J.*, ix. 451; *L.J.*, xiii. 189).

[4] Danby seems to have known some days earlier what was coming (*Reresby*,
pp. 135-6).

[5] *L.J.*, xiii. 184; *C.J.*, ix. 454-5; *Grey*, v. 223-47; *Reresby*, p. 136; Marvell, *Poems and Letters*, ii. 216-7.

were no doubt influenced by recent developments in the Upper
House. For a full year the Government, by its policy of
adjourning rather than proroguing Parliament, had made it
impossible for Shaftesbury to secure his release from the
ordinary courts of law,[1] with the result that the Earl had at
length determined to make a complete submission. Danby
interposed every possible obstacle. When Halifax presented
a petition from Shaftesbury on February 14 he took the lead in
securing its rejection, by informing the Lords that no proper
application had yet been made to the King, and reminding
them of the contempt of their jurisdiction shown in Shaftesbury's appeal to the King's Bench.[2] When further petitions
were presented on February 20 and 21 he took an active part in
the long debates of these days, arguing that Shaftesbury should
not be allowed to address the House on his own behalf. Finally
when the petitioner, in spite of his arguments, was permitted
to address the Lords on February 25, he instigated Lord
Arundell of Trerice to raise new matter in the shape of " words
spoken in the King's Bench by that Earl of a dangerous
nature." On investigation being made, however, the two
shorthand writers produced as evidence could not agree what
exactly the words were, and this charge fell completely flat.
Shaftesbury was then allowed to make his submission in terms
prescribed by the House, and Danby himself, with the other
Lords of the White Staves, was ordered to wait upon the King
to desire that he might be set at liberty.[3] On February 27 he
again took his seat among his peers.

The French ambassador did not hesitate to describe the whole

---

[1] The courts were quite clear that they could do nothing for Shaftesbury so
long as Parliament was actually in session. That this was one of the reasons
for the repeated adjournments is shown by Danby's memoranda in favour of
the adjournment at Easter 1677—" The lords continuation in the Tower "
(B.M. Add. MSS. 28042, f. 36 ; cf. Ormonde MSS., N.S., iv. 392).

[2] Hist. MSS. Com., ix. 2, p. 102 ; Ormonde MSS., N.S., iv. 404 ; Cal. S.P.
Dom., 1677-8, p. 647 ; Marvell, Poems and Letters, ii. 209.

[3] Ormonde MSS., N.S., iv. 408 ; Cal. S.P. Dom., 1677-8, pp. 673, 677, 680 ;
Christie, Life of Shaftesbury, ii. 257-9 ; Brown, Shaftesbury, p. 248. An effort
was made to induce the newly liberated statesman to go into retirement, but
without success. "Der König wünschte, dass er sich während dieser Sitzung
aufs Land begeben möchte ; allein er antwortete er wäre so an den Tower
gewöhnt dass er lieber wieder hineinkomme als sich entferne " (Schwerin,
Briefe aus England, p. 223).

affair as " une grande mortification " for the Lord Treasurer,[1]
and certainly the reappearance of Shaftesbury in the ranks of
the opposition came at a most inopportune moment. But once
Shaftesbury had definitely determined on submission his
continued imprisonment in the Tower became a practical
impossibility, and the decision of the Lords in favour of his
release did not in any way mean that they had turned against
the Court. In the quieter atmosphere of the Upper House
there was every reason to expect that the difficulties of the
Government would receive careful and even sympathetic consideration, and the appointment of March 16 as the day for a
discussion of the Commons' address was therefore a signal for
a great effort on Danby's part to secure some modification of
its terms.

By a fortunate chance the proceedings opened with one of
those trivial incidents which serve to maintain good humour
among large bodies of men. A proposal made by one of the
bishops, that in the shadow of impending war a day should be
appointed for a general fast, was seconded, probably in derision,
by the Duke of Buckingham, and adopted amidst much unseemly
hilarity. Lord Fauconberg then objected to the use of the
word " immediately " in the address, declaring that an immediate war would mean grave danger to the defenceless English
possessions in the West Indies, and Danby seized the opportunity to move that the whole House should go into committee
to consider what improvements in the wording of the address
could be made. Anglesey took the chair, and for two long days
the debate continued.

The principal speakers in favour of an immediate declaration of war were Essex, Halifax, Shaftesbury, Buckingham,
Holles, Clarendon and Wharton ; their principal opponents the
Lord Chancellor, the Lord Treasurer and the Duke of York. In
general estimation, however, the honours of the debate lay with
Danby, to whom alone the relevant facts, both of the foreign
and of the financial situation, were thoroughly familiar. " Beginning to tell them how distracted he found the Exchequer,
how little has been given since, how much he has done with
what there was, and yet how many parts of preparation are

---

[1] Barillon to Louis XIV, March 7, 1678.

wanting to so perilous an undertaking, he did extremely stagger
the House as to their keenness of going immediately on."
Already a debt of £500,000 had been incurred in preparations.
" If we jump preposterously into a war," he declared, " the
Allies will leave it upon our hands and obtrude unreasonable
conditions upon us." By these arguments the House as a
whole was convinced, and several amendments were made in
the address, the most significant of which were the omission of
all reference to the ambassadors, and the substitution for
" immediately " of the words " with all the expedition that
can possibly consist with the safety of your Majesty's affairs." [1]

Even to the representatives of the Allies then in London
these amendments seemed not unreasonable, and the Marquis
de Borgomaniero, speaking principally as Spanish ambassador,
but interpreting also in some measure the wishes of his colleagues, strongly urged upon his friends in the Commons the
desirability of accepting them.[2] The Commons, however,
greatly resented the interference of the Lords, and when the
amended address was returned to them on March 19 resolved
by 155 votes to 112 that the word " immediately " should be
retained. Not unnaturally in the circumstances their reasons,
presented to the Lords at a conference on March 22, failed to
make any serious impression, and a minor deadlock followed, for
which an adjournment seemed the only remedy. On March 26
the Commons petitioned the King for a short recess, and on the
following day Parliament was permitted to adjourn to April 11.[3]

Thus Danby's great scheme of reconciliation had produced
results the very opposite of what he had intended. Suspicion
had risen higher than ever before. Parliament dared not entrust the King with an army or an adequate supply of money
until he had actually become involved in a war. The King
with equal reason dared not entangle himself in a war until he
had been provided with the men and money necessary to carry

---

[1] *L.J.*, xiii. 185, 186 ; Schwerin, *Briefe aus England*, pp. 232, 233 ; *Ormonde
MSS.*, *N.S.*, iv. 132, 415-7.

[2] Schwerin, *Briefe aus England*, p. 233—" Der Marquis den Mitgliedern
desselben vorgestellt dass es nicht an der Zeit sei Erbitterung und Misshellig-
keit zu stiften."

[3] *L.J.*, xiii. 191-3, 196 ; *C.J.*, ix. 458-63 ; *Grey*, v. 257-65, 266-8 ; *Ormonde
MSS.*, *N.S.*, iv. 361, 417-20 ; Marvell, *Poems and Letters*, ii. 218-9.

it on. Distrust and division appeared everywhere, not only at home, in Parliament, in the ministry, and even between the royal brothers, but abroad as well. The only stable point in Europe appeared to be Louis XIV, against whom the whole scheme had been directed. Danby himself was greatly weakened. It is true he had found a firm if temporary supporter in the Duke of York, and a staunch ally in the Prince of Orange, but the one had an outlook very different from his own, while the other could scarcely fail to regard him as at least partly responsible for the disasters which had occurred. Meanwhile he was proving troublesome, and therefore unsatisfactory, to the King, and was coming to be regarded by Parliament as one of the chief advocates of a French connection which he had genuinely done his best to destroy. Like most exponents of conciliation he was threatened from both sides. The King inclined to blame him for the faults of Parliament, and Parliament held him responsible for the faults of the King.

Not unnaturally the Treasurer tended to consider the position of affairs from the standpoint of finance, and regarded in this way the outlook was gloomy indeed. The expenses of the forces required by the war for the period to Christmas 1678 would, he calculated, be at least £2,400,000. Towards this enormous total Parliament had provided rather less than nothing. It had, it is true, passed a Poll Bill, which might bring in, during that period, about £300,000, but it had attached to the Poll Bill a prohibition for three years of the principal commodities imported from France which would mean a reduction in the Customs duties of nearly £290,000 a year,[1] while the general fall of Customs and Excise due to a war would account for £100,000 a year more. In addition to this it had to be considered that the £200,000 which the King had been empowered a year earlier to borrow on the Excise had not been repaid, that the special duty imposed on wine and vinegar in 1670 was due to expire at midsummer, and that a sum of £40,000 was required for the dowry of the Princess Mary.[2]

[1] " Cette clause est proposée par les ennemis de la Cour, et impose une necessité a sa Majesté Britanique de continuer la guerre trois ans " (Barillon to Louis XIV, March 14, 1678).

[2] King's speech of January 28, 1678, in *Parliamentary History*, iv. 896; *Cal. S.P. Dom.*, 1678, p. 98 ; *Supplement to Lindsey MSS.*, p. 92.

With such a dismal balance sheet before him Danby was not
in a position to be particular about the source from which
money was obtained, and when Charles brought forward the
inevitable suggestion of a subsidy from France he could scarcely
resist. As early as the middle of February young Ruvigny,
when sent with terms of peace to Louis, had been entrusted
also with a commission, in the event of the terms being accepted,
to propose an Anglo-French alliance in return for the payment to Charles of £600,000.[1] At the time Louis replied only
with a vague offer of assistance once the peace should have
been concluded, but in this way was laid the basis of a
negotiation which in the hands of Barillon gradually assumed
a more definite shape. Instead of £600,000 the smaller sum
of 6,000,000 livres was suggested, and especially after the
violent sitting of the Commons on March 14 there seemed at
least a fair prospect that an agreement might be reached on
that basis.[2]

Here, however, Montagu again made his influence felt.
Barillon, he assured Danby, was a creature of Louvois, who
really wanted war. Colbert and the peace party in France,
with whom he was personally in touch, were willing to pay
much more highly for a satisfactory settlement.[3] The Treasurer, accordingly, with the object either of wrecking the whole
negotiation or of extracting the uttermost farthing from the
hated enemy, insisted that a single payment of 6,000,000 livres
would be insufficient to enable the King to do without
Parliament as long as would be necessary, and demanded the
same sum as an annual subsidy for three years.

Had Charles at this point resolutely thrown in his lot either
with France or with the Allies he might still have won through
to salvation ; but, as too often before, he endeavoured to make
the best of both worlds, with disastrous results to himself.
Immediately after the fall of Ghent, Godolphin had been
hurriedly dispatched to the Continent to ascertain what changes

---

[1] *Mignet*, iv. 536.

[2] *Ibid.*, p. 571. At the same time as he was given instructions regarding this
negotiation Barillon was authorised " à employer jusqu'à cent mille écus pour
déterminer le Grand Tresorier." The money was never used.

[3] Montagu to Danby, January 18, 1678, *infra*, ii. 321-4.

that event had produced in the attitude of the Allies.[1] On
March 21 he returned, fully informed regarding the terms of
peace which would now be accepted, but without any actual
authority for proposing them. The Council, accordingly,
through fear of offending Parliament by appearing to initiate
peace proposals, declined to advise the King to make them the
basis of a definite negotiation, and it was resolved only " to
find the pulse " of the French King regarding them by showing
them to Barillon and sending a copy to Montagu.[2] Continued
uncertainty as between peace and war, however, was the one
thing which Danby could not face, and he therefore acquiesced
in instructions which he received from the King to write
privately to Montagu, authorising him to put the terms forward as a definite proposition of peace, the acceptance of which
by Spain and Holland Charles was prepared to guarantee. On
March 25 the letter was dispatched, stating, almost as an afterthought, that if peace was concluded on the basis suggested the
English King would expect the subsidy of 6,000,000 livres a
year for three years for which negotiations were already in
progress.[3]

No more extraordinary document ever emanated even from
the divided counsels of Charles II. The terms of peace were by
no means specially favourable to France, and Danby frankly
declared that he did not expect they would be accepted. If the
peace itself was unattractive it is difficult to see why it should
have been imagined that the French King would pay a large
subsidy to the monarch through whose good offices it had been
obtained. In the event the proposal proved a complete failure.
The terms of peace were rejected by Louis,[4] the question of the

---

[1] Rightly or wrongly Danby was believed to be behind this move. " Mr.
Godolphin went this day [March 5] to the Prince of Orange, as some say, but
others say to the French camp, he taking his last instructions from my Lord
Treasurer, who seems to be alone in the secret of what is now transacting with
France, and was, they say, called out of his bed at one of the clock on Saturday
night to attend his Majesty and the Duke, who had been at a long conference
with the French minister " (*Ormonde MSS., N.S.*, iv. 412).

[2] B.M. Add. MSS. 28040, ff. 50-2 ; *Cal. S.P. Dom.*, 1678, pp. 61, 67.

[3] The letter is printed *infra*, ii. 346.

[4] The original proposals, with the alterations which the French demanded,
are printed *infra*, ii. 345-6.

subsidy did not arise,[1] and Charles was thrown back upon the prosecution of a war policy. Since the beginning of March he had been endeavouring to form a quadruple alliance of England, Holland, Spain and Austria, and in view of the speedy re-assembling of Parliament this was now pressed forward. So great, however, had become the distaste of the Dutch for the war that the powers entrusted to their representative, van Beuningen, proved insufficient for what was desired, and while fuller powers were being awaited a further adjournment of Parliament became necessary.

To secure this without raising once more the whole problem of adjournment by the King's command it was considered best that there should be a new Speaker unconnected with previous controversies. Seymour, accordingly, found himself incapaci-tated by a convenient attack of rheumatism, and when the Commons assembled on April 11 Sir Robert Sawyer was dis-covered waiting to be elected in his place. Rumour had already anticipated the course of events by declaring that Seymour and Danby were on bad terms, and a clamour was immediately raised against Sawyer as presumably the nominee of the latter. When Secretary Coventry formally proposed him as Speaker the No's were as loud as the Aye's; but the hope of the opposition that by a policy of delay they might retain the services of Seymour was shattered by grave reports of his condition, and on an actual vote being taken by the Clerk of the House only six declared against Sawyer. On April 15, having been presented to and approved by the King, the new Speaker intimated to the Commons his Majesty's pleasure that they should adjourn to April 29, and after some debate and the hearing of two or three motions the House reluctantly complied.[2]

During the fortnight thus gained Danby appears to have con-centrated on one more effort at the consolidation of an effective Court party in the Commons. Never very united at any time, his following had recently shown alarming symptoms of dis-integration. Some few had definitely gone over to the other

---

[1] Montagu to Danby, April 11, 1678, *infra*, ii. 350-3.

[2] *C.J.*, ix. 463-4 ; *Grey*, v. 268-76 ; *Cal. S.P. Dom.*, 1678, p. 106 ; *Ormonde MSS.*, *N.S.*, iv. 421-3 ; Marvell, *Poems and Letters*, ii. 220-1.

side.[1] Many more had deemed it prudent to display less zeal on his behalf. The speaking on the side of the Court had become unbelievably bad, and the adequate presentation of its case had come to depend almost entirely on the two Secretaries of State and Sir John Ernly.

For this the growing suspicion of the policy of the Court was largely responsible. Men even of royalist sympathies were showing themselves much less ready to accept the professions of Charles or Danby at their face value than they had been in 1675 and 1676. But much was also due to the intrigues of the foreign ambassadors on both sides, who to serve their own, often temporary, ends were constantly spreading baseless rumours, insinuating plausible conjectures, and distributing lavish bribes among members of Parliament. Largely as a result of these intrigues Danby was finding it more and more necessary to have recourse to questionable methods of holding his party together, and the use of such methods inevitably impaired his credit with the more reputable among his supporters. The secret service accounts for the year 1677 indicate a considerable increase in the distribution of money among members of Parliament, and give some support to the contemporary belief that distributions of this nature were regularly made at the beginning of each session.[2] The fact that the corresponding accounts for the year 1678 have vanished is itself a suspicious circumstance. Danby never denied that during his period of office secret service expenditure rose considerably, and it is difficult to believe that the entire increase can be accounted for by legitimate expenses which he found it convenient to meet in this way.[3] Such evidence as

---

[1] In the great debate of March 14 Sir Gilbert Gerard, one of the Excise pensioners, had taken a prominent part in opposition to the Court, and had been responsible for the motion in favour of a declaration of war on France. He was later to go further in the same direction (*Grey*, vii. 213-4).

[2] These accounts are analysed *infra*, iii. 50-6.

[3] Among the Leeds MSS. (Packet 4) are preserved three separate statements of money issued for secret service—during the last year of Southampton's treasurership, from Easter 1666 to Easter 1667 ; during the last year of the succeeding commission, from Michaelmas 1671 to Michaelmas 1672 ; and during the entire period of Clifford's treasurership, from November 1672 to June 1673. The totals shown are £24,145, £37,266, and £45,760. Danby, on the other hand, was charged with having spent on secret service a sum of £231,602 during the two years from Christmas 1676 to Christmas 1678, and

exists, in fact, suggests that he was reducing the legitimate expenditure passing through secret service channels in order to make less noticeable an increase in other expenditure the items of which he wished to conceal.[1]

Alongside these secret and dubious methods of party organisation there continued the more open and innocent methods which had been developing among all parliamentary groups since shortly after the Restoration. The parliamentary managers of the Court party, like those of the opposition, still met to discuss tactics beforehand, arranged for speakers in the debates, and endeavoured to bring up voters for the divisions. The rank and file of the party were regularly entertained to dinner during the session, and instructed as to what was expected of them.[2] But even here the Court organisation was failing to work smoothly. In assuming control, as he had recently done, of foreign and military no less than of financial affairs, Danby had undertaken a task more than sufficient to overwhelm any one man. His supervision of Parliament inevitably suffered, and as his most intimate followers were not men of capacity, and his relations with the Secretaries were never really good, his position in the Commons was greatly weakened. Nevertheless a fresh survey of his following showed a very satisfactory paper strength. No fewer than 219 members of the Commons, it was believed, could be relied upon, of whom 30 were credited with some capacity to speak.[3]

That this strength existed on paper rather than in reality, however, was clearly demonstrated when the projected quad-

---

himself admitted having spent £252,467 10s. 5d. in the three years from Lady Day 1676 to Lady Day 1679 (infra, ii. 75; B.M. Add. MSS. 28042, f. 61; Memoirs of the Earl of Danby, pp. 69, 122-3, 163-4, 202-3, where Sir Robert Howard declares that the real total for the three years was £309,556 11s. 4d.).

[1] Danby's own salary of £8,000, originally paid as secret service money, ceased to be paid in this way after July 1676 (Cal. Treas. Books, v. 269).

[2] The principal " keeper of the Treasurer's public parliamentary tables " was Sir Richard Wiseman, who was examined after Danby's fall as to the source of the money expended by him on this form of hospitality. He assured the Commons that the money came from his own tenants, but the House was not convinced (Grey, vii. 334). For the contemporary belief that each guest at these parliamentary dinners found a guinea beneath his plate there appears to be no foundation.

[3] The list is printed infra, iii. 111-20.

ruple alliance had to be abandoned, and the King on April 29 faced Parliament scarcely better prepared for war than he had been in the previous January. The Chancellor opened proceedings with a very reasonable review of negotiations abroad since foreign affairs had first claimed general attention in March 1677, indicated the problems that had arisen, and declared the readiness of the King to be governed in his attitude to them by the Parliament's advice. The Commons replied by complaining that while they had always pressed for war the Chancellor's speech was mainly about peace, insisted on examining the alliances which the Government had made, and on May 4 resolved by 166 votes to 150 that they were unsatisfactory in themselves and contrary to the addresses of the House.[1] In the hope of securing a more dexterous control of business the Court then persuaded Sir Robert Sawyer in turn to find himself incapacitated by a dangerous illness, and procured the re-election of Seymour as Speaker;[2] but the Commons merely turned to the subject of evil counsellors and proved as intractable as before. Trouble in Scotland had concentrated special attention on Lauderdale,[3] for whose dismissal it was resolved on May 7, by 137 votes to 92, that an address should be presented to the King; but Danby was also struck at by a more general resolution, carried the same day by 154 votes to 139, against those who had advised the King's answers to the Commons' addresses of May 26, 1677, and January 31, 1678.[4]

Such resolutions worried Danby little in comparison with the failure of the Commons to vote any supply; but even here his party consistently failed to muster the strength he had anticipated. As early as April 29 the question of finance had

---

[1] *C.J.*, ix. 475; *Grey*, v. 276-81, 289-334.

[2] May 6. Although Sawyer was perfectly well, and had been promised 3,000 guineas for his complaisance, " he desired the prayers of the House, and wase therupon prayed for " (*Hatton Correspondence*, i. 160).

[3] Barillon to Louis XIV, April 21, 1678. " Le Duc d'Hamilton fut hier entendu au conseil privé. Sa Majesté Britanique ny estoit pas. Il fit ses plaintes et celles de toute l'Escosse contre le Duc de Lauderdail. Je sçais qu'on commence a dire a la cour que ce ministre a abusé de son pouvoir et a porté les affaires a une trop grande extremité. M. le Duc d'York et Milord Tresorier disent néantmoins qu'il le faut soustenir."

[4] *C.J.*, ix. 477, 478; *Cal. S.P. Dom.*, 1678, pp. 158-60.

been indirectly raised by the report of a committee appointed
to prepare matter for a conference with the Lords on the growth
of popery. This report concluded by declaring it the intention
of the Commons not " to consent to lay any further charge
upon the people, how urgent soever the occasion be that require
it," until a more effectual remedy should be found for that evil.
In vain Danby's followers insisted that such a resolution was
wrong in itself, that it was beyond the competence of the committee that put it forward, and that it raised a point most
unsuitable for a conference with the Lords. So high had the
aversion to popery risen that they were defeated by 129 votes
to 89, and the report was adopted.[1]

Danby then strained all the resources at his disposal to increase his voting strength, and on May 10, when the address was
reported embodying the resolutions of May 7, made his great
effort. In three successive divisions, although by the narrowest
possible margins, the Court was defeated,[2] and the condemnation of the ministers having thus been accepted the not very
happy decision was reached that the only possible way to carry
a motion for supply was by surprise. Early on May 11, accordingly, " when the House was thin," Secretary Williamson
delivered a verbal message from the King insisting on his
immediate need for supply if he was not to disband his forces
and lay up his ships ; but the debate was prolonged till the
House filled,[3] and the matter was then quietly shelved by a
vote of 178 to 177 against adjourning it.[4] In the afternoon of
the same day the King declared the address of the Commons so
extravagant that he was unwilling to give it the answer it
deserved, and on May 13, after appealing to the Lords, he prorogued Parliament to May 23.

In face of such an attitude on the part of the Commons
even Danby and York could scarcely maintain that war was
feasible. The former was at his wit's end to find money to

---

[1] *C.J.*, ix. 471 ; *Grey*, v. 281-7.

[2] The figures for the divisions were 176 to 174, 170 to 167 and 169 to 166 (*C.J.*,
ix. 479). Marvell describes the first as " a division of the House the most
numerous that I remember of many years " (*Poems and Letters*, ii. 224).

[3] " None being willing to give a negative, but neither forward to an affirmative in the uncertainty of war or peace " (*ibid.*, p. 225).

[4] *C.J.*, ix. 480 ; *Grey*, v. 382-9.

maintain the forces which had been raised ; the latter was becoming increasingly uneasy at the animus exhibited by Parliament against the Catholics. Neither of them in consequence offered any resolute opposition when Charles went over more definitely than ever to the side of Louis and proceeded to work for peace, not as hitherto on terms obtained from the Allies, but on a basis suggested by France. Since March Louis had been negotiating with the peace party in Holland, and early in April had announced the terms on which he was prepared to come to a settlement. These terms Charles now accepted, and undertook, in return for a single year's subsidy of 6,000,000 livres, that if the Allies did not agree to them within two months he would disband his army, prorogue Parliament, and remain neutral.

Inasmuch as it was becoming increasingly apparent that neither the Dutch nor the Spaniards could be induced to fight any longer, this might be interpreted as a reasonable provision for English interests rather than a direct desertion of the Confederates. Such an interpretation, however, was not in the least likely to commend itself to Parliament, and Danby, whose part in the negotiation had mainly taken the form of interposing obstacles and pressing for better terms, deemed it prudent to seek some partner with whom to share the responsibility for what was being done. His suggestion, however, on the pretext of " son peu d'expérience dans les affaires de cette nature," that Temple might be associated with him, seemed scarcely to be seriously meant, and was in any case immediately negatived by that cautious diplomat taking to his bed, " faisant le malade ou l'étant effectivement." In these circumstances Danby refused all connection with the formal treaty, and on May 17 it was signed by Barillon and Charles himself.[1] The same day the Treasurer had the melancholy duty of writing by the King's command to William of Orange, advising him to make peace on the best terms he could obtain.[2]

This apparent conclusion of the foreign entanglement, however, at least enabled the Government to meet Parliament with

---

[1] *Mignet*, iv. 572-82.

[2] *Infra*, ii. 432-3.

more confidence. On May 22 a six-weeks truce was concluded between the Dutch and the French, and although Charles was not yet aware of this when the Houses reassembled on May 23 he could with perfect truth announce that everything pointed towards a general peace. A good peace, he insisted, could best be secured by keeping the army and navy at full strength ; but if such a course did not commend itself to Parliament he professed himself willing to agree to whatever should be determined concerning the forces.[1]

With much dissatisfaction the Commons accepted this statement of the position. Sacheverell voiced the general indignation " that the King should pass a bill for an actual war, and yet treat for peace." Michael Malet bitterly declared that if a peace was concluded it could only be " the peace of Herod and Pontius Pilate." But in face of the considerable army which the King now had at his disposal even the extreme members of the opposition were beginning to appreciate the wisdom of moderation. They were prepared for a war, which would engage the army abroad, or for a peace, which would make disbandment possible ; but they dared not say or do anything which would give the King an excuse for retaining the army in idleness at home.[2] Accordingly, after an ineffectual attempt to induce the King to state definitely whether there was to be war or peace,[3] they assumed that peace was certain, and in a remarkably short time made provision for the instant disbandment of all the forces raised since the close of the previous September. A supply of £200,000 was voted and strictly appropriated for the disbandment of the army ; a slightly smaller sum was found necessary to defray the extraordinary charges of the navy and ordnance ; provision was made for repaying the £200,000 which the King had been authorised a year earlier to borrow on the Excise, and also for the dowry of £40,000 for which he stood engaged to the Princess Mary. In all, taxation calculated to produce £619,000 was

[1] See the King's speech of May 23 in *L.J.*, xiii. 221, and his messages to the Commons of May 28 and June 7 in *C.J.*, ix. 484, 491. The speech was drawn up by Sir William Temple (*Hatton Correspondence*, i. 164).

[2] " If we have war 'tis a madness to disband the army, and if we have none as much to keep them."

[3] *C.J.*, ix. 483; *Grey*, vi. 3-26 ; Marvell, *Poems and Letters*, ii. 226-7.

imposed, and the expiring duty on wine and vinegar about which Danby had been so anxious was continued for a further period of three years.[1]

At this point prudence might have suggested to Danby that he was well rid of an adventure which had always been risky and which had brought him nothing but disappointment. But the Treasurer was now reaching a stage where the voice of prudence could scarcely make itself heard. Even in the event, an unlikely one in his opinion, of the French subsidy being paid, he did not believe that he could make the Crown financially independent on the basis of the existing revenue, and the prospect of any substantial addition to that revenue seemed remote indeed. One after another he had tried every means he could devise of conciliating Parliament, without inducing it to do more than provide some temporary relief for the most pressing needs of the Crown ; and meanwhile his very complaisance had encouraged the Commons to advance claims which constituted a serious menace to the royal prerogative. If the growing danger of parliamentary domination over the King was to be averted it was essential that a permanent and satisfactory solution of the financial problem should immediately be found, or that recourse should be had to other methods of maintaining the royal authority.

With considerable misgiving, accordingly, Danby resolved to use even this unpropitious moment to make a last bid for a sufficient revenue. On June 18 the King summoned both Houses of Parliament before him, and in the plainest language declared it impossible for him, even in time of peace, to maintain the interests of the country abroad, or live in any ease at home, without an additional supply of at least £300,000 a year. At the same time he undertook that if a grant of this sum was made he would give his consent to a bill appropriating

[1] *L.J.*, xiii. 288. The total expenditure on army, navy and ordnance in preparation for a war was estimated at £706,000 ; but from this was deducted the sum of £300,000 already provided by the Poll Tax for that purpose. Danby argued that if the return from the Poll Tax was thus to be taken into account a corresponding allowance should be made for the serious reduction in the Customs caused by the prohibition of the importation of French commodities contained in the Poll Bill. The Commons, however, by 202 votes to 145, refused to make good the loss involved (*C.J.*, ix. 487, 497, 500 ; *Grey*, vi. 202-3 ; *Hatton Correspondence*, i. 165-6).

£500,000 out of the royal revenue permanently to the use of the navy.[1]

In spite of the concession which accompanied it this statement was received with great disfavour. John Swynfen declared it " a most unusual thing to have new demands for money at the latter end of a session." Sir John Knight insisted that the existing revenue was sufficient, and that all that was required was that it should be better managed, and freed from the burden of pensions upon it. Lord Cavendish carried criticism a stage further by proposing that those who had advised the King's demand should be removed from office. Frequent reference was made to the poverty of the country, to the vast sums already granted, to " popery and arbitrary power," to " Normans and wooden shoes," to the probable disuse of Parliaments if the King were once freed from the need of applying to them for money. " The States of France," declared Sacheverell, " gave the King power to raise money upon extraordinary occasions till their next meeting ; and they never met more."

Nevertheless it is clear that Parliament itself was none too happy about the financial position, and the main contention of the Court, that the needs of the Crown ought at least to be examined, might possibly have been accepted had it been presented with reasonable care and skill. Unfortunately Danby in the midst of his many preoccupations entrusted the management of the affair to Williamson, and Williamson displayed a slackness and lack of tactical ability which raise doubt whether he really wished the King's demand to succeed. His initial and most serious mistake lay in failing to warn the leaders of the Court party beforehand of what was intended, with the result that they came unprepared to the debate, and had to leave the speaking almost entirely to the two Secretaries and Sir John Ernly.[2] In the debate itself he allowed himself to be entrapped

[1] *L.J.*, xiii. 252. On the same day Secretary Coventry wrote to Ormonde conveying the King's instructions that at the next meeting of the Irish Parliament every effort should be made to secure an increase of the Irish revenue to £300,000, and offering as an inducement a guarantee that the money should all be spent within Ireland (*Ormonde MSS., N.S.*, iv. 151, 181).

[2] " There were but very few who spoke, since those who use to be consulted on lesser occasions, and are wont to come prepared, were altogether surprised with this." According to Burnet the feebleness of the speaking on the Govern-

into a ridiculous position by seconding the motion of that firebrand of the opposition, Michael Malet, that thanks should be given to the King " for his gracious expressions in his speech ; " for Sir Robert Thomas and Lord Cavendish immediately proposed that he and Malet should jointly present the address of thanks, and the main issue had then to be abandoned while he desperately endeavoured to persuade the House that only Privy Councillors should be entrusted with such a task. Finally, seeing how badly the debate was going, he attempted to withdraw the Government's proposal, only to find that the opposition was now so confident of its strength as to refuse to let him do so.[1] Without a division it was resolved that the question should be put, and the proposal that the House should go into committee to consider the raising of the £300,000 per annum was then rejected, also without a division.[2]

This put an end to Danby's hope of independence for the Crown based upon a sufficient revenue, and forced him to give serious attention to other methods of securing his object. There is little doubt that at this stage he considered the possibility of maintaining the royal authority and his own supremacy by means of the army. There is no doubt whatever that the Duke of York favoured such a scheme, and that it received some countenance from the King. To all three, accordingly, it came almost as a relief when on the morning of June 19 news arrived that Louis had failed to abide by his original agreement, and had suddenly refused to surrender any of his conquests until his ally Sweden had recovered all she had lost during the war. Danby was immediately entrusted with the task of intimating the news to the Lords, who in turn passed it on at a special conference to the Commons.[3] On the plea that the maintenance

ment side was due to a feeling entertained by many of the Court party that if the revenue desired by the King were granted their services in support of the Government would no longer be required (*History of My Own Time*, ii. 150).

[1] " Resolving never to have this thing spring up more."

[2] *C.J.*, ix. 499-500 ; *Grey*, vi. 94-102 ; *Ormonde MSS.*, N.S., iv. 434-6 ; Marvell, *Poems and Letters*, ii. 232-3.

[3] *L.J.*, xiii. 254-5 ; *C.J.*, ix. 502 ; *Ormonde MSS.*, N.S., iv. 152, 439. The French announcement was kept back until the last moment, and was made on June 14, only three or four days before the peace between the French and Dutch was to be signed. The letter from Sir Leoline Jenkins, dated Nimeguen, June 15, 1678, on which Charles founded his message to the Lords, is printed in Wynne, *Life of Sir Leoline Jenkins*, ii. 383.

of the forces was now of vital importance the disbandment of the army was first suspended and then abandoned altogether. Temple was hurried over to Holland to arrange a fresh treaty with the States [1] ; additional troops were got ready for dispatch to Flanders ; and all the Allies were urged to renew the struggle.

The result was only a more dismal failure than ever. The Commons were not merely suspicious of this new development but thoroughly tired of their long attendance at Westminster, and made their dwindling numbers an excuse for refusing to reconsider the decisions they had already reached. The Lords so far recognised the new situation as to extend the final date for the disbandment of the army from June 30 to July 27 ; but the only effect of this was to raise a dispute between the two Houses over their power to amend a money bill. The King of France, who had no desire for a renewal of the conflict, was quickly convinced by the attitude of the English and Dutch that he had gone too far, and seized the first good excuse for abandoning the position he had assumed.

Thereupon the cry for peace burst forth more loudly than ever on the Continent, and nothing the English Government could do could check it. On July 31 a separate treaty of peace was signed at Nimeguen between France and Holland. On September 7 the treaty was formally ratified, and before the close of the year it was accepted by Spain. Until well on in the autumn Danby strove his hardest to rescue something from the wreck of his schemes, but without any success whatever. All he accomplished by this last misguided effort was to discredit the Government, flout the expressed wishes of the Commons, throw away the French subsidy, and incur great additional expense in connection with the forces. Parliament had been prorogued on July 15, but it could scarcely be doubted that when it met again a heavy reckoning would have to be faced for the events of the summer.

---

[1] He left England on July 2 (Temple to Danby, July 1, 1678, *infra*, ii. 490 ; Temple to Ormonde, July 2, and to Williamson, July 4/14, 1678, in Temple, *Works*, ii. 463-7). In all probability he was the bearer of Danby's letter to William of July 1, 1678, printed *infra*, ii. 435.

CHAPTER XIII

TITUS OATES AND RALPH MONTAGU, 1678-9

DURING the year 1677 and the early months of 1678 Danby had repeatedly come within an ace of complete success ; but his final failure left him floundering in a morass from which he could see little hope of extricating himself. As a guarantee of the domestic policy which it was his real ambition to carry through he had embarked upon an enterprise abroad which had almost immediately proved beyond his capacity to control. To support his attitude abroad he had raised a considerable army, which had become an absolute millstone round his neck, for he had the resources neither to maintain it nor to pay it off, and its very existence, especially since Parliament had voted for its disbandment, was a constant grievance with a large section of opinion in the country. To reconcile the opposition to the Crown he had brought down upon himself the unrelenting hostility of France, only to find the reconciliation at which he aimed still eluding his grasp, and the opposition much more ready to form an alliance with France than with the Crown or himself.

In these circumstances almost his only hope lay in Sir William Temple. The reputation which Temple had originally established by his successful negotiation of the Triple Alliance had never declined. Throughout the country he was recognised as one of the ablest diplomatists of his age, and almost the only whole-hearted supporter of the ideals with which that league in popular estimation was associated. If only he could be induced to accept the office of Secretary of State the Treasurer felt that expert advice in matters of foreign policy would no longer be lacking, and the country could hardly fail to be convinced that the Government's attitude in foreign affairs was what it professed to be.

Unfortunately Temple, while ready enough to face the trials and tribulations which confront the ambassador and diplomat, shrank from meeting the very similar troubles which are the lot of the politician.   From the summer of 1677 onwards Danby appears to have pressed him almost constantly to accept the promotion intended for him ; but the price which Henry Coventry demanded for the surrender of his post was a high one, and even when promised assistance from the King, Temple could with some justice declare that it was beyond his resources.   Thus his appointment was continually postponed, and although Danby frequently obtained his advice and assistance the ministry was deprived of the prestige which his inclusion in it would certainly have conferred.

Meanwhile trouble was inevitably brewing from the rival claims of Ralph Montagu.   At least as early as October 1677 Montagu had set his heart on the post of Secretary of State as the appropriate reward of his services to the Government ; [1] during his brief visit to England in November and December he had proposed his appointment to Danby himself, and for five or six months thereafter he continued to insinuate his pretensions, relying mainly on the support of Lady Danby and Charles Bertie. [2]   But however much the Treasurer might allow himself to be involved in the intrigues with France there was not the slightest chance of his favouring the appointment as Secretary of one who was so opposed to his own policy as the promoter of those intrigues.   Towards the close of May Montagu definitely put his fortune to the test by completing his own arrangements with Secretary Coventry and writing to Danby applying for his place. [3]   The answer appears to have been a decisive refusal, based upon the Treasurer's engagements to Temple, and although Montagu accepted his disappointment quite cheerfully, and exhibited no immediate hostility, it seems clear that he then came to the conclusion that his own advancement could be secured only by the removal from office of the

---

[1] His first slighting reference to Temple occurs in a phrase inserted as an afterthought in his letter to Danby of October 12, 1677 (*infra*, ii. 296).

[2] Montagu to Charles Bertie, March 29 and April 11, 1678, *infra*, ii. 344, 353.

[3] Montagu to Danby, June 4, 1678, *infra*, ii. 358.

patron to whom he had hitherto professed himself unalterably attached.[1]

The crisis in the relations between Danby and Montagu, however, arose out of an incident with which the former had no connection whatever. Early in the spring of 1676 the Duchess of Cleveland, despairing of further conquests in England, took up residence in France,[2] where she was later joined by her daughter Anne, Countess of Sussex. With Montagu she was soon on terms so intimate that if her word is to be believed he divulged to her all his political schemes ; but an intrigue into which she entered with the Marquis of Châtillon so roused his jealousy that he secretly sent information of her behaviour to Charles II. As a result when the Duchess visited England in the spring of 1678 she was very coldly received ; and the indignation which she naturally felt at Montagu's betrayal was converted to most bitter resentment when she discovered, on her return to France, that the ambassador had taken advantage of her absence to establish unduly familiar relations with her daughter, whom he had taken out of the monastery where she had been placed and entrusted to another which had " none of the best reputations." Without hesitation the Duchess sat down and wrote to King Charles one of the most venomous letters which history records. Every design that Montagu had ever imparted to her was set forth in the blackest possible colours. The sole object of that " most abomminable man," she declared, in endeavouring to become Secretary of State, was to drive the Treasurer from office, take his place, and by furnishing the King with all the money he needed " for his pocket and his wenches " get the Government practically into his own hands. The disrespectfulness of the expressions he had used regarding the King had been exceeded only by those he had employed concerning the Duke of York. His behaviour towards the Countess of Sussex had made " so great a noyes at Paris," that she had become " the holle disscores " of the town.[3]

[1] Montagu to Danby, July 1, 1678, and the remarks of the Duke of Leeds, *infra*, ii. 360, 371.

[2] *Cal. S.P. Dom.*, 1676-7, p. 25 ; *Rutland MSS.*, ii. 29.

[3] The letter, a masterpiece in its way, has been frequently printed, in the Appendix to W. Harris's *Charles II*, in P. W. Sergeant, *My Lady Castlemaine*,

These charges were far too near the truth to be safely ignored. As soon as Montagu heard of the Duchess's letter he made a desperate effort to recover the favour of the King and the Treasurer by endeavouring to carry out, through the agency of the latter, the marriage between his step-daughter, Lady Elizabeth Percy, and the Earl of Northumberland, which he knew Charles had very much at heart.[1] But nothing short of personal explanations, he believed, would serve to avert complete ruin, and on July 1, without waiting for permission from home, he set out for England.[2] There he found himself menaced not merely with dismissal from his offices but with imprisonment in the Tower, and appealed to Danby to procure him an interview with the King.[3] Probably with some reluctance the Treasurer complied,[4] and an ostensibly casual meeting was arranged at Hampden House. Charles, however, refused to listen to any explanations until Montagu had given an adequate reason for his unauthorised return home, and as Montagu's only reason was his desire to offer an explanation the interview brought him no satisfaction.[5] On July 12 his name was struck off the Council, his French embassy was entrusted to the Earl of Sunderland,[6] and his other places were immediately apportioned by popular rumour among the Treasurer's connections, that of Master of the Wardrobe to the King to Lord Dumblane and that of Master of the Horse to the Queen to the Earl of Plymouth.[7]

With both the King and the Treasurer against him Montagu's

p. 221, and from the original in the *Morrison Catalogue, Second Series*, ii. 233-6. The date, " Paris, Tuesday 28, [16]78," is not May 18/28, which was a Saturday, but June 18/28. The Duchess was not at Paris in May. Her pass to return to France is dated June 7 (*Cal. S.P. Dom.*, 1678, p. 614).

[1] Montagu to Lady Harvey, July 5, 1678, *infra*, ii. 362.

[2] *Hatton Correspondence*, i. 168. Apparently he was recalled on July 3 (*Cal. S.P. Dom.*, 1679-80, p. 157 ; 1683, p. 24).

[3] Montagu to Danby, July 8, 1678, *infra*, ii. 364.

[4] *Infra*, ii. 371.

[5] There is an account of the interview in *Ormonde MSS.*, N.S., iv. 443, where Montagu's own story of the whole affair is also given.

[6] P.C. Reg. 66, p. 370 ; *Cal. S.P. Dom.*, 1678, p. 287. Sunderland was on the best of terms with Danby, and at this particular moment was endeavouring to bring about a marriage between his own son Robert and Danby's daughter Sophia (*infra*, ii. 539-40 ; Barillon to Louis XIV, July 4, 1678).

[7] B.M. Add. MSS. 29573, f. 188 ; Carte MSS. 103, f. 230.

only hope of advancement lay in entering into relations with
the opposition, and to this he appears almost immediately to
have addressed himself. The prorogation of Parliament, however, made it dangerous if not impossible for him to take any
open step, and in the meantime the comparative quiet of the
autumn enabled Danby to forget for the moment his political
worries and devote himself to more personal concerns.

Among these the most sensational continued to be the affairs
of his prospective daughter-in-law, Bridget Hyde. The peculiar
position of that unfortunate lady, neither married nor single,
without parents, husband or acknowledged suitor to protect
her, made her an obvious target for the schemes of any adven-
turer who sought to improve his fortunes by a wealthy match.
The Emertons themselves had endeavoured to seize her, and
Sir Robert Viner apparently deemed it prudent to employ men
whose business it was to warn him of any further enterprise in
contemplation.[1] To the dangers of the preceding three years
the existence of a newly raised and ill-disciplined army now
added considerably by providing a large body of men from
which recruits for any deed of violence could readily be drawn.
It was from this quarter that the next attempt was to come.

On Sunday, July 21, at his country house at Ickenham, Sir
Robert Viner entertained to dinner a certain Henry Wroth, one
of the four pages of honour to the King, and also cornet to
Lord Deincourt's troop in the regiment of horse commanded by
Lord Gerard. This hospitality Wroth requited during the
course of an airing in Sir Robert's coach after dinner by drawing
a pistol upon his host and demanding the surrender of Bridget
Hyde, who was present with them. The arrival of six or eight
of his own troopers made resistance impossible, and Bridget,
hustled into a waiting coach, was rushed through Uxbridge and
Twickenham on towards Richmond ferry, where a four-oared
boat was waiting to carry her down the river.

Meanwhile Sir Robert rode for Whitehall, where he enlisted
Danby's assistance, and shortly before midnight obtained
warrants authorising the arrest of Wroth and his accomplices,
and closing the ports to all suspicious characters who might try
to leave the country. By that time, however, the danger was

---

[1] *Cal. S.P. Dom.*, 1676-7, pp. 545, 546 ; 1678, pp. 300-3 ; *Leeds MSS.*, p. 22.

really past. The country had risen behind the abductors, and just short of the ferry Bridget was rescued by the address (according to his own account) of a certain Thomas Hammon. Wroth was deprived of all his places in the King's service, but apparently contrived to evade arrest until the following February, when the Treasurer's power had greatly declined, and he probably escaped much more easily than might have been expected.[1]

Possibly Danby might have been more active in avenging the wrongs of one Bridget had his attention not been concentrated at the time on the fortunes of another, for his favour with the King was about to be crowned by the marriage of his own daughter Bridget to the only one of the royal children with whom he had established an intimate alliance, Charles, Earl of Plymouth. During July and August all sorts of rumours were current of the honours to be conferred upon the bridegroom and his future father-in-law. The Earl of Plymouth was to be made a Duke, Vice-Treasurer of Ireland, and captain of the Queen's troop of guards ; the Earl of Danby was to be given a similar step in the peerage.[2] In the end these rumours proved groundless, but the actual marriage ceremony, which took place with great splendour at Wimbledon on September 19, was justly regarded as marking the highest level which the private fortunes of the House of Osborne had yet attained.

Even before the conclusion of the marriage, however, the political situation had been transformed by an utterly unexpected development, the appearance of the portentous fable of the Popish Plot. On August 13 Christopher Kirkby, a

---

[1] Petition of Thomas Hammon to the Marquis of Carmarthen in B.M. Add. MSS. 28094, f. 138 ; Hist. MSS. Com., vii. 470 ; Cal. S.P. Dom., 1678, pp. 305, 330 ; 1679-80, p. 82, where the meaning of the torn passage is not beyond conjecture ; Dalton, English Army Lists, i. 203. In September four of Wroth's accomplices were charged with robbery, on the ground that Bridget Hyde had been deprived of some small articles, and three of them were convicted, though with what result does not appear (Hist. MSS. Com., xiii. 6, p. 10 ; Cal. S.P. Dom., 1678, p. 397).

[2] Hatton Correspondence, i. 167 ; Carte MSS. 103, ff. 228-9 ; Ormonde MSS., N.S., iv. 452, 454. " This young Earl must needs grow up into the expectation of any other great employment, when by his years he may be qualified thereunto, for his father-in-law shapes him and spurs him on to thoughts of business, and so everybody applauds the admirable endowments wherewith he is disposed thereunto."

T

gentleman whose interest in chemistry had secured him an appointment in the royal laboratory and ready access to the King's person, gave Charles the first warning of a conspiracy against his life. Two men named Pickering and Grove, he declared, were waiting to shoot him, and should their efforts fail he was to be poisoned by the Queen's physician, Sir George Wakeman. As authority for these statements Kirkby on the evening of the same day brought to Whitehall Dr. Israel Tonge, a fanatical London preacher, who produced a written narrative in forty-three articles of a vast Jesuit conspiracy against the King, the Government, and the Protestant religion. The origin of this document Tonge professed he did not certainly know, but he guessed the author to be a man who occasionally visited his patron Sir Richard Barker, in whose house he had found it.[1]

To Charles himself, who had some knowledge of the Catholics and their designs, the entire story, as well as the childishly mysterious manner in which it was being brought to his attention, appeared absurd. His purpose had been to go to Windsor on the following morning, and he declared he saw no reason for changing his plans. The Lord Treasurer could carry out whatever investigation was necessary. It is to Charles's credit that almost alone among the leading men of the day he discountenanced the Plot from the very beginning, and never at any time endeavoured to derive personal profit from it.

To Danby, however, who had all the prejudices of the average Anglican, the same story, repeated on August 14, appeared in a very different light. What seemed incredible to the King was quite possible or even probable to him. Moreover his personal interests were touched in a way in which those of Charles were not. If there was the slightest vestige of truth in Tonge's statements, and he failed to probe the matter to the bottom, it would certainly cost him his place, and very possibly his head.

But the chief determining factor in Danby's attitude was probably the idea which he entertained, if not from the first at least from a very early stage, that he might use the story of

[1] Danby's own account of the discovery of the Plot is given in *Memoirs of the Earl of Danby*, p. 30 *et seq*. This is to a considerable extent the basis of the narrative in Pollock, *The Popish Plot*.

the Plot to his own advantage. Little more than a year had
elapsed since he had expressed a hesitating wish for " some small
insurrection " as the best means of " getting into some condition of armes and money by the consent of the people, who
would otherwise not give the one and bee jealous of the other." [1]
The same advantages, it now appeared to him, might be
derived from an abortive Popish Plot. It would rally the nation
round the King, it would untie their purse strings, it would provide an excuse for the continued maintenance of the military
forces. Above all it would turn the hunt away from the Lord
Treasurer himself, and provide Parliament, when it met, with
something else to occupy its attention.[2]

It was with considerable energy, therefore, that Danby proceeded to investigate the Plot ; but his efforts met with singularly little success. His first object was to get into touch with
the original source of the information. Tonge, however, while
admitting three or four days later that he had ascertained
beyond doubt the identity of the person in question, refused to
disclose his name, lest it should lead to his assassination by the
papists. The next obvious step was to arrest Pickering and
Grove. These ruffians Tonge showed himself most anxious to
identify ; but they proved singularly elusive. Twice information was received that they were setting out for Windsor to
prosecute their nefarious designs, and arrangements were made
for seizing them. On both occasions they were prevented by
some unforeseen accident. Meanwhile Danby was kept busy
hurrying from Whitehall to Windsor to inform the King of
what was going on, from Windsor to Wimbledon to look after
his own affairs, and from Wimbledon back again to Whitehall
to continue his investigations.

According to one account the object of these tactics on the
part of the informers was to prolong the investigation until

---

[1] Memorandum of April 4, 1677, *infra*, ii. 68-9.

[2] *Lives of the Norths*, i. 211. So obvious were these considerations that it
was very generally asserted at first that the Plot was Danby's own invention
(*Burnet*, ii. 156). " Les gens opposés à la cour se moquent de toute cette accusation. Ils disent que c'est un artifice pour se faire un pretexte de garder des
troupes sur pied ; qu'on veut animer le Parlement contre les catoliques pour
l'empescher de traiter d'autres matieres " (Barillon to Louis XIV, October 10,
1678).

Parliament should meet, and so prevent the Plot from being stifled in the meantime.[1] In reality they probably represent nothing more than the natural efforts of uneducated men, by an affectation of mystery, to secure credence for a tale which had no solid foundation. In either case they came near to defeating their own object. The King's interest steadily declined. Fully realising that the only effect of a disclosure of the information received would be to produce a needless and dangerous panic he absolutely forbade Danby to divulge it to any one. Even the Earl began to grow lukewarm, and departed for Oxfordshire on business of his own, although still remaining in touch with events in London.

Realising that the whole Plot was in danger of dying a natural death the informers then resolved to take a further step. On August 30 Danby received information from Tonge that a packet of letters from Jesuits engaged in the Plot had been sent to the Windsor post-house for Father Bedingfield, the Duke of York's confessor. Immediately the Earl hastened to Windsor, only to learn that the letters had already arrived, that Bedingfield, alarmed at their contents, had shown them to the Duke, and that they had been recognised by both as impudent forgeries. Charles was thoroughly disgusted. In vain Tonge at length divulged the source of his information, and named the arch-informer, Titus Oates himself. The King would have nothing to do with any of them. It was probably with the idea that nothing more could be expected from the Court that Oates on September 6 swore to the truth of his statements before the well-known Protestant justice of the peace, Sir Edmund Berry Godfrey.

The Duke of York, however, had now also been inspired by the idea of turning the Plot to his advantage. The authenticity of the Bedingfield letters, he considered, could not possibly be maintained, and an open demonstration that they were forgeries would help to discredit the opponents of Catholicism and strengthen his own cause. He accordingly seconded Danby's arguments in favour of laying the matter before the Council, a course which the Earl had from the first advocated, if for no other reason than the desire to share his responsibility

---

[1] Lord Keeper Guilford's memoranda in *Dalrymple*, App., p. 320.

with others. Charles strongly disapproved of the suggestion, but as usual he had not sufficient resolution to withstand for long the combined importunities of his brother and his chief minister. On September 27 Oates and Tonge received a summons from the Privy Council, and on the following day, after Oates had again sworn to his information before Godfrey, and left a copy of his depositions with him, they appeared before the Council Board.

The Duke of York was speedily undeceived. To begin with the attitude of the Council to the whole story was one of amused incredulity, which even the brazen assurance of Oates and his ready answers in cross-examination did little to shake. But when the letters from which the Duke hoped so much were produced the situation immediately changed. Sir Robert Southwell, who was the clerk in attendance, was ordered to show the letters to Oates to see whether he could identify the handwriting, and made the task as difficult as possible by folding them so that only a line or two was visible. Nevertheless Oates at a glance named the author of each, and being asked why the writing bore so little resemblance to that which the authors customarily used, replied at once that it was their habit to write counterfeit hands which they might disown if occasion required.

This answer made a profound impression. By it the point which had told most heavily against Oates was suddenly converted into an apparent point in his favour, and a revulsion of feeling took place which made the Council ready to believe almost anything he said.[1] One result was to bring to light the essential divergence of interests between the Duke of York and the Lord Treasurer. The Duke had proposed to make his advantage out of the Plot by showing it to be false, but the Treasurer believed he would benefit by proving it to be true. Thus while James would now have liked to draw back, Danby insisted on pressing forward with the policy of precautionary arrests on which the Council at once decided. Armed with

---

[1] In an illuminating account of the rise of the Plot which he wrote more than four years later Sir Robert Southwell marks this answer as the origin of all the trouble. " This very thing took like fire, soe that what he said afterwards had credit " (B.M. Add. MSS. 38015, f. 278 ; see also the letter which Southwell wrote at the time to Ormonde, in *Ormonde MSS.*, N.S., iv. 455-7).

warrants and accompanied by a guard Oates went his rounds, seizing all whom he had accused.

The first arrests were effected on the night of September 28-9, and the alarm immediately began to spread. Whatever experienced statesmen might think of Oates, the people as a whole were prepared to believe all and more than all his depositions against the Catholics. Nevertheless the absurdity of his story might still have been demonstrated had nothing been found to substantiate his statements. On September 29, however, when the Council sat again, Oates made one of his luckiest shots by giving information against Edward Coleman, a busy intriguer, who had been Secretary to the Duke of York, and after having been dismissed more than once under pressure from Protestant interests had been taken into her service by the Duchess. A warrant for his arrest was accordingly prepared and signed ; but in the hurry of the moment no mention was made of his papers, and this omission might well have remained unrectified had not Danby at the last instant noticed it, insisted on the preparation of a fresh warrant, and procured the necessary signatures after the Council had actually risen. The Lord Treasurer's vigilance on this point was to have momentous consequences, and was an offence, as he later boasted, which the Duke of York never forgave.

Coleman's papers were seized the same evening, and were found to include a packet of letters of a highly incriminating character. Although revealing nothing like the grandiose scheme denounced by Oates they clearly showed that Catholic intrigues of a dangerous though somewhat nebulous type had for some time been in existence. Moreover the correspondence discovered was clearly only a fragment. Most of Coleman's papers had obviously been made away with, and it was assumed on all hands that the missing documents must have been of an even more treasonable character, documents which if found would have provided definite confirmation of Oates's assertions.

The effect of these discoveries was to convince the Duke of York that he had raised a devil which it might be very hard to exorcise, and he hastily endeavoured to repair his error. All possibility that the Plot might be stifled or laughed out of

court had vanished, but safety could still be sought in a
thorough investigation by the Council, which should prove its
baseless character before the meeting of Parliament could allow
the malcontents to get it into their hands.   Unfortunately the
King had arranged to set out for his autumn holiday at Newmarket on October 1, and in his absence it was not in the least
likely that the examination of the Plot would be vigorously pursued.   The result was the first serious dispute between the Duke
and the Lord Treasurer.   With the support of Lauderdale
James endeavoured to persuade Charles to put off his journey.
Danby, who had persuaded himself that his interest lay in a
parliamentary investigation, refused to join with them, and the
King accordingly set out.[1]

It may be questioned whether the King's going or staying
would have made much difference.   A complete investigation,
even in the most favourable circumstances, would have required some weeks, and events were soon to occur which made
any such delay impossible.   On October 12 Sir Edmund Berry
Godfrey was missing from his home.   Five days later his dead
body, bearing marks of strangulation, and with his own sword
driven through it from side to side, was found in a ditch at the
foot of Primrose Hill.   The efforts of countless investigators
have not yet succeeded in penetrating completely the mystery of
his death, but in the opinion of Protestant contemporaries there
was no mystery in it at all.   Godfrey was simply the first victim of the Catholic conspiracy, and unless precautions were
taken thousands more would soon share his fate.   An inde-
scribable panic seized upon London, and rapidly spread over
the whole country.   To deny the reality of the Plot became a
task from which the hardiest might shrink, and to refuse a
parliamentary investigation a course too bold for Charles to
contemplate.   James continued to insist that at all costs the
matter should not be permitted to fall into the hands of Parliament, and always blamed Danby for the fact that it was allowed
to do so, but Godfrey's death really left the Court without any
choice.

It was thus in a very heated atmosphere that Parliament
reassembled on October 21.   Danby had made such prepara-

---

[1] Clarke, *Life of James II*, i. 546.

tions as he could. He had somewhat relieved the financial difficulties of the Government by negotiating a new farm of the Hearth Money, which provided for advance payments of £150,000 before midsummer of the following year and an annual rent of £162,000 for five years thereafter.[1] He had made desperate efforts to strengthen his party in the House of Commons.[2] But with panic spreading everywhere the initiative no longer lay with the Court, and there was really little he could do until he had a clear idea what attitude Parliament was going to adopt.

Among the members of the two Houses the enemies of the Court were not perhaps appreciably more numerous than before. They still consisted of the same motley collection— opponents of arbitrary government, opponents of a despotic church, personal enemies of the Duke and the Lord Treasurer, disgruntled politicians who hoped to force themselves into office, and country squires who regarded Whitehall as a sink of iniquity and would have liked to drive all politicians out. But the discovery of the Popish Plot served to emphasise the one point which practically all sections of the opposition had in common, a hatred of Catholicism ; while the long drawn out investigation on which they immediately embarked helped to bring them together, and enabled them to exhibit a more united front than had hitherto been possible.

Nevertheless the chance of their effecting anything considerable against the triumvirate who controlled the Government seemed small. So long as Charles and James remained at one they concentrated in their persons all the sentiment of loyalty to the ruling house which was still a force of immense importance in England, and rendered any change in the accepted line of succession practically impossible. So long as the royal brothers and the Treasurer remained united they had at their disposal all the machinery of government and a secure

---

[1] Fortunately for Danby the terms of the farm had been agreed upon as early as August 17, before any rumour of the Plot had spread abroad. The warrant is dated October 30. As payment for the work of management the farmers were to retain all they collected beyond the annual rent of £162,000 up to the sum of £26,000, and 12d. in the £ on any overplus collected beyond that (*Cal. Treas. Books*, v. 1151).

[2] Barillon to Louis XIV, October 6, 1678 ; *Cal. S.P. Dom.*, 1678, pp. 398, 399.

majority, on any normal occasion, at least in the House of Lords. None of the three could be effectively attacked so long as he enjoyed the support of the other two, and the only real hope of the opposition therefore lay in breaking up their alliance. To this accordingly Shaftesbury and his fellows with some tactical skill addressed themselves.

Their original idea appears to have been to win over the Duke of York by promising him security for himself and the Catholics on condition that he would assent to the disbandment of the army and withdraw his support from the Treasurer.[1] With this object in view a rumour was even circulated that Danby was reviving Buckingham's old project of a divorce for the King. James, however, was not easily tempted into anything that savoured of disloyalty, and entertained the gravest doubt whether the promises of his opponents were within their power to perform. Before the close of the month, in spite of considerable pressure from his own followers, he had made it sufficiently clear that he would not be a party to any bargain such as that proposed.

The method then adopted was to reassure Charles and Danby while concentrating all the anti-Catholic zeal of the nation on the ruin of the Duke of York, and for a time this scheme seemed to have every prospect of success. By a vigorous prosecution of the Plot Danby hoped to reconcile himself with Parliament and with the nation, and support of the Plot was bound eventually to lead to a declaration against the Duke. In the early days of the session it was noted that the Treasurer's personal followers were among the most active in urging investigation, while old opponents of the Court, such as Littleton, Meres and Powle, held doubtfully aloof, still wondering whether the Plot was any-thing more than " un piege qu'on leur tend pour les engager a maintenir l'armée."[2]   On November 2, when Shaftesbury,

[1] " Le dessein des patriottes est de separer ce Prince des interests du Grand Tresorier, et je sçais qu'on luy offre de laisser les catoliques en repos et de donner de l'argent au Roy d'Angleterre si il veut abandonner la protection de ce ministre. On met toujours pour premier fondement que l'armée soit licentiée " (Barillon to Louis XIV, November 3, 1678, in *Campana de Cavelli*, i. 227).

[2] Barillon to Louis XIV, November 7, 1678. Even at this date, when the session was already a week old, the French ambassador could write of Danby and the Plot, " On soupçonne mesme que cest par son artifice et par celuy de l'Evesque de Londres que l'accusateur a esté suscité, et que son dessein est destablir son autorité et son credit par la perte de M. le Duc d'York."

supported by Essex, Halifax and the Bishop of London,
moved the House of Lords for an address to the King to exclude the Duke of York altogether from public affairs, Danby
spoke on the Duke's behalf, but in a way which raised
considerable doubt whether he meant what he said.[1] On
November 4, when Lord Russell went even further by moving
in the Commons that James should be removed from the King's
presence as well as from his councils, it was remarked that
the Treasurer's friends were not very active in opposing the
motion[2].

As the month advanced, however, Danby's zeal for the
prosecution of the Plot began to cool. Far from gaining any
credit by the discoveries for which he was responsible, he found
himself severely criticised for not making these discoveries
public at once, and it was even suggested that his failure for six
weeks to lay his information before the Council might justify a
charge of misprision of treason.[3] On November 9, in a speech
which Danby was believed to have drawn up,[4] Charles plainly
declared to both Houses that while he would accept any reasonable restrictions on a Catholic successor he would not desert his
brother ; [5] but the real test of Danby's attitude came a little
later, when a bill to exclude all Catholics from Parliament was
sent up by the Commons to the Lords. If the Duke of York
could be excluded from Parliament it was almost certain that he
would eventually be excluded from the throne. Nevertheless
the Treasurer, believing or professing to believe that the bill
would never be accepted by the Lords,[6] was not even present

[1] Clarke, *Life of James II*, i. 524 ; *Campana de Cavelli*, i. 228. " J'ay sceu
que ce ministre parla d'une maniere pour la deffence de M. le Duc d'York qu'on
ne sçauroit juger par son discours quelles sont ses intentions " (Barillon to
Louis XIV, November 14, 1678).

[2] *Grey*, vi. 133-49, 165-72. In a letter to Ormonde of November 5 Sir Robert
Southwell speaks of " it being taken for granted that the King and Lord
Treasurer are agreed not to resist any violent attempts " against the Duke
(Carte MSS. 38, f. 653).

[3] *Reresby*, p. 154 ; *Ormonde MSS., N.S.*, iv. 462, 470, 488.

[4] " On croit recognoistre le stile ordinaire de Milord Tresorier " (Barillon to
Louis XIV, November 24, 1678). Danby was at least familiar with the purport of the speech a day or two before it was delivered (*Reresby*, p. 157).

[5] *L.J.*, xiii. 345.

[6] *Reresby*, p. 158.

in the House when it passed its third reading.[1] To secure this result, however, the opposition lords had been compelled at the last moment to accept a proviso exempting the Duke of York from the operation of the Act, and the problem now came to be whether this amendment could be carried through the House of Commons. At this point Danby made his definite decision. On November 21 the entire debating and voting strength of his following in the Commons was exerted in the Duke's favour, with the result that the amendment was carried by a majority of two.[2]

In this way the alliance between James and Danby, which had been seriously shaken, was fully restored.[3] Despairing of more direct methods of ruining James, the opposition instigated Oates to accuse the Queen of complicity in the Plot, and in the hope of making way for another marriage for Charles procured from the Commons an address in favour of her removal from Whitehall ; [4] but Danby was one of the large majority in the Lords who ruined the scheme by refusing their concurrence.[5] The opposition then offered to prove that Charles had been married to the mother of the Duke of Monmouth before he met the Queen, and Colonel Birch made a special effort to secure

---

[1] *L.J.*, xiii. 364-6. " Le Grand Tresorier et M. le Duc de Montmouth n'estoient pas presens, et ont eu leurs raisons de ne s'y pas trouver. Cela fait douter des suittes " (Barillon to Louis XIV, December 1, 1678). A division list for the Lords about this time is printed *infra*. iii. 127-9.

[2] The voting was 158 to 156 (*C.J.*, ix. 543 ; *Grey*, vi. 240-54 ; Clarke, *Life of James II*, i. 526 ; Barillon to Louis XIV, December 5, 1678). " Das Unterhaus hat allen abwesenden Mitgliedern wissen lassen, sich ungesäumt einzustellen, und dabei beschlossen, dass nach 10 Uhr des Morgens niemanden gestattet sein soll, abzutreten. Dies ist, wie ich glaubwürdig berichtet worden bin, nur deshalb geschehen, weil der Herzog von York an demselben Tage nur durch zwei Stimmen von der Leistung des Testes entbunden worden ist, indem verschiedene Mitglieder sich entfernt, und wie verlautet hat des Königs Schatzmeister Tages vorher mehr als 100,000 Thaler vertheilt, um eine Stimmenmehrheit zu erhalten " (Schwerin to Frederick William, December 6, 1678, in *Briefe aus England*, p. 364). The charge of bribery, whether true or not, shows what Danby's attitude was believed to be.

[3] Barillon to Louis XIV, December 1, 1678.

[4] *Grey*, vi. 285-300.

[5] According to Sir Robert Southwell " there were not above five of the lords who stayed to vote that were for consenting to the address ; " while according to the Earl of Ossory there were eight (*Ormonde MSS.*, N.S., iv. 255, 484). In reality eleven lords voted for the address—Clare, Shaftesbury, Say and Sele, Halifax, Grey, Eure, Wharton, Paget, and the Bishops of Exeter, Lincoln and Oxford (Carte MSS. 81, f. 387).

Danby's support for this intrigue, " telling him it was in his power to bring that about which would make the kingdom happy and endear his memory for ever to it ; but the Treasurer tould him the King abhor'd the owning such an untruth." [1] In the early days of December Duke and Treasurer were believed to be more firmly united than for some time back,[2] and their union meant the continued strength of the triumvirate. Nearly two months after Parliament had met all the opposition had accomplished was the exclusion of a few Catholic peers from the Upper House and the impeachment and imprisonment in the Tower of five Catholic lords who had been accused by Oates.

While the Government was thus facing the storm surprisingly well, however, the Treasurer was growing increasingly uneasy about his own security. Apart from mere personal jealousy his enemies were inspired by many different motives. On the one hand were those who were interested in Irish affairs, and had been alienated by the support which he had accorded to Ranelagh and his associates. On the other hand were those who found a grievance in his reforms at the Treasury and his administration of the finances. But the most dangerous of all were those who denounced his recent conduct of affairs abroad, on the ground that it was designed, not to check France, but by securing an additional revenue and additional forces for the Crown to enslave the nation at home.[3] Between this group and the French King there was a real community of interests, for both were determined to secure the disbandment of the English army, and both were now convinced that their safety demanded the immediate ruin of the Treasurer. Throughout the autumn, accordingly, Barillon was entering into closer relations than ever before with Holles, Harbord, Littleton, Powle and others of the party, and was spending money lavishly to secure support for the objects which they had in common.[4]

[1] Clarke, *Life of James II*, i. 531.

[2] Carte MSS. 38, f. 678.

[3] An interesting account of Danby's personal enemies at this time is printed *infra*, iii. 6-7. It includes as possible enemies both the followers of Seymour and some of the supporters of the Duke of York.

[4] The progress of the intrigue can be traced in the French dispatches, from which a few extracts are printed by Dalrymple.

Had the matter gone no further Danby would have had no special cause for alarm ; but this particular group had a splendid weapon against him ready to hand in Ralph Montagu, who was in a position to produce apparently conclusive evidence of its main contention, that war with France had never been seriously intended. Probably in September Montagu entered into close relations with the group,[1] and during October he concluded a definite bargain with their ally the French ambassador, by which he undertook, in return for a sum of money, to produce letters in which Danby had instructed him to negotiate for a subsidy from France, and so drive the Treasurer from office.[2] Scarcely had Parliament met when by the united efforts of his associates he was returned to the House of Commons as member for the borough of Northampton,[3] and his personal safety was thus secured. Throughout November and December his scheme was being gradually perfected, and all that was needed was a favourable opportunity to put it in execution. The intention was that the Treasurer should not be attacked until the Duke of York had been finally disposed of, lest the appearance of a common danger should merely induce the triumvirate to unite together more closely than ever.[4]

Danby was perfectly well aware of what was going on,[5] but for a time deluded himself with the belief that Montagu would

---

[1] *Infra*, ii. 371-2.

[2] Barillon to Louis XIV, October 24, 27, November 3, 14, 1678.

[3] He first tried East Grinstead, but his overtures met with no encouragement there (*infra*, ii. 376). His success at Northampton was partly due to the Treasurer's excessive inclination to favour his own family. Danby first put forward his son-in-law, Lord O'Brien, whose father's death had caused the vacancy. Exception, however, was taken to him on account of his youth, and on his mother's refusal to let him stand he had to be withdrawn (Carte MSS. 103, f. 236 ; Earl of Northampton and John Willoughby to Danby, in Leeds MSS., Packets 10 and 16). Sir William Temple was then nominated, but his candidature began much too late, and he was defeated by 482 votes to 155 (*Records of the Borough of Northampton*, ii. 499). In spite of a certification to that effect from the Mayor, however, Temple was returned by the sheriff, and Montagu had to petition against the return. His petition was presented on November 6, and the House was sufficiently interested to examine the case itself on November 11, when without a dissentient voice he was declared duly elected and the sheriff was committed to the custody of the Serjeant at Arms (*C.J.*, ix. 533, 537-8 ; *Grey*, vi. 186 ; *Ormonde MSS.*, N.S., iv. 471).

[4] Barillon to Louis XIV, November 24, 1678.

[5] Notes of information which was reaching him in November are printed *infra*, iii. 8-9. *Cf.* also *infra*, ii. 377.

not dare to make public a transaction in which he had himself taken so prominent a part.[1] His confidence appears first to have been shaken by the arbitrary action of the Commons in sending Secretary Williamson to the Tower, which was generally interpreted as a prelude to a direct attack on the chief minister.[2] Even more ominous was the vote of December 2 for an address to the King " to represent the dangers of his adhering to private counsel and not taking the counsel of the Parliament."[3] Thereafter the Treasurer regarded an attack on himself as inevitable ; but he was by no means disposed to let his enemies choose their own time for making it. The Duke of York, he knew perfectly well, had repeatedly been tempted to abandon him, and might quite possibly succumb.[4] His obvious interest was to force Montagu out into the open while he had the King and Duke on his side, and while the Government was still strong enough to protect him.[5] Some information received through Sir Leoline Jenkins of secret conferences between Montagu and the papal nuncio was eagerly followed up, and enough was discovered, it was considered, to justify at least a formal investigation.

The particular incident which determined Danby's resolution, however, was connected with his own special province of finance. While granting a sum of £200,000 for the disbandment of the forces raised since September 1677, the Commons had insisted on providing against misappropriation of the money by a clause requiring it to be paid, not to the Exchequer, but to the Chamber of London. On December 16, when the bill of supply came up for its third reading, the full strength of the Court was exerted in an attempt to secure the deletion of this clause, with the result that a premature explosion nearly occurred. In the most emphatic manner the opposition declared their complete

[1] *Reresby*, pp. 158-9.

[2] November 18 (Barillon to Louis XIV, December 1, 5, 1678). Williamson was released, by order of the King, on the following day, which provided the Commons with a further grievance (*Cal. S.P. Dom.*, 1678, pp. 530, 531-2, 540 ; *Ormonde MSS.*, N.S., iv. 475-8 ; *Hist. MSS. Com.*, xii. 9, p. 72).

[3] *Grey*, vi. 301-15 ; *C.J.*, ix. 551 ; *Ormonde MSS.*, N.S., iv. 486. " My Lord Treasurer was struck at " (*Reresby*, p. 161).

[4] Barillon to Louis XIV, September 26, November 3, 1678.

[5] And possibly also before the army had been disbanded (Barillon to Louis XIV, January 5, 9, 1679).

lack of trust in those who had already kept the army embodied despite the Act for disbanding it. For the first time Danby was specifically named, and it was not obscurely hinted that future grants of money would be kept out of his hands as well.[1] Obviously the long-prepared attack was on the point of being delivered, and if he wished to anticipate it the sooner he moved the better.[2]

Early on the morning of Thursday, December 19, accordingly, an extraordinary meeting of Council was held, to which the King communicated the entire correspondence between Jenkins and Danby on the subject of Montagu's intrigues.[3] In view of such serious charges only one course of action was possible. An order was made for the seizure of Montagu's papers, and under the direction of the Clerks of Council his house was immediately surrounded by messengers.[4] No doubt one of the objects of the Court was to recover the letters which Danby and Charles himself had written to the ambassador ; but as they were well aware that some of these letters had already been widely read, and could guess that they might not all be in Montagu's possession, it is scarcely to be supposed that they expected by this means to stifle his information. Their real hope was that they might find sufficient confirmation of the charges brought against him to discredit him altogether, and if possible turn the hunt in the other direction.

Had Montagu not been a member of Parliament he would certainly have been arrested. At the moment when the Council took action, however, the Commons were actually sitting, Montagu was present in his place, and it was considered prudent simply to inform the House, through Sir John Ernly, of what

[1] Barillon to Louis XIV, December 26, 1678.

[2] *Ormonde MSS., N.S.,* iv. 490.

[3] The correspondence is printed *infra,* ii. 610-19. Williamson's notes of the meeting are printed in *Cal. S.P. Dom.,* 1678, p. 579.

[4] The order is recorded in P.C. Reg. 66, p. 483. As evidence of the interpretation placed upon Jenkins's information the preamble is significant— " Whereas the King had received information from his ambassador at Nimeguen that Montague, the late ambassador in France, had several private conferences with the Pope's nuncio, and did transact with him at unseasonable times in the night several matters in order to promote the Romish religion and, as it is violently to be suspected, tending to the advancing of the late damnable plott against his Majesty."

was being done. The debate on which the Commons were engaged, on the disorders committed by the army, was accordingly interrupted while Sir John delivered his message, that the King, having received information that Montagu, while ambassador in France, had held several private conferences with the Pope's nuncio there, had given orders for the seizure of his papers.[1]

The reception of this announcement by the House was of a very mixed character. On the one hand there was a general impression that any measures which might lead to discoveries in connection with the Plot should not be too readily called in question. " I wish the like proceedings had been in other cases," declared Serjeant Maynard ; " Coleman had time to sort his papers, and this diligence would have prevented it." Even Montagu's immediate confederates dared not risk the imputation of being favourers of the Plot by saying anything directly in his defence, and for a time took little part in the debate. On the other hand the Commons, as always, were very tenacious of their privileges. To seize a member's papers, it was argued, was much the same as to arrest his person, and neither could be justified except upon a charge of treason, felony or breach of the peace based upon information given in the proper legal way.

It was upon this point that the Commons ultimately concentrated, resolving after a long debate that they could come to no conclusion unless the King would be pleased to let them know what was the nature of the charge against Montagu and whether the information on which it was based was upon oath. With this vote Lord Cavendish and others were instructed to wait immediately upon the King ; while at the same time William Harbord was ordered to repair to Montagu's house to learn what actually had happened there. Harbord soon returned with the news that Montagu's papers had been carried off in four cabinets, which had been sealed up and were not to be opened until Montagu himself was present. But the House had long to wait before Lord Cavendish returned to report that the King was busy in the House of Lords, and had desired that they would attend him again at Whitehall when the House had risen.[2]

[1] C.J., ix. 559 ; Ormonde MSS., N.S., iv. 284-5.

[2] C.J., ix. 559 ; Grey, vi. 337-45.

This answer seemed the natural conclusion to the day's proceedings, and the Commons were on the very point of adjourning when Montagu himself spoke for the first time. During the period of waiting he and his confederates had been able to rearrange the plans which Danby's bold stroke had for the moment disconcerted, and they now delivered the attack which would have come in any case some days later. The whole object of the seizure of his papers, Montagu declared, was to secure some letters in his possession which would reveal the designs of one of the chief ministers. Immediately his friends took up the tale. Harbord asserted that the attack on Montagu had been intended for three or four days, but had failed to bring about the seizure of the incriminating documents. It was his knowledge of these documents which had made him so anxious to secure the election of Montagu to Parliament, and he considered them so important that he would rather forfeit £40,000 than the Government should have them. Lord Cavendish and Lord Russell, in somewhat more moderate language, also admitted their acquaintance with the papers in question and declared the importance of the secrets they would reveal.

In face of such testimony the somewhat apathetic attitude of the House changed to one of considerable excitement. The more moderate members proposed that Montagu's papers should be produced and examined on the following day. The extremists professed doubt as to what the morrow might bring forth, and desired to proceed at once. " For ought I know," declared Sir John Lowther, " Montagu may be served as Sir Edmundbury Godfrey was ; therefore I would not have him go out of the House for the papers. . . . I am of the opinion that we shall not sit here to-morrow. I move therefore to have the papers sent for now." Seconded by Sir Henry Capel this motion received the approval of the House, and the indefatigable Harbord was once more dispatched, along with three other members, to find the papers which Montagu believed he had put beyond the reach of the King's messengers.[1]

At the contents of the box with which he returned it is possible to hazard a guess. They presumably included not merely Danby's letters to Montagu of December 24, 1677, and

[1] *Grey*, vi. 345-7.

January 17, February 11 and March 25, 1678, but also the King's note of July 18, [1677].[1] As yet, however, Montagu had no thought of attacking the King, and when at the command of the House he selected from his box those letters which he considered would be of most service it was Danby's letters of January 17 and March 25 that he chose. With many hypocritical professions of regret at the painful duty that was being forced upon him he presented these to the Speaker, and they were immediately read.

The first letter produced little excitement, but the effect of the references contained in the second to peace and a subsidy from France was absolutely instantaneous. Member after member rose and moved that the Treasurer should be impeached of high treason. Harbord specially distinguished himself by the fury of his declamation, and by the wildness of his assertions about danger to the King's person, " poisons both liquid and in powders," and other horrors which Montagu, unless meanwhile made away with, would still reveal. But Danby's supporters were by no means silenced. Under the leadership of Sir Henry Goodricke they tried to confuse the main issue by concentrating on Harbord's extravagances and insisting that in a matter of such moment as the King's safety his statements should be investigated. Sir Thomas Higgons denied that there was anything to be ashamed of in concluding an honourable peace, or extorting money from a foreign ruler as a condition of it. " It is a very ordinary thing," he declared, " for Kings to get money from one another, as in Edward IV's and Henry VII's time, and there is no ground of this accusation of treason against this lord." Sir John Birkenhead went further and boldly carried the war into the enemies' territory. If the letters were treason, he pointed out, concealment of them was misprision of treason, and Montagu had been acquainted with their contents for six months.

The House of Commons, however, had received too severe a shock to reason calmly, or give such arguments the weight they deserved. Even Sir John Ernly's very reasonable demand,

---

[1] *Infra*, ii. 273, 304, 330, 334, 346. These are the letters which Montagu produced, together with those which still remain among the Montagu MSS. at Whitehall. It is not very certain what the " order from the Treasurer " is which Montagu offered to produce on December 21 (*Grey*, vi. 369).

made perhaps at Danby's suggestion, that Montagu's replies
to the incriminating letters should be produced, was practically
ignored. After a debate which continued until ten o'clock at
night it was resolved that there was sufficient matter of impeachment against the Treasurer, and a committee was appointed to draw up articles against him.[1]

Danby's counter-attack was a feeble one. He could easily
have shown, by means of the letters from Montagu in his hands,
that his accuser was deeply implicated in the French intrigues,
but only at the expense of bringing forward additional proofs
against himself. He accordingly tried to establish the fact that
a large section of the opposition were in league with France,
and with that object sent a note to the Speaker on the following
morning enclosing the two letters in which Montagu had given
him information of young Ruvigny's object in visiting England.[2] Unfortunately these letters were vague in their tenor,
and the only name they specifically mentioned was that of
Lord Russell, one of the most respected members of the House.
The reading of them must have given Montagu some uneasy
moments,[3] and certainly did not improve his reputation with
his associates, but on the general temper of the Commons they
had no effect whatever, and after debate it was resolved that
they should not be entered in the Journal.[4]

The impeachment thus proceeded unchecked, and on December 21 the committee appointed to draw up articles reported to
the House. The charges formulated against the Treasurer were
much more serious than those of 1675. On his letters to Montagu were based three accusations, all of which it was hoped to
maintain were treasonable—that he had " encroached to himself regal power " by conducting foreign affairs without reference to the Secretaries and the Council, and in defiance of the
wishes of the King and Parliament ; that he had endeavoured

[1] A division was taken on the proposal that the question should be put, and
carried against the Court by 179 to 116. See *C.J.*, ix. 559-60 ; *Grey*, vi. 337-
59 ; *Ormonde MSS.*, *N.S.*, iv. 284-5 ; *Reresby*, pp. 162-4 ; Carte MSS. 38, f. 682.

[2] Montagu to Danby, January 11 and 18, 1678, *infra*, ii. 318, 325.

[3] Grey records six speeches by the ambassador, which give a strong impression that he hardly knew what to say.

[4] The Duke of Leeds in later life firmly believed that the Commons had
refused even to read these letters, but he was certainly wrong (*C.J.*, ix. 561 ;
Grey, vi. 359-64 ; *Reresby*, pp. 164-5).

to introduce an arbitrary government, by raising an army on pretence of a war, and then continuing it in existence in spite of an Act of Parliament for disbanding it ; and that he had negotiated for a French subsidy to enable him to do without Parliament. To these were added the stock charges that he had wasted the King's treasure on pensions and secret service, and that he had procured great gifts for himself ; while an appeal to the passion of the moment was made by an absurd accusation that he was " popishly affected " and had concealed the Plot.[1]

Until ten o'clock at night the battle raged over these articles. Danby's supporters put up a good struggle, and forced no fewer than five divisions ; but they were beaten every time, and article after article was adjudged to provide sufficient ground for an impeachment.[2] Finally it was resolved that the articles should be engrossed, and should be sent up to the Lords when the Houses met again on the Monday, together with a clause desiring that the Treasurer should be sequestered from Parliament and committed to safe custody. On the afternoon of December 23,[3] accordingly, Sir Henry Capel appeared at the bar of the House of Lords, formally delivered the impeachment, and presented the request of the Commons.[4]

The short interval provided by the Sunday, however, had

[1] The articles of impeachment are printed *infra*, ii. 74-5.

[2] The Court party first concentrated on what they described as the irregular way in which the articles had been drawn up, and proposed that they should be recommitted. This was negatived by 179 votes to 135. They then endeavoured to secure the omission of the word " traiterously " from the first article, but were defeated by 179 to 141. The remaining divisions were less important (*C.J.*, ix. 562 ; *Grey*, vi. 366-87 ; *Ormonde MSS.*, N.S., iv. 286). The frequency with which the opposition vote reached one particular figure was much commented on. " The victorious side was alwayes 179, although there were some changed sides, and some went away, and others came in before every question, which has been looked upon as an omen—amongst them that wish it—that my Lord Treasurer is to loose his place in the year '79 " (*Hist. MSS. Com.*, xii. 9, p. 79). In reality the vote was not always the same.

[3] In the morning the time of the Commons had been partly occupied by the King's reply to their address desiring information about the accusation against Montagu. Charles sent them the correspondence between Danby and Jenkins, and the letters were read in the House, but they produced no effect whatever (*Grey*, vi. 387-9).

[4] The proper procedure was much in doubt, and the original idea seems to have been that after the articles had been presented and read Capel should make a speech explaining them. This idea, however, was abandoned (B.M. Add. MSS. 35865, ff. 64, 69).

enabled Danby to prepare his defence. At some time on that day he appears to have persuaded the King to inscribe a written authorisation on the drafts which he had preserved of the letters produced by Montagu, and with this to encourage him he rose as soon as Capel had left the House of Lords and delivered so convincing a speech [1] that when at the close he desired directions whether he should withdraw the House after a long debate resolved by a majority of twenty that he should not.[2] The hour being then late the whole matter had to be adjourned over

---

[1] Printed in *Memoirs of the Earl of Danby*, App., p. 40. The original notes for it are in B.M. Add. MSS. 28043, f. 3. This speech contains clear evidence that the note inscribed by the King on both drafts, " I aprove of this letter, C.R.," had already been written by the time it was delivered. That it had only recently been written seems to be the inevitable conclusion from a number of significant circumstances. (1) The actual letters sent to Montagu certainly did not bear the King's authorisation in any shape or form. These letters were presented to the House of Commons, entered in its Journal, read and copied by dozens of people, and printed in several pamphlets. It is incredible that if they contained a note in the King's handwriting there should not remain absolutely definite evidence to that effect. On the contrary the debate in the Commons seems to show that the only suggestion of the King's authority was that contained in Danby's own words in the second letter, " I am comanded by his Majestie to lett you know." If, however, the Treasurer did not think it worth while to ask the King to write his authorisation on the letters, he is hardly likely to have asked him to write it on the drafts at that time. (2) Although Danby retained drafts of many incriminating letters to Montagu not one of these bears a royal authorisation in any shape or form with the exception of the drafts of the two letters on which he was impeached. The conclusion would seem to be that the authorisation was written after the impeachment had commenced, when there was no longer any doubt which letters were to be used as evidence. Until then Danby could not know how many letters his messengers would recover, or even what letters Montagu had preserved. (3) The earlier of the two letters is so innocent in character that it is impossible to believe Danby thought of asking for any authorisation for it until he knew that it had been produced in Parliament. The absurdity of the authorisation, in fact, is so obvious that the Duke of Leeds, when publishing his *Letters*, omitted it altogether. (4) Although one draft was drawn up more than two months before the other the two notes of authorisation are precisely similar. It seems highly probable they were written at the same time, and that need not have been the time at which either draft was drawn up.

[2] *L.J.*, xiii. 432-4 ; *Reresby*, p. 166 ; *Ormonde MSS.*, *N.S.*, iv. 289, 491. Barillon declares that many even of the Court party were in favour of his withdrawing, but that the opposition were content to let him remain in his place " pour donner plus de matiere d'aigreur à la chambre basse " (Barillon to Louis XIV, January 5, 1679). It is impossible at this point, however, to trust Barillon where Danby is concerned. His idea seems to be disproved by the fact that Buckingham, Shaftesbury, Wharton and fifteen others protested. Lord Herbert explains the attitude of the House as due to " the King's pressing them and the Prince being present all the while the matter was debated " (*Hist. MSS. Com.*, xii. 9, p. 80).

Christmas Eve and Christmas Day to December 26, when the
Treasurer himself prayed for " a speedy way of dispatch, " and
the question of his commitment was taken into consideration.
To this, however, the Lords showed themselves strongly op-
posed, and after long debate it was resolved on December 27
that he should not be committed, that he should be allowed
counsel and a copy of the articles, and should be given until
January 3 to put in his answer. A quarrel between Lords and
Commons thus seemed imminent, when on December 30 the
King suddenly prorogued Parliament to February 4.[1]

The statement freely made at the time, and frequently
repeated since, that the object of the prorogation was to save
the Treasurer, is without foundation. Danby was well enough
satisfied with the way the impeachment was progressing, and
would have preferred that it should be carried through as
rapidly as possible. He frequently declared that the prorogation was not his work.[2] But Charles had become alarmed for
his own safety. Both Danby and Montagu knew so much that
he dared not allow a formal trial in which one would be the
accused and the other the principal witness. In the course of
the charges and counter-charges which were bound to be
made it was impossible even to conjecture what might be
brought to light.[3] The only way of escape seemed to be to stop
proceedings for the moment and try to bring about some
accommodation.

Further, there was a very definite practical reason for the
prorogation. The congestion of business at Whitehall was

---

[1] *L.J.*, xiii. 434, 441 ; *Ormonde MSS.*, N.S., iv. 492-5. " La délibération
qui s'y fit [i.e. in the House of Lords] il y a trois jours fut toute à l'advantage de
Milord Tresorier, et il passa d'un grand nombre de voix que ce ministre ne se
retireroit point et qu'il ne seroit point mis en prison. La chambre basse a
soustenu que tout cela estoit contre les regles et contre la justice, et prétendoit
poursuivre l'accusation encore plus vivement " (Barillon to Louis XIV, January
9, 1679). A division list for the Lords at this time is printed *infra*, iii. 129-33.

[2] " My Lord Treasurer laments more than any man the prorogation, which
hee everywhere declares that hee did with his utmost oppose, as making his
cause worse than any other aggravation could doe, and the King himself hath
freely spoken to the same effect " (Southwell to Ormonde, January 4, 1678/9,
in Carte MSS. 39, f. 1).

[3] Montagu's knowledge of the French intrigues went back to the Secret
Treaty of Dover, the truth about which he may possibly have known,
and he had in his possession at least one note in the King's handwriting
authorising his own negotiations.

becoming quite alarming The work of clearing up the confusion caused by the ill-starred military adventures of the
year would alone have been sufficient to occupy all the time of
the Government. When to this were added constant investigation into a constantly expanding plot, and the labour of carrying out the behests of a Parliament which sat every day and
often all day, officials were at a loss where to turn themselves.[1]
Some relief had been hoped from the usual Christmas recess,
but the Houses had been content with two days. The King
therefore took it upon himself to insist on a breathing space, in
which his servants might overtake their arrears of work, complete the disbanding of the army, and find, if possible, " the
bottom of the Plot." [2]

Meanwhile Charles, James and Danby embarked upon a
desperate effort to discover some way out of the maze into
which they had wandered. Charles as usual had recourse to
France, but Louis believed that his main object, the disbandment of the army, could more surely be obtained through
Parliament than through the King, and declined to give any
immediate assistance. James rested his hopes on the support
of the army, but Charles refused to countenance violent
measures. Danby inaugurated a fresh policy of retrenchment,
and with the defection of some of his own followers fresh in his
mind stopped the payment of all pensions for fifteen months ;
but it was clear that the relief secured by this means would
be quite inadequate.[3] Each of the three found himself driven
back upon the conclusion that the only way out of their difficulties was to come to terms with the opposition.

A month earlier this would have been practically impossible,
but the opposition had been seriously alarmed by the course of
events and by the prorogation of Parliament. The resisting
power of the Court had proved much greater than they had

[1] *L.J.*, xiii. 333 ; *C.J.*, ix. 531. A typical day in Sir Robert Southwell's
life at this time is described in *Ormonde MSS.*, *N.S.*, iv. 480. In a letter
written four years later he declares of the Popish Plot period that " during
that intervall I could have lived with more ease in a powder mill " (B.M.
Add. MSS. 38015, f. 279).

[2] His speech to Parliament is printed in *Grey*, vi. 400-1. The day after the
prorogation he spoke in similar terms to the Mayor and Aldermen of London
(Barillon to Louis XIV, January 12, 1679).

[3] Barillon to Louis XIV, January 12, 1679 ; *Ormonde MSS.*, *N.S.*, iv. 495.

anticipated, and their repeated efforts to break up the triumvirate which controlled the Government had resulted only in
uniting it more firmly than ever. A reconciliation between
Charles and the French King was always a possibility, and
might mean the complete ruin of their schemes. About the
middle of January, accordingly, Holles and the leaders of the
Presbyterian party [1] entered into negotiations with the Court,
and in a few days a definite agreement was reached. As regards
the general situation Charles undertook to disband the army,
dissolve the existing Parliament, and summon a new one, in
return for an immediate loan, to render the disbandment
possible, and a reasonable supply when Parliament should meet.
The Presbyterians, however, declared that it was impossible
to entrust the money to Danby or maintain him in his post,
and it was accordingly arranged that he should resign, but
should not be prosecuted. [2] Charles was thus freed from
his fear of what a trial might bring to light, and received
some assurance regarding the future ; Danby was provided
with an honourable way of escape from a difficult situation,
and the only person left unconsidered appeared to be the
Duke of York. But James had convinced himself that as far
as the Catholics were concerned no Parliament could be worse
than the existing one, and readily fell in with the idea of a
dissolution. [3]

So long as the negotiation continued the position was completely uncertain. On January 17 the King endeavoured to
secure more time for consideration by announcing in Council

[1] Burnet names Holles, Littleton, Boscawen and Hampden (*History of my
Own Time*, ii. 187).

[2] Holles declared that he was prepared to save " le Comte Danbi, mais non
pas le Grand Tresorier " (Barillon to Louis XIV, January 26, 30, February 9,
1679 ; *Burnet*, ii. 187-8 ; *Reresby*, p. 168). Shaftesbury was not a party to
this negotiation. At the time when it was going on he was conducting two
separate intrigues, one with Danby and the other with the Duke of York, in
the hope of setting them against each other (Robert Brent to Danby, January
21, 1678/9, in B.M. Add. MSS. 28053, f. 133 ; Thomas Knox to Danby, January 23, 1678/9, B.M. Add. MSS. 28047, f. 47 ; information of Lord Chandos,
February 20, 1678/9, in *Morrison Catalogue*, i. 181). Later, however, he
claimed credit for the result. " Of this dissolution my Lord Danby bore the
blame, thoe my Lord Shaftesbury gloried it was at his instance, when the other
desired to know what might appease his prosecutors " (Sir Robert Southwell
to Thomas Henshaw, November 22, 1682, in B.M. Add. MSS. 38015, f. 278).

[3] *Hist. MSS. Com.*, xv. 5, pp. 127-8.

a further short prorogation of the old Parliament to February 25,[1] and two days later a proclamation for proroguing was actually read and approved.[2] So widespread was the dissatisfaction aroused, however, that the speedy assembling either of the old or of a new Parliament was accepted as absolutely necessary, the proclamation was stopped, and after a period of painful hesitation the King on January 24, without submitting the matter to debate, announced a dissolution and the summons of a new Parliament to meet on March 6.[3] Immediately Danby began to make his preparations. He had already carried through a partial reconstruction of the ministry. The Solicitor-General, Sir Francis Winnington, who had been specially prominent in support of the impeachment, had been replaced by Heneage Finch, the second son of the Lord Chancellor.[4] Sir Stephen Fox and others who had voted with the majority had been dismissed from their employments.[5] The Earl of Salisbury had been admitted to the Privy Council.[6] One more effort had been made, though with the same ill-success as before, to induce Temple to accept Coventry's place as Secretary of State.[7] Now more strenuous measures were adopted. Secretary Williamson, who had proved too weak for a time of crisis, was dismissed to make room for the Earl of Sunderland,[8] and Temple, whose refusal of promotion was believed to have

---

[1] P.C. Reg. 67, p. 27 ; Cal. S.P. Dom., 1679-80, p. 37 ; Carte MSS. 243, ff. 363, 428.

[2] Williamson's notes in Cal. S.P. Dom., 1679-80, p. 41.

[3] " Le Roy d'Angleterre declara son intention vendredi au soir dans le conseil, et dit quil ne demandoit l'advis d'aucun de ceux qui estoient presens, parce qu'ils avoient tesmoigne en plusieurs occasions avoir plus d'esgard a ce qui pourroit plaire à la chambre basse et au peuple qu'a ce qui convient a l'autorité et à la dignité royale " (Barillon to Louis XIV, February 6, 1679 ; Cal. S.P. Dom., 1679-80, p. 52 ; P.C. Reg. 67, p. 46 ; Carte MSS. 39, f. 5 ; B.M. Add. MSS. 29557, f. 85 ; 29577, f. 181).

[4] Luttrell, i. 6-7.

[5] Barillon to Louis XIV, January 2, 1679 ; Ormonde MSS., N.S., iv. 284, 290-1, 496 ; Hist. MSS. Com., xii. 9, pp. 79-80.

[6] Hist. MSS. Com., xii. 7, p. 153.

[7] Danby to Temple, January 8, Temple to Danby, January 27, 1679, infra, ii. 505, 508.

[8] February 9 (Hatton Correspondence, i. 175 ; Luttrell, i. 9). Sunderland was sworn in on February 10 (P.C. Reg. 67, p. 87). His appointment was intimated beforehand by the King to Barillon and represented as a concession to France (Barillon to Louis XIV, February 16, 1679).

been partly based on hostility to Williamson, was commanded to return to England with a view to becoming Secretary.[1]

Danby's chief object, however, was to allay the general fear of popery which was at the bottom of all the trouble, and this meant a serious effort to solve the problem presented by the Duke of York. The happiest solution would have been the return of the Duke to the national Church, and with this in view the Treasurer instigated the Archbishop of Canterbury and the Bishop of Winchester to wait upon him and beg him to reconsider his position.[2] On the complete failure of their representations nothing remained but to press for the Duke's dismissal from Court. James himself considered the suggestion a fatal one, and believed it would prove a mere prelude to his exclusion from the throne ; but he asserted his willingness to go abroad if ordered to do so by the King, and a draft order was immediately supplied by Danby.[3] At the same time the Treasurer endeavoured to conciliate the Duke and ruin at least one scheme of his opponents by prevailing with the King to declare publicly that he had not been married to Monmouth's mother. James himself had been unable to obtain such a declaration, but Danby urged the matter so strongly that on March 3 the King formally declared in Council that he had never married any woman but the Queen, and all the Councillors present signed the declaration.[4] A few hours later the Duke and Duchess of York embarked for Holland.[5]

Meanwhile Danby had been doing all he could to influence public opinion and secure a favourable Parliament. At the very moment when the bishops were waiting upon the Duke a pamphlet containing the two letters from Montagu which he had sent to the Commons, together with his own speech in the House

[1] Danby to William of Orange, and to Temple, February 11, 1678/9, *infra*, ii. 441, 511.

[2] Barillon to Louis XIV, March 6, 1679, in *Dalrymple*, ii. 213 ; Clarke, *Life of James II*, i. 537-40 ; *Hatton Correspondence*, i. 177 ; *Clarendon Correspondence*, ii. 465-71.

[3] Danby's draft, endorsed, " I gave this to the King 26th of February [16]78/9," is printed in *Lindsey MSS.*, p. 401. The King's order, dated February 28, has been frequently printed.

[4] P.C. Reg. 67, p. 121.

[5] Clarke, *Life of James II*, i. 140-2 ; *Cal. S.P. Dom.*, 1679-80, pp. 95-6 ; *Hist. MSS. Com.*, xii. 7, pp. 156-7 ; *Ormonde MSS.*, N.S., iv. 341.

of Lords,[1] was being " cryed in the streetes." [2] Shortly afterwards a more elaborate defence appeared of the whole transaction with France.[3] At the same time an anxious eye was
kept upon the elections and Government candidates were
supported wherever that could safely be done.[4]

But as February drew to a close Danby's confidence began to
give way. On the 24th of the month Temple reached London,[5]
only to make it plain that he would not undertake the Secretary's office in such troublous times.[6] Still more ominous were
the election returns which were pouring in. No one had
seriously expected that they would be favourable to the Court,
but they proved much worse than had been anticipated.[7]

[1] *Two Letters from Mr. Montagu to the Lord Treasurer, one of the 11th, the
other of the 18th of January, 1677/8, which were read in the House of Commons,
together with the Lord Treasurer's Speech in the House of Peers, upon an Impeachment of High Treason, &c., brought up against his Lordship by the House of
Commons, December 23, 1678* ; London, Jonathan Edwin, 1679. This pamphlet was later called in question by the Commons, and it was proposed that
it should be burnt by the common hangman (*Grey*, vii. 32-50). The French
ambassador thought it worth suggesting to his own Court that an answer
should be published (Barillon to Louis XIV, March 13, 20, 1679).

[2] B.M. Add. MSS. 29557, f. 114.

[3] *An Explanation of the Lord Treasurer's Letter to Mr. Montagu, the King's
late Embassador in France, March 25th, 1678, together with the said Letter, and
the two Letters of Mr. Montagu which were read in the House of Commons, 1679.*
There is little doubt that Danby himself wrote this pamphlet.

[4] Danby to Newcastle, January 24, 1678/9, in *Portland MSS.*, ii. 153 ;
Danby to Latimer, February 3, 1678/9, in *Lindsey MSS.*, p. 401 ; Albemarle to
Danby, February 13, Lindsey to Danby, February 15, in Leeds MSS., Packet
10 ; *Reresby*, p. 169 ; *Hatton Correspondence*, i. 174 ; *Cal. S.P. Dom.*, 1679-80,
pp. 58, 59, 64, 65-6, 70, 75 ; *Further Correspondence of Samuel Pepys*, p. 347.
The methods adopted were often questionable, but no more so than those of
the opposition. In writing to Louis XIV on January 30/February 9 Barillon
urged the importance of the coming elections as a reason for a moderate
expenditure among his allies in the Commons. " Ils seront presque tous
esleus membres de la chambre des communes, et il leur en coustera pour se
faire eslire, car il faut en plusieurs endroits achepter les voix, et partout il faut
faire boire beaucoup ceux qui ont le droit de l'election."

[5] B.M. Add. MSS. 29557, f. 114.

[6] Temple, *Works*, i. 331-2, 479. The reason which Temple advanced, that
there ought to be at least one Secretary in the House of Commons, could
scarcely be refuted. The Government made every effort to secure his election,
but he took good care that the attempts should fail.

[7] *Burnet*, ii. 202. " Les elections des deputés de la chambre basse se font
presque partout avec un esprit d'aigreur contre la cour plus grand encore qu'on
ne l'avoit crû. Il suffit dans la plus part des lieux qui ont le droit d'eslire que
quelqu'un soit soupçonné d'estre dans les interests de sa Majesté Britanique
pour avoir une exclusion formelle " (Barillon to Louis XIV, February 27, 1679).

Lord Cavendish and Sacheverell were returned for Derbyshire
without spending a penny. Ralph Montagu, finding himself the
object of special opposition in Northamptonshire, hurriedly
accepted an invitation from the neighbouring county of Huntingdon, and "was chosen without trouble with one night's
stay." The Treasurer's relatives fared particularly badly.
Charles and Peregrine Bertie found themselves so ill supported
at Stamford that they retired from the contest. Henry Bertie
was defeated at Westbury. Lord Latimer nearly suffered the
same fate at Buckingham, where " the Duke of Buckingham
went himself to the town and made it his business to persuade
the people not to choose " him. In the entire House of Commons not another Osborne or Bertie was to be found.[1]

The effect was completely to upset the calculations not
merely of the Court but of the opposition leaders as well. While
the reduction of the placemen in the Commons to a mere hand-
ful [2] deprived the former of all control, the appearance of a
large number of new members who had no immediate association with the various factions of the previous Parliament, and
no knowledge of the engagements into which these factions had
entered, had much the same effect on the latter. Holles and his
fellows, one must suppose, were honourably desirous of fulfilling
the promises they had made to Charles and Danby, but they
were unable to do so. Such party discipline as they had built up
was shattered by the incursion of men who had never learned to
submit to it. The House of Commons was " resolved to venture
an hundred dissolutions rather then not ruin my Lord Treasurer ; " [3] and so long as it remained in that mood its leaders
could retain their positions only by submitting to its wishes.[4]

---

[1] *Hist. MSS. Com.*, xiii. 6, pp. 13, 14 ; *Ormonde MSS., N.S*, iv. 315, 317.
Dumblane was returned for Corfe Castle, but unseated on petition (*C.J.*, ix.
569, 594).

[2] Between 25 and 30 (*Ranke*, iv. 73). The French ambassador put the number on whom the Court could absolutely rely at 30 or 40 (Barillon to Louis XIV,
March 6, 1679).

[3] *Hatton Correspondence*, i. 178.

[4] " Les chefs des cabales et ceux qui avoient le principal credit dans l'ancien
Parlement ne sçavent ou ils en sont, car le grand nombre des deputés des
provinces qui n'ont aucune experience ny cognoissance des affaires prevaut
contre toutes les raisons, et personne n'ose les contredire ny s'opposer a leurs
mouvemens quelques irreguliers qu'ils soient " (Barillon to Louis XIV, April
6, 1679).

To an experienced parliamentarian like Danby the possibility of some such development was early apparent, and he lost no time in communicating his fears to his master. Unfortunately the measures to which King and minister had recourse in order to meet the danger were destined only to aggravate it. As a last barrier against the trial which he dared not allow Danby to face Charles persuaded him to accept a pardon of all offences committed before February 27, 1679.[1] The actual passing of the pardon presented some difficulty, for it was considered advisable to keep it secret, and it was doubtful whether any minister would venture to concur in it. All the preliminary offices were accordingly omitted, and the pardon having been engrossed Lord Chancellor Finch was commanded to bring the great seal and affix it. Finch, however, refused to do more than bring the seal, and the King therefore, having signed the pardon, handed it to the Chancellor's secretary, and commanded him to affix the seal in his presence.[2]

Danby himself, on the other hand, turned to Parliament. Of building up a real Court party in the House of Commons he had no hope whatever ; but in the chaotic situation which the absence of all party discipline would inevitably produce there, much, he knew, would depend upon the Speaker, and he therefore determined to secure the appointment of one upon whom he could rely. For some time he and Seymour had been drifting away from each other. Seymour had greatly resented the part which he had been required to play in bringing about the adjournments of 1677, and had been somewhat alarmed at the trouble in which they had involved him. In the spring of 1678 his defection from the existing Court party had been eagerly anticipated, and in the autumn he had endeavoured to reconcile himself with the opposition by advocating some of the most

---

[1] The pardon, dated March 1, 1679, is printed in *Memoirs of the Earl of Danby*, App., p. 12. It was a common thing in the reign of Charles II for statesmen to take out a pardon. All the members of the Cabal had done so before meeting Parliament in October 1673. Characteristically enough, Danby had never stooped to this course, and there is no good reason to suppose that he did so now. If he had wanted a pardon he would have obtained it in the previous December, when he knew that Montagu's attack was coming. The pardon was the King's contribution to the solution of a difficult problem.

[2] *C.J.*, ix. 575 ; *Finch MSS.*, ii. 46, 49-50.

extreme measures against the Catholics.[1] There was a general impression that he was too apprehensive for his own safety to be ready to do all the Court might require of him, while, as he had recently had a serious quarrel with Lady Danby, it was unlikely that he would risk anything for the sake of the Treasurer.[2] Probably for these reasons he had not been made a party to the bargain between Danby and the opposition, and had thus another grievance in the dissolution of Parliament, which had meant the exclusion from political life of many of his personal followers.[3] Danby accordingly looked for another candidate for the post of Speaker, and fixed upon Sir Thomas Meres, whose moderate attitude, it was hoped, would recommend him to all parties, and who, although not one of the group led by Holles, may possibly have had some share in the bargain which that group had made.

Seymour, however, had confidently expected to be Speaker, and was extremely reluctant to lose either the emoluments of the office or the dignity and importance it conferred. On the decision in favour of Sir Thomas Meres being announced to him by the Treasurer, with an intimation that the King believed he would be of more service out of the chair than in it,[4] he allowed both Charles and Danby to understand that he acquiesced, and then entered into negotiations with the opposition to secure his own appointment. Among the more extreme opponents of the Court a rumour of the intended changes had served only to spread a belief that Meres had been bought by the Government, and Seymour's overtures were given a ready welcome. The result was seen when Parliament met on March 6. The customary practice was for one of the Privy Councillors in the

---

[1] His attitude is well illustrated by his speeches in Grand Committee on November 22 (*Grey*, vi. 264-8 ; *Ormonde MSS.*, N.S., iv. 478-9).

[2] During the opening stages of the impeachment he had given " little satisfaction in the chaire to my Lord Treasurer's freinds " (Southwell to Ormonde, December 21, 1678, in Carte MSS. 38, f. 683) ; and as early as January 11 Danby was being warned not to rely upon him (B.M. Add. MSS. 28049, f. 30).

[3] *Cal. S.P. Dom.*, 1679-80, p. 77.

[4] This was not a new suggestion. In 1675 it had been proposed that Seymour should be made a peer in order to increase the debating strength of the Court in the House of Lords, and the intimation may therefore have been something more than a polite method of dismissal. Danby's announcement to Seymour was made on March 3 (*Hatton Correspondence*, i. 178 ; *Cal. S.P. Dom.*, 1679-80, p. 98).

Commons to propose as Speaker the candidate approved by the Court ; but before Sir John Ernly, who had been entrusted with the task of nominating Meres, could make any motion, Colonel Birch rose and proposed Seymour, whose name was received with acclamation. Amid noise and tumult which effectively drowned Ernly's belated efforts to speak, Sir Thomas Lee, Sir Richard Ingoldsby and others then carried Seymour to the chair, and after he had protested his unfitness in the customary short address the House adjourned for the day.

News of what had occurred filled Charles with a miserable uncertainty. Of Seymour's ability and general willingness to maintain the interests of the Crown there was not the slightest real doubt. Sir Thomas Meres was admittedly a poor substitute. When on the evening of his election the newly chosen Speaker presented himself at Court he was accordingly well received, and was given assurances which enabled him to assert, and possibly to believe, that the King approved of the choice the Commons had made. No uncertainty, however, existed in the mind of Danby. If a Speaker on whom he could rely had been desirable before, this foretaste of how the Commons were likely to behave only made such a Speaker more necessary and Seymour more objectionable than ever. Later on the same evening, accordingly, he in turn waited on Charles and persuaded him to abide by the original arrangement.

Probably Seymour knew or suspected that he had done so. On the following morning, in any case, when the Commons were summoned to the House of Lords to present their Speaker, he omitted the customary request to be excused, confining himself instead to a brief and, some considered, offensive statement that he had been unanimously chosen by the Commons and if approved by the King would do them and him the best service he could. In some confusion at this unexpected behaviour the Chancellor informed him that he was reserved for a different service, and required the Commons to make another choice ; but nothing daunted Seymour then turned to the King, and in a further interview obtained, so he said, a complete approbation for himself.[1]

[1] *Grey*, vi. 402-5 ; *Hatton Correspondence*, i. 178-81 ; Latimer to the Corporation of Buckingham, B.M. Add. MSS. 28087, f. 11 ; 29557, f. 121 ; *Ormonde MSS.*, N.S., iv. 346-7, 498-9 ; Barillon to Louis XIV, March 16, 20, 1679.

Danby was bitterly aggrieved. In the most outspoken manner he reproached the King with abandoning him, and urged the necessity of maintaining the royal right of approbation against the attempt of the Commons to get the choice of the Speaker entirely into their own hands.[1] For ten days a double battle raged, on the one hand a contest between Danby and Seymour at Court to secure control of the King, on the other hand a struggle between King and Commons over the right to nominate the Speaker. Seymour openly boasted that Charles was on his side, and that he did not " valew the Treasurer's power of a fidlestick." The King, however, when it came to the point, gave his support to his chief minister, and the dispute with the Commons ended in a compromise. Both Seymour and Meres were laid aside, and on March 15, after a short prorogation to enable a fresh start to be made, Serjeant Gregory was chosen Speaker.[2]

This was an unhappy beginning for a session on which so much depended, but worse was soon to follow. In undertaking to resign his offices Danby had not had any thought of going away empty-handed. He expected the customary " compensation " given to officials who demitted office with the approval and favour of the King, and not unreasonably, considering his great services to the Crown, put his pretensions fairly high. The original idea appears to have been that he should be given the post of Lord Steward of the Household, which Ormonde was to be induced to surrender, and this idea was carried so far that suitable compensation for Ormonde was in turn discussed ; [3]

[1] Memorandum printed *infra*, ii. 71-2.

[2] This solution of the difficulty was proposed by William Russell and Lord Cavendish in agreement with the Court. Sacheverell declared himself opposed to all compromise, but felt the House so little approved of his attitude that he offered to withdraw, and had his judgment immediately confirmed by shouts from all quarters of " Go, go " (*Grey*, vi. 405-39 ; vii. 1-4 ; *Hatton Correspondence*, i. 181-4 ; *Ormonde MSS.*, N.S., iv. 356-7 ; *Finch MSS.*, ii. 47). Gregory was approved by the King on March 17 (*L.J.*, xiii. 461).

[3] *Hist. MSS. Com.*, xiv. 7, p. 26 ; *Ormonde MSS.*, N.S., iv. 320, 324, 328, 340, " Il s'est respandu depuis deux jours un bruit que Milord Tresorier a dessein de se demettre de sa charge, qu'il acheptera celle de grand maistre de la maison de sa Majesté Britanique, que les finances seront administrées par des commissaires qu'il fera choisir luy mesme, et qui seront entierement dans sa dependance " (Barillon to Louis XIV, February 27, 1679). Danby's draft of the letter which the King was to write to Ormonde is printed in *Lindsey MSS.*, p. 401.

but the scheme had eventually to be abandoned, and when on March 13 the King called upon Danby for his promised resignation he was offered instead a pension of £5,000 a year for life, and the rank of marquis. The grant of the pension actually passed all the offices as far as the great seal, but was there stopped.[1] The warrant for the marquisate was drawn up, signed by Charles and Sunderland, and formally handed to the Earl at a meeting of the Cabinet Council on March 16.[2] At the same time the King declared his great satisfaction with his Treasurer's services, but announced that he thought it advisable to put his position into the hands of commissioners, who would take office on Lady Day.[3]

Even Holles and the Presbyterians can scarcely have given their assent to anything like this, and in the fury aroused among the other members of the opposition they found at least a fair excuse for receding from their bargain with the Court.[4] In the House of Lords the reported elevation of Danby was immediately attacked. Shaftesbury moved for an address to the King on the subject. Halifax, fixing his eyes upon Charles, who was present, declared that so offensive a step could not possibly have been proposed, and that Shaftesbury must be the victim of an unfounded rumour.[5] The general problem of the lords in the Tower had already been raised.[6] It was now resolved that in spite of the dissolution of the Parliament which had impeached them the impeachments were still in force,[7] and on March 20 Danby, whose position was the same as theirs, was ordered to put in his answer to the articles against him within a week.[8]

[1] According to Danby the Chancellor assured the King that he had put the great seal to it, but in actual fact he had only put the *recepi* (*infra*, ii. 113).

[2] The warrant, dated March 16, is B.M. Add. MSS. 28094, f. 47. The titles it proposed to confer were Marquis of Danby and Baron of Seaton Ross. Danby's original choice was Marquis of Carmarthen, but for some reason he abandoned this. Apparently he and his family were given place for several days in accordance with his new dignity.

[3] Danby's own notes in B.M. Add. MSS. 28043, f. 7 ; 29557, f. 128 ; *Cal. S.P. Dom.*, 1679-80, p. 103 ; Barillon to Louis XIV, March 27, 1679.

[4] *Burnet*, ii. 205.

[5] March 17 (*Ranke*, iv. 77 ; *Hatton Correspondence*, i. 183-4 ; *Ormonde MSS.*, N.S., iv. 359-60).   [6] *L.J.*, xiii. 457-8.

[7] March 19 (*ibid.*, p. 466). There are some rough notes of the debate on the matter in Carte MSS. 228, f. 229.

[8] *L.J.*, xiii. 469.

In the Commons a much more bitter atmosphere prevailed. In the light of the rewards showered upon the Treasurer every step taken by the Government was interpreted or misinterpreted so as to tell against him. The new Treasury Commission, it was declared, was simply a number of his own creatures, intended to act as a stop-gap until he could safely resume the position he was vacating.[1] The dismissal of the Duke of York, and the dissolution of Parliament, which he had hoped might be put to his credit, were asserted to be part of a scheme for securing entire control over the King and the Government, and it was freely suggested that they should be made the basis of additional articles of impeachment. With more justice the quarrel over the appointment of the Speaker was laid to his charge. On March 20, accordingly, the Commons resolved upon a message to the Lords to remind them of the impeachment against him, and to desire that he might be sequestered from Parliament and committed to safe custody.[2]

These proceedings on the part of the two Houses revived all the King's worst fears of an actual trial, with its consequent revelations, and before it could even be decided what effect should be given to the message of the Commons he made a further effort to postpone the evil day. Appearing in the House of Lords on March 22 he summoned the Commons before him and assured them in the most emphatic manner that Danby was innocent of the charges made against him, that the letters to Montagu had been written by his particular command, that he had given him a full pardon, and that if there was anything defective in the pardon he would repeat it, if necessary, ten times over.[3] The result was merely to add fuel to the flames. The Commons attacked the pardon, asking in what manner it had been obtained and questioning the power of the King to

---

[1] There were good grounds for this statement. The first intention was that such devoted followers of Danby as Lord Alington [not Lord Arlington] and Sir Edward Dering should be included in the commission, and even as eventually constituted it was composed almost entirely of partisans of the Court (*Cal. S.P. Dom.*, 1679-80, p. 109 ; *Savile Correspondence*, p. 76 ; *Hatton Correspondence*, i. 183 ; Barillon to Louis XIV, March 27, April 3, 6, 1679).

[2] *C.J.*, ix. 572.

[3] *Cal. S.P. Dom.*, 1679-80, p. 106 ; *Ormonde MSS.*, N.S., iv. 369-70 ; *Lindsey MSS.*, p. 404 ; *Grey*, vii. 19. The speech is not given in the Journals of either House.

pardon in such a case.[1]   The Lords, in the midst of the general exasperation, seemed little likely to adhere to their former resolution that Danby should not be confined. A brief respite, however, was provided by the week-end recess, and of this the King took advantage. On Sunday, March 23, he approached Danby in the Treasury Chambers and commanded him to go into hiding.[2]

The Earl appears to have hesitated. Until midnight he remained in consultation with his friends, many of whom were opposed to his withdrawing, but in the end he obeyed the King, and took refuge that night in his brother's house in town.[3] On the following morning the temper of the Lords was early apparent, and the King, who was in the House, sent a most peremptory note by the Earl of Bath, requiring Danby to be gone instantly, and to withdraw, if possible, out of England. The message was in a sense unnecessary, for the Treasurer was already safe ; but Charles had not misjudged the position. Within an hour Black Rod, in accordance with the orders of the Lords, was vainly searching for Danby to take him into custody. In the opinion of the French ambassador if he had been found at that moment he would certainly have lost his head.[4]

On March 25 the white staff of the Treasurer was delivered by Lord Latimer to the King,[5] and Danby's period of office came formally to an end. It had been a period of great achievements in finance, due almost entirely to the energy and initiative of Danby himself. The regular revenue had been substantially

---

[1] See the report on the pardon in *C.J.*, ix. 574-5, and the debate on the report in *Grey*, vii. 39-47.

[2] Danby's own notes in B.M. Add. MSS. 28043, f. 7.

[3] *Reresby*, p. 173. The " brother " is probably the Earl of Lindsey, but may be Charles Osborne.

[4] *L.J.*, xiii. 474-6 ; B.M. Add. MSS. 28043, f. 7 ; Barillon to Louis XIV, April 3, 1679. The statement which Christie bases on Barillon's dispatch (*Life of Shaftesbury*, ii. 319), that Black Rod reached Danby's house (not Wimbledon, of course, but the Cockpit) just an hour after he had fled, is certainly incorrect, and is hardly substantiated by the dispatch itself.

[5] Apparently Latimer had no specific authority for the surrender of the staff, and was not at the moment in direct touch with Danby. The staff was accepted by the King with many promises of favour to be shown to Danby and his descendants in better times (B.M. Add. MSS. 28040, f. 10 ; *Supplement to Lindsey MSS.*, pp. 63-4).

increased, without the help of any additional grant from Parliament. Considerable subsidies had been extorted from the French King.[1] About half the standing debt had been funded on equitable terms, and most of the remainder had been either liquidated or provided for in some semi-permanent manner. Expenditure had been brought under stricter supervision, and although not seriously reduced had at least been prevented from expanding at what for some time had been its normal rate.

Nevertheless the enemies who declared that Danby left the Government worse off financially than he found it were not without justification for their statement. During the last twelve or fifteen months of his treasurership circumstances over which Danby had no control had combined with his too adventurous foreign policy to undo much of his earlier work. The regular revenue had been considerably reduced by the prohibition of imports from France. All prospect of further subsidies from the French King had, at least temporarily, been renounced. Vast new debts had been incurred in preparation for a war which had never taken place. Expenditure had been increased by rebellion in Virginia, hostilities against Algiers, the development of a system of bounties on exported wheat, an extension of the pensions list, and a slackening of Danby's own control as his energies became engaged elsewhere and his personal influence with the King grew more precarious. At the beginning of 1679 the gap between income and expenditure was probably greater, and the anticipations on the revenue were certainly heavier, than in the summer of 1673.[2]

Despite the criticism directed against Danby's financial methods, however, it was the success of these methods rather than their failure that constituted his unpardonable crime in the eyes of the opposition. Only the most prejudiced among politicians seriously believed that Danby himself was inclined

---

[1] The total amount received from France during Danby's treasurership was approximately £300,000 (*Cal. Treas. Books*, iii. p. lxiv.).

[2] See *infra*, iii. 31-2, and the authorities there quoted. Even as late as the middle of April the part of the army which remained undisbanded was costing more than £400,000 a year, and it was anticipated that in the summer nearly £1,000,000 would be required to pay off the army and the fleet together (*Ormonde MSS., N.S.*, iv. 503).

to popery or to France ; but large numbers feared that Charles was so inclined, and still larger numbers were convinced that James was. By his resolute championship of the prerogative, and by his skilful management of finance, Danby had come near to enabling Charles, and presumably in due course James, to give effect to their inclinations, and his mere relinquishment of office was therefore insufficient to satisfy any of his opponents. The more moderate were determined to improve the occasion by ensuring that he should never be in a position to make a second effort in the same direction.[1] The more violent were equally determined to punish him severely for having come so near to success at his first attempt.

In the House of Lords moderation on the whole prevailed, partly because many of the members realised that Danby's case might easily at some future date be their own, partly because most of them took their judicial duties seriously, and could not find in the allegations made by the Commons any reasonable basis for a charge of treason. On March 22, immediately after the King's announcement of his grant of a pardon to Danby, the Lords had given instructions for the preparation of a bill disabling him from entering the royal presence, holding public office, receiving grants from the Crown, or sitting in Parliament. This bill they now amended, at the committee stage, so as to make it, in addition, a bill of banishment ; and in its new form it was read a third time and passed on March 26. In substance it provided that unless Danby should surrender himself to justice by May 1 he should suffer perpetual exile from that date, and in the event of his being found in England should incur the penalties of high treason without the possibility of pardon except by Act of Parliament.[2]

The Commons went considerably further. Their attitude to

---

[1] That he would make such an effort at the earliest opportunity was everywhere assumed, and the most extravagant schemes were attributed to him. According to one account he was meditating the sale of Tangier for £600,000, and of Jamaica for a similar sum, with the object of making the King financially independent. The answer of the Commons to this rumour was to give orders for the preparation of a bill " annexing Tangier to the imperial crown of England " (*C.J.*, ix. 588 ; *Grey*, vii. 97-101 ; *Ormonde MSS.*, *N.S.*, v. 38 ; Barillon to Louis XIV, April 17, 1679).

[2] *L.J.*, xiii. 471-81. The bill is printed, with the amendments shown, in *Hist. MSS. Com.*, xi. 2, pp. 95-7.

Danby was summed up in the articles of impeachment which they had undertaken to make good. By fleeing from justice, they argued, Danby had tacitly admitted the charge of treason contained in these articles, and the only logical course was to proceed against him as a traitor. On March 25, accordingly, they appointed a committee to draw up a bill summoning Danby to surrender himself, and in default attainting him. On March 26 the bill was introduced and given a first reading, and thereafter its progress was rapid and almost unopposed. The final date by which Danby might surrender was fixed at April 10, a clause was introduced making him incapable of pardon except by Act of Parliament, and with these amendments the bill was given a third reading and passed on April 1.[1]

Two very different solutions were thus propounded for the problem presented by Danby's flight, and the conflict between them began as soon as the bill advocated by each House reached the other. On March 27 the Lords' bill of banishment was delivered to the Commons, and was summarily rejected, without a division, on the second reading.[2] On April 1 the Commons' bill of attainder was delivered to the Lords, and received more courteous, though scarcely more respectful, treatment. Having been given a first and a second reading, it was then entrusted to a committee of the whole House with the remarkable instruction " that the attainder be left out of the bill." To this instruction the committee gave effect in a no less remarkable way, for it refrained from leaving the attainder out of the bill, but by means of two ingenious modifications ensured that it should apply only in the event of Danby being found in England after May 1. This practically meant a transformation of the Commons' bill of attainder into something substantially the same as the Lords' original bill of banishment ; and in this form the Lords passed it and returned it to the Commons on April 4.[3]

For ten days thereafter the rival merits of banishment and attainder continued to divide the political world and provide material for frequent conferences between the two Houses.

[1] *C.J.*, ix. 576-81 ; *Grey*, vii. 60. The bill is printed in *Hist. MSS. Com.*, xi. 2, pp. 110-12.

[2] *C.J.*, ix. 577-8 ; *Grey*, vii. 60-2 ; *Ormonde MSS., N.S.*, v. 9-10.

[3] *L.J.*, xiii. 493-7 ; *Ormonde MSS., N.S.*, v. 30-3.

The King was strongly in favour of banishment, which alone, he believed, offered an assured prospect that there would be no trial, but dared not press for this solution of the problem lest his motive should become too apparent. The Lords were both divided and uncertain. On the whole the moderate men on both sides appear to have supported banishment, and the extremists on both sides, for reasons directly contradictory of each other, to have supported attainder.[1] Danby, although still in hiding,[2] exerted himself to the utmost to rally his followers behind him,[3] and had no difficulty in mustering an imposing array of peers and bishops who were anxious to do what they could for him ; but he seems neither to have been clear what course he wished them to pursue nor to have been successful in inducing them to observe his directions.[4] Banishment was the lesser penalty, but for that very reason the more likely to be actually enforced. Attainder was much more serious, but was clearly intended by many of its advocates as a threat which they did not expect to have to carry out. Considerations such as these produced widespread bewilderment. Many of the peers changed from one side to the other during the course of the debates. Many more refused to give expression to their views at all.[5]

It was almost inevitable in these circumstances that the wishes of the Commons should prevail. Not merely had the

---

[1] *Finch MSS.*, ii. 48-9.

[2] Although pressed by the King to leave the country, Danby refused to do so unless provided with a yacht for the purpose, and so given official countenance in his departure. His place of concealment was a subject of much speculation. According to one rumour he was hidden in the palace of Whitehall ; and this was taken so seriously by the Commons as to induce them to give orders for an address to the King on the subject (*L.J.*, xiii. 508-10 ; *C.J.*, ix. 584-5, 589 ; *Grey*, vii. 80 ; *Reresby*, p. 175). According to another rumour he " lay concealed at Mr. George Montagu's in a low apartment which opens upon the river " (*Lindsey MSS.*, p. 406).

[3] His notes and calculations are printed *infra*, iii. 140-8.

[4] Danby later declared that he urged his friends to vote for the attainder, as a thing which would never in the end be allowed to take effect, and there is evidence in support of his statement (*infra*, ii. 77-8, 80) ; but it is doubtful whether this was more than an occasional expedient adopted by him, and there is little to suggest that his friends were prepared to accept the responsibility of following his instructions.

[5] The number of votes cast in divisions fell far short of what might have been expected from the importance of the issues at stake and the large attendance at each meeting of the House. Protests were many, but signatories few.

Commons the whole weight of popular opinion behind them, and the power of the purse in their hands, but they were also more united than the Lords, and had much the better logical case. The Lords indeed could find no legal justification at all for their version of the bill, and were reduced to admitting " that banishment is so far from being the legal judgement in case of high treason that it is not the legal judgement in any case whatsoever." The only plea they could advance was that of moderation and expediency ; but even here the Commons had the better of the argument. Neither moderation nor expediency, they declared, could justify the imposing of penalties on Danby for offences which he might not have committed. The true object of the bill before the Houses was not to punish him, either moderately or severely, for crimes as yet only laid to his charge, but to enable Parliament to ascertain the degree of his guilt by inducing him to appear and stand his trial ; and the heavier the penalty provided in the event of his remaining concealed the more likely he was to follow the course desired.[1]

This last argument the Lords apparently found unanswerable, and it was fully justified by the event. On April 14 the Commons' bill of attainder, substantially in its original form, was accepted by both Houses.[2] Owing to the delay in dealing with it the date by which Danby was required to surrender if he wished to escape the penalties it imposed had been altered, first to April 15 and then to April 21 ; but even so the interval allowed was recognised to be short, and the Lords accordingly presented a special request to the King that he would name an early day on which the bill might be tendered to him for his assent.

The prospect with which he was thus confronted, of having to take an active part against the minister who had served him only too well, was more than even Charles could face. The

---

[1] *L.J.*, xiii. 504-16 ; *C.J.*, ix. 588-94 ; *Grey*, vii. 85-97, 103-6.

[2] The final vote in the House of Lords was 39 to 36 in favour of the bill. It shows the confused state of parties on this issue that six bishops were believed to favour the bill, but left the House rather than vote for a penalty involving the shedding of blood, while seven remained and voted against the bill (*Hatton Correspondence*, i. 186 ; *Ormonde MSS.*, *N.S.*, v. 48). The division list is printed *infra*. iii. 148-51.

odium which his father had incurred through his behaviour
in very similar circumstances to the Earl of Strafford scarcely
required the representations of Danby's friends to keep it ever
present before him. While appointing April 16 as the day on
which the bill of attainder should be tendered to him he
accordingly gave Danby the permission he had several times
desired to surrender himself.[1] Late on April 15 Danby gave
himself up to Black Rod, and early on the following day he
was brought to the bar of the Lords. There he made the best
excuse he could for his failure to appear earlier, and put
forward a number of requests regarding his trial, the majority
of which were granted. He was then commanded to withdraw,
and in spite of his petition that he might be allowed, on account
of his health, to remain in the custody of Black Rod was
committed to the Tower.[2]

[1] B.M. Add. MSS. 28043, f. 7.

[2] *L.J.*, xiii. 520-1 ; *C.J.*, ix. 597. The notes for his requests to the Lords
are B.M. Add. MSS. 28043, ff. 13, 15, 98.

PART III

A STATESMAN OUT OF OFFICE

1679-89

CHAPTER XIV

IN THE TOWER, 1679-84

No sooner was Danby safely lodged in the Tower than his importance as a factor in the political situation to all appearance vanished, and the hue and cry of which he had so long been the object swept on unchecked after the Catholics and the Duke of York. The fallen statesman had many enemies, but few really wished to impose upon him any heavier penalty than loss of office and imprisonment, while a considerable number went in daily terror of the revelations which, if driven to extremity, he might make.[1] The animus hitherto displayed against him had been based largely on the fact that his ability alone had enabled the King and the Duke of York to withstand the wishes of Parliament. Now that he was apparently powerless the majority of the opposition would have been content to leave him in peace, and devote their time to the much more necessary work of dealing with the succession to the throne. The leaders of the Presbyterian party especially could not entirely forget that they had promised he should be gently used.[2] Thus the bill of attainder was allowed to drop, and even the impeachment for a moment halted in its course. A committee of secrecy, it is true, was forthwith appointed to take evidence and prepare additional articles against him,[3] but no such articles were ever produced.

Unfortunately an uneasy consciousness soon began to spread

---

[1] The possibility that Danby might tell all he knew, not only about the Court but also about the opposition, was never ignored (Barillon to Louis XIV, April 27, May 4, 15, 1679). Among moderate men there was also a genuine reluctance to involve the King as a continued prosecution of Danby was bound to do (*Ormonde MSS., N.S.,* iv. pp. xxi-xxii).

[2] " Il s'est fait un merite a leur esgard par la cassation du vieux Parlement, dont ils tesmoignent ouvertement de la reconnoissance " (Barillon to Louis XIV, July 13, 1679).

[3] April 17, (*C.J.,* ix. 598, 600, 602).

abroad that Danby's powerlessness was more apparent than real, and that even from the Tower he was exercising a most undesirable influence over the policy of the Court. The complaint that the ministry was still full of his friends and followers was partly met when Charles on April 21 completely remodelled the Privy Council, and introduced into it many of the leading members of the opposition.[1] But even then the Household remained untouched, and the frequent attendance of Lord Latimer upon the King as gentleman of the bedchamber evoked widespread disapproval.[2] In reality Danby was in constant communication with Charles, not merely upon his own affairs but upon those of the nation as well, and the growing feeling that further steps would have to be taken against him was only too well justified.

Moreover the line of defence which the Earl was compelled to adopt was one peculiarly fitted to exasperate the Commons and rouse suspicion of his good faith. Charles was still determined to prevent his trial altogether, or at least to defer it as long as possible, and with that object in view sent him positive orders to produce his pardon. At the same time his lawyers informed him that unless the pardon was put forward at the beginning of the proceedings it would automatically become void.[3] On April 25, accordingly, when brought before the Lords to answer to the articles against him, he formally pleaded his pardon in bar of the impeachment.[4] This caused an angry debate in the Commons. If impeachments could thus be evaded, it was pointed out, it would be impossible not merely to punish evil counsellors, but even to convict them of their guilt.[5] The whole problem of the form of the pardon, and the manner in which it had been obtained, was again raised. Motions were made that the prosecution of the Catholic lords should be laid

---

[1] *Burnet*, ii. 209-10. Even in the new Council the Earl of Bath and Sir William Temple were believed to continue Danby's influence (*Ormonde MSS.*, N.S., iv. 517).

[2] Barillon to Louis XIV, May 15, 1679.

[3] *Memoirs of the Earl of Danby*, pp. 45-7 ; *Burnet*, ii. 219.

[4] His plea, in which he protests his innocence of all the charges made against him and recites his pardon, is printed in full in *L.J.*, xiii. 537-40.

[5] " If great men do exorbitances with pardon, it takes away *culpa* as well as *poena* " (Sir Francis Winnington).

aside, and that no money should be granted until Danby had
been dealt with. Finally it was referred to the committee of
secrecy to consider the whole question of the plea and the
validity of the pardon.[1]

On April 28 Sir Francis Winnington reported that the
committee could find " no precedent that ever any pardon was
granted to any person impeached by the Commons of high
treason, or other high crimes, depending the impeachment,"
and another acrimonious debate followed. It was freely
assumed that pleading the pardon amounted to a confession of
guilt, and that if Danby decided to rely upon it he must stand
or fall by the decision regarding its legality. Accordingly a
resolution was taken to give the Earl an opportunity of withdrawing from such a dangerous position,[2] and a message was
sent to the Lords desiring them to enquire of him whether he
would " rely upon and abide by the plea of his pardon."[3] This
only caused further delay and exasperation. Danby desired
a week to decide upon his answer, and was given until May 3.
He then declared that on the advice of his counsel he would
insist upon the plea he had put in.[4] The Commons were greatly
incensed at what they considered an equivocal answer.[5] Sir
John Knight moved for a fresh bill of attainder, and received
considerable support. Members began to wonder what lay
behind all this evasion.[6] On the main point, however, that the
pardon was void, the Commons were practically unanimous,

---

[1] *C.J.*, ix. 602 ; *Grey*, vii. 133-7. The bewilderment and annoyance of
the Commons were well expressed by Colonel Titus. " This lord is like
Samson, who doth trouble us more att his death then in his life, nor doe I
beleeve his protestations more then the Earle of Danby doth, who professeth
innocense and declares guilt att the same breath " (B.M. Add. MSS., 28046,
f. 105).

[2] That this was at least the professed object of the Commons seems to be
made clear by Powle's speeches in *Grey*, vii. 156-7, 172-3.

[3] *C.J.*, ix. 606 ; *Grey*, vii. 152-7.

[4] *L.J.*, xiii. 544-5, 551-2 ; *Ormonde MSS., N.S.*, v. 71, 76-7.

[5] " Monsieur le Comte de Danby . . . declara qu'il prétendoit se servir de
son pardon. Il persista néantmoins a soustenir qu'il n'est point coupable. La
chambre des communes pretend que sa response n'est pas cathégarique, et qu'il
faut se confesser coupable quand on veut se servir de la grace du Prince "
(Barillon to Louis XIV, May 15, 1679).

[6] " There is some cunning man in his practice, that has advised this, and he
is laying a trap for you." Few probably realised that the " cunning man " was
Charles II.

and after two days' debate it was resolved that the whole House should proceed to the bar of the Lords, and on the ground that the plea advanced by Danby was no plea at all should demand immediate judgment against him.[1]

This demand of the Commons compelled the Lords to take the legality of the pardon into serious consideration, and as a necessary preliminary raised in a more acute form than ever the whole question of the bishops. As a result partly of their long association with Danby, partly of their general attitude to the prerogative, it was assumed that the bishops would vote in favour of the pardon,[2] and in the comparatively equal balance of forces among the lay peers would practically decide the issue. A determined effort was therefore made by the opposition in the Lords to maintain not merely that the bishops could not vote in cases involving blood, but that they could not vote on preliminary questions on which these cases depended. On May 6 the battle was fairly joined, and continued intermittently for three weeks thereafter.[3] Meanwhile the Commons became more and more extravagant. After they had voted the pardon illegal they considered it an insult that counsel should be allowed to argue that it was legal. They therefore objected to the order made by the Lords that Danby should attend with his advisers in Westminster Hall on May 10 to make good his plea before a Lord High Steward ; and when their own suggestion of a committee of both Houses to regulate procedure was rejected, they resolved on May 9 that any commoner who maintained the validity of the pardon should be accounted a betrayer of the liberties of the Commons of England. Danby immediately petitioned the Lords for relief and directions on the ground that his counsel were afraid to

---

[1] *Grey*, vi. 167-87 ; *C.J.*, ix. 611-2 ; *L.J.*, xiii. 553. The most bitter speech came from Seymour. " Whether the pardon or plea be good or not is not the question. The justice of the nation is abused. He has turned three kingdomes into an Aceldama. This answer is evasive. Hee'd have the pardon discoursed before he will insist. You ought to give no countenance to this shameful delay. You are wronged of eight weeks by this man " (B.M. Add. MSS. 28046, f. 119).

[2] Barillon to Louis XIV, May 18, 1679.

[3] There are very elaborate " Short Notes of the Debates in the Lords House concerning the Bishopps sitting in Case of Blood, May 1679," in Carte MSS. 81, ff. 561-8.

act, and the two Houses stood openly at variance with each other.[1]

Some such result as this was probably what Charles had anticipated or even desired. From Parliament the King had little to hope and much to fear. His one chance of preserving his authority and ensuring the succession to the throne for his brother lay in evasion, in the grant of specious but inadequate concessions, and in enticing his opponents into extravagances which would discredit them with the nation. As the quarrel between the two Houses became fiercer, and the Commons refused to proceed to the trial of the Catholic lords until judgment had been given upon Danby's pardon, or to admit of judgment upon the pardon until the bishops had been excluded from voting in all questions connected with the impeachment,[2] he may well have congratulated himself on the success of his policy.

To Danby, on the other hand, the position of affairs seemed gloomy indeed. In the exasperated temper of the House of Commons he had little hope of mercy if once he fell into their hands,[3] and the constant attacks made by them on the prerogative seemed to suggest that the defence on which he had been induced to place his sole reliance might give way at any moment. No department of government was free from parliamentary inquisition, and with the object of discovering what sums of money had been distributed among members an investigation was even being conducted into Secret Service expenditure, in the course of which pressure of every kind was being employed to wring information from Charles Bertie, Sir

---

[1] *L.J.*, xiii. 555-65 ; *C.J.*, ix. 614-8 ; *Grey*, vii. 199-213, 219-28. The principal grievance of the Commons was that in the proceedings at Westminster Hall they would occupy the ignominious role of spectators. As there was no charge to be maintained they could not act as accusers ; they were not judges ; and so there would be nothing for them to do but listen to Danby's counsel disputing their arguments about the pardon. Their opinion, so far as they had one, appears to have been that the Lords should settle the legality of the pardon in their own House, with the assistance, if necessary, of the judges, and without hearing Danby at all. If the pardon was declared invalid they expected judgment on Danby at once. If, on the other hand, it was declared valid, they proposed to proceed by bill of attainder (Barillon to Louis XIV, May 18, 1679).

[2] The final position adopted by the Commons is fully stated in *C.J.*, ix. 631-3, reprinted with a few omissions in *Memoirs of the Earl of Danby*, App., pp. 18-28. The Lords refused to accept their contentions.

[3] Barillon to Louis XIV, May 29, 1679.

Stephen Fox, and Sir Richard Wiseman.[1] As the month of May advanced, accordingly, Danby adjured the King, in increasingly urgent terms, to take more strenuous measures. The efforts of the Commons to regulate the militia, to interfere with the appointment of governors of fortified places, officers of ships, and judges, and still more to alter the course of the succession to the throne, clearly showed, he declared, that they were aiming at complete sovereignty, and " must either bee shortly dismiss't " or bring King and kingdom to ruin.[2]

The effect of these representations was seen on May 27, when Charles, completely ignoring his new Privy Council, unexpectedly prorogued Parliament to August 14, but even then Danby continued to make suggestions foreshadowing, or actually going beyond, the attitude which was to be adopted by the King two years later. Every care, he insisted, should be taken for the control, in the interests of the Court, of the navy, army and garrisons. The safety of the Tower should be secured, and provision should be made for dealing with a possible insurrection. A declaration should be published justifying the proceedings of the Government and appealing to the nation against the unreasonable conduct of the Commons. Parliament should be dissolved, and if a new one had to be summoned it should be required to meet in some other place than London.[3]

With characteristic courage Danby was quite prepared, if set free, to direct the policy of the Government himself along

[1] *Grey*, vii. 228-36, 315-36, 345 ; *Ormonde MSS., N.S.*, iv. 517-8 ; *Lindsey MSS.*, pp. 407-11 ; *Supplement to Lindsey MSS.*, p. 270 ; *infra*, ii. 84.

[2] A remarkable series of four letters from Danby to Charles (possibly all that were written at this time) illustrates his exhortations. The letters of April 28 and May 5 are printed in full in *Morrison Catalogue*, iii. 115-7 ; that of May 13 in *Campana de Cavelli*, i. 265-7 ; and that of May 21 *infra*, ii. 82-4. One of the most striking features about these letters is the thorough acquaintance which they show Danby possessed with all that was going on. Although in the Tower, he could still unravel the mysteries of an intrigue in the City, and send a private admonition to the Lord Mayor regarding his behaviour.

[3] " Memorandum " in Danby's handwriting, printed in Pollock, *The Popish Plot*, pp. 390-1. In a later hand this is dated [16]78/9, but the real date is almost certainly June 1679. Sir Richard Weston, whom it appears to mention, was not knighted until February 27 (Shaw, *Knights of England*, ii. 253), and the memorandum contains many expressions which seem to be repeated in Danby's letters of May and June. On the other hand Lord Robartes, whom it suggests as a fit person for " encouragement," was, very probably in consequence of this recommendation, created Earl of Radnor on July 23.

the lines he advocated, but the King, with greater insight or more timidity, refused to take any irretrievable step, or even maintain the legality of his own pardon so far as to set his former minister at liberty. In vain Danby set forth every possible argument in favour of his release, and indicated every conceivable method by which it might be accomplished—bail from the King's Bench, bail from the Council, permission to retire for a short time into the country, permission to retire for two or three years to the Continent.[1] The King expressed the greatest sympathy, and gave the utmost assurances of his favour, but it was only too apparent that he would not take the risk of doing anything at all.[2] Before the end of June Danby had practically abandoned hope of release until Parliament should again meet.[3]

As the King had neglected his advice " to have something writt to satisfy the people," Danby set to work to vindicate himself, and in June or July drew up an able defence of his conduct at the Treasury, in foreign affairs, and in connection with the Plot.[4] At the same time he appears to have carried through a very thorough rearrangement of his papers, which was to be of service to him in later years.[5] But in spite of these

---

[1] Danby to the Earl of Bath, June 3, 1679, *infra*, ii. 84-8. The Earl himself laid little stress on his first two suggestions, partly because he had no hope that any lawyer could be induced to argue publicly in favour of bail, or any judge or councillor to give it, partly because an admission that bail was necessary would be a " diminution " of his pardon. His principal hope was that the precedents set in the cases of Wharton and Salisbury might be followed, but, as he perhaps realised, Wharton and Salisbury had only offended the Lords, whereas he had offended the Commons. Failing any other solution he was quite prepared to go into exile. Temple pressed this last solution on the King (*Diary of Henry Sidney*, i. 11).

[2] Earl of Bath to Danby, May 29, June 4, 10, 15, 1679, in B.M. Add. MSS. 28049, ff. 50, 60 ; *Lindsey MSS.*, pp. 411, 412.

[3] Danby to Lord Norris, June 20, 1679, in *Morrison Catalogue*, iii. 117.

[4] *An Impartial State of the Case of the Earl of Danby in a Letter to a Member of the House of Commons*, London, 1679, reprinted in *Memoirs of the Earl of Danby*, p. 3. This pamphlet was certainly written before Parliament was dissolved, and almost certainly after it was prorogued, as it refers to many of the events of the session. Yet Charles Hatton on November 1 refers to it as " newly come out " (*Hatton Correspondence*, i. 200). Probably it was held back after the dissolution, and not published till the autumn. Contemporaries had little doubt as to the identity of the author (*Cal. S.P. Dom.*, 1679-80, p. 272). The notes on which it was based are B.M. Add. MSS. 28043, f. 157.

[5] Such memoranda as B.M. Add. MSS. 28044, f. 1, " Letters of importance to shew that I was not in the interests of France," were probably drawn up at this time. Where his letters have two endorsements the earlier seems to date from this period.

literary labours time hung heavy on his hands and his confinement proved increasingly irksome.   Early in May Thomas
Cheeke took the place of Sir John Robinson as Lieutenant of
the Tower,[1] and thereafter the treatment accorded him was
much more rigorous.   He was locked up in his house every
night, and it was even proposed to lock him up in his room.[2]
No one was allowed to visit him without permission, and a
careful watch was kept on those who frequented his company.[3]
The heat of summer proved very oppressive.   Never had he
felt " so sensible of the punishment of his imprisonment " as
when autumn began, and the time approached when in more
normal circumstances he would have been visiting Kiveton or
the country seats of his friends.[4]   In September he was troubled
by a serious illness.[5]   At the beginning of October a report
spread abroad that he was dying " of the jaundies," and it was
not until December that he fully recovered.[6]

Just when everything seemed at its worst an old temptation
assailed him with redoubled force.   Shaftesbury had never
ceased his attempts to sow dissension between him and the
Duke of York, and the resentment inspired in James by his
exile to the Continent had provided a golden opportunity.   By
skilfully playing on the Duke's suspicion that the exile was
really a subtle move on the Treasurer's part to get the King into
his own hands, Shaftesbury had persuaded him to throw his
weight against Danby in the later stages of the impeachment,
and especially after his own appointment as President of the
Council had even contrived to obtain some share of the Duke's
favour.[7]   Danby complained to James, but received only an

[1] *Cal. S.P. Dom.*, 1679-80, p. 137.

[2] B.M. Add. MSS. 28043, f. 8.   Cheeke was not inspired by sheer male-
volence.   He complained to the Council that Danby " kept such ill hours that
he could not secure him safe ; since which his lordship keeps better supping
hours and bed time " (*Hist. MSS. Com.*, vii. 473).   For his maintenance in the
Tower Danby had to pay Cheeke £2 4s. 5d. a week (B.M. Add. MSS. 34195,
f. 82).

[3] *Cal. S.P. Dom.*, 1679-80, pp. 131-2.   There was, of course, nothing unusual
in these regulations.

[4] Danby to Lord Norris, August 1, 1679, in *Morrison Catalogue*, iii. 117.

[5] *Luttrell*, i. 22.

[6] B.M. Add. MSS. 29577, ff. 199, 211 ; *Cal. S.P. Dom.*, 1679-80, p. 272.

[7] Duke of York to Colonel Legge, May 8, 1679, in *Campana de Cavelli*, i. 257-9 ;
Hist. MSS. Com., xi. 5, p. 32.

evasive answer, and considered he had a very real grievance indeed.[1]

On July 12, however, Charles dissolved Parliament and summoned another for October 7.[2] A few weeks later he fell seriously ill, and the Duke of York was hastily summoned home to England.[3] This made James a more serious danger than Danby, and Shaftesbury forthwith resolved to reverse his policy and ally with the latter against the former. Nothing, he believed, could be more damaging to the Duke than the revelations which Danby was in a position to make, and he accordingly entered into negotiations with him, through the medium of the Duke of Monmouth and Colonel Birch, to persuade him to divulge what he knew.[4]

There is no doubt that Danby succumbed to the temptation ; but the revelations which he was prepared to make were scarcely as startling as had been anticipated, while the terms on which he insisted were distinctly high. Under no circumstances would he act as an informer. Whatever he had to say against James he would say in his place in Parliament, and his own release was therefore a necessary preliminary to everything else. The expedient suggested was that the Commons, when Parliament met, should address the King for a fresh pardon, in order that the disputes about the old one might be removed ; but it is questionable whether an agreement was concluded on this basis.[5] In any case it soon became apparent that the Commons were not going to be permitted to assemble for some time, and the whole arrangement, if there was one, fell through. Instead of looking to the opposition Danby turned once more to the King. Since early in August he had been collecting the opinions of lawyers and enlisting friends in his

[1] Danby to the Duke of York, May 27, June ; Duke of York to Danby, June 14, 1679, *ibid.*, pp. 271-2, 277-81.

[2] *Cal. S.P. Dom.*, 1679-80, p. 195. It was suspected at the time that the dissolution was due to Danby's influence (Thomas Thynne to Lord Halifax, July 12, 1679, in Foxcroft, *Halifax*, i. 174).

[3] He arrived on September 1 (*Hatton Correspondence*, i. 191 ; *Hist. MSS. Com.*, xii. 7, p. 161.)

[4] Shaftesbury also had the idea of using Danby as a counterpoise to Halifax, who was proving one of the main obstacles in his path (*Ormonde MSS., N.S.*, iv. 566-7).

[5] Undated memoranda printed *infra*, ii. 88-93.

support,[1] and during September and October he made a determined effort to secure by some means or other his enlargement
from the Tower.[2] His attempts, however, proved completely
unsuccessful, and as one prorogation of Parliament followed
another he again abandoned the struggle.

His enforced leisure he employed once more in literary activity.
Early in 1680 Sir Robert Howard brought out a reply to his
published defence,[3] which he considered so important that he
not only prepared an answer,[4] but on its appearance in print
presented copies both to the King and to the Duke of York.[5]
Apart from that " all his study was for patience."[6] In April
he was reduced by sickness to a milk diet, and his misfortunes
seemed only completed by the death of Lady Latimer on May 1,
two days after the daughter to whom she had just given birth.[7]
Not merely was his family to be ruined, but it was apparently
to suffer premature extinction. Nevertheless before the meeting of Parliament drew too near he resolved on one last appeal
for liberty, and pressed the King so strongly that he was given
a definite promise of release.[8] On June 26 he believed that all
was settled, and was hastily seeing to his will and his estate in

[1] Danby to the Earl of Bath, August 5; to the King, August 5; to the Earl
of Sunderland, August 28, in B.M. Add. MSS. 28049, ff. 62, 66, 70.

[2] See his petitions, and drafts and copies of warrants for his release, in
B.M. Add. MSS. 28047, f. 61; 28049, ff. 78, 82; *Lindsey MSS.*, pp. 415-8.
Dates range from September 8 to late in November.

[3] *An Examination of the Impartial State of the Case of the Earl of Danby in a
Letter to a Member of the House of Commons*, London, 1680, reprinted in *Memoirs
of the Earl of Danby*, p. 52.

[4] *The Answer of the Right Honourable the Earl of Danby to a late Pamphlet
entituled An Examination of the Impartial State of the Case of the Earl of Danby*,
London, 1680, reprinted in *Memoirs of the Earl of Danby*, p. 109.

[5] Drafts of the letters which accompanied the pamphlets are B.M. Add. MSS.
28049, ff. 88, 89, endorsed by Danby, " Coppy of my letters to the King and
Duke about my booke, May, 1680."

[6] *Portland MSS.*, iii. 365. Under date January 26, 1680, Danby records in
his diary, " The Parliament mett and was prorogued to the 15 of April, on
which day I shall have been a compleat year in the Tower " (B.M. Add. MSS.
28040, f. 10). The note is one frequently struck in his letters.

[7] Grace Osborne, born and died on April 29. Mother and child were buried
together in Westminster Abbey on May 5 (*Westminster Abbey Registers*,
Harleian Society, p. 199).

[8] Danby to Charles II, May 22, June 20, 1680, in B.M. Add. MSS. 28049,
ff. 84, 93.

preparation for an immediate departure for Holland.[1]   But
the very next day brought disillusionment.[2]   The King had
given way to the representations of prejudiced or timorous
advisers, and after a struggle to obtain at least a short
holiday under guard at Wimbledon Danby resigned himself to
the inevitable.[3]

This meant looking to Parliament, and as soon as it became
known that the Houses would actually assemble on October 21
he began an energetic canvass of his friends among the Lords,
urging them to come up in good time and give him their assistance.[4]   It speedily became apparent, however, that Parliament
had no intention of wasting its energies on his concerns at all.
The immediate object of Shaftesbury and his associates was to
exclude the Duke of York altogether from the succession to the
throne, and failing that to revive the dwindling credit of the
Plot by a further investigation, and an energetic prosecution of
the Catholic lords in the Tower.   By the time the Exclusion
Bill had been rejected and Lord Stafford brought to his trial
the atmosphere had become much too heated for Danby's
claims to have even a chance of consideration.   At the very
beginning of the session he had prepared a petition to the Lords,
praying them, in view of his ill-health and long imprisonment,
and the unlikelihood of his being brought to a speedy trial, to
admit him to bail ;[5]   but this he did not venture even to present.
About the middle of November he appealed through the agency
of Lord Conway to the opposition, but Shaftesbury was not
disposed to be generous, and with some vehemence declared
that he " would not abate him an ace."   Not merely had the
opposition leader his own imprisonment of 1677 to remember,

[1] Autograph notes dated June 22 and 26, 1680, in B.M. Add. MSS. 28043,
f. 17.

[2] Danby to Charles II, June 27, 1680, in B.M. Add. MSS. 28049, f. 100.

[3] Same to same, with the accompanying petition, July 20, 1680, *ibid*, ff. 106-8.

[4] The proclamation requiring the attendance of members is dated August 26
(*Cal. S.P. Dom.*, 1679-80, p. 621), but most of Danby's letters were sent off
before that (B.M. Add. MSS. 29558, f. 70 ; *Rutland MSS.*, ii. 54).   Many of the
replies are preserved in B.M. Add. MSS. 28053, ff. 179-97.   As usual Lord
Conway was Danby's chief agent.

[5] The draft of this petition, in Danby's own handwriting, is in Leeds MSS.,
Packet 11.   It is undated, but as it refers to his imprisonment " above eighteene
months " it must have been drawn up about October 21, 1680.

but he was greatly incensed by the fact that Danby's friends had voted against the Exclusion Bill, while he had a shrewd suspicion that much of the King's firmness in support of his brother was due to Danby's secret counsels.[1]

The prorogation and dissolution of January 1681, therefore, found the position substantially unchanged. Danby once more had recourse to his pen, and published a reply to an attack made by Sir Robert Howard in the previous October on his administration of the Exchequer.[2] He also seriously considered the feasibility of bringing his case by Habeas Corpus before the King's Bench.[3] A reconciliation with Edward Seymour,[4] however, followed immediately afterwards by the appointment of Lord Conway as Secretary of State,[5] considerably improved his position both in the House of Commons and at Court, and about the middle of February he determined to rest his hopes on the Parliament which had been summoned to meet at Oxford on March 21. That the Commons in the midst of their zeal for exclusion could be induced to proceed with his trial he did not for a moment imagine ; but he could see no reason why the Lords, with the help of a little management, should not be

---

[1] Conway to Danby, November 15 and 19, 1680 (B.M. Add. MSS. 28053, ff. 203, 205); Danby to Conway, November 16, 1680 (B.M. Add. MSS. 28049, f. 127). In the draft of an otherwise unimportant letter from Danby to Charles II, the date of which is about November 20, 1680, the following passage has been struck out : " I will not presume to offer your Majestie any advice concerning the publique, because I hope your Majestie has much better ; but I thinke itt my duty, whatever becomes of mee, when I know itt to bee certainely true, to lett you know when you are betrayd, which I am sure you are every day to my Lord Shaftsbury, and by those who are in your greatest trusts, one of which told him within this 48 houres that the reason why your Majestie is so uncertaine in your resolutions of complying with your Parliament in everything they can aske is the correspondence I hold with your Majestie by writing, which though they do not see yett they can tell by your Majestie's being so changed of a sudden as they sometimes find you, and have done particularly in the concernes of the Duke " (B.M. Add. MSS. 28053, f. 224).

[2] *Sir Robert Howard's Account of the State of his Majesty's Revenue, as it was left by the Earl of Danby at Lady Day, 1679, in a Letter to a Friend*, dated October 13, 1680, reprinted in *Memoirs of the Earl of Danby*, p. 153. *The Earl of Danby's Answer to Sir Robert Howard* came out early in 1681 (*Memoirs*, p. 191).

[3] Danby to Charles II, February 3, 1681 (B.M. Add. MSS. 28049, f. 130).

[4] Conway to Danby, January 11, Danby to Conway, January 12, 1681 (B.M. Add. MSS. 28053, ff. 220, 222).

[5] January 31 (Conway to Danby, February 1, 1681, in B.M. Add. MSS. 28053, f. 236).

persuaded to allow him bail, and towards this object he concentrated all his energies.[1]

It is impossible not to admire the skill and completeness with which he made his arrangements. By individual letters [2] or by the personal solicitation of his friends he enlisted the support of every available peer,[3] and gave them all the same instructions, that they should be at Oxford at the beginning of the Parliament to support his application for bail. As they came up they were waited upon by Latimer or Dumblane, and induced to consult together regarding the best method of achieving this object. In the absence of the Earl of Lindsey the nominal leadership was assumed by Norris, Conway and Bath. Seven of the principal nobles in the land offered themselves as sureties, and in case the House of Lords should have any objection to peers acting in that capacity a number of the principal gentry of Oxfordshire were persuaded, if required, to take their places. Every conceivable detail was provided for, even to the speech which Danby was to deliver if summoned to Oxford, the coaches which were to carry him thither, and the lodgings which he and his guards were to occupy while there.

The one thing which Danby failed to do was to inspire some of his own resolution in his supporters. His plan was that at the first suitable opportunity when the temporal peers in his favour had a majority in the House [4] his petition for bail should be presented and put to the question, and under the anxious eye of Lord Latimer his instructions were carried out to the letter. On March 24 Lord Norris presented the petition,[5] under circumstances in which it should have been readily granted ; but as soon as it came to the point the hearts of many of the lords

[1] Autograph notes dated January 19, 1681, in B.M. Add. MSS. 28042, f. 83.

[2] What appears to be his standard letter is B.M. Add. MSS. 28049, f. 129, but it is clear that each lord was addressed in somewhat different terms. Replies are B.M. Add. MSS. 28053, ff. 238-49.

[3] At his instance Edward Noel, son of Lady Danby's brother-in-law, Viscount Campden, was summoned to the Lords as Baron Noel of Titchfield. He also urged the King to complete the grant of an English peerage to Lord Lumley in order that he might have one more vote (B.M. Add. MSS. 28049, f. 132), but this recommendation was not adopted at this time.

[4] It is improbable that this was due to any distrust of the bishops. Danby's fear was rather that if his majority depended on the bishops the vote might later be questioned.

[5] The petition is summarised in *Hodgkin MSS.*, p. 200.

failed them.   Halifax declared the petition was most ill-timed ;
Shaftesbury asserted that it should have been for trial, not for
bail ; and Danby's friends weakly allowed the matter to be
postponed without a question to March 28.[1]   This gave the
Commons time to take the alarm.   On March 25 they appointed
a committee to inspect the Journals relating to Danby's impeachment, and on receiving a report resolved immediately on
a message to the Lords reminding them that they had already
demanded judgment against the Earl, and desiring that a day
might be fixed when judgment should be given.   The consideration of this message was also deferred by the Lords to
March 28.[2]

Danby was well aware that the collapse of his original plan
would probably mean the failure of his whole scheme, but he
urged his supporters to make the most of the opportunity still
open to them, and as soon as the House assembled on March 28
Lord Norris once more raised the problem of his release.   Monmouth, however, tried to secure precedence for another petition,
and while this point was being decided the King delivered the
stroke which Danby seems to have known was coming, and had
quite possibly advised.   Only a few days earlier Charles had
concluded a three years' subsidy agreement with France, which
had greatly increased the strength of his position at home.
Going out from the Lords, where he had apparently been
present, he now returned in his robes, summoned the Commons
before him and dissolved Parliament.[3]

Two years earlier Danby had urged upon the King the
desirability of having a declaration published to justify the
royal actions to the nation at large.   He now drew up such a
declaration himself,[4] only to have the mortification of seeing it

---

[1] *L.J.*, xiii. 752.   According to the philosopher, John Locke, the petition
would certainly have been granted had it been pressed (Christie, *Shaftesbury*,
ii. p. cxv).

[2] *L.J.*, xiii. 755 ;   *C.J.*, ix. 708.

[3] The material for this curious episode in Danby's career is very full, and is
worth studying as an illustration of his methods.   See B.M. Add. MSS. 28042,
f. 83 ;   28043, ff. 25-34 ;   28049, ff. 132-5 ;   28053, ff. 251-4 ;   Carte MSS. 79,
f. 164 ;   *Lindsey MSS.*, pp. 421-32 ;   *Hodgkin MSS.*, pp. 199-200.   The " Instructions " to Lord Latimer are printed *infra*, ii. 93-7.

[4] The autograph draft, very liberally corrected, is in B.M. Add. MSS. 28091,
ff. 89-102.   It is, perhaps, the most unconvincing paper of its kind which
Danby ever drew up.

rejected in favour of a much shorter manifesto composed by Chief Justice Sir Francis North, which appeared in print early in April.[1] Taken in conjunction with the rather unfortunate moment selected for the dissolution this might seem to suggest that Charles was unfavourable to Danby's pretensions, but the Earl was immediately reassured on that point,[2] and in view of the probable abeyance of Parliament for some time devoted the next two months to a series of desperate efforts to secure his freedom. On April 15 he petitioned the King to release him on his own authority ; [3] but when the petition came to be discussed in Council the Lord Chancellor, Lord President and Chief Justice North all argued against granting it, and it was dismissed.[4] He then with the King's approval sued out his Habeas Corpus, and after a delay occasioned by illness was brought before the King's Bench on May 14, only to have the decision of the matter referred to the following term.[5]

Finally he appears to have considered the feasibility of being tried on his impeachment outside of Parliament ; [6] but here a fresh difficulty arose. Ever since his incarceration in the Tower his very helplessness there had made him the target of innumerable accusations from informers who wished to earn an easily won reputation, or scoundrels who hoped to save themselves by incriminating other people. On May 16 one of these, Edward Fitzharris, who had been impeached by the Commons and was now being prosecuted by the Crown, endeavoured to secure the postponement of his own trial by accusing him of being accessory to the murder of Sir Edmund Berry Godfrey ; and the

---

[1] Carte MSS. 222, f. 282 ; *Lives of the Norths*, i. 235-6 ; *Burnet*, ii. 288-9. This declaration is printed in *Memoirs of the Earl of Danby*, App., pp. 99-106.

[2] Danby to Latimer and to Lord Norris, April 3, 1681, in *Lindsey MSS.*, p. 432, and *Morrison Catalogue*, iii. 118.

[3] There is a draft of the petition in B.M. Add. MSS. 28047, f. 106, and draft warrants to the Lieutenant of the Tower to discharge the Earl or bring him before the King, *ibid.*, ff. 108, 110, and 28049, f. 175. The letters which Danby wrote to Charles almost every day at this time are in B.M. Add. MSS. 28049, ff. 139-66 *passim*.

[4] B.M. Add. MSS. 28040, f. 10 ; 28053, ff. 207, 257 ; 29558, f. 252 ; *Lindsey MSS.*, p. 433. The Council meeting was on April 27.

[5] There is a full account of the proceedings in B.M. Add. MSS. 28043, f. 36. See also B.M. Add. MSS. 28040, f. 10 ; 29558, ff. 259, 272 ; *Cal. S.P. Dom.*, 1680-1, pp. 262, 280, 284.

[6] B.M. Add. MSS. 28040, f. 10 ; *Lindsey MSS.*, p. 434.

grand jury of Middlesex, of which Godfrey's brother Michael was foreman, found a true bill against him.[1] This new charge obviously complicated the situation, and Danby accordingly petitioned the King for an immediate trial upon it ;[2] but Charles would not allow anything to obstruct the prosecution of Fitzharris himself, and the execution of the informer on July 1 left the Earl subject not only to his original impeachment but to an indictment for which there was not a scrap of real evidence.[3] Not until the beginning of December was he able to free himself from this new burden by obtaining a *nolle prosequi* from the Crown.[4]

By trying Fitzharris after he had been impeached the judges had incurred the risk of being called to account by a future House of Commons, and dared not at the same time face the danger of offending the Lords by admitting Danby to bail.[5] It was the summer of 1682, accordingly, before a definite decision was reached regarding his Habeas Corpus. On May 27 he was

---

[1] B.M. Add. MSS. 28049, f. 179 ; 28053, f. 261 ; 29558, f. 276 ; Carte MSS. 222, f. 307 ; *Cal. S. P. Dom.*, 1680-1, pp. 285, 310. " One reason why that point was chosen to be put upon him was said to be because the case of murder was not in his lordship's pardon " (North, *Examen*, pp. 224-5). There is a copy of the indictment in B.M. Add. MSS. 28047, f. 289. On a list of the jurymen Danby has noted, " When any of these jurymen were asked (as particularly Edward Boscowen, Esquire) how they came to give such a verdict upon the single and uncertaine evidence of Mr. Fitsharris, they all answer they did not find itt upon the evidence of Fitsharris but upon what Mr. Michaell Godfrey deposed. And yett the said Godfrey hath declared that hee never deposed anything against the said earle" (*ibid.*, f. 285).

[2] The petition was presented on May 19. There is a copy in B.M. Add. MSS. 28047, f. 112. *Cf.* Carte MSS. 222, f. 305 ; *Luttrell*, i. 87.

[3] In a last effort to save himself, Fitzharris offered, in return for a pardon, to declare who had instigated him to make his accusations (*Hist. MSS. Com.*, xii. 9, p. 86 ; *Luttrell*, i. 99 ; *Hatton Correspondence*, ii. 2).

[4] He first petitioned the King and Council for a *nolle prosequi* on October 19 (B.M. Add. MSS. 28047, f. 122). On November 22 Michael Godfrey was desired by the Attorney-General to state whether he had any evidence which would justify a prosecution, but required a few days for consideration (*ibid.*, 28040, f. 10). No satisfactory answer having been received by the end of the month an order in Council was made for a *nolle prosequi*, which was issued on December 2 (*ibid.*, 28047, f. 124. *Cf.* Danby's letter to Latimer in *Lindsey MSS.*, p. 418, the date of which is November 29, 1681).

[5] This is the main point brought out by Danby's own memoranda, " The substance of the discourse betwixt my Lord Bathe, Sir John Ernle and my Lord Chancellor about mee, 17th June, 1681, upon Lord Bathe and Sir Johns being sent to the Lord Chancellor by the King upon that occasion " (B.M. Add. MSS. 28043, f. 57).

brought before the King's Bench, and there argued his case in person for nearly two hours ; but three of the judges desired further time for consideration, and he was therefore remanded.[1] On June 29 he appeared again, supported by a dozen or more peers, and once more argued his case, only to be met with a decision that the Court could not give him any relief.[2]

As the King had plainly intimated through the Attorney-General his approval of the Earl being bailed the only possible explanation of the judges' conduct in Danby's eyes was that they were afraid that the Lords might resent any interference with their prisoner, and he forthwith set out to prove this fear to be groundless. During the autumn he was engaged in an elaborate canvass of the members of the Upper House, the object of which was to secure their signatures to a fresh petition which he intended to present, desiring that his case might be referred to the whole twelve judges.[3] A circular letter was sent to more than a hundred of the lords asking for their support, and copies of the petition were entrusted to Danby's friends and relatives, who travelled from one country seat to another asking for signatures.[4] The result was not unsatisfactory,[5] but the King disliked the idea of pressure being brought to bear on the Government in this way, and towards the close of the year the whole project was abandoned.[6]

With the failure of this scheme Danby's efforts to obtain his

[1] *Rutland MSS.*, ii. 74 ; *Luttrell*, i. 189-90. Danby's speech, together with some account of the proceedings, is printed in *Memoirs of the Earl of Danby*, App., pp. 49-98. The original draft of the speech is in Leeds MSS., Packet 11.

[2] Justice Raymond alone considered that he ought to be bailed. There is a 56 page account of the proceedings in Leeds MSS., Packet 11. See also *Hist. MSS. Com.*, vii. 405 ; *Luttrell*, i. 199-200.

[3] A copy of the petition is summarised in *Portland MSS.*, viii. 20.

[4] The original draft of the circular letter is in Leeds MSS., Packet 11, where can also be found eight copies in a clerk's handwriting, and a number of lists of lords used in the canvass. The lords were divided into four groups, those resident near London (51), those in the west (11), those in the north (20), and the bishops (25). Each group was entrusted to the care of two or three friends or relatives. Dumblane and Lord Lumley apparently took charge of the north.

[5] In Leeds MSS., Packet 11, is a copy of the petition with nineteen signatures (given in *Leeds MSS.*, p. 21), but these cannot be nearly all that were obtained, for no bishops are included among them.

[6] *Portland MSS.*, viii. 20-1 ; Danby to the King and to Lord Latimer, December 20, 1682, in Leeds MSS., Packet 11.

release practically came to an end. He had exhausted every
method he could think of, and none appeared to offer any
further hope. The King, it is true, professed the utmost desire
to set him free, if only some suitable expedient could be devised,
and in the spring of the following year he once more applied to
the King's Bench for bail ; [1] but there was no serious expectation that any result would follow, and his application was dismissed. For many months Danby's attention was much more
occupied with domestic worries than with the problem of his
own release. Since his fall from power he had found increasing
difficulty in securing recognition of his financial claims on the
Government, and was running short of ready money.[2] On
November 25, 1680, he had received official information of the
death of his son-in-law, Lord Plymouth, more than a month
earlier at Tangier..[3] In March 1682 Lady Danby had met with a
carriage accident which had nearly proved fatal. For a fortnight she lay dying, as it was believed, in her house at the
Cockpit, while her husband's most desperate efforts could not
secure him permission to visit her even under guard.[4] Scarcely
had she recovered when the death of young Lord O'Brien in
the wreck of the *Gloucester* frigate [5] threw the whole family into
mourning, and presented Danby with the difficult problem of
settling the affairs of his daughter Sophia.[6] A few months later
a serious quarrel between Lord and Lady Lansdowne presented

[1] *Hist. MSS. Com.*, vii. 362, 481 ; Carte MSS. 222, f. 318 ; Danby to Lord
Hatton, May 11, 1683, in B.M. Add. MSS. 29560, f. 9 ; *Luttrell*, i. 258.

[2] At the time of his resignation his salary as Lord Treasurer was £11,000 in
arrear, and effect had still to be given to several of the grants made to him.
According to his own account his enemies put every obstacle in his way (*Supplement to Lindsey MSS.*, p. 96 ; B.M. Add. MSS. 28042, f. 23 ; 28051, f. 100 ;
28053, ff. 167-77 ; Carte MSS. 243, f. 473).

[3] B.M. Add. MSS. 28053, ff. 201, 210. Lord Plymouth, who had gone to
Tangier as a volunteer, died there on October 17, 1680, and was buried in
Westminster Abbey on January 18, 1681 (*Westminster Abbey Registers*, Harleian
Society, p. 201).

[4] There is a full account of these efforts and their ill-success, drawn up by
Danby for Lord Conway, in "A Relation of my Proceedings in order to the
getting Leave to see my Wife " (Leeds MSS., Packet 11). See also Danby to
the King, March 19 ; Danby to Lord Conway, March 29 and April 1 ; Charles
Bertie and Lord Conway to Danby, March 30, 1682 (*ibid.*) ; B.M. Add. MSS.
37990, f. 53 ; *Rutland MSS.*, ii. 66-8 ; *Luttrell*, i. 176 ; *Cal. S.P. Dom.*, 1682,
pp. 144-5. Danby blamed Lord Halifax for what Charles Bertie, with surprising moderation, calls " a strange severity."

[5] May 6 (*Dalrymple*, App., i. 68-72).   [6] *Rutland MSS.*, ii. 72-3.

him with an even more difficult problem centring round his daughter Martha.[1]

But the greatest worry of all was that occasioned by the matrimonial tangle in which Dumblane was still involved. The matter was the more important inasmuch as Latimer, in spite of repeated negotiations for a second wife,[2] remained a widower without an heir. On July 5, 1680, the Court of Delegates for ecclesiastical appeals had at length decided almost unanimously that the marriage between Bridget Hyde and John Emerton was a good one ;[3] but a petition was immediately entered for a review of the cause, and much of Danby's energy during 1682 was devoted to securing that the review should lead to a reversal of the decision. The methods he employed were not unlike those which had won him fame as a party organiser in Parliament, and can be excused only by his own reiterated assertion that the decision against Dumblane was really inspired by political hostility to himself. In the end, however, all his careful preparation was nullified by the reckless conduct of the persons principally concerned. On April 25, 1682, Dumblane and Bridget Hyde were married in the church of St. Marylebone,[4] and on July 12 they announced their marriage to the Delegates at Serjeant's Inn.[5] This practically compelled Danby to force a decision in their favour within a few months or buy the Emertons off, and the former alternative having failed he had eventually to fall back on the latter. Popular report put the bribe at 20,000 guineas. Whatever it was it proved sufficient to induce the Emertons to withdraw their pretensions, and on April 20, 1683, the Delegates by a majority declared John Emerton's marriage with Bridget Hyde invalid.[6]

[1] " Lady Lansdown has left her Lord, whether willingly or not I will not determine. They say he will see her no more because of some letters that have passed between her and Mr. Leveson Gower " (B.M. Add. MSS. 29577, f. 503).

[2] *Infra*, ii. 100-4. There are many letters dealing with these negotiations in Leeds MSS., Packet 11.

[3] B.M. Add. MSS., 29558, f. 53 ; *Luttrell*, i. 52.

[4] Their marriage certificate is B.M. Add. MSS. 28050, f. 42.

[5] B.M. Add. MSS. 29577, f. 449 ; *Rutland MSS.*, ii. 75-6 ; *Luttrell*, i. 205.

[6] *Luttrell*, i. 255 ; Newdigate-Newdegate, *Cavalier and Puritan*, pp. 188-9. There is an enormous mass of correspondence dealing with this whole matter, in Leeds MSS., Packet 11 ; B.M. Add. MSS. 28051, 28072 *passim* ; 28050, f. 40 ; 28053, ff. 289, 293 ; 38849, f. 180 ; *Clarendon Correspondence*, i. 74-5 ; *Hodgkin MSS.*, p. 201. Danby, as usual, laid much of the blame for his disappointment on the shoulders of Halifax, who was one of the Delegates.

The settlement was thus much more costly than Danby had ever anticipated, or than it need have been ; but at least it set the Earl's mind at rest regarding the prospects of his own family, and enabled him not merely to rejoice in the growing strength of the Government but to find a certain grim satisfaction in the fate which was overtaking some of his former opponents. In July 1681 Shaftesbury had joined him in the Tower, from which he was released only to die some months later at Amsterdam. After the discovery of the Rye House Plot other Whig leaders, Russell, Sidney and Essex, became his fellow-prisoners for a yet shorter period. For Shaftesbury he can scarcely have had any pity, but with Russell and possibly Essex he had something of the nature of a reconciliation, and when the one had perished on the scaffold and the other by his own hand he could remain " temperate in what hee sayd of those gone thence afore him."[1] Perhaps he saw in their tragic fate an intimation that his own long imprisonment was drawing to a close.

[1] *Hatton Correspondence*, ii. 35.

CHAPTER XV

ON BAIL, 1684-5

THE immediate cause of the eventual release of Lord Danby was the decision taken by the King not to summon a fresh Parliament, as the law required, within three years of the dissolution of the previous assembly.[1]   On the one hand this made the Earl's case much the harder, by opening up before him the prospect of lifelong imprisonment ; on the other hand it partially freed those by whom that case was to be judged from the fear of the wrath of Lords or Commons which had hitherto made them turn a deaf ear to his appeals.   But beneath the surface other factors of a more potent character were working towards the same end.   The King, careless though he was, could not but resent the slight to his authority involved in the constant disregard of his pardon, and was sincerely anxious to give some relief to his former minister, provided it could be managed without danger or inconvenience to himself.   The Duke of York was a consistent advocate of the claims of the Catholic lords in the Tower, whose position was substantially the same as that of Danby, except that they had no pardon.[2]   In the party struggles at Court some of the ministers, notably Halifax, were beginning to consider the possibility of finding in the Earl a useful ally,[3] while it may well be the case that Charles had already conceived the idea of employing him to counterbalance the influence of others.   The popular clamour against him had long died

[1] As early as September 4, 1683, Danby was assured that there would be no Parliament (*Morrison Catalogue*, iii. 118).

[2] Danby had originally attempted to keep his case separate from that of the Catholic lords, insisting both upon his pardon and upon the fact that the offences with which he was charged could not be interpreted to be treason, or even felony ; but at this point he seems to have recognised the inadvisability of maintaining this attitude any longer (*Lindsey MSS.*, pp. 438-9).

[3] Charles Bertie to Danby, January 24, 1683/4, *ibid.*, p. 439 ; *Letters of Lord Chesterfield*, pp. 270-2.

down, and what might once have produced an armed insurrection could now be counted upon to rouse little more than a passing interest. The only serious opposition to his release, in fact, was likely to come from the French and their allies at Court, who might discern in it signs of an approaching change in England's attitude to foreign affairs.[1]

It was thus with some hope that in the early days of 1684 Danby embarked upon a fresh attempt to secure his liberty. A careful canvass of the judges served to show that Chief Justice Jeffreys and probably two of his brethren of the King's Bench were in his favour, and that the principal obstacle to the attainment of his desires was likely to be the influence of the Lord Keeper, Guilford, who wished to refer the matter to the whole twelve judges. A final effort was therefore made to enlist support,[2] and on the first day of term Danby moved the King's Bench for a hearing of his case.[3] The result was disappointing. Not until February 4 was he brought before the Court, and even then he was remanded while the judges took further time to consider. One delay followed another, and owing to the shortness of the term it seemed only too likely that it would come to an end without anything whatever having been accomplished.

Charles, however, had made up his mind,[4] and was supported by the majority of those about him. On February 9 he spoke in very plain terms to the Chief Justice, and two days later to the other judges. The effect was seen on February 12, when Danby was once more brought before the Court and all the judges declared that he ought to be admitted to bail. The Earl himself was bound in a recognisance of £10,000 to appear before the House of Lords on the first day of the next session of Parliament, and his four sureties, the Dukes of Somerset and Albe-

---

[1] The situation is clearly described by Barillon in his dispatch to Louis XIV of February 10, 1684.

[2] Danby to the Earl of Abingdon, January 11, 1684 (B.M. Add. MSS. 34079, f. 44), requesting him to come up to town and exert his influence with Sir Richard Holloway, the least favourable of the four King's Bench judges.

[3] January 28 (Barillon to Louis XIV, February 7, 1684).

[4] " Hee said . . . that if the judges would not baile you (which hee would see and speake with the judges to-morrow) hee would by God free you himselfe " (Latimer to Danby, February 4, 1683/4, in B.M. Add. MSS. 28049, f. 214). Latimer's letters make it quite clear that Danby's release was largely due to Charles.

marle, and the Earls of Oxford and Chesterfield, were similarly bound in £5,000 each. Before the day was out he was a free man once more.[1]

Freedom alone, however, was insufficient to satisfy Danby, and the last year of the reign of Charles was to prove a period of strenuous effort on his part to recover something of the power and prestige he had lost. His immediate object was the fulfilment of the promises made him at the time of his fall, partly for their own sake, partly as a public recognition of past services and an earnest of favours to come. His ultimate object was a restoration to office, if not indeed to his former post of Lord Treasurer.

The chief obstacle in the way of his designs was France. Louis XIV and the French ambassador had offered less opposition to his release than might have been expected, for they were assured that he would not be allowed to play any part in politics, and they saw in so conspicuous a disregard of Lords and Commons a further guarantee that Parliament would not be summoned for some time.[2] Nevertheless they were distinctly anxious. The situation in Europe, where war between France and Spain had just broken out, was very uncertain, and the three years' treaty between France and England had already run out. Not very much, it was feared, would be required to induce Charles to desert his ally, and should he do so the French designs upon Luxemburg would have to be abandoned, the Dutch and even some of the German princes might be encouraged to come to the assistance of Spain, and a serious check to French ambition would be the result. By comparatively open representations through his ambassador, and more secret pressure exerted through the Duchess of Portsmouth and the Earl of Sunderland, Louis accordingly did his utmost to check the pretensions of a statesman whose hostility to France, originally strong enough, had been made even stronger by the five years' captivity in which French machinations had involved him.

In this he had the willing assistance of the Duke of York.

---

[1] *House of Lords MSS.*, 1678-88, p. 89 ; *Lindsey MSS.*, pp. 438-42 ; B.M. Add. MSS. 28049, ff. 206-20 ; *Luttrell*, i. 297, 300-1. The Catholic lords were bailed at the same time.

[2] Barillon to Louis XIV, February 28, 1684.

Although to serve his own ends James had consented to Danby's release he had never forgiven the Earl for being the cause of his exile in 1679, or ceased to regard him as a dangerous rival for the control of the King and the Government. Since the discovery of the Rye House Plot, ascendancy at Court had been falling more and more into the hands of the younger and more extreme members of the Clarendonian party, who looked for guidance to the Duke and his brother-in-law, the Earl of Rochester. In accordance with their high Tory views Parliament had been suffered to remain in abeyance, and the Government had been maintained by means of subsidies received from France. Against the continuance of this policy, however, a constant struggle had been waged by the Marquis of Halifax, who enjoyed great personal influence with the King. Charles always disliked to bind himself to any one faction, and retained Halifax as Lord Privy Seal largely as a counterpoise to his own overbearing brother. An alliance between Halifax and Danby seemed therefore highly probable, and it appeared at least possible that such an alliance might bring over the King and lead to a complete change in the Government.

The chief difficulty came from the principals themselves. Halifax was accustomed to playing a solitary hand, and in the insecure position in which he was placed was very uncertain whether an alliance with Danby would strengthen or weaken him. Danby on the other hand could never trust Halifax. Rightly or wrongly he believed that the Marquis had been one of the causes of his long imprisonment and had almost to the last opposed his release. Only sheer necessity could combine two such suspicious partners in an effective alliance.

It was thus a very complicated situation with which Danby was called upon to deal, and his choice of a policy was made even more difficult by the fact that his release, coming suddenly after expectations had many times been disappointed, had roused a certain amount of excitement in political circles, and led to his every action being watched. Within a few hours of gaining his freedom he waited on the King in his bedchamber, and was cordially received. When he complained of his long imprisonment Charles replied that it was against his wishes. This the Earl thankfully admitted, and with doubtful sincerity expressed a desire, of which the King approved, to retire for some time into the country for the sake of his health. The meeting was not in private, and both King and Earl were probably acutely conscious that every word they said would be repeated.

Immediately thereafter Danby, as in duty bound, proceeded to pay his respects to the Duke of York, but met with a very different reception. James complained that Danby had been making disparaging statements about him. The Earl replied that although he had frequently differed from him in opinion he had never said anything against his person, and desired to know the source of the accusation. To this James would make no direct answer, and Danby retired in some disgust.[1]

As he was about to leave the royal presence Danby had chanced to meet Halifax, who was entering, and the two lords had saluted each other somewhat coldly. On the following day, however, Halifax sent a message by Sir John Reresby that his behaviour had been dictated solely by a desire to avoid provoking comment, and Danby declared in reply that he had been moved by much the same considerations, "the jealousie being great of a friendship between them." But this was by no means the whole truth. Both statesmen were fencing for position. Each was afraid to trust the other and doubtful of the value of an alliance. As early as February 20 Sir John Reresby was convinced that they understood each other, but if they did it was probably in a very different sense from what the diarist believed.

Danby in truth found himself at first in a stronger position than he had anticipated, and did not require Halifax's co-operation. The mere fact of his release had been a set-back for the French interest, and for a time it hesitated to raise its head. A considerable body among the opponents of James were completely distrustful of Halifax, and many of these were quite willing to accept Danby as a leader. The majority of the nobility waited upon him to compliment him. Sir Thomas Meres and Sir Peter Pett, at the head of a deputation from the " Loyall Clubb " which met in Fuller's Rents, attended him

---

[1] *Reresby*, pp. 330-1 ; *Portland MSS.*, iii. 377 ; Barillon to Louis XIV, February 24, 1684.

with congratulations upon his release.[1]   As early as February 25 he had joined with "divers other lords" in an offer "to farm all his Majesty's revenue at a great rent yearly, and half a million advanced."[2]

About the same time Danby had a second and presumably secret interview with the King, at which he boldly advanced his claims.   The most important were naturally for a confirmation of his marquisate and his pension of £5,000 a year, but with these was joined a third of somewhat different origin.   Early in the reign the reversion of the lucrative post of Master of the Rolls on the death of Sir Harbottle Grimston had been granted to Lord Colepeper.   In 1677, however, Danby had bought the reversion from him for his son Lord Latimer, and obtained a grant of it for life in the name of George Johnson.   The investment had not proved a profitable one, for Grimston clung to life with true Puritan tenacity ; but in addition serious efforts had been made since Danby's fall to invalidate the arrangement and defraud him of the reversion altogether.[3]   He therefore desired that a fresh grant should be made which should put the matter beyond all doubt.

The King's reception of these requests was most favourable. The state of his finances, he declared, made it impossible for him to confirm the pension, but as regards the title and the Rolls Danby might have his grants carried through as rapidly as he desired.   Rumours immediately spread abroad that the Earl was to become Marquis of Carmarthen, and a warrant was actually made out for a fresh grant of the reversion of the Rolls.[4]

But the French interest was very far indeed from being crushed, and this was more than it proposed to endure.   Urged

---

[1] B.M. Add. MSS. 28053, f. 390.   The club had been founded about the time of the Popish Plot to support the Government, and both Danby's sons were members.   There is a copy of the address in B.M. Add. MSS. 28051, f. 189.

[2] *Hist. MSS. Com.*, vii. 376.   This grandiose scheme had been originated a year earlier by Halifax, but it never came to anything. As Halifax abandoned it in January 1684, it seems not impossible that Danby was introduced by the other partners in his place (Foxcroft, *Halifax*, i. 385, and the authorities there cited).

[3] Carte MSS. 79, f. 114 ; B.M. Add. MSS. 29558, ff. 295, 300 ; *Cal. S.P. Dom.*, 1682, pp. 110, 113 ; *Luttrell*, i. 93 ; *Lindsey MSS.*, p. 421.

[4] Among the Leeds MSS. is an entire packet of papers and correspondence (Packet 9) dealing with this problem of the Rolls.   Danby estimated the value of the place at £10,000 a year.

on by the French ambassador the Duchess of Portsmouth
represented to Charles in the strongest terms the mistake he
was making. The grant of an increase of title to a man who had
only been released upon bail she declared to be most improper.
As regards the Rolls she adopted arguments supplied by Lord
Keeper Guilford, that a reversion could not be held in the name
of a deputy, and that a recent rule made by the King prohibited
all such grants for life. Both grants were in consequence
stopped, but as some compensation Danby was offered the
right of nomination to the first two vacancies among the Six
Clerks in Chancery.[1]

This was a severe blow, rendered all the more bitter by contrast with the high hopes which the Earl had for a moment
entertained. Early in March, when the Court went to Newmarket, he retired to Wimbledon,[2] and there drew up a final
appeal to the King, which he presented after the Court's return.
With faultless logic he pointed out that if he deserved some
compensation for the loss of his employments even before his
imprisonment, he deserved still more compensation after five
years' unmerited suffering in the Tower. Scarcely any other
minister, he declared, who had served the King faithfully and
demitted office with his favour, had been denied some recompense or the right to sell his place ; scarcely any other warrants
for titles or pensions had been granted and then rendered
ineffective. The argument that nothing should be done while
he continued under bail agreed ill with the course pursued in
the very similar cases of Edward Seymour and Sir William
Scroggs ; the suggestion that his grant of the Rolls for life
was invalid was beside the point, for the original grant had been
made before the rule against life grants had been adopted.
Nevertheless he desired to submit himself entirely to the King,
and if nothing could be done for him at the moment hoped he
might renew his requests at a more suitable time.[3]

This petition apparently produced no effect, but almost im-

---

[1] This is substantially Danby's own account as given in his letter of February
28, 1685, to Rochester (infra, ii. 113). The whole series of events took place
in the second half of February (Ormonde MSS., N.S., vii. 202, 207 ; Luttrell, i.
302 ; Barillon to Louis XIV, March 15, 1684).

[2] Hist. MSS. Com., vii. 376.

[3] The letter, dated March 27, is printed infra, ii. 110-2.

mediately afterwards a fresh opportunity seemed to offer for
Danby to play some part in political life.   Lord Dartmouth,
who had long been a favourite of the Duke of York, returned at
the very close of March from the expedition on which he had
been sent to evacuate Tangier, and on his appearance at Court
about the middle of April his alliance was sought by both of the
principal factions.   Dartmouth, however, refused to join with
either, and proposed to found instead a third party on a truly
national basis, " being avers to fenaticisme on the one hand,
and to popery and a French interest on the other."   This scheme
was so completely in accordance with Danby's ideas that on its
being made known to him by Dartmouth's brother-in-law, Sir
Henry Goodricke, he gave it his warmest approval, and no
doubt hoped to turn it to his own advantage.   But Dartmouth
was neither sufficiently able to make his plan a success nor
sufficiently feeble to become a mere puppet in another's hands ;
and in the end his design came to nothing.[1]

Meanwhile the French faction had not failed to profit by
the disunion among their opponents.   On April 14 they secured
the appointment of Godolphin as Secretary of State, and were
believed to be on the point of elevating Rochester to the post
of Lord Treasurer.   In May the Duke of York, although
excluded by the Test Act from all official positions, was practically restored to his old post of Lord High Admiral and allowed
to participate in the proceedings of the Privy Council.   Almost at
the same time the capture of Luxemburg by the French startled
the whole of Europe, and led in August to the conclusion of the
Truce of Ratisbon, by which the recent acquisitions of France
were provisionally surrendered to her for twenty years.

Danby thereupon gave up the struggle in despair.   His own
influence seemed to have dwindled to vanishing point, and a
final visit to Court which he paid at the end of July produced no
result whatever.   " The King is just as formerly, very kind in
words, but nothing more," he wrote to his wife, " and the Duke
very civill in appearance." [2]   When in August he retired for the
autumn to Kiveton the French interest seemed triumphant
both in England and abroad.

---

[1] *Reresby*, pp. 335-6.
[2] The letter, dated July 31, 1684, is printed *infra*, ii. 123.

The reception he met with in the north must have compensated in some measure for his failure in the south. Six years had elapsed since he had been among his Yorkshire friends, and " all the country to a very great distance " hastened to wait upon him. One circumstance on which he dwelt with peculiar satisfaction was the visit of Sidney Montagu of Wortley, second son of the first Earl of Sandwich and a distant relative of Ralph Montagu, " who told mee," he wrote to Lady Danby, " he was sorry that any of his relations (much more of his name) should have carried themselves so unjustly towards mee, and he hoped I woud not have the worse opinion of him for their ill behaviour." [1]

From such scenes Danby was recalled by the startling news of an impending revolution at Court. The very triumph of the French party had in the end proved their undoing. The Duke of York, always arrogant and overbearing, presumed too far upon the easy-going temper of the brother whom he secretly despised, and his attitude was only too faithfully imitated by the Earl of Rochester. Louis XIV, reassured as to the European situation, and confident of his control over English policy, ceased his efforts at conciliation and discontinued his pension. Charles thereupon inclined to the other side. Rochester, much against his wishes, was removed from the Treasury, and made Lord President of the Council. Godolphin lost his Secretaryship of State and had to return to the Treasury. The credit of Halifax obviously increased.

It seems clear from Danby's absence at Kiveton, and also from the character of his conversation at this time with Sir John Reresby,[2] that these changes were in no sense his work ; but it was unquestionably his part to endeavour to profit by them. Unfortunately he was detained in the north until the end of September by a severe illness, accompanied by a difficulty which had long troubled him of swallowing any food ; [3] and even when he returned to London his ill-health continued.

---

[1] The letter, dated September 6, 1684, is printed *infra*, ii. 124.

[2] *Reresby*, p. 344.

[3] Reresby, visiting him at Kiveton on September 25, " found him in bed extream weake," but sufficiently aware of the possibilities of the political situation to promise to do all he could for the diarist " if ever he lived to come into businesse " (*Memoirs*, pp. 345-6).

During the concluding months of the year an elaborate intrigue was in progress, the main objects of which were the exile of the Duke of York to Scotland, the return of Monmouth, and the elevation of Halifax to the post of chief minister of the Crown ; [1] but there is nothing to suggest that Danby was in any way involved in this. For the greater part of the time at least he was at Wimbledon, too weak to move, and his sole recorded intervention in politics, on behalf of the loyal party in the corporation of Leeds, had to be effected through Lord Latimer. [2]

Early on December 27, however, news reached him which roused him to activity. The Master of the Rolls had wakened speechless that morning, and was not expected to live. So changed by this time was the aspect of the Court that Danby had at least some hope of making his pretensions effective, and he immediately wrote to Lord Latimer desiring him to remind the King of his claim to the place. The chief obstacle in his path, it appeared to him, was Sunderland, whom he believed to be engaged in pressing the claims of the Lord Chief Justice Jeffreys, and in order to counteract this influence he determined on December 30, although still very weak, to come to town himself. His efforts, however, proved ineffective. On January 2, 1685, Sir Harbottle Grimston died, and although Danby when he waited upon the King was graciously received, Charles declared that he must have a lawyer for the post, and shortly afterwards nominated Sir John Churchill. There still remained the right to appoint to the first two vacancies among the Six Clerks, but even this, it appeared, was to be subject to a postponement. Lord Colepeper claimed the first vacancy, and after the matter had been heard before the Cabinet Council, Charles admitted that he had promised the Duke of York that he should have it, and declared he could not break his word to his brother.

Nevertheless these interviews were not productive only of disappointment. On being denied the Rolls Danby seized the opportunity to remind the King of the title which had been granted him, and was met by a promise that if he would only

---

[1] Miss Foxcroft has marshalled the somewhat scanty evidence for this intrigue in her *Life of Halifax*, i. 422-35.

[2] B.M. Add. MSS. 28050, f. 45 ; *Lindsey MSS.*, p. 445.

have patience it would not be long before he should both have that title confirmed and be restored to the Council. Two days after the unsatisfactory decision of the dispute between him and Lord Colepeper he again waited on the King to express a fear that this decision meant he was under the royal displeasure. Not only was he assured that such was not the case, but the same promises were in substance repeated to him. If he would only wait a little longer he would be restored to the Council with a particular mark of the royal favour.[1]

The obvious conclusion seems to be that in the new Government which Charles was endeavouring to set up Danby was to be assigned a part ; but the problem still remains what that part was to be. It could scarcely be a small one, for Danby was not the man to fill a subordinate role. In spite of his tragic fall he was the only one of Charles's ministers who had been really successful, and no one knew that better than the King himself. It is impossible to avoid the suggestion that Charles intended to use Halifax to clear the way, and then proposed to restore Danby to his old position of first minister of the Crown.[2]

If such was the royal intention it was probably never divulged to any one.[3] Danby did not again see Charles alive. On February 2 the King was seized with a serious illness, and after appearing to rally passed away about noon on February 6. It must have come as a severe blow to the minister who had served him faithfully, and maintained with him a very real if not very intimate friendship for nearly twenty years, to learn only a few days later that he had died a Catholic.[4] The fact augured ill for the new reign.

[1] Danby's own account of these transactions is given in his memorials of February 28 and July 6, 1685, to the Earl of Rochester and James II, printed *infra*, ii. 112-6.

[2] When it is remembered that finance was the main problem of the whole reign it seems clear that any system of government which involved a breach with France was bound to centre round either Danby or Godolphin, and the latter had scarcely the strength of character necessary to face a difficult situation.

[3] It seems plain that Danby himself had no suspicion of what was going on, or he would never have explained his connection with the plot to James, who was to be its chief victim.

[4] Alexander Sherburne to Danby, February 18, 1685, in *Morrison Catalogue*, iii. 119.

CHAPTER XVI

UNDER JAMES II, 1685-8

THE death of Charles II inevitably meant the return to power of the Clarendonians, with whom Danby had been almost constantly at variance since the beginning of his political career. The son-in-law of the old Chancellor ascended the throne as James II. Ten days later the Chancellor's second son Laurence, Earl of Rochester, was entrusted, as Lord High Treasurer, with the greatest office at the disposal of the English Crown. In the following September his eldest son Henry, Earl of Clarendon, having previously supplanted Halifax as Lord Privy Seal, was raised to similar eminence in Ireland as Lord Lieutenant.

The ascendancy of this faction, however, was by no means unquestioned. On the one hand it had to contend with those moderate Anglicans who, having no personal connection with the King, were not prepared to go so far in his support as his immediate relatives. On the other hand it was threatened, to a steadily increasing extent, by a Queen's party, which represented James's second and Catholic marriage with Mary of Modena as against his first and Protestant marriage with Anne Hyde. The most prominent statesman in the former group was the Marquis of Halifax, still retained in office as Lord President of the Council, who looked for support to Lord Keeper Guilford and to the aged and venerable Ormonde. The political leaders of the latter group were Sunderland, who remained Secretary of State ; Godolphin, who lost his seat on the Treasury Bench but was granted instead the position of Chamberlain to the Queen ; and to a much lesser extent Lord Chief Justice Jeffreys, who was already assuming some of the political functions of the Lord Chancellor.

The natural associates for Danby were the moderate Angli-

cans. Could he and Halifax have agreed to become joint heads
of that party their position in the country would have been
immensely strengthened, and the whole course of James's reign
might have been appreciably affected. Personal jealousies,
however, still made any such agreement impracticable. On the
other hand an alliance between Danby and the Queen's party
was impossible. Sunderland, Godolphin and Jeffreys, it is
true, had all at one time acknowledged great obligations to
him and professed attachment to his cause ; but since his fall
they had completely deserted him, and had shown themselves
ready to support policies of which he thoroughly disapproved.
Sunderland especially had become an admitted partisan of
France, and was more than suspected of an inclination towards
Catholicism.

It was therefore in an alliance with the Clarendonians that
Danby saw his best chance of restoration to favour. Nearly
twenty years had passed since he had assisted the Duke of
Buckingham to drive them from office ; his differences with
them had always been personal rather than political in character, and it seemed not unreasonable to hope that in a time of
difficulty, such as the reign of James promised to be, these
differences might be allowed to sink into oblivion. The King
himself had long forgiven the factious conduct of Sir Thomas
Osborne. It remained to be seen whether he could pardon the
behaviour of the Earl of Danby at the time of the Popish Plot.
Yet even here the prospect was not unhopeful. James was
admittedly a much more determined man than his brother, with
a very high idea of the royal prerogative. The failure of Charles
to stand by his Lord Treasurer had always been condemned by
him, and now that he was himself upon the throne he might be
expected, if only in his own interest, to rectify in some measure
the mistake which Charles had made.

On February 28, accordingly, only three weeks after the
beginning of the new reign, Danby addressed a memorial to
Lord Treasurer Rochester setting forth his pretensions.[1] Not
one of the compensations promised him by the late King, he
pointed out, had been made effective. He therefore prayed that
the patent for his marquisate might at length be allowed to pass,

---

[1] The memorial is printed *infra*, ii. 112-4.

and that if the condition of the Treasury rendered a pension impracticable he should at least have confirmation of his grant of the farm of exported coals, in reversion after Lord Townshend, which had lapsed with the death of Charles II.[1]

It does not appear that this petition produced any effect whatever, and it seems just possible that it was never even brought to the notice of the King.[2] That a Lord Treasurer should actively assist his predecessor in office and possible rival was perhaps too much to ask. In any case James, for the time being, was not in a position to grant any of Danby's requests. The greater part of the royal revenue had come to an end with the death of Charles, and in order to secure its renewal he had been reluctantly compelled to summon a Parliament to meet on May 19. At the very moment when he was apologising in the most abject manner to the French monarch for taking this unwelcome step[3] he could scarcely venture to show favour to the old enemy of France. So little chance had Danby at this time of receiving any countenance, and so low had his credit for good or ill fallen, that his name is not even mentioned in the French dispatches of the period.

The effect of this repulse appears to have been to inspire in Danby a fear that worse might be in store for him. Although released on bail he had not yet been freed from his impeachment, and if the King could not be relied on to protect him might still be relegated to the prison from which he had with such difficulty emerged. The attitude of the approaching Parliament was thus of the greatest importance to him, and he watched the course of the elections with the keenest anxiety. On the whole these were not unfavourable. The reduction of the once powerful Whig party to a group of thirty or forty members was entirely in accordance with his interests. His own followers were fairly successful. In Yorkshire Sir Henry

[1] The grant to Lord Townshend was one of 4/- per chaldron for twenty-one years from Michaelmas 1667 at a rent of £1,000 per annum. In February 1676 the same duty at the same rent was granted for a further period of thirty-one years to William Ettricke, of the Middle Temple, who presumably was Danby's nominee (*C.J.*, x. 109 ; *Cal. Treas. Books*, v. 109).

[2] That Danby suspected this is suggested by the concluding sentence of his memorial of July 6, printed *infra*, ii. 114-6.

[3] Barillon to Louis XIV, February 19, 1685, in C. J. Fox, *History of the Reign of James II*, App., p. xv.

Goodricke, Sir Edmund Jennings and Sir John Reresby were returned ; four Berties found seats in Lincolnshire, while other two were elected by Woodstock and Oxford City.[1]

But of the one election in which Danby was personally concerned the result was distinctly ominous. Among the prominent Exclusionists whom the Court was most anxious to debar from the House of Commons was Thomas Wharton, who had represented Buckinghamshire in the three preceding Parliaments, and again came forward as a candidate for the same constituency. To oppose him, accordingly, a certain Thomas Hackett was put forward, and the management of the election was entrusted to Jeffreys himself. Hackett's chances, however, were from the first regarded as slight, and in order to secure some return for his trouble and expense the Lord Chief Justice proceeded to arrange that if his protégé was defeated at the county elections he should stand for the town of Buckingham.

Here a curious situation had already arisen, which the threatened intervention of Hackett only rendered more complicated. Of the two Whig candidates Sir Richard Temple was in so strong a position as to be considered practically unassailable. The election lay with the mayor and twelve aldermen, and several of the latter having failed to take the oaths within the time appointed by law, he had contrived, by obtaining judgments against them, to get them completely into his power. Of the whole body of thirteen it was calculated that at least seven were absolutely bound to him. The other Whig, Sir Ralph Verney, however, had a much smaller interest, and Lord Latimer, who with the approval of the Lord Treasurer came forward to oppose him, had at first every prospect of success. But the intervention of a Tory was immediately followed by a combination of the Whigs, and Latimer was already feeling despondent even before the appearance of Hackett on the scene.

The strength of Hackett's position lay in the fact that the people of Buckingham were most anxious to have the Assizes held in the town, and for this they were almost entirely dependent on the favour of the Lord Chief Justice. On the other hand their only chance of securing the Assizes permanently lay in providing suitable accommodation, and for this they were

[1] *Return of Members of Parliament*, i. 553, 554, 556.

dependent on Lord Latimer, who had promised some years earlier to build them a town house.[1] Neither of these considerations, however, was in the least likely to prevail against Sir Richard Temple. If Hackett appeared, therefore, he and Latimer would be rivals for the chance of excluding Sir Ralph Verney, and one or both of them must be defeated.

The obvious course was to persuade the Lord Chief Justice to transfer Hackett elsewhere, and with that object in view Latimer called upon him and Danby wrote. But Jeffreys absolutely refused to alter his plans. He declared that he would put out the aldermen who were in Temple's power and secure the defeat of both Whigs. He asserted that if Latimer was not in as strong a position as he had hoped it was due to his failure to keep his promise regarding the town house. Further he had a serious complaint to make. In the county election the tenants of James Herbert, Danby's son-in-law, were all found to be engaged on Wharton's side. There must be no masquerade at such a time, he declared to Latimer ; if a remedy was not found it would reflect upon them all ; an idle Tory was worse than a trimmer. These expressions, faithfully reported to Danby, provoked from him a reply which considerably startled the Chief Justice, and led him to explain away most of what he had said.[2] But the original difficulty still

---

[1] The history of the town house is itself sufficiently curious. Latimer had obtained a grant of timber from Charles II for the express purpose of building it (*Cal. Treas. Books*, v. 620-1 ; B.M. Add. MSS. 28049, f. 102), but owing to financial difficulties and the unlikelihood of any Parliament being summoned had gone no further. His chief anxiety was to avoid building the house until he was sure of his election ; that of the Corporation to avoid electing him until they were sure of their house ; and that of both to refrain from giving any occasion for a parliamentary enquiry into corrupt practices in the borough. The arrangement eventually made was that Latimer should deposit £200 in the hands of a certain Mr. Carpender, that sum to be devoted to building the town house if the election turned out well, and repaid to Latimer if it did not. The money was duly deposited, and was returned in the following June. The town house was eventually built by Verney.

[2] Danby's explanation was that he had no control over Herbert, and that Herbert in addition had lost control of his tenants. From a letter of thanks written by Wharton to Danby, and dated February 16, 1684[/5] (*Morrison Catalogue*, vi. 405), it is, however, plain that Danby had favoured Wharton's candidature, and had spoken on his behalf not only to Herbert but also to Lord Carnarvon. Yet he could write, " I hope my Lord Chief Justice knows me too well to believe I shall promote any Whig's interest." Wharton's half-sister Elizabeth was the second wife of Danby's brother-in-law, the Earl of

remained.   On April 10 Hackett was defeated at the county election,[1] and all interest turned to the town.

There every possible scheme by which Latimer's election might be secured was being debated.   Of the thirteen members of the Corporation he could count only on six, including the Mayor.   Thus he was bound to be in a minority ; but even so the Mayor was prepared to return him, provided the matter of the town house could be satisfactorily settled.   Such a price, however, appeared to Latimer too high for an election which was certain to be disputed, and he inclined to consider another suggestion, that as Buckingham had originally elected its members by popular vote he should ignore the Corporation, throw himself upon the populace, who were friendly to him, and secure a return through them.   But as this course of action was bound to alienate the friendly Mayor, and likely to be regarded with disfavour by the Government, it was dropped.[2]

Finally Latimer endeavoured to destroy the credit of his adversaries' supporters.   At the original meeting of the Corporation held on March 4 to consider the representation of the town in Parliament, after the Mayor had proposed that they should choose loyal men, one of the aldermen, George Dancer, had risen and declared that he was not for loyalty.   This was sufficient, it was argued, to warrant his expulsion from his place, in which case the voting would be six on each side, and Latimer might hope to be returned by the Mayor's casting vote.   In spite of depositions and affidavits against him, however, Dancer was not put out, and when the election was eventually held, on May 15, it was the two Whigs who were returned.[3]

Lindsey ; Wharton's first wife, Anne Lee, was, like Danby himself, a great-grandchild of Sir John Danvers and Elizabeth Nevill (*supra*, p. 8, note 3) ; and Wharton is referred to by Danby as his cousin.

[1] *Return of Members of Parliament*, i. 551.

[2] The draft of a letter to Rochester, sounding him upon the attitude of the Government to this idea, is still extant (B.M. Add. MSS. 28087, f. 7) ;   but no reply has been discovered.

[3] The correspondence regarding this election has been very fully preserved. It is to be found in B.M. Add. MSS. 28053, ff. 314-9 ; 28087, ff. 3, 5, 16-70 *passim* ; *Morrison Catalogue*, ii. 338 ; *Lindsey MSS.*, p. 446.   Most of the letters are from Latimer or his agents.   Danby's letter of April 14, which admirably summarises the position, is printed *infra*, ii. 126-7.   There are some picturesque details about the election in *Memoirs of the Verney Family*, iv. chap. ix.   Latimer petitioned the Commons against the return, but failed to prosecute his case (*C.J.*, ix. 716, 760).

2 A   D.L.I.

That the various devices suggested by Latimer were all
abandoned in the end was at least partly due to the fact that
Danby did not consider his credit with the Government to be
good enough.   If a return was obtained by dubious means it was
almost certain to be questioned in Parliament, and the decision
there was only too likely to be unfavourable.   Rochester had been
polite, and Jeffreys at least civil ; but it was clear from their behaviour that the Government, while not exactly hostile, was
utterly indifferent to his personal interests.   In a House of Commons in the election of which the Court had played a part beyond
all precedent there was not in the end a single Osborne to be found.[1]

It was therefore with some trepidation that Danby looked
forward to the actual opening of Parliament ; but the worst of
his fears were soon proved to be without foundation.   In the
coronation ceremonies on April 23 he was assigned the place
appropriate to his rank,[2] and when he waited upon the King
shortly afterwards he was graciously received.   James readily
granted him access at all times to the royal presence, and in
view of possibilities during the session promised that if his
services were required he should be informed by the King himself.   " I find the King and ministers outwardly very civill," he
wrote to his wife on May 13, " and there will be no danger of
my going to our old quarter." [3]

At the moment this glimpse of royal favour was of some
practical importance.   Danby and the three Catholic lords were
still under recognizances to appear before the House of Lords
on the first day of Parliament to answer to their impeachment.
James was known to be most anxious that the Catholics should
be discharged, and it now appeared he was willing that Danby
should be similarly dealt with.   The effect was seen when on

---

[1] In view of this fact it is perhaps not without significance that of the protests later made in the Commons against the " management " of the elections
the first came from Edward Seymour, once Danby's ally, and the second from
his future associate, Sir John Lowther, who was seconded by Lord Willoughby
and his brother Peregrine Bertie (Barillon to Louis XIV, June 2 and 4, 1685,
in Fox, *James II*, App., p. lxxxix *et seq.* ; Lonsdale, *Memoir of the Reign of
James II*, ed. 1857, pp. 451-3).

[2] His wife for days beforehand was so busy making preparations that Danby
had to recall his coach from Buckingham, whither it had been sent to assist his
son.

[3] *Infra*, ii. 114, 127-8.

May 19 the Earl attended at the bar of the Lords and presented a
petition praying for relief, either by trial or by such other means
as the Lords should find convenient.   For the moment he and
the Catholic lords were ordered to continue their attendance on
the House ; but on May 22, the next day of meeting, the order
of March 19, 1679, which had declared that impeachments do not
lapse on the dissolution of parliaments, was reconsidered and
formally reversed.   So changed was the temper of the House
that only three peers had the hardihood to record a protest.[1]

After more than six years Danby was thus at last freed from
his impeachment ; [2] but although he resumed his place in
Parliament and took an active part in the proceedings of the
Lords no further evidence of royal recognition came his way.
Immediately after the adjournment of Parliament he accordingly drew up a further memorial, which on July 6 he presented
in person to the King.[3] Artfully reminding James that the
Parliament which had driven him from office was the same
Parliament as had endeavoured to pass the Exclusion Bill, he
reiterated his statement that of the compensations promised
him for the loss of his posts not one had been made effective,
and prayed for the King's bounty in connection with them.
Any favour shown him he hoped to deserve by strict observance
of the royal commands, which he was sure would " never
require any other sort of obedience but what is suitable to the
duty of an honest subject."

In spite of the somewhat ominous conclusion this memorial
seems to have inspired James with the hope that he might
secure the support of Danby for the schemes he was already
meditating, and sending for the Earl to Windsor he sounded
him on the question of the Test.   Of the answer he received no
record whatever remains, but that it was not satisfactory may
be judged from the fact that Danby's petition was not granted,
nor was any employment offered to him.[4] Danby, indeed, had

---

[1] *L.J.*, xiv. 7-12 ; J. E. T. Rogers, *Protests of the Lords*, i. 67.

[2] He and his bail were finally discharged on June 1 (*L.J.*, xiv. 24).

[3] The memorial is printed *infra*, ii. 114-6.

[4] The sole authority for this incident is a tantalisingly brief note made by
Danby on p. 439 of Kennet's *History* : " Memorandum his [i.e. James's] sending for mee in the July before [i.e. before November 1685] to Windsor, and what
hee said about the Test and my answer " (B.M. Add. MSS. 28042, f. 114).

made his advances to the Clarendonians on the assumption that James was prepared to let his religion remain a private matter, continue the tradition of Clarendon, and base his authority on the support of the " old Cavalier and truly loyal " party. Any suggestion of tampering with the Test made it plain that the Clarendonians themselves were no longer true to the principles of Clarendon, and rendered an alliance between them and Danby impossible.

As yet, however, the Earl exhibited no sign of disaffection. James's ecclesiastical policy had not gone far enough to give him serious offence, while the foreign policy of the Government, which seemed to be aiming at a real alliance with Holland, met with his warmest approval. To the pretensions of Monmouth he was unalterably opposed, and during the rebellions of the early months of the reign he remained conspicuously loyal. As Yorkshire was unaffected his own personal influence was not called into play ; but Lord Dumblane served with the Duke of Grafton in Feversham's army, was engaged at Philip's Norton, and was wounded in the shoulder, although not seriously, at Sedgemoor.[1] In the lengthy account of Monmouth's execution which Lord Latimer shortly afterwards sent to his father there is nothing to suggest that the Duke's fate was a matter for regret to either of them.[2]

Nevertheless during the summer and autumn of 1685 Danby was steadily drifting away from the Court and towards the moderate Anglicans, who were already beginning to form the nucleus of an organised opposition. The great increase in the army for which the King had found an excuse in Monmouth's rebellion he could scarcely, in view of his own past history, condemn ; but the grant of commissions in that army to Catholics was a very different matter. Where Catholics were once admitted it was to be feared that under the influence of James they would soon be in control, and a Catholic army was only too likely to prove the precursor of a Catholic state and a

---

[1] Two of Lord Dumblane's letters, giving some account of these engagements, are B.M. Add. MSS. 28050, ff. 46, 48. Immediately on hearing that he had been wounded Lady Danby, who had been in a fever of anxiety during the campaign, hastened away to join him ; but he was never in the slightest danger (*Rutland MSS.*, ii. 89-92 ; *infra*, ii. 128).

[2] The letter is partly printed in *Morrison Catalogue*, iii. 86.

Catholic church. Any hope that the employment of Catholics
might prove to be a mere temporary expedient due to an unforeseen crisis was soon dispelled by the King himself, who let
it be known in Council that it was his deliberate policy to secure
the repeal of the Test and Habeas Corpus Acts. In official circles
the chief opposition came from Halifax, who after the death of
Guilford on September 5 was almost the only representative of
the moderates. Elsewhere the royal proposals were received
with general uneasiness, which rapidly developed into settled
hostility. One result was to bring about a temporary association of Danby and Halifax, for although these two statesmen
could never unite in office they were not incapable of working
together in opposition. When Halifax, having refused all the
royal overtures, was eventually struck off the Council on
October 21, he was already in touch with a considerable group,
including Danby, Nottingham, Bridgewater, the Bishop of
London and all his brethren, who were concerting measures
together.[1]

The retention of Halifax for so long in the ministry had been
due to the King's desire to secure the benefit of his influence
with Parliament, which had been summoned to meet on
November 9 ;[2] and his dismissal had been decided upon with
some reluctance only when it became apparent that his support
could not be counted upon.[3] James thereupon seems to have
conceived the idea of replacing Halifax by Danby, whose
ability, determination and influence with the Church party
might prove an even greater asset on the side of the Government. Early in November, at any rate, immediately before the
reassembling of Parliament, he once more summoned the Earl
to his presence, showed him the speech which he proposed to
make in defence of the officers in the army who had not taken
the Test, and asked his opinion upon it.[4] Again Danby's

[1] The most reliable account of the situation at this time is given by Halifax
himself, in a letter written just after his fall, to Lord Chesterfield (*Letters of
Lord Chesterfield*, pp. 295-302). On the development of the opposition see the
lists printed *infra*, iii. 152-63.

[2] The proclamation announcing that it would meet came out on October 12
(*Luttrell*, i. 359).

[3] This is the impression created by the French dispatches of the period. See
those of October 29 and November 5 in Fox, *James II*, App., pp. cxxvii, cxxx.

[4] Notes on Kennet's *History*, B.M. Add. MSS. 28042, f. 114.

answer remains unrecorded, but it may be assumed that it was unfavourable. There is nothing whatever to suggest that he would have joined the Government upon the only terms which James would have considered.

When Parliament met on November 9, however, Danby, although present every day, was not prominent in opposition to the Court. By the House of Lords the speech upon which he had been consulted was received with submission, and the customary vote of thanks was adopted. Hostility at first manifested itself only in the Commons, and was not inspired to any appreciable extent by Danby's personal following.[1] Even when on November 19 the spirit of opposition spread to the Lords, and it was proposed to appoint a day for the consideration of the King's speech, he still remained in the background. According to the very imperfect reports of the debate which have survived the lead against the Court was taken by Devonshire, Halifax, Mordaunt, and Bishop Compton of London, who professed to be speaking for the whole bench of bishops. Danby is not recorded to have addressed the House at all.

The truth appears to be that Danby, as a result of his own experience in the reign of Charles II, was well aware that opposition to the King would only drive him into the arms of France, and so defeat its own ends. He may even have known, or at least guessed, that the opposition exhibited by the Commons was partly inspired by France. What he would have liked to do was to foster the inclination which James had recently been manifesting towards Holland, and for that a conciliatory attitude on the part of Parliament was necessary. Such at any rate is the conclusion suggested by the sole surviving evidence of his outlook at this time, a short but most carefully corrected speech written in his own hand, and obviously intended for delivery in the House of Lords. The main point of the speech is to propose that the claim of the King to

[1] Of those who declared against a standing army only Sir Edmund Jennings and perhaps Edward Seymour could be described as Danby's associates. That he took a great interest in the debates, however, is shown by his papers, which contain a copy in his own hand of the Commons' address of November 17 about the popish officers, together with the King's answer (B.M. Add. MSS. 28091, f. 83), another copy (*ibid.*, f. 117), and a list of the popish officers, 70 in number, whom it was proposed to indemnify for not taking the Test (*ibid.*, f. 121).

dispense with the laws forbidding the employment of Catholics should be referred to the judges.[1]

Whether the speech was ever actually delivered is uncertain. At the conclusion of their debate on November 19 the Lords resolved to appoint November 23 for a consideration of the address from the throne, and the probability is that the speech was immediately drawn up by Danby in preparation for that event. The resolution of the Lords, however, as well as the hostility of the Commons showed James that his schemes had no chance of parliamentary sanction, and on November 20 he prorogued Parliament to February 10. The policy to which it would not agree he proposed to carry through by means of the royal prerogative.

In a Government based on such a policy, however, there was no room for Danby, and with the prorogation of Parliament accordingly the Earl abandoned all hope of office and retired for two years into private life. Like many a discarded statesman he turned his thoughts from the sovereign of the moment to the sovereign of the future. Since 1679 he had had, as far as can be ascertained, no direct connection with William of Orange ; but both the Prince and the Princess were under considerable obligations to him, and on their accession to the throne, if he should live to see it,[2] he might hope to occupy a prominent position. By the close of February 1686 he was meditating a visit to the Continent, professedly " to the Spaw beyond sea, for to be releevd of his stoppage in his throat," [3] but really, one must suppose, with the object of making his court to the Prince of Orange, and re-establishing himself in his good graces. Three months later he had made actual preparations for an extensive tour through Holland, Flanders and Germany, and was hoping to set out, with Charles Bertie as his companion, in the course of a fortnight.[4] This sudden zeal for foreign travel, however,

[1] The speech is printed *infra*, ii. 132-3.

[2] It must be remembered that Danby was nearly two years older than James II.

[3] Charles Bertie to the Countess of Rutland, February 27, 1686, in *Rutland MSS.*, ii. 105. It may or may not be a coincidence that the Dutch ambassador, van Citters, had come over from Holland immediately before this, and had had his first audience with James on February 26 (*Ellis Correspondence*, i. 53).

[4] Charles Bertie to the Countess of Rutland, May 20, 1686, in *Rutland MSS.*, ii. 108.

on the part of one who had not been out of England for more than thirty years, could not fail to arouse suspicion. So cold was the attitude of the Court that Danby hesitated long before asking for permission to go, and when towards the close of July he made his request he was met by a formal refusal.[1] A possible alternative was to send one of his sons, whose presence at the Dutch Court would not be regarded as so significant ; but just as he was arranging to dispatch Lord Dumblane his whole scheme was shattered by a domestic calamity which was to distract his attention for some months.

Dumblane by his erratic disposition had long given him anxiety, and by his reckless proceedings in connection with his marriage had done not a little to bring about his fall. Since the first novelty of marriage had worn off he had been going from bad to worse. Falling into the hands of lewd companions he had not only squandered his own resources, but incurred debts sufficient to swallow up the greater part of his wife's fortune as well, and by the autumn of 1686 had reached the very end of his tether. On October 17 he wrote to his father a most affectionate letter, deploring the fact that his wife had just miscarried of a very fine boy, but rejoicing that she herself was out of danger.[2] Ten days later he had abandoned his wife and fled the country.

So destitute was Lady Dumblane that the Earl's first care was to send her a hundred pounds.[3] His next was to seek out and come to some reasonable settlement with his son ; but in this he was gravely hampered by the good-nature of both Lady Danby and Lady Dumblane, who were ready to offer almost any terms to induce the fugitive to return home. On November 1 Lord Dumblane dispatched from Calais a most submissive letter to his father, enclosing a full account of his faults and imploring forgiveness and assistance.[4] As he sent this letter by the hands of a common seaman, however, and apparently expected a reply through the same channel, Danby merely wrote in answer that while he was ready to give what advice

---

[1] Grenville to Leveson Gower, July 28, 1686, in *Hist. MSS. Com.*, v. 186.
[2] The letter is B.M. Add. MSS. 28050, f. 50.
[3] Danby to Lady Dumblane, October 27, 1686, *infra*, ii. 128.
[4] B.M. Add. MSS. 28050, f. 54.

or help he could he would do nothing until Dumblane gave an address and allowed of communication in a more reasonable manner.[1] Not until a month later was Dumblane, who had meanwhile moved on to Bruges, able to get over this new cause of offence by explaining that English visitors to Calais were not in the habit of giving addresses, but sent to the posthouse for their letters whenever the packet came in.[2] Towards the close of December Danby's emissary, Mr. Bonard, found Dumblane at Brussels, and early in January 1687 they set out for England together.[3] What exact terms were arranged between father and son is unknown, but they certainly left Dumblane's financial affairs very much under Danby's control. It is due to his escapades at this time that Dumblane for the remainder of his life was always in straits for money, and had to depend, first upon his father, and then after that father's death upon his own son.[4]

By the time Dumblane's affairs had been settled the whole position in England had become much more serious, and Danby found himself rapidly drifting into an attitude of real hostility to James. The disappearance of the moderates from the ministry at the close of 1685 had been followed a year later by the dismissal even of the extreme Anglicans who were ready to obey James in anything except the abandonment of their faith. Little cause though Danby had to love the Clarendonians he had yet regarded the presence of Rochester at the head of the Government as some safeguard for the interests of Protestantism, and the dismissal of the Lord Treasurer, accompanied as it was by the recall of his brother the Lord Lieutenant, in January 1687, destroyed any faith he yet had in the good intentions of the King. The places of the Hydes were given to Catholics, who not merely filled the army and the Privy Council, but even received appointments in the Church and the Universities. Lawyers, officials, and members of Parliament who refused their support to the royal policy were ruthlessly deprived of place

---

[1] Danby to Lady Dumblane, November 22, 1686, *infra*, ii. 129.

[2] Lord Dumblane to Danby, December 4/14, 1686, in B.M. Add. MSS. 28050, f. 58.

[3] Bonard's letter to Danby of December 28/January 7 is B.M. Add. MSS. 28051, f. 219, and Dumblane's of January 3/13 is B.M. Add. MSS. 28050, f. 60.

[4] *Leeds MSS.*, p. 43.

and pension. Finally on April 4 a Declaration of Indulgence was issued which on the King's sole authority suspended all penal laws against dissenters from the Church of England, and declared them capable of holding any office under the Crown without taking the prescribed oaths and tests.

By these developments Danby personally remained singularly unaffected. He had neither places nor pensions of which he could be deprived, for he had lost them all nearly ten years earlier. He was not moved as others were by the attack on the Universities, for he had never been a member of either of them. But the whole policy on which James was embarking violated every principle, religious or political, in which he believed, and his immediate friends and connections were badly hit by it. Scarcely had Parliament been prorogued in 1685 when the four Berties who held commissions in the army were dismissed.[1] Shortly afterwards Charles Osborne was deprived of his post in the Customs. The Bishop of London was first struck off the Council, and then in the summer of 1686 brought before a specially appointed Ecclesiastical Commission and suspended from his functions.

It was thus in a somewhat different spirit that Danby in the spring of 1687 again turned to William of Orange. As consort of the heiress to the throne William presumably would have it in his power to decide whether on the death of James the existing system in England should be continued or reversed. It was therefore essential to take precautions against his being won over to support James's measures. It was also desirable to induce him to use the influence with the King which his position gave him to press for the adoption of a more moderate policy.

A channel of communication was soon provided. The same events as had alienated Danby had seriously roused the apprehensions of William himself. Every step which James took away from his people was a step in the direction of France, for only to Louis XIV could he look for the support which might be necessary should their hostility become dangerous. All hope of an alliance between England and Holland had long since disappeared, and William was now faced with the need for pro-

---

[1] *Rutland MSS.*, ii. 97.

viding against a possible alliance of England and France. His
interest lay in conciliation, for he dared not quarrel either with
the King or with the opposition. One course might throw
England for the moment completely into the arms of France,
the other might endanger his own eventual succession to the
English throne.

Shortly after the fall of the Hydes, accordingly, William
dispatched his most skilled diplomatist, Dykvelt, to England,
partly to remonstrate with James on the policy he was pursuing
and appeal to the leading Catholics for greater moderation,
partly to reassure the Protestants as regards his own attitude,
convince them of their common interest against James, and
find out by conversations with the chief men of all parties what
the situation in England actually was. The negotiations with
the King were not a success, but those with the opposition
groups bore immediate fruit. At Dykvelt's desire a number of
meetings were held at the Earl of Shrewsbury's house in London, where Halifax, Danby, Nottingham, Devonshire and
other representatives of the various factions discussed the
whole situation and agreed upon the advice which should be
offered to the Prince. With this advice the Dutch envoy returned to Holland about the beginning of June.[1]

Among the opponents of the Court it was the Marquis of
Halifax to whom Dykvelt's credentials were chiefly directed,
but Danby was also specially named as one of those with whom
he should discourse, and his mission therefore marks the renewal from William's side of the long connection between Prince
and Earl which had been interrupted since 1679. Even to an
agent so well accredited, however, Danby hesitated to say all
he might have done, and the chief point of the letter from him
which Dykvelt carried back to Holland was to lament the lack
of any personal intercourse between the English malcontents
and the Prince.[2] To remedy this defect he made a further effort
during the summer to secure permission for a visit to Holland,
but in view of the suspicious attitude of the Court he considered
it prudent not to press his request. Such a visit, he feared,
would do more harm to him than it could be of service to the

---

[1] *Burnet*, i. 708-12.
[2] The letter, dated May 30, 1687, is printed *infra*, ii. 116-8.

Prince, and he accordingly turned aside to a round of country visits, in the course of which he discussed the situation with his immediate friends and relatives.[1]

From these he was recalled by the arrival in August of another envoy from Holland, Count Zuylestein, whose ostensible business was to offer condolences on the death of the Duchess Laura, mother of James's queen, but whose real object was to carry still further the work of Dykvelt. To Danby Zuylestein brought a most gracious letter from William, and the Earl and envoy discussed the situation at some length. Danby mentioned various possible contingencies and desired to know what the Prince's attitude in each case would be. Zuylestein gave the answers with which he had been entrusted, and these proved perfectly satisfactory. Before the envoy's departure early in September as good an understanding had been established on general points as was possible through an intermediary, but Danby continued to lament the lack of a still closer connection.[2]

Meanwhile James had been going from bad to worse. The attack on Magdalen College had nearly run its course, and before the close of the year that famous and wealthy foundation was to be turned into a Roman Catholic seminary. An attempt had been made to secure the admission of a Catholic to the Charterhouse, and Danby himself, who was one of the trustees, was involved in the successful resistance of that body to the royal mandate.[3] Bitter as was the resentment which such arbitrary acts produced, however, it would never have led to anything more than the legitimate constitutional opposition which had for some time been in existence. What altered the whole position of affairs in the autumn of 1687 was the comparatively sudden emergence of a possibility that James might succeed in making his hated system permanent.

On July 4 the King had marked his breach with the Anglicans by dissolving the Tory Parliament which he had kept in abeyance since the close of 1685. During the following six months

---

[1] *Rutland MSS.*, ii. 115.

[2] The letter which he entrusted to Zuylestein, dated September 4, 1687, is printed *infra*, ii. 118-9.

[3] *Macaulay*, ii. 942.

all the resources of the Government were devoted to preparing for the return of a more subservient Parliament based upon a combined Catholic and Dissenting interest. The corporations were remodelled again and again. In the counties all officials were required to answer a series of questions upon their willingness to support the royal policy. Those who refused were immediately dismissed, and their places were given to Catholics and Dissenters. Even the greatest nobles in the land were not exempt, and half of the Lords Lieutenants had to be dismissed, including Danby's own brother-in-law, the Earl of Abingdon. Once the officials in town and country were of his way of thinking James had little doubt of his ability to secure a Parliament to his mind.

While a serious possibility thus became apparent that the King might obtain formal legal sanction for his actions, a danger began to force itself upon public notice that he might be able to perpetuate his system through an heir of his own body trained in his own beliefs. In October it was whispered that the Queen was with child ; in November the news spread ; towards the close of December it was officially confirmed by a royal proclamation appointing a day of thanksgiving for the occasion. So long had the ultimate succession of Mary and her husband William of Orange formed the chief hope of the Protestant party and the chief fear of the extreme Catholics that the news never received a reasonable hearing from either side. On the one hand the Catholics hailed the expected birth as a miracle specially vouchsafed in aid of the true religion, and asserted their confidence that the child would be a boy. On the other hand the Protestants denounced the whole affair as a projected fraud, and adduced the divination of the sex of the child as proof of their contention.

The heated atmosphere to which this gave rise led to one curious incident which might have proved much more significant than it eventually did. On January 28, 1688, Danby received an anonymous letter written the day before apparently in a disguised hand. " I would not have a man to whome I have some obligations," the writer declared, " perish unwarned for a peevish obstinacy that will prove to noe purpose. Make your peace with the King, or be assured that after this 27 of January you have not many days to live. I should be overjoyed to heare this advice were so effectuall to make you repent before repentance be in vaine." Letters much the same in character were at the same time sent to Shrewsbury, Dorset, Halifax and Henry Sidney.[1]

By a strange coincidence some apparent confirmation of these letters was provided on January 31 with the discovery in Parker's Lane of the recently dismembered trunk of a man. Excitement rose high ; but the days of Sir Edmund Berry Godfrey had long passed away, and the murder was soon shown to have no connection with the letters or with the world of politics. On February 3 the dead man was identified as one Hobry, or Awbry, husband of a French midwife, who on being arrested and examined confessed the murder. On March 2 she was burnt in Leicester Fields, and the incident seemed to have closed.[2]

The natural conclusion was that the letters were merely the work of " some idle braines. " If so these brains must have been singularly acute, for they had guessed the fact that something of the nature of a conspiracy already existed, and had identified at least three of the conspirators. The mere rumour of the birth of a son and heir to James had destroyed the whole basis of the constitutional opposition which had long existed. The accession of Mary and William of Orange was postponed indefinitely ; such influence as they had with James completely vanished. Towards the close of 1687, accordingly, more vigorous methods of opposition began to be considered, the effect of which became apparent in the following spring.

It may well be questioned whether Danby ever seriously believed that James proposed to palm off upon the nation a supposititious child, but as early as March 1688 he had adopted that idea as part of his political creed, and resolved to throw in his lot definitely with William. On March 27, accordingly, he wrote both to the Prince and to the Princess making the very significant request that his daughter Lady Plymouth might be

[1] The letter to Danby is preserved in B.M. Add. MSS. 28053, f. 345. That to Dorset is printed, from a copy, in *Rutland MSS.*, ii. 117, and less accurately in *Luttrell*, i. 430.

[2] *Luttrell*, i. 430, 433 ; *Portledge Papers*, pp. 25-7 ; *Macaulay*, ii. 972-4.

admitted a lady of the Princess's bedchamber. For safety's sake the letters were entrusted to Lord Dumblane, who was to travel to Holland and, in case his actions were watched, deliver them indirectly through Dr. Stanley, the Princess's chaplain. Nevertheless it is clear that Danby hoped Dumblane and William might have some opportunity to discuss the political situation, with which he expressed himself as being on the whole satisfied. Resistance to the Catholic designs of the Court had been so general that he was sure they could not succeed except by violence. The public declaration of the Prince in Fagel's famous letter, that while thoroughly in favour of toleration he could not countenance any tampering with the Tests, had united the English nation in his support as never before.[1]

Suspicion at Whitehall, however, was more acute than Danby had supposed. Shortly after the letters were written Dumblane waited on the King to obtain leave to go abroad, and was somewhat roughly received. Leave was indeed granted, but with an express proviso that no visit must be paid to Holland. On the following day the King somewhat altered his tone, but still adhered in essentials to what he had said. He would trust Dumblane to go where he liked, but if he went only for curiosity he might as well satisfy that elsewhere as in Holland. In these circumstances it seemed to Danby unlikely that the King would allow Lady Plymouth to enter the Princess's service, and he accordingly wrote withdrawing his request. Dumblane was instructed to visit only Flanders, and was provided with a trustworthy servant who was to carry the letters from there to Dr. Stanley and receive any answers.

As regards the movements of Dumblane thereafter no information is available, but presumably the programme laid down by Danby was carried out, for the letters to the Prince and Princess were duly delivered, and very flattering replies were returned. Mary declared she would have been delighted to receive Lady Plymouth into her household, but admitted the validity of the reasons against her doing so, and proposed that

[1] The letter to William is printed *infra*, ii. 119-21. It is easy to read a great deal into many of its phrases, but the only point which emerges quite certainly is that Danby was trying to establish a permanent interest at the Dutch court, and with Mary rather than with William.

the matter should be postponed till some more favourable opportunity. Her obligations to Danby were great, especially for her own marriage, and she proposed to acknowledge them whenever she had the chance. William deplored the fact that he was to see neither the Earl himself nor his son.[1]

Before Dumblane with these letters could return from the Continent another and more important messenger was on his way to the Hague. The conferences at Lord Shrewsbury's house which Dykvelt had inaugurated had never come to an end, and towards the close of April Edward Russell, who was one of the group that met there, was sent over in the name of them all to ascertain what steps William was now prepared to take. The reply which he received was that it was impossible for the Prince to interfere in the affairs of England without formal and definite invitation from a sufficient number of men of quality there.

The England to which Russell returned with this answer was a very different England from that which he had left. During his absence the second Declaration of Indulgence had been issued, the Order in Council had appeared requiring it to be read from the pulpit on two successive Sundays, and the seven bishops had made their memorable protest. In the indignation roused by these events, strengthened as it was by the subsequent prosecution of the bishops, the project of inviting William over met with ready acceptance. Danby was one of the first to welcome the idea, and brought over with him both the Bishop of London and the Earl of Nottingham. The actual birth of a Prince of Wales on June 10 presumably confirmed the conspirators in their intentions. As early as June 18 the invitation was almost ready to be dispatched.[2]

The delay of nearly a fortnight which followed is probably to be accounted for by the concentration of all attention on the trial of the bishops. Danby was not intimately connected with ecclesiastical circles, and there is nothing to suggest that he took any part in the discussions which decided how the Declaration of Indulgence and the Order in Council should be met.

[1] Danby's letter, dated March 29, and the letters of Mary and William, dated respectively April 29 and April 30, are printed *infra*, ii. 121-3.

[2] *Dalrymple*, App., i. 227.

But as soon as the raising of a legal issue made the matter a political one he came to the front. At the trial of the bishops he was one of the many nobles whose presence struck terror into the hearts of the judges.[1] On the very night of their acquittal the famous invitation to William was drawn up, and entrusted for safe delivery to Admiral Herbert. Of the seven signatories Danby was certainly the most important on the Tory side.

[1] B.M. Add. MSS. 29563, f. 193 ; Carte MSS. 76, f. 28.

CHAPTER XVII

REVOLUTION, 1688

THE dispatch of the invitation to William was followed by a short breathing space. Zuylestein, who had been sent over from Holland to offer congratulations on the birth of the Prince of Wales,[1] was taken into their confidence by the conspirators, and requested to remain in England until a reply to the invitation could be received ; but in order to avert suspicion he was advised to go into the country for some days.[2] Presumably with the same object in view Danby joined his wife in a flying visit to his son-in-law James Herbert at Kingsey.[3] It was not desirable that the friends of William should be seen too frequently in each other's company.

On July 10 Danby was again in London ;[4] by that time the reply to the invitation had presumably arrived ; and during the following three weeks the main details of William's expedition were almost certainly arranged. According to the account which Burnet later obtained from Edward Russell[5] the advice on which the conspirators originally agreed was that William should come over with a large fleet but a small army. The argument which they advanced in favour of this was that his expedition must be prevented from assuming the appearance of a Dutch invasion ; but one may suspect their real motive to

[1] He arrived on June 23 (*Clarendon Correspondence*, ii. 178).

[2] Sidney to William of Orange, June 30, 1688, in *Dalrymple*, App., i. 231-2.

[3] The only evidence regarding Danby's movements at this time is to be found in two of his letters, dated July 7 and July 10 respectively, printed *infra*, ii. 134-5. These letters are by no means easy to interpret, or even reconcile with each other ; but the general fact of a visit to Kingsey seems to emerge from them quite clearly. Their main reference is to a lawsuit in which Lord Latimer was at this time involved.

[4] Zuylestein also was in London from July 12 onwards (*Clarendon Correspondence*, ii. 181-2).

[5] *Supplement to Burnet*, p. 292.

386

have been a fear that if he had a considerable force of his own he would become too independent of his English supporters. William, however, refused to jeopardise the success of his venture by accepting their proposals, and insisted that he must have a force of at least 10,000 foot and 3,000 dragoons.

The best place of landing, the conspirators strongly urged, was to be found in the north, either in Bridlington Bay or in the Humber below Hull. In his completed *History* Burnet ascribes this advice to the influence of Danby, who hoped to have " a share in the whole management by the interest he believed he had in that country." [1] There is no doubt whatever that Danby proposed to bring the revolution under his control, and with that end in view wished to establish himself from the first as the Prince's chief adviser. But in the eyes of landsmen the arguments in favour of a landing in the north were conclusive in any case. The south-west, as could readily be surmised, and as events were to prove, had been too thoroughly crushed after the failure of Monmouth's rebellion to be prepared for a second venture. Of the principal conspirators Devonshire in Derby and Nottingham, and Lumley in Durham possessed a local influence which equalled or even excelled that of Danby in Yorkshire. The north was specially well fitted to supply the lack of horses which was bound to be the chief difficulty of an invading force, and from it there was an easy and uninterrupted march on London. The only serious argument which could be produced on the other side was that an army operating from the north might be taken in the rear by forces coming from Scotland or Ireland.[2]

The opposition to the landing in the north came entirely from the seamen.[3] The east coast of England, they declared,

---

[1] *Burnet*, i. 777.

[2] " Les troupes d'Ecosses, qui sont de 5 à 6 mille hommes, ont ordre de se tenir sur la frontiére, pour estre prestes à marcher au premier signal, et elles ne seront pas éloignées de l'ennemy s'il paroit dans la province d'York. . . . Les forces d'Irlandes sont aussi toutes prestes pour passer la mer en cas de besoin " (Bonnet, October 2/12, 1688).

[3] In his Memoirs Burnet says " Herbert," in his *History* " Herbert and the other seamen." The point is of some importance as it leaves in doubt the attitude of Russell, who was Burnet's informant, and was presumably consulted from the very beginning. It would appear that he went with the landsmen.

was much too exposed for a large fleet at the late season of the
year when it might be expected that the expedition would set
sail. Further the presence of the fleet in the north would make
it possible for the French to throw reinforcements into England
just as they liked. To these arguments William, himself a
landsman, probably failed to give the weight they deserved.
He seems at any rate to have undertaken in the end to effect a
landing in the north, with the proviso that if circumstances
made it necessary he might land elsewhere.[1] Unquestionably
Danby expected William to land in the north, and equally
unquestionably he understood that if William were compelled
to land anywhere else he would send help in the shape of money
and munitions to his supporters there.

These arrangements having been completed the conspirators
about the beginning of August left London. Zuylestein returned to Holland, and was accompanied by Sidney. Shrewsbury and Russell, who could do little to promote a movement in
the north, prepared to follow. The remainder dispersed themselves over the country where they felt their influence would
most prevail, and proceeded to enlist as many as they dared in
support of their schemes.

Of Danby's movements at this time it is impossible to give a
connected account, for during the months of August and September he disappears almost entirely from view. Towards the
close of August he was certainly engaged in transmitting large
sums of money to the Continent, either for the service of the
expedition, or for his own use if compelled by the failure of the
conspiracy to retreat thither.[2] About the beginning of Sep-

---

[1] In S.P.Dom., James II, vol. 4, there is a double sheet of notes in William's
own handwriting headed, "Preventions necessaires pour le dessin de Juillet
1688," which probably gives his early reflections regarding the descent on
England. The notes on the place of landing are sufficiently vague—" Ou se
debarquer? En plusieurs lieus ou en un? S'il faut en mesme temps faire une
desente en Ecosse. Agir selon les occurances." Cf. Herbert's memorial, with
William's notes, in Correspondentie van Willem III en Bentinck, part i., i. 46-7,
and Albeville's information in Hist. MSS. Com., xi. 5, p. 178 et seq.

[2] Between August 21 and August 24 he sent over £2,500 in the form of bills
of exchange payable at Amsterdam in October (B.M. Add. MSS. 28042, f. 104).
Reresby was later informed that he had lodged a great sum of money in the
Bank of Holland (Memoirs, p. 521). In this respect Danby was by no means
alone. The French ambassador at the Hague estimated the total sum sent
over from England at £4,000,000 (Negotiations of Count d'Avaux, iv. 197,
214-5, 219, 221-2, 231-2).

tember he appears to have been engaged in putting all his affairs into order.[1] Later in the same month he is said to have drawn up " a full scheme of advices, together with the heads of a declaration," which Shrewsbury and Russell carried with them when they finally set out to join William.[2] But where he was at the time, and upon what other activities he was engaged, cannot be determined. Rumour declared that he was in Holland,[3] but for this there is not the slightest evidence, and the report is of importance only as suggesting that he was in retirement. The presumption is that after the close of the term he fulfilled his original intention of leaving London for the north,[4] and under pretence of a series of friendly visits spent his time " going about the country, to prepare and solicit the gentry." [5] At Whittington, a little Derbyshire village not far from Chesterfield, a formal conference was held, where in the presence of Colonel John Darcy he was reconciled with the Earl of Devonshire, the manager of his impeachment.[6] Tradition still indicates the Cock and Pynot as the inn to which the three conspirators retired in order to escape a shower of rain, but of the results of their deliberations no record whatever remains. How many similar conferences were held about the same time between Danby and other malcontents one can only surmise.[7]

As the autumn advanced, however, and the expected arrival of William drew nearer, the preparations of his supporters to receive him took more definite shape. During the course of September those who were to accompany him in his invasion

[1] Autograph notes endorsed, " Memorandums, 6 September [16]88," in B.M. Add. MSS. 28042, f. 102.

[2] *Burnet*, i. 766.

[3] Lady Plymouth to Lady Danby, October 11, in Leeds MSS., Packet 13b.

[4] *Rutland MSS.*, ii. 119.

[5] Clarke, *Life of James II*, ii. 231.

[6] *Infra*, ii. 251. Much ingenuity has been expended in trying to fix the date of this famous meeting. The most probable date would appear to be some time in September.

[7] The most remarkable illustration of Danby's activities is his extraordinarily outspoken letter to Lord Chesterfield printed *infra*, ii. 135. The date of that letter unfortunately has not been preserved, but internal evidence suggests that it cannot have been written before the last few days of September, while it is difficult to believe that Danby came as far south as Leicester at any time after the beginning of October.

were steadily drifting over to Holland.[1] Towards the close of
the same month, under pretence of drinking the sulphur waters
of Knaresborough, Danby, accompanied by Lord Dumblane
and Charles Bertie, took up his abode at Ribston Hall, the
family seat of the Goodrickes, where Sir Henry was then
amusing his leisure and providing for possible eventualities by
turning his garden into a small fortress.[2] The mansion was
most conveniently situated on the north bank of the river Nidd,
sufficiently isolated to be free from constant inspection by
curious eyes, and yet within easy striking distance of York.
Its central situation made it an ideal place for the reception by
Danby of complimentary visits from the Yorkshire gentry, some
of whom were entrusted with a knowledge of the great design.
For the next month it was to be the principal headquarters of
the English movement in favour of William.

On October 1 the whole series of conferences and discussions
in the north came to a head. There is reason to suppose that
about that time the Bishop of London took part in them.[3]
Much more important was the arrival of the Earl of Devonshire,
" pretending to see his estate." On September 29, after a long
journey, Devonshire reached Wetherby, where he was detained
by indisposition and presumably by the calls of business for
nearly two days. On the afternoon of October 1, having
heralded his coming by a brief note, he visited Ribston, and
arranged with Danby the final details of their rising. The
landing of William was to be the signal for the seizure of York
by the one and of Nottingham by the other. As York had a
governor and a garrison, while Nottingham was only an open
town, Danby was to act first in order to have the benefit of the
surprise. His arrangements made, Devonshire then left
Ribston, and had a conference the same night with Thomas

[1] On October 5 the Polish ambassador at the Hague wrote home, " Les
Anglois arrivent icy en foule pour s'embarquer avec M. le Prince d'Orange, et
il n'est pas possible d'en dire le nombre " (B.M. Add. MSS. 38495, f. 26 ;
cf. Negotiations of Count d'Avaux, iv. 235, 243).

[2] Hist. MSS. Com., xi. 5, p. 138. That the fortifications were something more
than mere toys is apparent from an old print of Ribston reproduced in C. A.
Goodricke, History of the Goodricke Family, p. 32.

[3] When James II summoned the bishops to meet him on September 28 " the
Bishop of London could not be found, being gone, it is thought, to his sisters
in Yorkshire " (Ellis Correspondence, ii. 224).

Wharton, who was also in the neighbourhood. Later he spent
some time in York, and visited Ripon before returning south.
His object in this, one may conjecture, was to establish relations
with the Whigs of the north, with whom Danby was not so
closely associated.[1]

Immediately Devonshire had departed Danby brought his
own preparations to a conclusion. His will was completed and
entrusted to his wife. All his horses were brought to Ribston,
and so many of his servants were summoned to follow him that
he had to apologise to Lady Danby for leaving her so ill
attended. Spies were sent out to report the movements of
troops, Danby being apprehensive both of the reinforcements
for James's army at that time pouring south from Scotland,[2]
and of the troops which were being pushed northwards towards
Newark to provide against any landing in East Anglia or
beyond the Humber.[3]

That these meetings and preparations should entirely fail to
rouse suspicion was scarcely to be expected. Early in October
Lord Fairfax of Emley, the Catholic Lord Lieutenant of the
North Riding, visited Danby, and was so alarmed by what he
saw and heard that he hastened immediately to York and laid
before Sir John Reresby, the governor of the city, all he had
been able to learn. Sir John had already exchanged courtesies
with Devonshire in York, and now deemed it advisable to call
upon Danby at Ribston ; but " their carriage appeared very
innocent," and " not believeing that men of that qualitie and
estate could design anything prejudiciall to the Government or
dangerous to themselves " he rejected Lord Fairfax's suggestions as absurd.[4]

If the Governor of York was satisfied, no one else was likely
to interfere, for the entire local administration of Yorkshire,

---

[1] *Lindsey MSS.*, p. 447 ; *Reresby*, pp. 514-5. Devonshire's note of October
1 from Wetherby is printed *infra*, ii. 137.

[2] *Hist. MSS. Com.*, xii. 7, pp. 215-6. The Scottish troops, more than 3,000 in
number, crossed the Border on October 1, and reached the neighbourhood
of London on October 25. The horse and dragoons, who marched by the east
coast route, entered York on October 15, and left four days later (Scott,
British Army, p. 194 ; *Reresby*, pp. 517-20 ; Lonsdale, *Memoir*, ed. 1857,
p. 478 ; Dalton, *English Army Lists*, ii. 210).

[3] Danby to Lady Danby, October 2, 1688, *infra*, ii. 136-7.

[4] *Reresby*, pp. 514-5.

like that of England as a whole, was in confusion. All three
ridings had Catholic Lords Lieutenants, whose authority, on
account of their failure to take the Test, was questioned at
every turn. Lord Langdale and Lord Fairfax of Emley were at
least capable and energetic ; but Lord Thomas Howard, to
whom the West Riding had been entrusted, was absent in
Rome, and had left as his representatives three deputy lieutenants, of whom only one was a Protestant, and only two
were immediately available.[1] The situation in many of the
towns, the administration of which was in process of reconstruction, was even worse ;[2] while the militia after years of
neglect was almost completely unorganised.[3] Moreover, there
was no lack of legitimate reasons for Danby's activity. James
had announced his intention of summoning a Parliament for
November 27,[4] and the gentry everywhere were engaged in
conferences and discussions to further the interests of their
candidates. On September 28 it was resolved that the writs
for this Parliament should be recalled ; but at the same time
the King issued a proclamation calling upon all his subjects
to arm for the defence of their country, and Danby, as one of
the leading men in the north, was naturally expected to take
some action upon it.[5]

The inefficient administration which had allowed the conspiracy to come to a head, however, became, as soon as it was
formed, an obstacle in its path, for so long as the existing
officials retained their places the conspirators could not themselves secure any control over the machinery of county govern-

[1] *Reresby*, pp. 511-2.

[2] The confusion in York City itself, where the magistrates were changed
more than once, is well described by Reresby (*Memoirs*, pp. 364-8, 389, 508-12,
521-2).

[3] " The militia here is in greate disorder by the late removall of the chiefe
gentry out of commission who were officers and commanders in it, and being
informd musters were not pleasing to your Majestie they have mett but once
since your coronation " (Earl of Lindsey to the King, Grimsthorpe, September
27, 1688, in S.P. Dom., James II, 4, f. 78). Danby makes it clear that the militia
of Yorkshire was in at least as bad a condition as that of Lincolnshire.

[4] The decision was taken as early as August 24, but the writs were very slow
in being issued.

[5] *Infra*, ii. 136. As many as 2,000 gentlemen in Yorkshire were believed to
have volunteered for the defence of the country (*Ellis Correspondence*, ii. 241).
There is no doubt that many of these were conspirators, who found in the call
to arms a cloak for their own designs.

ment. It was therefore determined to aim at a reconstruction
of the administration, and with this end in view it was resolved
on October 2, with the full approbation of the Sheriff of Yorkshire and of Sir John Reresby, that a mass meeting of the
Yorkshire gentry should be held on the following day. As the
city was filled with gentlemen who had come up to receive the
writs for the expected parliamentary elections,[1] the meeting was
well attended. Danby and Sir Henry Goodricke rode in from
Ribston, and the latter took the lead, pointing out how impossible it was that the gentry and the militia could render effective
service to the King while the Lords Lieutenants, being Catholics,
were men under whom they could not lawfully serve at all. To
both the loyal and the disloyal among his hearers his speech,
for different reasons, was thoroughly acceptable, and Sir John
Reresby himself seconded him. A representation of the situation was immediately drawn up and hastily dispatched to the
King, Reresby sending on in advance a letter of explanation,
in which he excused the part he had taken, but insisted that
what was desired was for the royal service.[2]

The prominent part played by Goodricke inevitably raises
the suspicion that what the conspirators were really hoping for
was the appointment of Danby as Lord Lieutenant of the
West Riding. So strong were the Earl's claims that the King,
had he retained separate Lords Lieutenants for the three
ridings, might have found it difficult to resist them. Military
considerations, however, suggested in any case the consolidation
of the three Lord Lieutenancies, and while accepting graciously
and without delay the representation that had been made to him
James evaded Danby's trap by nominating the Duke of Newcastle Lord Lieutenant of all three ridings. The appointment
reached Newcastle at Boroughbridge on October 9, and by the
evening of the same day the Duke was in York exerting himself
to the utmost to put the county machinery into working order.[3]

[1] According to one account more than 6,000 electors had come to York to
vote for Lord Clifford and Sir John Kaye as knights of the shire (" Journal of
Castilion Morris," in *Yorkshire Archaeological and Topographical Journal*, x. 161).

[2] This account is based upon a comparison of Reresby's narrative (*Memoirs*,
p. 512) with Danby's letter of October 2, printed *infra*, ii. 136. The petition
to the King apparently received 70 signatures (*Hist. MSS. Com.*, xii. 7, p. 215).

[3] Newcastle to Sunderland, October 10, 1688, in S.P. Dom., James II, 4,
f. 113 ; B.M. Add. MSS. 10039, f. 4 ; *Reresby*, pp. 515-6.

Danby of course could not himself serve under Newcastle, but he had every hope of securing the appointment of many of his followers to subordinate posts. So strong was the opposition of the gentry to the grant of any commissions to Catholics that Newcastle was induced to obtain permission from the King to leave them out altogether ; and of the deputy lieutenants and other officials whom he nominated a very large number were more or less intimately associated with the conspiracy.[1] But having thus established themselves in the very heart of the fortress which it was their intention to assault, the conspirators were now called upon to face a long period of waiting which must have tried their resolution to the utmost. Rumour followed rumour with unwearying persistence, but the Dutch fleet still delayed its coming, and meanwhile no man could tell when the Government might not decide to embark upon the policy of precautionary arrests which it had for some time had in mind. Danby was certainly among those under suspicion ;[2] but although " invited up to London by my Lord Belasis and the Kings order " he contrived to excuse himself with a vague offer of his services and protestation of his fidelity.[3] Lord Lumley was actually marked out for arrest, but evaded the officers sent to seize him.[4] It was probably with a view to disarming the suspicion of the Government that Charles Bertie returned to London and Danby once more took up his abode at Kiveton.[5] When tidings arrived of William's abortive start on October 19 it must have appeared for a moment that the

---

[1] A list of the deputy lieutenants, taken from the State Papers, is given in *Reresby*, pp. 520-1.

[2] The French ambassador mentions Halifax, Danby, Shrewsbury and Nottingham (Barillon to Louis XIV, October 18, 1688).

[3] Barillon to Louis XIV, October 21, 1688 ; B.M. Add. MSS. 34512, f. 115; *Reresby*, p. 520.

[4] *Reresby*, p. 524 ; Ralph Cole and John Duck to Sunderland, October 26, 1688, in S.P. Dom., James II, vol. 4. The first move of the Government against the conspirators appears to have been the issue of a warrant for the arrest of Lord Lovelace on October 6 (*Hist. MSS. Com.*, xii. 7, p. 213). About the same time efforts were made to secure Sir John Guise (Duke of Beaufort to Sunderland, October 13, 15, 1688, in S.P. Dom., James II, vol. 4). The surprising thing is that the conspirators in the north were so little molested.

[5] They both left York about October 18 ; but Dumblane remained in the city (Goodricke to Danby, October 20, in Leeds MSS., Packet 13b ; *Lindsey MSS.*, p. 447).

whole undertaking would have to be postponed to the following year, and ruin must have stared the conspirators in the face.[1]

Such was the position when news began to filter through that the Prince had once more set sail on November 1, but that after endeavouring for some time to steer northwards he had turned to the west and gone down the Channel. The first report, which came on November 4 from Hull, was to the effect that William had landed near Southampton, that London had risen, and that the King and Queen were preparing for flight ; [2] but this was soon contradicted by more official news. On November 7 it was known in York that the landing had really taken place at Torbay two days previously.[3]

The news was received by the conspirators with dismay. To attempt an insurrection without the assistance of some covering force from abroad would have been sheer madness. There were garrisons at York, Chester, Carlisle, Berwick, Tynemouth and Scarborough. Two regiments of foot were stationed at Hull.[4] Others were quartered in the midlands, and were known to have orders to unite at Newark and march on the north if trouble threatened in that quarter.[5] At any moment still more troops might be ordered south from Scotland,[6] or brought across from Ireland and landed at Chester. If the danger of being caught between two fires was a serious argument against William's landing in the north, it was a still more serious argument against any unaided insurrection in the same district.

Nothing therefore remained for Danby and his followers but to wait with what patience they could for the assistance in the

---

[1] Echard has preserved some curious anecdotes, which may have an element of truth in them, of the methods employed by Danby at this time to keep up the courage of his associates (*History of the Revolution*, pp. 170-2).

[2] B.M. Add. MSS. 28053, f. 349.

[3] *Reresby*, p. 524.

[4] It is difficult to be quite certain regarding the strength or exact disposition of the forces in the north, but there appear to have been at least four battalions there and some horse as well (Clarke, *Life of James II*, ii. 191).

[5] *Ibid.*, pp. 205-6.

[6] The idea that a large force of Scottish militia and Highlanders might be brought south to oppose William, or to keep the northern counties of England in check, was constantly being suggested (Balcarras, *Memoirs touching the Revolution in Scotland*, p. 11 ; *Hist. MSS. Com.*, xii. 7, p. 221).

shape of officers, money and munitions which William, in the event of his landing elsewhere, had promised to send them, or at the very least for some indication of what the Prince, in the circumstances that had arisen, desired that they should do. But days passed, and not a sign reached them. The truth no doubt is that William was determined to keep the revolution under his own control, and so long as things went well in the south had no desire to start an independent and possibly rival movement in the north.

Had the Government understood William's attitude it might have been readier to withdraw its troops from Yorkshire, but for some time after the landing at Torbay rumours were current that part of the Dutch force was making for the Humber. Thus there was little relaxation of pressure from Whitehall, and the only hope of the conspirators lay in an increasing slackness of the local administration due to the ineptitude of the Duke of Newcastle. Convinced that the landing of the Dutch so far away had removed all immediate danger and made his presence at York unnecessary, the Duke, who had returned to Welbeck on October 30,[1] insisted on remaining there, and Sir John Reresby, although he did his best, had neither the rank nor the official position necessary to enable him to take a real lead in county affairs. The result was seen when in the absence of Newcastle a meeting of deputy lieutenants was held at York on November 13 to concert measures for the maintenance of the peace. Without difficulty it was agreed that the entire militia horse should be called out, and that at least two troops of horse and one regiment of foot should remain permanently in garrison at York. But thereafter the meeting was dominated by Sir Henry Goodricke, who proposed on his own authority that a summons should be issued to all the gentlemen and principal freeholders to attend at York on Thursday, November 22, to prepare more adequate measures and to draw up a loyal address to the King. So innocent in appearance was this proposal that it received the hearty support of Reresby himself, and the notices were immediately sent out. Yet there can be no reasonable doubt that Goodricke was acting as the agent of the conspirators, who intended to use the meeting for their

---

[1] *Reresby*, pp. 523-4.

own purposes when they had made up their minds what exactly they intended to do.[1]

Long before November 22, although not a word had yet been heard from William, they had determined at whatever risk to themselves to take action. If anything was required to inflame still further their hostility to James it was provided by the arrival just at this moment of a new commission of the peace which omitted the names of Sir Henry Goodricke, Sir John Kaye, Christopher Tancred and at least twenty of the principal gentlemen of the West Riding, introducing in their place men who were most unfitted for the post.[2] Alarming rumours began to spread abroad that it was intended at the meeting on November 22 to petition for a free Parliament,[3] if not to take some even more extravagant steps. Sir John Reresby attempted to probe these rumours to the bottom, but was for the moment reassured.[4]

Meanwhile encouragement and an incentive to immediate action had reached the conspirators from outside. On November 15 Lord Delamere, as impatient of delay as Danby, and with much less sense of responsibility, summoned his tenants in Warrington, Manchester and Ashton to join him, and declared for the Prince of Orange. On the following day he held a general rendezvous on Bowdon Downs in Cheshire, and at the head of some 200 men rode south to Newcastle-under-Lyme, and then on towards Derby and Nottingham. Although there is no evidence that Delamere had any direct connection with Danby, or even perhaps with Devonshire, his rising was bound to set the whole north in a flame.[5]

---

[1] *Ibid.*, pp. 525-6. See also Reresby's letter of November 13 to Lord Preston in *Hist. MSS. Com.*, vii. 415.

[2] According to Reresby one of them could neither read nor write (Reresby to Newcastle, November 14, 1688, printed in *Memoirs*, pp. 583-5).

[3] Among the Kenyon MSS. (*Hist. MSS. Com.*, xiv. 4, p. 208) there is a petition for a free Parliament, dated November 17, from the nobility and gentry of Yorkshire.

[4] *Reresby*, p. 526.

[5] Delamere apparently acted entirely on his own initiative. His immediate connection lay with the Earl of Derby, who had been engaged in the conspiracy since early in October, and hoped to use his official position in Lancashire and Cheshire to further the conspirators' aims. Yet Delamere simply wrote to Derby that he was rising, and proceeded to do so. A full account is to be found in *Kenyon MSS.*, pp. 197-207. *Cf.* also the letter of Peter Shakerley, Governor of Chester, to William Blathwayt, November 21, 1688, in B.M. Add. MSS. 38695, f. 86. ; *Le Fleming MSS.*, pp. 220, 222.

Thus it was an extremely difficult, if not indeed a hopeless situation which confronted Newcastle when at length on November 19 he made his tardy appearance at York. Far into the night he and Reresby sat discussing ways and means, but beyond a resolution that they would not join in any but the most loyal of petitions they could come to no decision at all. On the morrow they were reinforced by the arrival in the city of the newly appointed sheriff of Yorkshire, Sir Richard Graham, uncle of Lord Preston, the Secretary of State. But when a meeting of deputy lieutenants was hastily summoned to consider the situation these three found that they stood alone. Sir Henry Goodricke plainly stated that at the larger assembly two days later he intended to follow the example already set by the bishops and lords in London and petition for a free Parliament, and his fellow deputies agreed with him. Newcastle then declared that he would not remain in York to be over-ruled by his own subordinates, but would return to Welbeck on the following day. No more unfortunate decision, as Reresby fully realised, could have been taken. So long as Newcastle remained at his post his rank and high official position were bound to secure him the first place in men's minds. With his undignified exit, according to his promise, on the evening of November 21, the stage was clear for the Earl of Danby.[1]

Meanwhile the last meeting of the conspirators had been held, and what they believed to be their final resolutions had been taken. On Wednesday, November 21, York was to be secured by Danby. The Duke of Newcastle and Sir John Reresby were to be seized. The five hundred militia horse and two regiments of militia foot stationed in the city would, it was calculated, go over in a body to the insurgents. The gentlemen who had come up for the meeting on the following day would be persuaded to declare for the Prince. At the same moment Nottingham was to be occupied by Devonshire, and in both centres of the insurrection manifestoes were to be published setting forth the reasons for the whole movement. While Newcastle was quarrelling with his deputies Danby was busily

---

[1] *Reresby*, pp. 527-8 ; Sir Richard Graham to Lord Preston, November 22, Reresby to the same, December 8, in *Hist. MSS. Com.*, vii. 417, 420.

engaged in gathering his forces together to give effect to these designs.[1]

Notice of what was intended had naturally to be sent to William of Orange, and Danby accordingly drew up a series of memoranda which served as instructions for a messenger whom he dispatched about this time to the Prince.[2] Much disappointment, he declared, had been occasioned by the failure of the invading force to send either men, arms, or money to the north, and it was still hoped that some of these might be forthcoming. Nevertheless it had been determined to make the attempts on York and Nottingham, and it was absolutely essential that instructions should be received from the Prince regarding the course which he considered should be pursued thereafter. The insurgents might either march to join him with what horse they could raise, which would be about 2,000 men, or they might remain in the north and enlist a much larger body of foot. If the latter alternative was preferred it was specially necessary that arms and money should be dispatched, and that a general should be sent under whom such a very mixed assemblage would be willing to serve. If any difficulty arose Danby's messenger was to address himself specially to Shrewsbury and Russell, to whom he was to represent the very bad effects produced by the Prince's neglect of his northern supporters. He was also to get into touch with Lord Abingdon, and if the latter found it impossible to get safely to the Prince was to invite him to come to Nottingham with Lord Northampton and their followers.

At the last moment, however, the unexpected resolution of the Duke of Newcastle to leave York led to a slight change of plan. The seizure of the city was postponed until after his departure, and the conspirators resolved to base their whole scheme upon the mass meeting of gentlemen and freeholders, at

[1] Danby's own statement is perfectly explicit. He took up arms on November 20 (Danby to William of Orange, December 11, printed *infra*, ii. 150). One may guess that the muster was at Ribston.

[2] The memoranda, without date or explanatory heading of any kind, are printed *infra*, ii. 139 ; *cf. Leeds MSS.*, p. 30. Information about the various messengers he sent to the Prince is given by Danby in his letters of December 1 and December 11 (*infra*, ii. 144, 150) ; but it is not very clear and possibly is inaccurate. It seems probable that this particular messenger was Peregrine Bertie.

which it was now clear that his restraining influence need not be feared. When exactly Danby himself came into York is not clear, but he was certainly there some hours before Newcastle's departure. So little were his intentions even then suspected that one of the last official acts performed by the Duke was to send him a commission appointing Lord Latimer a deputy lieutenant in the North as well as in the West Riding.[1] Yet at that very moment Danby's followers were engaged in winning over the officers of the militia and arranging their programme for the following day.

Early on November 22 about a hundred gentlemen assembled, in accordance with the notices which had been issued, in the Common Hall at York. Sir John Reresby, who now thoroughly disapproved of the meeting, refused to attend, and the lead was taken by its original promoter, Sir Henry Goodricke. In a speech of some length Goodricke declared that the only remedy for recent invasions of the law and attempts to introduce popery lay in a free Parliament. The proper course for the meeting, he asserted, was to petition the King for such a Parliament, and as a model for their petition he produced and read the petition already presented by the lords in London. Opposition immediately manifested itself, some considering that the terms of the petition should be modified, others that it should be accompanied by a loyal address. Nevertheless a petition on the lines proposed by Sir Henry was adopted, and many of the dissentients having retired in disgust the gentlemen present began to sign.

By this time it was one o'clock in the afternoon, and everything was ready for the serious business to which this was a mere preliminary. While Goodricke was playing his part at the meeting Danby had remained at his lodgings, gathering together his friends and retainers. These included Lord Lumley, Lord

---

[1] Danby to Latimer, November 21, *infra*, ii. 141. In October Newcastle had offered Latimer the position of deputy lieutenant in the West Riding and also a commission as colonel of one of the four militia regiments of foot ; but Latimer on his father's advice declared that as he was detained in London by legal business of his own it would be improper for him, in a time of such difficulty, to accept the latter (*ibid.*, p. 138). Newcastle, after the revolution was accomplished, was furious at the way in which he had been deceived, and sent to Sir John Reresby a whole batch of letters which he had received at this time from Danby, Devonshire and Goodricke, " all flattery, lies, and pretentions of loyalty " (*Reresby*, p. 545).

Dumblane, and Lord Willoughby, and numbered in all about a hundred horsemen. Scarcely had two signatures been appended to the petition in the Common Hall when Danby's messenger rushed in and gave the pre-arranged signal by crying out that the papists had risen and had fired on the militia. Without pausing to reflect on the complete absurdity of the statement the whole meeting rose, and, headed by those who were in the secret, poured out into the open. At the same moment Danby swept up at the head of his horsemen to the cry of " A free Parliament, the Protestant religion, and no popery." His allies jumped on their waiting horses and joined him. The four militia troops, whose captains had all been gained, went over in a body. The main guard of the company of Cornwall's regiment then in garrison was immediately overpowered. Sir John Reresby, hastening out to take horse and bring up the rest of the regulars, was intercepted by Sir Henry Belasyse at the head of thirty troopers and forced to surrender. In a few minutes the city was won.[1]

There still exists a sheet of paper on which Danby jotted down, at odd intervals throughout this day, notes of the matters for which he had to provide.[2] The first entry is the most ominous—" The Scotch batallion ; the foot granadiers ; scouts to both." Even after the success of their initial movement the position of the conspirators was highly precarious. Ten miles to the south-west of York, at Tadcaster, lay the grenadier company of Colonel Cornwall's regiment under Henry Villiers. Thirty miles to the south-east, at Hull, lay not only the normal garrison, consisting of the greater part of Lord Montgomery's regiment, which would probably be content with maintaining its hold over the fortress, but also a Scottish battalion, which might at any moment take the field. Scattered throughout Yorkshire and the north were many small bodies of regular troops, some engaged in changing stations, others in

[1] *Reresby*, pp. 528-30 ; Reresby to Preston, December 8, in *Hist. MSS. Com.*, vii. 420 ; Sir Richard Graham to Preston, November 22, *ibid*, p. 417.

[2] Leeds MSS., Packet 13a. The sheet has neither heading nor endorsement, but there can be little doubt either of its date or of the significance of its contents. Accompanying it is a similar series of notes, endorsed, " Memorandums, 28 November," which begins with the highly characteristic entry, " The preists to bee sent to the gaole to-morrow."

process of recruitment and as yet imperfectly armed. A considerable force of these was even in York itself. At the very moment on the evening of November 21 when Newcastle was moving out of York his own newly-raised regiment of foot was marching in, and during the night six companies of the regiment, under the major, Jeremy Mahoney, with difficulty found quarters in the city.[1] There they met a single company of Colonel Skelton's regiment under Thomas Witham, and all seven companies were certainly still in York immediately before, if not actually during, Danby's seizure of the government.[2] Had Newcastle acted with any foresight and energy, or Lord Langdale, the Catholic Governor of Hull, proved willing to forsake the shelter of its walls, it is difficult to see how the rising could have escaped disaster.

Fortunately for the insurgents nobody on the King's side had the ability and resolution to piece together the various elements out of which an efficient army in support of the government might have been organised, and Danby was left to deal with them in detail. After an insignificant scuffle, in which Captain Witham was knocked down and deprived of his sword, his company joined the rising.[3] Of Newcastle's men some probably followed their example or deserted,[4] and the remainder apparently were allowed to march to Hull. A day or two later the grenadiers at Tadcaster were challenged by some troops of horse sent out for that purpose, and immediately "laide downe their armes and joyned the horse, declaring for a free Parliament and the Protestant religion."[5] In the end the Hull

---

[1] Mahoney to Thomas Radcliffe, lieutenant-colonel of the regiment, and Ensign Thomas Errington (in command of Radcliffe's own company) to the same, York, November 22, in Leeds MSS., Packet 13b, partly printed in *Leeds MSS.*, p. 26. "The captain-lieutenant [William Jennison] marches into Yorke with six companys of his Graces regiment."

[2] Newcastle's regiment were under orders to march to Hull on November 22, but it is not clear when they went, or whether they all went.

[3] *Leeds MSS.*, pp. 25, 26 ; *Reresby*, p. 531, where, however, there is some confusion between Witham's company and that commanded by Villiers. On December 10 Danby was considering " if it can be contrived how to mount Captain Withams his company of foote and to cloathe them."

[4] Desertions had been very frequent even before they reached York. One company had lost 16 men in the march from Durham, and Errington boasted that with 52 men his ranks were better filled than those of any of the other five company commanders.

[5] *Hist. MSS. Com.*, xiv. 4, p. 209.

garrison proved to be the only real danger, and against it Danby adopted defensive measures. A careful watch was kept upon its movements. The repair of the walls of York was taken in hand, in order that the city might, if necessary, stand a siege, and an estimate was obtained of what it would cost to put them temporarily in good condition.[1]

Meanwhile every effort was made to build up an efficient field army, which might be used to crush the royalists in the north, or, if that seemed the better course, march to the assistance of William in the south. A solid nucleus for such a force already existed in the eight troops of militia horse, of which Danby constituted himself colonel in place of Newcastle, assuming also, in accordance with the practice of the day, the command of one of the troops, and entrusting the other seven to officers upon whom he could safely rely. All "principals" who had failed to send their quota to the muster were summoned to do so, deserters were called to account, and the discipline and training of the whole body were improved.[2] Several other troops were created out of gentlemen volunteers and their servants ; some foot companies were formed out of regular soldiers and others who had joined the cause ; and the foot regiments of the Yorkshire militia were hastily reorganised. But of this last body it is clear that Danby had not much hope. So completely had the militia foot been neglected that within the time likely to be available it seemed impossible to raise it to even a moderate level of efficiency.

The principal difficulty was that of securing arms. The small store at York Manor was seized, and all who failed to join the insurgents, especially the Catholics, were required to surrender what weapons and horses they had, even Welbeck, much to the Duke of Newcastle's disgust, being subjected to a

---

[1] *Hist. MSS. Com.*, xii. 7, p. 227. Paper in Leeds MSS., Packet 13a, headed, "An estimate off the present repaire off the breaches in the citty walls convenient for present security," and endorsed, "Estimate of repairs of the city walls at Yorke, December the 2nd, [16]88." The total shown is £177.

[2] An elaborate return, preserved in Leeds MSS., Packet 13a, gives full details of the eight troops as they stood on December 1, 1688. The troop commanders are Lieutenant-Colonel Lord Fairfax ; Major James Moyser ; Captains Charles Tancred, William Robinson, Sir Thomas Gower, Thomas Fawkes, Sir Richard Osbaldeston ; Captain-Lieutenant Henry Hitch. Most if not all of these had held the same positions under Newcastle.

raid by Lord Dumblane.[1] But the only considerable store of
munitions obtained came from Scarborough Castle, which was
seized on November 28, and provided not merely muskets,
bandoliers and pikes, but twenty-two pieces of cannon as well.[2]
To administer these to the best advantage an official store-
keeper was appointed, and a magazine was formed within the
Castle of York.[3]

Finance constituted a further difficulty, but here Danby's
knowledge and experience were of immediate service to his
followers. Under his direction voluntary contributions were
invited, goods belonging to some Catholics were seized and sold,
and all collectors of the revenue were required to continue in
office and transmit what balances were in their hands to the
insurgents.[4] The first sum so transmitted was one of £253 8s. 7d.,
paid in as early as November 24 by Nicholas Sugar, receiver of
the temporalities of the vacant see of York ; and this was
shortly followed by smaller sums from local postmasters and
collectors of Hearth Money. But thereafter the financial main-
stay of the rising, apart from voluntary contributions,[5] was the
Excise. From these and other sources sufficient was raised to
pay for all services which were not rendered free, and for its
efficient administration a military chest was established at York
in charge of Sir Stephen Thompson and Sir Henry Goodricke,
appointed Governor of the city.[6]

---

[1] *Hist. MSS. Com.*, xii. 7, p. 227.

[2] *Lindsey MSS.*, pp. 450, 453.

[3] Paper endorsed, " List of armes and amunition in the custody of Mr.
Buttler, store-keeper of the armes at Yorke, 12th of December 1688," in Leeds
MSS., Packet 13b. The list is divided into sections, showing the source from
which the arms came. From the main guard of the regular foot company at York
were obtained " 6 colours, 37 firelocks, 37 collars of bandaleers, 40 muskets."
As early as November 30 Lord Fauconberg sent from Ousebridge " 74 suits back
and breast, 59 pair of pistolls, 20 musquetts and carabins, 75 headpieces."
From Welbeck on December 5 came " 34 musquets, 12 headpieces, 20 swords."
Later a very considerable contribution was made by Hull.

[4] " About all collectors, and particularly of bishops revenue here " (Danby's
notes of November 22).

[5] The principal voluntary contributions were apparently £500 from Sir John
Hewley, £200 from Alderman Thompson of York, and £500 from Lord Fauconberg. The first two of these were repaid, and probably the last as well.

[6] Paper in Leeds MSS., Packet 13a, endorsed by Danby, " An account of
moneys received for the use of the government att Yorke, 18th December
1688. From Sir Henry Goodrick." This statement was presumably drawn
up just before Danby's departure for London, and shows in detail receipts

So successful did all these measures prove that by the close of November Danby felt ready to tackle his most serious problem, that presented by Hull. On the last day of the month he drew up a letter to his most trusted friend in the garrison, Sir John Hanmer, lieutenant-colonel of Lord Montgomery's regiment, urging him to assist in the surprise of the fortress, and offering him, if he would do so, the help of 1,000 men and a reward of £5,000.[1] For some reason the letter was not dispatched at once, but probably on December 3 it was at length sent off, and Danby awaited the result with some confidence.

Meanwhile the Earl had not forgotten his allies to the south. Among his memoranda of November 22 is included the significant reminder, " A letter to Nottingham," where Devonshire was anxiously waiting for news of his success. When precisely Devonshire took up arms cannot be determined, but he must have done so almost immediately after the movement of Lord Delamere had given the first alarm. His earliest venture was by no means a success. Having gathered together a small body of friends and dependants he marched to Derby, read there the Prince's declaration and a manifesto of his own,[2] and proceeded to keep open table for all who came to join him. The number who appeared, however, was not great, and the news of events

---

totalling at that time £1,987 4s. 11d. Some three weeks later it was brought up to date, receipts to January 7 being added to make a grand total of £4,559 9s., and expenditure being deducted to show a balance, as Goodricke in his own handwriting notes, " in cash in Sir Stephen Thompsons hand at York, in a strong chest, about 1,277 l." Finally at some unknown date, no further sums having been received, all outstanding claims were met, and the financial organisation of the chest was dissolved with the respectable sum of £22 18s. in hand. Individual items of expenditure, which this statement does not give, are set forth in the somewhat similar statement later required from Goodricke by the Government of William III (*Cal. Treas. Books*, ix. 409-10, 944). The two statements, however, are by no means strictly parallel. That laid before Danby deals with all payments, of whatever character, made into or out of the military chest at York, but with nothing else. That presented to the Government deals only with royal revenues placed at the disposal of the insurgents, but includes these whether in actual fact they reached the military chest, or, as frequently happened, were paid away by Goodricke's authority in the district where they were collected. Thus Goodricke accounts to the Government for £3,610 of Excise, but to Danby only for £2,519 16s. 6d. From a comparison of the two statements it would appear that Goodricke in about six weeks disposed of well over £6,000.

[1] The letter is printed *infra*, ii. 142.
[2] Printed in *Parliamentary History*, v. 17.

in the south was so contradictory as to encourage the royalists in the town to form a plot to seize him. Only a somewhat hurried flight to Nottingham enabled him to escape.[1]

On his arrival in that town he found awaiting him a messenger from Danby, who presumably carried news of the final resolutions of the Yorkshire conspirators, and this messenger he immediately sent back with a letter of his own explaining his position and intentions.[2] Already his prospects had greatly improved. Many of the neighbouring gentry had joined him, and more were shortly expected. Lord Delamere on his march south had reached Derby, and intended to be in Nottingham on the following day. The Earl of Stamford had come in, with a commission to inform the Earl of Manchester, Lord Grey of Ruthin, and others, of what was intended, and a gentleman had been dispatched to desire them to come to Nottingham, where the best course of action would be discussed. All that was wanted was news of events at York and an answer to a message which Devonshire somewhat earlier had sent to the Prince of Orange.

One cannot fail to derive from this letter the impression that the attempt to synchronise the movements at York and Nottingham was not taken very seriously in the end. Whether by accident or design, however, it was on November 22, the day of the seizure of York, that the irrevocable step was taken by the lords at Nottingham. A declaration of their objects was drawn up and numerously signed, and the nobility and gentry of the midlands began to draw together to form a considerable if somewhat disorderly army.[3]

Even to the Nottingham movement William was slow in sending his approbation, but recognition and encouragement were soon to come from another quarter. While the majority of the conspirators, as William's coming drew near, had either gone over to Holland or retired to the more remote parts of

---

[1] J. Grove, *Lives of the Earls and Dukes of Devonshire*, pp. 197-8.

[2] The letter, dated " Nottingham, Tuesday night, 7 a clock," is printed *infra*, ii. 139. In *Leeds MSS.*, p. 27, it is catalogued under date December 4 ; but the real date is clearly a fortnight earlier, November 20.

[3] *Parliamentary History*, v. 17-18. Devonshire kept Danby informed of his proceedings by letters dated November 24 and 28, partly printed in *Hist. MSS. Com.*, ix. 2, p. 460, and in *Morrison Catalogue*, ii. 35.

England, the Bishop of London had resolutely clung to his post in the City, in order to be at hand to provide for the safety of the Princess Anne. On November 25 the expected need for his services arose. In the afternoon a courier arrived with the news that Lord Churchill, the husband of Anne's favourite, had gone over to the Prince, and that the King was returning from his army to London and would be at Whitehall on the following day.[1] Some restraint on the Princess's movements was almost bound to ensue, and measures were hastily taken to get her away while there was yet time. Lady Churchill hurried to the Bishop of London, who undertook to prepare for Anne's reception in the City and to have a hackney coach in waiting for her shortly after midnight. About one o'clock in the morning the Princess, accompanied by her favourite and two attendants, stole down the back stairs, walked to the coach, which she found guarded by Compton and the Earl of Dorset, and drove away.[2] Her escape was none too soon, for Lord Churchill had been followed within twenty-four hours by her own husband, Prince George, and James had dispatched orders that guards should be posted round her lodgings. The guards were actually in position within two hours of her departure, but their presence proved in the end an advantage, for it spread a comfortable assurance that she must be within, and so prevented her flight from being discovered till ten the next morning.[3]

The remainder of that adventurous night was spent by Anne in the Bishop's residence in Aldersgate Street, and on the following morning she set out for Dorset's mansion in Epping Forest. There Dorset took his leave, but the small company still pressed northwards until on the evening of November 28 they reached Castle Ashby, where they were received by Compton's nephew, the Earl of Northampton. Thence by somewhat easier stages they proceeded by Market Harborough to Leicester, where they were given a civic reception. At the former town Anne at length disclosed her identity, and the gentry, led by Sir Charles Shuckburgh and Lord Cullen,

---

[1] *Clarendon Correspondence*, ii. 207.

[2] *Conduct of the Duchess of Marlborough*, p. 17 ; *Burnet*, i. 792.

[3] This is the Bishop of London's own account given in his letter to Danby of December 2 (*Hist. MSS. Com.*, ix. 2, p. 461).

began to come in to join her. It was thus at the head of an imposing cavalcade that the Bishop of London rode out of Leicester on December 1 and entered Nottingham on the afternoon of the following day.[1]

Even then, however, it was not considered that Anne was safe. Notice of her presence was immediately sent out to the neighbouring nobility and gentry, about a hundred of whom, led by Lord Chesterfield and Lord Ferrers, came to wait upon her, thereby raising in the assembled company a certain amount of discord between those who were in rebellion against James and those who professed to be merely in personal attendance on Anne.[2] At midnight an express was hurried off to the Prince of Orange to explain the situation to him and ask for his instructions.[3] A few hours later a messenger was dispatched to Danby, announcing the arrival of Anne, and asking him to send if possible some troops of horse for her protection.[4]

The request reached Danby at a most inconvenient moment. Hull he believed to be almost within his grasp, but the force at his command was not sufficiently large to enable him to send help to Anne and at the same time provide for the reduction of the town. While asserting his readiness to obey any orders which the Princess might send him he therefore urged the vast importance of securing the fortress, and the advisability of a few days' delay for that purpose before he marched south. If any danger threatened Nottingham, the best course, he suggested, might be for Anne to come to York. Her mere presence there would secure the whole of the north for the insurgents, and in the very unlikely event of York itself being seriously threatened a secure retreat was at hand in the fortress of Scarborough, from which, if necessary, the Princess might retire by sea to whatever place she pleased.[5]

---

[1] *Hatton Correspondence*, ii. 118-9.

[2] *Letters of Lord Chesterfield*, pp. 48-51 ; *Hastings MSS.*, ii. 211.

[3] The letters sent to William by the Bishop and Devonshire are printed in *Dalrymple*, App., i. 334-5.

[4] Compton's letter to Danby, dated December 2 and printed in *Hist. MSS. Com.*, ix. 2, p. 461, was probably written only a few hours earlier than Devonshire's letter, dated December 3 and printed *infra*, ii. 145. Both were probably carried by the same messenger.

[5] Danby's letters to Compton and to the lords at Nottingham, dated December 4, are printed *infra*, ii. 145-6.

Even before the letters containing these arguments had been written the difficulty which was the ostensible cause for them had been solved. On the night of December 3 Sir John Hanmer and Captain Copley, the Lieutenant-Governor of Hull, combining with the Protestant officers of the garrison, some of the magistrates and a number of seamen from the port, surprised Lord Langdale and Lord Montgomery and declared for the Prince. All the Catholic officers and soldiers were secured, as well as a number of Catholic gentlemen who had fled to Hull for safety, and the town was placed in the hands of the Lieutenant-Governor.[1]

Nevertheless, Danby showed no desire to march south. In response to his suggestions Anne and her advisers had declared that they must be guided in their actions by the instructions received from William ;[2] but in the disturbed state of the country it was doubtful whether William would propose that she should attempt to join him, and if he did not the offer of an asylum at York might well be accepted. The prospect of having Anne in his hands had many attractions for Danby. As her adviser and representative he might become all-powerful

---

[1] " Hull is certainly taken . . . in this manner. Captain Copley, Deputy Governer, was informed on Munday night last that Lord Longdale the Governor, Montgomery and Lord Dunbar had framed a design to seize the Captain and all the Protestant officers and souldjers in garison on Tuesday night, which design he communicated to the mayor, aldermen, and the principle inhabitants, who all resolved to be armed at the time, and the Captain ordered that at the beat of the drum all windows should be illuminated. In the evening they observed the Governer to bring in boates all the popish souldiers out of the fort into the town, but tooke no notice of it. At 10 of the clock the tatoo beat, immediatly upon which the Captain and all his company were at the guard, and all the windows were full of lights, which startled the Governer, who was advanceing in the darke with about 400 popish souldiers to execute his design. But upon his first approach the Captain went up to him and took him by the cravat, saying, My Lord, you are my prisoner ; and the Protestant souldiers seized his party and disarmed them and turned them out of the town, and comitted his Lordship and principle of his party. In the meane time the seamen gott into the fort, so all was over and without any bloud in two hours time " (Ballard MSS. 45, f. 20. See also Clarke, *Life of James II*, ii. 230-1 ; *Reresby*, pp. 535-6 ; newsletter of December 8 in B.M. Add. MSS. 34487, f. 46 ; Sir John Hanmer to Danby, December 4, Danby to Hanmer and to Lady Danby, December 5, *infra*, ii. 147-9). Hanmer's account certainly suggests that the actual seizure of the town was not inspired from York, and that Danby's letter of November 30 did not reach him until the morning after the event.

[2] Devonshire to Danby and the Bishop of London to Danby, December 5, *infra*, ii. 146-7.

in the north, and eventually, in virtue both of his military strength and his influence with one of the immediate heirs to the throne, might be in a position to dictate the settlement of the kingdom. He had already expressed to Sir John Reresby his fears of what might follow a complete success on the part either of James II or of William.[1] In his own interposition as a powerful mediator he probably saw the solution of that difficulty.

The coming of Anne to York, however, was bound to be followed by that of many nobles who would question Danby's pre-eminence in his own province, and the Earl accordingly attempted to anticipate this by securing from William some authority for the position he was endeavouring to assume. Already the insurgents at Hull had offended him by dismissing their Catholic prisoners and putting forth a declaration which was not in accordance with his policy. On December 7, accordingly, he dispatched Lieutenant Pullen, one of his most trusted subordinates, to William, with a request for a commission not merely to be Governor of Hull but to be Lieutenant-General of the five northern counties, with power to raise and officer both horse and foot regiments, and authority to nominate commissioners to manage the revenue within the same area.[2]

William, however, had no intention of surrendering so valuable a political counter as the Princess Anne, or of delegating to any one the extravagant powers which Danby claimed. Two days before Lieutenant Pullen set out to find him he had replied to the lords at Nottingham, sending them some English and Huguenot officers and expressing his desire that they should march immediately with the Princess Anne to join him at Oxford. His instructions, which reached Nottingham on December 8, would scarcely permit of evasion, and, although with some regret on the part of the Bishop of London, preparations were made to begin the march south on the following day. William's own letter was hurriedly passed on to Danby, and

[1] *Reresby*, p. 521.

[2] Danby's letter, dated December 7, is printed *infra*, ii. 149. Apparently he endeavoured to extend his authority over the counties of Lancaster, Nottingham, Lincoln and Rutland as well (*Cowper MSS.*, ii. 346). At one time it was believed that William was sending Prince George " to the north to command there in chief to prevent any disputes amongst the lords " (Ballard MSS. 45, f. 19), and this appointment is perhaps what Danby wanted.

notification was given him of the route which the forces from Nottingham intended to take.[1]

The departure of Anne from Nottingham destroyed completely Danby's vision of himself as a northern general holding the balance in her name between James and William, and for the moment he could think of no better course than to fall in with the plans of his allies and march south himself. On December 11, in a final letter to William,[2] he announced his intention of setting out to join him two days later at the head of 600 horse. Three days' march, he calculated, would take him to Nottingham, after which he proposed to follow in the wake of Anne to Oxford.[3]

Scarcely had this letter been written, however, when news received from London altered the whole situation. Since his return to his capital on November 26 James had been in a pitiable state of indecision. At the back of his mind lay always the idea of flight to France ; but he had also with more or less sincerity sought the advice of the peers in London on what concessions he should make, and entered into negotiations with the Prince. One result of this was the reissue of writs for the Parliament which had been so often talked about and had never been elected. The writs for Yorkshire reached Danby's hands on the evening of December 11, and although he had little hope of Parliament actually assembling he naturally wished to use the influence he then possessed to secure the return of his own followers. At York itself the election was fixed for December 17, when he expected that Lord Dumblane and Alderman Thompson would be chosen ; but other elections could not be so early. At the very least he calculated that three or four days must elapse before he could move.[4]

---

[1] William's letter to Bishop Compton, dated Salisbury, December 5/15, is printed in *Hist. MSS. Com.*, ix. 2, p. 460. The letters of Compton and Devonshire to Danby, dated Nottingham, December 8, are printed *infra*, ii. 151.

[2] Printed *infra*, ii. 150.

[3] In Packet 13a of the Leeds MSS. are two papers endorsed by Danby, " Memorandums, December the 10th, [16]88," and " Memorandums, 12 December [16]88," which note innumerable small details necessary to be provided for in connection with this march.

[4] Danby to Lady Danby, December 12, *infra*, ii. 152. At the same time the borough of Buckingham was being canvassed in the interests of Lord Latimer (Francis Wycliffe to Latimer, December 9, 11, 1688, in B.M. Add. MSS. 28087, ff. 75, 76).

Moreover James had also seriously considered the possibility of retreating northwards and throwing himself on the support of Danby. So far was this idea carried that Charles Bertie was appointed as his envoy,[1] and formal instructions were drawn up to guide him in arranging terms. On December 12, the very day on which he should have begun his march south, Danby was still at York, expecting the arrival of his brother-in-law the following day or the day after that.

Charles Bertie, however, never came, and his instructions never left the Secretary's office.[2] Early on the morning of December 11 James, having already sent away his wife and the Prince of Wales, cancelled the writs for Parliament, and issued orders for the disbandment of the army, had fled from London, and the whole Government was in confusion. Some rumour of what was happening must have reached York on December 13, for all through the night James Herbert sat up waiting on confirmation. About six o'clock the next morning the post rode in with a full report. Not only were the royal family gone, but several of the more obnoxious officials had accompanied them ; the lords in London had taken the government into their own hands, and the Prince of Orange had been invited to the City. In the dark of a winter's morning Danby proceeded to dictate an account to his wife, and explain the change in his plans which this would involve.[3]

His main idea was now to get to London as quickly as possible, for there it seemed inevitable that the concluding scenes in the Revolution would be staged. Some time, however, was neces-

---

[1] A letter of December 6 from London speaks of Bertie as " ambassador to the Northern Lords, where my Lord Danby is Regent, and dispatching to-morrow upon his Majesty's errand " (*Hist. MSS. Com.*, xi. 5, p. 225).

[2] According to Sir John Reresby Danby later told him that Bertie did come, and that his answer to the King's proposals was " that his own force, which he depended upon in the north, was not sufficient to trust to ; but if his Majesty would bring a considerable party with him, and come without the papists, he would sooner loos his life then his Majesty should be injured." One can only surmise that this represents what Danby thought of saying, or what perhaps he actually did say to some other and less formal messenger. It is quite possible that James renewed his proposals after his return from his first flight, but even then it cannot have been through the agency of Charles Bertie (*Reresby*, pp. 550, 557-8 ; Charles Bertie's letters in *Lindsey MSS.*, pp. 451-6).

[3] Danby to Lady Danby, December 14, *infra*, ii. 153.

sary to settle affairs at York, an address had to be procured
from the city to the Prince of Orange,[1] and Dumblane's election
had to be considered. It was therefore not until the morning of
December 18 that he proposed to set out ; but in case the
country should prove disturbed arrangements were made for
Sir Henry Belasyse with a troop of horse grenadiers to push on
ahead.[2] Meanwhile Lady Danby was urged to provide immediately for a general removal to London, and for the opening
up of Lindsey House.

In the midst of these preparations arrived the first recognition from the Prince of Orange which Danby had received
since the landing at Torbay. According to the Prince the first
of Danby's messengers to reach him was Lieutenant Pullen,
who found him on the evening of December 11 at Abingdon
and delivered the letter of December 7. Next day Lord Lumley
arrived with the letter of December 11, and William replied
to both at much the same time. His answers,[3] however, were
singularly colourless. A general acknowledgment of the
service rendered him was followed by a request for Danby's
presence and advice, and permission for the Earl to disband
his forces. Clearly if Danby had made no greater impression
on the Prince than these letters suggested the sooner he was in
London the better.

Unfortunately for himself and possibly for his country
Danby's intentions were not immediately to be carried out.
Scarcely had his letter to Lady Danby been dispatched when
news of the most alarming character began to arrive from all
quarters. Towards midnight on December 14 an express rode
in with an urgent summons for help from the Mayor of Chesterfield. Seven thousand papists and Irish, he declared, had

---

[1] A draft of the address, dated December 14, with alterations in Danby's
handwriting, is in Leeds MSS., Packet 13b.

[2] Paper in Leeds MSS., Packet 13a, endorsed by Danby, " Marching route
for the Granadeers from York under Sir Henry Bellasyse, 16 December,
[16]88." It shows a force of 42 grenadiers at 2s. a day, 3 corporals at 2s. 6d.,
2 drums at 2s. 6d., 2 sergeants at 3s. 6d., a quartermaster at 5s., and a lieutenant at 7s., making a total of £5 15s. 6d. a day. The route laid down is :
16th, Ferrybridge ; 17th, Bawtry ; 18th, Newark ; 19th, Coliford ; 20th,
Stilton ; 21st, Caxton ; 22nd, Ware.

[3] Dated Abingdon, 12/22 December, printed *infra*, ii. 150, 152.

burned Birmingham and come as near as Derby.[1] Almost at
the same time what appeared to be confirmation arrived from
Philip Bertie at Grimsthorpe. A body of fifteen hundred horse,
he wrote, burning and slaying wherever they went, had come
as far as Northampton. The Berties and their followers would
make as good a stand as they could, but it behoved the main
army at York to be on the alert.[2]

Within less than twenty-four hours panic had seized upon
the whole of Yorkshire. At 11 p.m. on December 14 a courier
from Chesterfield reached Rotherham. The news he carried
was immediately passed on to Doncaster, and there at 1.30
p.m. on the following day the Mayor was writing to give the
alarm once more to York.[3] By 2 p.m. the panic had reached
Pontefract and by 4 p.m. Leeds. At that time Sir Thomas
Gower with his troop of horse was in the latter town, but
under orders to march to York. The Mayor and Corporation of
Leeds immediately dispatched a request to Danby that the
troop might be allowed to remain for their defence, and Sir
Thomas agreed to defer his departure until the Earl's pleasure
was known.[4] The request was granted, but by the time Danby's
assent arrived a new danger had been conjured up. During the
night letters had come in reporting an outbreak of papists in
Lancashire, and before dawn on December 16 the Corporation
of Leeds were praying for further assistance to defend themselves against a force which they asserted to be only a few miles
away.[5]

One may well marvel that such foolish tales secured any
credence whatever ; but in the heated atmosphere of the day
almost anything might pass for truth. It is at least to Danby's
credit that he realised whence the danger, if danger there was,
must come, and took energetic steps to deal with it. Chester-

[1] The letter is in Leeds MSS., Packet 13b. The Mayor of Chesterfield got his
information by express from Sir William Boothby, who had it in turn from
William Eyre of Holme and others (Mayor of Doncaster to Danby, December
15, *ibid.*). Into the mists of its origin it is impossible to penetrate farther.

[2] Philip Bertie to Danby, December 14 (*ibid.*).

[3] Mayor of Doncaster to Danby (*ibid.*).

[4] Mayor and Corporation of Leeds to Danby, Sir Thomas Gower to the same,
December 15 ; Mayor of Pontefract to the same, December 16 (*ibid.*).

[5] Mayor and Corporation of Leeds to the lords at York, December 16,
6 a.m (*ibid.*).

field, Birmingham and the south might safely be left to the care of the Earl of Devonshire and William of Orange. His business, as self-appointed commander-in-chief in the north, was to watch the Catholics of Lancashire and especially to stop the gap through which the supporters of James in England might maintain communication with the Catholics in Ireland. All available forces were set in motion towards the west. Within thirty-six hours of the first alarm Captain Tancred with one troop of horse had been dispatched to Ferrybridge ; William Belasyse with another troop and Sir Henry with the grenadiers had been sent to Wakefield, and Sir Richard Osbaldeston had been ordered to take three troops to the relief of Sir Thomas Gower at Leeds. Danby himself at York was meanwhile hastening the embodiment of the three West Riding regiments of foot, and proposed to march on December 17 with five more troops of horse in whatever direction events might dictate.[1]

On the morning of that day news arrived from Sir John Lowther that he had intercepted an express from Lord Tyrconnel in Ireland to James II in which he pressed for the immediate dispatch of arms to him from Carlisle. This seems to have confirmed Danby in the conclusion to which he was in any case inclining, that the cause of all the alarms was the advance from the south of the Irish troops whom James had brought over to use against William, and that there was a formed design to march these troops north and ship them over to the aid of Tyrconnel.[2] With thirteen troops of horse and four regiments of foot he resolved to march on Rochdale and frustrate any such scheme.[3]

Scarcely had his resolution been taken, however, when more reassuring news began to come in. On the first alarm a small force of some 500 ill-armed horse and a rather larger number of foot had been gathered together at Sheffield by Sidney Wortley, one of the deputy lieutenants for the West Riding, assisted by John Gill and William Jessop, justices of the peace ; but no

---

[1] Danby to the Mayor of Pontefract, December 16, *infra*, ii. 155.

[2] The Governor of Chester believed that eight or nine thousand Irish were advancing upon him from London (B.M. Add. MSS. 38695, ff. 103-4).

[3] Danby to Latimer, December 17, *infra*, ii. 156 ; Charles Bertie to Danby, December 20, in *Lindsey MSS.*, pp. 455-6. Bertie speaks of Danby's total available force as amounting to 1,500 horse and 7,000 foot.

enemy appeared for them to fight. Jessop accordingly took horse for Chesterfield to seek confirmation of the original report, and was passed on from there to Derby. At Derby there had been a similar muster under the direction of Anchitell Grey and the Mayor, but although scouts had been sent out twenty miles round no cause for alarm had been found. Touch had been established with other scouts from Coventry, who had scoured the country round Birmingham with the same negative result. The report which Jessop brought back to his colleagues, and which they in turn transmitted to Danby, was that Birmingham was still standing, no Irish could be found, and all the local levies were being disbanded.[1]

The collapse of one rumour was followed by the collapse of the other. From Leeds Sir Thomas Gower reported that the Lancashire alarm was without foundation. The march of the horse was immediately stopped and the embodiment of the foot countermanded.[2] It is not clear whether Danby ever actually began his march from York, but if so he certainly did not advance very far. By December 19 he had abandoned all thought of military operations, had ordered the disbandment of the militia horse, and in spite of continued rumours of Irish marauders retired to Kiveton to prepare for his journey to London.[3]

Meanwhile the work of securing the whole north for the Prince of Orange had continued almost unchecked. The surrender of Hull had put an end to all resistance in Yorkshire. On December 5 Lord Lumley had made a rapid dash northwards to Durham, and had gained the support of that county for the insurgents.[4] Unfortunately on his return he was almost immediately dispatched to William of Orange,[5] and in his absence the reduction of Northumberland proved unexpectedly difficult. The agent on whom Danby was relying, Thomas

[1] S. Wortley, John Gill and W. Jessop to Danby, December 17, in Leeds MSS., Packet 13b. There is a very similar letter written by the officials at Doncaster to those at Leeds in B.M. Add. MSS. 10039, f. 51.

[2] W. Belasyse to Danby, dated Monday [December 17] at 3 p.m., in Leeds MSS., Packet 13b.

[3] Sir Henry Goodricke to Danby, December 19 (*ibid.*) ; *Reresby*, p. 540.

[4] *Lindsey MSS.*, p. 450 ; Lumley to Danby, Durham, December 5, in Leeds MSS., Packet 13b.

[5] December 11, *infra*, ii. 150.

Love, lieutenant in the company of grenadiers taken at Tadcaster, was seized at the critical moment by an illness which nearly proved fatal, and the other opponents of the Government hesitated to move until they had established communication with Lumley.[1] Not until Danby, in the name of the Prince of Orange, had formally summoned Berwick to surrender, did the Governor, Lord Widdrington, hand over his charge to Rupert Billingsley, lieutenant-colonel of the regiment then in garrison, and retire into the country.[2] A similar summons was prepared for Tynemouth, which was garrisoned by one company of Newcastle's regiment under William Tempest; but before the summons could be delivered the Lieutenant-Governor, Captain Henry Villiers, had sent his submission to the Prince, and had written to Danby to put his stores at his service.[3]

A more complicated problem was that presented by Cumberland and Westmorland. Carlisle had a Catholic governor in the person of Francis Howard of Corby,[4] and especially after the fall of Hull had become the principal refuge for all the Catholics of the north. The garrison, however, amounted only to three companies of Colonel Cornwall's regiment of foot, and Danby's ally Sir John Lowther of Lowther considered that he would have had no trouble in reducing it had it not been for the conduct of a rival faction in the county, headed by Sir Christopher Musgrave and Sir George Fletcher, who placed so many obstacles in his path that he could not secure even the embodiment of the militia. Finding his own friends and tenants insufficient for the task confronting him, he appealed to Danby for a few troops of horse; but the Earl refused to send any part of his force so far away as Carlisle, and when on December 15 Carlisle eventually surrendered it was by an agreement between Howard and Musgrave, effected through the agency of Jeremiah

---

[1] Thomas Love to Danby, December 14; Philip Bickerstaffe to Danby, December 15, in Leeds MSS., Packet 13b.

[2] Draft summons, dated December 15; Danby to Billingsley, December 15; Billingsley to Sir Charles Porter, December 16 (*ibid.*). The surrender took place on the morning of December 16.

[3] Summons to Tynemouth Castle, December 19; Villiers to Danby, December 18 (*ibid.*).

[4] Appointed in October 1687 (*Luttrell*, i. 419).

D.L.I.

Bubb, the senior captain of the garrison, and Lowther was ignored altogether.[1]

Danby, however, was well enough pleased that the surrender had taken place in any shape whatever. On December 19, immediately after his return to Kiveton, Sir Henry Goodricke was able to write to him that "nothing now remains in the north out of the Prince's hands." [2] It was thus untroubled by any anxiety for his own province that a day or two later he set out on his journey to the south. On the evening of December 26 he entered London and prepared to deal with the problems that awaited him there.[3]

[1] Lowther to Danby, December 5, 12 ; Musgrave to Danby, December 17, 18 ; Captain Bubb to Danby, December 18 ; Goodricke to Danby, December 20, in Leeds MSS., Packet 13b. See also *Hist. MSS. Com.*, xi. 5, p. 245 ; xii. 7, pp. 223, 226.

[2] Goodricke to Danby, December 19, in Leeds MSS., Packet 13b.

[3] *Clarendon Correspondence*, ii. 236.

CHAPTER XVIII

SETTLEMENT, 1688-9

EVEN before Danby's arrival in town the first steps had been taken towards a national settlement. During the night of December 23-4 King James, having been brought back after his first flight, had absconded for the second time, and with the connivance of the Prince of Orange had got safely out of the country. On the following day the peers had adopted two addresses, the one inviting the Prince to assume the executive government until a Convention could assemble on January 22, the other requesting him to provide for the meeting of that Convention by issuing letters to the constituencies desiring them to elect members in accordance with the usual forms. Forty-eight hours later an anomalous assembly, consisting of all available members of Charles II's Parliaments and certain representatives of the Corporation of London, had followed their example. Danby himself was only in time to hear the Prince on December 28 accept the responsibilities which had been offered him.

To the politicians in the capital, however, his arrival, tardy though it might be, was an event of considerable importance. In the struggle which was obviously impending between Tories and Whigs, between those who aimed at some kind of accommodation with James and those who proposed to abandon him altogether, it needed no great discernment to see that the balance was likely to be decided by the eloquence of Halifax or by the energy and parliamentary ability of Danby. The attitude of the former could at least be surmised ; but the latter was a completely unknown quantity. His well-known loyalist principles would have marked him out as a partisan of James, had not the prominent part he had taken in the recent rebellion suggested equally strongly that he was a partisan of

William. How many were ready to follow any lead he should give it was difficult to say ; but among the number were certain to be included most of his own relatives, some of the bishops, and a considerable number of the representatives to be elected in Yorkshire and the north.

Among the Tories the impression was already gaining ground that the best solution of all their difficulties was to entrust the royal authority to William as Regent while leaving to James the actual title of King. On the afternoon of December 27, accordingly, the Bishops of Norwich and Ely, having first dined and discussed the matter with the Earl of Clarendon, waited upon Danby in order to ascertain what prospect such a scheme had of securing his support. They were met, however, by an impenetrable reserve, and had to return to Clarendon with the report that they could make nothing of him.[1]

To so premature an application a vague answer was inevitable. As a late-comer on the political scene Danby before he could commit himself had first to ascertain the exact position of affairs, and weigh with practised glance the chances of contending factions. At the very least he had to get into touch with his own relatives and immediate supporters, most of whom he had not seen for some time. But his hesitation was much more deeply rooted than these considerations alone would suggest. He had no affection for James, he cordially detested the schemes with which that monarch had identified himself, and he knew by bitter experience the hopelessness of expecting from him any change either of heart or of policy. On the other hand he had been greatly irritated by the casual treatment meted out to him during the last two months by William, and in view of the hazards which he and his followers had run was much incensed by the favour which he found the Prince showing to rival politicians, especially Halifax, who had risked nothing to promote the Revolution.[2] The Regency project must have seemed to him quite impracticable ; but the alternative proposals of the Whigs, involving what was really an elective monarchy, were repugnant to every political instinct

[1] *Clarendon Correspondence*, ii. 236-7.

[2] *Cf.* the " Memorandums att my first coming out of the North to the Prince att St. James," printed *infra*, ii. 159-61—" notwithstanding . . . that the Prince knew that hee had laught att us for medling in that undertakeing."

he possessed. Even as late as January 1, in consequence, when his own brother-in-law, the Earl of Abingdon, approached him (again, one may surmise, in the interests of the Regency party), he either could not or would not declare his intentions.[1]

Three days later, however, he at length took a step which indicates the lines on which his mind was working. In a letter to the Princess of Orange, dated January 4, 1689, he expressed his entire devotion to her " personall intrests " in view of the coming " trialls of mens minds and humors " among them, strongly urged the absolute necessity for her speedy arrival in England, and renewed the request which he had made nearly a year earlier that his daughter Lady Plymouth might be admitted a lady of her bedchamber. For making this request he claimed to have the Prince's sanction, but for the granting of it he and Lady Plymouth wished to be obliged only to the Princess herself.[2]

So colourless are the terms of the letter that it is difficult to read into it any great significance. Nevertheless in the light of later events it must be taken as marking, not merely Danby's definite abandonment of the cause of James, but his first step towards setting up, on behalf of Mary, an interest separate from those of her father and husband alike. Personal ambition combined with his political principles to urge upon him the desirability of Mary's accession to the throne. For her he seems to have had a real affection ; on her gratitude he considered himself to have special claims ; and under the rule of a woman he, as chief minister, might expect to exercise unusual power. Moreover if, as was generally believed, the Prince of Wales was supposititious, and if, as many were prepared to declare, James by his flight had abdicated the government, there could be no question of Mary's title. As the next in the succession she already was Queen and required only to be proclaimed. The absurd device of a regency need not be adopted ; hereditary right need not be abandoned ; the dangerous doctrines of the Whigs need not be called in.

Already the claims of Mary, whether at Danby's instigation or not, had been definitely put forward. In the assembly of

---

[1] *Clarendon Correspondence*, ii. 239.
[2] The letter is printed *infra*, ii. 156.

peers which met on the morrow of James's flight it had been
proposed by Lord Paget to solve all difficulties by an immediate proclamation of Mary as Queen ; and this proposal
had been seconded both by Lord North and (significantly perhaps) by the Bishop of London.[1] But the suggestion had not
received much support. The typical Tory was too reluctant to
abandon James, the typical Whig too much wedded to his idea
of a vacant throne and an elected monarch, to give it any
countenance. Long experience of Parliament, however, had
taught Danby how easily a small but determined group, which
holds the balance between two larger parties, may force the
acceptance of its own policy, and he by no means despaired of
success.

The one essential was that he should have at his disposal a
compact body of followers in each House, and to the elections
to the Convention he accordingly turned his attention. Those
of his adherents who had already been returned on the writs
issued by James had again to submit themselves to their con-
stituents,[2] but this seems to have produced no practical result
beyond a certain amount of inconvenience. Lord Latimer,
abandoning all hope of Buckingham, where his agents found
the burgesses almost unanimously in favour of Sir Richard
Temple and Sir Ralph Verney, was returned for Knaresborough.[3] Lord Dumblane and Alderman Thompson were once
more elected at York. Sir John Lowther obtained a seat in
Westmorland, Sir Henry Goodricke at Boroughbridge, John
Darcy at Richmond and Sir Jonathan Jennings at Ripon. The
Berties, although not quite so prominent as usual, secured the
return of five members of their family, including both Lord
Willoughby and Lord Norris. In a House of Commons which
was predominantly Whig Danby's seemed likely to prove the
strongest individual Tory group.

---

[1] *Clarendon Correspondence*, ii. 235.

[2] At the meeting of peers on December 24 it was proposed that instead of
William issuing letters to the constituencies the members already chosen should
meet and provide for the election of their fellows, " but this was slighted "
(*ibid.*, ii. 235).

[3] " By Sir Henry Goodrack good help." The election nevertheless cost £80
(Christopher Jackson to Lord Latimer, January 14, 1689, in Leeds MSS.,
Packet 14).

Scarcely had the group been formed, however, when a series of unforeseen events gravely reduced its effective strength. John Darcy died actually before his election,[1] and it was not until a month later that his place was filled by his brother Philip. Lord Latimer's opponent, Thomas Fawkes, prevailed upon the bailiff to return him also for Knaresborough, and there being thus a double return neither claimant of the seat could take his place in the House until some decision of the dispute had been reached.[2] No decision was arrived at until March 21, when Fawkes was declared to have been duly elected ; but as far as Danby was concerned the matter was unhappily settled a month earlier by the sudden death of Lord Latimer on February 15. This left the nominal leadership of the group to Lord Dumblane, who had little interest in parliamentary affairs and rarely spoke in the House. In other circumstances his place might have been taken by Lord Willoughby or Lord Norris ; but the Berties were hopelessly distracted by the fact that while the Earl of Lindsey was ready enough to follow Danby's lead the Earl of Abingdon had definitely thrown in his lot with the Regency party. So far as the group had a leader in the Commons it was apparently Sir Henry Goodricke.

Nevertheless the opening day of Parliament found Danby not ill prepared to make his attempt on behalf of Mary, and if anything more inclined to it than ever. The policy pursued by the Prince of Orange during the four weeks' interregnum had not met with his approval. Whatever settlement was adopted by England could not, he fully realised, be permanent unless it was adopted by, or forced upon, Scotland and Ireland as well. From the former, he was informed by his Scottish correspondents, little trouble need be expected ; but the latter constituted in his eyes a very serious danger indeed. The whole island seemed about to fall into the hands of the Catholics ; and if once the Protestant and English interest were completely extirpated it would be very difficult to re-establish.

---

[1] His death occurred on January 6, and was officially declared to the Commons on January 28. The election was on January 10 (*C.J.*, x. 14 ; *Return of Members of Parliament*, i. 563).

[2] *C.J.*, x. 13, 14. Neither Latimer nor Fawkes questioned the election of William Stockdale as one of the members for the borough.

Yet William appeared singularly indifferent, and refused to take any responsible adviser into his confidence as regards the measures which were being adopted. On a rumour spreading abroad that Richard Hamilton, colonel of one of the Irish regiments brought to England by James, was to be sent to Dublin to negotiate with the Catholic leaders, Danby approached the Prince with a protest, and urged that a squadron of ships should be sent instead. All the answer he received was that the fleet could not be trusted, and that the business of Ireland was in a fair way to being settled.[1]

This attitude on the part of the Prince Danby later attributed, as he attributed most of the shortcomings of the Government immediately after the Revolution, to the malign influence of Halifax. Lord Tyrconnel, the Catholic Lord Lieutenant, he declared, " sent several messages to King William, that he was ready to deliver up Ireland, if he would but give him a decent excuse, by sending anything that looked like a force to demand it ; but Lord Halifax told him, that if Ireland was quiet, there would be no pretence for keeping up an army, and if there was none, he would be turned out as easily as he had been brought in ; for it was impossible to please England long, and he might see they began to be discontented already." [2] If, however, Danby was entirely excluded from the Irish negotiations, this story cannot have been based on personal knowledge, and it is almost certainly untrue.[3] William as a foreigner probably underestimated the importance of Ireland, and hesitated to dispatch to the relief of the Protestants any forces on which he could rely, lest by so doing he should make himself too dependent on his own supporters in England, and lose control of developments there. The secrecy which gave such offence both to Danby and to Clarendon [4] was necessary if his negotiations through Hamilton were to have any chance of success. In the end his policy was to prove a complete failure, but it is not clear that in his own interests, or even in those of England, he could have done any better.

[1] " Memorandums," *infra*, ii. 159.

[2] Dartmouth's note in *Burnet* (ed. 1833), iii. 369.

[3] See Miss Foxcroft's discussion of this whole problem in her *Life of Halifax*, ii. 76-80.

[4] *Clarendon Correspondence*, ii. 238 *et seq*.

Danby, however, was much disgusted, and it was with his zeal for the Prince considerably abated that he approached the meeting of the Convention on January 22. In the absence of any Lord Chancellor or Government officials both Houses of Parliament were left absolutely free to choose their own Speakers, and the first trial of strength between parties took place over the elections. That the Commons would choose a Whig Speaker was almost a foregone conclusion, and the election of Henry Powle in preference to Sir Edward Seymour can scarcely have caused Danby either surprise or regret. In the Lords, however, he was himself a serious candidate for the post, and the election of Halifax was a considerable mortification to him. It left him free, however, to accept the chair when the House went into committee, and in this way, while enjoying much less dignity, he had perhaps more real influence than his rival.

For the first few days the House of Lords was occupied mainly with preliminaries, and in these Danby took a prominent part. He was chairman of the committee appointed to draw up an address of thanks for the letter to both Houses in which the Prince of Orange gave an account of his administration and inaugurated the session. It is possible to discern his influence in the fact that the address adopted by the Lords and subsequently approved by the Commons, while desiring William to continue at the head of the Government until a permanent settlement could be reached, laid special stress on the problem of Ireland. He was also a member of the original committee charged to investigate the circumstances of the death of the Earl of Essex, and of the committee appointed to devise measures against papists in London and Westminster. So fully was his time occupied with the work of these bodies that his attendance at the House itself became distinctly irregular.[1]

It is a significant fact that when on January 25 the Lords turned to the main question with which they had been summoned to deal Danby was not present.[2] As there was no chance of his own solution of the succession problem securing im-

---

[1] *L.J.*, xiv. 102-7.

[2] As the House was called over the same day, and he is not included among the absent, it may be supposed that he was still engaged with his committees

mediate acceptance the Earl's obvious policy was to remain in
the background until the two main parties had exhausted
themselves in a struggle with each other, and then press for
the recognition of Mary as a compromise between them. One
of the features of the early debates in both Houses, in consequence, is the almost complete absence from them of his
recognised supporters.[1] On the motion of the Earl of Devonshire the consideration of the state of the nation by the Lords
was postponed to January 29, and the House of Commons were
thus enabled to take the lead. There the main points at issue
were fought out on January 28, and the famous resolution was
adopted which declared that James had abdicated the government and that the throne was vacant.

On January 29 this resolution was reported to the Lords,
but not immediately taken into consideration. Instead the
Lords resolved themselves into committee, with Danby in the
chair, and proceeded to consider their own solution of the
problems at issue. After long debate the advocates of a
Regency forced a consideration of their expedient by proposing
the question, " Whether a Regency, with the administration of
regal power under the style of King James the Second, during
the life of the said King James, be the best and safest way to
preserve the Protestant religion and the laws of this kingdom." [2]
The voting was bound to be close, and Danby may well have
surmised that he held the balance in his hands. His first idea
appears to have been to take the affirmative side, and so bring
about an immediate contest between the friends of James, as
represented by the Lords, and the friends of William, as represented by the Commons ; but the undesirability of combining
such a struggle with a contest between the Houses made him
incline the other way,[3] and in the end he and Halifax were

---

[1] Sir John Lowther spoke once or twice in the Commons, and on January 29
Sir Joseph Tredenham and Lord Dumblane, probably with Danby's long
imprisonment in mind, indicated the " exorbitances of Westminster Hall "
as a national grievance (*Hardwicke State Papers*, ii. 412, 423, 424) ; but none
of them made any material contribution on a controversial subject.

[2] *L.J.*, xiv. 110.

[3] This seems the simplest explanation of the otherwise incomprehensible
statement made by Halifax and quoted by Miss Foxcroft from his " note
book " that Danby had promised the Earl of Abingdon an hour before the
division to vote on the other side (*Life of Halifax*, ii. 49). It was a matter of
parliamentary tactics.

largely responsible for securing the defeat of the Regency scheme by 51 votes to 49.[1]

On the two following days the Lords, still in committee, took into consideration the resolution of the Commons, and dealt with it clause by clause. The word " abdicated " was altered to " deserted," but otherwise the resolution was accepted until it came to the last clause, which declared the throne to be vacant. Here if ever Danby had to make a stand, and he accordingly came definitely forward as the champion of the Princess Mary by pronouncing against it. After debate it was first of all proposed to substitute for the clause a simple statement that " the Prince and Princess of Orange be declared King and Queen ; " but on the previous question being moved this was defeated by 52 votes to 47. A division was then taken upon the vacancy of the throne itself, and the clause declaring it was even more decisively rejected by 55 votes to 41.[2]

The real difficulty, however, as Danby well knew, still remained to be faced. Unless the concurrence of the Commons could be secured the vote of the Lords was bound to prove ineffective, and of that concurrence there seemed little prospect. Not merely had the Commons shown themselves overwhelmingly in favour of their own original resolution,[3] but when on February 2 the amendments made by the Lords were reported to them these amendments were rejected with little debate and without a single dissentient voice.[4] Nevertheless Danby did not despair. None of his supporters served on the committee appointed by the Commons to draw up reasons why they could not agree with the Lords ; and when the report of the committee was presented on February 4 an attempt was made at his instigation to secure a reconsideration of the whole problem

[1] With the majority went the Bishop of London, while the Bishop of Bristol spoke on the same side, although he " modestly withdrew when they came to vote." The debate was an unusually acrimonious one for the House of Lords, " insomuch that my Lord Wharton desired my Lord Clarendon might be called to the barr for calling the Civil War a rebellion ; and my Lord Winchelcy in the twilight stood up and said, My Lords, I perceive these lords (meaning the Regency lords) intend to tire us with long debates, but I hope God will give us courage and witt to maintaine the debate against them " (Ballard MSS. 45, f. 25).

[2] *House of Lords MSS.*, 1689-90, p. 17 ; *L.J.*, xiv. 112-3.

[3] *Luttrell*, i. 499.   [4] *C.J.*, x. 18 ; *Grey*, ix. 46-9.

at issue, Sir Joseph Tredenham declaring that although he considered the throne to be " vacant," presumably as regards
James II, he could not agree that it was " entirely vacant,"
such a thing being impossible in a hereditary monarchy.

The attempt proved premature. At the instance of Sir
Thomas Lee the Speaker ruled that the question of the vacancy
of the throne was no longer before the House, Tredenham had
to acquiesce, and neither Danby nor any of his followers took
part in the formal conference later in the day at which the
Commons submitted their arguments to the Lords.[1] This,
however, only involved a slight change of plan. On the effect
of the conference being reported to the Lords, Danby first
assisted in determining the decision of that body to adhere to
their amendments, and then agreed to serve, along with the
Bishop of London, on the committee appointed to draw up
reasons for their attitude. Although acceptable enough to the
advocates of a Regency who constituted the majority of the
committee, the reasons adopted were substantially those on
which Danby based his case. A vacancy of the throne, it was
pointed out, could not be admitted, because that would make
the monarchy elective, whereas by the constitution of England
it was hereditary. No act on the part of the King alone could
destroy the right of his heirs, and therefore if the throne were
vacant as regards James, allegiance would necessarily be due
to the person who came next in the succession.[2]

These reasons, submitted at another conference of the two
Houses on February 5, and reported to the Commons the same
day, achieved the object at which Tredenham had aimed, of
reopening the whole question of the vacancy of the throne.
Sir Thomas Clarges, originally one of the foremost champions
in the Commons of the Regency scheme, took the lead in recommending what seemed to him the next best solution of the
national problem. " These reasons of the Lords," he declared,
" seem to me to be so cogent that they deserve to be seriously
weighed. . . . By this vacancy I understand only that the King
has abdicated from himself, . . . and that the government comes
to the next Protestant heir in succession, . . . the Princess of

---

[1] *L.J.*, xiv. 115 ; *C.J.*, x. 18-19 ; *Grey*, ix. 49-50.
[2] *L.J.*, xiv. 116-7.

Orange." Tredenham returned to the charge. " There is no other way to have peace and quiet," he insisted, " but by recognising the Princess, who has no natural nor legal impediment." Until late in the afternoon the debate continued, the friends of James and the supporters of Mary combining to maintain that an " absolute vacancy " could not be admitted ; but when eventually the question was put, whether the House should agree with the Lords in their second amendment, it was resolved in the negative by 282 votes to 151. With the minority went practically all Danby's followers—his son Dumblane ; his brothers-in-law Charles, Henry and Peregrine Bertie ; his nephew Lord Norris, as well as Sir Jonathan Jennings, Christopher Tancred, Sir Robert Cotton and Sir Joseph Tredenham.[1]

Had the last word really lain with Parliament Danby might conceivably have struggled on a little longer. While these debates and conferences had been taking place, however, the ultimate decision had been virtually determined by a series of events outside of Parliament, the dates of which unfortunately cannot be discovered, and even the precise sequence of which remains in some doubt. As early as December 30 Halifax had been informed by William that he would not accept anything short of a life tenure of the throne ; [2] but Danby's realisation of the Prince's attitude came much later. At a great meeting of the anti-regency party held at the Earl of Devonshire's a determined effort was made to decide between the claims of the Prince and the Princess. The chief speakers on opposite sides were Halifax and Danby, and the former at length considered it expedient to play what he knew to be a trump card by suggesting that William's own sentiments should be ascertained. At the meeting was one of the Prince's confidants, who under pressure at length gave it as his opinion that William would not like to be his wife's gentleman usher. Danby thereupon broke up the meeting, disgusted, one may suspect, not so much by William's attitude as by this fresh proof of the superior part which Halifax had in his confidence.[3]

[1] C.J., x. 19-20; Grey, ix. 53-65. A list of the members of the Commons believed to have supported the Lords' amendments is printed infra, iii. 164-72.

[2] Spencer House Journals in Foxcroft, Halifax, ii. 203-4.

[3] Dartmouth's note in Burnet (ed. 1833), iii. 393-4.

Even in face of this statement Danby would almost certainly have persisted in supporting Mary's claims had it not been that she herself refused to give him any countenance. Some time after his first tentative offer of January 4 he had dispatched a special messenger to the Princess with an account of the political situation and an assurance that if she approved he could have her placed alone upon the throne. He now received " a very sharp answer," in which she declared " that she would take it extreme unkindly, if any, under a pretence of their care of her, would set up a divided interest between her and the Prince." At the same time she sent both Danby's letter and a copy of her own reply to William.

Possibly it was this which inspired the Prince to make at length a formal statement of his own attitude. Summoning before him Halifax, Danby, Shrewsbury and two or three more of his supporters, he declared he would be neither regent nor prince consort, but if anything less than the kingship for life were offered him would simply return to Holland.[1] This made it plain that no intermediate course was possible between the restoration of James on the one hand and the elevation of William on the other. As early as February 4 a growing realisation of this fact had reduced the majority in the Lords against the vacancy of the throne to a single vote.[2] Now with Danby's admission of it, made probably on the evening of the following day, the balance was to be thrown over to the other side. Late on February 5 Sir Henry Goodricke, who had not voted with the rest of his party against the vacancy of the throne, was selected as one of the managers to maintain the case of the Commons at a free conference which they desired with the Lords.[3] On the following morning Danby and his friends remained conspicuously aloof from the unusually large body of managers nominated by the Lords in response.[4] There is little doubt that during the interval the Earl had been engaged in that process of canvassing which he understood so well, confirming some peers in their readiness to follow his leadership and inducing others to absent themselves. The result was seen

[1] *Burnet*, i. 819 ; *Ranke*, iv. 507.
[2] The division was 54 to 53 (*House of Lords MSS.*, 1689-90, p. 17).
[3] *C.J.*, x. 20.   [4] *L.J.*, xiv. 118.

later in the day, when the substance of the conference was reported to the Lords. The debate was long ; but with Danby and his following throwing in their lot with the Whigs the division was decisive. By 65 votes to 45 the abdication and the vacancy of the throne were accepted,[1] and lest Danby's own change of attitude in the Lords should not have been rendered sufficiently clear something of the nature of a public recantation was made immediately afterwards by his son in the Commons. " I ask pardon," declared Lord Dumblane on February 7, " for my mistake the other day in my vote that the throne was not vacant. I have great obligation to the Prince, and have showed my duty to him. You cannot do too much for him." [2]

This speech, made in a debate on the settlement of the crown, might seem to indicate that, having abandoned the idea of maintaining Mary's interest independently of William, Danby was now inclining towards those who would have maintained William's interest independently of Mary ; but for this suggestion there is no real evidence. If Halifax is to be believed, indeed, Danby always declared that " it had been happy if the King would have been content with the regency." [3] Practical man that he was, the Earl readily appreciated the desirability of the regal power being in William's hands ; but in the interests of the hereditary succession he would have preferred that it should be exercised in Mary's name. According to one account [4] it was he who made the formal proposal in the Lords that the Prince and Princess of Orange should be declared King and Queen ; and whether this be so or not the resolution to that effect, adopted without a division by the Lords on February 6 and agreed to by the Commons on February 8, represents the compromise which in the end he was prepared to accept.

---

[1] *House of Lords MSS.*, 1689-90, p. 18. " After the conference was over the Earle of Danby made an excellent speech in the House of Lords, and then the vote being put whether or no they should agree with the vote of the House of Commons of the 28 January that the King had abdicated the government it was carried by three voyces, and that the throne was vacant by twenty voyces " (Rawlinson MSS. D. 1079, f. 12). Clarendon was very bitter about the methods used in carrying this vote (*Clarendon Correspondence*, ii. 260-2).

[2] *Grey*, ix. 73.

[3] Halifax's " note book," quoted in Foxcroft, *Halifax*, ii. 49.

[4] *Mazure*, iii. 357.

Even after the passing of this resolution a few preliminaries had still to be settled. Many of those who had opposed the elevation of William and Mary were yet quite prepared to recognise them as *de facto* rulers. To such people, however, the existing oaths of supremacy and allegiance, which referred to the occupant of the throne as " lawful and rightful " sovereign, were bound to prove a stumbling-block. This difficulty was brought out with much eloquence in the Lords by the Earl of Nottingham, who proposed that the oaths should be modified to suit the circumstances of the moment. The proposal was seconded by Danby, but vehemently opposed by Halifax, who declared that any alteration in the oaths would throw ridicule on the title of the new sovereigns as well as on their own proceedings, and tried to use the authority of the chair to beat down opposition. Such tactics were dangerous, however, when applied to a man like Danby, and a scene of fierce recrimination followed, the ill-feeling between the two statesmen which had been increasing for weeks suddenly finding vent. " Does that lord in the chaire intend to argue me into perjury," Danby bitterly enquired, " and in short schooled him so shamefully that my Lord Hallifax did not open his mouth ; and lett him know he would handle him for the time to come without mittins." The Earl's contention was that though they had resolved to make William and Mary King and Queen upon the existing crisis of affairs " yet no man could affirme they were rightfully so by the constitution," [1] and with this the Lords so far agreed that they resolved to proceed next day to a reconsideration of the oaths.[2]

On February 7 the Lords in committee with Clarendon in the chair proceeded to draw up two new oaths, which were adopted by the House. At the same time the Commons were engaged in defining more fully and precisely the succession to the throne, and in hastily drawing up a statement of the conditions on which it was to be offered. After some days spent in adjusting

[1] Ballard MSS. 45, f. 27a. Miss Foxcroft has somewhat mistranscribed the ill-written lines. The words she conjectures to be " hooted " and " next " are certainly " schooled " and " not " (*Life of Halifax*, ii. 55). That Danby resented the whole affair very keenly is shown by the account of it he gave some three weeks later to Reresby (*Memoirs*, p. 558).

[2] *L.J.*, xiv. 119.

details between the two Houses the succession, the conditions, and the oaths were embodied on February 12 in a single document ever since known as the Declaration of Right. At five o'clock on the same evening Princess Mary, who had been summoned to England about the middle of January but had been delayed by adverse winds, reached Whitehall.[1] Ten o'clock on the following morning was fixed for the final scene.

At eight o'clock on February 13 Danby was in his place in the House of Lords, from which, after the necessary business of the day had been transacted, Lords and Commons together proceeded to wait upon the Prince and Princess in the Banqueting House at Whitehall. There Halifax in the name of the Convention presented the Crown and the Declaration, which were thankfully accepted. William and Mary were then immediately proclaimed King and Queen.

---

[1] Admiral Herbert with the convoy for her arrived in Holland on January 22/February 1, but she could not put to sea until February 10/20 (*Doebner*, pp. 7-9). According to Echard the summons to her was advocated by Danby (*History of the Revolution*, p. 228).

PART IV

CARMARTHEN AND LEEDS

1689-1712

CHAPTER XIX

DISAPPOINTMENT, 1689-90

THE proclamation of the new sovereigns seemed to place the highest offices in the state once more within Danby's grasp. William and Mary were under great obligations to him. The marriage between them, which had done so much to strengthen the position of both, was pre-eminently his work. In the recent rebellion, intended to vindicate their title to the Crown, he had played a prominent, if not indeed the leading part. Throughout the debates of the Convention he had consistently advocated their claims, although the precise form in which he had originally done so had not met with the approval of either of them. For a period of fifteen years, broken by only one serious gap, he had maintained with them a friendly correspondence, and he was widely believed to be more in their confidence than any other leading statesman of the day.

Moreover in a political world which, as William was already beginning to realise, was composed mainly of furious and impracticable partisans, Danby occupied a middle position. Owing to his long imprisonment in the Tower and his subsequent retirement from public affairs he had been associated neither with the Whig extravagances of the Exclusion Bill period nor with the Tory reaction which followed. No considerable party thirsted for his blood ; nor had he, on the other hand, any recent injuries which he wished to avenge. To William this was a powerful recommendation, for the new King desired above all to avoid becoming the mere head of a faction, and even had he been prepared to do so would have found difficulty in determining to which faction he should give his adhesion. The Whigs supported his title but opposed his prerogative. The Tories supported the prerogative but viewed his title with doubt.[1] Danby almost alone was an assured supporter both of the prerogative and of the new régime.

It is not surprising, therefore, that popular opinion anticipated Danby's elevation to his old post of Treasurer,[2] or that the Earl himself confidently expected not merely some such advancement, but the fulfilment at length of the promises made him by Charles II at the time of his fall. William, however, had other ideas. Probably he distrusted Danby's managing spirit, and feared that if he elevated him to any influential post his own inexperience of English affairs would throw a dangerous amount of power into his hands.[3] More certainly he exaggerated Danby's unpopularity, and shrank especially from restoring him to the very office from which he had been so conspicuously hurled. Whatever the reason, he had decided as early as the beginning of February that the Treasury should be entrusted to commissioners,[4] although his neglect of Danby's pretensions did not become publicly apparent until later in the month.

That such neglect was possible was due to the fact that William had found, as he imagined, an abler and less exacting adviser in the Marquis of Halifax. It is impossible to deny a grim sense of humour to the Fates who so frequently brought these statesmen together in alternate friendship and hostility, and who compelled two such different men to pursue policies which bear such a constant superficial resemblance. While Danby held a middle position owing to his failure for some time to associate himself definitely with either political party, Halifax did so no less because he had alternately associated himself with both. He had thus the same claim to William's favour as his rival, and could do more to justify it, for while Danby's non-party position was the result of purely temporary circumstances his own was due to settled conviction.

In the race for the new King's favour, however, the decisive

---

[1] Onslow's note in *Burnet* (ed. 1833), iv. 5.

[2] Philip Musgrave to Lord Dartmouth, December 26, 1688, in *Hist. MSS. Com.*, xv. 1, pp. 142-3 ; newsletter of February 14, 1689, in *Cal. S.P. Dom.*, 1689-90, p. 2.

[3] " Note, a great jealousie of being thought to bee governed " (Spencer House Journals in Foxcroft, *Halifax*, ii. 203).

[4] *Reresby*, pp. 547-8. William later declared to Halifax that there were two places which should always be in commission, the Admiralty and the Treasury.

factor was Halifax's success in establishing his position nearly a month before Danby appeared on the scene at all.[1] The Earl had completely miscalculated the course of the revolution, and a year's unceasing effort was to be required before he could recover the ground he had lost. In his whole life there were few more bitter disappointments than the preference shown at this time to Halifax, who had hindered rather than helped the movement against James. Instead of the Treasury there was offered to him the post of Lord President of the Council coupled with one of the Secretaryships of State, the former " a place of credit and place but of small profit," [2] the latter a position in which any minister was bound to be overshadowed, at least as regards foreign affairs, by the King himself. With some reluctance he allowed himself to be appointed President ; but at the same time Halifax by his own choice was given the much more lucrative post of Lord Privy Seal, and so obviously secured the ascendancy that Danby was quite unable to conceal his mortification.[3]

The new Privy Council was sworn in, and the principal appointments were made, on or shortly after February 14. The result was a not unreasonable compromise between the claims of contending factions. On the Treasury and Admiralty Commissions places were found for a strange collection of Whigs and Tories. One Secretaryship of State went to the Whig Shrewsbury, the other to the Tory Nottingham. The balancing policy on which these arrangements were based seemed to Danby a complete mistake,[4] but there is nothing to suggest that he regarded it as involving any injustice to himself or his associates. His own loss of the Treasurership was a disappointment rather than a grievance, and the claims of his relatives

---

[1] Earl of Lindsey to Lady Danby, December 10, 1688, in *Lindsey MSS.*, p. 452 : " My L[ord] H[alifax] sent my friend down into the north to fight whilst he and Nottingham intended to be the great men in the south." There was no deliberate policy on the part of Halifax, but this represents what occurred.

[2] *Reresby*, p. 555. The salary eventually granted, however was £1,500 a year (*Cal. Treas. Books*, ix. 139).

[3] *Reresby*, p. 557 ; *Supplement to Burnet*, p. 313.

[4] According to Halifax he declared that William had better put himself into the hands of the fanatics than continue trimming (Foxcroft, *Halifax*, ii. 212, note 1, quoting the Devonshire House note book. On William's early preference for a policy of trimming see *ibid.*, ii. 65, note 2).

and friends were adequately recognised. The Earl of Lindsey remained Great Chamberlain. Lord Willoughby scored a sentimental triumph by his appointment [1] to the Chancellorship of the Duchy of Lancaster, the possession at one time of that stout rival of the Berties, Sir Robert Carr. The Earl of Bath, Lord Lumley, the Bishop of London and Sir John Lowther were admitted, along with the Lord Chamberlain, to the Privy Council.

But as regards the disposal of the minor offices, to which he considered that his followers were entitled to be preferred, Danby felt he had a very distinct grievance indeed. The basis of the allocation in this sphere was the proclamation of February 14, which permitted all Protestant sheriffs, justices of the peace, collectors, receivers and others connected with the revenue who had held office at the beginning of the previous December to continue in possession.[2] Unfortunately Danby's followers, almost without exception, had been deprived of their offices either in 1679 or during the reign of James, and they thus started under an initial handicap against which their patron found he was unable to contend There were many claimants for few posts, and his influence with the King was not sufficient to secure for them that share in the spoils of office which he considered the fitting reward of their services in the north.

So early did this become apparent, and so rapidly, one may surmise, were all desirable positions appropriated, that within five days of the opening of the new reign Danby found it necessary to write to William a letter of remonstrance.[3] It is to his credit that in that letter he asks nothing for himself, and lays his chief stress on the claims of his second in command in the northern rising, Sir Henry Goodricke, whose services as yet had received no recognition whatever, and who seemed in danger of being completely ignored. When it is considered that Danby had given the King a full account of the operations in the north it is difficult to find any reasonable justification for this neglect. The Earl suggested that Goodricke might be appointed a Commissioner of Customs. This, however, was denied, and it

---

[1] On March 1 (*Cal. S.P. Dom.*, 1689-90, p. 12).

[2] *Ibid.*, p. 1.

[3] Dated February 18. It is printed *infra*, ii. 161.

was not until April 2 that he was rewarded with a grant of the office of Lieutenant-General of the Ordnance.[1] With more doubtful taste Danby next put forward the claims of his own rather futile brother Charles, who had been a Commissioner of Customs for a short time under Charles, but had lost all his posts under James. William, however, failed to do anything for him, and Danby had eventually to find him a place himself.[2]

The reception accorded to this remonstrance could scarcely therefore be described as favourable, and it certainly did nothing to diminish the Earl's discontent. His failure to advance his followers was a serious blow to his prestige, which was rendered all the heavier when it was found that the same men, by applying through other channels, could secure their objects.[3] The King, in fact, seemed almost to be inspired by an actual aversion to the Osborne family. Lord Latimer, who had been personally well known to him since his visit to Holland in 1674, was denied the position of Gentleman of the Bedchamber, which he had held for many years under Charles II. Lord Dumblane was rewarded by a warrant under the sign manual for the somewhat inappropriate position of Postmaster-General ; and yet shortly afterwards, without a word of warning or explanation, that office was granted to Major John Wildman, the notorious republican. Lady Plymouth's desire to become Lady of the Bedchamber to Queen Mary remained apparently ungratified.[4]

Moreover on one particular point Danby had a very serious grievance of his own. For eight years he had striven to secure the fulfilment of the promises made him in 1679, and especially the confirmation of his grant of a marquisate. What he desired was partly the increase in dignity, but partly also the admission, which such a confirmation would more or less imply,

---

[1] Almost at the same time Charles Bertie, whose claims were also strong, was made Treasurer and Paymaster of the Ordnance (*Cal. S.P. Dom.*, 1689-90, pp. 49, 56).

[2] In Leeds MSS., Packet 14, there is a letter dated December 22, 1689, from Charles Osborne to the Lord President, in which he complains of his low condition generally and expresses his disappointment that the King had done nothing for him. It bears a note in Danby's handwriting, " I did hereupon give my brother 100 l. on the 23th ditto."

[3] Danby mentions in particular Mr. Roberts, Sir Robert Cotton, and Sir Jonathan Jennings (*infra*, ii. 160). Jennings was appointed Sheriff of Yorkshire, but what preferment was given to the others is not clear.

[4] *Infra*, ii. 160-1.

that he had been unjustly accused. For that very reason, however, the King hesitated to take any action, and either definitely refused to confirm his patent or at least postponed a decision. The bitterness which this aroused was rendered all the greater by the fact that Danby attributed it, along with his other grievances, to the machinations of his rival Halifax. In conversation with Sir John Reresby the Marquis expressed his resolve to give the Earl " noe just occasion of difference," and for the breach between them, which was proving highly injurious to the Government, William entirely freed Halifax from blame ; but it is painfully evident that the Lord President had another tale to tell.[1]

Such personal matters, however, by no means formed the sum and substance of Danby's complaints. On February 28 Sir John Reresby dined with him and had to listen to a vigorous indictment of the Government.[2] The principal charge was still the ineptitude of the policy being pursued towards Ireland. William's attempt at negotiation through the agency of Richard Hamilton had, as Danby had anticipated, proved a complete and even shameful failure. Hamilton had betrayed the Government he had undertaken to serve, and Tyrconnel, reassured as to William's weakness, had become more aggressive than ever. James was known to have sailed from Brest with French troops to assist the Catholics in the island, and Parliament had just been officially informed of the fact.[3] In Londonderry and Enniskillen the Protestants were still with difficulty holding out, but no active measures seemed in preparation for their relief, and unless help was speedily sent it was practically certain that the whole of Ireland would be lost. On February 14 a special Committee for the Affairs of Ireland had been

---

[1] Miss Foxcroft, relying mainly on the Spencer House Journals, presents the case for the Marquis (*Life of Halifax*, ii. 62 *et seq.*) ; but if Halifax really had as much influence with William as these Journals suggest it is difficult to believe that there was not something in Danby's complaint. It is always well, while admitting the great abilities of the Lord Privy Seal, to remember the words with which that stout Cavalier the Earl of Chesterfield broke off his long and intimate friendship with him. " I had rather," he declared to him before company, " be a plaine honest country gentleman than a cunning, false court knave " (*Letters of the Earl of Chesterfield*, p. 55).

[2] *Reresby*, pp. 556-9.

[3] *C.J.*, x. 36 ; *Parliamentary History*, v. 150.

appointed, of which Danby himself was a member; but so great was his disgust at William's failure to give effect to his repeated representations that after their first meeting on February 15 he had not once attended.[1]

The second point in his indictment was, as might have been anticipated, the encouragement given by the King to the Presbyterians, and his neglect of the Anglican interest. Like many feebler men Danby had no sooner carried through the Revolution than he began to feel the reaction. Under stress of a common danger he had consented to an alliance with the Whigs in the interests of Protestantism in general; but his association with such men as the Earl of Devonshire in the northern rising had done little to prepare him for the presence in the ministry of some of those who were now his colleagues. That concessions must be made to those who had done so much to put William on the throne he could not reasonably deny; but under his suspicious scrutiny the significance of all concessions was greatly exaggerated, and what appeared to the King to be only elementary justice appeared to him to be evidence of a settled policy of favouring the Whigs.

Nevertheless it is not easy to make out what precisely Danby objected to. The main grievance of the Tories was the continued sitting of the Whig Convention, and the introduction of a bill declaring it to be a Parliament.[2] Only a fresh assembly, they asserted, regularly summoned by writs issued by a king, could effect a permanent settlement; only fresh elections, they whispered, could secure the Tories the representation they might justly claim. But it is impossible to believe that Danby, whose main object was to galvanise the Government into some activity, gave his countenance to a contention which was bound to be productive of confusion and delay. A grievance which appealed to a smaller section among the Tories was the provision made by the Act declaring the Convention to be a Parliament, that the recently adopted oaths of allegiance and supremacy should be taken by all members of both Houses after March 1. But Danby thoroughly approved of the oaths, and

---

[1] A return of the attendances is printed in the *House of Lords MSS.*, 1689-90, p. 179.

[2] *Burnet*, ii. 5-6. The bill was first introduced in the Lords on February 18 and received the royal assent on February 23 (*L.J.*, xiv. 128, 132).

expressed some contempt for those who scrupled to take them.[1]
A further cause of discontent, especially among the Hydes and
their connections, was the fact that in the settlement of the
succession the claims of the Princess Anne were postponed to
those of William. But Danby was so little in sympathy with
the views of this party that he was specially selected by Anne
herself to intimate, at a formal meeting with the Archbishop of
Canterbury, her entire satisfaction with what had been done.[2]

The real basis of his attitude seems to have been a strong
suspicion, if not actual knowledge, of the intention entertained
by William to secure some relaxation of the Test in favour of
Protestant Dissenters. To such a concession Danby, for
political as well as religious reasons, was completely opposed,
and his fear that it was the ultimate goal of the King's policy
made him suspicious of every other concession to Dissenters.
It is probably not without significance that only an hour or
two before he unburdened himself to Sir John Reresby the
Toleration Bill had been read for a first time in the House of
Lords.[3] The bill had the support of the bishops, it was drawn
up and introduced by that pillar of orthodoxy, the Earl of
Nottingham, and there is nothing to suggest that Danby
opposed it ; but it must have roused in him the liveliest apprehensions of what might follow.[4]

Where Danby was dissatisfied more extreme Tories were
thoroughly disgusted. Within a fortnight of his accession, indeed, William, while failing to conciliate the Whigs, had
succeeded in completely alienating the Tories. So serious did
the position appear that Danby doubted whether the new
system would be of long continuance. The King and Lord

---

[1] As Lord President, Danby was the first to take the oaths on March 2 after
the Speaker of the House, Lord Halifax, had done so (*L.J.*, xiv. 136).

[2] The meeting took place on March 1 (*Clarendon Correspondence*, ii. 267, 270).

[3] *L.J.*, xiv. 134 ; *House of Lords MSS.*, 1689-90, p. 34.

[4] A letter-writer a few days later describes the general situation in words
which Danby himself might have employed. " The Queen is very zealous for
the Church of England, but declines always to declare herself till she have
heard the King's opinion, who I find is sett upon a comprehension. It is his
misfortune to fall in with a few men and to espouse their interest whose credit,
God knowes, is not very good, such as Dev[onshire], Del[amere], Lov[elace],
Hamp[den], &c., and to neglect those officers and men of interest and quality
that not only contributed most to the late revolution but could have prevented
it " (Ballard MSS. 45, f. 31a).

Halifax, he declared, " were strangly conceited of their security ; " if only James " would quitt his papists it might possibly
not be too late yet for him." So gloomy a view was no doubt
the result partly of his personal disappointments and partly of a
prolonged attack of ill health induced by over-exertion at the
time of the Revolution ; but that there was considerable
ground for it cannot be questioned.[1] Unfortunately Danby had
played so prominent a part in the expulsion of James that he
could expect nothing but ruin in the event of a restoration.
Uncertain whether to support the new Government or to
oppose it, he accordingly made his sickness an excuse for a
temporary retirement. As Lord President he was untroubled
by departmental duties, and so long as William himself was in
England his presence even at the meetings of Council was unnecessary. From the beginning of the reign to March 20 he
rarely attended even the House of Lords.[2]

Meanwhile he endeavoured to build up for himself a power
in the north which should put him in a position, in the event of
a counter-revolution, to extort favourable terms from the new
Government. On March 12 the Lords Lieutenants were appointed, and Danby, as was to be expected, was restored to his
old post at the head of the West Riding of Yorkshire.[3] Apart
from the large body of militia which it provided, however, this
was in a military sense the least important of the three ridings.
It contained no fortress, nor as a rule any considerable body of
regular troops. Danby accordingly made it his object to secure
in addition control of Hull, the greatest fortress and garrison

---

[1] Halifax, in spite of his " conceit " of his security, shortly afterwards
expressed much the same opinion (*Reresby*, p. 564). So bad was William's
health, and so great was believed to be the danger of his assassination, that it
was scarcely expected he would live to the end of the year.

[2] Halifax accused Danby of malingering, but for the reality and seriousness
of his illness there is the impartial testimony of Reresby (*Memoirs*, pp. 557,
565). It is certain, however, that he was quite content to remain for a while
in the background. Between January 22 and February 13 he was absent
from the Lords only on three occasions ; between February 15 and March 19
he was present only on three occasions, and even for these attendances there
were special reasons.

[3] *Cal. S.P. Dom.*, 1689-90, pp. 20, 21 ; *Luttrell*, i. 512-3. The expectations
of his friends and relatives were gratified at the same time. Lindsey became
Lord Lieutenant of Lincoln, Abingdon of Oxford, Lumley of Northumberland,
and Sir John Lowther of Westmorland.

town north of the Humber, the governorship of which usually
went with the lieutenancy of the East Riding. The task proved
somewhat difficult, for William looked with disfavour on his
request, but on April 1 a commission was drawn up appointing
him Governor.[1] Two months later his associate in the northern
rising, Lionel Copley, was reappointed Lieutenant-Governor,
with power to act in his absence.[2]

In spite of this success, however, Danby's relations with
William in the spring of 1689 were thoroughly bad. The auto-
cratic monarch could ill endure the dictatorial attitude of his
minister. Not merely did Danby continually pester him with
the claims of his followers, but he required the satisfaction of
these claims as a right rather than a favour, and probably made
it only too plain that he had a good deal of justification for so
doing.[3] Not merely did he deliver his opinion on all sorts of
topics with such insistence that, as he himself confessed, " he
was uncivil in pressing it," but his advice, even when William
could not or would not follow it, only too often proved to be
sound.

On one particular point, also, Danby gave great offence to
the King. In order to gratify Marshal Schomberg, who had
served as second in command of the expedition to England,
William proposed to confer upon him the Garter formerly in
the possession of James.[4] Danby then consulted with other
members of the order, including the Earl of Rochester, and
with four or five of them waited upon the King in order to

---

[1] Spencer House Journals in Foxcroft, *Halifax*, ii. 211 ; *Cal. S.P. Dom.*,
1689-90, p. 48. Halifax and Reresby, who were both in a position to know,
were in agreement " that the Earl of Danby had gott the goverment of Hull
as a place of retreat, and wherby to make his terms, should ther be any change
of times " (*Reresby*, p. 571).

[2] The appointment is dated June 4 (*Cal. S.P. Dom.*, 1689-90, p. 137).

[3] Spencer House Journals in Foxcroft, *Halifax*, ii. 210. Danby has so
constantly been accused of unduly favouring his followers that it is necessary,
while admitting the general justice of the charge, to remember the other side
of the picture as shown by the answer made by Reresby when Halifax reflected
on the Earl's importunity. " I tooke upon that the confidence to say," he
tells us, " that I did not know what that lord lost with the King by it, but he
gained much upon others ; for it was generally said that noe lord made it their
business to doe good offices for their contrimen but my Lord President "
(*Memoirs*, p. 577).

[4] " Knight Companion as well as Sovereign of that most honourable order "
(Ballard MSS. 45, f. 35a).

inform him that James's ribbon was not vacant. Such a contention seemed to cast some doubt on William's title to the
throne, and perhaps on that account it was overruled at a
meeting of the Chapter on April 3, where Schomberg was duly
elected ; but the incident left a good deal of bitterness behind.[1]

In these circumstances it was inevitable that King and Earl
should find themselves at variance in Parliament. From March
20 onwards Danby's attendance at the House of Lords became
quite regular again, a fact which it is difficult to avoid connecting with the rise to prominence of several problems in which
the interests of the Church of England were involved.   On
March 11 a Comprehension Bill, aiming at such concessions as
would induce the moderate Dissenters to join the Church, was
introduced in the Lords by the Earl of Nottingham. On March
14 the Comprehension Bill and the Toleration Bill were read a
second time and entrusted to the same committee, and a further
bill was introduced to determine the oaths and tests which
should be taken by all persons admitted to office under the
Government. On March 15 the Lords resolved that the taking
of the sacrament should not be part of the test required by
this last bill ; and on the following day the King himself, on
the advice of Richard Hampden and without apparently consulting his ministers, strongly urged in a speech to both Houses
that any oaths and tests laid down should be such as to admit
to office all Protestants able and willing to serve.[2]

It is highly improbable that Danby at this time had strong
views on toleration or even on comprehension ; but as regards
the Test he was adamant, and in the debates on these bills he
made his attitude absolutely clear. At the beginning of the
revolution, he declared, only Church of England men had been
engaged in it ; but others were now coming forward and endeavouring to qualify themselves for office. In the case of these
men it was essential to ensure that they were such as would not
constitute a danger to a monarchical government and an epis-

----

[1] Halifax's notes in Spencer House Journals, Foxcroft, *Halifax*, ii. 211-2 ;
Danby to Lady Danby, April 2, 1689, *infra*, ii. 218-9 ; *Luttrell*, i. 517. So
bitterly did Clarendon resent the insult to James that he reproached Rochester
for condescending even to attend the installation of Schomberg on May 14
(*Clarendon Correspondence*, ii. 276).

[2] *L.J.*, xiv. 145-50.

copal Church, and it was necessary therefore that all persons should be required " both to take an oath of fidelity to the King and receive the sacrament as a declaration of their being in communion with the said Church." Nothing less, he insisted, would suffice to preserve the existing constitution.

The lead thus given was readily followed. The Whig Earl of Devonshire went even further than Danby, declaring not merely that the sacramental test should be retained but that all should be required to take the sacrament kneeling, and that the use of the surplice by the officiating clergyman should remain compulsory. The Tory Earl of Nottingham, although responsible for both the Toleration and the Comprehension Bill, entirely concurred, and produced historical examples to show how easily a government could be overturned once it admitted to office those of contrary opinions. The question being put whether kneeling at the sacrament and the wearing of the surplice should be continued, " it was carried in the affirmative by more then three to one ; " and on March 21 a clause providing that the sacramental test should be abrogated was formally rejected.[1]

William was deeply disappointed, and in this is probably to be found the origin of his bitter outburst to Halifax—" For Lord Danby, hee knew not what to make of him. All his kindred and dependence voted against him. Hee could not live with a man at that rate." The King, indeed, seems to have gone so far as to remonstrate with the Lord President, but if so without success. In language strangely reminiscent of the previous reign Danby informed him that " he would serve him in everything but against the Church." [2]

At the moment this estrangement between King and Earl was distinctly unfortunate, for the day of the coronation was approaching, and it was assumed that the King would signalise that event by conferring peerages on the most prominent of those who had assisted him to gain the throne. Among these Danby considered that he came first, not merely because of his great services at the Revolution, but also because he had now

---

[1] Ballard MSS. 45, f. 58 ; *L.J.*, xiv. 156.

[2] Notes of conversations between William and Halifax on March 28 and April 4 in Spencer House Journals (Foxcroft, *Halifax*, ii. 206, 211-2).

had a warrant for a marquisate in his possession for more than
ten years. On rumours of William's intentions as regards others
reaching him he accordingly wrote to the King setting forth
his own claims. Assuming throughout that in virtue of Charles
II's patent he already was a Marquis, he hinted in studiously
vague language at his desire to be made a Duke. Halifax, he
pointed out, with ready suspicion of the source from which
opposition might come, could not fairly object, because his
elevation to the rank both of Earl and Marquis had preceded
that of the Lord Privy Seal.[1]

The reception accorded to this request was not favourable.
William absolutely refused to make Danby a Duke,[2] or to
confirm his earlier grant of a marquisate. On the other hand
he was at length persuaded to make a fresh grant advancing
him one step in the peerage. By a patent dated April 6 Danby
was created Marquis of Carmarthen. Five days later he enjoyed the precedence above all the nobility assigned at the
coronation to the Lord President, while his son Dumblane,
henceforth to be known as Earl of Danby, his son-in-law Lord
Lansdowne, and his nephew Lord Willoughby acted as train-
bearers to the King. On April 24 he was introduced under his
new title in the House of Lords.[3]

So far, however, were these honours from satisfying him
that two days later illness, disappointment and disgust had
combined to force upon him a fresh retirement. Nobody knew
better than he did how completely the immediate success and
ultimate stability of the settlement just effected depended upon
a proper adjustment of revenue to expenditure ; yet of such
an adjustment he could see no sign whatever. The offer made
by the King at the very beginning of his reign to surrender the
hated Hearth Tax must have seemed to him an act of foolhardy
generosity, the failure of the Government thereafter to give any
clear financial guidance to Parliament ineptitude at its very
worst. So far as he had any influence of his own he appears

---

[1] The letter, dated April 5, is printed *infra*, ii. 162.

[2] Probably with this incident may be connected the brief note in Halifax's
record of his conversation with the King on April 21—" Gave his word L[ord]
P[resident] should never bee a D[uke] " (Foxcroft, *Halifax*, ii. 216). Danby's
fear of Halifax's opposition was not ill-founded.

[3] *L.J.*, xiv. 190.

to have exercised it in favour of a grant to William of the entire revenue enjoyed by James,[1] but without result. On April 25, after more than two months of bewilderment, confusion and delay, the Commons fixed the ordinary peace charge of the government at £1,318,680, a figure to which experience clearly indicated it could not possibly be reduced, and which in any case greatly exceeded the revenue the House had undertaken to provide.[2] At this rate, he gloomily declared, things could not long continue as they were, and establishing himself at Wimbledon he remained throughout the greater part of May absent from Council and Parliament alike.[3]

The choice of a retreat so near the capital was deliberate, for the Lord President not only wished to continue his general supervision of affairs, but was already anxiously watching one particular development in which he was personally very much interested. Since the collapse of the Popish Plot scare Titus Oates had fallen on evil days. He had had judgment given against him for defamatory libel at the suit of James, and had further been convicted of perjury and subjected to a flogging from which only his hardy constitution had enabled him to escape alive. On April 4 these judgments were brought by separate writs of error before the House of Lords, and five days later April 18 was fixed for hearing arguments upon them.[4] The Lords, however, proved very reluctant to deal with the case. It was not until after several postponements that on April 26 Oates's counsel were at length heard in favour of a reversal of the judgments, and not until after still more postponements that on May 17 the judges who had given those judgments were heard in support of them.[5]

It is a significant fact that throughout this period Carmarthen's attendance at the House of Lords coincided almost exactly with the days on which Oates's case was down for a

---

[1] See especially Sir John Lowther's speech of February 27 in *Grey*, ix. 124.

[2] *C.J.*, x. 56, 80, 104.

[3] *Reresby*, pp. 576-7. Between April 27 and May 23 he was present in the Lords only on four occasions, and attended Council the same number of times.

[4] *L.J.*, xiv. 167, 172. Oates had petitioned the Lords for redress as early as March 11 (*House of Lords MSS.*, 1689-90, p. 47).

[5] *L.J.*, xiv. 180, 184, 191, 193, 194, 201, 202, 203, 209, 213 ; *House of Lords MSS.*, 1689-90, pp. 76-8.

hearing. So intimately was the Popish Plot connected with his own impeachment that he feared at every moment the old charges against him might be given a new lease of life, and desired to be present in his own defence. His apprehensions were soon justified. On May 23 Oates, impatient at the continued delay, not merely presented to the Commons a petition for redress, but published a statement of his case, in the third paragraph of which reference was made to letters " produced by a person of quality, by which the Government was satisfied of the underhand dealing of a great minister of state at that time, in order to procure a great sum of money, to put off the Parliament." Carmarthen was immediately aroused ; but so no less were the Lords as a body, for this appeal to the Commons on what was a purely judicial question they regarded as a serious breach of privilege. On May 25, accordingly, after deliberation, the Lords resolved that Oates should be committed to the Marshalsea. Carmarthen took a prominent part in the debate, declaring with more truth than discretion that there was only one sense in which Oates's sentence should be reversed. Whereas he had formerly been whipped from Newgate to Tyburn he ought now to be whipped from Tyburn to Newgate.[1]

It was an ill-advised speech. William declared to Halifax that Carmarthen must have been mad when he made it ; [2] but the displeasure of the King, whose efforts at conciliation it upset, was the least of the troubles in which it involved the Lord President. Hitherto the part he had played at the Revolution had protected him in some measure from the animosity of the Whigs. Of the twenty-eight heads under which the Commons on February 2 had defined the things necessary for securing the religion, laws and liberties of the country only two could be considered as reflecting specially

---

[1] *C.J.*, x. 144 ; *L.J.*, xiv. 219-21 ; North, *Examen*, p. 224 ; *House of Lords MSS.*, 1689-90, p. 78 ; Ballard MSS. 45, f. 39. The exact occasion on which Carmarthen's speech was delivered is not quite clear, but this seems the most likely. Miss Foxcroft says May 16 (*Life of Halifax*, ii. 218, note 4) ; but Oates's case was not considered that day, and Carmarthen was not in the House.

[2] Spencer House Journals in Foxcroft, *Halifax*, ii. 218. These alone would seem to date the speech between May 22 and May 27.

upon him.[1] A tacit indemnity had been granted for the non-resisting test and for his intrigues with France. Even his elevation to a prominent place in the Government had been accepted without serious complaint. But the old hostility was never very far from the surface, and this incident brought it once more to light.

On May 31 the judges were consulted as regards Oates's writs of error, but although they were unanimously of the opinion that the judgments against him were illegal the Lords resolved by 35 votes to 23 that the judgment for perjury should not be reversed. Nor in spite of his submission would they release Oates from the Marshalsea.[2] The Whig majority in the House of Commons were bitterly incensed at this treatment of a man whom some of them regarded, and others professed to regard, as a martyr in his country's cause, and not unnaturally they found vent for their fury in an attack on Carmarthen. On June 1 it was moved by John Howe, one of the most in-temperate of the Whig politicians, that an address should be presented to the King requesting him to remove from his presence and counsels all persons who had ever been impeached in Parliament. Even among those not specially hostile to the Lord President this motion met with some support. The Com-mons as a whole were in a very critical mood, and disposed to welcome any method of expressing their resentment at the supineness of the Government and the continued miscarriage of affairs in Ireland. During a debate which continued inter-mittently for three days many echoes of 1679 were heard, and members who had entered Parliament since that year were enlightened as to the exact course of Danby's impeachment and the precise nature of a " stamped pardon by creation." In the end, however, it was the pardon, not the impeachment itself, that engaged attention, and the sole result of the debate was a resolution, adopted without a division, that a pardon was not pleadable in bar of an impeachment in Parliament.[3]

[1] Those which declared that the too long continuance of the same Parliament should be prevented, and that no pardon should be pleadable to an impeach-ment in Parliament (*C.J.*, x. 17).

[2] *L.J.*, xiv. 225-9 ; *House of Lords MSS.*, 1689-90, pp. 78-80 ; *Luttrell*, i. 540. The judgment for defamatory libel was reversed on June 1.

[3] *C.J.*, x. 162, 163, 165 ; *Grey*, ix. 276-86.

For this indecisive outcome William himself was partly responsible. Not only did he send Dykvelt to expostulate with Howe, but, although with some reluctance, he used all the influence he had in favour of his minister.[1] The real reason, however, for the failure of the attack seems to have been that Carmarthen and the Whigs still had one common interest in their detestation of Halifax. The Whigs could never forgive the statesman who had secured the defeat of the Exclusion Bill and had formed the chief prop of the ministry of 1681 ; the Lord President could never pardon the rival who had outstripped him at the time of the Revolution. A tacit bargain was therefore struck, which was to remain a factor in the political situation for some time. Howe's motion was quietly dropped. Carmarthen on his part reconsidered his attitude to Oates, and on June 6 moved the Lords to petition the King that the remainder of the arch-impostor's sentence might be remitted. To many members of the House this seemed a happy way of escape from the highly illogical position they had assumed, and the Lord President was readily appointed chairman of a committee to draw up the necessary address, and one of the deputation entrusted with the duty of presenting it to the King.[2]

Unfortunately the opposition in the Commons were by no means satisfied with what seemed to them a mere evasion of the point at issue, and Carmarthen soon found himself compelled to go further than perhaps he desired in the effort to conciliate them. Towards the bill in which they endeavoured to secure by legislative means what the Lords in their judicial capacity had refused his attitude appears to have been merely that of a mediator between parties. As chairman of the subcommittee which drew up the Lords' amendments, and later as one of the managers of a conference between the two Houses, he made a genuine attempt to reach a compromise which all could accept, though without success.[3]

In another connection, however, his conduct is more open to

---

[1] *Macaulay*, iv. 1674-5 ; Spencer House Journals in Foxcroft, *Halifax*, ii. 219.

[2] *L.J.*, xiv. 234, 236 ; *Luttrell*, i. 544, 545.

[3] *House of Lords MSS.*, 1689-90, pp. 259-61 ; *L.J.*, xiv. 276.

criticism. No one knew better than William how precarious his own life was, and how much it was to be desired, in the interests both of England and of the great European schemes which he had at heart, that the succession to the throne should be explicitly defined beyond the power of a few unexpected deaths to place it in doubt. On a Bill of Rights being sent up by the Commons to the Lords he had therefore commissioned the Bishop of Salisbury to propose as an amendment to the clause defining the succession to the throne that the Princess Sophia and her descendants, the nearest undoubted Protestants, should be added to the entail.[1] Carmarthen, to whom such practical considerations always appealed, had firmly supported the amendment in its unimpeded passage through the Lords, and continued to do so even at a later stage.[2] Yet when on June 19 it came up for discussion in the Commons his followers united with the opposition in securing its rejection. " This looks like a kind of perpetuity," declared Sir John Lowther. " There may be revolutions and changes ; this Princess of Hanover may turn Catholic. Queen Elizabeth would not determine the succession, and she was a wise princess. Till I am better convinced, I cannot agree to it." [3]

In these arguments there seems to be reflected something of the extreme reluctance which Carmarthen had always shown to deviate any further than was absolutely necessary from the direct line of succession ; but it is very doubtful whether such semi-legitimist principles had for the moment any influence upon his policy. Many of the Whig opposition in the Commons were intent on keeping the succession at least partially open with a view to increasing the power of Parliament. Many more were so incensed at the conduct of the Lords towards Oates as to be ready to oppose any measure coming from the Upper House. Open defiance of the prevailing current of opinion would certainly have endangered Carmarthen's understanding

[1] *Burnet*, ii. 15-16 ; *House of Lords MSS.*, 1689-90, pp. 345-6. The amendment was proposed in committee on May 22 and accepted by the House on May 24.

[2] *L.J.*, xiv. 278. " Your Lordship having shewed yourself so much a friend to her Highness's being named in the succession, her Highness entends to write her own sence of itt to your Lordship " (W. D. Colt to Carmarthen, Hanover, July 30, 1689, O. S., in B.M. Add. MSS. 28054, f. 211).

[3] *Grey*, ix. 345.

with the Whigs, and Lowther's speech was probably little more than a piece of parliamentary tactics intended to strengthen that understanding.

If so it was singularly well-timed, for danger was already threatening from a quite unexpected quarter. Unknown to the Lord President the Earl of Danby, whose erratic genius was now finding an outlet on the sea, had procured a small but unusually swift vessel, which with the assistance of the Duke of Schomberg, Master-General of the Ordnance, he had fitted out as a privateer. Probably through Sir Henry Goodricke, the Lieutenant-General of the Ordnance, news of this perilous venture reached Carmarthen, and was received by him with some dismay. For his son he had little regard, but for the future of his family he had much. Nevertheless if left to himself he might not have interfered. In an evil moment, however, he gave way to the solicitude of his wife, and applied to his friend Nottingham, as Secretary of State, for a warrant for Danby's apprehension. This was granted, the armed vessel being held to justify a suspicion of treasonable practices,[1] and Danby was brought before the Secretary; but on his undertaking to appear again when summoned no further steps were taken.

Immediately the House of Commons was up in arms for its privileges. On June 22 it ordered the Earl of Danby to attend in his place in the House at their next meeting to give an account of the matter. On June 24 accordingly the Earl attended, and to his credit made light of the whole occurrence. The House, however, was not satisfied, and insisted on interrogating the messenger who had served the warrant, and on appointing a committee to enquire from the Earl of Nottingham on what information the warrant had been issued, and how Lord Danby had been dealt with. During the debates the privileges of Parliament, the rights of Privy Councillors, and eventually the relations of parents and children were the subject of much heated discussion. Sir Henry Goodricke was the Lord President's chief apologist, and in the face of what threatened to become a dangerous situation thought it best to divulge the whole inner history of the affair, so far as he knew it. Reasonable counsels then prevailed. On June 28 the Commons

---

[1] The warrant is dated June 20 (*Cal. S.P. Dom.*, 1689-90, p. 159; *C.J.*, x. 197).

resolved that the granting of a warrant to arrest the Earl of
Danby was a breach of their privileges, and there the matter
was allowed to rest.[1]

That the enemies of Carmarthen did not endeavour to make
further capital out of this singular incident was probably due
to the fact that the movement against Halifax was at length
coming to a head. The real cause of hostility to the Lord
Privy Seal was partly resentment at his conduct during the
concluding years of Charles's reign and partly jealousy of the
high position which he occupied in the favour of William; but
the pretext for the attack now delivered against him was the
misconduct of affairs in Ireland, where the Protestants of
Ulster still looked in vain for effective succour. The weakness
of the Government's Irish policy had always been one of Carmarthen's chief grievances; but in supporting the outcry
which arose he was probably influenced less by public spirit
than by a desire to injure his rival and turn the hunt off himself. On July 13 the Commons were so incensed at William's
evasion of their request to be permitted to inspect the minute
books of the Irish Committee that the persons who had advised
him to it were declared to be enemies of the kingdom, an
address was proposed for the removal of both Halifax and Carmarthen from his councils, and only the adjournment of the
debate saved them.[2] When on August 2 the attack was
renewed, however, Halifax alone was aimed at, and in the long
debate which took place on the following day Carmarthen's
son and followers were among those who voted against him.
The Lord President tried to explain this away as being due to
personal resentment on Danby's part at Halifax's attitude in
the trial of his marriage petition;[3] but there can be little
doubt that he was really working in conjunction with the
Whigs for the overthrow of his old enemy.[4]

[1] *C.J.*, x. 193-200; *Grey*, ix. 356-9, 361-2, 368-75.

[2] *C.J.*, x. 217; *Letters of Lady Russell*, ii. 5; *Luttrell*, i. 558. A letter from Carmarthen to Halifax on this occasion is printed in Foxcroft, *Halifax*, ii. 86, note 1.

[3] Spencer House Journals, *ibid.*, ii. 229; *Clarendon Correspondence*, ii. 284-5.

[4] According to Burnet the alliance was maintained through the Earl of
Monmouth, over whom Carmarthen had great influence (*Supplement*, p. 313).
William realised that the Lord President had conciliated his adversaries, but
believed he had done so by offering to resign (Spencer House Journals in Foxcroft, *Halifax*, ii. 221, 232).

Although the motion against Halifax was defeated by eleven votes William was supremely disgusted. For weeks he had been waiting with ill-concealed impatience for Parliament to effect a settlement of the revenue and pass immediately necessary legislation, only to find such important work constantly neglected for the sake of factious controversies and attacks on his ministers. He would willingly have got rid of Carmarthen, who seemed to be both an inspirer of the factions and an object of their attack ; but the Marquis refused to go unless actually dismissed.[1] He would gladly have prorogued or even dissolved Parliament, but hesitated to do so while any possibility of a satisfactory settlement still remained in sight.[2] On August 20, however, the futility of longer delay had at length become apparent to him, and the Houses of Parliament were required to adjourn for a month, with the prospect of further adjournments until winter.[3]

Carmarthen, who had been completely exhausted by the long session, immediately obtained leave to retire into the country ; [4] but for a few days he was detained in London by the requirements of the situation abroad. On May 7 William, with the full approval of his Lord President, had formally declared war on France, which was already supporting the deposed King James in Ireland.[5] Twelve days later Carmarthen, Halifax, Wharton and the two Secretaries of State had been appointed to negotiate an offensive and defensive alliance with the Dutch. So intricate were the various points that arose that discussions continued for three months, but on August 24 the treaty was at last signed, and for the first time for nearly a year Carmarthen found himself comparatively at leisure.[6]

The few weeks of retirement in which he indulged, however, gave him little rest. Ill-health, from which he had never been

[1] Spencer House Journals, *ibid.*, ii. 230.

[2] As early as July 10 he was arguing with Halifax in favour of a recess (*ibid.*, ii. 224).

[3] *C.J.*, x. 271.

[4] Spencer House Journals in Foxcroft, *Halifax*, ii. 232.

[5] Sir Henry Goodricke was chairman of the committee of the Commons which drew up the address in favour of war with France adopted on April 24 and presented to the King on the following day (*C.J.*, x. 101, 104).

[6] Foxcroft, *Halifax*, ii. 73, note 2.

free since the opening of the new reign, continued to trouble him. A combination of domestic and political calamity was added with the death on September 1 of his daughter Lady Lansdowne, which weakened still further the already failing alliance between the Osborne-Bertie group and the followers of the Earl of Bath.[1] The claims of business were never far away, and on September 18 he had to drag himself painfully from Mimms to Wimbledon in order that he might attend the King on the following day at Hampton Court and give his advice about the meeting of Parliament. The effort proved unavailing, for he was unable to be present at Council, and on September 20 he was again too ill to attend in his place in the House of Lords ; but the further adjournment of Parliament for a month was entirely in accordance with his wishes.[2]

Nevertheless during this period his prospects were steadily improving. For some time the inner circle of advisers had consisted of a singularly well-balanced group, Halifax and Carmarthen, the Whig Shrewsbury and the Tory Nottingham, with Lord Portland to represent the Dutch interests of William.[3] But the events of the past session had done not a little to weaken both the ascendancy of Halifax within that group and the King's confidence in the principles on which the group was based. Unpopular though Carmarthen might be,[4] William had found that Halifax was more unpopular still. Injurious to the royal dignity and authority though reliance on one party alone might prove, it seemed doubtful whether it could produce worse results than the delay and confusion which appeared inseparable from the policy of balancing. As early as July William, who was thoroughly disgusted with the violence of the Whigs, was toying with the idea of basing his Government chiefly on the support of the Church party, and thereafter Halifax

---

[1] *Luttrell*, i. 582.

[2] *L.J.*, xiv. 319 ; Carmarthen to Nottingham, September 17, 1689, in *Finch MSS.*, ii. 246-7. The Lord President did not attend Council at all between September 2 and October 14 (P.C. Reg., vol. 73).

[3] *Luttrell*, i. 568. These five are referred to as the English Junto in *Hist. MSS. Com.*, xiv. 3, p. 118.

[4] On William's rather extravagant ideas on this point see his remark to Halifax as late as February 1690 [surely not 1689 as Miss Foxcroft suggests] that the Lord President " could never keep of a year from being attaqued " (Spencer House Journals in Foxcroft, *Halifax*, ii. 220).

watched with jealous eyes the development of the project.[1]
During the autumn recess the possibility of a dissolution of
Parliament was being openly discussed.[2] There could be little
doubt that this would mean a modification of the royal policy
in the direction desired by the Tories and the Church interest,
and as early as August 27 Shrewsbury, the first of the Whigs
to take alarm and the least attached to the Government by
any considerations of personal interest, was offering his resignation to the King.[3]

It was therefore in a somewhat different frame of mind that
Carmarthen approached the next meeting of Parliament on
October 19, and the events of the session soon justified his
hopes. Lord Halifax considered it advisable to decline the
office of Speaker,[4] and as the Great Seal was in commission the
King appointed Sir Robert Atkyns, Chief Baron of the Exchequer, to perform the duties of Lord Chancellor in the House
of Lords.[5] But the rancour of the Whigs was no whit allayed.
The operations of the summer in Ireland, at sea and on the
Continent, had met with little success, and the Houses made it
their chief object not merely to hunt down those who were to
blame, but to discover the authors of past offences such as the
attack on the town charters and the executions of 1683. Every
effort was made to implicate Halifax, again, one may suspect,
with the connivance of the Lord President. The attempt was
a complete failure, but the inevitable result of the constant
strife between Halifax and the Whigs was to weaken the
credit of them both, and to raise correspondingly that of Carmarthen and the Tories. On November 23 a vigorous effort
was made in the House of Lords to add to a new Bill of Rights
a clause declaring all pardons invalid in cases of impeachment ;
but this appears to have been the only attack directed against
the Lord President during the whole course of the session, and

---

[1] *Ibid.*, p. 227, and *passim* thereafter ; *Clarendon Correspondence*, ii. 296-7.

[2] *Finch MSS.*, ii. 247.

[3] His letter, pleading illness, is printed in *Shrewsbury Correspondence*,
pp. 6-9.

[4] His demission of this office and his early retirement were anticipated by
October 10 (*Clarendon Correspondence*, ii. 292).

[5] *L.J.*, xiv. 319-20.

it was heavily defeated.[1] Early in December a report was
current that Carmarthen was to be made Lord Treasurer and
his ally Nottingham Lord Chancellor ; and though William
assured Halifax that he would never put the Treasury in Carmarthen's hands the report fairly reflects his altered standing
with the Government.[2]

In truth William was utterly tired of his Whig Parliament.
The animosities which had wrecked so much business in the
spring had suffered no diminution during the recess. In
spite of all the pressure he could bring to bear, the bill of
indemnity for past offences, which alone, he considered, could
provide the basis of a stable settlement, showed no sign of
passing the Commons. The supplies voted had been quite
insufficient for the needs of the Government, and in the midst
of the incessant wrangling there seemed little prospect of getting
any more.

About the middle of December, accordingly, the King
desired Shrewsbury to provide him with a speech requiring
Parliament to adjourn for a month. The reason put forward,
which had the support of Nottingham, was that so many of
the Tory country gentlemen had retired from town to spend
Christmas with their families that the business of the Commons
could not be properly conducted. On this very ground, as well
as that of expediency, Shrewsbury combated the proposal,
insisting that a lengthy adjournment would practically mean a
declaration in favour of the Tories and an abandonment of the
true policy of alliance with the Whigs.[3] In his attitude he had
the support of a certain section of the Tories themselves, who,
foreseeing not an adjournment but a dissolution, argued that
William before taking any step should make a further effort to
secure sufficient supplies to tide over the period till a new
Parliament could be elected.[4] William allowed himself to be
persuaded and Parliament for the moment continued.

[1] After long debate the voting was 50 to 17 against the clause. Among the
twelve peers who protested were both the Earl of Bath and his son Lord
Lansdowne (*L.J.*, xiv. 351 ; *House of Lords MSS.*, 1689-90, p. 345).

[2] *Luttrell*, i. 617 ; Spencer House Journals in Foxcroft, *Halifax*, ii. 242.

[3] His letter to the King, dated December 22, is in *Shrewsbury Correspondence*,
pp. 14-15.

[4] Trevor's letter in *Dalrymple*, App., ii. 80-4.

His leniency, however, was ill-requited. On January 2 William Sacheverell proposed to add to the bill then before the Commons restoring the charters which had been forfeited under Charles and James a clause excluding from municipal office for seven years all officials who had played any part in the surrender of these charters. So scanty was the attendance of country gentlemen that this immense proscription of Tories was carried by a majority of two to one, and the bill was ordered to be engrossed.[1] Two days later the third reading was appointed for January 10, and this short delay, though obtained with the greatest difficulty from the triumphant Whigs, was deemed so little likely to lead to a change in the attitude of the Commons that Carmarthen, apparently with the approval of the King, began to muster his forces with a view to securing the rejection of the obnoxious clause in the Lords.[2]

Fortunately his efforts proved unnecessary. By the appointed day so great a muster of country gentlemen had taken place that in a debate lasting till after ten o'clock in the evening the Tories more than held their own. At an early stage Sir Walter Yonge roused much ill-feeling by declaring that nobody could be against the clause except " such as approved of all the villainies of the surrenderers." Sir Henry Goodricke was so incensed as to threaten to withdraw from the House, and would have called the offender to the bar had he not been restrained by the argument that his objections, coming some time after the offence, were too late. " Yonge is a young gentleman," declared Sir Thomas Clarges, and with this feeble jest the incident was allowed to pass. Nevertheless the main practical point made by Goodricke, that the clause was so widely drawn as to exclude nearly all those who normally served on corporations, was felt to be sound, and under the leadership of Sacheverell himself, who had never gone as far as some of his followers, the Whigs endeavoured to meet it by suggesting various modifications. One after another, however, these were voted down, the original Tory majority of five steadily increasing on each occasion ; and when eventually the

---

[1] *C.J.*, x. 323.   The voting was 133 to 68.
[2] *Clarendon Correspondence*, ii. 301.

clause itself was put to the vote it was rejected without a division.[1]

In William's eyes this outburst of Whig fanaticism was the last straw. At home no settlement appeared possible so long as the existing Parliament remained. Abroad everything was going wrong, and yet he was denied the means to put things right. When he proposed to go in person to Holland all the ministers to whom he declared his intention, Carmarthen among them, protested in the strongest possible manner.[2] When in view of their remonstrances he resolved instead to take charge of the campaign in Ireland he was informed that both Houses of Parliament would vote addresses against his doing so. On January 25 the expected address was moved in the House of Lords, and the debate upon it was adjourned to January 27.[3] Before the discussion could be resumed on that day the King appeared in the Lords, summoned the Commons before him, and prorogued Parliament to April 2. On February 6 Parliament was dissolved, and another was summoned to meet on March 20.[4]

[1] *C.J.*, x. 329 ; *Grey*, ix. 510-20. A contemporary list, giving the names of those who were believed to have supported the Sacheverell Clause, is printed *infra*, iii. 164-72.

[2] *Burnet*, ii. 39-40. At one time, apparently, it was suggested that Carmarthen himself should go to Holland, accompanied by Nottingham, to meet the confederate ministers at the Hague (*Luttrell*, i. 601).

[3] *L.J.*, xiv. 425-6. Halifax was informed by the Duke of Bolton that Carmarthen drew up the address and then spoke against it (Foxcroft, *Halifax*, ii. 244, note 7). If there is any truth whatever in the story the probable explanation is that Carmarthen was using such credit as he still had with the Whigs to lure them to their destruction.

[4] *L.J.*, xiv. 428-9.

CHAPTER XX

SUCCESS, 1690–3

THE first year of the new reign had been a period of dissatisfaction and disillusionment for all concerned. Of the enthusiasm with which the Revolution had at first been acclaimed scarcely a trace at the beginning of 1690 remained. The Whigs were furious at being baulked of their revenge for the persecution of the previous eight years. The Tories were indignant that after the sacrifices they had made in the common cause they should be reproached with the misdeeds of the Government they had helped to overthrow. Both parties were aggrieved that they had not been allowed to monopolise the administration under the new system. William bitterly accused his new subjects of ingratitude, and as he surveyed the condition of Ireland, where Ulster alone recognised his authority, wondered gloomily whether in the Continental struggle on which his heart was set his recently acquired kingdoms were to prove an asset or a liability. The English people retorted by denouncing William as a foreigner who had established himself as ruler of their country simply in order to serve his own ends. The very evils which the Revolution had been intended to abolish, they declared, had been magnified. The standing army had increased ; the Habeas Corpus Act, only threatened by James, had been suspended by William ; the Church seemed in as much danger from Dissenters as it had previously been from Catholics. Discontent as a result spread everywhere ; the higher clergy refused to recognise the new sovereigns ; Jacobitism stalked unchallenged in the streets.[1]

From this depressing chaos emerged clearly the one salient fact that the methods of government advocated by Halifax and adopted by William had proved quite impracticable. A

---

[1] *Ranke*, iv. 579–80.

policy of trimming based upon a coalition ministry would probably have broken down in any case ; but William had neither the tact and personal charm, nor the knowledge of the English constitution and of English politicians, which would have been necessary to give it even a chance of success. Efficiency in government, it was plain, could be secured only by placing greater reliance on one or other of the principal political parties, and William's task was simply to determine which should be preferred.

It shows how thoroughly the Whigs had alienated him by their extravagances that although they were his own firmest supporters, although they were admittedly more in favour of the war than their political opponents, and although he habitually exaggerated their importance and strength in the country, it was yet to the Tories that he turned. The main reason for his decision, however, is probably to be found in the influence of Carmarthen. William was still too inexperienced to take the internal affairs of England into his own hands, and in view of his probable absence in Ireland or on the Continent required a minister on whom he could absolutely rely. Granted that Halifax was impossible, Carmarthen, as a year earlier, was the only alternative. Although now definitely associated with the Tories, he was not as obnoxious to the Whigs as many of his fellows, and about him there was no trace of Jacobitism. Moreover for the system of government which William proposed to adopt he was specially fitted. Without Halifax's fertility in devising expedients and reconciling discordant views, he possessed in a much higher degree the determination necessary to fix upon one settled course of action and the energy to carry it into effect ; while in the art of marshalling a parliamentary party in support of his policy he was absolutely without a rival.

The first serious step in the direction of a Tory Government was the prorogation and dissolution of the Convention, for which contemporaries, probably with justice, believed that Carmarthen was largely responsible ; [1] but more significant was the resignation of Halifax on February 8. In that event

---

[1] *Evelyn*, January 12, 1690. William confided his intention to prorogue to one person only, who was probably Carmarthen (*Macaulay*, iv. 1792).

was involved not merely the triumph of one statesman over his rival but the victory of one system of government over another. William would greatly have preferred to retain Halifax in office. His acceptance of his resignation was a practical admission that he could not both incline to the Tories and continue the policy of balancing in which he had hitherto placed his confidence. As early as December Carmarthen appears to have anticipated events by offering the Privy Seal to the Earl of Chesterfield, and on Chesterfield's refusal he is said to have made the same offer to the Duke of Bolton ;[1] but in the end Halifax's place had to be supplied by commissioners, of whom two were Tories and one a Whig.[2]

Other changes soon followed. Realising at last that the post of Lord High Treasurer was quite beyond his power to obtain, Carmarthen contented himself with securing an indirect influence over finance through the appointment of Sir John Lowther as First Lord of a reconstituted Treasury Commission. At the same time he was personally gratified by the admission of Sir Henry Goodricke to the Privy Council. The Admiralty Commission was remodelled in the Tory interest, the Earl of Pembroke being placed at its head, while similar alterations were effected in the local administration, the lieutenancy of London especially being purged of Whigs by the Lord President's ally Bishop Compton, in whom the refusal of Sancroft to recognise the new sovereigns had revived the hope of himself becoming Archbishop of Canterbury.[3]

In advocating these alterations Carmarthen had been relying upon a favourable result for the Church party at the coming general election. Probably at his instigation, a mass meeting of Tory members of Parliament held immediately after the prorogation had made a formal offer of their services to the King ; while William for his part seized every opportunity of declaring his steadfast determination to support the established laws and religious institutions of the country.[4] The results

---

[1] Foxcroft, *Halifax*, ii. 109-15.

[2] William Cheyne, Sir John Knatchbull, and Sir William Pulteney.

[3] *Burnet*, ii. 40-1 ; *Luttrell*, ii. 21, 25.

[4] *Evelyn*, January 12, 1690 ; *Clarendon Correspondence*, ii. 304.

of the alliance thus cemented were soon apparent. The factious conduct of the Whigs had alienated not merely the King but also popular opinion throughout the country, and at the polls a tendency speedily became manifest to elect moderate men inclining towards the Tory side. Some of Carmarthen's personal following, it is true, were seriously embarrassed by the tactics of the Whigs in publishing the names of the " Jacobites " who had voted with the minority on February 5, 1689, against declaring the throne vacant ;[1] and it was at least partly on this account that the Earl of Danby found it advisable to abandon his candidature both in Hertfordshire and in York City.[2] But the Lord President's brother Charles was returned at Hull ; many of his henchmen were elected in Yorkshire ; and the Berties as usual secured several seats in Lincolnshire, Oxfordshire and Wiltshire.[3] The whole character of Parliament was changed, and instead of being predominantly Whig it became at least moderately Tory.

Of these developments it was Carmarthen's function to make the most he could in the interests of the Government, and even before the elections had been completed he had returned once more to the familiar task of party-building. In the Lords, he estimated, some 45 peers and 5 bishops might be expected to follow his lead, while 34 peers and 3 bishops would probably join Halifax in opposition. Of the situation in the Commons he was by no means so certain, for many years had elapsed since he had been in really close touch with that body ; but there was at least a solid block of about 50 members,

[1] *A Letter to a Friend upon the Dissolution of the late Parliament and the Calling of a new one ; together with a List of those that were against making the Prince and Princess of Orange King and Queen.* The list of names is printed *infra,* iii. 164-72, with a note of those who lost their seats at this time. The general inclination to favour the Tories is shown by the fact that out of the total of 150 only 56 failed to secure re-election for the same constituency, and even of these 9 were elected elsewhere. The Tories later carried the condemnation of the pamphlet in the House of Commons by 180 votes to 156 (*C.J.*, x. 398).

[2] *Hist. MSS. Com.*, vii. 482 ; George Prickett to Carmarthen, February 19, and to Christopher Tancred, February 22, Richard Sheldon to Charles Osborne, February 17, and Robert Waller to Carmarthen, March 12, 1690, in Leeds MSS., Packet 14.

[3] *Return of Members of Parliament*, i. 567, 568, 570.

including his own relatives, on whom he felt he could safely rely.[1]

The real problem of the Court party in the Commons, however, was in Carmarthen's eyes one not so much of numbers as of leadership and organisation. Both Secretaries of State and nearly all the Tory members of the Privy Council were in the Lords. Lowther and Goodricke had shown little capacity for party management, and were in any case superior to the more sordid tasks which it was apt to involve. Henry Powle as Speaker had inclined too much towards the Whigs, and was known in any case to be in danger of being unseated on petition. Recourse was therefore had to Sir John Trevor, " a bold and dexterous man," who had frequently been of service to Carmarthen during his period of power under Charles II, and who now undertook to manage the Court interest, " provided he was furnished with such sums of money as might purchase some votes." In the reign of James similar activities had earned for him an unsavoury reputation, and when on March 20 Sir John Lowther proposed to the newly assembled House of Commons that he should be chosen Speaker the motion accordingly roused some outcry among the Whigs ; but the majority was so obviously on his side that it was not considered worth while to challenge a division, and he was immediately conducted to the chair by his proposer and Sir Henry Goodricke.[2]

At the same time as Carmarthen was thus providing for the conduct of Government business in the Commons he was endeavouring by every means in his power to improve still further the position in the Lords. Doubtful peers were systematically canvassed, and some even of those considered hostile were approached. The Earl of Danby was summoned to the Upper House as Baron Osborne of Kiveton, took his seat on the first day Parliament met, and for a time attended with exemplary regularity.[3] Somewhat later Lord Willoughby

---

[1] The two lists are printed *infra*, iii. 173-8. From the names included it is clear that Carmarthen, while looking for support mainly to the Tories, had no thought of abandoning all association with the Whigs.

[2] *C.J.*, x. 347 ; *Burnet*, ii. 42 ; *Ranke*, iv. 583-4 ; Foxcroft, *Halifax*, ii. 136, note 1.

[3] The warrant for his summons is dated March 3, and the summons itself March 14, 1690 (*Cal. S.P. Dom.*, 1689-90, p. 492 ; *L.J.*, xiv. 431).

de Eresby was similarly called up, and surrendered his seat in the House of Commons to a younger brother, Peregrine Bertie.[1]

Having thus prepared the way, Carmarthen boldly attacked what both he and the King considered the vital problem, the problem of finance. On March 21 the King in his opening speech to both Houses strongly emphasised the desirability of a settlement of the revenue, and on March 22, immediately the speech had been formally reported to the Commons, Sir John Lowther moved that the House should go into committee to consider it. The procedure suggested was generally considered too precipitate, but on the main point there was little opposition, and it was in a sympathetic and helpful spirit that the House on March 27 eventually took up the general question of supply. The official Court motion, repeatedly brought forward by Lowther, was that the regular revenue should be granted to William and Mary for their lives, and in support of this proposal Carmarthen marshalled his entire following. In a particularly vehement speech Sir Edmund Jennings declared that any failure to settle a sufficient revenue on the King would mean either " popery and slavery on the one hand or anarchy on the other." William Ettricke reflected bitterly on the suggestion that the King should be kept " as it were at board wages," and argued that the House could not " in justice and gratitude do less for him than for his predecessors." Sir Henry Goodricke's attitude to the revenue was the same. " You settle it," he declared to the House, " only for the lives of your deliverers."

Had measures as determined and energetic as these been adopted by the Government a year earlier it is at least possible that they might have proved successful ; but the debates in the Convention had given such currency to the idea of a revenue limited to a period of years that there was now little hope of it being abandoned. Probably Carmarthen himself recognised this, for the King's speech included an offer, against which he must otherwise have protested, to allow the revenue to be used as a fund of credit for supply for the war. It was one of the accepted maxims of the time that such a fund required a revenue for a fixed period, and on this point all who were

---

[1] *L.J.*, xiv. 468 ; *Return of Members of Parliament*, i. 567.

afraid of going too far in support of the King inevitably concentrated. Even Sir Robert Cotton, while expressing his
gratitude to William, declared that " there must be some
certain number of years to have a fund." The final decision,
in consequence, was of the nature of a compromise. On
March 28 the Commons resolved that the hereditary revenues
enjoyed by James II were vested in William and Mary, that
the parliamentary Excise should be granted to them for life,
but that the Customs should be granted only for a period of
four years from the following Christmas.[1]

Second in importance in William's eyes only to the problem
of the revenue was that of indemnity for past offences, to which
emphatic reference was also made in the speech from the
throne. On this point the Lord President was in entire agreement with his sovereign ; and throughout the many debates
on the subject in the Convention he had consistently thrown
his weight on the side of a reasonable settlement.[2] He was
now given the honour of presenting in the House of Lords an
Act of Grace, which granted a free pardon to all but a small
number of specially culpable individuals. Without serious
difficulty the Act secured the single reading which such a
measure required in the Lords, and shortly afterwards was
similarly approved by the Commons.[3]

These were substantial successes, and bear witness both to
the skilful management of the Lord President and to the
general disgust with the previous conduct of the Whigs in
connection with the issues involved. There were other issues,
however, where it was the attitude of the Tories that required
justification, and by bringing these forward the Whigs were
able to put Carmarthen's capacity to an even more severe test.

On March 26 the Duke of Bolton introduced in the Lords a

---

[1] *C.J.*, x. 358-9 ; *Grey*, x. 4-23 ; *Burnet*, ii. 42-3.

[2] See especially the debates of March 25, May 14, June 15, 1689, and
January 21, 1690, in *Grey*, x. 186-8, 244-52, 313-27, 538-47.

[3] *L.J.*, xiv. 502-6 ; *C.J.*, x. 423 ; *House of Lords MSS.*, 1690-1, p. 87.
There was some opposition in the Lords, but only from the Earl of Huntingdon
and the Bishop of St. David's, who were themselves among those excluded by
the Act (*Clarendon Correspondence*, ii. 313). The Commons objected to the
unusual procedure of the Lords in informing them that they had accepted the
Act *nemine contradicente*. A conference between the two Houses was desired,
but the adjournment taking place at this time nothing more was heard of the
matter.

bill declaring the Acts of the Convention " to be of full force
and effect by the laws of the realm," and recognising William
and Mary as " rightful and lawful " King and Queen. Immediately the more rigid Tories were up in arms. Acts passed
by an assembly which had not been summoned by royal writ
could not, they maintained, be laws ; nothing done by such
an assembly could give any one a lawful title to the crown ;
and the existing occupants of the throne could not in any case
be described as " rightful " sovereigns. The attitude of the
extreme Tories thus remained substantially what it had been
a year earlier, but, as was soon to appear, with a significant
difference, shown in the fact that the real weight of their attack
was directed exclusively against the first clause in the bill.
Now that William had thrown in his lot with the Church
interest there was not the same inclination to cast doubt on
his title. What the Tories wished to question was the legal
competence of the previous Whig Parliament rather than the
constitutional right of the previously Whig King.

With this attitude Carmarthen unquestionably had some
sympathy, and he began by opposing the bill ; but his object
in doing so was not so much to bring about its rejection as to
secure amendments which would make it more generally
acceptable. On April 3 he himself proposed as a substitute
for the first clause an entirely different form of words by which
the Acts of the Convention were to be "ratified, confirmed and
enacted and declared to have the full force and strength of Acts
of Parliament." To this, however, the Whigs would not
agree. On April 4 they rejected the word " confirmed " by
34 votes to 25, and insisted on the retention of the word " declared " by 33 votes to 27. The Lord President then abandoned his amendment, and on April 5 voted with the majority
when a Whig version of the clause worked out in committee
failed by 36 votes to 30 to secure the assent of the House.

Having thus maintained the ascendancy of the Tories and
prevented the division which was constantly threatening to
appear in their ranks, Carmarthen immediately thereafter
allowed the dictates of common sense to prevail, and in the
strongest possible terms indicated to the Lords the evil consequences which must follow a rejection of the bill. Between one

body of men who considered the Acts of the previous Parliament to be lawful, and another body of men who were quite prepared to make them lawful, agreement, he insisted, should not be difficult to reach. So impressed were the Lords by his reasoning, and so bewildered, perhaps, by four days of " politick distinctions," far exceeding " as to nicenes . . . the philosophicall distinctions of the schollmen," that without a division they declared it their opinion " that all the Acts passed in the last Parliament . . . were and are good laws to all intents and purposes whatsoever."

On the basis of this resolution a compromise was quickly effected. Apparently without dispute it was agreed that the clause recognising William and Mary should be modelled on that in the Bill of Rights, and with this object in view the original Recognition Bill was entirely recast. The Whigs accepted the word " enacted " instead of " declared," and the omission of the phrase " rightful and lawful " applied to the sovereigns. The Tories on their part rather illogically agreed to the use of the words " were and are " in the case both of the sovereigns and of the laws. On April 8 the amended bill passed the Lords and was sent down to the Commons. Among the nineteen peers who protested Carmarthen noted with relief as many opponents as supporters of the Government.[1]

In the Lower House a bitter struggle was anticipated, and expectations were so far fulfilled that on the second reading of the bill on April 9 much criticism was directed by Clarges, Musgrave, and even Sir Joseph Tredenham against the use of the words " were and are." Lowther and Goodricke had difficulty in holding the Court party together, and were reduced to vague exhortations that all should " lay hands to the Government," and that " disputes ought to be avoided." But the representative chamber was much more affected than the peers by the practical argument, set forth by Wharton, and more ably by the Solicitor-General, Sir John Somers, that if the Acts of the previous Parliament were invalid the Parliament then in session had no legal existence. As a result Lowther, who had previously moved for a third reading on the following

---

[1] *L.J.*, xiv. 438-60 ; *House of Lords MSS.*, 1690-1, pp. 1-7 ; *Hatton Correspondence*, ii. 146-7 ; *Portland MSS.*, iii. 446.

day, owned himself convinced that it should be taken at once, and without a division the bill was accepted as it stood.[1]

Scarcely had this difficulty been surmounted, however, when the whole controversy was in substance renewed by another Whig measure, introduced by Thomas Wharton in the Commons on April 25, requiring all officials formally to abjure King James. Many Tories who were loyal supporters of William and Mary would have refused to take any oath to that effect, and the prospect was thus raised that the Government might be discredited if the bill were rejected, while the Tories would almost certainly be divided if it passed. Fortunately the opponents of the bill could argue with considerable justice that the main principle it contained was already embodied in the oath of allegiance, and that the multiplication of needless oaths was strongly to be deprecated. " Where you put a buttress," declared Clarges, " there the building is weak. . . . Nothing will tend more to bring in King James than this bill." By 192 votes to 178 the motion to commit was lost, and by the same number of votes to 165 the bill itself was rejected.[2]

With this summary dismissal of Wharton's proposals Carmarthen was by no means in entire agreement, and there are clear indications that he considered they might, with judicious modification, have formed the basis of a valuable measure.[3] On May 1, accordingly, probably at his instigation, a somewhat similar bill was introduced in the Lords, the feature of which was the abandonment of an actual abjuration of James, and the substitution for it of a declaration, which it was hoped Whigs and Tories alike would be prepared to make, recognising William and Mary as sovereigns " of right . . . by the laws of the realm," and undertaking to stand by them and their Government against James.[4] Almost immediately, however, it became apparent that the Tories had already given away

[1] C.J., x. 371, 373 ; Grey, x. 45-52 ; Burnet, ii. 41-2. "The leaders of the Tory party drew in their followers (before they were aware of it) to consent to it " (Supplement to Burnet, p. 340).

[2] C.J., x. 388-91 ; Grey, x. 73-87 ; Burnet, ii. 43-5 ; Portland MSS., iii. 447.

[3] " The Church party would have alter'd it and framed it better, but that was oppos'd by the other side " (Luttrell, ii. 35).

[4] See in particular Lowther's speech of April 26 in the Commons, where he claims to have Carmarthen's authority for what he is saying (Grey, x. 84). The speech seems clearly to foreshadow this bill.

their case. With bland effrontery Lord Wharton now came
forward with the argument that the multiplication of needless
declarations was strongly to be deprecated. The Earl of
Macclesfield entirely concurred.   In vain the Bishop of London
endeavoured to reconcile a general opposition to unnecessary
oaths with support of this particular declaration.   His ingenuous admission that " there was not, nor could be made, an
oath to the present Government that he would not take " was
greeted with shouts of derisive laughter, and even the presence
of the King at the debates could not secure the passage of the
bill in a form which the Tories could accept.[1]

At an early stage the original declaration was rejected by
38 votes to 35 ; but on May 8 Carmarthen secured the adoption
of a new declaration drawn up by himself.   To this, however,
the opposition insisted on adding a definite repudiation of
allegiance to King James ; while on May 12 they also carried
a proposal that the declaration should be required of all
ecclesiastics as well as of civil and military officials and members
of Parliament. The task of drawing up a clause imposing the
declaration in accordance with these resolutions was entrusted
to a committee which included the Lord President ; but it is
clear that the alterations effected had greatly diminished his
zeal for the measure. William was equally disappointed and
withdrew his support, the committee never reported to the
House, and the bill died a natural death.[2]

If this was a failure on Carmarthen's part it was a small one,
and constituted scarcely a blemish on his general conduct of
the session.   So successful had his tactics proved in getting rid
of the spirit of factious opposition prevalent in the previous
Parliament that from first to last only one serious attack was
made upon the ministry, and even that had a somewhat
ignominious issue. On May 14 the Commons resolved themselves into committee of the whole House to consider means of
securing the safety of the kingdom during the King's impending
absence, and soon found themselves on dangerous ground.
Sir John Thompson moved that all those who had advised the

---

[1] Dartmouth's note in *Burnet* (ed. 1833), iv. 79.

[2] *L.J.*, xiv. 481-501 ; *House of Lords MSS.*, 1690-1, pp. 38-44 ; *Supplement
to Burnet*, p. 342 ; Foxcroft, *Halifax*, ii. 127.

King to dissolve the last Parliament should be dismissed from his Council. Charles Hutchinson considered that ministers who had been impeached were not fit to be near the King. It was left, however, to Carmarthen's own relative, John Grenville, second son of the Earl of Bath, to mention him by name, and in a speech which raked up all the old charges against him to propose that he should be removed.[1] Shadrack Vincent retorted rather neatly by moving that the Earl of Bath should also be dismissed for his conduct in the reign of James II ; but when Sir Edward Seymour, with all the rancour of a friend turned enemy, supported Grenville's motion the position began to look more serious.[2] The general sense of the House, however, was entirely opposed to the course which the debate was taking, and after some warm speeches had been made in the Lord President's defence the whole matter was quietly dropped.[3]

In singling out Carmarthen in this way the malcontents did no more than recognise the position which he had built up for himself. Since the resignation of Halifax his supremacy within the Government had become steadily more and more assured. In February his growing influence at Court was marked by his removal to the apartments in St. James's Palace formerly occupied by the King and Queen.[4] In March it was popularly reported that he was to be made a Duke, and his ally Lord Nottingham a Marquis.[5] In April and May his

---

[1] For some months the Grenvilles had been acting with the Whigs, but their extreme hostility to the Osbornes at this time was almost entirely the result of some family quarrel proceeding from old disagreements between Lord and Lady Lansdowne (*infra*, ii. 161). In the autumn the King's guards and the authority of the House of Lords scarcely sufficed to prevent a duel between Lansdowne and Danby (*L.J.*, xiv. 527-40 ; *House of Lords MSS.*, 1690-1, p. 151 ; *Luttrell*, ii. 118 ; *Portledge Papers*, p. 91).

[2] Seymour's hostility was purely personal, and inspired largely by jealousy of Carmarthen's power and influence. As early as March 27, during the debates on the revenue, he had declaimed with indecent violence against the authority exercised in turn by Halifax and Carmarthen. " As this the last Parliament," he declared, " so another governs this ; the White Horse rides one stage, the Black another." Goodricke retorted in kind by suggesting to him that dislike both of a white horse and of a black horse was no reason why he should ride upon an ass (*Grey*, x. 14).

[3] *C.J.*, x. 413 ; *Grey*, x. 139-45 ; *Hatton Correspondence*, ii. 149 ; *Luttrell*, ii. 42.

[4] Foxcroft, *Halifax*, ii. 112, note 5.

[5] *Cal. S.P. Dom.*, 1689-90, p. 517.

credit rose as the parliamentary session proved more and more
favourable to the Court, and with the beginning of June his
triumph seemed complete when the Earl of Shrewsbury, the
last important Whig and his own chief rival in the ministry,
resigned in disgust at his growing ascendancy.[1] On the very
day on which the seals were delivered the King finally
nominated the Council of Nine on whose advice the Queen
was to rely during his absence, and presented them to Mary.
Among the nine the Lord President was the person whom
he specially recommended to her.[2] For the next three years
Carmarthen was to remain unquestionably the first minister of
the Crown.

His second period of power, however, bore little resemblance
to his first. Never at any time was he able to dominate
William III as he had dominated Charles II. His colleagues
in the ministry were no longer the mere creatures of his power,
but statesmen of real or pretended ability who strongly resented
any suggestion of subordination to him. Above all he was
deprived of the prestige which he might easily have won by the
successful administration of a department of his own, and
compelled to justify his claim to pre-eminence by his general
capacity as a counsellor. This was the most unfortunate
feature of his position, not merely for himself but for his
country. As a " minister without portfolio " he was not in
his proper sphere, for with the main problems of policy which
confronted the Government he was scarcely competent to deal.
His knowledge of foreign affairs was elementary. He had never
had any real experience of warfare either on land or on sea.
It is even to be suspected that the new financial problems to
which operations of unprecedented magnitude were soon to
give rise were beyond his capacity to solve. Thus his appropriate function in the ministry might seem to have been that
of uniting and inspiring the efforts of men who possessed more

[1] Foxcroft, *Halifax*, ii. 250-1 ; *Burnet*, ii. 45 ; *Clarendon Correspondence*,
ii. 316. According to Queen Mary the immediate cause of Shrewsbury's
resignation, which had been impending for some time, was " a dispute he had
had with Lord President before the King, in which the King followed Lord
Presidents advise before his " (*Doebner*, p. 28).

[2] At the same time as William advised Mary to rely on Carmarthen he
advised Carmarthen how to conduct himself towards Mary (Dartmouth's
note in *Burnet*, ed. 1833, iv. 241 ; *Doebner*, pp. 28-9).

specialised ability than himself. But for this task he was almost completely unfitted. His relations with the majority of his colleagues were bad. Some had old causes of enmity with him ; many were suspicious of his policy, and nearly all were jealous of his ascendancy within the Government.

In the spring of 1690, however, the essential weakness of Carmarthen's position was not yet apparent, and William had scarcely left London to conduct his campaign in Ireland when the old statesman made a bold effort to get the control of affairs entirely into his own hands. Queen Mary, who had been entrusted with the executive government during the King's absence, was young and inexperienced, dreadfully afraid of the responsibilities she was being called upon to face and of the day of judgment which awaited her if she failed to play her part with success. Over her mind the " undertaking spirit " of the Lord President seemed destined to establish a complete ascendancy. Whatever problems might arise he always be- lieved he had the correct solution, and always had the energy and determination to put his solution in force. From the very first he was in constant attendance on the Queen, anxious to save her the smallest inconvenience and to monopolise her entirely himself.[1]

In the end, however, as Carmarthen well knew, Mary's attitude was bound to be dictated by William, and he therefore endeavoured to bring all the regular channels of communication with the King under his own supervision. Mary had her own private correspondence with William, but her account of affairs he might hope, by judicious representations, to influence. Nottingham, sole Secretary of State since the resignation of Shrewsbury, conducted the official correspondence of the Government ; but Nottingham was one of his allies, and might be trusted in ordinary circumstances to represent his side of the question. Nevertheless to make assurance doubly sure he instituted a regular correspondence of his own, in which he was encouraged by the King, who, one may surmise, was only too glad to obtain a lucid survey of events unencumbered

---

[1] " Lord Carmarthen is upon all occasions afraid of giving me too much trouble, and thinks by little and little to do all " (Queen Mary to the King, June 26/July 6, 1690, in *Dalrymple*, App., ii. 122).

by official verbiage on the one hand or by terms of endearment on the other.[1]

It is difficult to avoid connecting with this the attack made by Carmarthen upon the integrity of Major Wildman, the Postmaster General. The quarrel between them was, it is true, an old one. Although they had once been associated as followers of Buckingham, Wildman was a Whig of the extreme type which Carmarthen specially detested. He had been prominent under the Commonwealth, and had made a fortune out of the estates of Cavaliers ; he had favoured the schemes of Monmouth ; he had endeavoured to use the Revolution as a weapon against the Church. Above all he was occupying at that very moment a post which had been promised to Lord Danby. But there was more in the matter than this would suggest. The Lord President, in his own interest and that of the Tories, was endeavouring to control the correspondence of the Government with the King, with Scotland, and with statesmen elsewhere ; and Wildman was bent upon tapping it in the interest of the Whigs.

Serious trouble had begun a year earlier, when Lionel Copley, then newly appointed Lieutenant-Governor, had taken it upon himself to stop and examine the mails at Hull. The local postmaster, George Mawson, very properly obtained from Wildman a letter requiring Copley to desist from this practice ; but the only result was that he himself was seized by a sergeant and four musketeers, carried to the guard-room, and there tied neck and heels for more than two hours. With these arbitrary proceedings, which were later inquired into and condemned by the House of Commons,[2] it is impossible to

[1] While all William's letters to Mary and Carmarthen and some of his letters to Nottingham have been lost, the majority of the letters to William in all three series have been preserved. Mary's letters are in S.P. Dom., King William's Chest, and have been printed, not always quite accurately, by Dalrymple. Copies of Nottingham's letters are among the Finch Papers at Burley-on-the-Hill, and have been calendared in *Finch MSS.*, vol. ii. Carmarthen's letters, also in King William's Chest, are partly printed by Dalrymple and very badly calendared in *Cal. S.P. Dom.* They are now for the first time printed in full (*infra*, ii. 163 *et seq.*). The earliest letter in each series appears to have been written on June 4, the day of the King's departure from Kensington, and dispatched by Sir Robert Southwell, who delivered it to William at Chester on June 8 (*Finch MSS.*, ii. 287-92).

[2] *C.J.*, x. 191, 265-8.

believe that Carmarthen had any direct connection, and such evidence as exists renders it doubtful whether he had authorised even the seizure of the mails.[1]   Yet it is scarcely to be supposed that Copley would have gone as far as he did unless he had reason to expect some countenance from his official superior, and it is significant that although he was shortly afterwards removed from his command it was only in order to be appointed to the lucrative post of Governor of Maryland.[2] Whatever may be the precise explanation of this curious affair its effect was certainly to increase still further Carmarthen's aversion to Wildman and his desire to have him dismissed. It was even declared, and apparently with good reason, that the Postmaster was tampering with the King's own correspondence. The Lord President was accordingly able to secure the support of Nottingham, Portland and the Queen herself in urging that he should be deprived of his office, although this was not actually done till nearly a year later.[3]

Thus Carmarthen's attempt to establish an exclusive influence over William was only a partial success, and in his dealings with Mary he fared little better.   In the Queen's character were depths which had scarcely yet been sounded, and which came as a surprise to all but her most intimate acquaintances. At whatever cost of trouble and anxiety to herself she refused to become a mere puppet in the hands of any one man or faction, insisted on hearing all sides, applied as well as she could the ideas or instructions of William, and even upon occasion trusted her own judgment.[4]   Nevertheless the Lord President's influence was undoubtedly very great.   In her private memoirs Mary, while acknowledging her obligations to him, notes that he was " of a temper I can never like ; " but when compared with what she has to say of the other members of her Council of Nine this brief comment might almost be

---

[1] Carmarthen to Copley, June 20, 1689, in Leeds MSS., Packet 14.

[2] *Cal. S.P. Dom.*, 1690-1, p. 12 ; *Cal. Treas. Books*, ix. 1431, 1836.

[3] *Correspondentie van Willem III en Bentinck*, part i, i. 123-58 ; *Finch MSS.*, ii. 316, 392 ; Carmarthen to the King, June 13, 16, 26, 1690, *infra*, ii. 163-6, 169 ; Queen Mary to the King, June 26/July 6, July 7/17, 1690, in *Dalrymple*, App., ii. 120-1, 133.

[4] Queen Mary to the King, June 26/July 6, July 10/20, 1690, in *Dalrymple*, App., ii. 122, 136-7.

described as effusive flattery. Devonshire was "weack and obstinate, made a meer tool by a party;" Dorset "to lazy to give himself the trouble of bussiness, so of litle use;" Pembroke "as mad as most of his family;" Nottingham "suspected by most as not true to the Government;" Monmouth "mad," and governed by "his wife who is mader;" Lowther "very honest but weack."[1] In truth Carmarthen was the one thoroughly capable and reliable man in the ministry, and by his energy and determination alone prevented it from breaking down altogether.

This, however, could be accomplished only by unwearied labours, and the summer of 1690 was for him a period of ceaseless activity. Not a department of government was free from his anxious supervision. Jacobite conspiracies, the affairs of Scotland, recruiting for the navy, the operations of the fleet, the raising of the ready money so urgently required both by Mary in England and by William in Ireland, were matters with which he was incessantly concerned.[2] Not content with his duties as Lord Lieutenant of the West Riding, he kept an eye on the local administration everywhere, allaying the discontent of the tinners of Cornwall, urging his relative the Earl of Rutland to accept the Lord Lieutenancy of Leicester, and himself forming one of a temporary commission appointed to act as Lieutenants of Somerset.[3]

On June 30 the defeat of the combined English and Dutch fleet off Beachy Head threw the whole country open to invasion by the French, and in the dark days that followed Carmarthen's efforts were redoubled. Had the Queen not absolutely forbidden him he would himself have gone down to Dover to examine into the condition of the beaten fleet and investigate the cause of its ill-success.[4] When no agreement could be

[1] *Doebner*, pp. 29-30.

[2] *Luttrell*, ii. 48, 79-80 ; Carmarthen to the King, *infra*, ii. 163-89.

[3] Hist. MSS. Com., *Various Collections*, viii. 69-70 ; *Finch MSS.*, ii. 300; *Rutland MSS.*, ii. 129 ; *Cal. S.P. Dom.*, 1690-1, p. 39 ; *infra*, ii. 170-1, 176.

[4] Mary sent Devonshire and Pembroke instead. " I told Lord President, when I named them, that he could not be spared ; but I saw he looked ill satisfied, so that when the council was up I spoke to him, and bid him remember how necessary he was. He said he did not look on himself as so tied but he might go away upon occasions. I told him if he were not by place, yet being the person you had told me whose advice I should follow and rely the most on I could not spare him " (Queen Mary to the King, July 3/13, 1690, in *Dalrymple*, App., ii. 127).

reached as regards a successor to the defeated Admiral Torrington he offered to serve as one of a commission of three to whom
the supreme command should be entrusted.[1] He was among
the first to realise that the French might endeavour to cut off
all communication between England and Ireland, and with
the Queen's consent urged William most strongly to return
home with some of his troops before it was too late.[2] In
raising additional forces for the defence of England he took
a prominent part, his son Danby accepting the command of a
regiment of dragoons which the City of London undertook to
provide.[3] The hurry and confusion of those terrible days is
reflected in the very handwriting of his letters to the King.
From the usual carefully written fair copies they degenerate
for a time into hastily scribbled drafts, for which he considered
it necessary to apologise.[4]

In the end the crisis passed without producing any of the
disastrous results which had been anticipated, but Carmarthen's
activity in meeting it had greatly enhanced his reputation for
loyalty and ability, and immensely strengthened his position
at Court. So completely were his interests now identified
with those of William that before the Irish campaign was over
he decided upon a step which amounted almost to a permanent
guarantee of his devotion to the Revolution settlement. On
the last day of July, while the French fleet was still upon the
coast, the grandson whom he had so long desired was born,
and no sooner had the fear of invasion died away than he wrote
to the King desiring him to stand godfather and give his name
to the child.[5] The actual ceremony had to be postponed for
a month, and the King had eventually to be represented by
the Earl of Pembroke, but it was as William Henry that the
infant Lord Latimer was at length christened on September 12,

---

[1] *Dalrymple*, App., ii. 145-50 ; *Finch MSS.*, ii. 378-9, 382-3 ; *infra*, ii. 173,
176, 183-5. The problem of the command was much complicated by points
of precedence, and by the tendency of nearly all concerned to regard it from a
party standpoint.

[2] Carmarthen to the King, July 6, 7, 9, 13, 15, 1690, *infra*, ii. 173-81.

[3] *Luttrell*, ii. 75, 76 ; *Finch MSS.*, ii. 354-5, 416 ; *Cal. S.P. Dom.*, 1690-1,
pp. 68-70 ; Carmarthen to the King, July 2, 15, 1690, *infra*, ii. 173, 181.

[4] *Infra*, ii. 179.

[5] Carmarthen to the King, August 12, 1690, *infra*, ii. 187.

to become immediately the centre of his grandfather's hopes for the future of his House.[1]

The effect of this, however, as well as of the general policy pursued by the Lord President, was to relegate him to some extent to the middle position which he had occupied during and immediately after the Revolution, and to bring down upon him the enmity of the extreme men of both parties. As early as April Rochester and the high Tories had been alienated by his failure to support that exclusive Anglican domination of which the King's adhesion to the Church interest had given them a fleeting hope.[2] During the summer the extreme Whigs had been similarly alienated by his resolute opposition to the proposals they repeatedly brought forward for a dissolution of Parliament. So confident were the Whigs of a majority at a general election that they offered the Queen an immediate loan of £200,000, to be repaid out of money voted by the new Parliament, on the sole condition that she should effect a dissolution. Mary, however, refused to take so important a step without express instructions from William, and in this determination she was encouraged by Carmarthen, who argued on the one hand that the existing Parliament was perfectly satisfactory, and on the other that a general election would produce nothing but turmoil and inconvenience, as the same men would almost certainly be re-elected.[3] The session which began on October 2, accordingly, shortly after the King's return from Ireland, was marked by a series of attacks upon the Lord President, inspired by very different motives, and coming from very different quarters in the political world.

The particular grievance put forward by the malcontent Tories was the imprisonment of Lord Torrington, whose failure at Beachy Head had been followed by his commitment to the Tower. This was denounced as a base attempt on the part of

[1] Carmarthen to Lady Danby, September 3, 1690, *infra*, ii. 221-2 ; *Luttrell*, ii. 103.

[2] " The White Marquis and I are quite out, so I thinke he is with Lord Nottingham, and that he is (I mean the White) quite struck up with the Dissenters, and all the fine promises concerning the Church and the good bishop quite vanished " (Rochester to Clarendon, April 15, 1690, in Hunterian MSS. at Glasgow University).

[3] Queen Mary to the King, July 15/25, August 7/17, 12/22, 1690, in *Dalrymple*, App., ii. 141, 157, 159.

the Government to propitiate the Dutch, who declared that their squadron in the allied fleet had been deliberately left to bear the brunt of the contest ; and an ill-assorted coalition in the Lords, led by Halifax and Rochester, endeavoured to use it as a weapon against the whole Council of Nine, and especially against the Lord President. Although national feeling, however, and concern for the privileges of the House enabled them to carry in the Lords, by a majority of 32 to 17, a resolution against the commitment, they were unable to proceed any further, and their proposal that the Nine should be formally censured was not even seriously considered.[1]

The attack of the Whigs upon Carmarthen was more personal and more dangerous in character. Immediately after the Revolution the Earls of Peterborough and Salisbury had been committed to the Tower, and in the autumn session of 1689 they had both been impeached of high treason in joining the Church of Rome. On the first day Parliament met they now petitioned the Lords to be discharged, on the ground partly of the Act of Grace which had meanwhile been passed, and partly of the intervening dissolution and prorogations of Parliament, as a result of which they maintained their impeachments had lapsed. This was immediately seized upon by Shrewsbury and the Whigs as a pretext for raising once more the problem in which Carmarthen was so vitally interested, whether impeachments were in any way affected by a dissolution or prorogation, and a practical decision that they were not affected was reached when it was resolved that the Earls should not be discharged but should be admitted to bail.[2]

The only effect was to enable Carmarthen to give an exhibition of his skill in the art of parliamentary management. On the King he knew he could rely, for William was interested in maintaining his Act of Grace, and in any case was opposed to severity towards Catholics or punitive measures of any kind. A division list of the Lords on the question whether the Earls should be discharged was accordingly taken, and every conceivable method of influencing those who had voted in the

---

[1] *L.J.*, xiv. 525, 527 ; *House of Lords MSS.*, 1690-1, pp. 93-6 ; Bonnet, October 24/November 4, 1690, in *Ranke*, vi. 152.

[2] *L.J.*, xiv. 515-8 ; *House of Lords MSS.*, 1690-1, pp. 91-2 ; *Burnet*, ii. 68-9

negative was considered and put in force. At the same time
absent peers who might be expected to support the Government were hastily summoned to attend.[1] The result was seen
on October 30, when a committee appointed to examine into
the question of impeachments made its report, and the whole
problem was debated. Precedents as far back as the reign of
Edward III were quoted, and the resolutions of 1679 and 1685
were read and discussed ; but the decision ultimately reached,
that Peterborough and Salisbury should be discharged from
their bail, amounted to a declaration against the continuance
of impeachments, and only eight peers thought it worth while
to protest.[2]

In spite of this double failure on the part of the malcontents
William was anxious to conciliate the two main sections of
the opposition, and it was probably with this object in view
that he effected at this time a further readjustment within the
ministry. In November the Treasury Commission was once
more remodelled, the Tory Godolphin, who had been a member
of the first Commission, being reintroduced and given Lowther's
place at its head, although the former First Lord continued to
sit at the Board. In December the long vacant Secretaryship
of State was conferred upon the Whig Sidney. These changes
can scarcely have been pleasing to Carmarthen, and illustrate
the limits of his political influence. They were based upon
the policy of " trimming " which he had repeatedly denounced.
Neither Godolphin nor Sidney was in any sense a friend of his,
and about the appointment of the latter he had not been
consulted or even informed beforehand.[3] Yet the practical
effect of their inclusion in the ministry was probably to
strengthen his hand, by emphasising the middle position into
which his hostility to Jacobitism was forcing him, and helping
to identify his supremacy with moderate counsels.

Certainly no loss of royal favour was implied, for with
Parliament in session the Lord President was thoroughly in
his element, and was giving almost daily proof of his capacity

---

[1] The list is printed *infra*, iii. 179-81.

[2] *L.J.*, xiv. 536-8 ; *House of Lords MSS.*, 1690-1, pp. 96-108 ; *Luttrell*,
ii. 123.

[3] Dartmouth's note in *Burnet* (ed. 1833), iv. 8. Godolphin was one of those
who voted on October 6 against discharging Peterborough and Salisbury.

to serve the Crown. In organising the House of Lords to secure the desired decision of the impeachment question he had apparently been engaged in a purely temporary improvisation ; but for weeks before Parliament assembled he had been actively employed in consolidating a party in the House of Commons, which should be prepared to vote the supplies necessary for the operations of the following year. The central feature of his organisation was a body of seven " managers of the King's directions," led by Lowther and Goodricke, whose function it was to get into touch with all the supporters of the Government in the House, confirm them in their good inclinations, and hold general meetings at which the tactics they should pursue should be determined. In addition, members of Parliament who were also Privy Councillors were required to render their assistance, particular individuals were appealed to in all sorts of different ways, and the King through the Treasury and Admiralty Commissions brought pressure to bear on all revenue officials, all officers in the army and navy, and all pensioners, to vote for supply.[1] As a result the Commons were induced to face in a serious fashion the responsibilities of England as a member of a great European coalition, and to vote with alacrity the unprecedented sum of four million pounds for the armed forces.[2]

This alone would have given Carmarthen a sufficient claim upon the royal gratitude, but just before the session came to an end chance enabled him to strengthen that claim, and at the same time commend himself to the nation at large, by unmasking a dangerous Jacobite conspiracy. On November 28 an anonymous letter reached him, warning him of a second Gunpowder Plot against King and Parliament which appeared to have its headquarters in a house in the Old Palace at Westminster. The alarm proved to be a false one, for although he immediately informed the Lords, and Black Rod was instructed to make a thorough search of the premises indicated, nothing suspicious could be found.[3] The uneasiness produced, however, was not readily allayed, and inevitably led to further

---

[1] A rough draft of the scheme of operations is printed *infra*, iii. 178-9.

[2] Burnet to James Johnston, October 14, 1690, in *Tindal*, iii. 160, note 1.

[3] *L.J.*, xiv. 570-2 ; *House of Lords MSS.*, 1690-1, p. 192 ; *Luttrell*, ii. 134.

alarms. Within a fortnight information was brought to the Lord President by Nicholas Prat, a boatman, of some doubtful characters, professing to be smugglers, who had engaged his services to take them over to France.

Fortunately one of the racing yachts with which the Earl of Danby delighted to experiment was available, and under the command of Christopher Billop, who had previously been a captain in Danby's regiment of dragoons, this was sent down the river to intercept Prat's vessel when it was actually at sea and escape from it was impossible. On the last night of the year, by arrangement between Prat and Billop, the operation was successfully carried out. Prat's passengers were arrested, and proved to be Lord Preston, John Ashton and Edmund Elliot, all of them supporters of the exiled monarch. With them were seized important papers indicating a conspiracy to restore James as soon as William and the bulk of the English army were sufficiently engaged on the Continent.[1]

This discovery made an immense impression, and greatly increased the prestige of the Lord President. For weeks he was, if not the most popular, at least the most generally acclaimed figure in the country. A movement against him, which had for some time been gathering strength in the Commons, collapsed as soon as the arrest of Preston was known.[2] Never since the days of Charles II had his credit stood so high or his position seemed so secure. When on January 6, 1691, William set out for the Hague men could reassure themselves by noting that he left " the Marquesse of Caermarthen behind him," who was to " preside as cheif minister in his absence." [3]

Probably it was at the desire of the Lord President himself that his reward largely took the form of an increase of his influence in his own county. In the previous July his control of the fortress of Hull had been strengthened by the appointment of his brother Charles as Lieutenant-Governor there in

[1] *Macaulay*, iv. 1960-7 ; *Burnet*, ii. 69-70 ; *Luttrell*, ii. 152-3.

[2] The day appointed for " hunting the white elephant " was January 2, 1691 ; but when the time came " no motion was made." Robert Harley described the scheme of the malcontents as " a very weighty affair and set on foot by men of trick " (*Portland MSS.*, iii. 456).

[3] *Luttrell*, ii. 137.

place of Lionel Copley.[1] Now in February 1691 he was
admitted High Steward of the borough in succession to Lord
Kingston, and entrusted with the lieutenancy of the East in
addition to that of the West Riding.[2] The popular expectation
was that he would be placed at the head of all three Ridings,
and in February of the following year this was actually
done.[3]

Gratifications of a different character, however, were by
no means lacking. Lord Danby was rewarded for his share
in the defeat of the conspiracy with the command of the first
marine regiment, of which Lord Torrington had been colonel,
and was also appointed captain, first of the *Suffolk* and then
of the *Resolution*, both 70-gun men-of-war, in which he was
to see active service during the summer.[4] The long-desired
dismissal of Major Wildman [5] was followed by the appointment
as Postmasters General of Sir Robert Cotton and Thomas
Frankland, the former of whom at least was among Carmarthen's most faithful followers.[6] A pension of £3,500 a year for

---

[1] *Cal. S.P. Dom.*, 1690-1, p. 68.

[2] *Ibid.*, pp. 254, 286. Subordinate officials in the East Riding who were
" whiggishly inclined " were immediately dismissed (*Luttrell*, ii. 230).

[3] *Cal. S.P. Dom.*, 1690-1, p. 311 ; 1691-2, p. 155.

[4] *Cal. S.P. Dom.*, 1690-1, p. 199 ; *Luttrell*, ii. 155 ; B.M. Add. MSS. 36662,
f. 113. A curious incident in which Danby was at this time involved caused
some comment. As he was returning home along the Strand towards midnight on January 27 a body of men pretending to be pressmasters endeavoured
to press the servants in attendance on his coach, and when the Earl with
drawn sword came to their assistance knocked him down and injured him.
The rioters, whose object probably was to extort money, were later tried and
convicted ; but at Danby's intercession they were pardoned, with the exception of two who were condemned to stand in the pillory (*Luttrell*, ii. 21, 167,
184 ; *Portledge Papers*, pp. 99-100 ; *Hist. MSS. Com.*, v. 381 ; *Hodgkin
MSS.*, pp. 330-1). Possibly as a result of his reckless generosity and uncertain
behaviour Danby always enjoyed great popularity with the seafaring classes.
On his appointment as captain two hundred seamen from Suffolk " went in
a body with a ships pendant displaying before them " to offer him their
services, and were rewarded with " five guineas to drink the Kings health "
(*Luttrell*, ii. 186).

[5] Not only was Wildman dismissed, but Carmarthen had the satisfaction
of telling him that " it was his Majesties express order from Holland " (B.M.
Add. MSS. 29565, f. 16).

[6] According to Sidney Carmarthen disapproved of the choice on the ground
that one of the new Postmasters was a Whig and the other a Tory. Both,
however, were moderate men (*Cal. S.P. Dom.*, 1690-1, p. 283). The extreme
Whigs were much aggrieved at the change (*Portland MSS.*, iii. 461).

life was offered to the Lord President, and in view of his age
altered by special favour to one for a fixed period of twenty-one
years.[1] Rumour incessantly declared that he was to be
created Duke of Pontefract;[2] while in the spring it was
even reported that he was to be restored to his old place of
Lord High Treasurer.[3]

Such eminence inevitably brought trouble in its train.
Apart from a flying visit at the end of April William was out
of England from the beginning of January 1691 to the close
of October, and for nearly ten months accordingly Carmarthen
was called upon to shoulder the principal burden of government.
In some ways his position was easier than in the previous year.
The absence of the King was no longer regarded as altogether
abnormal, and in itself caused little difficulty. Queen Mary
had now some experience of the duties of her position, and her
advisers had become more accustomed to working with each
other. No desperate crisis had to be faced such as that which
had followed the disaster of Beachy Head. But the situation
as a whole was very unsatisfactory. In spite of William's
victory at the Boyne in the previous summer Ireland seemed as
far from settlement as ever. Great indignation had been
aroused in England by the ill-treatment of the episcopal clergy
in Scotland, and by the establishment of an advanced presbyterian system there. Ready money was so scarce that the
Government was at its wits' end how to find even the most
immediately necessary supplies.

With unwearied energy and unabated confidence Carmarthen
tackled these and all other problems that came his way.
Ireland as usual had a foremost place in his thoughts, for on
events in that country he considered the fate of the whole
Revolution settlement still depended. So diligent was his
attendance at the Committee for Irish Affairs that with the
support of Sir Henry Goodricke he was able practically to

---

[1] *Cal. Treas. Books*, ix. 1135; B.M. Add. MSS. 34095, f. 290; *Portland
MSS.*, iii. 465; v. 202; *infra*, ii. 194. There was a good deal of criticism of
so large a grant at such a time. Godolphin and other members of the Treasury
Commission were induced to sign the warrant only by the Queen's express
command (*Cal. S.P. Dom.*, 1695, pp. 168, 169).

[2] *Cal. S.P. Dom.*, 1690-1, p. 311; *Luttrell*, ii. 197, 304.

[3] *Cal. S.P. Dom.*, 1690-1, p. 350.

dominate its decisions.[1] So careful was his supervision of the
minutest details even of its military organisation that Marlborough felt impelled to protest to William against what he
considered unwarranted interference.[2] So convinced was
he of the inefficiency of the system of government by Lords
Justices set up by the King, and of the need for a really capable
Lord Lieutenant, that although tormented by frequent attacks
of illness he offered, if no abler man could be found for the post,
to undertake the administration of the country himself.[3]

In Scotland his interest was less direct. Distasteful to him
though the proceedings of the dominant faction in that country
were, he could scarcely maintain they were a real danger to the
Revolution settlement except in the sense that any approval of
them by William might alienate the Church interest in England.
Nevertheless he felt bound to represent to the King in the
strongest terms the threat to the royal authority which they
involved, and the obvious danger that they might lead to civil
war.[4] For finance he disclaimed all responsibility, declaring
himself " wholly ignorant of the methods taken " at the
Treasury. Yet here also he had his contribution to make,
urging the King to seek some immediate relief by borrowing
from the Dutch what remained unpaid of the £600,000 voted
to them for their assistance at the Revolution, and playing
his customary part in negotiating temporary loans from the
city of London.[5]

In smaller matters, especially those in which the Queen was
personally interested, he was incessantly active. He was
appointed Governor of a " new corporation for setting the poor
at work by a joint stock throughout England," and a member
of two commissions for the reformation of hospitals and houses
of charity.[6] On him fell such ungrateful tasks as that of

---

[1] Carmarthen, Goodricke and Sidney were the only members who attended
regularly (*Cal. S.P. Dom.*, 1690-1, p. 264 ; *infra*, ii. 197).

[2] *Cal. S.P. Dom.*, 1690-1, p. 262.

[3] Carmarthen to the King, January 23, February 20, 1691, *infra*, ii. 190,
195-7 ; *Luttrell*, ii. 165.

[4] Carmarthen to the King, February 27, May 22, July 14, 1691, *infra*, ii.
198, 200-2.

[5] Carmarthen to the King, February 3, 27, 1691, *infra*, ii. 191, 197 ; *Cal.
S.P. Dom.*, 1690-1, pp. 241-3, 272, 277-8 ; *Luttrell*, ii. 181, 249.

[6] *Cal. S.P. Dom.*, 1690-1, pp. 240-1, 422, 473.

soothing the wounded feelings of the Spanish ambassador when one of his servants, arrested for debt, failed to secure his release from the Privy Council.[1] For vacant posts he was always ready with a suitable candidate, though his recommendations were by no means always accepted. The appointment of Tillotson instead of Compton to the see of Canterbury must have been a disappointment to him,[2] and the King's general policy of promoting Low Churchmen to bishoprics can hardly have been regarded by him with favour.[3] On the death of William Jephson, Secretary to the Treasury, he put forward the claims of Charles Bertie ; but the appointment went to Henry Guy.[4] On the death of Sir Peyton Ventris, Puisne Justice of the Common Pleas, he recommended William Ettricke to be a Baron of the Exchequer ; but the recommendation was ignored.[5]

Carmarthen's influence in the summer of 1691 was thus all-pervasive rather than all-powerful ; but this distinction was little regarded by contemporaries, most of whom were in a thoroughly discontented frame of mind and anxious only to find somebody to blame for the shortcomings of the Government. The main grievances were on the one hand the heavy taxation, and on the other the miserable return provided by the operations of the year, especially at sea. For neither of these was Carmarthen directly responsible ; and he had

---

[1] Blancard, May 19/29, 1691, in *Hist. MSS. Com.*, vii. 197-8. Diplomatic privilege and domestic issues were both involved. The debt for which the servant was arrested, and for which he had made himself responsible, was really one of the ambassador's personal debts. The creditor was an Irish papist, who was believed to be the tool of " quelque caballe Jacobite." In order to silence him the Government took proceedings against him as a recusant, only to be confronted by opposition from the ambassador, who regarded this as persecution of his own faith.

[2] According to one rumour Compton was to be consoled for his loss with the hand of Carmarthen's daughter, Lady Plymouth, in marriage (*Portland MSS.*, iii. 467 ; *Portledge Papers*, p. 110) ; and it was very generally believed that his failure to attend at Tillotson's consecration, and again at his admission to the Privy Council, was due to disgust (Carte MSS. 79, ff. 350, 358). Carmarthen himself, however, was present at Tillotson's consecration (*Luttrell*, ii. 238).

[3] The ecclesiastical appointments made in the spring of 1691 should be compared with those anticipated in the autumn of the previous year (*Luttrell*, ii. 95, 215).

[4] Blancard, June 9/19, 1691, in *Hist. MSS. Com.*, vii. 199 ; *Luttrell*, ii. 242, 250.

[5] Carmarthen to the King, March 13, 1691, *infra*, ii. 199.

certainly done as much as was within his power to ensure an active naval policy.[1] Yet such was his position in the Government that the blame for everything was almost inevitably laid at his door. Had his colleagues stood by him he might have been able to share the responsibility with them ; but the majority were only too glad to see him made the scapegoat, and those who were ready to help were not in a position to do so. Until the close of March Nottingham and the Bishop of London were with William on the Continent. Lowther was first alienated by some grievance of his own, and then incapacitated by a wound received in a duel.[2] It was thus on the foremost minister alone that the whole weight of the growing popular discontent fell, and " Tom the Tyrant " was savagely denounced in countless pamphlets and lampoons which found only too much matter for invective in his past career.[3]

Never deficient in courage the Lord President faced the storm of obloquy with the same resolution as he had displayed in similar circumstances before ; but his attempt to meet the popular clamour had an increasingly disastrous effect on his policy. In his relations with the King it induced him to lay quite unwarranted stress on the desirability of conciliating English popular opinion. His advice on the major problems then before the Government, in consequence, never very good at the best, rapidly degenerated, and became distinctly offensive to William, who resented most bitterly the suggestion that his great schemes of European policy should be subordinated to the dictates of an ignorant English Parliament.[4] In his

---

[1] Carmarthen to the King, February 10, May 22, August 28, 1691, *infra*, ii. 193, 200, 205 ; Blancard, August 7/17, 11/21, 14/24, September 11/21, 1691, in *Hist. MSS. Com.*, vii. 202 ; viii. 565-6.

[2] B.M. Add. MSS. 34095, ff. 295, 325 ; *Portland MSS.*, iii. 463 ; *Luttrell*, ii. 150, 210.

[3] Carmarthen was fully conscious of the extent to which he was deserted by his colleagues. The substance of his complaint, of which glimpses can be caught in many of his letters to the King, is embodied in the concluding paragraph of his letter of August 28, 1691 (*infra*, ii. 206).

[4] The intrusion of this political element in Carmarthen's advice is apparent all through his letters to the King during 1691. See especially those of February 20, May 22 and July 18 (*infra*, ii. 195, 200, 202). It is significant that from the spring of 1691 the number of his letters which have been preserved rapidly declines. William's practice apparently was to keep only those which he deemed important, and Carmarthen's letters were losing their importance to him.

relations with his political opponents, on the other hand, Carmarthen was induced to lay far too much stress on petty parliamentary tricks which, whatever immediate victories they might win him, could hardly be made a permanent basis for his power. Throughout the spring and summer of 1691 he was constantly engaged in investigating the plot he had discovered, with the object not so much of preventing any Jacobite movement as of finding a useful weapon against his enemies. The papers which had been seized implicated some ; the confessions of Lord Preston incriminated others. With these in his hands he hoped to be able to " breake the teeth " of the opponents of the Government when Parliament met.[1]

In this he was not unsuccessful. Long before the opening of the new session on October 22 both Whigs and extreme Tories had begun to muster their forces for an attack upon him,[2] and a proposal had even been made that supply should be refused as long as he remained at the head of the Government.[3] So formidable did the coalition against him appear that it was rumoured he was on the point of retirement, or would at least exchange his English offices for the lucrative and dignified post of Lord Lieutenant of Ireland.[4] At the critical moment, how-ever, news of the capitulation of Limerick,[5] involving the successful conclusion of the Irish campaign, greatly improved the political situation, encouraged his friends, and determined his resolution, which probably had never wavered, to stand his ground.

Scarcely had Parliament met when rumblings of discontent made themselves heard in the Commons, and Sir Thomas Clarges reflected bitterly on the failure of the fleet to achieve

---

[1] Carmarthen to the King, February 3, 1691, *infra*, ii. 192.

[2] As early as the middle of July Carmarthen was being threatened on the one side by Rochester, who was aiming at the post of Lord Chamberlain and a dominant position in the Government, and on the other side by " une si forte caballe contre luy qu'on le ruinera au Parlement et peut être meme à la cour " (Blancard, July 14/24, 1691, in *Hist. MSS. Com.*, viii. 1, p. 562).

[3] Blancard, without date, in *Hist. MSS. Com.*, vii. 201. This letter must have been written between July 31, when Dartmouth was sent to the Tower, and October 25, when he died there.

[4] Blancard, October 13/23, 16/26, 1691, in *Hist. MSS. Com.*, vii. 203, 204 ; Bonnet, October 30/November 9, 1691, in *Ranke*, vi. 160-1.

[5] Limerick surrendered on October 3, and the official news reached London on October 12.

any substantial success during the summer.[1] But it was not
until November 3, when the House resolved itself into committee to consider the state of the nation, that the real attack
on the Government began.   At first criticism was impersonal,
and was confined almost entirely to alleged malversation and
miscarriages in the armed forces.   The army was the subject of
debate on November 3, and the navy on November 7.[2] But in
a very short time a more ominous note began to be struck.
Seymour, who had been absent at the beginning of the session,
made his appearance in the Commons, and attacked the King's
opening speech as involving a breach of the privileges of Parliament.   A small group of Tories, including Seymour, Clarges,
Sir Christopher Musgrave and Paul Foley, endeavoured to
secure for the Commons the right to nominate the principal
officers of the fleet, and were checked only by an impressive
speech from Sir John Guise, in which it was pointed out that
this would mean giving not advice but directions to the King.
Carmarthen's old enemy, John Howe, made a violent attack on
the Cabinet Council, which he denounced as a secret body
unknown to the constitution, and criticised the composition of
the Privy Council, many of the members of which he declared
to be unworthy of their places.   His speech was not followed
up, but it was highly significant of the direction in which the
opposition was tending, for the first part of it was generally
interpreted as a personal attack upon Carmarthen, and the
second part as an attack upon Goodricke.[3]

So far as the Lord President was concerned all this criticism
had at least one beneficial result.   Just as it emphasised the
danger that he might be made the scape-goat for all the failings
of the civil administration, so it made it clear that Admiral
Russell might be held solely responsible for the ineffectiveness
of the fleet.   A tacit alliance in consequence sprang up between
the groups supporting these two statesmen, which was to

---

[1] Blancard, October 23/November 2, 1691, in *Hist. MSS. Com.*, vii. 204 ;
Bonnet, of the same date, in *Ranke*, vi. 159-60.

[2] *C.J.*, x. 545, 547 ; *Grey*, x. 162-7.

[3] Blancard, October 30/November 9, November 3/13, 6/16, 1691, in *Hist.
MSS. Com.*, vii. 204-6 ; Bonnet, November 3/13, 6/16, 1691, in *Ranke*, vi.
161-3.

prove of considerable service to them both.[1] But the formation
of a coalition among those whose conduct was called in
question was almost inevitably followed by the formation of a
similar coalition among their critics. In the House of Commons
the friends of Halifax, Rochester and Godolphin gave full
support to Seymour, Clarges and their fellows ; Lord Brandon
and other Whigs came to the assistance of Howe ; and the Lord
President was in a position of real peril[2] when an apparently
fortuitous incident suddenly engrossed all attention and gave
him at least a respite.

Shortly after the capitulation of Limerick Sir Ralph Delavall,
cruising with his squadron in the neighbourhood of the Scilly
Isles, had taken a French packet boat sailing from Brest to
Ireland, and had found on board her a number of papers,
among them a copy of a letter from General Ginkel, commander-
in-chief in Ireland, to Sir Ralph, referring to a letter which
Ginkel had received from the Earl of Nottingham. Most of
the papers were in French, and as Sir Ralph did not understand
that language he showed them to a number of his captains,
including the Earl of Danby, before dispatching them, in a
sealed packet, to Whitehall. From this originated, on the one
hand a rumour, the authorship of which it is impossible to
discover, that among the papers were copies of instructions
sent by Nottingham to Sir Ralph, some of which Sir Ralph had
never received, and on the other hand a plain statement made
by Danby to some members of Parliament that the papers
included copies not merely of the letter from Ginkel to Sir
Ralph but also of a letter from Nottingham to Sir Ralph. On
November 16 one of those to whom Danby had spoken, George
Rodney Bridges, member for Haslemere, laid the whole matter
before the House of Commons.

So promising an opportunity of finding damaging evidence
against the Tory Secretary of State,[3] the son of the Tory Lord

[1] " On juge qu'il s'est fait quelque accord secret entre les chefs de ces deux
grands partis . . . les Camarthens et les Russels " (Bonnet, November 10/20,
1691, in *Ranke*, vi. 163-5).

[2] " Il faut qu'il ayt beaucoup d'amis pour se maintenir contre un si grand
nombre d'ennemis " (Blancard, November 10/20, 1691, in *Hist. MSS. Com.*,
vii. 206).

[3] " Importing no less than the betraying his Majesty's most secret counsels
and orders " (*C.J.*, x. 554).

President, and a Tory admiral, was not to be neglected by the Whigs, and the information obtained from Bridges was eagerly followed up. The investigation, however, proved unexpectedly long and tedious, and the results disappointing. The individuals concerned were nearly all seamen, whose attendance as witnesses could not readily be secured. Danby himself, being a member of the Lords, could not be summoned before the Commons, and his information had to be obtained by the clumsy method of conferences between the two Houses. The papers on which everything turned had never been seriously examined before they reached the Secretary of State's office, and it was difficult to prove that none had been abstracted at an early stage. Not until December 15 did the investigation end in a general agreement that the rumour of actual instructions from Lord Nottingham among the papers was without foundation, and that even Danby's story of a letter from Nottingham had no other origin than the mention of a letter from Nottingham in the letter from Ginkel.[1]

There is no proof that Carmarthen had any connection with this incident. Not merely did he refrain from joining in the investigation in the Lords or serving among the managers of the conferences with the Commons, but for the greater part of the time the investigation continued he was not even present in Parliament. Yet it is hard to believe that a mare's nest so opportunely discovered by his own son was not in some sense of his contrivance.[2] If in fact the whole story was part of a

[1] *L.J.*, xiv. 649-61, 674-5, 685 ; *C.J.*, x. 554-60, 587-8 ; *House of Lords MSS.*, 1690-1, pp. 327-34 ; *Grey*, x. 175, 181-3 ; Blancard, November 17/27, December 8/18, 1691, in *Hist. MSS. Com.*, vii. 207, 210 ; Bonnet, November 17/27, 1691, in *Ranke*, vi. 167-8.

[2] On November 16, when the Commons rejected by 186 votes to 66 a proposal that Danby should be directly interrogated about the papers taken on the French packet boat, the tellers for the minority were Carmarthen's supporter, Sir Jonathan Jennings, and Henry Herbert (*C.J.*, x. 554). On December 15, the very day on which the investigation came to an end, Carmarthen, after having been most irregular in his attendance in the Lords, suddenly began to attend with perfect regularity. It is difficult to be sure how to interpret these facts, but the general impression they make is that while Carmarthen was anxious that he should have no personal part in the investigation he was also anxious that the investigation should be vigorously pursued. Contemporaries realised that Danby's apparent mistake might be deliberate. " On void que my Lord Danby s'est meconté, s'il n'a pas eu de dessein " (Blancard, November 24/December 4, 1691, in *Hist. MSS. Com.*, vii. 208).

plot to sow confusion in the ranks of the opposition it certainly
succeeded in its object. The grand attack upon the Government from which so much had been anticipated was broken up
before it had time to develop, and the opposition was exposed
to the counter-stroke which Carmarthen had all along meditated.
On November 16, the very day on which Bridges gave his
information to the Commons, Carmarthen's friends moved that
the confessions and examinations of Lord Preston should be laid
before the House, and as no convincing reason could be urged to
the contrary the motion was adopted without a division. On
December 2 the documents involved were formally delivered to
the Commons, and a week later the examination of them began.[1]

Preston's confessions were not particularly startling ; but
they implicated, in greater or less degree, so many of the
malcontents, both Whigs and Tories, that the opposition as a
body was effectively silenced, and a comparatively easy
passage was secured for the financial legislation which in
Carmarthen's eyes was the main purpose of the session. For
four weeks Lowther and Goodricke, reinforced by Sir Richard
Temple, had striven their hardest to secure an immediate grant
of supply, but with little success ; and Lowther in particular
was becoming heartily sick of his ungrateful task. On
December 3, indeed, when the capacity of the Commissioners
of the Treasury was questioned in the Commons, he was to
cause a painful scene by declaring that he was not fit for his
place and would be happier out of it. But already the situation
was improving. On November 19 a vote was carried for an
army of 65,000 men for the following year. On November 28
this figure was substantially increased by a resolution that the
word " men " in this connection did not include officers.[2] In

[1] *C.J.*, x. 554, 558, 571, 580 ; *Portland MSS.*, iii. 482.

[2] *C.J.*, x. 557, 565 ; *Grey*, x. 167-70, 175-80, 183-8, 191-200. The Commons
were very ready to vote in general terms that they would grant what was
necessary for the prosecution of the war, but extremely slow to fix upon a
specific sum or descend to details. Possibly the Government weakened its
own case at the very beginning by allowing the Master of the Mint, Thomas
Neale, to propose on November 6 that a grant of £4,000,000 should be made.
As Neale was believed to have run through two fortunes of his own there was
little inclination to accept his guidance in financial matters. " Il eut eté bon
qu'un autre membre eut dit la meme chose " (Blancard, November 6/16,
1691, in *Hist. MSS. Com.*, vii. 206 ; Bonnet, of the same date, in *Ranke*, vi.
163).

vain Clarges, Musgrave, Foley and Robert Harley maintained that so large a force was both unnecessary and dangerous, endeavoured to regulate the precise number of troops to be maintained in England, Scotland, Ireland and Flanders respectively, and put every difficulty they could think of in the way of the Government. In vain Foley reminded the Commons of King John of France, who was captured by the English at Poitiers, and pictured the crushing burden of taxation which the country would have to bear if William were similarly captured and held to ransom.[1] With remarkably little trouble in the end the Commons were induced to vote even greater supplies than in the previous year.

Unfortunately his successful use of Preston's depositions inspired Carmarthen to adopt similar tactics in dealing with similar statements coming from a much less reputable source. At the very beginning of December William Fuller, a young man who had risen to affluence as an informer and had then fallen on evil days and been imprisoned for debt, appealed to Tillotson, in whose household he had once served, and through the agency of the Archbishop's son-in-law, James Chadwick, informed the Commons that he had additional matters of great moment to discover. As Fuller was an associate, if not indeed a disciple, of Titus Oates, his statement was received with considerable scepticism, and it was not until December 9 that he was actually heard at the bar of the House ;[2] but his cunning in giving Halifax a prominent place in his list of conspirators immediately secured him the support of Carmarthen,[3] and this in turn made his revelations a real factor in the political situation. Throughout the greater part of January

---

[1] Blancard, November 20/30, November 24/December 4, December 1/11, 1691, in *Hist. MSS. Com.*, vii. 207-9 ; Bonnet, November 24/December 4, December 1/11, 1691, in *Ranke*, vi. 169-71. Seymour had also intended to speak in favour of a considerable reduction in the number of troops, but was restrained by the attitude of his own reputed partisans from the south-west, the district most exposed to French attack, who insisted " une centaine à la fois " that the question should be put without further debate, and loudly declared that 100,000 men would be better than 65,000.

[2] *C.J.*, x. 571, 573, 580 ; *Grey*, x. 202-6 ; Blancard, December 11/21, 1691, in *Hist. MSS. Com.*, vii. 210.

[3] " The discovery made by Fuller is under the management of the White Marquis. It is supposed chiefly to be directed by him against the Black Marquis " (*Portland MSS.*, iii. 485).

and February the Commons waited, with what patience they could muster, for the two witnesses whom he undertook to produce ; but no witnesses were forthcoming, and as one delay followed another belief in his revelations steadily declined.[1] On February 24, 1692, the House of Commons resolved " that William Fuller is a notorious imposter, a cheat, and a false accuser ; "[2] and the whole affair came to an end with considerable loss of reputation to all concerned.

Thus the adjournment of Parliament on the same day as this resolution was adopted found the political situation substantially unchanged. If Carmarthen's parliamentary tactics had done something to discredit the opposition they had certainly done nothing to strengthen the Government. A determined effort was accordingly made to silence the more dangerous among the Tory malcontents by admitting them to office.[3] On March 1 Rochester and Seymour were sworn of the Privy Council, and on Seymour in particular, whom it was considered specially necessary to conciliate, additional favours were showered. Before departing for the Continent William formally recommended him to Mary as one on whose advice she might fully rely. On March 18 he was admitted to the Cabinet, and three days later he was appointed to the Treasury Commission in place of Lowther, who willingly resigned.[4]

Promotions were accompanied by dismissals. As early as January 10 Marlborough, who had not merely intrigued, like so many others, with the exiled James II, but had ostentatiously posed as the champion of national resentment at William's reliance on Dutchmen and other foreigners, had been deprived of all his posts. On March 3 Sidney was required to deliver up his seals to the King, and the nation was again left with only one Secretary of State. On March 15 John Howe had to surrender his post of Vice-Chamberlain to Carmarthen's nephew, Peregrine Bertie. On June 23 four lords who had already been

---

[1] *C.J.*, x. 605, 610, 681-5 ; *Grey*, x. 224-6.

[2] *C.J.*, x. 693.

[3] Extensive changes in the Government were being anticipated as early as the end of January (B.M. Add. MSS. 36662, f. 297 ; *Portland MSS.*, iii. 488).

[4] B.M. Add. MSS. 36662, f. 346 ; *Luttrell*, ii. 372, 375, 391.

deprived of their offices, Halifax, Shrewsbury, Marlborough and Torrington, were all struck off the Privy Council.[1]

There is little doubt that these changes were largely due to the influence of Nottingham, between whom and Carmarthen an original difference of outlook had been tending to develop into something approaching antagonism. Nottingham had greatly resented the position in which he had been placed by Danby's statements with regard to the letters seized by Delavall, and disapproved as strongly of Carmarthen's connection with some of the moderate Whigs[2] as Carmarthen in turn disapproved of his connection with the semi-Jacobites among the Tories.[3] But from whatever quarter they were inspired the changes were sufficiently disastrous in their effect on the Government. The disgrace of Marlborough, which the King made no effort to explain or justify to the nation, and which caused a serious estrangement between the Queen and Princess Anne, roused a good deal of discontent.[4] Rochester and Seymour were not men of high character, and their policy had too obviously been dictated by a spirit of faction and self-interest for them to have any large following. Their inclusion in the ministry, in consequence, did little to satisfy the malcontent Tories, while it did much to alienate the Whigs. Unwilling though Carmarthen would have been to admit it, the chief strength of his ministry had hitherto lain in the fact that while inclining strongly to the Tory side it had never broken with the moderate men of the other party. The extreme Tories could not be conciliated, and the purely Tory ministry which he professed to be his ideal was, as he probably half realised, an

---

[1] B.M. Add. MSS. 36662, f. 328 ; Carte MSS. 76, f. 78.

[2] Blancard in his dispatch of November 24/December 4, 1691, specifically mentions Sir Robert Howard and Major Wildman (*Hist. MSS. Com.*, vii. 208). It is impossible to believe that Carmarthen had more than an indirect connection with such men, but any connection at all would have been enough to alienate Nottingham.

[3] *Burnet*, ii. 86.

[4] It also gave a good deal of satisfaction in certain quarters. " Il n'y a presque personne qui n'en soit bien aise, et qui ne deteste son ingratitude et son extreme avarice. L'une et l'autre passent l'imagination." According to Blancard the immediate objects Marlborough had in view in exercising pressure on the King were purely personal, the title of duke for himself and the office of Master General of the Ordnance (letter of January 26/February 5, 1692, misdated 1693, in *Hist. MSS. Com.*, vii. 220).

impossibility. By inclining still more towards the Tory side his ministry was merely courting destruction.

What made the position worse was that the sole success of the year 1692, the defeat of the French fleet off La Hogue, was the work of the Whig Admiral Russell. Popular opinion demanded that the victory should be followed up by a descent on the French coast, and Carmarthen, whose son Danby had won distinction for the whole family by the part he had taken in the operations,[1] supported the popular attitude by every means in his power. In vain, however, did he write in the most urgent terms to William, offer to pledge his own credit in order to raise the necessary funds, personally supervise the preparation of a great armament, and go down to Portsmouth to discuss measures with the commanders.[2] Not until two months after La Hogue was the expedition ready, and even when it put to sea it accomplished nothing more than a futile display, returning home with all its objects unfulfilled. For this the Tories naturally blamed the pusillanimity of the Whig admiral, while the Whigs equally naturally blamed the dilatoriness of the Tory Government, concentrating their invective mainly upon Nottingham, who had certainly taken into his hands a much greater part of the naval administration than either his abilities or his official position warranted. Some sacrifice would clearly have to be made to appease Parliament, and the main political problem of the autumn was to determine what that sacrifice should be.

On August 16 Rochester, now in his own eyes a serious candidate for the position of chief minister, tackled this problem in a memorial which he dispatched to William. The root cause of the trouble with Parliament, he declared, was the continental war, which was extremely expensive to maintain, and which appeared to be waged in the interests of the Allies rather than of England. Greater stress should therefore be laid on the war at sea, and less on the war on land. If this were done William himself would be able to spend more of his time in England, and in particular would be able to return to London earlier

---

[1] *Luttrell*, ii. 465, 469.

[2] Carmarthen to the King, June 14, July 14, 1692, *infra*, ii. 208-12 ; *Rutland MSS.*, ii. 136 ; *Luttrell*, ii. 528 *et seq.* ; *Cal. S. P. Dom.*, 1691-2, pp. 394, 399

that autumn, so as to make better preparation for the conduct of his business in the Commons than he had done in the previous session, and yet meet Parliament before the enthusiasm roused by the victory at La Hogue had entirely faded away.

In this advice there was little that was palatable to William, and he immediately transmitted the memorial to Carmarthen for his opinion. So far as Parliament was concerned Carmarthen substantially agreed with Rochester. The coming session, he admitted, was bound to be a difficult one, and only the more optimistic among the ministers believed that the necessary supplies would be forthcoming. The King's presence at an early stage would certainly be a help. But as regards the war Carmarthen entirely refused to support Rochester. Failure to continue active operations on the Continent he indignantly described as " sitting still and letting the French King take what he will." Rochester, he declared, had done his best to frustrate Russell's projected descent on France in the summer, and his advice on this point was only a continuation of the same obstructive attitude.[1]

It seems probable that the impression made upon William by this controversy between the two Tory leaders destroyed any chance Rochester may have had of ousting Carmarthen from his place of chief minister ; but the rejection of Rochester's proposals left the problem of Parliament as far from solution as ever. The essential factors in that problem, as Carmarthen saw it, were on the one hand the lack of any solid body of supporters on whom the Government could rely,[2] and on the other hand the tacit understanding between the extreme men of both parties whom their enemies disparagingly referred to as Jacobites and republicans.[3] To meet the dangers involved the only practicable course seemed to be to bring pressure to bear on individual men, and this he proceeded to do, though without much hope of satisfactory results. Government officials in

---

[1] Rochester's memorial is printed, together with Carmarthen's marginal comments, in *Dalrymple*, App., ii. 240-3.

[2] " There being now no such thing as any particular interest that is considerable enough to do good."

[3] " Those who would subvert your government and those who would governe your Majestie in itt." Carmarthen's views are set forth in his letter to the King of September 9, 1692, *infra*, ii. 212-4.

Parliament were urged to support the administration. All members of the ministry who had any personal or local influence likely to be of service were called upon to use it. By these means an ill-assorted coalition was built up which was all the Government could look to for support when the new session of Parliament opened on November 4, 1692.[1]

In the end, however, the situation, serious though it was, proved less serious than had been anticipated. By a strange perversion what should have been a great national question debated between parties was transformed into a purely personal question contested by the two Houses of Parliament. Each House felt bound to stand by its own member. The Lords supported Nottingham, the Commons supported Russell, and in the resulting confusion much of the popular animus against the Government failed to find a mark. Bills to restrict the authority of the King and resolutions censuring his ministers and officials were brought forward in unprecedented abundance ; but no irretrievable disaster occurred, supplies for the war were not denied, and the ministry, whether by luck or skilful management, escaped with a bad shock.

Nevertheless it was made clear that Nottingham and Russell could not both be retained in the service of the Government, and a decision had to be reached as to which should be dismissed. The problem was a difficult one, and there can be little doubt that Carmarthen had sufficient influence to secure whichever solution he preferred. But he was extremely reluctant to use his influence. To come to the assistance either of Nottingham or of Russell would mean engaging himself much more definitely than he desired on the side of the extreme Tories or the Whigs. Moreover he had his own safety to consider. In the attack on the ministry which occupied the early days of the session violent criticism was directed against both Carmarthen and Nottingham ;[2] but the debates soon brought to light the essential difference in their positions. The real charge against Carmarthen was that he and his immediate associates in the Cabinet

---

[1] Details are given in two lists printed *infra*, iii. 182-7.

[2] " Le Marquis de Camarthen, Président des Conseils, et le Comte de Nottingham, seul Secretaire d'Estat, ne furent pas nommez, mais on les désigna si bien que personne ne les méconnut " (Bonnet, November 29/ December 9, 1692, in *Ranke*, vi. 187).

had monopolised the government, to the exclusion of the Privy Council, which was the recognised organ of administration. But the absurdity of trying to revive the Privy Council, especially in time of war, was clearly demonstrated by Sir Richard Temple in a brilliant speech in which he pointed out that one of the acknowledged reasons for the success of the French, and even of the Dutch, was that they entrusted their most secret counsels only to a few men.[1] The real charge against Nottingham, on the other hand, was that he was either incapable or disloyal, and to this charge it proved much more difficult to find an effective answer. Thus Carmarthen was tempted to dissociate himself from Nottingham, while he experienced little inclination towards a closer alliance with Russell, whose ability and integrity were also being called in question.

So long as the mutual recriminations of Nottingham, Russell and their partisans engrossed the attention of Parliament Carmarthen was thus relegated somewhat to the background ; but especially after the Christmas recess the ordinary business of the session came more to the front, and in dealing with this he showed himself as active and decided as ever. He assisted in defeating a Place Bill which the Commons sent up to the Lords, although in doing so he found himself in opposition to both of his brothers-in-law, Lindsey and Abingdon.[2] He encouraged his friends in the Commons to oppose a Triennial Bill which the Lords had passed and sent down to them.[3] He stoutly resisted such extravagances as the demand made by some discontented peers that the surrender of Ostend and Nieuport should be required as some security for English operations on the Continent, asking whether any guarantee had been given that the Commons would provide the money

[1] Bonnet, November 29/December 9, 1692, in *Ranke*, vi. 187-8. Lowther drove the point home in a manner which cannot have been very gratifying to some of his hearers. " I have heard foreign ministers say," he declared, " that 'tis better for their affairs in England than anywhere else, because once a year the Parliament sits, and without the charge of intelligence they know all affairs " (*Grey*, x. 277).

[2] *L.J.*, xv. 169, 172 ; Blancard, January 3/13, 6/16, 1693, in *Hist. MSS. Com.*, vii. 212 ; Bonnet, January 6/16, 1693, in *Ranke*, vi. 200.

[3] *Grey*, x. 299-308 ; Bonnet, February 10/20, 1693, in *Ranke*, vi. 212.

to maintain these places.[1] Throughout these proceedings he continued to have the support of the moderate Whigs who still held office under the Government.

Thus the contest between Nottingham and Russell was determined without his intervention, and in the end Nottingham proved to have sufficient credit with the King to prevent his own dismissal. On January 22, 1693, Russell was allowed to resign, and the command of the fleet for the following summer was entrusted to Killigrew, Delavall and Shovell. As the first two of these were suspected of Jacobitism, and all three were regarded as Tories, their appointment was generally attributed to Nottingham.[2] How exactly Carmarthen regarded it cannot with certainty be determined. It was the final step towards his ideal of a Tory Government served by Tory officers ; but it is at least doubtful whether he approved.

[1] Bonnet, January 13/23, 1693, in *Ranke*, vi. 202-5.
[2] *Burnet*, ii. 103.

CHAPTER XXI

DECLINE AND FALL, 1693-1702

THE fall of Carmarthen was a gradual process, and was primarily due, not to any personal failure on his part, but to the inability of the ministry of which he was the most prominent member to bring the war with France to a successful conclusion. Although the struggle had now lasted for four years, not a single success had been won on the Continent which could provide any compensation in English eyes for the vast expenditure incurred ; while at sea the victory of La Hogue had been more than balanced by the incessant depredations of French privateers, against which the navy seemed unable to offer any effective protection. For this unhappy state of affairs the party which had been steadily tending to monopolise the Government naturally had to bear the blame, and when in the early days of 1693 the Tories were given almost complete control it was only in order that they might have one last chance of justifying their position by securing some decisive victory.

The result was almost unrelieved disaster in every sphere of operations, and a shock to the credit of the ministry from which it was impossible that it should recover. The capture of Heidelberg by the French in May, the fall of Rosas and the growing threat to Barcelona during the summer, the defeat of the Savoyards at Marsaglia in September, all might have been condoned by an English public who had little appreciation of the significance of events in distant theatres of war. But the failure of William himself at Landen in the middle of July was an entirely different matter. So great was the repercussion of that event that the Lord President hastened home from Bath, whither he had gone for a month's holiday by permission of the Queen, with the object of confronting any danger that might threaten from abroad and quietening the popular clamour at home ; and although the defeat proved much less disastrous than had at first been reported the clamour continued unabated.[1]

The principal cause of discontent, however, was found as usual in events at sea. Whether through incompetence, divided counsels, or treachery, the newly appointed Tory admirals were responsible for the greatest disaster that had yet befallen English commercial interests. The vast Smyrna fleet, numbering nearly 400 sail of merchant vessels, for the safety of which it was one of their main duties to provide, was escorted by them only some two hundred miles beyond Ushant, and then allowed to continue its voyage towards the Mediterranean with a comparatively small convoy, on the assumption, which nothing had been done to confirm, that the bulk of the French fleet was still in harbour at Brest. In reality the French, having left Brest before the English had put to sea, were waiting in the neighbourhood of Lagos, and the vessels of the Smyrna fleet, sailing straight into the trap intended for them, were scattered, captured, or destroyed. To counterbalance this catastrophe not a single success was gained by the English navy during the whole of the year.

For the failure at sea Carmarthen was not in any sense responsible. As early as the end of April he had warned William of the disunion, mistrust and lack of enterprise which made any real success at sea unlikely, and had recommended as the only remedy the issue of precise and imperative instructions by the King himself.[2] Not only so, but his son Danby, as was revealed by a commission of enquiry, had strongly urged the importance of sending a squadron to discover the true position at Brest, and on the argument being advanced that it was dangerous to detach any considerable number of ships for that purpose had offered with one single vessel to undertake the

[1] Carmarthen to Blathwayt, August 8, 1693, *infra*, ii. 223 ; Carte MSS. 233, ff. 180, 231 ; *Rutland MSS.*, ii. 140. While at Bath the Lord President was " serenaded " by the Jacobites, who sang seditious songs beneath his window (*Luttrell*, iii. 125, 140, 153, 189).

[2] Carmarthen to the King, April 28, 1693, *infra*, ii. 214. In May the Lord President, accompanied by other lords of the Council, paid an official visit to the fleet at Portsmouth, with a view to promoting greater unanimity among those responsible for its movements (*Cal. S.P. Dom.*, 1693, p. 134; *Luttrell*, iii. 97, 100).

task himself.¹ It was unlikely, therefore, that the storm threatening the Government would fall with any special severity upon the Lord President,² and from the first he was able to watch its progress with a certain degree of detachment.

In the circumstances that had arisen it was practically inevitable that Russell should be recalled to the command of the fleet, and the recall of Russell was bound to mean the disappearance of Nottingham from the ministry. The problem was to determine what further changes should follow. As early as March the first signs of a Whig revival had appeared when Sir John Somers was appointed Lord Keeper of the Great Seal, and Sir John Trenchard was elevated to the Secretaryship of State left vacant more than a year before by Sidney.³ During the autumn it was rumoured that both Nottingham and Carmarthen would retire,⁴ and when the former, after refusing to resign voluntarily, was summarily dismissed on November 6, it was generally assumed that he would be succeeded by Shrewsbury, and that further favours would be showered upon the Whigs.⁵

Shrewsbury, however, in spite of much pressure, excused himself at first from accepting the seals,⁶ and Carmarthen was thus given an opportunity of retrieving the situation. The

---

¹ Apparently the matter went so far as to lead to a serious quarrel between Danby and Killigrew, and to the suggestion later on that the animus shown against the admirals was inspired by Danby (L'Hermitage, October 6/16, 10/20, 1693).

² According to Burnet " the Marquis of Carmarthen was much suspected " (*History of My Own Time*, ii. 116) ; but the impression left by contemporary correspondence is rather that he remained remarkably free from censure.

³ The appointment of Somers was announced on March 18, and he and Trenchard were sworn in on March 23, 1693 (B.M. Add. MSS. 34096, ff. 312, 315). By a curious chance it was upon Carmarthen that the duty fell of pressing Somers to accept his new post (*Luttrell*, iii. 58-61). The relations between the great Whig lawyer and the Lord President, however, appear to have been not unfriendly (*Morrison Catalogue*, vi. 151).

⁴ B.M. Add. MSS. 28878, f. 125.

⁵ Carmarthen to Abingdon, November 7, 1693, *infra*, ii. 224 ; L'Hermitage, November 7/17, 1693 ; Blancard, November 7/17, 10/20, 1693, in *Hist. MSS. Com.*, vii. 213-4 ; *Hatton Correspondence*, ii. 196-8, where Somers, Russell and Trenchard are already reported to be " the governing men." There are indications that Carmarthen recommended Sir John Lowther for Nottingham's place, but if so it cannot have been with much hope of success, as Lowther was anxious for a reduction rather than an increase of his official responsibilities.

⁶ *Shrewsbury Correspondence*, p. 18 *et seq*.

dismissal of Nottingham was not altogether unwelcome to him. For some time they had been drifting apart, and Carmarthen could not but feel that it was Nottingham's preference for the extreme Tories which was largely responsible for the crisis he was now facing. Freed from his former ally's influence he might retrace the steps he had taken in the last few months, expel the semi-Jacobite element from the ministry, and re-establish the tacit understanding with the moderate Whigs which had served him so well before.

The pursuit of such a policy, however, required the greatest care and circumspection, and in the session of Parliament which began on November 7 Carmarthen both spoke and acted with extreme caution. The speech from the throne, for which he may in some measure have been responsible, gave general satisfaction by promising the punishment of those who had not done their duty at sea ; [1] but it is difficult to show that either he or his satellites took more than a formal part in the investigations by both Houses which followed.[2] When serious discontent arose in the Lords over the King's reply to a request for information as to what had passed in Council concerning the fleet it fell to him to smooth away the difficulty by explaining that there was no intention of withholding what was desired.[3] To the Lords he commended himself by taking a prominent part in the rejection of a Treason Bill which the great majority of them viewed with disfavour ; [4] to the Commons by encouraging

[1] *L.J.*, xv. 295.

[2] Sir John Lowther in particular seems to have exercised a moderating influence. " Miscarriages have been unfortunate, but must be proved, and then I shall concur to punishments. But do not judge men before they be heard " (*Grey*, x. 314-5, 325, 327 ; Blancard, November 21/December 1, 1693, in *Hist. MSS. Com.*, vii. 215).

[3] *L.J.*, xv. 319, 331-2, 340-3 ; *House of Lords MSS.*, 1693-5, p. 101. " L'adresse que les seigneurs firent presenter jeudy au Roy estoit pour suplier Sa Majesté de leur faire communiquer le tems que le conseil de cabinet avoit eu avis que la flote de France avoit mis à la voile, et le jour qu'il en avoit informé les commissaires de l'amirauté pour le faire savoir aux amiraux ; et le Roy fit reponse qu'il prendroit en deliberation leur adresse. Il y eut la dessus quelque dispute, ce qui fit naistre la question sy la chambre s'ajourneroit pour un mois ; mais Mylord Camarthen assura que l'intention de Sa Majesté estoit d'accorder ce qu'ils demandoient, et l'adjournement ne fust que jusqu'a lundy " (L'Hermitage, January 16/26, 1694).

[4] In this he was supported by Halifax and opposed by Nottingham (L'Hermitage, February 27/March 9, 1694).

his followers in opposing a Triennial Bill which the hereditary chamber, to their intense indignation, endeavoured to thrust upon them ; [1] and to both Houses by his successful mediation between them in a dispute over the details of the Mutiny Act.[2]

Only where the King's interests were directly concerned, indeed, was he prepared to risk adopting a determined attitude, and on these occasions good fortune as a rule attended his efforts. As befitted a responsible minister at such a crisis he laid great stress on the necessity of adequate supplies for the armed forces, even giving his countenance to proposals which were violently denounced as foreshadowing the introduction of a general Excise ; [3] and the session proved remarkable for the large sums granted during its course.[4] Like many landowners he disapproved of the Whig proposals for raising a loan of £1,200,000 by incorporating the subscribers in what was to become the Bank of England, believing that this would lead to a fall in rents, and a disuse of the practice of lending upon mortgage. Yet having made his attitude clear to the Lords he pointed out in the most emphatic manner that any refusal to accept the scheme would mean the postponement for an indefinite period of the King's departure to take charge of the campaign on the Continent, and on this purely practical basis secured the acceptance of the so-called Tonnage Bill, in which the proposals were embodied, by 43 votes to 31.[5] The attempt made by the House of Commons to call in question the King's conduct in rejecting a new Place Bill passed by Parliament was viewed by him with great disfavour, and Lowther, Goodricke and

---

[1] *Grey*, x. 368, 370.

[2] *L.J.*, xv. 380-8, 405-8 ; *C.J.*, xi. 119-20, 144 ; *House of Lords MSS.*, 1693-5, pp. 366-7.

[3] Lowther's speech of December 11, 1693, in *Grey*, x. 360 ; Bonnet, February 23/March 5, March 16/26, 1694, in *Ranke*, vi. 240, 243 ; Blancard, December 15/25, 1693, in *Hist. MSS. Com.*, vii. 219.

[4] Rather more than £5,000,000. " Sa Majesté n'aura jamais eu de plus grosses sommes ni plus réelles que celles que la session du Parlement qui a paru la plus chagrine luy aura données " (Bonnet, April 20/30, 1694, in *Ranke*, vi. 247).

[5] *L.J.*, xv. 421-5 ; Bonnet, April 24/May 4, 1694, in *Ranke*, vi. 247 ; L'Hermitage, April 24/May 4, 1694 ; *Luttrell*, iii. 298-9. It shows the extent to which Carmarthen on this occasion abandoned his usual allies that with the exception of the Archbishop of Canterbury all the bishops present in the House voted with the minority.

Sir Robert Cotton all spoke warmly upon the subject.[1] When Parliament was prorogued on April 25, 1694, it could scarcely be denied that he had largely contributed to the success of the session, not so much by the advocacy of any specific policy, as simply by an avoidance of unnecessary controversies, and a readiness to co-operate with any party and support any measure in either House which was likely to be of assistance in the conduct of affairs.

Had Carmarthen's advice been as essential to the King as in earlier days these tactics might well have achieved the end in view, and the Lord President might again have consolidated his position at the head of a moderate ministry composed mainly of Tories. But in his search for a non-party statesman who should guide him through the labyrinth of English politics William was already turning to another adviser. Where Halifax had proved too little of a practical politician, and Carmarthen too much of a Tory, the Earl of Sunderland, he hoped, might prove to be just what was required. Although discredited beyond any other leading statesman by the lengths to which he had gone in support of James II, Sunderland had already contrived to secure the countenance and favour not merely of the King, who was more interested in his possible usefulness than in his previous record, but of several of the most determined among his former opponents. During the months preceding the assembling of Parliament he had been entrusted with much of the work of organising a body of Government supporters which would normally have been supervised by Carmarthen, and his name had been freely mentioned as that of a likely successor to Nottingham.[2]

In other circumstances an alliance of Carmarthen and Sunderland at the head of a composite ministry would have been at least a possibility. Not only, however, was Sunderland con-

[1] *Grey*, x. 377-84. Lowther pointed out that the Bill had been carried by a majority of only ten in the Commons, and declared that even this small majority was misleading, inasmuch as " les biens, et par conséquent la consideration dans le Royaume du moindre nombre de ceux qui avoient esté pour rejetter le Bill estoient trois fois plus grands que de ceux qui l'avoient fait passer " (Bonnet, January 30/February 9, 1694, in *Ranke*, vi. 237).

[2] *Macaulay*, v. 2386-91 ; Foxcroft, *Halifax*, ii. 171-3 ; Feiling, *Tory Party*, pp. 295-6 ; *Correspondentie van Willem III en Bentinck*, part i., ii. 38-40 ; *Portland MSS.*, iii. 528-9 ; *Burnet*, ii. 108, 123-4 ; L'Hermitage, September 19/29, 1693.

vinced that the best course the King could pursue at the moment was to look for support to the Whigs, but he owed his rehabilitation to his alliance with a group of statesmen, Shrewsbury, Godolphin and Marlborough, who were inspired both by the same idea and by resolute opposition to Carmarthen's ascendancy.   Thus the Lord President's whole scheme had in the end little chance of success, and its definite failure was marked by the eventual decision of Shrewsbury, under continued pressure from his supporters, to accept the Secretaryship.   On March 2, 1694, the appointment was made, to be followed almost immediately by those of Russell as First Lord of the Admiralty and Charles Montagu as Chancellor of the Exchequer.   The whole ministry began to assume a distinctly Whig complexion.

Nevertheless Carmarthen continued to be treated with the greatest consideration.   By the dismissal of Nottingham the Church interest had been deprived of one of its stoutest champions, and it was too dangerous to risk alienating it further by giving offence to the Lord President.   As the political influence of the old statesman declined, accordingly, the private honours conferred upon him and his relatives if anything increased.   In January 1693 he had been appointed Lord High Steward at the trial of Lord Mohun for the murder of William Mountfort, and had created quite a sensation by the size of his coach and the splendour of his liveries.[1]   At the same time his son had been given command of the *Royal William*, a 100-gun man-of-war, with an independent flag.[2]   Later in the year Lord Danby was advanced to be Rear-Admiral of the Blue, was a serious candidate for the honour of convoying the King back to England after the close of the campaign on the Continent, and was for a time entrusted with the command of a special flotilla of bomb-vessels and fireships designed for an attack on St. Malo.[3]

---

[1] *L.J.*, xv. 207-14 ; *Cal. S.P. Dom.*, 1693, p. 14 ; *Hatton Correspondence*, ii. 188-9.   The appointment carried with it a fee of £1,000 and an allowance of £500 a day while the trial lasted (*Luttrell*, iii. 26-9).

[2] *Luttrell*, iii. 18, 87, 89.

[3] L'Hermitage, September 29/October 9, October 6/16, November 3/13, 1693 ; Carte MSS. 79, f. 508 ; 233, f. 196 ; *Cal. S.P. Dom.*, 1693, pp. 216, 355 ; *Luttrell*, iii. 135-217.   The command of the convoy was eventually given to Rear-Admiral David Mitchell, while that of the special flotilla, which had been delayed to so late a season in the year as to lose much of its importance, was transferred to Captain John Benbow.

In November, at the request of the Lord President, the Earl of Abingdon was made Chief Justice in Eyre south of the Trent, with Charles Bertie as his secretary.[1] A few weeks later, on the resignation of Sir John Lowther, the post of Vice-Chamberlain to the King was given to Peregrine Bertie.[2] Finally in May 1694, with the object no doubt of reconciling him to the ministerial changes which were taking place at the same time, Carmarthen was given his final step in the peerage and created Duke of Leeds.[3]

No one realised more clearly than the new Duke, however, how precarious his position was becoming, and in the months following the grant of this last honour his efforts to avoid committing himself were redoubled. Scarcely had Parliament risen when he set out on a three months' tour of the midlands and the north, in the course of which he endeavoured to revive his political influence by formal visits to no fewer than eighteen principal seats of the nobility and gentry.[4] On his return to London at the end of July he found himself immediately confronted with the most serious problem of policy then before the ministry, the problem whether the main English fleet, which had been sent into the Mediterranean to the relief of Barcelona, should be ordered to continue its protection of that city by wintering at Cadiz, or should be allowed to return home. No evasion was possible, for considerations of domestic no less than of foreign policy were involved. The absence of so large a part of the fleet was bound to cause great dissatisfaction at home ;

---

[1] Carmarthen to the King, September 30, and to Abingdon, November 7 1693, *infra*, ii. 216, 224 ; B.M. Add. MSS. 18675, f. 31 ; *Cal. S.P. Dom.*, 1693, p. 404 ; *Luttrell*, iii. 223, 231. The secretary's place alone was said to be worth £500 a year.

[2] L'Hermitage, February 20/March 2, 1694 ; *Luttrell*, iii. 270-1.

[3] Burnet, slightly anticipating events, says it was " to colour the dismissing him from business with an increase of title " (*History of My Own Time*, ii. 155). The warrant was signed on April 30, and the patent is dated May 4, 1694 (*Cal. S.P. Dom.*, 1694-5, pp. 121, 125). The Duke was introduced in the House of Lords on November 12, 1694 (*L.J.*, xv. 431). Popular expectation was that his title would be Duke of Pontefract (*Luttrell*, iii. 280). According to his own statement his preference for Leeds was due to the fact that the town was " the most considerable place (York being appropriated to the royal family) for trade, &c.," in the county with which he was so intimately associated (*Thoresby*, ii. 109).

[4] *Rutland MSS.*, ii. 155 ; *Lonsdale MSS.*, p. 105.

its recall was only too likely to lead to disaster abroad. Yet when on August 2 the crucial debate took place in Council the Lord President " declared he would give no opinion, but managed his arguments so well for and against " the recall of the fleet that his colleagues were quite unable to determine which policy he favoured.[1]

That it was possible for him to be so long absent from London,[2] and to adopt so indeterminate an attitude on a matter of vital importance, shows the extent to which his personal participation in affairs had declined. Yet his reputation still stood high. His recovery from a serious illness in the autumn elicited a congratulatory letter from the King himself,[3] and in November his influence was strong enough to secure for Sir Ralph Delavall restoration to favour and a promise of employment in the following year.[4] Once again his son Peregrine, now known as Marquis of Carmarthen, proved a genuine asset to him, raising the credit of the whole family by his spirited conduct at the disastrous conflict in Camaret Bay,[5] and probably in recognition of his services there being at length accorded the honour of bringing William home to England.[6] Where political controversies were not immediately concerned the Lord President's age, experience, rank and official dignity secured for him among the younger men who were now coming forward a position that was almost unique. In the dark days at the close of the year, when Queen Mary's illness was followed

[1] *Shrewsbury Correspondence*, p. 66.

[2] He was recalled at least once, however, during his absence (*Luttrell*, iii. 332).

[3] The letter, dated October 21, 1694, when the King was in Holland, has unfortunately been lost (*infra*, ii. 446).

[4] Carte MSS. 76, f. 538.

[5] L'Hermitage, June 15/25, August 28/September 7, 1694 ; Carte MSS. 79, f. 534 ; *Luttrell*, iii. 328, 329 ; *Cal. S.P. Dom.*, 1694-5, pp. 168-70, 183 ; 1703-4, p. 389 ; *Portland MSS.*, viii. 41-2. Carmarthen's own *Journal of the Brest Expedition* appeared at the beginning of July (Carte MSS. 79, f. 542 ; *Portland MSS.*, iii. 551).

[6] Carte MSS. 79, ff. 631, 635 ; *Cal. S.P. Dom.*, 1694-5, pp. 315-6 ; *Luttrell*, iii. 377. Unfortunately the convoy of which Carmarthen was in charge, after crossing to the coast of Holland, was incessantly hampered by contrary winds, and although the Admiral does not appear to have been seriously at fault the long delay to which the King was thus subjected did not improve his favour at Court. His letters describing his difficulties are in B.M. Add. MSS. 34351, ff. 7-40.

by her untimely death, and William lay incapacitated by grief, it was to the Lord President that the nation turned as its temporary head, and it was he who, at the special request of the Privy Council, attended upon the King, urged him to take more care of his own health, and endeavoured to remind him that the interests of the living should not be uselessly sacrificed to the memory of the dead.[1]

Largely no doubt as a result of the prestige which Leeds enjoyed, and of the circumspection of his behaviour, Whig hostility was for a time held in check, and the animus against him, which might have been expected to accompany the political revolution then taking place, was not immediately apparent. Sooner or later, however, it was certain that the Whigs would endeavour to take advantage of their growing strength to deliver a general attack on the Tories still in office, and when that time came Leeds could hardly fail to be involved. No great political foresight was required to see the danger of some such development in the parliamentary session which began on November 12, 1694, and from the very first Leeds sought to safeguard himself by a more conciliatory attitude towards his opponents than he had ever yet been prepared to show.

As in several previous sessions the principal measures on which the Whigs had resolved to concentrate their energies were a Triennial Bill, a Place Bill, and a Treason Bill, all of which were introduced in the House of Commons at the earliest possible date. Mindful perhaps of his own long imprisonment during the abeyance of Parliament under Charles II, Leeds risked offending the King by giving his vote for the Triennial Bill, which on this occasion passed both Houses and received the royal assent.[2] In the case of the Place Bill a similar change

---

[1] P.C. Reg. 76, p. 16; L'Hermitage, December 28/January 7, 1694/5; Bonnet, December 28/January 7, 1694/5, in *Ranke*, vi. 263; *Lexington Papers*, p. 34.

[2] According to his own account Leeds was warned by the King that he would live to regret his complaisance, and later appreciated the justice of the remark (*infra*, ii. 253). While accepting the general principle that Parliaments should be both frequent and of limited duration, however, the Lord President showed no anxiety for a dissolution of the existing Parliament, in which he still had many friends. The Commons were much divided on the question how long that Parliament should be allowed to continue, and it was

of front could hardly have been effected without rousing too much comment ; but happily that bill failed to reach the House of Lords, and the Lord President's chief anxiety was thus the policy he should adopt towards the Treason Bill.

In the long struggle over that measure the natural conflict of principles between Whig and Tory was complicated by an even more bitter conflict of interests between Lords and Commons. The Whigs were anxious to protect the innocent subject against a possibly arbitrary Government by a strict definition of law and procedure, the Tories equally anxious to strengthen the Government against a probably guilty subject by leaving it as free as justice could permit. On the other hand each House had specially in mind the grievances of one particular class of subject. The Commons were interested in the ordinary citizen, who was much at the mercy of the ordinary courts ; the Lords were interested in the peerage, who were even more at the mercy of the Crown, working through the Court of the Lord High Steward. In addition there was a divergence of opinion between those in office, who wished to postpone all fresh restrictions on the Government until after the conclusion of the war, and those out of office, who saw no reason why action should not be taken at once.

Several times already this conflict of interests and opinions had led to the rejection of valuable amendments in the law of treason, and on this occasion Leeds seems to have tried to evade the whole problem by giving his support to an entirely different measure, introduced in the Lords by the Marquis of Normanby, the object of which was to make wilful perjury a capital offence, and so strike at the very root of the evils so apparent in treason trials. The judges on being consulted, however, gave it as their opinion that the main effect of the

largely due to the influence of Sir John Lowther that the extreme date eventually fixed upon was November 1, 1696, rather than November 1, 1695. In the Lords the Earl of Pembroke, possibly with the support of the Lord President, argued unsuccessfully that in order to avoid retrospective legislation the existing Parliament should itself be given a further three years of life, and that the date should therefore be November 1, 1697. This reluctance to face a speedy dissolution was fully shared by many members of the Whig Government, but not by the Whig rank and file, who were confident that a general election would result in the return of a definitely Whig Parliament (Bonnet, December 4/14, 11/21, 14/24, 18/28, 1694, in *Ranke*, vi. 252-60).

bill would simply be to discourage prosecutions, and on this ground the motion that the bill should be engrossed was met by a negative against which Leeds could only record his protest.[1]

The difficulties of the Treason Bill had therefore to be faced, and on the whole Leeds advocated the acceptance of that measure. It is true that he insisted on an amendment introduced by the Lords reforming the Court of the Lord High Steward,[2] upon which the two Houses found it impossible to reach agreement, and which therefore caused the loss of the bill. It is equally true that many who were secretly opposed to the bill also supported that amendment in the expectation that some such result would follow. But Leeds appears to have declared himself in favour of the general principles of the bill as well as of the amendment, and on January 23, in the very important debate on the question whether it should come into force on March 25, 1695, or March 25, 1698, he certainly argued strongly in favour of the earlier date, which was rejected by only one vote.[3]

On this last point Leeds had made common cause with the Tory malcontents in opposing the wishes of what was mainly a Whig Government. Yet two days later he performed a signal

---

[1] In thus dissenting from the opinion of the House he had the support not merely of Normanby but also of Bolton and Devonshire (*L.J.*, xv. 443-66 ; *House of Lords MSS.*, 1693-5, pp. 410-12 ; Bonnet, December 11/21, 1694, in *Ranke*, vi. 257).

[2] It is probably significant that this amendment was introduced into the Treason Bill immediately after the Perjury Bill had been rejected (Bonnet, January 22/February 1, 1695, in *Ranke*, vi. 267).

[3] *L.J.*, xv. 448-72 ; *House of Lords MSS.*, 1693-5, pp. 416-20. " Ce jour-là, Mecredy, les Seigneurs entendirent le rapport du comité touchant le bil des procez de haute-trahison, et il y ut de grandes disputes sur la clause qui y a été ajoutée, que le bil ne pourroit être en usage, ou n'auroit force de loy, qu'en l'année 1698. Le Duc de Leeds, President du Conseil, s'etendit fort sur l'importance du bil, et sur l'avantage qui en reviendroit a la nation, et aux pairs en particulier, et dit qu'il ne s'en etoit point encore proposé de plus considerable que celui-la ; et d'autres ayant dit qu'il etoit bon, comme il avoit déja été arrêté, qu'il n'ut lieu qu'apres la paix, parce qu'il se pourroit faire que des malintentionnés dans la conjoncture presente abuseroient des priviléges que cet acte leur donneroit, mais il repliqua que pour lui il ne vouloit pas faire du prophète en determinant le temps que la guerre dureroit, si ce seroit deux ou trois ans, et qu'il étoit d'opinion que dès celle-ci le bil seroit mis en pratique. Mais la question ayant de nouveau été agitée là-dessus, il y ût 44 voix contre 42 pour en renvoyer l'usage en 1698 " (L'Hermitage, January 25/February 4, 1695). It should be noted that Leeds was not one of the twenty-four lords who protested against the vote.

service for that Government by assisting it to withstand what was mainly a Tory attack. Encouraged no doubt by the narrowness of the majority recorded against him, Nottingham on January 25 put himself at the head of all the discontented elements in the House of Lords, and moved what amounted to a vote of censure on those in control of affairs. Beginning his vicious onslaught [1] by enumerating some dozen grievances of the first importance, including the absence of the fleet in distant waters, the mismanagement of the attack on Brest, the establishment of a Bank which was injurious both to the commercial and to the landed interest, the drain of money overseas, and the bad condition of that at home, he made it his principal point that William should be urged to include in the ministry " des personnes de bon sens et qui ne fussent pas odieuses à la nation ; " and ended by proposing a petition to the King that he should not go to Flanders that year, or if he deemed it essential to go that he should declare immediately to whom the Government was to be entrusted in his absence. Halifax then continued the attack by declaiming against the Bank, Torrington by denouncing misconduct at sea, and Rochester by arguing that the sitting Parliament, having been summoned by William and Mary, could have no legal existence now that Mary was dead.

On behalf of the Government Godolphin made a rather feeble speech, consisting largely of apologies for Shrewsbury, who was too ill to attend and answer for himself. Devonshire and Normanby also spoke for the Government ; but it is clear that the main burden of the defence fell upon Leeds, who acquitted himself so well as to secure the rout of the malcontents. In order to give point to what threatened to be a very long and rambling debate it was resolved to concentrate on one particular grievance, and the grievance selected was the evil effects said to be produced by the Bank. On a formal proposal being made that a day should be appointed to take these into consideration it was rejected by 33 votes to 23, and the attack on the Government collapsed with it.[2]

[1] " La harangue la plus envenimée qu'il fut possible contre le Gouvernement."

[2] *L.J.*, xv. 471 ; *House of Lords MSS.*, 1693-5, p. 459 ; L'Hermitage, February 1/11, 1695 ; Bonnet, January 25/February 4, 1695, in *Ranke*, vi. 268 ; *Luttrell*, iii. 431-2.

By these temporising tactics Leeds no doubt succeeded in postponing for a few months the evil day when he himself should be assailed ; but a postponement was all it was possible for him to achieve, and as the parliamentary session drew to a close the inevitable crisis at length developed. A seemingly unimportant petition from the town of Royston in Hertfordshire,[1] concerning some exactions made by an infantry regiment which had been defrauded of its pay, induced the Commons to embark upon an investigation into corrupt practices which speedily assumed alarming dimensions. Inasmuch as the Tories had almost monopolised the Government for some years previously the majority of the revelations naturally affected members of their party, and were seized upon with avidity by the Whigs and pressed to the utmost. Henry Guy, the Secretary to the Treasury, was accused of receiving a bribe of 200 guineas for procuring payment of the arrears due to a regiment, and was sent to the Tower.[2] Sir John Trevor, Speaker of the Commons, was discovered to have taken 1,000 guineas from the City of London for assisting the passing of a local bill, and was expelled from the House.[3] Finally it began to appear that even greater men might be implicated if a sufficiently exhaustive investigation could be made into the affairs of the East India Company.

During the two previous years that Company had been hard put to it to defend its charter, and an examination of its accounts for the period showed disbursements amounting to nearly £90,000 for which there was no satisfactory explanation. The obvious assumption was that the money had been distributed as bribes among statesmen and courtiers, and the governor of the company, Sir Thomas Cook, through whose hands it had passed, was required to state what had become

---

[1] Presented on January 12, 1695 (*C.J.*, xi. 202).

[2] February 16 (*C.J.*, xi. 236).

[3] March 16. On the previous day the Commons had proceeded to the election of a new Speaker, and by 179 votes to 146 had chosen Paul Foley in preference to Sir Thomas Littleton. It is probably indicative of Leeds's desire to remain on good terms with responsible Whig opinion that Littleton, a recognised Whig proposed by Wharton as the Government candidate, was seconded by Sir Henry Goodricke (*C.J.*, xi. 272, 274 ; *Cal. S.P. Dom.*, 1695, p. 318).

of it. On his refusal to do so he was sent to the Tower,[1] and a bill was rapidly rushed through the House of Commons imposing very heavy penalties upon him if he persisted in his attitude.[2]

When this bill was received by the Lords the Duke of Leeds was not in the House, and had been very irregular in his attendance for some time ; but on April 9, the day fixed for the first reading, he came forward to deliver a most vehement attack upon it, and thereafter was present in the House practically every day. In the heated atmosphere of the moment to speak against the bill at all was dangerous, and rumour immediately asserted that he had been paid £10,000 for doing so ; but with characteristic confidence he declared upon his honour that his hands were entirely clean, offered to take an oath to that effect, and insisted that his sole reason for opposing the bill was the shock to public faith involved in compelling a member of any society to reveal its innermost secrets.[3] The obstructive tactics which he and his friends adopted, however, proved unavailing, and Sir Thomas Cook deemed it prudent to come to an agreement with both Houses that in return for an indemnity he would reveal all he knew.[4] His revelations, made to a special joint committee of Lords and Commons on April 23, proved extremely difficult to interpret ; but as a result of exhaustive investigation it was clearly established that

[1] March 26 (C.J., xi. 283).

[2] The bill, introduced and read a first time on March 28, passed the Commons and was sent to the Lords on April 6 (C.J., xi. 285, 295-6). It is printed in House of Lords MSS., 1693-5, pp. 548-9.

[3] L.J., xv. 532, 534 ; Parliamentary History, v. 911. " Le Duc de Leeds, qu'on avoit dit avoir reçû 10,000 l. en s'opposant au bil contre le chevalier Cook, dit qu'il suffiroit de se mettre en devoir de le faire rejetter pour être incontinant accusé d'être du nombre des gratifiés, mais qu'il declaroit sur son honneur qu'il n'y avoit aucune part, et que si cela ne suffisoit pas il etoit prêt de s'en purger par serment ; que n'y ayant donc aucun interêt particulier, celui du public lui faisoit dire que ce seroit violer la foy publique que d'obliger un membre d'un corps a reveler les secrets de sa societé " (L'Hermitage, April 16/26, 1695).

[4] Leeds professed to welcome this change of front, as meaning that the bill which he " esteemed to be of so pernicious a nature " would no longer be necessary, but urged that for the sake of the reputation of the House Cook should be required, before the indemnity was granted, to declare upon oath whether his revelations would implicate any of its members (Parliamentary History, v. 912). At the same time the Duke was giving every assistance to other peers, such as Normanby, whose conduct had been called in question during the general investigation (L'Hermitage, April 19/29, 1695).

Cook had enlisted the support of the Duke of Leeds through
the agency of Sir Basil Firebrace, who in turn had employed
an intermediary named Charles Bates, and that in recognition
of this a sum of 5,500 guineas, in two notes of 3,000 and 2,500
guineas respectively, had been paid.

The real problem was to determine whether the money had
ever actually reached Leeds himself.　The story told by Bates
was that he had offered it to the Lord President, who had told
him to keep it ; but that being very bad at counting money
he had obtained permission for the Duke's Swiss servant, John
Robart, to cash the notes for him.　Robart had accordingly
done so, but had immediately handed the coin over to him,
and he had kept it until shortly before the investigation, when
in view of the outcry that was beginning he had returned the
greater part of it to Sir Basil Firebrace.　On cross-examination,
however, Bates had to admit that this was not strictly true,
and that in reality Robart had retained the money until
immediately before the repayment was effected.[1]

This was a highly suspicious tale, and when on April 27 the
report of the joint committee was laid before the Lords the
Duke felt it necessary to defend himself.　In substance he confirmed the story told by Bates, protesting his own complete
innocence of corruption and yet taking credit for generosity in
assisting another to procure so substantial a reward.[2]　Meanwhile, however, the report had also been laid before the Commons by Thomas Wharton, the chairman of the committee,
and there after some bitter speeches it was resolved that Leeds
should be impeached.[3]　A message whispered in his ear gave
him news of what was happening, and breaking off his address
to the Lords he hurried across, with their permission, to confront the greater danger in the Commons.

---

[1] *L.J.*, xv. 565-79 ; *House of Lords MSS.*, 1693-5, pp. 549-61.　The Duke's
explanation was that he was quite unaware the money had been left in his
house.　" Ayant deja declaré dans la Chambre des Seigneurs qu'il n'avoit
point reçû d'argent, et qu'il étoit prêt même d'en faire serment, il a dit à
quelques uns de ses amis qu'ayant appris depuis que ces 5,000 l. avoient été
portées chez lui il les a renvoyées au chevalier Cooke " (L'Hermitage, April
26/May 6, 1695).

[2] *Parliamentary History*, v. 934.

[3] *C.J.*, xi. 327.　The only argument advanced in his defence appears to have
been that there was no law against taking money at Court.

The speech which he there delivered, although it lasted about half an hour, was almost certainly impromptu, and was generally regarded as one of his less happy efforts. Reminding his hearers of the injustice with which he had been accused in 1678, he assured them that if he had been the kind of man he was then said to be they would not have been sitting in Parliament to pass judgment upon him. The latest accusation, he insisted, was as baseless as the earlier one, and inspired by nothing but personal animosity. Firebrace had been promised an indemnity in return for accusing him. His own services in the marriage of William and Mary and at the time of the Revolution should have been sufficient evidence of his honour and good faith.

Nevertheless what he said carried considerable weight, and there was a general feeling that if he could have spoken before the impeachment was voted it might not have been voted at all. But having made their decision the Commons refused to entertain his suggestion that they should reconsider it, and showed themselves much readier to accede to his alternative request, that the matter should be brought to a determination as speedily as possible. Immediately after Leeds had withdrawn the impeachment was carried up to the Lords by Wharton, and a committee was appointed to prepare formal articles against him.[1]

The articles presented by this committee and approved by the Commons on April 29 [2] bore little resemblance to those of

---

[1] The account given in the contemporary *Collection of Debates and Proceedings in Parliament in 1694 and 1695*, reprinted in *Parliamentary History*, v. 935-6, is confirmed in substance by L'Hermitage. " Les Communes en ayant été averties [*i.e.* of the Duke's desire to be heard] firent mettre un siége au dedans de la barre, et étant arrivé il fit un discours d'une demie heure. Il dit que c'etoit pour la seconde fois qu'il comparoissoit devant cette Chambre pour répondre aux calomnies de ses ennemis ; qu'il y avoit deja plusieurs années qu'on l'avoit accusé d'avoir le coeur François, mais que l'evenement avoit fait voir le contraire, voulant donner à entendre que c'etoit lui qui avoit le plus contribué au mariage du Roy, ce qui étoit fort opposé a l'esprit dont on vouloit qu'il fut animé ; et il ajouta que s'il avoit été tel qu'on vouloit qu'il fut il pouvoit dire que cette assemblée ne seroit pas formée comme elle est presentement, et qu'il y en avoit beaucoup qui n'auroient pas l'avantage de s'y trouver, mais que cependant il voyoit bien que ses ennemis ne se lassoient point, et qu'il voyoit qu'il y avoit une grande cabale contre lui ; et il fit extremement valoir les services qu'il croyoit avoir rendu, et d'une manière même un peu forte " (L'Hermitage, April 30/May 10, 1695).

[2] Printed *infra*, ii. 237.

1675 and 1678. They made no mention of treason, but only of high crimes and misdemeanors, and amounted to little more than a statement that the Duke had betrayed his trust as a Privy Councillor by entering into a corrupt contract to procure for the East India Company the charter they desired in return for a sum of money. But on that very account they were the more dangerous. There could be little real doubt that Leeds was guilty, and the studied moderation of the charge only made it more difficult for his friends to disguise the issue by concentrating on any absurd accusations against him.

In their haste to vote the impeachment, however, the Commons had failed to provide for securing the necessary evidence, and when the Duke entered a formal plea of not guilty, and the Commons endeavoured to substantiate their charge, they discovered that John Robart was not to be found.[1] This practically brought matters to a standstill, probably to the secret satisfaction of all parties, for no one knew what facts a thorough investigation might bring to light. The Commons naturally blamed Leeds for the disappearance of Robart. The Duke very properly replied that it was not his business to produce witnesses for his accusers, insisted on his right to a speedy trial, and even moved, though unsuccessfully, that if the Commons could not proceed before the close of the session his impeachment should be dismissed. On April 30 his followers endeavoured to hold up a money bill in the Commons until the impeachment should be proceeded with. On May 3, after repeated complaints of a delay which he declared to be de-

---

[1] The articles of impeachment were carried up to the Lords by Wharton on April 29, and were denounced by Leeds in a speech in which he reiterated his statement that they were the result of a plot contrived against him some time before. On April 30 the Duke entered his plea of not guilty, declaring on his honour and conscience that he had great wrong done him in the accusation (*L.J.*, xv. 582-4 ; *Parliamentary History*, v. 938). The importance of Robart lay in the fact that he alone could establish any direct connection between Leeds and the money, a matter on which the most diverse opinions prevailed. " Personne ne deposant avoir donné cet argent au Duc de Leeds, quelques uns veulent qu'il n'ait point û connoissance qu'il ait été porté chez lui, et que c'est madame sa femme qui l'a reçû à son insçû ; mais tout le monde n'est pas disposé à faire un si favorable jugement, n'y ayant pas autant d'apparence qu'il seroit à souhaiter pour lui que cet argent ait demûré si longtemps dans sa maison sans qu'il en ût aucune connoissance, ayant été compté par un officier de sa maison " (L'Hermitage, April 30/May 10, 1695).

liberate,[1] Leeds threatened to hold up the same bill in the Lords. In vain the Lords remonstrated with the Commons. The Commons could only reply at a special conference that without Robart they could not proceed, and the Lords saw no remedy but a petition to the King requesting him to issue a proclamation for stopping the ports and seizing Robart.[2] The same day the Parliament, which had already remained in session unduly long, was prorogued without any conclusion having been reached.[3]

The offence of which Leeds was accused was characteristic of the age rather than of the man, and few even among his accusers had any right to cast a stone at him ; but the penalties of being found out were almost as heavy in the late seventeenth century as in more upright times. Owing to the death of Mary it was necessary on this occasion that during William's absence on the Continent the royal power should be delegated to a commission of regency, of which Leeds in happier circumstances would almost certainly have been a member.[4] Now his inclusion in the commission was practically impossible ; and if he was not to be one of the regents, or Lords Justices, it was difficult to see how he could continue to preside at meetings

---

[1] " Alledging that the impeachment was only to load him with disgrace, and that they never intended to try him." Leeds reminded the Lords how easily his case might be theirs. " Il leur representa que cette affaire les regardoit tous en quelque manière aussi bien que lui, et que si on permettoit aux Communes d'accuser qui ils voudroient sans se mettre en devoir de justifier ce qu'elles avançoient il ne tiendroit qu'a elles de suspendre de leurs emplois ceux qui en auroient " (L'Hermitage, May 3/13, 1695).

[2] Leeds made no opposition to the petition, supplied Robart's full name, and described the circumstances which had induced him to seek refuge in Switzerland (L.J., xv. 584-9 ; C.J., xi. 329-33 ; House of Lords MSS., 1693-5, p. 581 ; Parliamentary History, v. 938-41 ; Burnet, ii. 146-7 ; L'Hermitage, May 3/13, 1695). Letters were immediately issued to the authorities at all the ports requiring them to secure the fugitive (Cal. S.P. Dom., 1694-5, p. 460).

[3] According to one account, after the conference " the Lords had a long debate about throwing out the impeachment, and precedents were searched, but none coming pat in the matter it was offered by the Duke of Shrewsbury that in the common courts of justice upon the like accounts it was the common practice to suspend a trial. The House took up the notion, and it was passed with common consent that his Grace should stand impeached till the next meeting of Parliament " (Cal. S.P. Dom., 1695, p. 328). There is no record, however, of any such resolution.

[4] " Il y a apparence que le Duc de Leeds auroit été parmi ces gouverneurs, s'il n'avoit pas été accusé par la Chambre des Communes " (L'Hermitage, May 7/17, 1695).

of the Council, which these Lords Justices would necessarily attend. Rumour accordingly anticipated his immediate dismissal, and named the Earl of Sunderland as his successor.[1]

William, however, still hesitated to alienate the Church party by removing the one prominent minister in whom they had confidence,[2] and was also reluctant to inflict so signal a mark of his displeasure on a statesman to whom Mary at least had always professed great obligations. A private intimation was therefore given him that he should not appear in Council at all while the Lords Justices were in office, and the problem of his position was thus shelved until a more convenient season.

With doubtful wisdom Leeds interpreted the royal instructions in the narrowest and most literal sense. Until the King actually left England he not only continued to frequent the Court but persisted in attending the Council, and on May 9 had thus both the pleasure of welcoming his nephew Peregrine Bertie to the Board, and the mortification of giving his approval to the proclamation desired by the Lords ordering the arrest of John Robart, the principal witness against himself.[3] During the summer he allowed no doubt to be entertained that although in temporary retirement he was still Lord President, insisting on taking precedence on formal occasions even of the Lords Justices, unless the full quorum of four were present which alone entitled them to represent the King.[4] Immediately

---

[1] *Luttrell*, iii. 466, 467.

[2] It was believed that Leeds was deliberately trying to bring the Church into the quarrel and " breake his fall upon their backs " (*Portland MSS.*, ii. 173).

[3] P.C. Reg. 76, p. 130 ; *Cal. S.P. Dom.*, 1694-5, p. 465 ; *Luttrell*, iii. 470 ; L'Hermitage, May 10/20, 1695. It was noticed as significant at the time that the proclamation made no mention of any reward (Carte MSS. 76, f. 679). In the middle of August, on information that Robart had appeared in London, the Lords Justices issued a similar proclamation, offering a reward of £200 for his apprehension (L'Hermitage, August 16/26, 1695 ; *Cal. S.P. Dom.*, 1695, pp. 45, 344 ; *Portledge Papers*, p. 210).

[4] " Madame la Princesse alla Dimanche à la chapelle de Whithall, ce qu'elle n'avoit pas fait depuis la mesintelligence. Il y ût un grand concours de monde. Le Duc de Leeds s'y trouva, qui ne voulut pas perdre l'occasion d'y prendre sa place selon son rang de President du Conseil, se mettant au dessus du Duc de Sommerset, et même de deux Lords Justice, qui n'étoient pas toutefois regardés comme tels, n'étant pas quatre, qui est le nombre suffisant pour representer le corps de la regence ; ainsi ils n'êtoient pas en droit de le preceder. Il laissa seulement les places de l'Archevêque et du Garde des Seaux, et prit la troisième " (L'Hermitage, June 4/14, 1695).

William returned from the Continent he came forward and proposed to attend the Council once more.[1]

Other ideas, however, were now in the ascendant. In the Continental war the campaign of 1695 had proved more favourable to the Allies than any which had previously been conducted, and the success of English arms at Namur and in the Mediterranean had inspired the King and his advisers with the resolve to risk a dissolution,[2] in the hope that a Whig Parliament would be returned, and that Whig Parliament and Whig ministry might then co-operate wholeheartedly in the prosecution of the war. Of such a policy the restoration of Leeds to his former position clearly could form no part, especially as the discredit into which the Lord President himself had fallen had been appreciably augmented by an unhappy error committed during the summer by his son. Placed in command of a separate squadron for the protection of English trade in the Channel and the Irish Sea, Carmarthen had been engaged in bringing home the Cadiz fleet of some eighty sail when he mistook a number of outward-bound West Indiamen, accompanied by some warships which he had been ordered to add to his own fleet, for a French force under the Marquis of Nesmond, and feeling he was not strong enough to protect his convoy retired with it to Milford Haven.[3] Not only so, but having once got into port he was prevented by contrary winds from getting out again. The result was a long delay to the Cadiz

---

[1] *Luttrell*, iii. 537.

[2] As early as the beginning of September a dissolution was anticipated (*Portland MSS.*, iii. 565-6 ; *Luttrell*, iii. 523, 524).

[3] Carmarthen was guilty of nothing worse than an error of judgment, and had given so many proofs of his courage that even his enemies charged him with no more than lack of enterprise due to dissatisfaction at the treatment of his father. In this very expedition he had again given a display of that headlong disregard of consequences which so endeared him to the men he commanded, and which was at once his greatest virtue and his most serious weakness. " On écrit aussi d'Irlande que le feu ayant pris au *Devonshire*, vaisseau de guerre, dans le tems que les gens de l'equipage nettoyoient leurs armes dans la chambre d'un canonnier, un mousquet qui s'en étoit allé par hazard ayant mis le feu à des bandolières et à de la poudre, ce qui avoit tué et blessé trente hommes, et que dans le tems que le reste s'eloignoit en diligence de crainte de subir le même sort le Marquis de Carmarthen y accourut en personne, et par son exemple et ses exhortations fit éteindre le feu de manière qu'il y aura peu de dommage " (L'Hermitage, July 26/August 5, 1695).

fleet,[1] serious losses among other ships which during his enforced inactivity remained insufficiently protected, and a general outcry which compelled the Government to recall him to London.[2]

In these circumstances the real danger seemed to be that if the Whigs secured control of Parliament they would waste their time in factious attacks on Leeds, Carmarthen and other Tories, instead of devoting their energies to the European conflict. Scarcely had William returned to England, accordingly, when a tacit bargain was struck. The King refrained, at least for the time, from offering Carmarthen any further employment at sea, and renewed his instructions to Leeds to remain absent from Council. The Whig leaders on their side undertook to prevent any revival of the " business of the East India Company." [3] A dissolution was then proclaimed,[4] and the country was plunged into the first general election it had known for five years.

Until the returns were completed the position inevitably remained somewhat uncertain ; but it was soon abundantly clear what the general character of the new Parliament was going to be. Leeds himself was not specially badly hit. His brother Charles was once more returned at Hull ; his Yorkshire followers retained their seats ; and the Berties were more successful than ever.[5] But the Parliament elected was strongly Whig,[6] and his continued participation in affairs was thus made impossible. No open disgrace followed. The King remained quite friendly. The University of Oxford chose this as the most

---

[1] " La flotte du Detroit . . . ayant demûré si longtems à venir qu'on dit que les fruits qui se trouveront parmi ces marchandises seront gates, y ayant entr'autres beaucoup d'oranges et citrons " (L'Hermitage, August 2/12, 1695).

[2] *Luttrell*, iii. 478-507 ; L'Hermitage, July 30/August 9, 1695 ; *Portledge Papers*, p. 209 ; *Burnet*, ii. 155 ; *Portland MSS.*, iii. 564 ; *Cal. S.P. Dom.*, 1695, p. 38.

[3] This seems to be the obvious interpretation of Shrewsbury's letter to Somers of October 31, 1695 (*Shrewsbury Correspondence*, pp. 399-400).

[4] On October 11 (*L.J.*, xv. 596).

[5] *Return of Members of Parliament*, i. 574, 575, 577. Leeds took a keen interest in the elections, and at Westminster gave " a great deal of roast beef against Mr. Montagu," though without result (*Buccleuch MSS. at Montagu House*, ii. 246).

[6] The contemporary estimate was that more than 150 new members were elected, most of them Whigs (*Burnet*, ii. 160 ; *Luttrell*, iii. 548).

opportune moment to confer upon him the degree of D.C.L.[1] During William's reign, however, he was never again to appear in Council.[2]

A less resolute man might have accepted this courteous relegation to obscurity as the end of his political career ; but Leeds was constitutionally incapable of submitting tamely to a stroke of adverse fortune, and embarked at once on a determined effort to recover the power and prestige he had lost. Since the death of Mary and the growth of Whig influence at William's court many of his Tory friends had inclined to consider the possibility of a Jacobite restoration. He, on the other hand, turned to the next occupant of the throne according to the Revolution settlement and endeavoured to establish himself in the good graces of Anne. For some years his determined championship of William had caused the Princess to regard him with suspicion ; but his relatives among the Berties had always enjoyed her confidence,[3] and more than once since the disgrace of Marlborough and the estrangement of Anne from her royal sister he had been looked to as the man best fitted to effect a reconciliation.[4] Now when the death of Mary had partly healed the breach he arranged to surrender to the Princess his rooms in St. James's Palace, paid her formal visits at Windsor, and succeeded at least in overcoming any hostility she had formerly felt for him.[5]

That he was unable to advance any further and form, as perhaps he intended, an anti-Jacobite Church party in her favour, was no doubt due to the influence of Marlborough, who declined any co-operation with him. Nevertheless he did not immediately go into opposition to the existing Government. Not only were he and his son the holders of several lucrative offices which they were reluctant to endanger, but they were both anxious to retain the favour of the Court as some protection against a possible attack by Parliament ; and although,

[1] On November 9, 1695, when the King, in the course of a lengthy progress, visited the University.

[2] As late as November 12 it was considered worthy of note that he was not summoned to a Council meeting (*Luttrell*, iii. 550).

[3] *Infra*, ii. 220.

[4] B.M. Add. MSS. 36662, f. 415 ; *Luttrell*, ii. 438.

[5] *Burnet*, ii. 149 ; *Luttrell*, iii. 475, 510.

in accordance with the wishes of the King, the assault on Leeds was not renewed, it was scarcely likely that Carmarthen would remain unaffected by the inevitable enquiry into the losses at sea during the summer.

On December 6, 1695, only a fortnight after Parliament met, the question of these losses was raised in the House of Lords, and on December 27, the Admiralty Commission having meanwhile made its answer to all the complaints brought forward, January 4 was appointed for a general consideration of the matter. Characteristically enough on that day Carmarthen, on whom the Admiralty had thrown much of the blame for all that had gone amiss, did not even take the trouble to attend,[1] and might have been condemned in his absence had not Torrington and Leeds secured some delay by arguing that a satisfactory investigation could be conducted only by a special committee and not by the whole House. With his usual audacity, indeed, Leeds insisted on being a member of the committee, declaring that he would be among the most active in examining Carmarthen, and one of the readiest to condemn him if he were guilty. Happily it soon appeared that apart from his one serious error Carmarthen had conducted his operations with ability,[2] and could make out quite a good case against the Admiralty, which had supplied him neither with sufficient forces, nor with reliable information, nor even with intelligible instructions. On February 6, after interminable debates, the Lords resolved " that the Lord Keviton hath behaved himself in the last summer's expedition at sea with courage, conduct and fidelity," and the incident was officially closed.[3]

The fundamental reason, however, for the Lord President's reluctance to go into opposition went much deeper than these personal considerations. As a result of nearly forty years' con-

[1] " Au lieu de se trouver à la Chambre pour respondre il s'absenta, et on trouva que s'estoit une ireguliarite fort extraordinaire, et chacun y fit ses reflections." The general opinion was that Carmarthen " estoit peut-estre plustot occupé de quelque nouveau plaisir qu'embarasé de sa deffence."

[2] " Il parut qu'on le croyoit moins coupable que l'absence qu'il avoit fait le jour qu'il devoit respondre n'avoit donné lieu de le croire."

[3] *L.J.*, xv. 606 ; *House of Lords MSS.*, 1695-7, pp. 64-117 ; L'Hermitage, January 7/17, 14/24, February 7/17, 1696 ; *Luttrell*, iv. 1-14. The attack on Carmarthen was generally regarded as being also an indirect attack on Leeds (*Hastings MSS.*, ii. 256).

nection with the Government, half of which had been spent in positions of the highest trust, Leeds had had indelibly impressed upon him the outlook of the official, and was incapable of irresponsible obstruction. His experience of opposition was extraordinarily limited. In spite of the many vicissitudes of his stormy career he had never once taken the lead in Parliament against the Government, and indeed had scarcely appeared in opposition at all since the days of Clarendon. Moreover he was not greatly attracted to any section among the malcontents of the day. With the new Toryism which was beginning to grow up under the leadership of Foley and Harley he had little sympathy, while too many of the older Tories appeared to him to be infected with Jacobitism.

Thus his main activities in the parliamentary session of 1695–6 were still directed towards assisting the Government to deal with the many difficult problems confronting it. During the previous summer alarm at the rapid deterioration of the silver currency had reached a height which made immediate action imperative. The lack of a milled edge had encouraged clipping and paring until an average silver coin contained little more than half the amount of metal it was supposed to contain, and the ordinary process of buying and selling had become a highly speculative transaction. Unfortunately it was easier to recognise the evil than to find a remedy which would spread the cost of a restoration equitably over all, and while avoiding too serious a dislocation in financial matters would yet refrain from providing the clippers and parers with further opportunities for illicit profits. Somers, it is true, proposed in Council an ingenious scheme by which all unmilled coin was suddenly and without warning to be called down to its value by weight, while at the same time holders of such coin who immediately surrendered it to be tested were to be given notes promising payment of the difference between its nominal and its real value. But this scheme proved too daring for the Council to consider without parliamentary sanction, and the initial step was thus left to be taken when the Houses assembled later in the year.[1]

As a man well versed in financial affairs Leeds was better able to appreciate the full gravity of the situation than most

---

[1] *Burnet*, ii. 147.

of his contemporaries, and seems also to have been much impressed by the simplicity and boldness of the proposals advanced by Somers. It was not improbably at his instigation that the Lords took the whole problem into consideration at the very beginning of the session,[1] and agreed upon a somewhat colourless address to the King, which they transmitted to the Commons for their concurrence with the obvious purpose of stirring that body into action.[2] But the Commons in their debates, in the resolutions they adopted, and in the bill which was eventually founded on these resolutions, were guided rather by the Chancellor of the Exchequer, Charles Montagu, and the scheme they adopted differed in certain essential respects from that of Somers. After May 4, 1696, clipped money was no longer to be received as legal coin of the realm. In the interval before that date all holders of such money were to be invited to surrender it to the Government, receiving in return, as quickly as it could be produced, good money of the same nominal value. The loss involved in the transaction was to be borne by the nation.[3]

The commercial dislocation necessarily produced by the shortage of coin under this scheme, although less violent than that under the other, was bound to be of much longer duration. When the Coinage Bill came up from the Commons to the Lords, accordingly, Leeds proposed as an amendment what, although now shorn of the element of surprise, was essentially Somers's scheme. It is not clear that Somers himself now supported it ; but its origin was probably known, and few among the Lords were inclined on such a matter to oppose their opinion to that of the greatest lawyer of the day supported by a former Lord Treasurer. Almost without question the proposal was accepted, and a clause giving effect to it was drawn up and embodied in the bill.[4]

[1] On December 2, 1695, the first day real business was done.

[2] All that is certain is that Leeds was a member of the select committee which drew up the address, and one of the managers of the conference at which it was communicated, with reasons, to the Commons (*L.J.*, xv. 603-5).

[3] *C.J.*, xi. 354-9, 363-4, 367-70 ; *Burnet*, ii. 161.

[4] The bill was received by the Lords and read a first time on December 27. Leeds made his proposal on the second reading on December 30, and was appointed a member of a select committee to draw up a clause embodying his ideas. On December 31 the clause was reported and approved, and the whole bill was referred to the same committee in order that the necessary

Possibly the Commons really feared the extreme confusion of the few days during which, according to Leeds's proposals, the bulk of the coinage of the nation would have to be handed over to be tested.[1] Possibly they doubted whether it was practicable to let money pass by weight.[2] More probably they were animated by nothing more than their usual dislike of any interference by the Lords in financial affairs. In any case they refused to accept the alterations made in their scheme, and rather than cause delay by raising a quarrel between the two Houses Leeds very properly acquiesced in their decision.[3] Somewhat later in the session trouble arose over the inflated value of the gold guinea, which in the depreciated state of the silver coinage was being accepted as the equivalent of 30 shillings. Montagu's remedy was a bill arbitrarily fixing the price of the guinea at 22 shillings. Whether out of sympathy with those whose interests lay in maintaining the value of the guinea, or as a result of an appreciation of the fact that a reform of the silver coinage would automatically produce the reduction desired, Leeds also opposed this measure, but on being defeated in the Lords again acquiesced.[4]

adjustments should be made in it. On January 2, 1696, the bill, so adjusted, was reported, and on January 3 it was approved and passed (*L.J.*, xv. 622-8). " Au reste, sur la seconde lecture de ce bill, le Duc de Leeds proposa hier dans la Chambre des Seigneurs de fixer un tems ou chacun seroit oblige de porter son argent dans des bureaux, qui seroient establis dans tout le royaume, ou il y auroit des personnes qui seroient preposées, et qui auroient fait serment, lequels peseroient l'argent qu'on leur porteroit et le remettroient ensuite entre les mains des propriaiteres ; et que sy £100 sterling ne pesoient, par example, que la valleur de £60, on donneroit des billets ou talleys pour recevoir dans un autre tems £40 sterling avec l'interest, et que cette monoye ronguee auroit encore cours dans le commerce selon ce qu'elle peseroit jusqu'a ce qu'elle peut estre eschangee. . . . Ce nouveau projet fut generallement aprouve, a la reserve de trois ou quatre seigneurs qui sy oposerent " (L'Hermitage, December 31/January 10, 1695/6).

[1] The last day for this, according to the Lords' amendment, was January 25, 1696.

[2] " La Chambre des Communes . . . a trouvé qu'il y avoit tant de difficulte pour mettre en execution le projet des Seigneurs, de prandre la monoye au poids, qu'elle n'y a pu y acquiesser " (L'Hermitage, January 7/17, 1696).

[3] In the conferences between the two Houses Leeds, although a manager, does not appear to have taken a prominent part. The Commons eventually got over all difficulties by bringing in a new bill, to which the Lords offered no serious opposition (*L.J.*, xv. 632-46 ; *House of Lords MSS.*, 1695-7, pp. 128-31)

[4] The supplementary Coinage Bill fixing the price of guineas was sent up by the Commons to the Lords on March 28, and in spite of the efforts of

One reason for this unusual self-effacement on his part was that in the meantime there had arisen a threat to the Government of a different but much more alarming character. Since the death of Mary a general feeling had spread abroad that in the life of William was to be found the only serious obstacle to a Jacobite restoration, and while loyal subjects thus became daily more apprehensive for his safety the disloyal were encouraged in conspiracies aiming even at deliberate assassination. On Friday, February 21, 1696, full details of the most dangerous of these conspiracies, which provided not merely for the assassination of William, but also for insurrection at home accompanied by invasion from abroad, were betrayed to the Government. On the following day most of the conspirators were seized. On Monday, February 24, in a formal speech from the throne, William laid the matter before both Houses of Parliament.[1]

It says much for the reputation still enjoyed by Leeds that in this crisis of affairs his advice and support were immediately and eagerly sought. When the Cabinet Council was hastily assembled on the intervening Sunday to consider what action should be taken a special summons was sent to him,[2] and in

Nottingham was read there a first and second time on March 30. The real debate took place in grand committee on March 31, when " outre ce comte l'on a eu a soutenir les efforts du Duc de Leeds et du Comte de Rochester, secondez par 30 autres lords et animez par tout ce qu'il y a d'orfevres, marchands, et autres personnes interessées, sans parler de plus de 50 membres des Communes." The main argument advanced was that guineas were worth more than 22 shillings even in new money in Holland, and would therefore be exported ; but after a discussion lasting five hours the regulation passed by the Commons was approved by 53 votes to 33. Nottingham, Rochester, Abingdon, the Bishop of London and eleven other lords protested ; but Leeds did not join them (Bonnet, March 31/April 10, 1696 ; *L.J.*, xv. 720-3 ; *House of Lords MSS.*, 1695-7, pp. 234-5).

[1] *L.J.*, xv. 679. Leeds was a member of the committee which drew up the address in reply, thanking the King for his speech, congratulating him on his escape, and promising full support both at home and abroad.

[2] The meeting lasted for two hours and a half in the morning, and was resumed after dinner. " Le Duc de Leeds fut apellé en particulier." The others summoned were the Lords Justices of the previous summer, Prince George of Denmark, and Sir William Trumbull, who had succeeded Trenchard as Secretary of State (L'Hermitage, February 25/March 6, 1695/6). A fortnight earlier Leeds had been sent for by the King (*Hastings MSS.*, ii. 255), and it seems highly probable that this was in connection with the first report of the conspiracy, received by the Government on February 11, which was regarded with some scepticism at Court.

the prompt and effective measures adopted it is possible to see reflected his resolute and determined spirit.[1] Nevertheless the discovery of the assassination plot marks, to a much greater degree than his own impeachment, a turning point in his attitude to the Government. Almost from the beginning the Whigs endeavoured to make party capital out of the wave of horror that swept the country, grasping eagerly in particular at a proposal, first advanced in the Commons by Sir Rowland Gwyn, that members should follow the precedent of Elizabeth's reign by entering into an Association to defend William, their " rightful and lawful " King, against " the late King James and all his adherents." The result, as was intended, was to confront the Tories with the same dilemma as had caused them so much trouble in 1689 and 1690. If they opposed the Association they ran the risk of being branded as Jacobites. If they accepted it they would have to reckon with disunion in their own body, for the more rigid among them certainly would not take it.

In the Commons, where the project of an Association was brought forward on February 24, its acceptance was almost a foregone conclusion. The opposition of such men as Sir Edward Seymour and Sir William Williams served only to inflame the Whig majority, and the more moderate counsels of Sir John Lowther, obviously inspired by Leeds, were ignored.[2] In the Lords, however, where the Association was not brought forward till February 26, the atmosphere was somewhat calmer, and there Leeds himself took charge of the attempt to find a way of escape from the trap which the Whigs had set.

His first effort was directed towards securing the abandonment of the Association on the ground that it was altogether needless. Nobody, he declared to the Lords, could doubt that they were already virtually associated to maintain the Government, and the only effect of an attempt to give more precise definition to that fact would be to create division where no division yet existed. Finding, however, that this argument

---

[1] As Lord Lieutenant of the three ridings of Yorkshire Leeds took his part in giving effect to these measures (Hist. MSS. Com., *Various Collections*, viii. 81).

[2] *C.J.*, xi. 466-7 ; *Hastings MSS.*, ii. 259.

would not prevail, he reverted to the attitude he had adopted
when the same dilemma had been propounded before, and
endeavoured to prevent disunion by devising a formula which
could be accepted by as many, especially among the Tories, as
possible. The main difficulty was the recognition of William
as " rightful and lawful " King, vehemently opposed by
Nottingham, Rochester, Normanby and Ferrers, and as vehemently insisted upon by Monmouth, who with some show of
reason challenged those who denied that William was rightful
king to say plainly who it was that they considered to be the
rightful sovereign.[1] Finally, after an exhausting debate, Leeds
proposed that for the obnoxious words " is rightful and lawful
King of these realms " should be substituted " hath a right by
law to the crown of this realm, and that no other person whatsoever hath any right to the same." Devonshire and Portland
immediately intimated their approval, and the amendment was
on the point of being carried when Earl Rivers cast the balance
somewhat the other way by proposing, as a more exact form
of its final clause, the words " that neither the late King James
nor the pretended Prince of Wales nor any other person hath
any right whatsoever to the same." In this form, towards ten
o'clock in the evening, the Association was accepted by 60 votes
to 34.[2]

It was soon apparent that the apprehensions entertained by
Leeds and his allies were not without foundation. In the
Commons, where the original wording of the Association had
been retained, about a hundred members refused to sign ; in
the Lords about twenty.[3] Even the group of relatives who

[1] Monmouth spoke for two and a half hours, and insinuated that Rochester
at least had in mind neither James nor his son but the Princess Anne.

[2] *L.J.*, xv. 683 ; *House of Lords MSS.*, 1695-7, pp. 204-5 ; L'Hermitage,
February 28/March 9, 1695/6 ; *Burnet*, ii. 169-70 ; *Hatton Correspondence*,
ii. 221. According to one account Leeds adopted a much more extreme
attitude. " The President of the Council said that he would neither subscribe
him to be lawful or rightful King, to which Dr. Burnet replied that if he were
of the same sentiment he could very well have been one of the assassins in
the proclamation ; the first replied upon him that that doctrine was impious
and heretical in the pulpit, howsoever he broached it in that House " (*Hastings
MSS.*, ii. 259). The first part of this statement, however, is almost certainly
based on some misapprehension.

[3] The attitude of individual members of both Houses to the Association is
indicated *infra*, iii. 187-213.

followed Leeds himself were divided, the Osbornes and Lincolnshire Berties taking one side, while the Oxfordshire and Wiltshire
Berties took the other. Nor was this the worst. Almost of
its own accord the Association spread throughout the land, and
was signed with such alacrity that the Whigs were encouraged
to introduce a bill giving it legal recognition and making the
signing of it compulsory for all officials and members of Parliament. Divided in mind between dislike of those who advocated
this new test and contempt for those who scrupled taking it,
Leeds strongly opposed it in the House of Lords, and yet when
the final stage was reached was prevented by a real or pretended illness from appearing and voting against it.[1]

Thus the prorogation of Parliament on April 27 found the
Duke very far from satisfied with the course events were taking.
Had he been given a place among the Lords Justices and permitted to exercise once more the functions of Lord President
his resentment at the growing dominance of the Whigs would
no doubt have been diminished ; but any hopes he may have
had in that direction were shattered when William on April 30
nominated the same Lords Justices as in the previous year.[2]
Possibly by way of compensation Sir John Lowther, whose
influence had been increasing for some time, was created Viscount Lonsdale,[3] and Leeds himself was given an extension of
one of the many valuable grants made to him in the reign of
Charles II.[4] But the Duke's dissatisfaction was too deep-rooted

---

[1] The resolutions on which the bill was based were adopted in the Commons
on April 2, and the bill itself was introduced there two days later. On April 8
it was passed and sent to the Lords, where it was given a first reading the
same day. On April 14 it was passed by the Lords with some amendments
which were readily accepted by the Commons (C.J., xi. 543, 545, 553, 556 ;
L.J., xv. 730, 731, 735 ; House of Lords MSS., 1695-7, pp. 245-7). The great
debate in the Lords on April 13 lasted until nine o'clock, and every article
in the bill was opposed by Nottingham. " Il estoit apuyé par le Comte de
Rochester, par l'Evesque de Londres et par quelques autres ; mais deux de
ceux qui se seroient joint à eux, le Duc de Leeds et le Marquis de Normanby,
se trouverent indisposez et leur manqueront " (Bonnet, April 14/24, 1696).

[2] The inclusion of Leeds among the Lords Justices was certainly regarded
as a possibility. Writing to the States General, the official Dutch corre-
spondent in London, after giving the names of those appointed, adds, " Le
Duc de Leeds reste President du Conseil, mais sans en faire les fonctions, non
plus que ce qu'il a fait depuis un an " (L'Hermitage, May 5/15, 1696).

[3] Cal. S.P. Dom., 1696, p. 153.

[4] Infra, p. 553.

to be seriously affected by such bribes. Early in July he retired in disgust to Bath, and from that city proceeded to Yorkshire, not returning to London till the middle of October.[1]

While he was in the north the series of events was taking place which was to determine his political attitude beyond hope of change. Of the prisoners arrested in connection with the assassination plot the most important was undoubtedly Sir John Fenwick, and it was to Fenwick accordingly that all looked for information regarding the still greater men who were generally believed to have been behind the conspiracy. Every inducement was held out to him to reveal all he knew, and on August 10 he at length submitted a paper of information for the consideration of the King. To the consternation of the Whig Government, however, which had been expecting revelations incriminating the Tories, the principal persons implicated by his statements proved to be Shrewsbury, Russell, Marlborough and Godolphin, all members of their own body ; and the fate of Fenwick was thus immediately transformed into a party question. The Whigs dared not show any leniency towards him lest that should be interpreted as implying that his confession was accepted as true. The Tories could not be severe lest that should be interpreted as implying that his confession was regarded as false. During the summer the expectation was that Fenwick would be tried in the ordinary courts ; but lack of sufficient evidence against him made a conviction there highly improbable, and in the autumn it was accordingly resolved to place the matter before Parliament and proceed against him by bill of attainder.

Leeds had no personal reason for coming to the aid of Fenwick, and little inclination to show favour to any Jacobite conspirator ; but his indignation at the use of the assassination plot as a party weapon to weaken and divide the Tories inevitably inspired him with a desire to retaliate in kind by using Fenwick's statements to discredit the Whigs. It was thus, in all probability, with his mind already made up to show Fenwick what countenance he could that he came south to the meeting of Parliament on October 20 ; and if anything was needed to confirm his resolution it was provided by the acclamations with

[1] *Luttrell*, iv. 83 ; *Hastings MSS.*, ii. 285.

which he was received by a section of the London mob on his entry into the city.[1] The Tory cause, as he had always believed, did not lack supporters among the populace.

On November 6 Admiral Russell, the principal member of the Commons accused by Fenwick, acquainted the House with the charges made against him and his associates ; the papers of information were presented and read ; Fenwick was personally examined ; and on his failure to withdraw his " false and scandalous " accusations, and make a " full and ingenuous discovery " of the conspiracy, it was ordered that a bill of attainder should be brought in against him. As the motion in favour of the attainder was carried by a majority of nearly three to one Leeds was early confirmed in his belief that there was little chance of securing its rejection in the Commons ; but this did not deter him from making the best fight he could. Under the guidance of his own nephew, Lord Norris, Nottingham's brother, Heneage Finch, and such outstanding Tories as Sir Edward Seymour, Sir Richard Temple and Sir Christopher Musgrave, a storm of criticism was directed against the bill, and the majority in favour of it was substantially reduced at every stage. Nevertheless on November 25 it was eventually passed and sent to the Lords, where it was generally recognised that the real struggle would take place.[2]

Unfortunately for Fenwick the result of that struggle had already to some extent been prejudiced by events in the Commons. Owing to the large number of Low Church appointments made by William it was assumed that the vote of the bishops would on the whole go against Fenwick, and a proposal had accordingly been made to suggest their exclusion from voting by omitting the words " Lords Spiritual " from the enacting clause of the bill of attainder. This proposal, however, had been decisively defeated by 159 votes to 94, and the bishops hostile to Fenwick, some of whom might otherwise have

---

[1] *Hastings MSS.*, ii. 285.

[2] *Parliamentary History*, v. 998-1149 ; *Vernon Correspondence*, i. 46-50. The principal divisions in the Commons were, on the motion for a bill of attainder, 179 to 61 ; on the second reading of the bill, 196 to 104 ; on the motion for committing the bill, 182 to 128 ; on the motion for engrossing the bill, 125 to 88 ; on the motion that the bill do pass, 189 to 156 (*C.J.*, xi. 577-98).

refrained from voting, were thus not merely encouraged to vote, but warned that they might be endangering one of the rights of their order if they failed to do so.[1]

Even with the assistance of the bishops' vote it was seriously doubted at first whether the bill of attainder would be accepted by the Lords.[2] The opponents of the bill had the better case, the better speakers, and, it was believed, the larger number of voters actually in attendance on the House. Had Leeds been in charge of the opposition the rejection of the bill might have been carried at once. On November 14, however, the Lords had issued a special summons to absent members to attend,[3] and as the House gradually filled, and pressure was brought to bear by the Government on the less resolute among its opponents, the position changed. It was regarded as a great success for the Government that the use of proxies in connection with the bill was forbidden, and that consideration of it was postponed from November 26 to December 1, and then after a first reading to December 15.[4] During the interval it was believed that the majority turned decisively against Fenwick,[5] and when the struggle began this belief appeared to be justified. Preliminaries were concerned mainly with the question what evidence should be admitted, and on these preliminaries the voting went steadily in favour of the Government. Cardell Goodman, the principal witness, had been bribed by Fenwick's friends to abscond, and it was proposed to accept as evidence depositions which he had already made. Leeds stoutly resisted this proposal, but was defeated by 73 votes to 53, and could only

[1] *Parliamentary History*, v. 1111-2 ; Bonnet, November 20/30, 1696. The proposal that the bishops should be excluded was made by Lord Spencer (*Vernon Correspondence*, i. 69).

[2] " Cela pourra grossir le nombre de ceux qui seront pour ce dernier bill, mais d'ailleurs on aprehende beaucoup qu'il ne passe pas dans leur Chambre."

[3] *L.J.*, xvi. 12-13.

[4] *L.J.*, xvi. 19-20, 26, 34. " On crut avoir gaigné beaucoup hier dans la chambre haute, en faisant renvoyer l'affaire du Chevalier Fenwick à mardy prochain, au quel jour il y comparoistra, parce que lundy le Duc de Schrewsbury, qui y est si interessé, le Duc de Newcastel et d'autres bien intentionnez pour la Court doivent arriver. Mais cela n'empeche pas qu'on ne doute extrémement du succés que cette affaire y aura " (Bonnet, November 27/December 7, 1696).

[5] " Quelques uns calculent que le parti contre luy y est de 14 plus fort, sans les eveques " (Bonnet, December 8/18, 1696).

record his protest. John Clancy, a man of bad character who had been sentenced to the pillory for complicity in the bribery, was believed to have something to say in Fenwick's favour. Leeds urged that he should be heard, but the Lords decided that he was incompetent to act as a witness. On December 18, after a debate which continued until midnight, the second reading of the bill of attainder was carried by 73 votes to 55, and again Leeds could do no more than join with others in recording a protest.[1]

At this point, however, a reaction set in. Many peers who had been ready enough to vote against Fenwick in the early stages of the proceedings shrank from doing so when the end came in sight. Devonshire, Dorset and Pembroke, three of the Lords Justices during the previous summer, openly declared that they had hitherto voted for the bill of attainder only with the object of frightening Fenwick into a confession, and that in future they would oppose it.[2] Ormonde, Somerset, Lord Willoughby de Eresby, Lord Fitzwalter and others also changed sides. With characteristic skill Leeds made the path easy for such converts by suggesting that some milder penalty might be found for Fenwick, of whose substantial guilt nobody had any real doubt.[3] As a result the concluding stages of the bill were marked by more bitter controversy than ever ; but in the end the influence of the Court prevailed. On December 23, after a debate lasting till eight in the evening, the third reading was

[1] *L.J.*, xvi. 39-44 ; *House of Lords MSS.*, 1695-7, pp. 274-82 ; *Vernon Correspondence*, i. 126-34. The late sittings occasioned by the bill were regarded with great disfavour by the older peers. " Le Duc de Leeds dit que ceux qui estoient regles dans leur maniere de vivre ne pouvoient soutenir une si grande fatigue ; que pour les jeunes, qui opinoient à faire durer plus longtems la seance, pouvant souper à deux heures apres minuit, ils n'en seroient pas indisposes, mais qu'il valoit mieux s'assembler plus matin pour des affaires d'une telle importance et n'y demeurer pas si tard ; qu'alors tous les vieillards, dont l'avis devoit estres d'un plus grand poid que celuy des autres ne manqueroient pas de s'y trouver " (L'Hermitage, December 18/28, 1696).

[2] Of the four remaining Lords Justices Godolphin also voted against the bill, Shrewsbury was absent, and Somers was not a peer. Only the Archbishop of Canterbury " spoke for the bill to admiration," and eventually voted for it (*Vernon Correspondence*, i. 140).

[3] " Le Duc de Leeds disoit qu'on pouvoit convertir la peine du Chevalier Fenix à une prison perpetuelle, et le punir par une autre voix que celle du bil d'un suplice aussy rude que la mort " (L'Hermitage, December 25/January 4, 1696/7).

carried by 68 votes to 61, no fewer than 53 members of the
House, including Leeds, recording their protest.[1] On January
11, 1697, William gave his assent, and on January 28 Sir John
Fenwick was executed.

The effect of this controversy on the political outlook of the
Duke of Leeds was far-reaching. On the one hand it put an
end to the connection he had long maintained with the more
moderate among the Whigs ; on the other hand it led to a
reconciliation between him and the semi-Jacobites among the
Tories. During the course of the struggle his regular associates
had been Nottingham, Rochester, Normanby, and his old
friend the Bishop of London, who had been converted by
personal disappointments from a zealous Whig into one of
the highest of high Tories. With these and other like-
minded politicians he was to be connected for the remainder of
his life.

In this association lay the main cause of his eventual dismissal
from office. During the summer of 1697 negotiations for a
European peace were being conducted, partly in formal
congress at Ryswick and partly in private discussions between
the personal representatives of William III and Louis XIV. In
September these negotiations found their appropriate conclusion in the treaty of Ryswick, and the political situation in
England experienced another change. The Whig ministry so
necessary for the prosecution of the war commenced to show
signs of dissolution, and William began hesitatingly to look to
the Tories again. But it was not to the group who followed
Nottingham that the King turned, and the change was thus
actually harmful to the Duke of Leeds. Hitherto he had been
retained in office largely with the object of reconciling the
Church party to the existence of a ministry which otherwise was
almost exclusively Whig, and as the Whig element in the
ministry declined his presence became less and less necessary.
For some months rumour was busy nominating his successor.

---

[1] *L.J.*, xvi. 48. A division list, not quite accurate, is printed in *Parliamentary
History*, v. 1154-5. Of the twenty-six bishops five were excused attendance ;
twelve, mainly those recently appointed, voted for the bill ; and nine, mainly
those of earlier appointment, voted against the bill. It was considered matter
for surprise that the Archbishop of York, the Bishop of Bath and Wells and the
Bishop of Hereford were among the nine (*Vernon Correspondence*, i. 134).

He was to surrender his place to the Duke of Shrewsbury, to the Earl of Sunderland, to the Earl of Tankerville.[1]

In these rumours there was certainly an element of truth, for with the change in his party connections Leeds was being tempted into opposition as never before, and was making himself distinctly obnoxious to the King. A foretaste of his new attitude had been given as early as the winter of 1696-7, when he had abandoned his studiously non-committal attitude of three years earlier, and joined with the Marquis of Normanby in delivering a violent attack on a proposal to raise money by prolonging and extending the privileges of the Bank of England.[2] With the reassembling of Parliament on December 3, 1697, his hostility to the Government grew more pronounced, and his attitude on the main controversies of the day became one of steady opposition.

Chief among these controversies was that raised by Charles Duncombe, a zealous Tory, who had been dismissed from his post of Cashier of Excise by the Whig Charles Montagu, now First Lord of the Treasury as well as Chancellor of the Exchequer. Early in January 1698 Duncombe sought revenge by accusing Montagu and the whole Treasury Board of serious peculation in connection with the recently instituted Exchequer Bills, only to find the charge not merely dismissed but retorted on his own head. The result was to place him in substantially the same position as Sir John Fenwick had occupied. The Whigs felt bound to inflict upon him some signal punishment, the Tories equally bound to bring him off as safely as they could. On February 1 it was ordered by the Commons that a bill of pains and penalties should be brought in against him, and on February 26 the bill, sentencing him to forfeit two thirds of his enormous fortune to the public service, passed its third reading by 138 votes to 103 and was sent up to the Lords.[3]

---

[1] *Shrewsbury Correspondence*, pp. 434, 480, 502 ; L'Hermitage, March 12/22, 1697 ; Bonnet, April 20/30, 1697 ; *Luttrell*, iv. 212-3, 354.

[2] " Les Seigneurs ont aussi délibéré aujourdhuy sur ce mesme etat de la nation, et la matiere s'est bornée à la banque, contre laquelle le Marquis de Normanby a declamé de toutes ces forces, l'accusant d'achepter elle mesme ces propres billets, et apellant sa conduite une vraye banqueroute. Le Duc de Leeds est celuy qui l'a apuyé le plus " (Bonnet, November 27/December 7, 1696).

[3] *C.J.*, xii. 78-133.

There preparations had been made to receive it, and it was immediately assailed by Leeds, Nottingham, Rochester, Peterborough and Bolton. A strong appeal to the class prejudice of the Lords was made by the argument that the Commons should have proceeded by impeachment, and that in unnecessarily having recourse to a bill they were virtually assuming to themselves the powers of a judicial tribunal. Much was made of the penalty imposed, which, it was declared, was altogether out of proportion to the offence. As a result the second reading of the bill was carried only by 48 votes to 36, and Leeds with 19 others recorded a protest. The more convincing argument was then brought forward that there was no real proof of the charges advanced by the Commons except some incriminating admissions which Duncombe himself had been surprised into making, and the opponents of the bill were thus able to secure two conferences with the Commons to enquire into the evidence on which they had acted. Leeds was one of the managers, and Rochester reported the results, which proved so little satisfactory to the Lords that the party opposed to the bill was considerably strengthened. On March 15, in consequence, the proposal to commit the bill was defeated by 48 votes to 47, and the bill itself was rejected.[1]

So prominent was the part taken by the Duke of Leeds in this contest that his enemies were able to secure some credence for the assertion that in the final division the numbers were equal, and that he was responsible for deciding the issue by means of " his casting vote." [2] An even more important part seemed destined to be his in another contest begun a few weeks later with a renewed attack on the East India Company. Not merely was Leeds as a leading Tory practically bound to defend the existing Company, but he had been impeached for corruption

[1] *L.J.*, xvi. 222-35 ; *House of Lords MSS.*, 1697-9, pp. 128-30, 135-8 ; *C.J.*, xii. 147-54 ; L'Hermitage, March 8/18, 15/25, 1698 ; Bonnet, March 8/18, 1698 ; *Luttrell*, iv. 351-6. Of the fourteen bishops in the House eight voted against Duncombe and six for him.

[2] *Complete History of England*, iii. 743. Leeds was particularly bitter about this statement, which seemed to depict him as the most resolute defender of a man whose guilt was generally admitted (*infra*, ii. 445). The attitude of Leeds to Duncombe was substantially the same as his attitude to Fenwick—not that he was innocent, but that the procedure adopted in dealing with him was unjustifiable, and that in any case he was no worse than his accusers.

in connection with his previous efforts in that direction, and h
impeachment was still in force. On June 27, accordingly, whe
a bill setting up a new East India Company was delivered b
the Commons to the Lords, he rushed with characteristi
impetuosity into the fray, and on the second reading of the bil
which took place on July 1, delivered an impressive speecl
denouncing it as contrary to the liberty of the subject and a
infringement on the prerogative of the sovereign.[1] A situatio
might easily have developed comparable to that which had bee
produced by his equally unwise denunciation of Titus Oates nin
years earlier ; but just as on that occasion the King personall
interposed and persuaded him to be silent. The second readin
of the bill was carried by 65 votes to 48 ; but Leeds did no
even sign the protest which followed, and remained absen
from Parliament for the brief remainder of the session.[2]

As so often before, however, the most worrying controversie
in which Leeds became involved were those connected with hi
own son. Since his vindication by the House of Lords in th
early days of 1696 Carmarthen had been in favour but generall
out of employment. Full pay as Rear-Admiral of the Blue hac
been continued to him, and in April 1697 had been granted t
him as a regular pension.[3] In the autumn of 1696 he had bee
accorded the honour of bringing the King back from th
Continent in the *Royal Transport*, a heavily armed yacht buil
for that purpose under his own special direction.[4] In the summe

[1] " Le Duc de Leeds, qui fut celui qui avoit employé son credit aupres d
Roy pour obtenir à la vielle compagnie la chartre qu'elle a eue, soutenu de tou
les evéques presens et de plusieurs seigneurs séculiers, fit tous ses efforts pou
prouver que ce bill, ainsi qu'on l'avoit dressé, étoit contraire aux loix et au
libertés des sujets ; qu'il étoit opposé à la justice, puisqu'on ruinoit par l
plusieurs familles sans sujet, et qu'on faisoit une atteinte aux prérogatives d
Roy, qui est d'accorder des chartres ; que sa Majesté n'ayant pas retiré cell
qu'elle avoit accordé à la vielle compagnie le Parlement n'étoit pas en droit d
la casser " (Bonnet, July 5/15, 1698).

[2] *L.J.*, xvi. 329-43 ; *House of Lords MSS.*, 1697-9, pp. 257-8 ; Tallard t
Louis XIV, July 12, 1698, in *Grimblot*, ii. 61-5. In the following autumn, how
ever, the old Company was still relying on the support of " le Duc de Leeds, le
Sieurs Musgrave, How, Greenville, et toute leur cabale " (Bonnet, Septembe
26/October 6, 1699).

[3] *Cal. S. P. Dom.*, 1696, p. 153 ; 1697, p. 135 ; 1702-3, p. 22 ; 1703-4
pp. 30-1, 388-9.

[4] Carmarthen, however, did not command the convoy. " Les dernier
lettres ayant apris que sa Majesté faisoit estat de repasser bientost en Angle
terre, l'on a donné les ordres necessaires pour le départ des yachts, et ils son

1697 an 80-gun man-of-war already on the stocks had been
completed in accordance with his instructions, and he had been
given command of her with an independent flag.[1]   Now in the
early days of 1698 his experience of naval affairs was to earn
for him a brief prominence in the commercial and political
world.

During the previous autumn King William had complimented
the Czar Peter, who had reached Holland in the course of his
travels in the west, by presenting him with the *Royal Transport*,
" the best sailer " he had.[2]   So pleased was the Czar with the
vessel that on his arrival in England in January one of his first
objects was to seek out her designer, and between him and
Carmarthen a considerable degree of intimacy soon grew up.[3]
Carmarthen repeatedly entertained the Czar and discussed
naval affairs with him.[4]   In conjunction with Admiral Sir David
Mitchell he organised a mock battle of some thirty vessels at
Portsmouth, which gave the Czar peculiar pleasure.[5]   Towards
the close of April Leeds and Carmarthen combined to give a

---

soit descendus à la Baye du Nord, où l'Amiral Ailmer se rendra demain pour
   conduire en Hollande avec quelques vaisseaux de guerre.   Le Marquis de
Carmarthen sera aussi de la partie, non pas comme officier de pavillon, mais
comme capitaine d'un bastiment de nouvelle fabrique, dans lequel sa Majesté
y a promis de passer, et qui fut basti il y a un an sous la direction de ce
Marquis, expressément pour ce sujet, et est nommé de la le *Royal Transport*.
est non seulement plus viste qu'un yacht, allant à voiles et a rames, mais est
aussi de beaucoup plus de defense, ce qui n'est pas à mespriser dans un temps de
brouillards, où l'on se peut trouver écarté des vaisseaux de guerre " (Bonnet,
September 22/October 2, 1696).

[1] *Cal. S. P. Dom.*, 1697, pp. 155, 168 ;   *Downshire MSS.*, i. 739.
[2] *Luttrell*, iv. 290 ;   *Portland MSS.*, iii. 590.
[3] " Comme il apprit que Milord Carmarthen étoit celui sous la direction de
qui ce vaisseau avoit été fait, il fut lui rendre visite pour discourir avec lui de
la marine.   Ce Milord, ravis d'avoir un si grand hôte en sa maison, fit venir
plusieurs sortes de liqueurs pour les luy presenter, et entre les santés que ce
Seigneur luy porta il en but une au bon succès de l'entreprise de sa Majesté
Czarienne sur Constantinople.   Le Czar répondit à cette santé par ces paroles,
le succès vient de Dieu, et je tacherai d'en pouvoir être l'instrument.   Ce
Milord demanda au Czar la liberté de luy rendre visite, mais le Czar la lui refusa,
& lui dit que par contre il le viendroit voir souvent " (Bonnet, January 21/31,
1698).
[4] " Personne n'a mieux s'en ménager l'esprit de ce Prince que le Marquis de
Carmarthen."
[5] " Rien n'a plus attaché les yeux de ce Prince que de voir comme chaque
vaisseau avançoit et obeissoit aux ordres au moindre signal " (Bonnet,
March 29/April 8, 1698).

magnificent dinner to the Czar and his retinue at Wimbledo
with " musitians and singing men to divert him." [1]   In retur
the Czar, before leaving for Holland a few days later, granted t
Carmarthen the sole privilege of importing tobacco into Russi
a privilege which Carmarthen immediately sold to a body o
English merchants interested in the eastern trade.[2]

   The jealousies aroused by these transactions, not merely a
Court but also among rival groups of merchants, were a caus
of serious annoyance to William, and this annoyance wa
intensified by the simultaneous reappearance of the problem o
a successor to Sir Robert Howard in the lucrative office o
Auditor of the Exchequer.[3]   Nearly a quarter of a century ha
now elapsed since that problem had ostensibly been settled by
grant of the reversion of the place to Carmarthen ; but th
grant had repeatedly been challenged, and the position sti
remained uncertain.   Against Carmarthen's pretensions it ha
been argued, on the one hand that he was personally unfit fo
the post, and on the other that his grant was invalid, inasmuc
as the appointment lay with the Treasury and not with th
King.[4]   About the truth of the first of these contentions ther
could be little doubt, for at the very moment when the matte
was under discussion Carmarthen's creditors were being held a
bay only by the fact that his father had a mortgage over all hi
real estate, and within a few months Leeds was to be givin
Lady Carmarthen instructions what to do if the bailifi
endeavoured to seize her husband's personal property.[5]   A
regards the second contention a decision seemed inevitabl
when Sir Robert Howard eventually died on September 3, 169
   Probably Carmarthen's claim would have been opposed i

---

[1] *Luttrell*, iv. 342, 357-61, 371.

[2] The Czar's grant appears to have been one of importing 3,000 hogsheads o
tobacco the first year, 5,000 the second year, and 6,000 annually thereafte
subject to an import duty of 4½d. per lb., an immediate advance of £12,000 o
that duty, and a gift of 1,000 hogsheads to the Russian Court.   Carmarthen
arrangement with the merchants appears to have been that they shoul
provide the £12,000, and should pay him a lump sum of 1,000 guineas, with
pension of £1,500 per annum for life (Bonnet, April 22/May 2, April 26/May
1698 ;   *Luttrell*, iv. 363, 372).

[3] As early as December 1697 Sir Robert was believed to be on the point o
death (*Luttrell*, iv. 313).

[4] Godolphin to the King, March 20, 1691, in *Cal. S. P. Dom.*, 1695, pp. 169-7

[5] Leeds to Lady Carmarthen, July 23, 1701, *infra*, ii. 226-7.

y case ; but the opposition was rendered both more certain
d more serious by the fact that in the general decline of Whig
fluence Charles Montagu had fixed on Howard's place as the
e to which he would himself retire to escape the pursuit of his
emies. On September 5, with the support of two other
ommissioners of the Treasury, Sir Thomas Littleton and John
mith, Montagu conferred the post of Auditor of the Exchequer
a his brother Christopher, who was to hold it until he was
ady to take it himself, and thus threw on Leeds and Carmar-
en the onus of substantiating their claim. This Leeds found
imself unable to do, for before he could take any steps the
ontagus had engaged all the best counsel in town on their side,
d soon made it obvious that they proposed in addition to en-
ench themselves behind their parliamentary privilege. By
e spring of 1699 the Duke had decided, at least for the time,
to let the affair drop.[1]

By an unhappy coincidence Carmarthen was simultaneously
isappointed of another lucrative post, the reversion of which
e had held for an even longer period. Towards the close of
arch 1699 Sir Richard Piggott, Clerk of the Patents in the
ourt of Chancery, died, and Carmarthen immediately
dvanced his title to the place. Lord Somers, however, insisted
at the right of appointment belonged to him as Lord Chancel-
or, and conferred the post upon his own brother-in-law, Charles
ocks.[2] In vain Leeds and Carmarthen carried the tale of their
rongs to the King. William was merely exasperated by these
ickerings over reversions granted long before he ascended the
hrone, and refused to interfere.[3] All he would do was to take
ito consideration the arrears of the pension of £500 which
harles II had granted to Carmarthen until the Auditorship of

---

[1] Correspondence and memoranda in B.M. Add. MSS. 28086, ff. 1-43 ;
'Hermitage, September 9/19, 1698 ; Bonnet, September 9/19, October 4/14,
698 ; *Cal. Treas. Books*, xiv. 7, 176, 189, 222, 323 ; *Luttrell*, iv. 423-33.
Iontagu's anxiety to avoid a trial appears to have been due, not to any doubt
f the decision which the judges would give, but to a fear that the House of
ords, if the case came before them on appeal, would decide in favour of their
wn member (*Cal. S. P. Dom.*, 1698, p. 393).

[2] *Luttrell*, iv. 500, 501, 507 ; *Cal. S.P. Dom.*, 1699-1700, p. 191.

[3] Blathwayt to Leeds, September 16/26, 1698, in B.M. Add. MSS. 28086,
18 ; L'Hermitage, September 30/October 10, 1698 ; Carte MSS. 79, f. 674 ;
uttrell, iv. 427, 433.

the Exchequer should become his, and even these arrea
amounting by this time to more than £9,000, were dealt with
a very unsatisfactory way. Authority was given for the co
struction of a special galley, to be called the *Peregrine*, und
Carmarthen's directions,[1] and this he was to have in settleme
of the arrears. William, however, liked the vessel so well th
he refused to part with her, and granted instead a pension
£1,000 a year, which in turn was not paid.[2]

The resentment felt by Leeds and his relatives not unnatu
ally found expression in Parliament, where the general electi
of 1698 had produced a situation distinctly unfavourable to t
ministry and the Whigs.[3] His immediate aim was revenge
the Montagus and their associates, and with this in view
instigated an investigation by the Commons into the workir
of an Act of 1695, by which they had forbidden their member
with certain exceptions, to take any part in the managin
farming or collecting of any tax. But while this led to t
expulsion of several guilty members from the House, Christoph
Montagu was able to escape by pleading that in spite of t
offices he held he had not in actual fact done anything contra
to the Act since taking the oaths,[4] and Leeds had for the mome
to rest content with the general discredit which he had manag
to cast on his enemies.

His ultimate object is less obvious, and it is even doubtf
whether he had one. The burning question of the moment w
the reduction of the army to the numbers which had suffice
the reign of Charles II, and on this point his attitude seems

---

[1] She was of about 190 tons burden, was classed as a sixth-rate, carried
guns, and had a complement of 58 men (*Cal. S.P. Dom.*, 1699-1700, p. 21
1700-2, p. 302 ; *Luttrell*, iv. 525).

[2] *Cal. S.P. Dom.*, 1703-4, pp. 30, 389.

[3] Memorandum of December 2, 1698, in *Grimblot*, ii. 190-200.

[4] " La veritable origine de tout ce manege a sa source dans la jalousie q
le Duc de Leeds porte à Monsieur Montaigu, de ce qu'il suplanta l'été passé
Marquis de Carmarthen, son fils, en la charge d'Auditeur de l'Exchiqui
ainsi qu'il a été dit. Le dit Duc, voulant se vanger à present du Sieur Montaig
a fait en sorte que la Chambre s'est souvenue de cette loix, dans l'espérance q
Monsieur Montaigu y seroit enveloppé ; mais lors qu'on est venu à examin
le cas de son affaire on a vû qu'il n'avoit fait aucune fonction de sa char
depuis le moment qu'il avoit preté les serments de fidelité à la Chambre,
sorte qu'il n'y avoit aucune prise sur lui, et c'est sur quoy le Duc de Lee
n'avoit pas réfléchi " (Bonnet, February 17/27, 1699).

have been a mixture of practical good sense, insular patriotism'
and personal ambition. His whole outlook in domestic and
foreign affairs was opposed to any undue weakening of the
army, and the moderate reduction already effected after the
conclusion of the treaty of Ryswick had been regarded by him
with disfavour, if for no better reason than that it involved the
disbandment of Carmarthen's regiment of marines.[1] When the
fateful division was now taken in the Commons on the third
reading of the bill restricting the army to 7,000 men his brother
Charles, presumably by his directions, voted against it.[2] But
whatever number of men was to be allowed he was clear that
they must all be Englishmen. In the House of Lords, where
there was more personal sympathy for William than in the
House of Commons, a resolution was carried by 54 votes to 38
expressing a willingness to consider any expedient which might
enable the King to retain the Dutch guards in whom he had
such trust ; but Leeds declared himself entirely opposed to the
resolution, and along with the other members of the minority
signed a protest against it.[3]

It is scarcely surprising, therefore, that after the prorogation
of Parliament on May 4 William at last set himself to solve the
problem which he had repeatedly postponed since the impeachment of Leeds four years earlier. Recent events had made a
reconstruction of the ministry inevitable, and at a time when
posts were few and claimants many it was impossible that a
Lord President who never exercised his functions, or even
attended Council meetings, should be maintained indefinitely
in office. Faced with a choice between dismissing Leeds and
making him again an effective minister of the Crown, William,
not unnaturally in view of his Lord President's recent conduct
and increasing age, decided upon dismissal. On May 18 Leeds
was required to surrender his post to the Earl of Pembroke,

---

[1] *Lonsdale MSS.*, p. 108. William decided to retain the four junior regiments
of marines, but to disband the two senior regiments commanded by Carmarthen
and Sir Clowdisley Shovell. " Des qu'ils ont seu leur sort ces deux colonels se
sont abandonnés au murmure, et principalement le premier, qui n'avoit pas
l'autre employ du Roy, et qui d'ailleurs n'étoit pas déja trop avant dans les
interets de la Cour " (Bonnet, August 9/19, 1698).

[2] The division took place on January 18, 1699, and the voting was 221 to
54 (*C.J.*, xii. 440). A list of the minority is printed *infra*, iii. 213.

[3] February 8, 1699 (*L.J.*, xvi. 377 ; *House of Lords MSS.*, 1697-9, pp. 284-5).

whose office of Lord Privy Seal was in turn transferred to Lord Lonsdale.[1]

The almost simultaneous ejection of Leeds from his three lord lieutenancies and from the governorship of Hull [2] is less easily explained. Leeds himself fully appreciated the extent to which he had fallen under the displeasure of the King, and in anticipation of his dismissal at Hull petitioned that he might be paid the arrears of his salary there, and that his brother Charles might be allowed to remain lieutenant-governor of the fortress.[3] But a man of his rank and reputation was rarely excluded from all local offices except for some very special reason, and it seems almost certain that his dismissal at least from the lieutenancies was due to a misapprehension. During the summer of 1699 he was so ill that his life was for some time despaired of,[4] and William, who was in Holland, appears in the end to have granted away his offices under the impression that he was either dead or dying.[5] The step had no sooner been taken, at any rate, than it was felt to be a mistake, and the Court endeavoured, with complete lack of success, to spread the impression that he had voluntarily resigned.[6] Carmarthen was again given a naval command, and allowed to entertain some hope of being sent ambassador to Russia. Leeds was well received by the King after his return to England, and it was even suggested that the post of Lord President might be restored to him, Pembroke being compensated with a Garter.[7]

That nothing of this nature was actually done appears to have been due to Leeds himself. The political situation in the

---

[1] *Cal. S.P. Dom.*, 1699-1700, p. 181 ; *Luttrell*, iv. 517-8. Leeds was not struck off the Council, although he still remained absent from its meetings.

[2] In August (*Cal. S. P. Dom.*, 1699-1700, pp. 243, 254).

[3] Leeds to Lonsdale, May 19, 1699, in *Lonsdale MSS.*, p. 113.

[4] *Luttrell*, iv. 540, 543, 559 ; L'Hermitage, July 21/31, August 1/11, 18/28 1699.

[5] *Luttrell*, iv. 545. " Le fait est que le Duc de Leeds étant ici fort malade, on rapporta en Hollande à sa Majesté qu'il étoit mort. Le Roy la-dessus dispose de ses employs. Quelque tems apres, ayant appris qu'il étoit relevé de maladie sa Majesté contremanda l'ordre qu'il avoit donné d'en favoriser quelqu'autre (Bonnet, October 20/30, 1699).

[6] *Hist. MSS. Com.*, xv. 9, p. 110.

[7] Bonnet, October 31/November 10, 1699 ; Carte MSS. 228, ff. 328, 341 *Luttrell*, iv. 567, 574. The idea that Leeds might again become Lord President persisted as late as November 1700 (*Portland MSS.*, iii. 635).

closing years of William's reign was extremely perplexing, and
the Duke may not have been altogether sorry that his loss of
office enabled him to retire to the fringes of the political contest
and refrain from making any clear declaration of his own policy.
From the autumn of 1699 onwards his attendance in Parliament
became distinctly irregular, and was on the whole confined to
occasions on which matters of special interest to himself were
in debate. The problem presented by the relations of England
and Scotland, at that time rendered particularly difficult by
controversies over the Scottish settlement in the isthmus of
Darien, was one of which he had long experience, and for the
greater part of February 1700 he was busily engaged in assisting
the deliberations of the Lords upon it.[1] As a man whose fortune
was largely built upon grants from the Crown he was naturally
inclined to oppose proposals for the resumption of such grants,
and signalised himself by his hostility to the motion adopted in
the Commons on February 13 for the resumption of all grants
made since the accession of James II.[2] Later in the same
session, however, when the Commons sent up to the Lords a
money bill to which they had tacked provisions for the resumption of grants in Ireland, his attitude was less clear. He was
little inclined to countenance the Irish grants, which had gone
to William's foreign favourites rather than to himself or to his
friends, and he fully sympathised with the Government's wish
that the bill of supply should pass. On the other hand he

[1] *L.J.*, xvi. 491-530 ; *House of Lords MSS.*, 1699-1702, pp. 68-73. The
motion " that a day may be appointed for taking into consideration the present
posture of affairs in Scotland relating to the business of Darien " was made in
the Lords on January 10. At that time, although the session was already two
months old, Leeds had only twice appeared in the House ; but as soon as the
Scottish problem was seriously embarked upon his attendance became quite
regular. On February 8, along with Abingdon, Normanby, Nottingham, the
Bishop of London and others, he signed a protest against the putting of the
motion, " that the settlement of the Scotch colony at Darien is inconsistent
with the good of the plantation trade of this kingdom," on the ground that no
time had been allowed in which to decide a matter of such difficulty and
importance ; and he appears to have given his full support to the proposals
later brought forward to settle the whole problem by a union of the two
kingdoms.

[2] *C.J.*, xiii. 208. " Le Duc de Leeds et le Comte de Rochester, qui sont bien
avant interessés dans les liberalités que fit le Roy Jacques, et qui sont des
bonnes tetes de la chambre haute, ne feront pas difficulté de se joindre à ceux
qui ont receu des dons de sa Majesté à present regnante, quoyque de sentimens
opposés " (Bonnet, February 16/26, 1700).

objected on principle not merely to resumptions in general but still more to tacking. He accordingly spoke for the bill, but ended by opposing it ; and yet, when the King desired the Lords to let it pass, acquiesced in their decision to do so, and did not even join in the protest recorded by Lonsdale, Pembroke and others among his associates.[1]

Probably as a result of the moderate, if not very decided, attitude which he adopted on these and other points, Leeds was repeatedly pressed during the summer and autumn of 1700 to give his support to the interests of the Court ; but he refused to commit himself in any way, and especially after the death on July 10 of Lord Lonsdale, who had been his chief connecting link with the Government,[2] insisted on remaining aloof from the political struggle. Nevertheless he continued to enjoy considerable influence both with the King and in Parliament, where he displayed during the spring session of 1701 the same irregular activity as in the previous year. The malcontent Whigs who helped to hound Somers from office would have had him replaced by John Methuen, Lord Chancellor of Ireland ; but Leeds was successful in demonstrating to the King Methuen's lack of legal training, and Sir Nathan Wright was appointed Lord Keeper instead.[3] The malcontent Tories who denounced the partition treaties in which William III and Louis XIV had provided for the dissolution of the Spanish Empire were

---

[1] *L.J.*, xvi. 567-76 ; *House of Lords MSS.*, 1699-1702, pp. 141-2. " Le Duc de Leeds fit un assés long discours pour montrer la necessité de ce bill, mais il finit par l'y oposer a cause des clauses. La deliberation n'est pas expliquée à son avantage " (Bonnet, April 9/20, 1700).

[2] " On a avis que le Vicomte de Lansdale a taché inutilement de ramener le Duc de Leeds dans les interets du Roy, dans une entrevue qu'ils ont eû ensemble à la campagne " (Bonnet, June 28/July 9, 1700). That Leeds and Lonsdale were still on the friendliest terms with each other is shown by a letter written by the former to the latter only four days before his death (*Lonsdale MSS.*, p. 116).

[3] *Le Neve*, p. 144. " Le tems qui dévelope toutes choses a apris qu'une des raisons pour laquelle on a attaqué si souvent le dernier Chancelier étoit la faction de quelques uns qui vetiloient l'éloigner de ce poste pour y avancer le Sieur Methuwin, Chancelier d'Irlande. Et tout indigne qu'il en est, le choix seroit peut-être tombé sur sa personne dans la facheuse conjoncture des affaires, si le Duc de Leeds n'eut exposé à tems aux yeux de sa Majesté l'insuffisance de cet homme, ce qui fut confirmé et apuyé peu de momens apres par le Chef de Justice Holt. Ce n'est pas ici le moindre avis que le Duc de Leeds aye donné " (Bonnet, May 7/18, 1700).

steadily supported by him ; [1] but when they went further, and proceeded to impeach the ministers whom they held responsible, he withdrew his support, and ceased to attend the House of Lords.[2] Possibly as a result of his forbearance, when the Lords eventually dismissed the impeachments, on the ground that the Commons had failed to prosecute them, his own impeachment of 1695 was dismissed for the same reason along with them.[3]

Thus the Act of Settlement passed through the House of Lords without help or hindrance on his part. Its provision " that no pardon under the great seal of England be pleadable to an impeachment by the Commons in Parliament " can scarcely have been very palatable to him, and two at least of its constitutional provisions must have been regarded by him with serious disfavour ; but its further regulation of the succession and the strongly nationalist character of many of its clauses were so thoroughly in keeping with his own ideas that it can scarcely be doubted his support would have been forthcoming had it been required.[4] Like many others he was simply marking time, waiting for the new reign which it was obvious could not be long postponed, and meanwhile occupying himself with things of little moment. In September it was noted as significant that he was for an hour with the King in private ; [5] and in December he was giving offence to the Earl of Burlington by presenting an address from the town of Leeds which the Earl considered should have been presented by himself.[6] Yet when the last Parliament of the reign assembled on December 30 he did not even trouble to attend,[7] and the death of William on March 8, 1702, found his position in the political world still as indeterminate as it had been ever since 1699.

[1] *L.J.*, xvi. 622-9, especially the protests signed by Leeds on pp. 623, 624, 629.

[2] His last appearance in the House was on May 16. Carmarthen voted with the majority for the acquittal of Somers on June 17, though nearly all Leeds's allies voted on the other side (*House of Lords MSS.*, 1699-1702, p. 300).

[3] On June 24, the last day of the session (*L.J.*, xvi. 769).

[4] The bill passed through all its stages in the House of Lords without serious opposition between May 14 and May 22, and received the royal assent on June 12 (*L.J.*, xvi. 681-99, 738 ; *House of Lords MSS.*, 1699-1702, p. 374).

[5] *Hist. MSS. Com.*, xi. 5, p. 293.

[6] *Ibid., Various Collections*, viii. 85.

[7] He was actually present on the first two days, but did not take the oaths.

CHAPTER XXII

CLOSING YEARS, 1702–12

To the accession of Anne the Tories had long looked forward as the event which would enable them to enter into their own again, and it soon appeared that their expectations were not going to be disappointed. However sincerely the new Queen might profess her determination to make no distinction among her faithful subjects, to whatever party they belonged, it was well known that her High Church inclinations were so strong as to make real impartiality impossible for her. The keynote of her whole attitude was struck in her final speech to the Parliament sitting at her accession, in which she expressed her firmness to the interests and religion of the Church of England, and her determination to countenance those who had the truest zeal to support it.[1]

With such sentiments the Duke of Leeds was completely in sympathy, and his attitude secured to him from the very beginning a considerable degree of personal intimacy with the Queen. His relatives also were influential at Court. The young Countess of Abingdon was specially intimate with Anne, and after her own appointment as lady of the bedchamber [2] contrived to secure minor positions not only for her husband but for her husband's uncles as well.[3] Nevertheless in the reconstructed ministry, while the associates of the Duke of Leeds in the last years of William's reign were all given important posts —Rochester as Lord Lieutenant of Ireland, Nottingham as

[1] May 25 , 1702 (*L.J.*, xvii. 150).

[2] April 10, 1702 (B.M. Add. MSS. 29567, f. 149).

[3] The Earl of Abingdon succeeded Lord Lucas as Constable of the Tower and Lord Wharton as Lord Lieutenant of Oxfordshire, and was sworn of the Privy Council (*Cal. S.P. Dom.*, 1702-3, pp. 389, 488). Captain Henry Bertie became his nephew's deputy in the Tower, and Charles Bertie was made Treasurer of the Ordnance (*Luttrell*, v. 164, 180).

Secretary of State, Normanby as Privy Seal, and Sir Edward Seymour as Comptroller of the Household—the Duke himself had to be content with the honorary dignity of a Privy Councillor.

The explanation of this possibly lies in a quarrel which came to a head at this time between the Duke and the Queen's uncle, the Earl of Rochester, who during the temporary absence of Marlborough on a mission to Holland played a large part in the formation of the ministry. In 1696 the Duke had obtained from King William an extension for thirty-one years of a grant made him by Charles II of certain manors, liberties and rents, amounting in value to some £600 per annum, and including a rent of £40 per annum for Wychwood Forest payable by the Earl of Clarendon.[1] Before the warrant for the renewal could be signed, however, the Earl of Rochester, who disliked the idea of this particular rent being granted away from his family and hoped to get it for himself,[2] persuaded the Duke to have it omitted from the warrant, on the understanding that £400 should be paid him as compensation. Unfortunately Rochester had been so completely out of favour with William III, and the making of unnecessary grants had roused so much trouble in the House of Commons, that he had not even attempted to get the £40 rent for himself, and claimed that on that account he could not be required to pay the compensation. Leeds on the other hand insisted that the compensation ought to be paid whether Rochester obtained his grant or not.

An immediate settlement of the dispute had been rendered unnecessary by the fact that the original grant made by Charles II was for the life of the Queen Dowager, who was still living in Portugal. The period of thirty-one years therefore had not yet begun, the Duke was still receiving the rent from Wychwood Forest, and his loss amounted to no more than the interest on the £400 which had not been paid. No sooner had Rochester's standing at Court, however, been altered by the accession of

---

[1] The warrant for the original grant, dated July 10, 1678, the docquet of the original grant, dated March 19, 1679, and the warrant for the later grant, dated April 21, 1696, are printed in *Cal. Treas. Books*, v. 1047, 1288; xi. 98.

[2] As early as the close of 1674 he had entered a caveat that nothing should pass concerning Wychwood Forest without notice to him (*Cal. S.P. Dom.*, 1673-5, p. 474).

Anne than he demanded that a settlement must be reached, and it was agreed to refer the whole question to the arbitration of the Earl of Nottingham.[1]

No record of any decision has been preserved, and the £400 remained a subject of dispute as late as 1710, five years after the death of the Queen Dowager.[2] But the mere fact that Leeds and Rochester could have recourse to arbitration at all suggests that the quarrel between them was not a very bitter one, and the main reason for the absence of the former from the ranks of the ministry is probably to be found in family troubles and in increasing age and infirmities.[3] His failure to secure any Government position is no more remarkable than his continued absence from the House of Lords. During the first eight years of Anne's reign he was scarcely ever present in Parliament, and at the beginning of 1705 he actually went so far as to entrust his proxy to his son Carmarthen.[4] In August 1703 it was confidently reported that he had died at Bath ; in November of the same year his wife, who had never quite recovered from a second carriage accident in 1698, was dragging out the last weeks of her life at Wimbledon.[5]

Even when his troubles were at their worst, however, Leeds was still capable, when occasion arose, of a temporary incursion into the political arena. The machinations by which his son had been defrauded of the Auditorship of the Exchequer had never been forgiven by him, nor had the loss of that office itself been accepted as final. No sooner had Godolphin been appointed Lord High Treasurer, and the ministry reconstructed on a definitely Tory basis, than he consulted the Attorney-

[1] The two statements presented to Nottingham by Leeds and Rochester, dated respectively April 18 and April 27, 1702, are in B.M. Add. MSS. 29587, ff. 93, 95. It is difficult to read them without feeling that Rochester, if not technically in the wrong, was at least guilty of very sharp practice.

[2] B.M. Add. MSS. 28041, f. 25.

[3] According to a contemporary authority Leeds on accepting the position of Privy Councillor " declined any other public post " (Le Neve, p. 145). It is a little difficult to picture him adopting this self-denying attitude, but he may have been temporarily disinclined to press his claims.

[4] B.M. Add. MSS. 28041, f. 2. The recorded attendances of the Duke of Leeds in the House of Lords during the first seven winters of Anne's reign are as follows—1702-3, 29 ; 1703-4, 1 ; 1704-5, 1 ; 1705-6, 9 ; 1706-7, 1 ; 1707-8, 19 ; 1708-9, 5.

[5] B.M. Add. MSS. 29568, ff. 130, 149.

General, and on his advice presented a memorial to the Treasurer, setting forth the case and praying that Carmarthen might be admitted to the office of Auditor as his patent directed. For some time a dispute between father and son delayed proceedings ;[1] but on July 3 Carmarthen and Charles Montagu, now himself Auditor of the Exchequer and recently created Lord Halifax, were both heard at the Treasury, the patent presented by the former was read, and his admission was denied until he had made good his case at law.[2] Leeds then proceeded by bill in the Exchequer, praying the assistance of the Barons in obtaining the place ; but after many delays Halifax brought in a demurrer, and this being allowed by the Barons after argument on July 2, 1703, the Duke found himself, as far as he could ascertain, without any legal remedy whatever. In vain he appealed to the public in a printed pamphlet, supported the attacks which the Tory House of Commons was then delivering against Halifax, and voiced his grievance in the House of Lords. The Auditorship of the Exchequer was lost for ever.[3]

The only other thing which could draw Leeds from his retirement was a summons to the support of the Church. In each of the three sessions of Anne's first Parliament a bill to disqualify occasional conformists from office was sent up from the Commons and debated in the Lords, and every time there seemed the faintest prospect of it being carried the Duke, at whatever inconvenience to himself, attended to give it his support. In the final debate on the first bill he grew so bitter as to inform Halifax publicly " that his family was raised by rebellion, but his own suffered by it," and a duel between Carmarthen and the injured nobleman was prevented only by

[1] Leeds insisted that before help could be given his son must abandon his vicious way of life and assign the auditorship in trust to him, presumably as some security for his debts.

[2] " My Lord Treasurer does not think it reasonable for him to interpose by granting an admission in prejudice of an officer that hath been more than three years in possession, and thereby to create a confusion in the affairs of the Exchequer, especially since the counsel of either side have admitted that if there be a right there is a remedy at law " (B.M. Add. MSS. 28086, f. 58).

[3] B.M. Add. MSS. 28086, ff. 44-77 ; *The Marquess of Carmarthen's Case, upon the Contest of his Title with the Lord Hallifax to the Office of Auditor of the Exchequer* ; Luttrell, v. 185, 190-1, 290, 308-9, 314.

the exercise of the authority of the House.[1]   When the second
bill came up he insisted on being present although his wife was
actually dying at the time.[2]   During the debates on the third
bill a different issue was raised by a proposal in the Commons
to override the opposition of the Whig Lords by tacking it to
a money bill.   It is perhaps evidence of the practical good sense
which tempered the fiercest party passions in Leeds that his
followers voted with the majority against the tack,[3] and that
he himself did not even attend the purely formal debate which
the Lords accorded the bill before they rejected it.

That this did not imply any reconciliation on his part to the
practice of occasional conformity was shown soon afterwards
when the dissolution of 1705 was followed by the return of a
Whig House of Commons, and the Queen in her speech from
the throne gave some offence by referring in unfavourable terms
to those who fomented animosities and were " so very malicious
as even in print to suggest the Church of England as by law
established to be in danger." [4]   Like the majority of the Tories
Leeds was convinced that the Church was in very real danger,
and he was greatly irritated by the action of Lord Halifax,
who, in the hope of gaining some tactical advantage by forcing
the Church party to substantiate their rather wild declamation
on the subject, challenged them to a formal debate on the state
of the nation.   On December 6, the appointed day, he accordingly emerged once more from his retirement to set forth his
views on the gravity of the situation.   In reply to Lord Wharton,
who enquired whether the danger was supposed to come from
the Queen or from some other source, he declared that the real
danger was the practice of occasional conformity, that the
Queen was in entire agreement with him on this point, but that

---

[1] L.J., xvii. 185, 188 ;   Hist. MSS. Com., xii. 9, p. 96 ;   Luttrell, v. 245 ;
Thoresby, iii. 426-7.

[2] L.J., xvii. 348.   Protests were recorded by the Tories against the refusal
of the Lords to give the bill a second reading, and also against their decision
to reject it.   Leeds did not wait to sign either protest, but Carmarthen signed
both.   A list of the lords who voted for and against the bill is given in Parliamentary History, vi. 170-1.

[3] Most of the Berties, however, voted for the tack.   The division list printed
in Parliamentary History, vi. 362-7, suggests that opinion was much divided
on the point.

[4] October 27, 1705 (L.J., xviii. 8).

" if deer-stealers were got into his park he should think his deer in danger though he had no suspicion of his keeper."

Some more bitter, if scarcely delicate, allusions enabled Leeds to silence Wharton ; but the Tories had no chance of carrying their main contention, and the debate ended in a resolution, against which Leeds and Carmarthen both protested, that the Church was " in a most safe and flourishing condition," and that whoever suggested it was in danger was " an enemy to the Queen, the Church and the kingdom." [1] Once more a duel between Halifax and Carmarthen was with difficulty averted,[2] while Leeds in disgust resolved to abandon politics altogether. His natural associates in the ministry had resigned or been dismissed early in the reign, Rochester in 1703, Seymour and Nottingham in the following year. During the course of 1705 his immediate relatives had lost the minor posts they held.[3] Marlborough and Godolphin, the mainstays of the ministry, were no friends of his ; Harley, who had succeeded Nottingham as Secretary of State, belonged to a younger generation of Tories of whom he did not approve ; to the increasing favour which their determined championship of the war was gaining for the Whigs both at Court and in the country he was unalterably opposed.

When excluded from politics in 1679 the Duke had turned instead to literary labours, and he pursued the same course now. Some part in determining his resolution was no doubt played by the appearance in 1702 and the following years of the Earl of Clarendon's *True Historical Narration of the Rebellion and Civil Wars in England*,[4] for between that great statesman and the Duke of Leeds there existed a resemblance of which the latter could not but be aware. The real determining factor, however, was the death at Wimbledon, on January 6, 1704, of the Duchess of Leeds. In spite of the ill-natured sneers of opponents the married life of Duke and Duchess had been a distinctly happy one, and this dissolution of their partnership

[1] *L.J.*, xviii. 43-4 ; *Parliamentary History*, vi. 479-507 ; Dartmouth's note in *Burnet* (ed. 1833), v. 242.

[2] *Luttrell*, v. 621-2 ; *Hist. MSS. Com.*, vii. 506.

[3] Charles Bertie was dismissed in May and the Earl of Abingdon in October. The Countess of Abingdon resigned in November (*Luttrell*, v. 546, 600, 609).

[4] The first part was presented to the Queen on May 25, 1702 (*Luttrell*, v. 177).

appears to have broken the thread of the Duke's life, reminded
him of his own approaching end, and inclined him towards
composing some kind of memoir of the part he had played
during his long political career.[1]

As materials to work upon he had not only his own volu-
minous correspondence, but a journal which he had kept during
his first year of office as sole Treasurer of the Navy,[2] various
minor journals of important events during his life,[3] and a series
of pocket almanacs in which from 1666 onwards he had jotted
down notes of contemporary occurrences. Even when he began
to write, three of the most important of these almanacs, those
for 1676, 1677 and 1678, had already gone amissing ; [4] but from
those that remained he proceeded to extract, probably about
the beginning of 1704, a series of " memorandums," which were
presumably intended to form the basis of a more notable work.[5]
At the same time he began a regular diary, which he continued,
largely in his own handwriting, until the end of his life.[6]

It is this diary which forms the chief authority for the Duke's
activities during the reign of Anne. The greater part of his
time was clearly devoted to personal and family affairs. His
financial transactions, notes of which constitute about half the

[1] It is significant that the first entry in the autograph portion of Leeds's
diary records his wife's death (B.M. Add. MSS. 28040, f. 64).

[2] B.M. Add. MSS. 28040, f. 11.   [3] These have all been noticed above.

[4] All the almanacs have since disappeared, and in spite of diligent enquiry
no trace of them can be found.

[5] These memorandums, so far as they now exist, are B.M. Add. MSS. 28040,
ff. 1-10. Although they include nothing later than 1681 there are several
reasons for assigning their composition to the year 1704. (a) On f. 8 is the
endorsement in the handwriting of the Duke of Leeds, " Abstract of Memorandums from 1666 to 1704." (b) The memorandums are written throughout
in a clerk's handwriting ; but until the eighteenth century the Duke of Leeds
rarely employed an amanuensis, and had they been drawn up in the seventeenth century it is scarcely to be imagined he would have failed to write
them himself. Further there are many autograph notes on the memorandums,
and these are all in a handwriting which it is impossible to date earlier than
1704. (c) The continuous autograph diary begins in 1704.

[6] One fragment of this diary is B.M. Add. MSS. 28040, ff. 64-7. It covers
the whole of January, February and March, 1704. For some reason Leeds
seems then to have temporarily abandoned it, and the bulk of the diary, which
is B.M. Add. MSS. 28041, makes a fresh start on January 1, 1705. The heading
of this part, on f. 1, would suggest that the Duke's original intention was to
go back to midsummer 1702 and start practically with the accession of Anne
but if so the idea was abandoned.

diary, were of the most varied and extensive character. He was deeply interested in the Company of Mine Adventurers, of which he became Governor, and for the ill-success of which he had to bear much of the blame.[1] He lent large sums both to the Government and to private individuals. His chief interest, however, lay in his estates at Wimbledon [2] and in Yorkshire. During his period of power under Charles II he had purchased the manors of Harthill and Todwick. To these he now added Wakefield, and North and South Anstan ; and pulling down the old home of the Osbornes at Kiveton erected in its place a mansion which remained intact until 1811.[3]

More exacting than such material cares were his responsibilities as head of a large and ever growing family. Since his fall from office in 1679 the matrimonial alliances of his children had scarcely maintained the same brilliant level as before that event. His daughter, Lady Anne Coke, had contracted something of a mésalliance by marrying as her second husband, in March 1691, Captain Horace Walpole, the uncle of the future Whig Prime Minister ; [4] and this was only partially counter-

---

[1] The Corporation of the Governor and Company of the Mine Adventurers of England was formed in 1698 to exploit certain mines in South Wales previously belonging to Sir Carbery Pryse. The real promoter was Sir Humphrey Mackworth, who became Deputy-Governor, and on the failure of the undertaking was accused of peculation, voted guilty of " many notorious and scandalous frauds " by the House of Commons, and proceeded against by special bill (C.J., xvi. 391 ; Luttrell, iv. 434, 489; vi. 564-6). Le Neve is characteristically cautious in his comment on Leeds's connection with the enterprise. " The Duke had been Governor of the Company of Mine Adventurers a long time, but whether to his honour or profit I cannot determine. Sure I am that some have suffered considerably by it, but that may more justly be laid at the doors of some others than his Graces " (Lives of Illustrious Persons, p. 146).

[2] " March 23th, [1703/4], I signed articles with James Cendy of Fulham, gardner, for the keeping my gardens att Wimbledon by the yeare for the sums of 200 l. a yeare to bee paid quarterly, and 18 l. a yeare more to bee paid halfe yearely to the keeper of my orange garden there " (B.M. Add. MSS. 28040, f. 66).

[3] Hunter, South Yorkshire, i. 144.

[4] " To the great dissatisfaction of all her relations " (B.M. Add. MSS. 34095, f. 305 ; Luttrell, ii. 201) ; " to the no small grief of her ancient father the Duke of Leeds " (Verney Letters of the Eighteenth Century, i. 218). Lady Anne failed to win her father's approval of the marriage, but Walpole later showed himself not unwilling to support the Tory interest, and in January 1712 the Duke was so far reconciled as to solicit a place for him from the Earl of Oxford (Portland MSS., iii. 462 ; v. 137).

balanced by the union on March 5, 1692, of Sophia, widow of Lord O'Brien, with Sir William Fermor, newly created Lord Leominster.[1] In August 1706, also, Lady Plymouth gave considerable offence to her relatives by marrying her own chaplain, Dr. Philip Bisse, who however was later promoted to the episcopate.[2] All these alliances increased the ramifications of the House of Osborne and multiplied the patriarchal responsibilities of the Duke of Leeds, for while the more undesirable among them, probably to his secret satisfaction, proved to be without issue, this was by no means the case with the others, and many of the children of the earlier marriages were now reaching an age when their position in life had to be seriously considered.

Of the two sons and one daughter born to Lady Anne by her first husband only the heir, Edward Coke, had survived infancy, and on this, his eldest, grandchild Leeds had lavished much of his attention ever since he had been left fatherless at the age of three in 1679. The remarriage of Lady Anne had increased his feeling of responsibility, and in 1696 he had found Edward a bride in the person of Cary, daughter of Sir John Newton of Barr's Court, a young lady of fifteen with a fortune estimated at £40,000. Now he found himself confronted with a fresh set of responsibilities, for both Edward and Cary died in 1707, leaving a large family, of whom the eldest, Thomas, later to be Earl of Leicester, was barely ten years old. By amicable agreement the actual guardianship of the children was left to Sir John Newton, Charles Bertie, and two others; but young Thomas at least remained a frequent visitor at Wimbledon and a constant object of his great-grandfather's care.[3]

More directly burdensome were the affairs of the Herbert family, for the death of Leeds's son-in-law, James Herbert, on November 11, 1704, was followed by that of Catherine Herbert on December 8, 1708, and the Duke thus found himself principal executor of a heavily encumbered estate[4] and guardian of a number of youthful grandchildren. His special interest

[1] B.M. Add. MSS. 29578, f. 290; 36662, f. 331; *Luttrell*, ii. 346.

[2] *Luttrell*, vi. 76, 548, 558, 643.

[3] C. W. James, *Chief Justice Coke*, pp. 135-78.

[4] The other executors were the Earl of Abingdon, Thomas Carter and Mr. Clark; but they left the Duke to act alone (B.M. Add. MSS. 28041, f. 2).

naturally lay in the eldest son and heir Thomas,[1] the settlement of whose affairs caused him much anxiety ; but he had also to bestir himself to send the second son James to sea under Captain Peregrine Bertie,[2] and to enter the youngest, Philip, first at "Eaton Schoole"[3] and then at St. John's College, Cambridge. The girls, Elizabeth, Catherine and Jane,[4] spent most of their time with him, and in 1708 he successfully negotiated a marriage between the eldest and Sir John Cotton.[5]

On the two sons and four daughters of Lady Leominster Leeds also bestowed much of his attention. Although Lord Leominster had been married twice already the elder boy, born on March 23, 1697, was heir to the title, and as he had been given the name of Thomas was presumably one of the Duke's many godsons.[6] Lord and Lady Leominster, however, were well able to look after their own children, and in the last resort the descendants of all his daughters were at most a secondary consideration to Leeds. Inevitably it was in those who might inherit his own title and fortune that the Duke's real interest lay. Of these his son was still a source of constant anxiety owing to his unstable character and permanently impecunious condition. In the spring of 1705 Carmarthen was given command of the squadron which was to convoy the Duke of Marlborough

---

[1] Born on July 5 and christened on July 18, 1687, when Leeds and the Earl of Pembroke were godfathers (*Rutland MSS.*, ii. 115).

[2] "1706, April 16th, I gave five guineas on executors' account to James Herbert, who went this day to sea in the *Ruby* with Captain Peregrine Bertie, which is repaid to mee. . . . 1707, June 20th, James Herbert had a commission to bee 2nd leiutenant in the ship *August*, Captain Scott commander. They were to sayle for Lisbon the 29th, and I sent 10 l. to him by note the 26th by the said Captain Scott, who was then att London" (B.M. Add. MSS. 28041, ff. 9, 14).

[3] "I gave him two guyneys for play money and two guyneys to the master for entrance money and three guyneys to Mr. Davis who went with him" to see him entered (B.M. Add. MSS. 28041, f. 3).

[4] Jane died on December 10, 1705. Another granddaughter, Charlotte Herbert, had died before her father on March 12, 1704 (B.M. Add. MSS. 28040, f. 66 ; 28041, f. 7).

[5] The marriage took place at Wimbledon on July 4, and three days later Leeds presented the young couple to the Queen at Windsor (B.M. Add. MSS. 28041, ff. 15, 17).

[6] The younger boy, born on March 13, 1704, and called William after his paternal grandfather, has not generally been noticed. One of the daughters, Sophia, died at Holborn on March 9, 1708 (B.M. Add. MSS. 28040, f. 66 ; 28041, f. 15).

and his fleet of transports to Holland ; but before he could set
out he had to borrow £50 from his father " to bee repaid out
of his first pay." [1] The new reign brought him fairly regular
employment for a time, and the rank of Vice-Admiral of the
Red ; [2] but it was clear that little reliance could be placed upon
him to maintain the honour of the family in years to come.

Thus the hopes of the aged Duke rested mainly on his grandsons, William Henry, Earl of Danby, and his younger brother
Peregrine Hyde. On William Henry he settled the greater part
of his estate,[3] while to both boys he took the place of their
somewhat neglectful father. Towards the close of 1706 he made
arrangements for the completion of their education by a period
of residence abroad, and on December 1, in company with their
governor M. Berard, they departed for Holland.[4] For the next
five years, with Utrecht as their centre of operations, they were
to spend their time studying foreign languages and conditions
of life on the Continent. The expense in which this involved
the Duke fell little if at all short of £1,000 per annum, but his
generosity was in some measure repaid by a regular series of
letters in which his grandsons and their governor kept him
informed of political developments abroad.[5]

Meanwhile his life was spent in a comparatively regular round.
Every autumn he took up his residence at Kiveton and entertained there his relatives and friends. Throughout the rest of
the year he lived at Wimbledon, except for a few weeks during
the session of Parliament, when he came into London itself.
Until 1708 he resided, while in town, in Holborn, but in the
spring of that year he let his house there on a lease which was

---

[1] B.M. Add. MSS. 28041, ff. 3, 4.

[2] In the summer of 1703 it was even anticipated that he would be made
Admiral of the Blue. He was also allowed to continue the experimenta
building of light naval craft in which he was specially interested (*Cal. S. P
Dom.*, 1703-4, pp. 28-31, 388-90 ; *House of Lords MSS.*, 1704-6, p. 29 ; *Luttrell*
v. 136, 212-9, 262, 275, 277, 287, 308 ; vi. 458, and *passim*).

[3] Leeds appears from his diary to have been constantly altering his will
but his intention to make his grandson his heir remained permanent throughout

[4] B.M. Add. MSS. 28041, f. 12.

[5] Twenty of Danby's and ninety-four of M. Berard's letters were in th
Morrison collection and are partly printed in *Morrison Catalogue*, ii. 3 *et seq*
iii. 120 *et seq*. Others were among the papers at Hornby Castle. A few ar
among the Leeds MSS. in the British Museum. The Duke's replies have no
been preserved.

to run to the close of 1714,[1] and apparently resigned himself to living out of town altogether.

Scarcely, however, had he thus signalised his continued determination to abstain from politics when his whole attitude began to change. In 1706, like many other Tories, he had been greatly incensed by the publication of the third volume of the anonymous *Compleat History of England,* the Whig author of which was almost immediately identified as Dr. White Kennett. So completely did the Duke consider his own conduct to be misrepresented in that volume that instead of the memoir which he had hitherto been contemplating he conceived the project of writing a criticism or reply, and drew up with that object in view a list of passages on which he proposed to comment.[2] The reply apparently was never even begun, but an idea which the Duke had long entertained, of publishing in his own justification some part of his correspondence, was taken up instead, and arranged so as to embody to some extent the remarks which he had thought of making. Probably in 1708 the work of compilation was commenced, and an introduction and notes were written reflecting severely on Dr. Kennett.[3]

The work proved to be unexpectedly well timed. Before it could be published the Whig ministry which the war had produced was beginning to break up under the strain of war weariness, and a wave of reactionary feeling was setting in which was to carry the Tory party to power. To the old Duke the mere suggestion of any such development was a call to action, and roused in him a fresh interest in politics which is apparent on every page of his diary from 1709 onwards. At Michaelmas of that year, scarcely more than twelve months after he had let his own house in Holborn, he took a lease of Lindsey House, and on November 18 removed into it with his family in order to be nearer the scene of operations.[4] A few days earlier Dr. Henry Sacheverell had delivered at St. Paul's his famous fifth of November sermon on " the perils of false brethren in Church

---

[1] B.M. Add. MSS. 28041, f. 15. The rent was £110 a year.

[2] " Remarks taken out of Dr. Kennet's History of England " (B.M. Add. MSS. 28042, f. 112).

[3] The curious slip made by the Duke in writing ' 1708 ' instead of ' 1678 ' (*infra,* ii. 373) suggests that it was in the former year he was actually writing.

[4] B.M. Add. MSS. 28041, ff. 20-1.

and State," and had roused such a storm of indignation among the Whigs by his insistence on the doctrine of non-resistance and his denunciation of toleration and occasional conformity that it was obvious a crisis was imminent.

By such an experienced politician as Leeds the decision of the Whigs to impeach Sacheverell must have been recognised as a grave tactical error, and he immediately set himself to exploit it to the utmost. Lest the Doctor himself might feel inclined to modify his opinions he united with other Tory peers in sending him every encouragement to make a firm stand.[1] On January 10, 1710, just two days before the articles of impeachment were carried up from the Commons to the Lords, he resumed his place in Parliament after an absence of nearly a year. Throughout the three weeks of the trial he continued regularly in attendance, raising every obstacle which might retard proceedings, and signing protest after protest against the resolutions adopted by the Whig majority.[2] On March 20, when the lords were called upon individually to give their verdict, he and Carmarthen voted with the minority in favour of acquittal.[3]

The main difficulty with which he had to contend was that of reconciling support of Sacheverell with his own conduct at the time of the Revolution, and this he endeavoured to accomplish in a long speech which he delivered on March 16. Admitting his share in the movement against James II he solemnly declared " he never thought that things would have gone so far as to settle the crown on the Prince of Orange, whom he had often heard say that he had no such thoughts himself ; that they ought to distinguish between resistance and revolution, for vacancy or abdication was the thing they went upon, and therefore resistance was to be forgot ; for had it not succeeded it had certainly been rebellion, since he knew of no other but hereditary right." [4]

[1] *Downshire MSS.*, i. 886.

[2] The supporters of Sacheverell protested on eight occasions. Leeds signed six of the protests, and Carmarthen all of them.

[3] Carmarthen, who rarely spoke, is recorded to have addressed the Lords on Sacheverell's behalf, and Leeds is said to have been moved to tears by the eloquence of the Doctor's own defence (*L.J.*, xix. 29-118 ; *Portland MSS.* iv. 535 ; *Luttrell*, vi. 551-61). The voting was 69 to 52. A division list is printed in *Parliamentary History*, vi. 886-7.

[4] *Parliamentary History*, vi. 847.

Almost at the same time as this speech was made the Duke's collection of letters came out,[1] and was so well received that he ventured on a second edition,[2] and authorised the republication in book form of the pamphlets which he and Sir Robert Howard had written at the time of his impeachment under Charles II.[3] For some months he was an outstanding politician, constantly in attendance on the Queen, and introducing to her numerous loyal addresses from districts and towns in the north.[4] With unshakable optimism he even looked beyond the lifetime of the sovereign on the throne, opened up correspondence with Hanover, and instructed his grandsons on the Continent to pay a complimentary visit to the Electress and Elector.[5]

There is no doubt that Leeds sincerely wished for a Tory revival, but there is equally little doubt that he hoped out of that revival to gain something for himself. His pension of twenty-one years on the Post Office was coming perilously near its end, and he desired to have it renewed for life. He also aimed at the recovery of the three lord lieutenancies in Yorkshire of which he had been deprived, and even hoped that in the reconstructed ministry which the Tories began to build up after the prorogation of Parliament he might be entrusted with the privy seal.[6]

As far as the pension was concerned little trouble arose. The Queen readily consented to its renewal, and when a first grant proved void another was obtained after some delay.[7] But the

---

[1] *Copies and Extracts of some Letters written to and from the Earl of Danby (now Duke of Leeds) in the years 1676, 1677 and 1678, with particular remarks upon some of them,* advertised in the *London Gazette,* No. 4662, March 7-9, 1709/10.

[2] Substantially identical with the first, apart from the correction of some errors.

[3] *Memoirs relating to the Impeachment of Thomas Earl of Danby (now Duke of Leeds) in the year 1678.* London, 1710.

[4] B.M. Add. MSS. 28041, ff. 23-7, 35, 37; *Wentworth Papers,* p. 139; *Portland MSS.,* iv. 642-3.

[5] The correspondence is printed *infra,* ii. 234-7.

[6] *Portland MSS.,* iv. 563; *Luttrell,* vi. 633. " 18th [July], I went to Windsor and spoke to the Queen to be restored to my lieutenancy of Yorkshire and warden of Sherwood Forest. . . . 22th [July], Duke Hamilton came to Wimbledon to aske mee if I pretended to the Privy Seale, because in that case hee would not pretend to itt " (B.M. Add. MSS. 28041, f. 30).

[7] B.M. Add. MSS. 28041, ff. 24, 25, 27; Leeds to the Earl of Oxford, August 11, 1711, July 12, 1712, in *Portland MSS.,* v. 72, 202.

new ministers showed themselves extremely unready to burden themselves with a statesman whose day was past, and whose career contained only too many unfortunate episodes which might later be brought up against them. In the end all that was offered to Leeds was the place of Justice in Eyre north of the Trent, and the Lord Lieutenancy of the East Riding. The latter he declined, on the ground that the Governorship of Hull, which usually went with it, was not being offered at the same time ; and his suggestion that the Lord Lieutenancy of the West Riding or of Nottingham should be given him instead was ignored.[1] Towards the close of 1711 the Duke received his patent as Justice in Eyre, the last official appointment he was ever to hold.[2]

Possibly the rebuff to his more extravagant hopes was a blessing in disguise. Leeds was now a very old man, scarcely capable of performing real official duties. Yet it almost seemed as if he would outlive not merely his friends and contemporaries, but the majority of his descendants as well. Goodricke had died on March 5, 1705, Seymour on February 17, 1708, and now Charles Bertie followed on March 22, 1711. The years of Tory revival were fatal years in the personal history of the Osborne family. On August 10, 1709, Thomas Herbert, on whom the Duke had lavished so much attention, passed away shortly after his twenty-second birthday.[3] James then became the heir, and Leeds with unwearied energy proceeded to fulfil his part as executor of a fresh settlement. To avert the possible extinction of the Herbert line a marriage had to be hastily arranged, and on September 15, 1710, James Herbert was united to Sarah, daughter of Sir James Hallett.[4]

The supreme tragedy, however, was yet to come. In the autumn of 1711 William Henry, Earl of Danby, a youth who, so far as can be judged from his letters, might well have justified the high hopes his grandfather rested upon him, celebrated his

---

[1] Leeds to the Earl of Oxford, September 6, 21, 1711, in *Portland MSS.*, v. 87, 92.

[2] B.M. Add. MSS. 28041, f. 32.

[3] *Ibid.*, f. 20.

[4] Her portion was £10,000. On June 15, 1711, she had a son, to whom Leeds gave the name of James, and on May 24, 1712, another son, Thomas, who died shortly afterwards (B.M. Add. MSS. 28041, ff. 25, 29, 35).

majority at Utrecht. A few days later he contracted smallpox,
and died on August 16. Immediately on news of his illness
reaching England his brother Peregrine Hyde was ordered home,
but in the spring of 1712 he also was attacked by the disease
and only with difficulty saved to become in due course third
Duke of Leeds. [1]

By these events, which threatened the destruction of all he
had tried to achieve, it is probable that the old Duke was badly
shaken. For some years he had felt his health failing him,[2]
and although his activity never flagged he must have known
the end was drawing near. Contemporaries believed that it
was his intention on his eightieth birthday to retire altogether
from public life ; [3] but there is nothing to suggest that he made
any attempt to do so, and in the spring of 1712 he was still in
constant attendance on the Queen. In the early days of July
he introduced three addresses at Court, from Leeds, Pontefract,
and Lichfield ; [4] and shortly thereafter set out on his customary
journey to Yorkshire. Before he had covered half the distance,
however, he was seized by an attack of convulsions at Easton
Neston in Northamptonshire, the seat of his daughter Lady
Leominster, and passed away there in his eighty-first year on July
26, 1712. He was buried in a vault which he had himself con-
structed on the north side of the church at Harthill.

Appropriately enough the marble tomb beneath which he
rests bears inscribed upon it a record of his honours and employments rather than a panegyric upon his virtues.[5] It is impossible to depict the first Duke of Leeds as a great and admirable
character. Pride and ambition were his ruling passions through
life. He is accused on all sides of untruthfulness and corruption.
His capacity has probably been exaggerated both by friends
and by enemies. His ideals never give the impression of being
specially high, his knowledge of being specially wide, or his

---

[1] Just before the smallpox attacked him Leeds had recognised the new
position occupied by Peregrine Hyde by making him an allowance of £300 a
year (B.M. Add. MSS. 28041, ff. 30, 34).

[2] Leeds to Dr. Hans Sloane, January 15, 1705, January 10, 1707, printed
infra, ii. 229, 231.

[3] Le Neve, p. 145.

[4] B.M. Add. MSS. 28041, ff. 36-7 ; Thoresby, ii. 125-7.

[5] The inscription is printed in Hunter, South Yorkshire, i. 146-7.

reasoning of being specially profound. He was a man of real ability, but not a genius; a fluent and pointed speaker, but not a great orator; a shrewd and energetic man of business, but not a great financier; an able and efficient man of affairs, but not a great statesman.

Yet when all this has been said the worst has been admitted, and the voice of calumny was so busy in his own lifetime that it is more necessary to modify than to emphasise the verdict of contemporaries. In courage, energy and resolution, the virtues which distinguish the man of action rather than the thinker, Leeds has been surpassed by few. If he was not of those who rise superior to the age in which they live, at least he never consciously fell short of the standard it required. His outlook undoubtedly was not an exalted one; but in this he differs from only too many of his contemporaries, that to the principles he had he remained almost unswervingly loyal.